A Power User's Quick Reference

WORD 2000 IN A NUTSHELL

A Power User's Quick Reference

Walter Glenn

O'REILLY®

Beijing • Cambridge • Farnham • Köln • Paris • Sebastopol • Taipei • Tokyo

Word 2000 in a Nutshell
by Walter Glenn

Printed in the United States of America.

Published by O'Reilly & Associates, Inc., 101 Morris Street, Sebastopol, CA 95472.

Editor: Troy Mott

Production Editor: Madeleine Newell

Cover Designer: Hanna Dyer

Printing History:

August 2000: First Edition.

Library of Congress Cataloging-in-Publication Data

Glenn, Walter J.
Word 2000 in a nutshell : a power user's quick reference/Walter Glenn.--1st ed.
p. cm.
ISBN 1-56592-489-4
1. Microsoft Word--Handbooks, manuals, etc. 2. Word processing--Handbooks, manuals, etc. I. Title.

Z52.5.M52 G57 2000
652.5'5369--dc21 00-057988

ISBN: 1-56592-489-4
[M]

Table of Contents

Part 3: Beyond the Basics

Part 4: Appendixes

Preface

In the years since its creation, Word has grown from a simple word processor to a complex program with more functions than any one person could ever want. Word has consistently topped the list of the really great applications around. One of the best things I can say about it is that you can fire it up, start typing right away, and produce a pretty nice document—no experience necessary. There is also no end to the amount of functionality you can uncover if you feel like digging.

Of course, Word has its problems. It can be slow. It crashes sometimes (it even crashed while I was writing this preface). The interface is often frustratingly complex. Error messages are not helpful and the help system leaves a lot to be desired.

I've been using Word since it was created, and during the year I've spent writing this book, I've used it a *lot*. I considered myself a pretty savvy Word user when I started work on the book, but I quickly found out just how wrong I was. Like most of the people I've worked with, I had no idea of Word's full potential.

I have tried my best to create an accurate, no-nonsense reference that covers not only how to accomplish various tasks, but also why you might want to accomplish them.

Organization of This Book

Word 2000 in a Nutshell is structured in three parts.

Part 1, *The Big Picture*

Part 1, *The Big Picture*, is an overview of the interface and a look into the inner workings of Word. It is intended to give the reader a solid understanding of Word's basic dynamics.

Chapter 1, *Word Overview*, is a quick reference to the basic Word interface that is aimed at getting a user up to speed quickly. Chapter 1 also includes a Task List, which functions as a sort of information desk for the book. It provides a quick reference to the most common tasks in Word and shows where in the book those tasks are detailed.

Chapter 2, *How Word Works*, is a critical chapter. It starts with a description of how Word builds its interface each time it starts and what environmental variables affect that process. From there, it opens Word's hood and examines the nuts and bolts that make it work (and sometimes not work).

Chapter 3, *Customizing Word*, covers the two primary tools used to customize Word's operations and its interface: the Tools → Options and Tools → Customize commands.

Part 2, *Menu Reference*

Part 2, *Menu Reference*, is the part of the book that should keep you coming back for more and will likely end up with the most dog-eared pages. The chapters are organized according to Word's menus. Each chapter is organized by the commands on the menu it covers.

Chapter 4, *File*, details the menu commands used to start, save, close, and print documents, edit document properties, and exit the Word program.

Chapter 5, *Edit*, details the commands used for selecting and manipulating content and for searching documents.

Chapter 6, *View*, details the commands used for changing the way a document window looks and works.

Chapter 7, *Insert*, details the commands used for inserting fields, footnotes, cross-references, graphics, and other objects into a document.

Chapter 8, *Format*, details the commands used for formatting content.

Chapter 9, *Tools*, details commands used for setting options, customizing Word, and accessing other tools that just don't fit into Word's other menus.

Chapter 10, *Table*, details the commands used for building and manipulating tables.

Chapter 11, *Window*, details the commands used for controlling document windows.

Chapter 12, *Help*, details the commands used for getting help.

Part 3, *Beyond the Basics*

Part 3, *Beyond the Basics*, brings the topics discussed earlier in the book to bear on actual tasks. In these chapters, you look over my shoulder while I walk through many of the interesting things you can do in Word.

Chapter 13, *Collaborating*, looks at several different tools Word offers for collaborating on documents with other users.

Chapter 14, *Creating a Template*, walks through the creation of a sample template.

Chapter 15, *Fields and Forms*, examines the use of fields in Word and also walks through the creation of an electronic form.

Chapter 16, *Creating a Web Page*, looks at tools Word includes for designing web pages and some methods for cleaning up the often messy HTML code that Word generates.

Chapter 17, *Using Master Documents*, shows how master documents can be used to group collections of documents for global formatting and printing.

Chapter 18, *Working with VBA*, looks at the tools and methods for using Visual Basic for Applications to extend Word's functionality to new levels.

Part 4, *Appendixes*

This section includes supplemental reference information and several quick-reference lists.

Appendix A, *Keyboard Shortcuts*, is a comprehensive reference to Word's keyboard shortcuts, arranged by function.

Appendix B, *Registry Keys*, details the common registry keys used by Word.

Appendix C, *Converters and Filters*, details the text converters and graphics filters included with Word 2000.

Appendix D, *Tip Reference*, is a complete list of all of the numbered tips included in the book.

Conventions Used in This Book

The following typographical conventions are used in this book:

`Constant width`
: Is used to indicate command-line computer output and code examples, language constructs such as VBA statements, and constants.

`Constant width italic`
: Is used to indicate variables in examples. It is also used to indicate variables or user-defined elements within italic text (such as path names or filenames). For instance, in the path *\Windows*`username`, replace `username` with your name.

`Constant width bold italic`
: Is used to indicate replaceable user input in examples.

Italic
: Is used to introduce new terms and to indicate URLs, variables in text, user-defined files and directories, commands, file extensions, filenames, directory or folder names, and UNC pathnames. Italic is also used to highlight chapter titles, and in some instances, to visually separate the topic of a list.

Tips, notes, and warnings

The following formats are used to indicate tips, notes, and warnings:

TIP # 1

Tip Title

This is an example of a tip, which gives specific instruction on how to use a given Word element that the author feels is important and beneficial to the user.

This is an example of a note, which provides valuable and timesaving information.

WARNING

This is an example of a warning, which alerts users to a potential pitfall in the program. Warnings can also refer to procedures that might be dangerous if not carried out in a specific way.

Path Notation

We use a shorthand path notation to show you how to reach a given Word or Windows user interface element or option. The path notation is relative to a well-known location. For example, the following path:

Insert → Picture → WordArt

means "Open the Insert menu (in Word), then choose Picture, then choose the WordArt command."

Keyboard Shortcuts

When keyboard shortcuts are shown (such as `Ctrl-Alt-Del`), a hyphen means that the keys must be held down simultaneously, while a plus means that the keys should be pressed sequentially.

How to Contact Us

We have tested and verified the information in this book to the best of our ability, but you may find that features have changed (or even that we have made mistakes!). Please let us know about any errors you find, as well as your suggestions for future editions, by writing to:

O'Reilly & Associates, Inc.
101 Morris Street
Sebastopol, CA 95472

800-998-9938 (in the U.S. or Canada)
707-829-0515 (international/local)
707-829-0104 (FAX)

You can also send us messages electronically. To be put on the mailing list or request a catalog, send email to:

info@oreilly.com

To ask technical questions or comment on the book, send email to:

bookquestions@oreilly.com

We have a web site for the book, where we'll list examples, errata, and any plans for future editions. You can access this page at:

http://www.oreilly.com/catalog/word2000ian/

For more information about this book and others, see the O'Reilly web site:

http://www.oreilly.com

Office Service Release 1 (OSR-1) was released just prior to this book's publication. While it fixes many small bugs in Word 2000, we did not find that the update greatly impacted the information or advice in this book. You may want to check Microsoft's Office Update site (http://www.officeupdate.com) for complete details on this service release.

Acknowledgments

I worked on this book for a very long time. I'm both glad that it will finally be put to use and sad to close such an interesting chapter in my life. Since I started this book, three children were born: Troy Mott's son, Luke, Tom Syroid's son, Landon, and my own daughter, Maya. It is to them I'd like to dedicate this book, along with my son, Liam. He spent far too many nights without his dad.

As is always said, no book is written alone.

Before anyone else, I would like to thank Troy Mott, my editor at O'Reilly. He has this marvelous and often infuriating ability to pat a writer on the back with one hand while tearing apart a manuscript with the other. His insights and guidance have pushed this book far beyond anything I could have done without him. He's wanted to see this book written for a long time and it is as much his as anyone's.

Thanks to Katie Gardner at O'Reilly, who organized everyone's efforts, made sure I knew what I was doing, and slaved over all the figures in the book. She also took over much of the project development while Troy was out with his new son.

Thanks to Helen Feddema for writing an excellent chapter on VBA (Chapter 18, *Working with VBA*) on such short notice and for her review of other parts of the book.

Thanks to Laurie Ulrich for taking up the gauntlet and contributing to much of this book during a rough stretch of my own.

I would also like to thank Tom Syroid for a grueling technical review of the book (my eyes were bleeding, too). He had just finished his own book, *Outlook in a Nutshell*, and I'm sure he enjoyed giving mine both barrels. He even worked on it during his vacation. Thanks to Tom English (my brother) and Lue English (my mother) for their reviews, as well.

Finally, I want to thank my wife, Susan. While I was writing this book, she went through a pregnancy, gave birth, and started a new job. Throughout it all, she gave me nothing but support.

—Walter Glenn
May 2000

Part 1

The Big Picture

Chapter 1

Word Overview

You can find a better program to perform almost any single function that Word offers. Excel is better at graphs and expressions, Illustrator is better for creating images, and many programs are better for creating web pages. However, it's hard to find another program that offers as much broad-ranging utility as Word.

To start with, it's certainly good at word processing, a phrase that means a lot more today than it did just a few years ago. Word provides professionally designed templates for creating business and personal letters, proposals, reports, newsletters, flyers, and even brochures. Layout and formatting tools are better than ever. Word can also create drawings, tables, HTML, forms, and even custom programs.

And that's really the design philosophy behind Word. It is a tool that is meant to put a host of different features into the hands of people who mainly need to do simple word processing, but also need extra features occasionally.

This chapter is like an information desk for the rest of the book. It examines the Word interface in general and briefly shows how to type, edit, and format documents. It also includes a task list that covers the common uses and keyboard shortcuts for all of the Word menus and shows you where in the book to go for more detail.

The Word Interface

At first glance, you won't notice many significant changes in Word 2000 from previous versions of Word. Aside from the fact that the default setting now combines the Standard and Formatting toolbars on a single line, it's difficult even to tell whether you are running Word 2000 or Word 97.

One very significant change in Word 2000 becomes obvious when you open more than one document. Word now boasts a *single document interface* (SDI), in which each open document has its own window completely separate from other documents (Figure 1-1). Each document also appears on the taskbar as a separate button. Switch between documents with the Window menu (in any of the open documents) and by clicking the taskbar buttons.

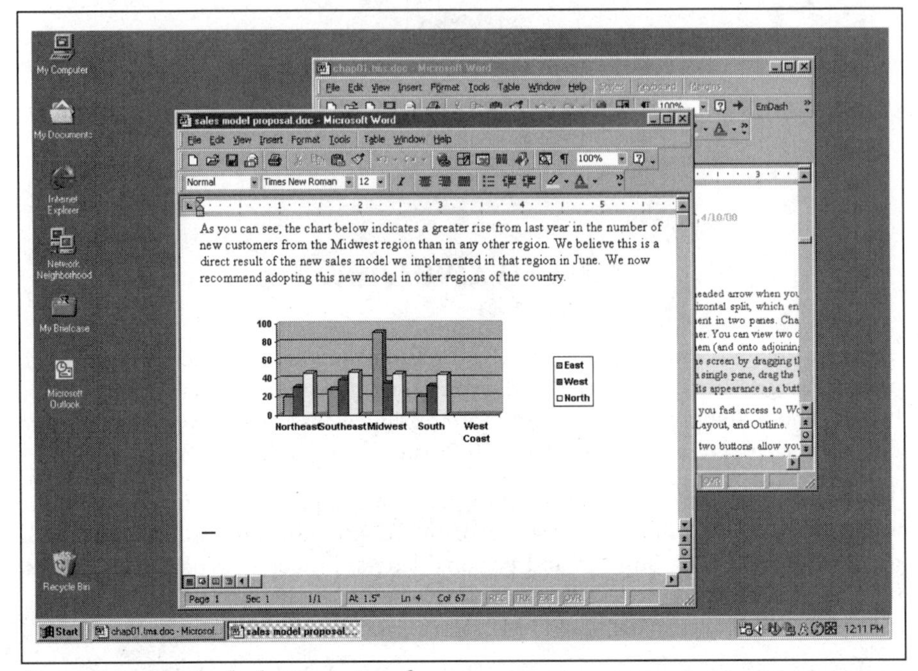

Figure 1-1: The single document interface

TIP # 1

Switch Between Documents with Alt-Tab

The Alt-Tab and Alt-Esc keyboard shortcuts, normally used for switching between applications, also switch between open Word documents. The SDI behaves as if each open document is a distinct application. However, the core Word program files are only loaded into memory once.

Title and Command Bars

In previous versions of Word, menus and toolbars were distinct. In Word 2000, menus and toolbars are both a type of *command bar* (Figure 1-2). Commands on these bars, whether they are buttons or word commands, are treated the same by Word. This change means a couple of things. You can now drag the menu bar to undock it and make it float anywhere in the Word application. Also, customization of menus and toolbars is now the same. Add buttons to traditional menus and add full menus right beside buttons in toolbars. You'll learn more about this in Chapter 3, *Customizing Word.*

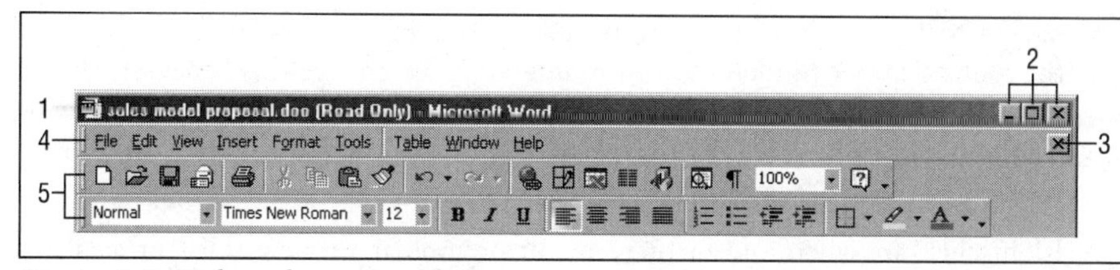

Figure 1-2: Title and command bars

The following numbered list details the essential title and command bar interface elements:

1. *Title bar.* The title bar shows the name of the active document and the application. Word also uses the title bar to denote a document's state. For example, if you open multiple windows of the same document (using Window → New Window), Word indicates this by numbering each window. :1 denotes the original, :2 the second copy, and so on. If a document is opened as read-only, that information appears in parentheses beside the document name.

   Double-click the title bar to maximize the document window or to restore it to its pre-maximized state. Right-click the title bar to display a context menu for closing the document or changing its size. Right-click the document's taskbar button to access this same context menu.

2. *Sizing buttons.* The Minimize, Maximize, and Close buttons affect only the active document. The Close button affects only the document and not Word, unless only one document is open at the time (see the next bullet).

3. *Close Window button.* If only one document is open, a separate Close Window button is added to the far right of the menu bar. Click it to close the document but leave Word itself open. Use the regular Close button on the title bar to close both the document and Word.

4. *Menus.* Word's new *adaptive menus* show only the basic commands (as decided by Microsoft) and the most frequently used commands on both menus and toolbars.

TIP # 2

Turn Off Adaptive Menus

Experienced Word users often find adaptive menus annoying. Turn them off using Tools → Customize → Options → "Menus show recently used commands first." Adaptive menus may also hinder new users, making it hard to find commands by scanning menus.

5. *Toolbars.* Word 2000 combines the Standard and Formatting toolbars into a single row of tools. This does provide an extra bit of space in the document window, but usually doesn't leave enough room to show all buttons. And

having to select the More Buttons option (the down arrow at the far right of the toolbar) to see hidden buttons is annoying. To change this behavior, choose Tools → Customize → Commands → Options → "Standard and Formatting Toolbars share one row." You can also drag one of the toolbars to another level yourself (shown in Figure 1-2) and this feature turns off automatically.

Right-click anywhere on an open menu or toolbar to view a list of available toolbars. Click any toolbar on the list to toggle it on or off.

Rulers

Word's rulers control the margins and indentation of the text in a document and are good for measuring and lining up text. The horizontal ruler (Figure 1-3) appears directly above the main document window in all of Word's views except for Outline view. The vertical ruler appears to the left and only in Print Layout view. For the most part, the vertical and horizontal rulers behave the same way, so we're only going to take a close look at the horizontal ruler here.

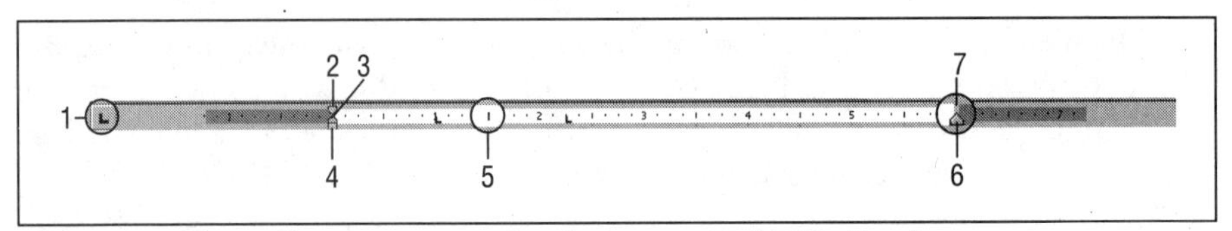

Figure 1-3: Controlling margins and indentations with Word's rulers

1. *Tab selector. Click the button to* cycle through the different available tab types. Types include:
   - *Left.* Left tabs are Word's default and the type most users think of when they think of tabs. Text is aligned against the left edge of the tab stop.
   - *Center.* Center tabs align the text around the center of the tab stop.
   - *Right.* Right tabs align text against the tab stop's right edge and are a great way to align the rightmost digits of lengthy lists of numbers as you enter them.
   - *Decimal.* Decimal tabs align numbers (or text) based on decimal points. They are great for aligning currency figures. Be careful, though. Text is also aligned on decimals, so if you type a sentence with a period, the period will align on the tab stop.
   - *Bar tab.* Bar tabs do not create an actual tab stop. Rather, they create a vertical line at the position they are inserted. This is great for putting vertical lines between tabbed columns in instances where you would rather not use a table.

- *Indents.* Select first line and hanging indent options and then click anywhere in the active ruler space (the white area) to place the indent there. This is the same as dragging the indent markers (described in the following list).

TIP # 3

Move the Pointer for a Moment to See Tab Type

Once you select a tab type, move the pointer away for a moment and then move it back to display a ScreenTip with the name of the tab type.

2. *First line indent.* This indicates the indent used by the first line of a paragraph. Like other indents, you can place this indent anywhere, including outside the margin of the page.
3. *Hanging indent.* The hanging indent specifies the indent used by subsequent lines of the paragraph. When you move a hanging indent marker, the first line indent marker does not move. This can change the relationship of the first line indent as the rest of the paragraph changes.
4. *Left indent.* The left indent indents all of the text in the paragraph from the left margin. If the paragraph also contains a first line indent, the first line indent marker moves along with the left indent marker to maintain the appropriate first line indent.
5. *Default tab stops.* Word maintains default tab stops every inch. When you place a custom tab stop, all default stops to the left of the new custom stop disappear, but the ones to the right remain.
6. *Right indent.* The right indent marker indents all of the lines in a paragraph from the right margin.
7. *Margin markers.* These are the thin light gray strips where the dark gray and white areas of the ruler meet. Drag the margin markers to change left and right margins for a paragraph.

TIP # 4

Double-Click the Ruler for Different Effects

Double-click the active area of the ruler below the measurement markings to place a tab of the selected type and open the Tabs dialog box (Format → Tabs). Double-click above the measurement markings or anywhere outside the margins to open the Page Layout dialog box (File → Page Setup → Layout).

Main Document Window

Word's main document window (Figure 1-4) contains the document itself and a number of interface elements for changing how the document is displayed.

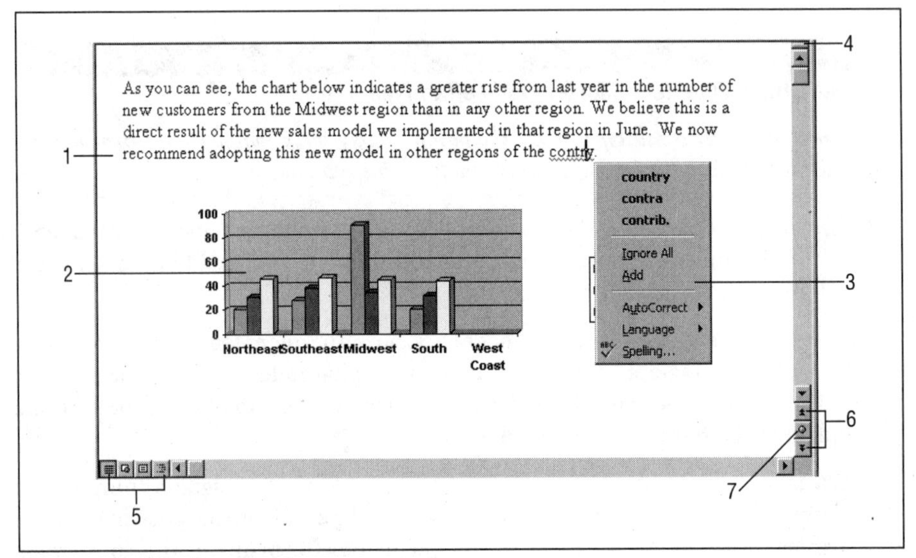

Figure 1-4: Word's main document window

The following list shows the important elements of the document window:

1. *Main Text Window.* When you first open a blank document, you can just start typing. Your text automatically appears within the blank document template's preset margins, so little or no preparation is required.

   A Word document is actually composed of several different layers. Two drawing layers positioned behind and in front of a main text layer let you control the placement of floating objects such as drawings and text boxes to a greater degree than if they were inserted directly inline with the text. You can find more on document layers in Chapter 2, *How Word Works.*

2. *Objects.* You can insert all kinds of objects into a Word document aside from text and formatting. Different types of objects are inserted on different layers of a document. Graphics, for example, can exist in a drawing layer or in the text layer itself. Right-click any object to display a context menu with options for managing and formatting the object.

3. *Context menus.* Right-clicking any element in Word displays a context menu that offers options for working with the element. Context menus offer quick access to pertinent commands from Word's menus. For example, right-clicking a misspelled word offers a list of language and spelling options. Context menus

are one of the many things in the Word interface that can be customized (Chapter 3 covers this in detail).

Microsoft now refers to the contextual menus that open when you right-click an object as shortcut menus. I prefer to call them context menus for two reasons. First, it helps distinguish them from other types of shortcuts in Word and Windows. Second, it better describes their use, which is to provide quick access to commands based on context.

4. *Screen split handle.* Drag this slim handle down to split the document window into two separate panes. Changes made in one pane appear instantly in the other and selections can even be dragged between panes. This is a great way to work on two different parts of a document at once. Once the split is made, drag the handle to adjust the pane size. Drag the handle to its original location to close the extra pane.

5. *View buttons.* These buttons give you fast access to Word's four primary views: Normal, Web Layout, Print Layout, and Outline. Each of the following views is covered in detail in Chapter 6, *View.*

   – *Normal* provides a larger workspace, but you must rely on the status bar to see where you are in the document. One plus to working in Normal view is that page and section breaks are more visible, represented by a horizontal line and text indicating the type of break.

   – *Web Layout* shows any background color or graphic (Format → Background) added to the page and shows the position of text and graphics as they should appear in a web browser.

   – *Print Layout* adds an extra vertical ruler on the left side of the page and allows you to see the physical edges of the paper, a major help in laying out a document and monitoring pagination.

   – *Outline* displays the document as a hierarchical list of headings and supporting paragraph text. Use this view for planning and structuring document headings.

6. *Browse buttons.* By default, these two buttons move through a document page by page. Default Page browsing is on if the color of the triangles on the buttons is black. If they're blue, you're browsing by another document element, as described in #7.

7. *Select Object button.* To choose how the browse buttons operate, click the Select Object button and choose an element from the palette that appears. You can browse by Page, Section, Comment, Footnote, Endnote, Field, Edit, Heading, Graphic, or Table.

   When browsing with an object selected, the arrows on the Browse buttons turn blue. In addition, the ScreenTip that appears when you mouse over the Browse buttons specify which object is set.

TIP # 5

Perform Find Next with Browse Buttons

When using the Edit → Find feature to search for a particular word, phrase, or element (for example, a style) within a document, you can close the Find window and use the Browse buttons to perform Find Next and Find Previous instead. The Browse buttons retain this function until reset with another element.

Click and Type

Word 2000 boasts a new feature named Click and Type that allows you to quickly insert formatted text, graphics, tables, and other items into a blank area of a document by simply double-clicking. It does this by automatically selecting a text alignment based on the position of the pointer. The pointer icon changes to indicate that Click and Type is available and what alignment is set with its use. The pointer icons used look very much like the left, center, and right alignment buttons on the Formatting toolbar.

For example, create a title page by double-clicking in the middle of a blank page and typing the centered title or insert text to the right of an existing paragraph without having to manually add a tab stop.

Word normally aligns the insertion point according to the paragraph alignment or tab stops, but when working with a single-column layout in Print Layout or Web Layout view, Click and Type lets you add text and align it in a stroke.

Note that Click and Type does not work in areas with more than one column, within bulleted or numbered lists, or next to floating objects. Click and Type is also not available while recording a macro. Click and Type is enabled by default. Disable it using Tools → Options → Edit → Enable click and type. The Edit tab on this same dialog also lets you choose the default paragraph style to use with Click and Type.

Status Bar

Word's status bar (see Figure 1-5) shows the location of the insertion point and of the current view in a document, indicates the settings of certain options, and shows when Word is performing certain background operations.

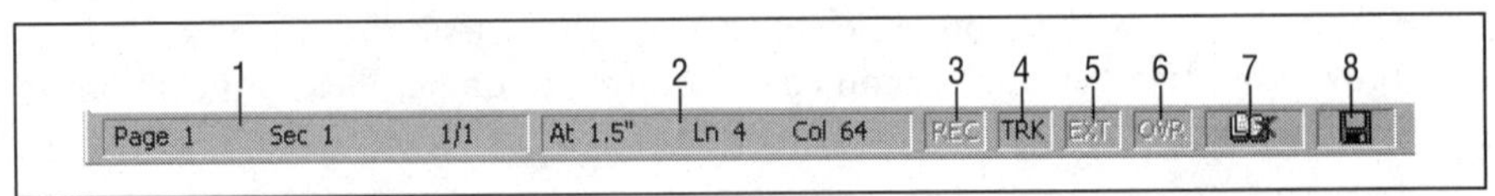

Figure 1-5: Using Word's status bar

The following list shows the important elements of the status bar:

1. *Page and section location.* This section of the status bar displays the page and section number of the current document view and shows how many pages the document contains. This does not show the position of the insertion point, just the location of the page currently shown in the window. Note that the page number refers to the physical page, not the numbered page (page numbers can be affected by page number format settings and the renumbering of sections in a document), and the section number refers to naturally occurring and forced section breaks throughout your document. See Chapter 2 for more information on sections.

   Double-click anywhere in this section to open the GoTo tab of the Find and Replace dialog box (Edit → Go To). Use the dialog box to go to any page or section in the document.

2. *Line and column location.* This section displays the location of the insertion point in the document:

   - The "At" number indicates the position relative to the vertical ruler, moving down the page.
   - The Line (Ln) number refers to the vertical position of the insertion point on the page. Word doesn't count blank lines, only lines containing text. Rows in a table do count as lines, whether they contain text or not.
   - The Column (Col) number indicates the horizontal position of the insertion point from the left margin.

3. *REC.* This refers to Macro Recorder. Double-click this block to open the Record Macro dialog box (double-click the block). When recording, REC turns bold to indicate that a recording is in progress. Double-click the block to stop the recording.

4. *TRK.* Word's Track Changes feature allows two or more people to maintain separate revisions on a document. Accepted changes are made a permanent part of the document. Rejected changes are deleted, restoring that portion of the document to its pre-edited state.

   If Track Changes is on, TRK is bold on the Status bar. Double-click the block to toggle Track Changes on and off. Right-click the block to open a context menu for working with Track Changes. Learn more about this and other collaborative features in Word in Chapter 13, *Collaborating.*

5. *EXT.* Double-click the Extend Selection block to toggle EXT on and off. While EXT is on, clicking the mouse selects all text between the insertion point and the place you click.

6. *OVR.* While the Overtype feature is on, any text typed mid-sentence wipes out an equal amount of the adjoining text. When OVR is off, text typed in

mid-sentence is inserted, and the text following the insertion point is moved to accommodate the new text (the default setting). Toggle this feature by double-clicking the OVR block or by pressing the Insert key.

TIP # 6

Watch the Overtype Indicator

Be sure Word is not in OVR mode when doing text insertions—it's a dangerous and destructive mode to work in, and with the ability to select text with your mouse and type replacement text, there are few practical applications for OVR mode.

7. *Spelling and grammar status.* If grammar and spell-checking is enabled, a book appears in this block, representing the spell-check process that occurs as you type. A small pencil moving over the book's pages indicates that text is being checked, a red X indicates that errors have been discovered, and a red check-mark indicates that text has been checked and no errors have been found.

   If spell-checking as you type is disabled, the book disappears. To hide spelling and grammar errors, or to set other spelling and grammar options, right-click the block and choose from the context menu. Double-click the block to jump to the next error in the document after the insertion point and automatically open a context menu with correction suggestions.

8. *Background save.* This area remains blank until you save a document, at which time a small picture of a 3.5" disk appears in the box. The disk also appears in this box during a background save. Background saves update the temporary version of the open file—the actual file is not updated until you choose File → Save or click the Save button.

   To control how often (and if) background saves are performed, choose Tools → Options → Save → "Allow background saves." Consider turning this feature off when working with large documents, as the time required for background saves may become inconvenient.

Installing Word

When you insert the Office 2000 CD-ROM, the installation program starts automatically and displays a series of installation dialog boxes that confirm the name and company name, ask for the CD key from the back of the CD case, and offer components to install.

Most of this is standard stuff, but Office 2000 does use the newly designed Windows Installer. The new installer provides a better way of selecting components to include in the installation and makes it easier to maintain installations later. The list of components to install is accompanied by a Windows Explorer–like system showing expandable sections under each main component (Figure 1-6).

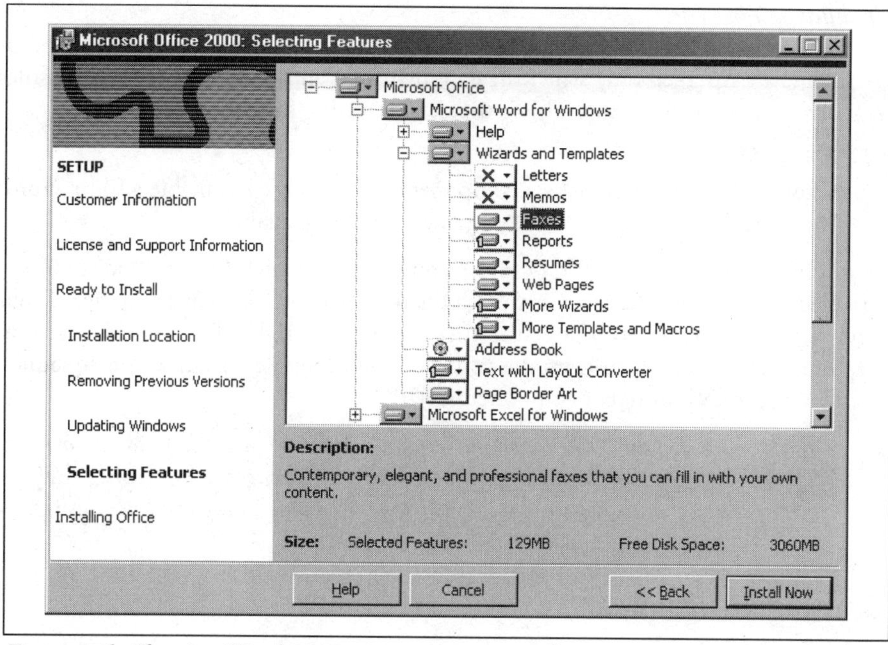

Figure 1-6: Choosing Word 2000 components to install

Install each component in a number of ways:

Run from My Computer
: This option installs the component on the local hard drive.

Run all from My Computer
: This option sets all components in a branch to install to the hard drive.

Run from Network
: You won't see this if you're installing on a PC that isn't networked. This option lets you run Word from a network server instead of from the local drive. Choose this only if you have continuous access to the network server.

Run all from Network
: This option installs every component of the selected branch on the network, not just the main program.

Run from CD
: This option causes the component to be run from the CD instead of from the hard drive each time it is used.

Run all from CD
: This option makes the selected branch of components run from the CD.

Installed on First Use
: This is a good option if you're not sure which components to choose. Components are installed only when they are first used and the Office installation files are required at that time. This is the default setting for many components.

Not Available
: Choose this option to make a component completely unavailable within Word. If you decide you want it later, you must run Setup again.

If you insert the Office 2000 CD into a computer on which Office 2000 is already installed, the autorun feature on the CD acts as if it will launch Setup again, but does not. To launch Setup after the first installation, right-click the CD drive in Explorer and choose Open from the context menu. Double-click *setup.exe* to launch it and add, remove, or repair components.

The Repair Office option reinstalls software according to its original configuration, repairing any corrupted or changed files. Word's Help → Detect and Repair command does the same thing and is covered in Chapter 12, Help.

Starting a Document

By default, Word opens a new, blank document each time it starts. This document contains many default settings, such as business-standard margins, single line-spacing, left-aligned tabs set to every half-inch, and a standard font (Times New Roman, 12 points).

Double-click an existing document in Windows Explorer to start the Word application and open the selected document directly. If the document is one you've worked on recently, check the *Documents* folder on the Start menu for a shortcut.

TIP # 7

Create Shortcuts to Documents

Storing documents on the Windows desktop seems like a good idea because it makes them instantly available for review, editing, or printing. However, it also makes them hard to organize. Instead, store the document in a better location and create a shortcut to the document on the desktop. To create a shortcut on the desktop, choose File → Open. In the dialog box that opens, right-click the document. Choose Send to → Desktop (Shortcut).

Major Word Sections and Task Lists

Word offers nine standard menus. The commands found within each one are described in detail throughout the various chapters of this book. The following sections present a mini-synopsis of each menu, the useful functions the menus provide, and where in the book to go for details.

File

Use the File menu to control Word files. Start, save, close, and print documents, edit document properties, and exit the Word program. The File menu's most frequently used commands are included as the first six commands on the Standard toolbar. These six commands also contain some anomalies. Normally, the menu command and the toolbar equivalent perform the same task in the same way. Not so with the New button and File → New, and the Print button and its menu companion, File → Print. In both cases, the menu command opens a dialog box for setting options and the button performs the command using default actions.

TIP # 8

Use the Shift Key for More File Menu Options

If you press and hold the Shift key before opening the File menu, the Close command becomes Close All (meaning all open documents) and the Save command becomes Save All. Use these changes to close and/or save all open documents without repeatedly opening the File menu.

Keyboard shortcuts

Create a new document: Ctrl-N
Open a document: Ctrl-O
Save a document: Ctrl-S
Save a document with a new name (Save As): F12
Print a document: Ctrl-P
Close the active document: Ctrl-F4
Exit Word: Alt-F4

File task list

Create a new document: Chapter 4, page 99
Open a document or search for a document: Chapter 4, page 101
Save a document: Chapter 4, page 107
Save as a document as a web page: Chapter 4, page 108
Save multiple versions of a document: Chapter 4, page 108
Preview a document before printing: Chapter 4, page 115
Preview and print a document: Chapter 4, page 116

Edit

The Edit menu offers the ability to undo previous actions (and redo any undone actions), select the entire document, delete content, and search your document for a particular word, phrase, or code, such as a paragraph mark or a non-breaking space.

The Edit menu's Cut, Copy, and Paste commands move document text around inside and between documents. In addition, you can paste objects from other applications, such as a section of an Excel worksheet or a PowerPoint chart, to a document and create a link to the source content by using the Paste Special command. The Edit menu also provides a way to maintain this linked content (Edit → Links), and to edit the linked object (Edit → Object).

Keyboard shortcuts

Undo last action: Ctrl-Z
Redo last undone action: Ctrl-Y
Cut content: Ctrl-X
Copy content: Ctrl-C
Paste cut or copied content: Ctrl-V
Select the entire document: Ctrl-A
Find specified text or formatting codes: Ctrl-F
Browse (Find) next item: Ctrl-Page Down
Browse (Find) previous item: Ctrl-Page Up
Replace found content with new content: Ctrl-H
Go to a particular page or section: Ctrl-G (or F5)

Edit task list

Undo the last action: Chapter 5, page 131
Cut, copy, and paste content: Chapter 5, page 132
Paste linked content: Chapter 5, page 134
Select an entire document: Chapter 5, page 137
Search a document for a particular word, phrase, or code: Chapter 5, page 137
Replace a word, phrase, or code with another: Chapter 5, page 140
Move to a particular page or section in a document: Chapter 5, page 141
Update or remove links to a document: Chapter 5, page 142

View

The View menu provides a series of commands for changing the way a document window looks and works. Choose from four main views, or turn off all onscreen tools and elements, showing only the document itself in Full Screen view. Toggle views of the ruler, comments, or any of Word's toolbars.

Finally, use the View menu to change the display size of a document. Zoom in close to make intricate changes in the position of a graphic, or zoom out to see a document's "big picture." The Zoom feature's Whole Page view is a great alternative to Print Preview, in that you can both see and edit the entire document.

Keyboard shortcuts

Change to Normal view: Alt-Ctrl-N
Change to Outline view: Alt-Ctrl-O
Change to Page Layout view: Alt-Ctrl-P

View task list

Change to Normal view: Chapter 6, page 146
Change to Print Layout view: Chapter 6, page 149
Change to Web Layout view: Chapter 6, page 148
Build a document outline: Chapter 6, page 151
Display various toolbars: Chapter 6, page 153
Turn on the ruler: Chapter 6, page 153
Open the Document Map: Chapter 6, page 154
Create a header and/or footer for a document: Chapter 6, page 155
View comments for a document: Chapter 6, page 159
Change to Full Screen view: Chapter 6, page 160
View multiple pages of a document, or use zoom on a single page: Chapter 6, page 161

Insert

The list of items you can insert in a document is extensive—everything from the date and time, to a scanned image, to a link that accesses a web site when clicked.

One of the Insert menu's most powerful commands is Insert → Object, which inserts content from another application. Add a blank object and build it using the native application's tools (which appear within the Word application window), or add an object from an existing file.

Keyboard shortcuts

Insert a page break: Ctrl-Enter
Insert a Bookmark: Ctrl-Shift-F5
Insert AutoText: F3 or Alt-Ctrl-V
Insert a Hyperlink: Ctrl-K

Insert task list

Force a page break within a document: Chapter 7, page 164
Insert page numbers: Chapter 7, page 166
Create or insert an AutoText entry: Chapter 7, page 169
Insert a field: Chapter 7, page 173
Insert a special character or symbol: Chapter 7, page 174
Create a footnote or endnote: Chapter 7, page 177
Place a caption with a figure or table: Chapter 7, page 178
Generate a table of contents or index: Chapter 7, page 181
Add clip art or other graphic elements: Chapter 7, page 186
Create a cross-reference to another part of a document: Chapter 7, page 179
Insert an object from another application: Chapter 7, page 195
Bookmark your document: Chapter 7, page 196
Insert a hyperlink to another file or a web site: Chapter 7, page 197

Format

There are several levels of formatting in Word. Format individual characters by applying different fonts, text colors, and font sizes. Format paragraphs by applying indents, tabs, and styles. Format sections with page layout and margin settings.

The Format menu also customizes the way Word automatically formats a document (a.k.a. AutoFormat)—making such changes as converting fractions to symbols (1/2 to ½), displaying web addresses as hyperlinks, and automatically numbering or bulleting lists as you type.

While the most commonly used formatting commands are represented on the Formatting toolbar, you'll find that the Format menu's dialog boxes provide an extensive set of tools for changing fonts, setting alignments, and applying colors and borders to text. The toolbar equivalents are often faster to use, but they don't offer the options and the same degree of control over how the formats are applied.

Keyboard shortcuts

Open the Font dialog box: Ctrl-D
Change the case of text: Shift-F3
Perform an AutoFormat: Alt-Ctrl-K

Format task list

Format characters and words: Chapter 8, page 201
Format paragraphs: Chapter 8, page 205
Apply character and paragraph styles: Chapter 8, page 231
Set indents, alignment, and line spacing: Chapter 8, page 205
Change bullet character, size, and color: Chapter 8, page 208
Apply custom borders and shading: Chapter 8, page 211
Convert paragraph text to columns: Chapter 8, page 214
Set custom tabs: Chapter 8, page 216
Change the case of selected text: Chapter 8, page 220
Apply a background to a web page: Chapter 8, page 221
Choose a theme for a document: Chapter 8, page 224
Apply and customize Word's AutoFormat settings: Chapter 8, page 230
Format the selected graphic, text box, AutoShape, or other object: Chapter 8, page 235

Tools

The Tools menu provides access to most of the commands in Word that don't involve inserting objects, formatting text, using tables, or working with files. These commands include spelling and grammar checking, online collaboration tools, mail merge, and macros.

The Tools menu also contains commands for setting various Word options and for customizing Word's menus and toolbars. The multi-tabbed Tools → Options dialog, for example, contains settings that control the way Word looks and works. The Options Dialog controls the basics, such as where files are saved, and which application window elements are displayed, as well as the settings that are a matter of personal taste and need, including how and when the spelling and grammar checking feature works.

Keyboard shortcuts

Spelling and Grammar: F7
Open the Thesaurus: Shift-F7
Open the Macros dialog box: Alt-F8
Open the Visual Basic Editor window: Alt-F11
Open the Microsoft Script Editor window: Alt-Shift-F11

Tools task list

Spell-check a document: Chapter 9, page 243
Find a synonym with the Thesaurus: Chapter 9, page 247
Change the language settings for Word: Chapter 9, page 246
Get a word count for a document: Chapter 9, page 249
Create an automatic summary: Chapter 9, page 250
Create or edit an AutoCorrect entry: Chapter 9, page 251
Change AutoFormat settings: Chapter 9, page 251
Collaborate with coworkers: Chapter 13, page 319
Merge different versions of a document: Chapter 13, page 331
Use mail merge to create form letters or labels: Chapter 9, page 257
Record a new macro: Chapter 18, page 399
Customize Word's interface: Chapter 3, page 78
Change Word's application and document options: Chapter 3, page 56

Table

Use the Table menu to control complex lists, create forms, or even provide layout for a page. Create formulas that reference cells within the table, referring to the cells by their column letters and row numbers, just like in an Excel worksheet.

Rather than setting indents to control the horizontal and vertical flow of text, create a table to house the text, and use the easily adjusted width of the table columns to control where text falls on the page.

The Table menu contains commands for drawing "freehand" tables or inserting a specified number of uniform columns and rows. There are also tools for changing the size and appearance of table columns and rows, and for converting tabbed text to tables.

Keyboard shortcuts

None

File task list

Draw a cell or block of cells: Chapter 10, page 277
Insert a uniform table: Chapter 10, page 278
Delete rows or columns: Chapter 10, page 282
Delete a table: Chapter 10, page 282
Insert columns or rows: Chapter 10, page 279
Merge table cells: Chapter 10, page 284
Split table cells: Chapter 10, page 285
Format a table automatically: Chapter 10, page 286
Convert between text and table format: Chapter 10, page 290
Sort table rows: Chapter 10, page 292
Perform a calculation within a table: Chapter 10, page 293
View and edit table properties: Chapter 10, page 295

Window

Use the Window menu to switch between open Word documents and choose how to display multiple open documents. The New Window command creates a duplicate window for the active document. Work in either window and scroll to view different portions of the same document.

Keyboard shortcuts

Switch between open documents: Alt-Esc or Alt-Tab

Window task list

Open a duplicate window of the active document: Chapter 11, page 300
Arrange a group of windows for easier viewing: Chapter 11, page 301
Split a document window into separate panes: Chapter 11, page 302
Switch between open documents: Chapter 11, page 304

Help

By default, help comes through an animated Office Assistant in which you type a question and choose a help topic from those offered in response. Alternatively, turn the Assistant off and use a more traditional help window. If none of the articles offered meet your needs, search for help on the Web from Microsoft's tech support site.

Other help features include special tools for WordPerfect users, a What's This feature that opens ScreenTips explaining interface elements and character formatting, and the Detect and Repair command, which searches for problems in Word's application files and attempts to fix them.

Keyboard shortcuts

Open Word Help: F1
Activate What's This? Help: Shift-F1

Help task list

Start Word Help: Chapter 12, page 305
Hide the Office Assistant: Chapter 12, page 310
Invoke What's This? Help: Chapter 12, page 310
Run Detect and Repair: Chapter 12, page 315
View the Word version and System information: Chapter 12, page 315
Go to the Microsoft Office help pages on the Web: Chapter 12, page 311

Chapter 2

How Word Works

It's surprising how many Word users I know (and I mean long-time, sophisticated users) who still get annoyed with many of Word's little quirks and yet never try to figure out what Word is really doing. Instead, they accept these quirks as a matter of course and almost subconsciously correct any errors that result.

For example, try selecting two consecutive paragraphs by dragging the pointer over them, cutting (or copying) them, and then pasting them somewhere else in the document. Notice that Word doesn't copy the formatting of the second paragraph, but does for the first paragraph. Many users do this over and over again, get annoyed by it, and fix it each time by manually reapplying the style or formatting to the second paragraph. There is a pretty easy way around this (and you'll learn it later in the chapter), but until you learn what Word is doing, it's not easy to see the solutions to these kinds of problems.

This chapter takes an under-the-hood look at Word. Among other things, it covers:

Global architecture
: Each time you start Word, it actually creates a new interface, based on built-in program information, global templates (like *normal.dot*), user-defined templates, and document settings.

Files
: All kinds of information besides text are stored in Word files, including graphics and inserted objects. Every Word document also has an attached template file that controls the styles, toolbars, and macros in that document. In addition, Word uses temporary (*.tmp*) and AutoRecover files to help ensure that documents are kept safe while editing.

Parts of a document
: Word maintains separate layers for text and drawings. Various types of objects can be inserted in these different layers. Within the text layer, Word breaks documents down into three parts for formatting purposes: sections, paragraphs, and characters. Styles are used to quickly apply formatting to both characters and paragraphs.

Word's Global Architecture

When using Word, you are looking at the program through several layers, the current document being closest to you. All of these layers combine to form Word's *global layer*, the overall interface that is built and presented each time Word starts and a document is created (or opened). Basically, the global layer is built like this:

1. When Word first starts, it begins to build the interface based on the built-in application layer. The basic Word interface and all of the menus, toolbars and commands are programmatically loaded on the screen based on settings in the program files and the Windows Registry.

2. Word then finds the *normal.dot* template and adds it into the interface. Any custom commands, toolbars, and options override those in the application layer.

3. Word then looks at files in *\Program Files\Microsoft Office\Office\Startup* (the default location—change it using Tools → Options → User Location). It first loads any *.dot* (template) files in alphabetical order and then any *.dll* and COM add-in files, also in alphabetical order. Any customizations in these files override those built so far. For example, if a file named *a.dot* and a file named *b.dot* both exist in the startup folder, *a.dot's* customizations are loaded and then *b.dot's* customizations are loaded, overriding *a.dot's*.

4. Once these three steps are complete, Word has officially loaded, assuming Word starts without opening a document at the same time. At this point, additional templates and add-ins can be manually loaded using Tools → Templates and Add-Ins → Add.

TIP # 9

Start Word Without Loading Components

Launch Word from the command line using the /a switch (word.exe /a) to start up without loading normal.dot, templates in the Startup folder, add-in libraries, or user settings stored in the Registry. See the sidebar "Starting Word from the Command Line," later in this chapter, for details on other switches and how to use them.

5. After adding any templates and add-ins manually, Word's global layer is pretty much built. Create a new document (or open an existing document) and any templates attached to that document are loaded. For example, start a new contemporary letter using Word's built-in template, and *Contemporary Letter.dot* is added to the global layer. Open an existing document, and any template attached to it is loaded.

6. Finally, when opening an existing document, any customizations within the document itself (as opposed to within the template attached to that document) are loaded.

Any customizations, styles, etc. applied to the current document override those found in the current template, which in turn override settings found in *normal.dot*, which in turn override those found in the application itself.

Consider this example: the key combination Ctrl-N has the built-in effect of creating a new blank document. This is part of the application layer. You could customize that keystroke to do something different (like apply a certain style) and save that customization as part of *normal.dot*. Whenever you used the key combination in any document in Word, it would now apply that style. If, however, you customized Ctrl-N to do something different (like switch to Outline view) and saved that customization as part of the document template (assuming the document template is not *normal.dot*), then the key combination would have that effect in any document to which the template is attached. In other words, customizations in the current template would override customizations in *normal.dot*. Likewise, customizations in the current document would override even customizations in the document template.

I can almost hear you saying, "Great—but what's it mean to me?" When customizing the Word interface, creating custom templates, or creating macros or custom scripts, this basic understanding of how Word builds itself can help solve any number of weird events.

Word Files

When starting a new document, Word creates a temporary *AutoRecover* file in the *\Windows\Temp* folder, which is used to recover document information should Word crash. The first time a new document is saved, Word also creates two other files. The first is the document itself, which takes an extension based on the type of document you create (*.doc* for Word files, *.dot* for templates, *.rtf* for rich text files, and so on). Next, Word creates a temporary file in the same folder as the document. It holds all of the work done inside a document between saves.

Documents

You are probably most familiar with the *document* file. A document file is created and named whenever a new document is saved for the first time. There are lots of things you can do with a file in Word, mainly by using the File menu. For detailed information on manipulating files with Word, check out Chapter 4, *File*. In this section, though, we're going to take a look at what goes into a file (how Word itself uses the file) and what can be done with the file from *outside* Word (i.e., from Windows itself).

A document file contains the text you type, but it can also contain:

- Characters that are typed and characters that aren't, such as paragraph marks, tab marks, section marks, and more. These are covered a bit later in the chapter.
- Formatting applied to those characters, whether it is applied directly through character formatting or indirectly through paragraph formatting.

Starting Word from the Command Line

Like most programs, Word can be started from the Windows command line (Start → Programs → "MS-DOS Prompt" in Windows 95/98 and Start → Progams → Accessories → "Command Prompt" in Windows 2000). At the prompt, just type *winword.exe* to launch Word normally. There are also a number of startup switches that affect how Word launches:

/a Start Word and prevent add-ins and global templates from loading. The switch also locks the settings files, so that no settings may be modified when Word is started with this switch.

/l addinpath
Start Word normally and load a specific add-in or global template. For example, using `winword.exe /l c:\word\newglobal.dot` would load a template named *newglobal.dot* found in the *c:\word* folder.

/m Start Word without running any AutoExec macros, which are macros set to run when Word starts or when a particular document opens. This can also be done by holding down the Shift key while starting Word normally.

/m macroname
Start Word without running any AutoExec macros and have Word run a specific macro on starting.

/n Start a new instance of Word with no document open. Documents opened in each instance of Word will not appear as choices in the Window menu of other instances.

/q Start Word and suppress the slash screen. This switch is new in OSR-1.

/t template name
Start Word with a new document based on a template other than *normal.dot*.

/w Start a new instance of Word with a blank document. Documents opened in each instance of Word will not appear as choices in the Window menu of the other instances.

Another way to use startup switches is to create a shortcut to the *winword.exe* executable in Windows (in any open folder, choose New → Shortcut). Once the shortcut is created, right-click it and open its Properties dialog from the context menu. In the Target field, add the switch to the end of the executable path. Whenever you launch that shortcut, Word starts with the assigned switch.

- Formatting applied to the sections in a document. This includes section location and page layout information such as margins and alignment.
- Styles defined in the document itself or copied from the template the document is based on.
- Customizations made in the document or copied from the template the document is based on.
- Macros defined in the document or in the template attached to the document.
- Different versions of the document created using the File → Versions command.
- True Type fonts used in the document if the Tools → Options → Save → "Embed True Type Fonts" option is enabled.
- Form fields and the data entered in them.
- A preview picture of the document if the File → Properties → Summary → Save Preview Picture option is enabled.
- Graphics embedded in the document using the Insert → Picture command.

Obviously, a lot of stuff is (or can be) saved in a document file. This helps explain how document files can quickly grow to a large size even when you haven't written very much.

A document file can hold many of the same items as a template. In fact, documents usually do contain all of the customizations, macros, etc. that exist in the template they are attached to. All of that information is copied to the document file. The only thing that a document cannot contain but a template can is formatted AutoText entries.

Why, then, even use templates? There are two reasons. First, it is much easier to base a new document on a template than on another document. Second, you can quickly attach new templates to existing documents. All of this is covered in the section on templates later in this chapter.

There are a few things that can be done with a document file outside the realm of Word. For starters, double-click the file to launch Word and open the file. Issue the print command from the file's context menu to quickly open the file, print it using Word's default print settings, and then close it again. This is just like choosing the Print button on the Standard toolbar. Finally, open a file's property sheet by right-clicking the file and choosing Properties from the context menu. One of two things happens on opening the property sheet:

- If the file is not currently open in Word, property pages are shown that duplicate the ones available within Word by choosing File → Properties. In addition, a General tab is added that includes the file's Windows properties.
- If the file is currently open in Word, the property sheet has only a General tab. Word properties are not available outside Word while the document is open.

All of Word's property sheets are detailed in Chapter 4. The General tab shows standard Windows information about the file, including the name, type, location, and size, as well as the dates that the file was created, last modified, and last accessed (Figure 2-1). At the bottom of the tab are options to make the file Read-only (you can open the file, but not save any changes), Hidden (not visible in the Windows folder unless View → Folder Options → View → Show all files is turned on), and Archive. The Archive option is used by backup programs and other software to determine whether a file has been changed.

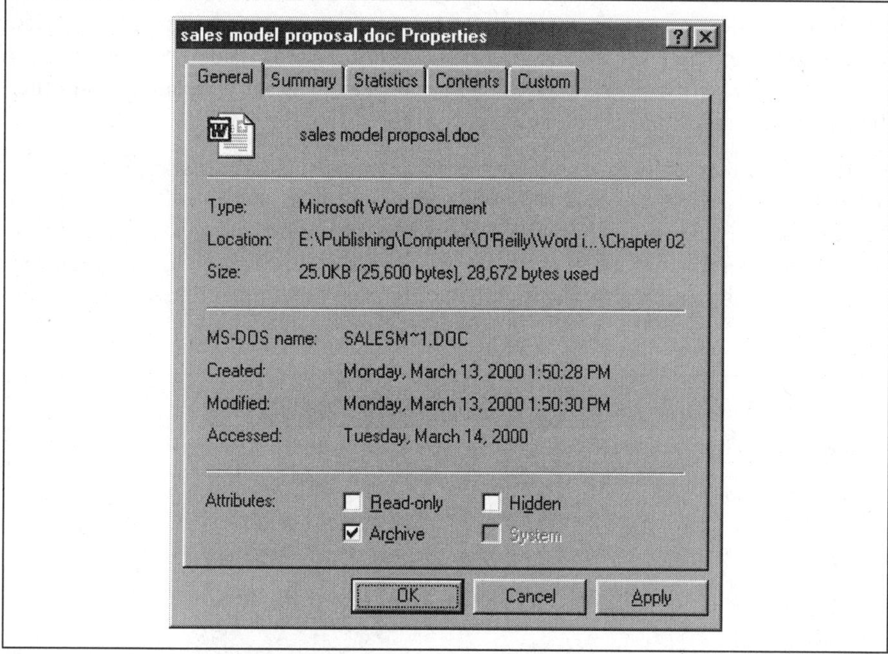

Figure 2-1: Viewing a document file's property sheet

Templates

Every document in Word is based on a *template* (a file with a *.dot* extension) or, as is said in Word, each document has a template *attached* to it. Create a new default document by clicking the New button on the Standard toolbar or using File → New and choosing the Blank Document template. Word creates that new document based on the global template *normal.dot*. Documents can also be based on a number of other built-in Word templates or on custom templates you create yourself.

By default, a template has a *.dot* extension and can contain styles, macros, formatted AutoText entries, customizations, and boilerplate text—to name just a few things. Starting a new document based on one template and then attaching another template to it instead changes styles and everything else associated with the template in one shot.

Word uses several different types of templates, including *normal.dot*, other global templates, and user and workgroup templates. When working with templates, though, it is important to keep in mind that there is really no structural difference between the different types of templates. A template is just a file with a *.dot* extension and they are all basically the same. Templates differ not in what they are, but in how they are used.

Global templates

Global templates are loaded into Word's global layer and are not necessarily attached to a document. To make all of the juicy elements of a template (styles, macros, etc.) available to all documents currently loaded, load the template as a global template. There is really nothing special that makes a template global other than that it is loaded in this manner.

There are two ways to load a global template: manually, or automatically each time Word starts. To load a global template manually, open Tools → Templates and Add-Ins (see Figure 2-2). Click the Add button to browse for any *.dot* file. Click OK and that template is added and becomes a global template (which, as you can see now, really just means that it is globally available to all open documents as long as it is loaded).

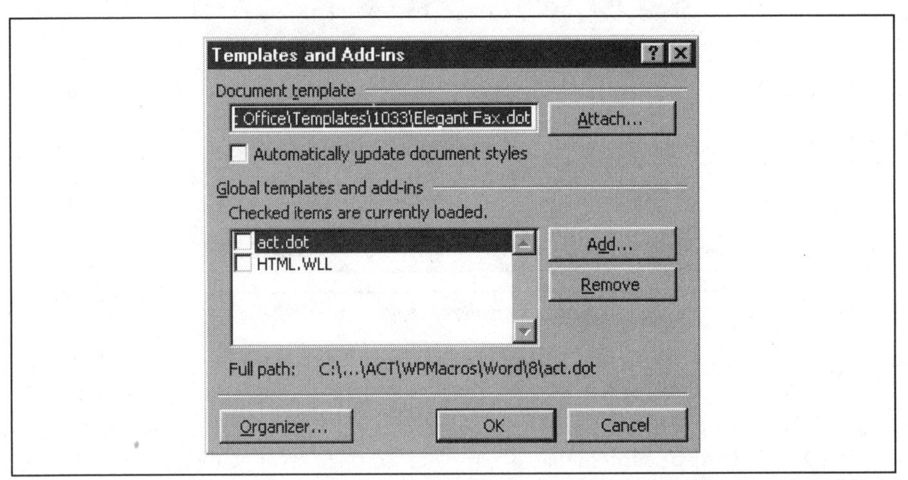

Figure 2-2: Loading a global template manually using Tools → Templates and Add-Ins

Other actions available in the Templates and Add-ins dialog include:

- Unload a global template by selecting the template from the list and clicking Remove.
- Temporarily deactivate a global template by clearing the checkbox beside it.
- Attach a different document template to the current document by clicking attach (more about this a bit later).

- Have Word automatically update any styles in the document whenever the styles in the template attached to the document are updated (also more on this later).
- Open Word's Style Organizer, which is discussed in Chapter 8, *Format*.

TIP # 10

Load Global Templates Automatically When Word Starts

To have Word automatically load a global template every time the application starts, just put it in the \Program Files\Microsoft Office\Office\Startup folder or whatever startup folder is designated using Tools → Options → User Locations.

Normal.dot

As you've no doubt surmised, *normal.dot* is an awfully important template. At its heart, though, it is really no different from any other Word template. In fact, you can create a new template, name it *normal.dot*, replace the old file with the new one, and Word uses it with no problems.

What distinguishes *normal.dot* from other templates is, again, how it's used. It is the default global template loaded with Word and, in fact, is loaded every time Word starts. It is not loaded via the startup folder or the Templates and Add-ins dialog; instead it is loaded programmatically. You can't deactivate or unload it as you can with other templates. Delete it from the hard drive and Word just creates a new one the next time it starts up. Make a customization and save it in *normal.dot* and that customization is available in all documents all the time. It is the primary filter through which you work with the Word application.

WARNING

While it's true that Word creates a new normal.dot if you delete yours, don't try this without backing up your normal.dot first. When Word creates a new one, it does so based on default settings and you will lose all customizations you may have made to the old file (and this usually means most customizations made with Word in general).

In addition to all of this, *normal.dot* also receives some other special treatment:

- AutoCorrect entries that have any formatting or pictures applied to them are stored in *normal.dot*. This means that after reinstalling Word or moving to another computer, you can bring files along to hold on to these entries. It also means that if you use a lot of long, formatted AutoCorrect entries, the *normal.dot* file quickly swells to a significant size. This can adversely affect Word performance, as pretty much everything done in Word somehow relates to *normal.dot*. AutoCorrect is covered in detail in Chapter 9, *Tools*.

Only formatted AutoCorrect entries (and those with pictures) are stored in normal.dot. Unformatted entries are stored in an access control list (.acl) file named for your Windows username—something like username.acl. This allows unformatted entries to be made available to other Office applications. Formatted entries are only available within Word.

- AutoText (that's AutoText, not AutoCorrect) entries are stored by default in *normal.dot*. This can also increase file size, but AutoText entries can easily be moved to another (or even their own) template to load and unload when you want. If a document is based on a template other than *normal.dot*, AutoText entries can be saved to it instead. AutoText is covered in Chapter 7, *Insert*.
- Since *normal.dot* is a permanent global template and it is loaded first, customizations performed on *normal.dot* are always available (unless overridden) in other documents and templates. Also, remove any functionality from *normal.dot* (say, by removing a menu command) and that functionality will be missing from other templates and documents unless specifically added to them.
- Since many options and customizations are stored in *normal.dot*, Word must save the file each time Word closes or discard any unsaved changes. By default, Word saves *normal.dot* automatically when the program closes. If you want some control over this process, turn on the Tools → Options → Save → "Prompt to save normal template" option. This makes Word open a dialog each time it closes asking whether it should save changes. Unfortunately, Word does not show you what those changes are; you just have to remember. Personally, I use the default setting and just let Word handle things.

Document templates

Document template is simply the name given to the template attached to the current document. The items within this template are available only within that document (of course, the template could be loaded globally, providing its items to all open documents, or attached to another specific document).

Every new document is based on a template. Create a new blank document and it is based on *normal.dot*. Create a different style of document using Word's File → New command (Figure 2-3), and the document is based on whatever template that type of document is assigned to. Create a template based on one of Word's wizards, and Word asks for some information and then creates the document using a template.

Most of the items in the File → New dialog are actually templates. Selecting one creates a new document based on the template. The templates appearing in the New dialog are either built-in Word templates or exist in either of two folders: a user templates folder or a workgroup templates folder. Word actually classifies document templates into two basic categories based on these locations, though there is no real difference between the templates. Here's the rundown:

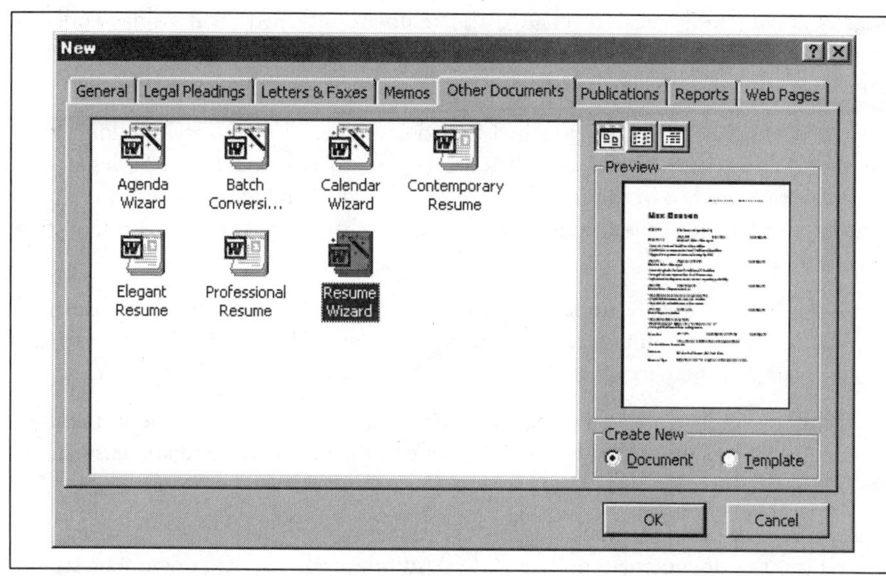

Figure 2-3: Creating a new file with File → New

- User templates are intended to be templates that an individual user stores on his or her local computer. By default, Word stores these templates in the *\Windows\Application Data\Microsoft\Templates* folder or the *\Windows\Profiles\UserName\Application Data\Microsoft\Templates* folder, if the computer is configured for multiple users. Any template stored in this location appears on the General tab along with the standard blank templates. Any folder (or shortcut to a folder) created in this directory that includes at least one template becomes a tab in the new document dialog box. Change the default user templates folder using Tools → Options → User Locations.
- Workgroup templates are intended to be templates stored on a network server and be available to all members of a workgroup. By default, no specific folder is assigned for workgroup templates, though you can assign one using Tools → Options → User Locations. Other than the fact that it is intended for use by multiple users, the workgroup templates folder works the same as the user templates folder.

TIP # 11

Set Templates to Read-Only

It's usually a good idea set up templates in a workgroup folder as read-only, both to prevent modification and to allow more than one person to use a template at once. To do this, right-click the template in Windows Explorer and choose Properties from the context menu. On the General tab of the dialog that opens, select the "Read-Only" option.

Once a document is created, change the template attached to it using Tools → Templates and Add-Ins (see Figure 2-2). Click the Attach button to pick any template to attach to the current document.

When a new template is first attached to a document, all of the styles (along with macros, toolbars, etc.) in the template are copied to the document. Styles in the document that are not in the template are unaffected. If the template and the document have styles that have the same name but have different properties, one of two things happens:

- If the "Automatically update document styles" option on the Templates and Add-ins dialog is not selected, nothing happens. The conflicting style in the template is not copied to the document and the document keeps its style.
- If the option is turned on, the style in the template *replaces* the style in the document. This is important because the style in the document and any customizations made to it are lost.

Thereafter, style changes made within the document do not affect (and are not affected by) the document template *if* the "Automatically update document styles" option is off. Turn it on to have the styles in the document updated based on those in the template *each time* the document is opened.

Temporary Files

Whenever a file is opened or created, Word creates a temporary version of the file that exists only while the document is open. It contains all of the work done since the file was opened or created. Save the document and the original version of the file is updated to include changes to that point. Close the document at this point and the temporary file is deleted.

If Windows Explorer View → Folder Options is set to show hidden objects, you can see the temporary files while documents are open (Figure 2-4). They appear on the right side of the Windows Explorer window and have the same name as the open files. The only difference is that the first letter of the filename is replaced by a tilde (~) and the second letter is replaced by a dollar sign. The file icon also appears dimmed, indicating that it is hidden. If the temporary files remain in a folder after the document is closed (normally due to Word crashing while files are open), delete them. Word won't allow the deletion of a temporary file for an open document.

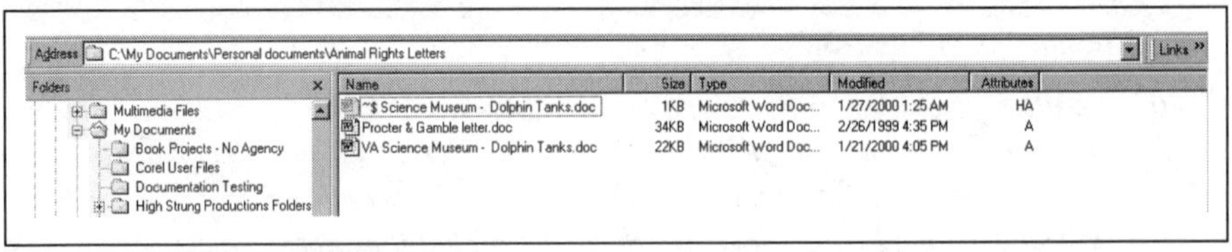

Figure 2-4: Viewing temporary files

TIP # 12

Can't Open or Save a File?

Word often leaves .tmp files lying around (after a crash, for example). If you find that a document won't open or save, try looking in the document's folder for a left-over .tmp file and deleting it. Word also uses temporary files to determine the state of a document. If a .tmp file for a document exists in the folder with a document, Word assumes the file is in use. Try to open the file and Word tells you the file is in use and offers to open a read-only copy instead. You can't save the file in the same location with the same filename. If you try, Word opens the Save As dialog instead.

AutoRecover Files

In addition to the normal temporary file, an AutoRecover version of each open document is saved in the *\Windows \Temp* folder. Word deletes AutoRecover files, like *.tmp* files, when the document is closed. The AutoRecover version of the file is updated based on the AutoRecover setting found under Tools → Options → Save (Figure 2-5). Enter a period in minutes (the default is 10) to adjust the frequency. If these automatic saves are slowing things down (if memory is at a premium, Word may pause briefly while the save is occurring), turn AutoRecover off by removing the checkmark next to the option.

I recommend leaving AutoRecover on, given the frequency with which Word tends to crash. If you are working on an important document (and perhaps on a flaky system), set the AutoRecover frequency lower and live with the inconvenience. I also recommend making it a habit to press Ctrl-S once in a while to save the document normally.

If Word does crash while a document is open, the best recourse is just to restart Windows itself and then restart Word. Word detects that it closed improperly and opens any existing AutoRecover files. These files should have all of the work done up to the time of the last AutoRecover save.

Unlike *.tmp* files, AutoRecover files are named according to an internal mechanism and it is often difficult to tell which file goes with what document. However, since Word deletes AutoRecover files whenever a document is saved, the chances are there won't be too many AutoRecover files to sift through. Your best bet is to turn on the Details view in Windows Explorer and check the modification times when searching for a specific document. Better yet, just open all the files.

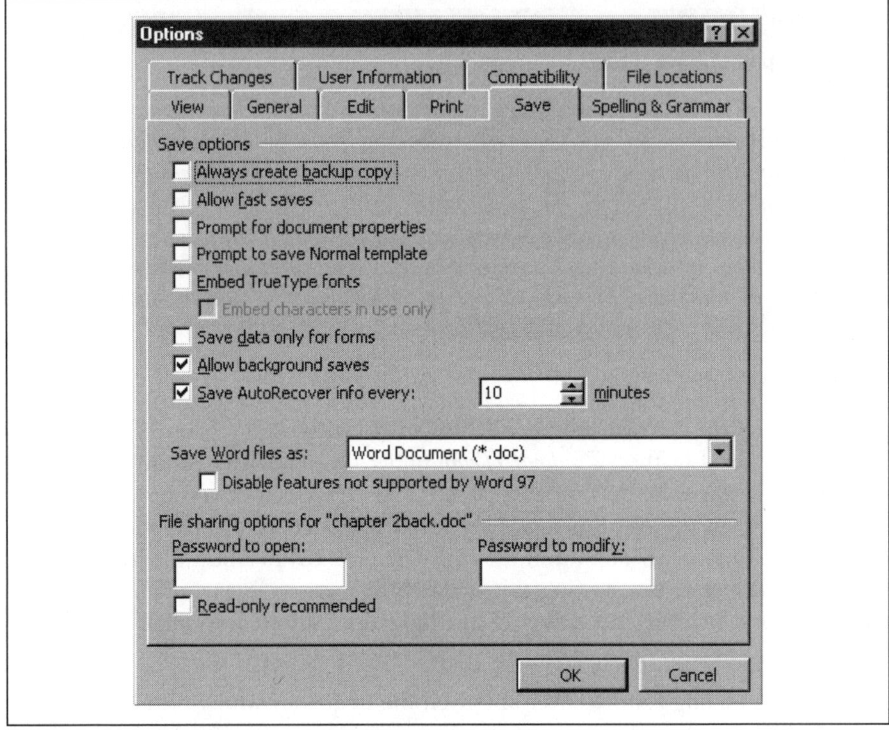

Figure 2-5: Adjusting the timing of AutoRecover saves

TIP # 13

Allowing Fast Saves

Another option in Tools → Options → Save is "Allow fast saves." This feature speeds up saving by recording only the changes made in a document during the current session. When you have finished working in the document, clear the "Allow fast saves" checkbox to force Word to perform a full save, which may decrease the file size of the document. See Chapter 3, Customizing Word, for more on using this feature.

The Word Document

As discussed earlier, whenever a document is opened or created, Word creates a global layer as the application starts up. Documents themselves also contain a number of layers that are unrelated to Word's global layer. After the document is established, you'll interact with text, drawing, and header/footer layers for the purposes of building content. In this section, we'll take a look at the interaction of those layers and then delve deeper into the parts of the document.

Document Layers

Every Word document contains six different layers that when stacked on top of one another produce a page similar to the illustration shown in Figure 2-6.

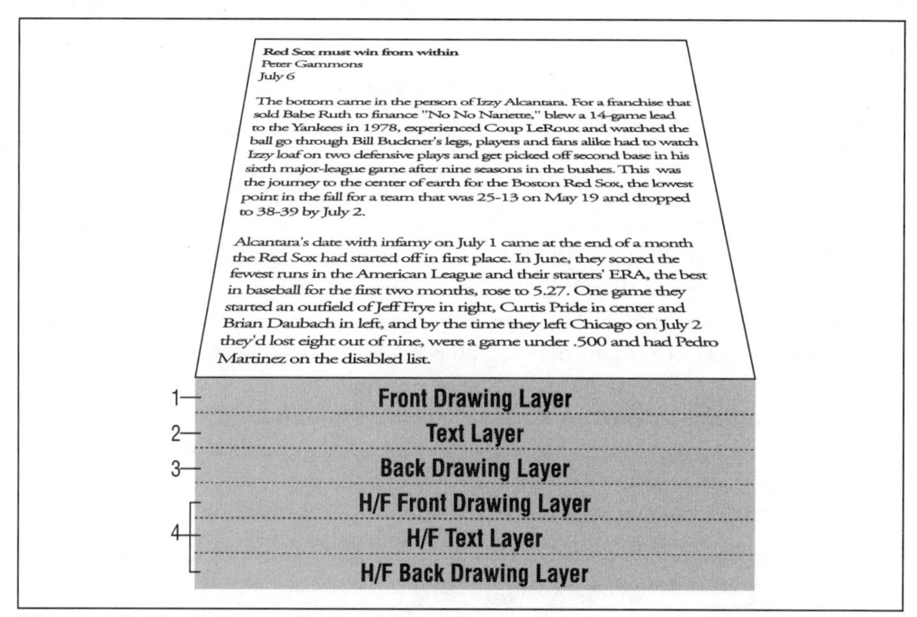

Figure 2-6: The six layers of a document

The following list shows the layers of a Word document from top to bottom:

1. *Front Drawing Layer.* Think of this layer as a transparency laid on top of the text layer of a document. Only floating objects, such as drawings or text boxes, exist in this layer. If an object is in this layer, it appears in front of the text of the document.

2. *Main Text Layer.* This layer usually contains the text of a document, though text is often placed in floating text boxes in drawing layers. In addition to text, you can place inline and framed objects in this layer. These objects are discussed in the next section.

3. *Back Drawing Layer.* This is the transparency laid behind the text layer of your document. Only floating objects exist in this layer. If an object is in this layer, it appears behind the text of the document.

4. *Header/Footer Layers.* These three layers work identically to the three main layers, except that they are positioned behind the main back drawing layer. This means that any objects or text in the main drawing or text layers will always obscure objects and text in the header/footer layers.

Objects

Object is a generic term used to describe something other than text inserted or pasted into a document. Common objects include pictures, drawings, PowerPoint slides, and so on. In Word 2000, there are three basic types of objects: floating, inline, and framed.

This section is intended to provide a basic understanding of the way objects are used in a Word document. For specific procedural information on using these objects, see Chapter 7.

Inline objects

Inline objects appear in line with the text in the main text layer and behave as though they were a single character. The insertion point moves over an inline object just like it moves over a character. Text does not wrap around inline objects. With the exception of text boxes and drawing objects (WordArt, Charts, etc.), all objects are inserted as inline objects by default. For example, use the Insert → Picture → From File command to insert a separate graphic file into a document, and that graphic is inserted as an inline object. To verify this, right-click the graphic and choose Format Picture from the context menu. On the Layout tab (Figure 2-7), the "In line with text" wrapping style is selected, indicating an inline object.

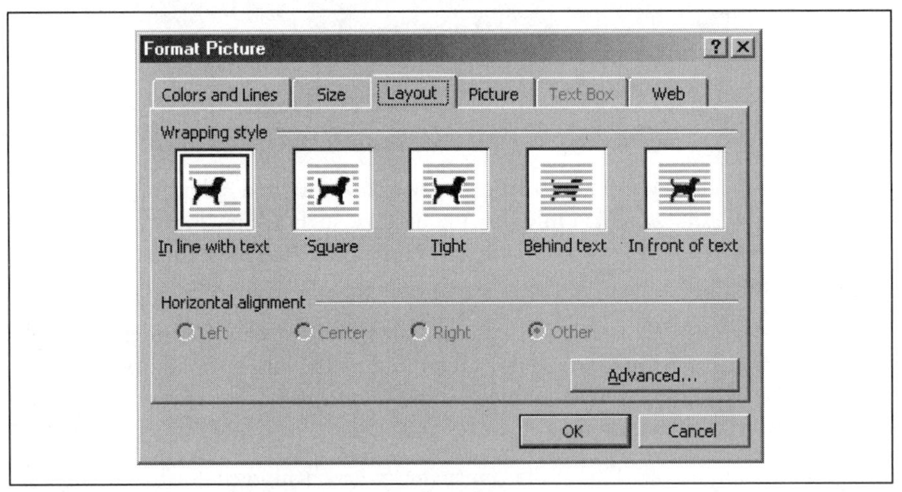

Figure 2-7: Viewing the wrapping style of an object

Inline objects are best used when the object should behave as a character, since inline objects can be moved and formatted in the same way as characters. For example, you might want to format the object using tabs, indents, and paragraph or character formatting.

Framed objects

Like inline objects, framed objects appear only in the main text layer. However, in contrast to inline objects, text always wraps around framed objects. Framed objects are really a holdover from previous versions of Word that did not include any drawing layers and for general use, floating objects have replaced framed objects. However, since framed objects can include addressable field codes, they are still quite useful at times.

Floating objects

Floating objects exist only in Word's drawing layers and can be dragged around and placed pretty much anywhere. In addition, floating objects can be stacked on top of one another within a layer. For example, suppose there are two objects in the back drawing layer (behind the text): one a background graphic for a newsletter and the other a text box with an advertisement. Those two objects could be stacked so that the graphic appeared behind the textbox, creating an additional layering effect even though both objects are on the same drawing layer (Figure 2-8).

Figure 2-8: Stacking floating objects within a layer

Floating objects are often tacked to the text layer through the use of *anchors*. If, for example, you draw a shape or create a piece of WordArt, the image is anchored to the paragraph containing the insertion point at the time the item is created. Drag the shape or image to another spot in the document, and the image anchors to the text in the new location.

This may sound fine, but if you then move the paragraph to which the image is anchored—say by adding text in front of it—the image moves with the paragraph, which may not be the desired effect. Sometimes, objects can even obscure text (Figure 2-9). You can change the behavior of an object (including unlocking the anchor to the surrounding text) by selecting the object and choosing Format → Object. The use of objects and anchors is detailed in Chapter 7.

TIP # 14

View Drawing Layer Object Anchors

View drawing layer anchors (and therefore anticipate their effect on text and drawn images as a document is edited) by choosing Tools → Options → View → Object Anchor. Use the Print Layout view to get an idea of how images will look in a printed document. In Figure 2-9, an anchor character in the margin shows the paragraph the selected image is anchored to.

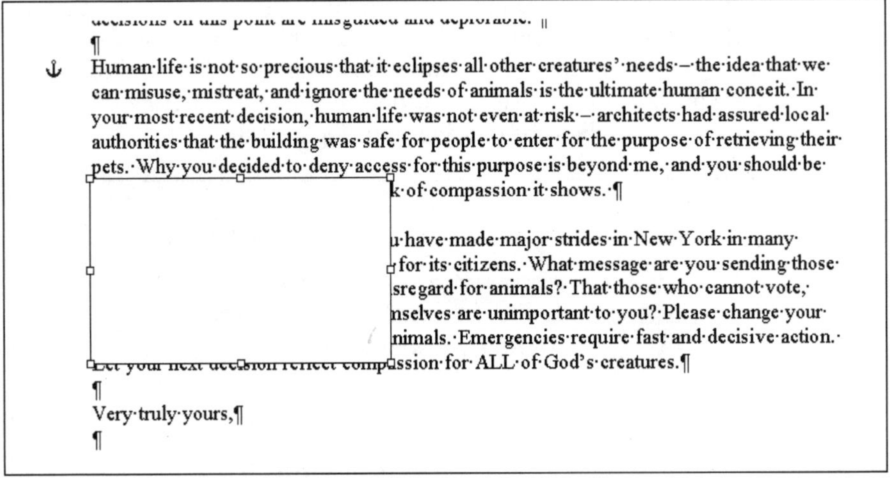

¶
Human·life·is·not·so·precious·that·it·eclipses·all·other·creatures'·needs·—·the·idea·that·we·can·misuse,·mistreat,·and·ignore·the·needs·of·animals·is·the·ultimate·human·conceit.·In·your·most·recent·decision,·human·life·was·not·even·at·risk·—·architects·had·assured·local·authorities·that·the·building·was·safe·for·people·to·enter·for·the·purpose·of·retrieving·their·pets.·Why·you·decided·to·deny·access·for·this·purpose·is·beyond·me,·and·you·should·be·
k·of·compassion·it·shows.·¶
u·have·made·major·strides·in·New·York·in·many·
for·its·citizens.·What·message·are·you·sending·those·
sregard·for·animals?·That·those·who·cannot·vote,·
nselves·are·unimportant·to·you?·Please·change·your·
nimals.·Emergencies·require·fast·and·decisive·action.·
ssion·for·ALL·of·God's·creatures.¶
¶
Very·truly·yours,¶
¶

Figure 2-9: Text obscured by a floating object in the front drawing layer

Format floating objects either to allow or not allow text to be wrapped around them. To change the way the text and drawing layers interact, right-click the drawn shape and choose Format AutoShape from the context menu. The context menu command varies depending on what element is selected—it may appear as Format Text Box, or Format WordArt. In the Layout tab (see Figure 2-7), choose the wrapping style that you need. Text can wrap around the item, fitting closely to it or forming a square around it, or it can go behind the text to create a watermark.

TIP # 15

Format Drawing Layer Items Before Placing Them Behind Text

When placing a drawing layer item behind text, be sure that it isn't so dark that reading the text becomes difficult or impossible. Before placing the item behind the text, choose a fill color and an outline color that won't compete visually with the text layer, and then put the item in the back drawing layer. Place the drawing behind the text prematurely and you may not be able to select it again without difficulty.

Floating objects are powerful and flexible enough that I use them most of the time. However, floating objects do have a number of limitations that often force me to use one of the other two object types, inline and frame (discussed previously), on occasion. For the most part, these limitations include the use of fields. Fields in one layer do not recognize fields in other layers. If you need to be able to access information from a field, it is best to put that field inside a frame in the text layer. For example, it is best to use a frame when the object includes a field that needs to capture information such as captions, table of contents entries, or index entries.

Fields

A field is a set of instructions that inserts information into a document automatically. For example, Word includes a field named *Date* that always displays the current system date. Many of Word's sexier commands, such as Insert → Index and Tables, Insert → Headers and Footers, and Tools → Mail Merge, rely on fields to provide their functionality. The Insert → Field command also offers a way to insert various types of fields into a document manually.

This section is intended to provide a general overview of how fields are used in a Word document, both by users and by Word itself. For specific procedural information on using fields, check out Chapter 15, Fields and Forms.

Normally, when a field is inserted into a document, Word displays only the results of that field. For example, insert a date field into a document and Word displays the date and time using the same character and paragraph formatting used by the surrounding text. Select the results of the field, though, and Word highlights the entire field in gray, one way to indicate that it is a field and not normal text. Right-click the field and choose Toggle Field Code from the context menu to display the actual field code behind the results. Field codes are programmatic sequences of instructions that tell Word what information to display as a result of the field.

Figure 2-10 shows a sentence with a field in it (the field results are highlighted in gray) and the same sentence with the field code displayed. The following list describes the components of the figure:

1. *Field results.* Results are the information created by the field. Clicking a result highlights the entire field in light gray.

2. *Context menu.* Right-clicking a field opens a context menu with commands for toggling the field code display on and off and for updating the field results.

3. *Field markers.* Field markers mark the beginning and end of a field when field codes are displayed. These look like the curly brackets inserted with the keyboard, but they aren't. Every field is contained in markers.

4. *Field name.* Every field has a name. The field in Figure 2-10 is named DATE. Automatic fields have names assigned by Word. Inserted fields are assigned names manually, as described in Chapter 15.

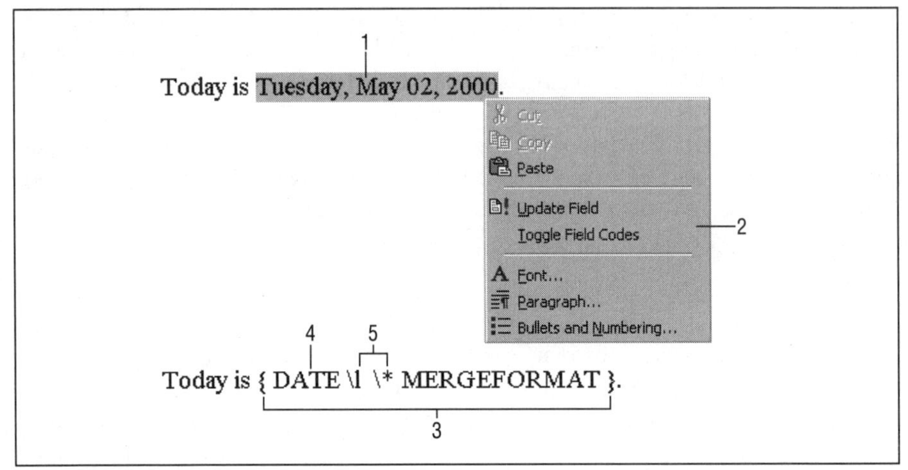

Figure 2-10: A field result is shown in the first sentence; the code behind the result is shown in the second sentence

5. *Switches*. Switches are preceded by a backslash (\) and apply various options to the field, depending on the type of field. There are many switches available for fields in Word. A complete list of switches is available in the Word help file. Many common switches are covered in Chapter 15. The field in Figure 2-10 uses two switches:

   l
   : This switch causes Word to format the field using the same format used the last time a date field was inserted with Word.

   * *MERGEFORMAT*
   : This switch specifies that any character formatting applied directly to the field should be preserved during updates to the field. The * Lower switch overrides the * MERGEFORMAT switch for case formatting.

TIP # 16

Show the Codes for All Fields in a Document

Instead of toggling field codes on one at a time, display codes for all fields in a document using Tools → Options → View → Field Codes. While this option is on, the Toggle Field Codes command on a field's context menu works as normal.

Fields are inserted in documents in one of two ways:

- Manually, by using the Insert → Field command, which opens the Field dialog box (Figure 2-11). Select a field from a list of field categories and names. Manually inserted fields appear by their codes within a document.
- Automatically, by creating other document elements such as an index, bookmark, or table of contents. Many of these commands work using predefined

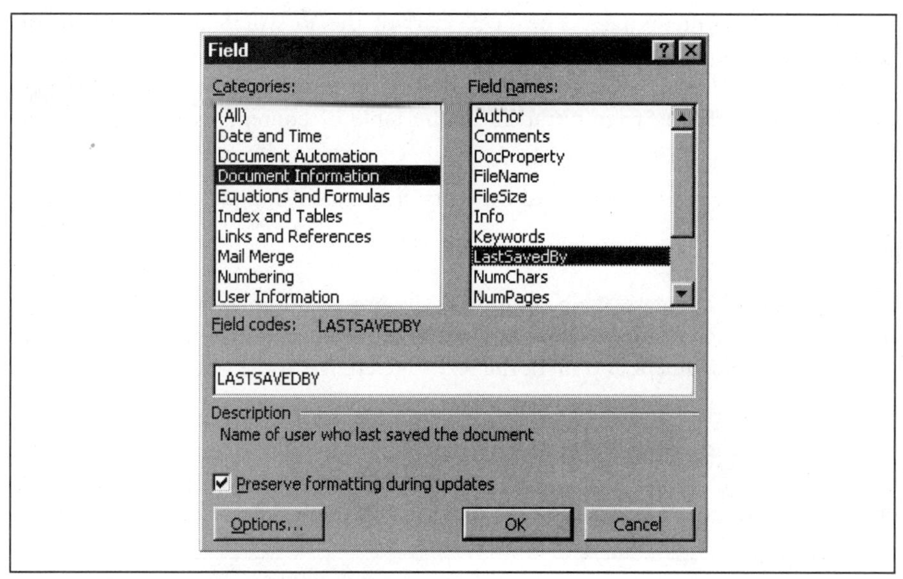

Figure 2-11: Choosing a field and field options

fields. Some fields generated by these commands work the way fields are supposed to. You can update them, modify the field code, and format the results. Some, such as the hyperlink field, work a bit differently, as described below.

TIP # 17

Use ScreenTips to Find Out What Fields Do

Click the What's This help button (?) in the Field dialog box and then click on a field. A ScreenTip pops up, often displaying a better description for the selected field than what is shown in the Description area of the dialog.

Table of contents

A table of contents is created using paragraphs in a document formatted with heading styles. After using the Tables → Table of Contents command, Word goes through the document searching for all of the paragraphs that use Word's built-in heading styles (or any styles you specify), notes the page on which the text is found, and builds the table of contents. The list of headings is converted to a style configured in the Index and Tables dialog box, normally followed by a dot-leader tab that leads up to the page number. Edit the document after creating the table of contents and you can update the table by selecting it and pressing F9.

Turn field codes on in the document and you'll see that the table of contents is represented by a single code that looks something like `{·TOC·\o·"1-3"·\h·\z·}`. This code builds a table of contents using options set by three switches. The \o switch tells Word to use outline headings instead of using paragraphs marked with special table of contents tags. The "1-3" part of the \o switch tells Word to use heading levels 1-3. The \h switch causes Word to create hyperlinks in the table of contents so that clicking an entry jumps to that part of the document. The \z switch tells Word to hide the page numbers in the table of contents when viewing the document in Web Layout view.

Learn more about creating a table of contents in Chapter 7.

Index

Unlike a table of contents, which automatically uses existing text in a document to create itself, an index and the text it will cite must be created manually. You have to go through the document and mark the text to reference in the index.

When text is marked as an index entry, Word inserts a field code. These codes are then used to build the index, much like the table of contents is built from Word headings. Display field codes in the document to see the codes for each marked index entry (Figure 2-12) and the code for the index itself (Figure 2-13).

Buying·Cruelty-Free·Cosmetics{·XE·"Cosmetics"·}¶

Read·labels.·If·the·words·"Not·tested·on·animals"·or·words·to·that·effect·don't·appear,·put·the·product·back·on·the·shelf.·Better·yet,·ask·the·store·to·stop·carrying·products·that·are·tested·on·animals,·or·suggest·that·the·cruelty-free·products·be·placed·together·on·a·shelf·to·make·them·easier·to·find.·This·will·tell·them·that·you·care·about·this·aspect·of·a·product's·manufacturing,·and·let·them·know·that·people·are·paying·attention.·Writing·to·manufacturers·that·still·test·on·animals·is·another·important·part·of·the·compassionate·life·—·your·responsibility·doesn't·end·with·simply·cutting·animal·products·out·of·your·life·—·make·your·voice·heard·whenever·and·wherever·you·can.¶

¶

¶

Figure 2-12: Marking an index entry and inserting an index field code

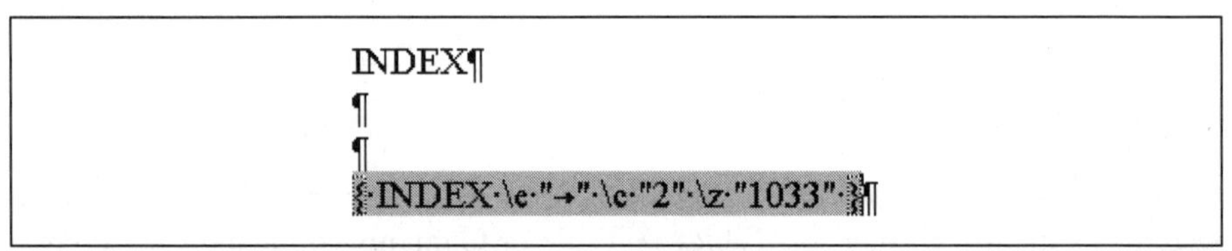

INDEX¶

¶

¶

{·INDEX·\e·"→"·\c·"2"·\z·"1033"·}¶

Figure 2-13: A single code representing the entire index

TIP # 18

Control How an Index Is Created

Edit the quoted text in an index entry field to adjust the entry that appears in the index. The \t switch is followed by whatever "See Also" text is entered in the Mark Index Entry dialog box. The text following the colon (:) is the subentry for the main marked index entry. This, too, can be edited. For more on using indexes, see Chapter 7.

Hyperlinks

Hyperlinks are deceiving in that they are a type of field, but they really don't act like other fields. When a hyperlink is inserted, information about that link is stored in the document. Pointing to the link afterward pops up a ScreenTip with the name of the file or the name of the web address to which the hyperlink points. Display field codes and the hyperlink code is clearly visible (Figure 2-14).

METHYLCOBALAMIN

{ HYPERLINK "C:\My Documents\Medical Info\B12Forms.doc" }is the neurologically active form of vitamin B12. The liver does not convert cyanocobalamin, the commonly available form of vitamin B12, into adequate amounts of methylcobalamin, which the body uses to treat or correct neurological defects. Animal studies have shown that high doses of methylcobalamin are effective in neuron regeneration and that there is no known toxicity at these doses.

Figure 2-14: Viewing the field code for a hyperlink

However, in most respects hyperlinks don't act like other fields. For one thing, although the quoted text in the field code can be edited, this does not actually change the hyperlink in any way. Type in a new URL manually and the hyperlink still points to the old URL. Editing the URL manually also does not change the ScreenTip that displays when pointing to the hyperlink. For more on using hyperlinks, see Chapter 7, and Chapter 16, *Creating a Web Page*.

Document Formatting

When writing a document (a letter, a proposal, or even a chapter for your new Word book), it is convenient to think in terms of conventional grammatical constructs. Letters form words, words form sentences, sentences form paragraphs, paragraphs form pages, and pages form documents. These constructs work great during what I call the creation phase of a document—when you are basically thinking of, and writing down, all of the information that a document will contain.

When it comes to formatting a document, however, these conventional constructs just aren't that important in a word processing program like Word. When formatting, it helps to understand how Word sees a document.

To Word, all documents consist of three parts:

- A document has one or more *sections.*
- A section has zero or more *paragraphs.*
- A paragraph has one or more *characters.*

Word also has three types of formatting: section, paragraph, and character—one for each of the three parts. While Word's interface often makes it seem like formatting can be applied to an entire document, formatting is really just being applied to every section of the document. You're about to have a good look at each of these parts of a Word document and see both how the formatting of the various parts works and how Word's construction of a document really affects the way a document turns out.

Sections

Start a new document from the Blank Document template and the result is a document consisting of one section. Everything typed and all formatting applied are part of that section. That section grows to contain the entire document until you do one or more of the following:

- Insert a section break manually, by choosing Insert → Break. The Break dialog box presents four different types of Section breaks to choose from.
- Change the orientation of an individual page or range of pages in a document.
- Change the margins for a single page or range of pages by choosing "From this point forward" or "Selected text" from the "Apply to" drop list in the Page Setup dialog box (Figure 2-15).

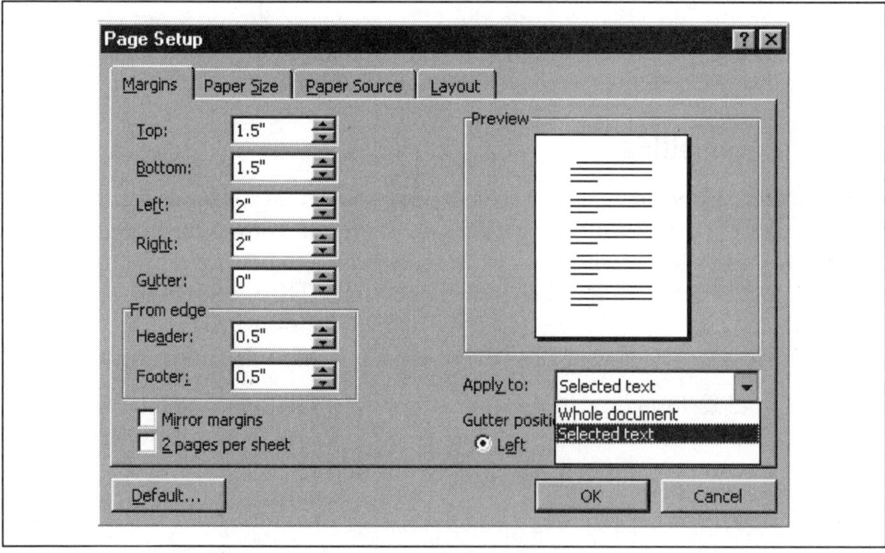

Figure 2-15: Section breaks resulting from layout settings

Insert section breaks manually to have different formatting for different portions of a document. For example, you might want:

- A page to be set as even or odd if using different page numbers for even and odd-numbered pages

- A large section in the middle of the document to be formatted with different margins than the rest of the document
- A title page to have no page number and print using different printer settings

If the section break occurs automatically, Word inserts a break so that portion of the document can be treated differently.

Word shows the section of a document that contains the insertion point by number on the status bar (see Figure 2-16).

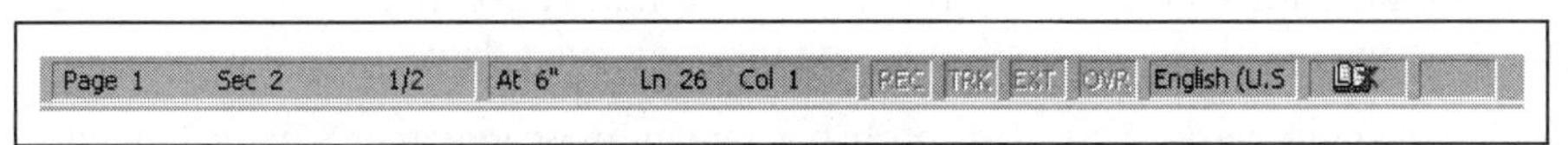

Figure 2-16: Determining the active section with the status bar

Make section breaks visible in a document one of two ways:

- Switch to Normal view using View → Normal. This shows section breaks where they occur in a document along with text indicating the type of break (Figure 2-17). I always recommend working in Normal view when using a document with multiple sections.

Life·in·Captivity¶

¶

→ Study·after·study·shows·that·the·life·span·of·marine·mammals·in·captivity·is·just·30%·of·the·life·expectancy·in·the·wild.·Considering·that·"the·wild"·includes·exposure·to·pollution,·other·animal·predators,·and·hunters,·this·makes·the·life·span·statistic·even·more·staggering.·Take·away·these·significant·threats·and·still·their·lives·are·horribly·short·in·captivity.·Life·in·a·tank·is·torture·for·these·animals,·driven·mad·by·the·reverberations·of·their·own·sonic·navigation·systems.·Scientists·most·familiar·with·the·effect·of·captivity·on·dolphins·have·declared·a·moratorium·on·the·capture·of·dolphins,·even·for·the·purposes·of·study.·Much·more·can·be·learned·by·observing·them·in·the·wild.·There·is,·therefore,·no·valid·argument·for·the·capture·and·captivity·of·dolphins.¶

::::::::::::::::Section Break (Continuous)::::::::::::::::

¶

→ Perhaps·you·feel·that·using·already·captive·and·therefore·"non-releasable"·animals·makes·your·intended·tank·a·humane·solution.·Let's·take·that·concept·and·place·it·in·human·terms.·Imagine·a·child·who·due·to·disability·cannot·be·allowed·to·live·on·its·own·when·it·reaches·the·age·of·majority.·If·you·read·that·the·child's·parents·locked·it·in·a·room·with·five·or·six·other·similarly·disabled·children·and·allowed·them·to·reproduce,·creating·more·disabled·children,·you'd·be·outraged.·That's·the·same·thing·as·placing·six·breeding-age·male·and·female·dolphins·in·the·same·tank.·They've·been·raised·in·captivity·(if·you·end·up·using·the·animals·you·claim·to·be·using),·and·therefore·cannot·be·released·into·the·wild·(the·jury·is·still·out·on·that·fact,·by·the·way),·and·they'll·give·birth·to·more·dolphins·that·"can't"·be·released.·Those·offspring·will·then·end·up·in·tanks·somewhere·else,·delighting·more·idiots·who·come·to·see·the·"fish"·and·be·entertained.¶

¶

Figure 2-17: Viewing section breaks in Normal view

- Turn on the Show/Hide option (Standard toolbar) when in other views. This also shows where the breaks occur and what type they are, but I find it more difficult to use as Word tends to cram the horizontal line up against the preceding paragraph instead of giving it a line of its own.

TIP # 19

Create a Document, Then Break It into Sections

It's a good idea to type an entire document and then break it into sections. This makes it easier to control the effect of sections on pagination (the flow of text over page breaks).

Paragraphs

The simple paragraph is one of the most important concepts in all of Word. The ultimate success of every bit of formatting in a document depends on the paragraph.

The paragraph mark. You were probably taught in school that a paragraph is a group of sentences with a common topic. When working with Word, however, an additional definition is needed. In Word, a paragraph is a paragraph mark (¶) plus all of the text preceding that paragraph mark up to, but not including, the previous paragraph mark or the beginning of the document (Figure 2-18). The paragraph mark contains all of the formatting information (both character and paragraph formatting) for a paragraph. The number of paragraph marks in a document is equal to the number of paragraphs. Every time you press the Enter key, a new paragraph is created and a new paragraph mark is placed in the document.

Life in Captivity¶
¶
Study after study shows that the life span of maring mammals in captivity is just 30% of the life expectancy in the wild. Considering that "the wild" includes exposure to pollution, other animal predators, and hunters, this makes the life span statistic even more staggering. Take away the significant threats and still their lives are horribly short in captivity. Life in a tank is torture for these animals, driven mad by the reverberations of their own sonic navigation systems. ¶
Scientists most familiar with the effects of captivity on Dolphins have declared a moratorium on the capture of dolphins, even for the purposes of study. Much more can be learned from observing them in the wild. There is, therefore, no valid argument for the capture of dolphins.¶

Figure 2-18: Selecting a whole paragraph, including the paragraph mark

TIP # 20

Turn Paragraph Marks On

To create a well-formatted document, you must be able to see Word's paragraph marks. You can make Word show them in a document using the Show/Hide button on the Standard toolbar. However, this also turns on a lot of other hidden characters (like spaces and tabs) that many people find distracting. Instead, use Tools → Options → View → Formatting to turn on just the formatting characters you want to see. Even if you only turn on paragraph marks, your life in Word is about to become a lot better.

For the most part, the paragraph mark is a character like any other character in Word. It has a font, a size, and a color. You can move it, copy it, and even delete most of them (the final paragraph mark in a document can never be removed). But the paragraph mark is also special. The paragraph mark:

- Holds all the formatting information for that paragraph, including character formatting—fonts, sizes, style, color, indents, outline level, bullets, and any tabs that were pressed in the paragraph as well as any tab settings put into effect within the scope of the paragraph. Unless overridden by applying manual character formatting (Format → Font), every character in the paragraph takes on the formatting applied to the paragraph mark.

While paragraph formatting is contained in the paragraph mark, you cannot adjust a paragraph's format by selecting the mark and applying new formats directly to it. This action just applies character formatting to the paragraph mark itself.

- Is the end of a paragraph. No text may be typed after the paragraph mark. Using the right arrow to move over it causes the insertion point to move to the beginning of the next paragraph. The End key jumps to the end of any line, but if that line contains a paragraph mark, it jumps to a position right in front of the mark.
- Always ends a document. The final character in a document is always the paragraph mark. Word associates a wide variety of formatting with the final paragraph mark, especially section and style formatting.
- Can't be overtyped. In overtype mode (indicated by the OVR button on the status bar), any character in a document may be typed over except a paragraph mark.

TIP # 21

Select the Paragraph Mark to See Its Formatting

To see some of the formats contained in a paragraph mark, select it by double-clicking and look at the Formatting toolbar and the ruler. The Font, Size, any tabs, and the indents set for the text in that paragraph appear there. After selecting a paragraph mark, it can be copied and pasted over other paragraph marks to transfer formatting to other paragraphs. The Format Painter button on the Standard toolbar can also be used to copy formatting. You can also see elements of the paragraph formatting using the Help → What's This? command described in Chapter 12, Help.

Creating new paragraphs. Every time the Enter key is pressed, Word starts a new paragraph by putting a new paragraph mark in the document. Most of the time, paragraph formatting is carried over to the next paragraph. If you are typing along in Normal style and hit Enter, a new paragraph is created using the Normal style and whatever manual formatting was used in the previous paragraph.

What really happens when you hit Enter at the end of a paragraph (the insertion point is directly in front of the paragraph mark for that paragraph) is a bit more complicated. Word looks up the style defined in the Format → Style → any style → Modify → "Style for following paragraph" option to determine what the style of the new paragraph will be. The default following style for the Normal style is Normal.

If you are in the middle of a paragraph and hit Enter, both the old and new paragraph are formatted using the same style as the old paragraph, including any manual formatting applied.

Manipulating paragraphs. Entire paragraphs can be selected in a number of ways. When selecting a paragraph by clicking and dragging, often only the text of the paragraph is selected and not the paragraph mark. This is great for moving the text into another paragraph (whether by drag-and-drop or cutting and pasting) and having it take on the recipient paragraph's formatting. Also note that wherever the selected text is moved, it has to become part of an existing paragraph. It cannot become a paragraph on its own, because it does not include the paragraph mark. You can quickly make it its own paragraph using the Enter key, but this still don't bring any of the previous formatting along with it.

To quickly select an entire paragraph along with the paragraph mark and all the formatting it contains, triple-click the paragraph or double-click in the margin beside the paragraph. Move the paragraph (again by drag-and-drop or cutting and pasting) and it becomes a paragraph on its own complete with formatting.

In the introduction to this chapter, I brought up an interesting quirk whereby selecting two consecutive paragraphs by dragging the pointer over them causes Word not to copy the formatting of the second paragraph, but to copy the formatting of the first paragraph. The reason for this is that the paragraph mark for the second paragraph is not included, but the mark for the first paragraph is included because it is dragged over in the selection process. The workaround for this is a simple one. Triple-click to select the second paragraph, then click at the beginning of the first paragraph while holding down the Shift key. This adds the first paragraph to the selection—a selection that now includes both paragraph marks. Having paragraph marks visible in Word eliminates most of these nasty quirks.

Tabs. As I mentioned earlier, the paragraph marker at the end of a paragraph holds any tab settings for that paragraph (Figure 2-19). To adjust tabs for a paragraph, the entire paragraph, including paragraph mark, must be selected first. Drag the tab stop on the ruler to adjust tabs for the selected paragraph.

This section discusses tabs as they apply to paragraphs and paragraph marks. For a full discussion of using tabs, see Chapter 8.

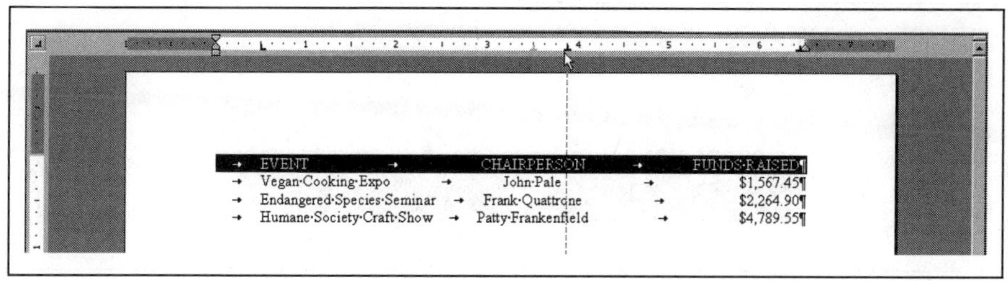

Figure 2-19: Getting control over tab settings using paragraphs

Merging Paragraphs

Here's an interesting thing. Merging two paragraphs works the way you would intuitively think it would, but does not work the way it should according to how Word normally handles paragraphs.

Suppose there are two consecutive paragraphs, each using a different format. If you merge the two paragraphs by placing the insertion point at the start of the second paragraph and hitting Backspace (or at the end of the first paragraph and hitting Delete), the second paragraph is brought up into the first paragraph and takes on the first paragraph's formatting. Intuitively, this is what you would expect to happen, since you are really moving the text from the second paragraph up into the first paragraph.

However, given the way that Word uses paragraph marks, this doesn't quite make sense. It would seem that both paragraphs would take on the formatting of the second paragraph, since the paragraph mark for the first paragraph is being deleted and the new joined paragraph now ends with the paragraph mark that belonged to the second paragraph. And, logically, this would be right. In fact, this is how it worked in versions of Word before Word 97. Then Word's designers decided that, while it made sense if users understood and used paragraph marks, it didn't make sense if they didn't. So the designers built in code that actually applies the formatting stored in the first paragraph mark to the second paragraph mark.

When changing tab settings for text in a document, be sure not to select the lines above or below the tabbed text. Since different tab settings can exist in paragraphs throughout a document, you risk selecting lines from two different sets of tab stops, making it difficult to make any adjustments. Figure 2-20 shows the ruler when paragraphs with different tab settings are selected at the same time. Note that the tab indicators are dimmed, so no adjustments can be made.

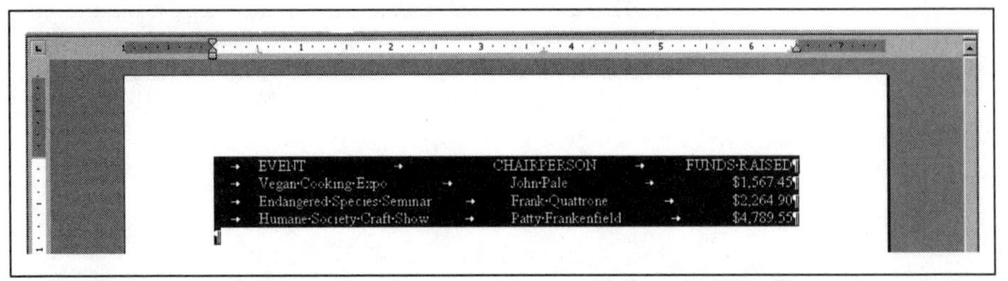

Figure 2-20: Dimmed tab stops on the ruler, showing paragraphs with different sets of tab stops are selected

Characters

Characters are the smallest pieces of a document. This is a significant fact to bear in mind when selecting and formatting text. A single character in a word, a single word (a collection of characters) in a paragraph, or even a blank space can be formatted simply by selecting the text and applying a different format to it.

To Word, every key pressed inserts a character. Some characters appear as printable text, others as non-printing characters. Tabs, returns, spaces, page breaks, and section breaks are all characters in a document. Select, move, or delete them just like any other character. This very fact explains a lot of the strange things that go on in Word. Use the Show/Hide tool to display these non-printing characters in a document (Figure 2-21).

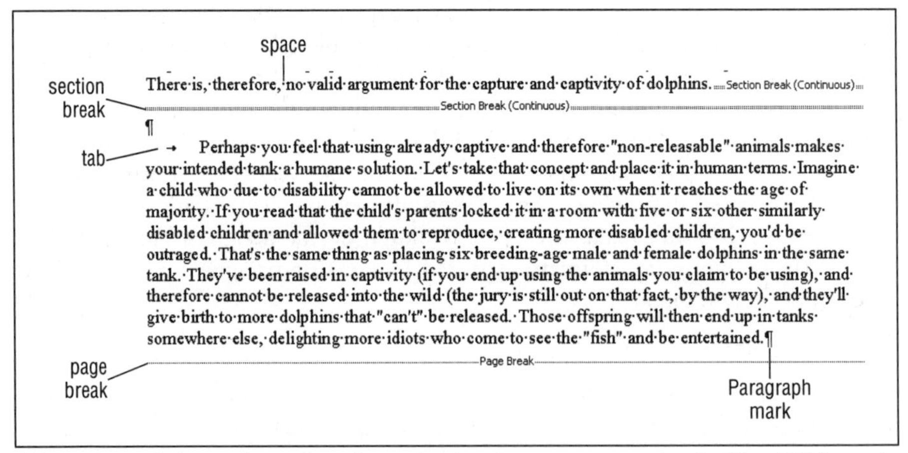

Figure 2-21: Paragraph marks, tabs, and space characters appearing in Show/Hide mode

Styles

It's surprising how many advanced Word users are unfamiliar with styles and all of their uses. Styles have gained the unfortunate reputation of being complicated to create and use. The truth is that styles are pretty straightforward.

A style is simply a collection of formatting information that has been given a name. Applying a style applies all the formatting in that style at once. There are two types of styles in Word:

Paragraph styles
: Contain formatting that is applied to an entire paragraph. Paragraph styles can include paragraph formatting (such as tabs, line spacing, and indenting), character formatting (such as font, size, and color), and formatting that applies to either characters or paragraphs (such as borders or languages).

Character styles
: Contain formatting that is applied only to selected characters within a paragraph. Characters within a paragraph can have their own style even if a paragraph style is applied to the paragraph as a whole. Character styles can only include character formatting.

Apply either type of style by selecting it from the Style drop-down list on the Standard toolbar (Figure 2-22). Paragraph styles are noted with a paragraph mark (¶) and character styles are noted with an underlined letter *a*.

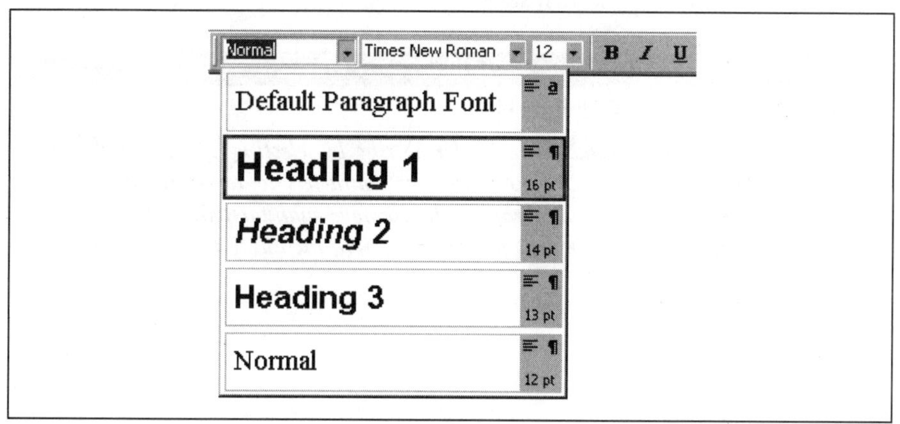

Figure 2-22: Applying paragraph and character styles

Applying a style is as simple as placing the insertion point where the new style should start or selecting a range of characters or paragraphs to format and choosing the style from the drop-down Style list.

TIP # 22

Use Character Styles for Characters

When applying styles to characters in a paragraph, be sure that the style is a character style—otherwise, it will apply to the entire paragraph containing the formatted text.

Here are some interesting points about applying styles:

- Character styles override paragraph styles. Applying a paragraph style to an existing paragraph changes all of the paragraph formatting to that specified in the style. This includes line spacing, tabs, indents, etc. It also changes the format of all of the characters in the paragraph to match that specified in the style, *except* for characters that have formatting applied directly to them. For example, suppose you have a paragraph formatted in the Normal style and you add special formatting to one word in the paragraph (say italicize it and make the font red for emphasis) by either applying the changes directly or using a character style. If you then apply a new paragraph style that uses a different font, all the characters in the paragraph would change except for that word.
- Paragraph style can be applied either by placing the insertion point within a paragraph and choosing the style or by selecting the paragraph and applying the style. Both actions do the same thing.
- Apply a character style while text is selected and the style is applied to that text. Apply it without text selected and the style is applied at the insertion point. Anything typed will be in that style.

TIP # 23

Remove Manual Formatting from Text

Quickly remove all manual character formatting by selecting a range of characters and pressing Ctrl-Spacebar. This causes the characters to revert to the character formatting defined in the paragraph style. Remove manual paragraph formatting from a paragraph by selecting the whole paragraph, including the paragraph mark, and pressing Ctrl-Q.

Chapter 3

Customizing Word

Word is something like the Swiss Army knife of document creation products. It boasts a lot of functionality for doing almost anything, from basic typing and formatting to indexing, creating tables, charts, pictures, web pages, and even serving as its own little programming platform. As soon as you fire up Word and poke through the interface, the abundance of menus, toolbars, and commands reflects this functionality. Many of Word's functions are used quite frequently, others less frequently, and still others not at all. Fortunately, Word lets you customize almost every facet of its menus and toolbars, and even some of its basic operations, to suit your style.

Customization is a pretty big topic and encompasses a lot of the actions taken in Word. Creating custom themes and styles, recording macros to automate tasks, turning off the Office Assistant, and creating AutoText entries are all ways to customize the Word environment. These actions are all covered in this book. This chapter is mainly concerned with two of Word's more intricate and powerful commands:

Tools → Options
: This command opens a dialog containing ten separate tabs for setting options ranging from what components of a document are visible onscreen, to what components print, to how Word handles spelling and grammar checking. The first section of this chapter details all of the options on the Tools → Options tabs, what those settings affect, and how to implement them. Many of the settings on the tabs apply to Word's application layer and affect any document displayed. Other options are applied only to the active document.

Tools → Customize
: This command opens a dialog with three tabs—one for creating and managing command bars, one for customizing the commands on those bars, and one for setting some general options specifying how the command bars work.

This chapter begins by describing where Word saves all of these customization settings and how to transfer customization between documents and templates. From there, it moves into using the Tools → Options command and then the Tools → Customize command. The chapter ends with a look at some of my favorite customizations.

Saving and Moving Customizations

The two different types of customizations covered in this chapter, those done using Tools → Options and those done using Tools → Customize, are saved in different ways. Tools → Options and Tools → Customize → Options settings are saved in the Windows Registry. Tools → Customize → Commands settings, custom toolbars, and custom key combinations are saved in a template or document.

Tools → Options and Tools → Customize → Options Settings

In Word 2000, all user options are stored in the Windows Registry in the registry subkey HKEY_CURRENT_USER\Software\Microsoft\Office\9.0\Word\.

Several subkeys exist under the main Word subkey:

Data key
: This key holds information concerning Word's most recently used (MRU) lists.

Options key
: This key holds information about options you set in Word using Tools → Options.

Stationery key
: This key contains the default location for the template for WordMail and the links to find the template.

Table of Authorities key
: This key stores the Category list that appears in the Table of Authorities list when you press Alt-Shift-I or use Insert → Index and Tables → Table of Authorities → Mark Citation, as described in Chapter 7, *Insert.*

Wizards key
: All wizard defaults are stored here. These settings are created the first time a wizard is run.

Copy settings to another computer or back up settings using the export feature of the Registry Editor. Just set it to export the branch you want to copy (such as the Options subkey).

This section serves to introduce the Word registry structure in a very general way and show the major keys under which Word stores settings. A detailed list of registry entries can be found in Appendix B, Registry Keys.

Commands, Toolbars, and Keystrokes

Whenever you create a custom toolbar, assign key combinations to a command, or customize the commands on toolbars and menus (as described later in this chapter), those changes are saved in a template (*.dot*) or document (*.doc*) file. You'll specify where to save them when performing the customization.

Toolbars

When creating a new toolbar using Tools → Customize → Toolbars → New, the dialog that opens has an option for making the new toolbar available to either *normal.dot*, to the current document, or to the template attached to the current document. If made available to *normal.dot*, the toolbar is available in any document opened. Create the new toolbar in a different template instead, and the toolbar would be available to all documents based on that template, or to all documents if that template were loaded globally.

TIP # 24

Transferring Toolbars Between Documents

Word makes it easy to move toolbars between templates and documents. Open Tools → Templates and Add-Ins and click the Organizer button. Use the Toolbars tab of the dialog that opens to transfer toolbars between files. Learn more about using the Organizer tool in Chapter 8, Format.

Commands

Customize commands using the Tools → Customize → Commands. At the bottom of that tab, a drop-down list defines whether to save any customizations in the current document or in *normal.dot.*

WARNING

Watch out for the default choice for saving customizations in the Tools → Customize dialog boxes. The first time the tab opens, the default choice is normal.dot. Thereafter, the default is whatever choice you made during the last customization.

Key combinations

On the dialog used to create key combinations, another drop-down menu defines whether to save key customizations in the current document or in *normal.dot*.

Once you have saved customizations to a template or document file, it is easy enough to move them to another computer, send them to another user, or back them up in case you need to reinstall Word.

In Chapter 14, *Creating a Template*, I walk you through the generation of a custom template (one that includes some customizations) and show different methods of distributing and using that template. Chapter 2, *How Word Works*, also includes a detailed look at how Word uses templates to build its interface and to govern document creation.

Configuring Word with Tools → Options

The Tools → Options command is used to change Word's settings. Use it to specify what components of a document are viewed onscreen or printed. Set user information (name, address, and all that), file locations (for example, where templates are found and the location documents are saved by default), and even control Word's interface to some extent. There are ten tabs on the Tools → Options dialog and we'll be examining them all in the upcoming sections.

Tools → Options → View Tab

The View tab (Figure 3-1) controls the on-screen display of a document. Turning off some of the display options can make Word redraw and scroll documents more quickly. Some of the options, like displaying the formatting marks, are turned off by default, but may be valuable when enabled. It's awfully hard to use Word well if you can't see half of what it's doing. The options on this tab only apply to the active document and to new documents created after the options are set, but not to any existing documents, even if they're currently open.

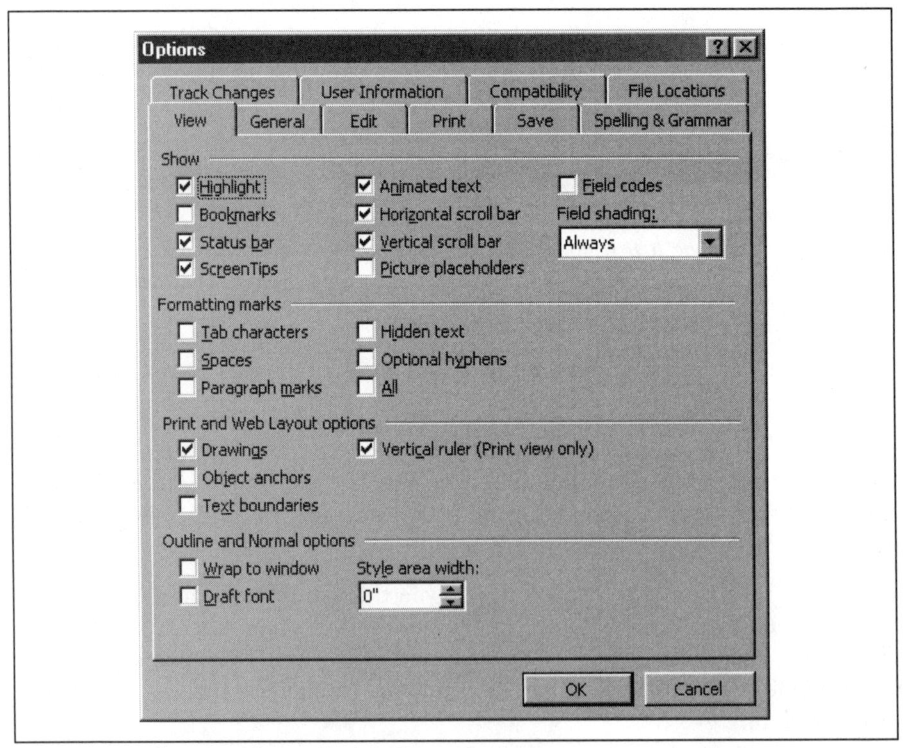

Figure 3-1: Choosing what is displayed in a document

The Tools → Options → View tab is broken down into four sections: Show, Formatting marks, Print and Web Layout options, and Outline and Normal options.

Tools → Options → View → Show

The Show section of the View tab (Figure 3-2) controls how Word displays certain interface elements and special objects in a document.

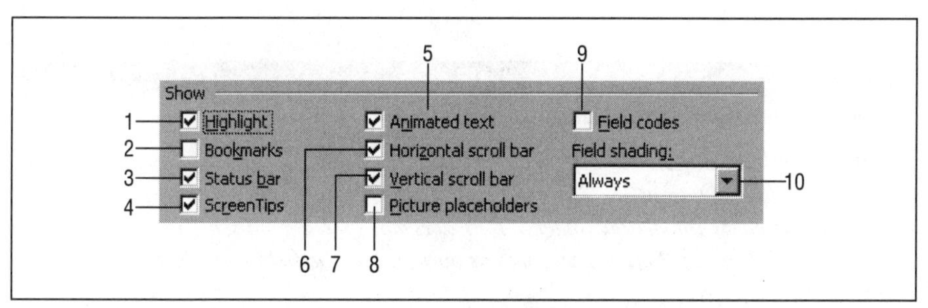

Figure 3-2: Controlling interface and document object display

1. *Highlight*. This option turns on or off the display of highlighted text onscreen and in printed documents. Highlight text using the Highlight button on the Formatting toolbar.

2. *Bookmarks*. This toggles the display of bookmarks and their links in documents. Bookmarks are discussed in detail in Chapter 7.

3. *Status bar*. This option toggles the display of the status bar at the bottom of the Word window. I recommend leaving this option on; the status bar (detailed in Chapter 1, *Word Overview*) provides a lot of important feedback on the current location of the insertion point and the document view. It also clues you in to some of the background settings and activity in Word, such as whether Track Changes is turned on (see Chapter 13, *Collaborating*) and the spelling and grammar status (see Chapter 9, *Tools*).

4. *ScreenTips*. This option enables or disables the pop-up ScreenTips that appear when the pointer is held over an interface element for a moment.

5. *Animated text*. Format → Font → Text Effects puts cute little text animations in the text layer of documents. This option toggles the display of these animations, though the animations themselves remain.

6. *Horizontal scroll bar*. This toggles the display of the horizontal scrollbar at the bottom of the Word window and the four view buttons to its left. Personally, I can't think of a good reason to turn the horizontal scrollbar off.

7. *Vertical scroll bar*. This option toggles the display of the vertical scrollbar, the split screen handle above it, and the browse buttons beneath it.

8. *Picture placeholder.* This option displays pictures as empty boxes. Depending on the types of pictures used, this can speed up display and scrolling. This option affects any pictures inserted with the Insert → Picture submenu, except for WordArt and AutoShapes. There is no way to turn off the display of these objects.

9. *Field codes.* When this option is not selected, the results of fields are shown in a document. Turn it on to show the field codes instead. See Chapter 15, *Fields and Forms*, for details.

TIP # 25

Display Field Codes When Linking Objects

When linking objects (like figures or Excel spreadsheets) into a Word document, turn Tools → Options → View → Field Codes on to have Word display the field codes instead of the actual images. This does not give a good sense of the size of the images, as does the Picture Placeholders option, but the field code does show the filename of the object.

10. *Field shading.* This turns on shading for field results, making them easier to find. Options are When Selected (meaning a field is shaded only when the field itself is selected), Always, and Never.

Tools → Options → View → Formatting Marks

Use the "Formatting marks" section of the Tools → Options → View tab (Figure 3-3) to toggle the display of hidden formatting characters in a document.

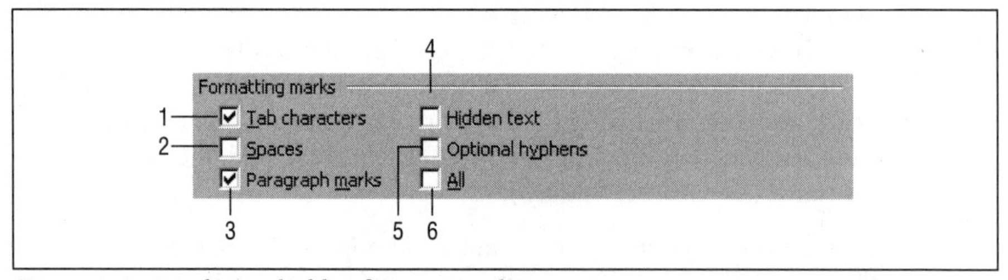

Figure 3-3: Displaying hidden formatting characters

1. *Tab characters.* When selected, tabs are displayed as arrows. As with most formatting options, I recommend leaving tabs displayed at all times. This makes it easy to distinguish between tabs, series of spaces, and indentations. Tab characters (along with other formatting characters in this section of the dialog) are not printed even if their screen display is turned on. For more on how tabs work, see Chapter 2.

2. *Spaces.* When selected, spaces are shown as small, gray dots. Many users find this helpful in distinguishing between single and double spaces. I find this

option marginally useful, since double spaces are one of the few things that Word's grammar checker is really good at finding.

3. *Paragraph marks*. When this option is selected, paragraph marks are shown at the end of each paragraph. Keep this option on at all times. Word's paragraph mark is the source of most of the formatting that goes on in Word and being able to see it is essential. For more on why the paragraph mark is so important, see Chapter 2.

4. *Hidden text*. Hide text by selecting it and choosing Format → Font → Hidden. Hidden text is not displayed on screen or printed by default (make Word print hidden text using Tools → Options → Print → Hidden Text). When this option is turned on, line breaks and pagination in a document change on screen, but not in the printed document.

5. *Optional hyphens*. This turns on the display of optional hyphens—the hyphens manually inserted (using Ctrl-Hyphen) to indicate where a word should break if it falls on the end of a line. See Chapter 9, for more on using hyphens.

6. *All*. This option turns on or off all of the formatting displays (#11–14). It is the same as using the Show/Hide button on the Standard toolbar.

TIP # 26

Set Formatting Options with Tools → Options → View and Toggle Them with Show/Hide

Set any formatting options (like paragraphs and tabs) using the Tools → Options → View tab and then use the Show/Hide button on the Standard toolbar to toggle between showing all formatting and just those you've enabled in Tools → Options.

Tools → Options → View → Print and Web Layout Options

The Print and Web Layout options section of the Tools → Options → View tab (Figure 3-4) controls how certain objects are displayed in Word's Print Layout and Web Layout views. The options are as follows:

1. *Drawings*. Uncheck this option to turn off the display of objects created with Word's drawing tools (WordArt and AutoShapes) when you are in Print Layout or Web Layout views. Normally, it's best to leave these on, as they do not significantly slow down display or scrolling.

2. *Object anchors*. When this is selected, object anchors are displayed in Print Layout and Web Layout views to indicate which paragraphs objects are anchored to. Anchors are discussed in Chapter 2.

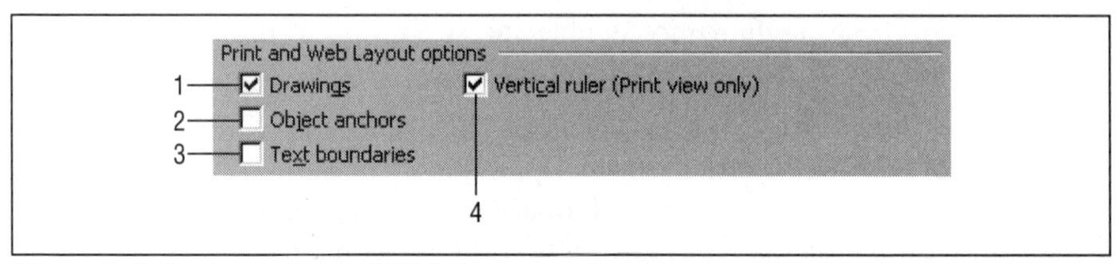

Figure 3-4: Setting Print and Web Layout options

3. *Text boundaries*. When this option is selected, Word displays dotted lines on the screen around page margins. This only works in Print Layout or Web Layout views and is a handy way of laying out margins for a document.

4. *Vertical ruler (Print view only)*. This toggles the display of the vertical ruler that appears in Print and Web Layout views. Word's vertical and horizontal rulers are discussed in Chapter 1.

Tools → Options → View → Outline and Normal Options

The Outline and Normal options section of the Tools → Options → View tab (Figure 3-5) controls how certain objects are displayed in Word's Outline and Normal views.

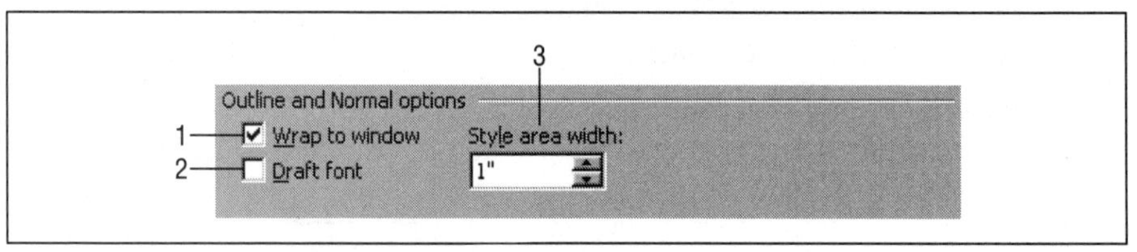

Figure 3-5: Setting Outline and Normal options

1. *Wrap to window*. This option only applies to Outline and Normal views. When selected, Word wraps text from one line to the next based on the size of the document window rather than on the document's margins. I recommend using View → Zoom to make the document representation itself fit into the window instead of using this option.

2. *Draft font*. This only applies to Outline and Normal views. When selected, Word substitutes a single font for all of the different fonts in a document. Most types of formatting are represented by bold or underlining, and graphics placeholders are used. All of this is an attempt to speed up a document's display, particularly on slower machines.

3. *Style area width*. This option sets the width used on the left page margin for displaying paragraph styles in Outline and Normal views. The default is 0, meaning that nothing is displayed. Figure 3-6 shows a document with the Style area width set to 1".

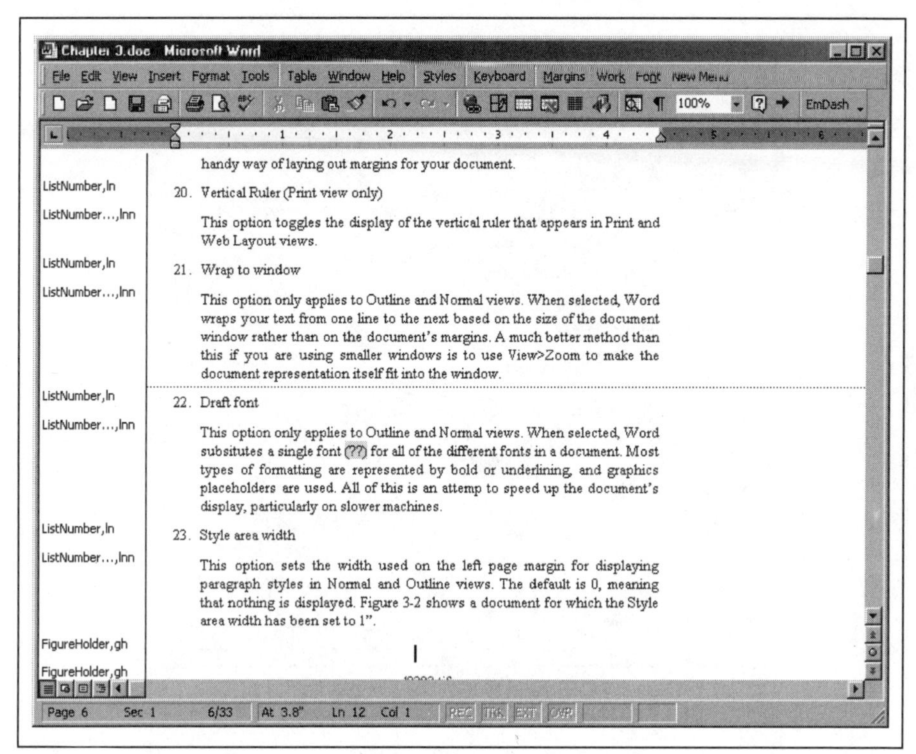

Figure 3-6: Viewing paragraph styles in the style area

Tools → Options → General Tab

The General tab (Figure 3-7) sets options that apply to the Word application in general, not just to the active document. The following list describes these options:

1. *Background repagination.* When this is selected, Word recalculates line and page endings and page numbers as you work. If this behavior slows down the document display too much, turn it off. Be aware, however, that while working on a document with background repagination off, the current state of the document is not shown accurately. Also, this option is not available if the Tools → Options → Edit tab is opened while a document is in Print or Web Layout view. Pagination always occurs in Print and Web Layout views, regardless of how this option is set.

2. *Blue background, white text.* There are actually two different reasons to view documents as white text on a blue background. The first is that former Word-Perfect user are often just used to it. The second is that many people, especially those with reading disorders like dyslexia, find it easier to work in this mode.

3. *Provide feedback with sound.* Word comes with sounds associated for almost every event. By default, these sounds are turned off, but can be enabled here.

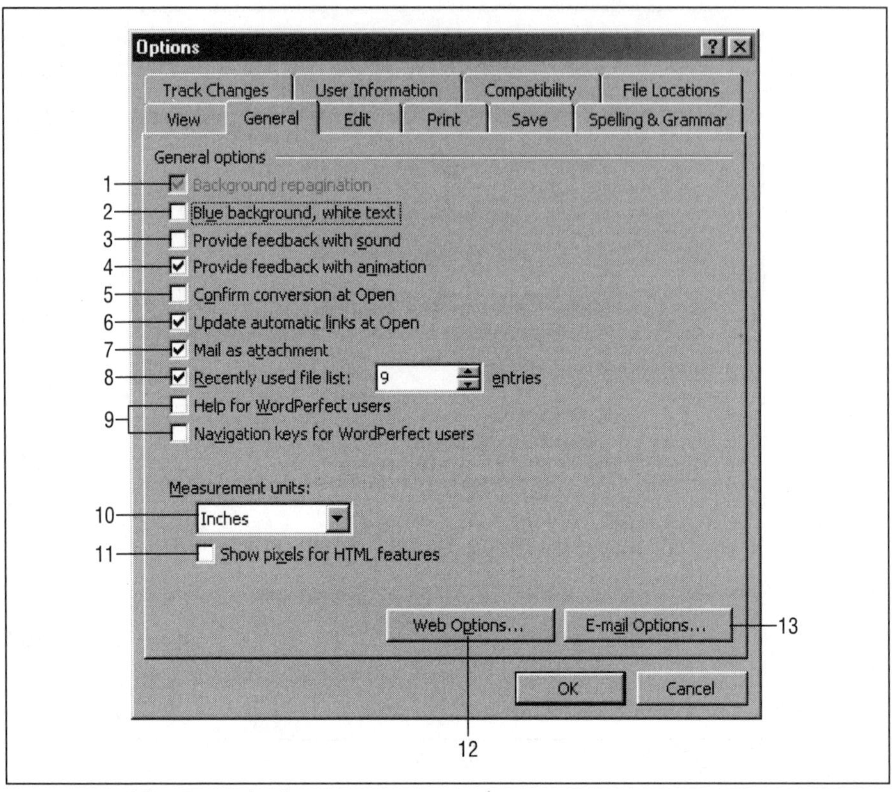

Figure 3-7: The General tab

4. *Provide feedback with animation.* Many of the actions Word performs are accompanied by cute little animations, such as the pen writing on the book icon on the status bar when Word checks spelling in the background. Turn those off here if they are annoying.

5. *Confirm conversion at Open.* When this option is not selected (the default), Word chooses converters when opening a document that is not in a native Word format. When this is selected, a dialog box for selecting a converter appears on opening such a document. For a list of native formats and available converters, see Appendix C, *Converters and Filters*.

6. *Update automatic links at Open.* When this is selected, any objects in a document that are linked to external files are updated on opening the document. This option is on by default, and you'll probably do best to leave it on. Turn it off (perhaps because some documents open too slowly) and you'll have to update your links manually using Edit → Links (this is covered in Chapter 5, *Edit*).

7. *Mail as attachment.* When this option is selected, Word documents sent by email (using File → Send To → Mail Recipient) are sent as attachments. When this is not selected, documents are sent as the body of the message. I recommend

finding out what the preference of the intended recipient is before making this decision. If the recipient doesn't have Word, sending an attachment might not make sense. On the other hand, if a recipient's email program does not support viewing highly formatted information in a message's body, sending an attachment might be necessary.

8. *Recently used file list*. By default, Word displays the four most recently used (MRU) documents near the bottom of the File menu for quick access (Figure 3-8). Enable and disable that function here and set the number of documents displayed from 0 to 9. Setting this option to 0 disables the option and prevents the display of the list, but Word still tracks recently used documents.

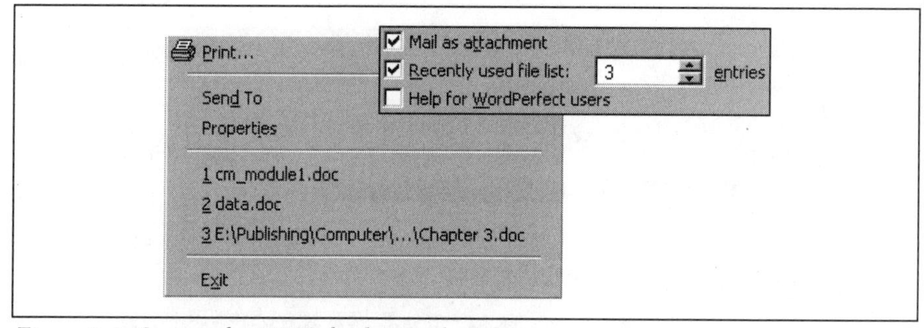

Figure 3-8: Setting the MRU display on the File menu

9. *WordPerfect options*. These options (Figure 3-9) are somewhat misplaced, in my opinion. "Help for WordPerfect users" turns on WordPerfect key combinations in Word, but is highly dependant on other settings that can only be made using the Help → Word Perfect Help dialog. "Navigation Keys for WordPerfect users" sets the Page Up, Page Down, Home, End, and Esc keys to their WordPerfect equivalent. All of this is covered in Chapter 12, *Help*.

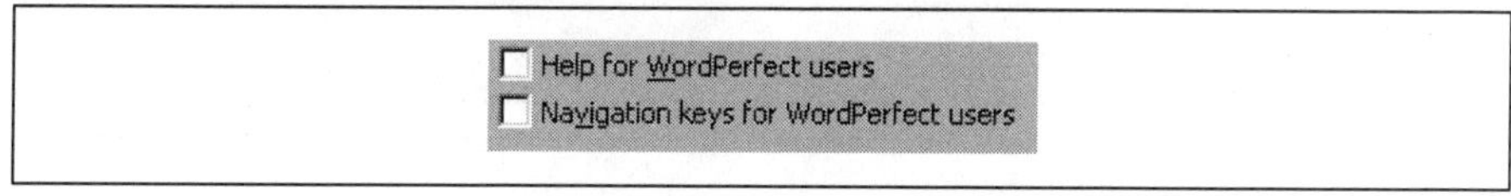

Figure 3-9: Word Perfect options on Tools → Options → General

10. *Measurement units*. This option sets the default unit of measure in Word. Options include inches, millimeters, and points. Override this unit of measure on an item-by-item basis in most of Word's dialogs that call for measurements.

11. *Show pixels for HTML features*. When this is selected, measurements in dialogs that are related to HTML (Web) creation are displayed in pixels, a more accurate representation for documents designed to be seen onscreen. See Chapter 16, *Creating a Web Page*, for more.

12. *Web Options*. This button opens the Web Options dialog, which we'll look at more closely in Chapter 16.

13. *E-Mail Options*. This button opens the E-Mail Options dialog. The E-Mail Signature tab (Figure 3-10) creates a personal signature that is added automatically to the end of any new message sent from Word. Use the Personal Stationery tab to choose a Word theme (see Chapter 8 for more on themes) to serve as the background for messages. Use this tab to specify default fonts for new mail messages and for replies. Finally, mark any comments added during a reply with your name (the name configured on Tools → Options → User Information). See *Outlook 2000 in a Nutshell* for details on using Word as the email editor in Outlook.

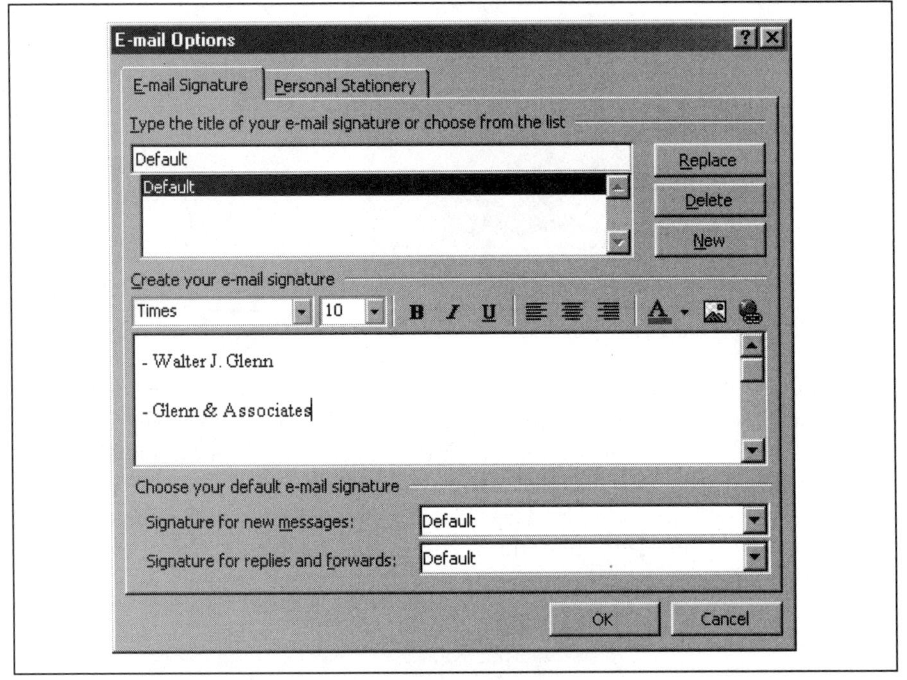

Figure 3-10: Email options

- *Title*. Enter a name for the signature to create. The title box shows the name of any selected signature.
- *List of Signatures*. This window shows a list of existing signatures.
- *Add/Replace*. This button is normally labeled Add, and is used to add a new signature to the list after typing in a title and the signature text. If an existing signature is selected and the signature text is modified, the button becomes Replace and is used to replace the signature text under the existing name.

TIP # 27

A Better Way to Drag-And-Drop Edit

If you are a fan of dragging and dropping to edit a document, try dragging with the right mouse button instead of the left. Releasing a selection dragged in this manner opens a menu for specifying whether to copy or move the selection.

3. *Use the INS key for paste.* Normally, the INS (or Insert) key toggles between Overtype and Insert mode. If this option is enabled, the INS key is used for pasting instead.
4. *Overtype mode.* In Insert mode (the default), text entered at the insertion point is inserted between any existing characters without modifying them. In Overtype mode, each character typed overwrites the character directly following it. Switch between these two modes using this checkbox, the INS key (unless you use the INS key for pasting, as described previously), or by double-clicking the OVR box on the status at the bottom of the Word window. Most people find that Insert mode is more intuitive, although those used to typewriters may find Overtype more familiar.

TIP # 28

Use Your INS Key for Pasting

Consider using the INS key for pasting instead of toggling between Overtype and Insert mode using Tools → Options → Edit. Many people accidentally hit the INS key once in a while and find themselves typing over text they wish they hadn't. Using the key for paste instead cures this common headache.

5. *Use smart cut and paste.* When this option is selected, Word automatically removes extra spaces left over when text is cut and adds spaces when text is pasted. Without this option, cutting text from the middle of a sentence often leaves spaces at the beginning and the end of that text, creating a double space. I find this feature pretty useful, even though Word doesn't always get it right. Word's grammar checker is good at picking up extra spaces and words that are "misspelled" due to a missing space.
6. *Tabs and backspace set left indent.* When selected, left margins can be applied using the Tab key and undone using the Backspace key. Turn this function off if you often change the margin without meaning to. Tabs and indents are covered in Chapter 8.
7. *Allow accented uppercase in French.* This option causes Word's spell-checker to suggest accent marks to uppercase characters when typing in French. If you aren't working in French, leave this one off.

- *Signature text.* Enter signature text of any length here. Signatures can also include pictures or hyperlinks (use the buttons on the formatting bar to insert these using typical Word dialogs).
- *Signature for new messages.* Choose the default signature that is attached to all new messages created in Word.
- *Signature for replies and forwards.* Choose the default signature that is attached to all replies made to messages in Word.

Tools → Options → Edit Tab

The Edit tab (Figure 3-11) changes some of the basic ways you interact with a document.

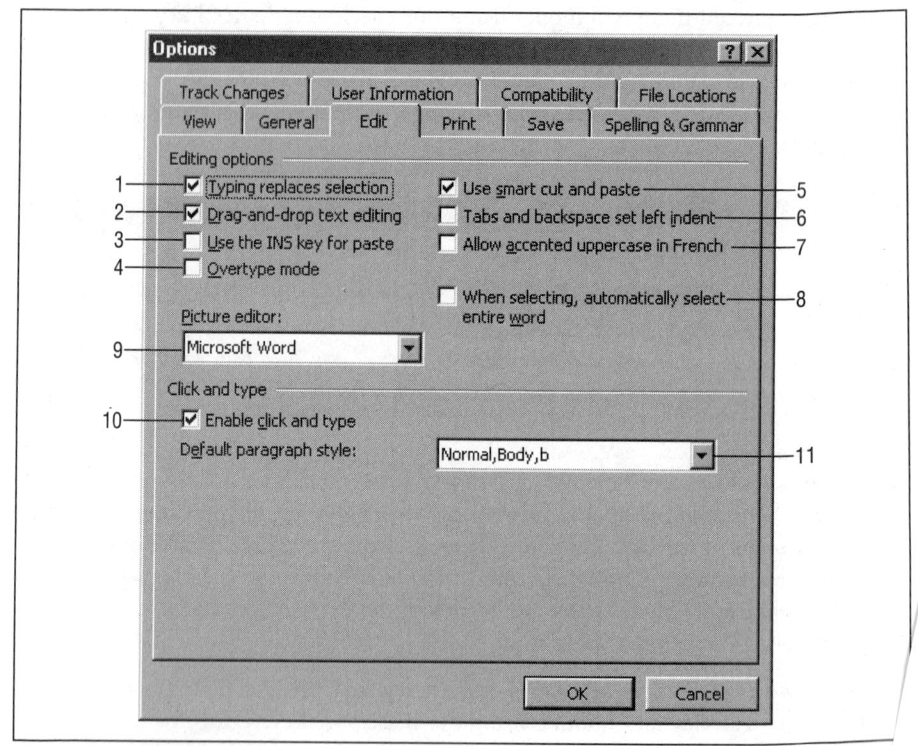

Figure 3-11: The Edit tab

1. *Typing replaces selection.* By default, typing text in a document replaces any currently selected. When this option is disabled, new text appears dir before the selection instead of replacing it. I recommend leaving this on.
2. *Drag-and-drop text editing.* When this option is enabled, drag any selectio document to another location in the document or to another docum move it. When this is disabled, selections may not be dragged.

8. *When selecting, automatically select entire word.* With this option on, dragging the mouse to select text causes Word to automatically select entire words and any trailing spaces.

TIP # 29

Finer Selection Control While Dragging

The Tools → Options → Edit → "Select entire word" option often makes it hard to select exactly the desired text, but there is a way around it without turning the option off. First drag the mouse to select a word. As soon as Word automatically selects an entire word, back the mouse up just a bit to deselect the word and then drag over that word again. This time, individual characters are selected instead.

9. *Picture editor.* The picture editor is the program used by default to edit pictures in a Word document. This list is supposed to display available graphics programs that you can make the default editor. While this sounds great in theory, the feature doesn't really work well. None of the graphics programs I have tested (including Microsoft's own PhotoDraw 2000) bothers to register itself in the registry as being able to work with Word 2000. At this point, there is no real workaround for this problem.
10. *Enable Click and Type.* Click and Type is a new method of automatically applying certain types of formatting to blank lines depending on where the mouse pointer is on the screen. The details of Click and Type are covered in Chapter 1. This option turns Click and Type on and off.
11. *Default paragraph style.* Use this option to select the default paragraph style that Word should use with the Click and Type feature. Note that Click and Type must be enabled for this option to have any effect.

Tools → Options → Print Tab

The Print tab configures a number of different settings that govern how and what parts of documents are printed. Detailed coverage of this tab is in the section on printing in Chapter 4, *File*.

Tools → Options → Save Tab

The Save tab (Figure 3-12) controls Word's automatic saving features and specifies some additional components to save with documents. The following list describes the Save tab options:

1. *Always create backup copy.* Normally, saving an open document commits any changes to the document file, replacing whatever was there before. With the "Always create backup copy" option enabled, Word renames the current file using the *.bak* extension before saving the current changes to the *.doc* file. For example, Word would turn a file named *work.doc* into a *work.bak* file and then

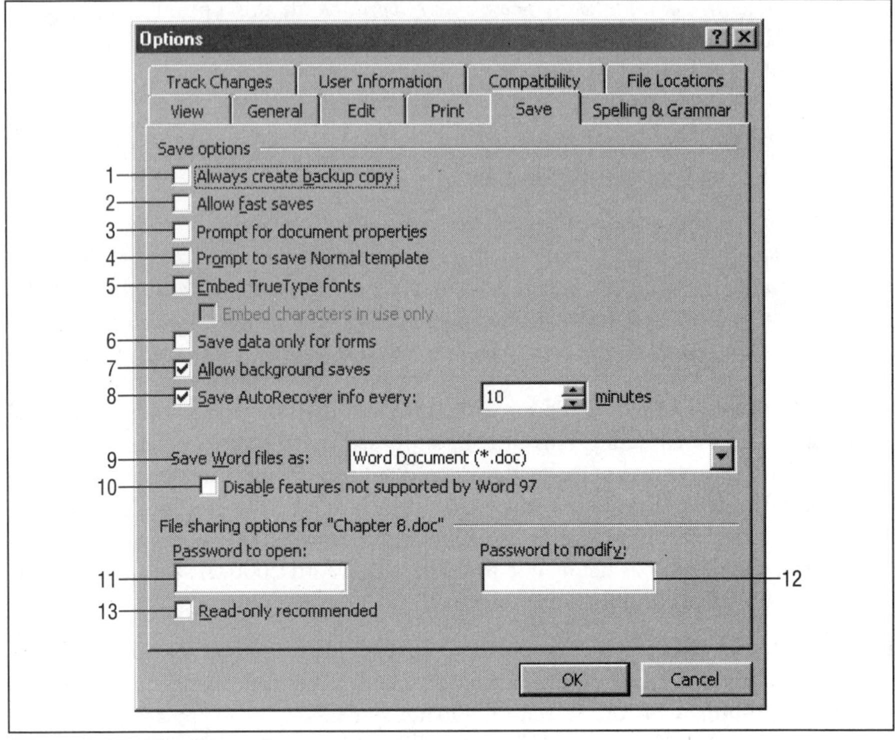

Figure 3-12: The Save tab

save any changes made as part of the *.doc* file. This preserves the document in its previous state in case the changes you make turn out not to be what you want.

2. *Allow fast saves.* During a normal (full) save of a document, the physical order of characters stored in the file is identical to the logical order of characters in the document that the file represents. In other words, changes to the file are incorporated into the contents of the file in the specific location where the change was made. During a fast save, changes to the file are appended to the end of the file instead. While this allows for faster saving, it also greatly increases the size of the file, as changes are appended instead of incorporated.

WARNING

I recommend not using fast saves at all when working with documents that contain sensitive information that has been deleted, because the information is not really deleted until a full save incorporates all changes.

When this option is selected, Word performs fast saves or full saves when you issue the File → Save command depending on a number of criteria:

- When you close the document, Word performs a full save.
- Every fifteenth save, Word performs a full save instead of a fast save, incorporating all changes into a document.
- Word also performs a full save when a lot of changes have been made to a document. Microsoft does not specify how many changes within a document it takes to make Word do a full save instead of a fast save, but there is a point at which Word does a full save of the document to incorporate changes.
- When the document is saved using a different format from that currently used, Word performs a full save.
- When working with a file over a network (i.e., a file on someone else's system or a company server), Word always performs a full save on the document regardless of whether fast saves are enabled.

TIP # 30

Do a Full Save Before Transferring Documents

I recommend leaving fast saves turned on, because it does speed the saving of a document enough to be noticed. Be sure to turn the option off and force a full save to help shrink the size of the file before sending it to someone else (especially through email).

---

3. *Prompt for document properties.* When this option is selected, the Summary tab of a document's properties (File → Properties → Summary) is automatically opened whenever a document is saved. This is useful when you must modify comments or keywords every time a document is saved. Otherwise, it's easy enough to open the properties yourself using File → Properties.
4. *Prompt to save Normal template.* With this option enabled, Word opens a dialog at every save, asking whether to commit any global changes made to *normal.dot.* By default, this option is turned off and these changes are saved automatically. I recommend leaving this option turned off during general use, though it may prove useful when creating or moving custom templates. Word's use of *normal.dot* is detailed in Chapter 2.
5. *Embed TrueType fonts.* When this option is selected, Word saves any fonts used in a document to the document file. Keep in mind that this setting affects only the current document, not all documents. The advantage to this is that other users can see the document exactly as intended, even if they don't have the fonts. The disadvantage is that this tends to increase the size of documents *significantly.* Since Word makes a pretty good representation of a document even without the correct fonts, the increase in file size is only a good tradeoff when using really uncommon fonts.

6. *Save data only for forms.* When this is enabled, only the actual data entered within a form field is saved, not the fields themselves. The document is saved as a text file. Fields in the document are delimited by commas. This is particularly useful when saving data that may be incorporated into a database or other program.

7. *Allow background saves.* With this option enabled, you can continue working in Word after issuing a Save command without waiting for the save to finish. Word usually handles this pretty well and I'd only recommend turning this option on if you find that working while saving is too slow or causes problems.

8. *Save AutoRecover info every: . . . minutes.* Use this option to have Word automatically save the AutoRecover information for open documents every specified number of minutes. Note that this does not mean that changes are being committed to the actual *.doc* file, just to the temporary AutoRecover file. Close a document without saving changes and all changes since the last Save command are discarded. For more information on how Word handles files, see Chapter 2.

9. *Save Word files as.* By default, Word saves all documents as Word 2000 documents unless otherwise specified. Use this drop-down list to make any of Word's native formats the default (Figure 3-13). I strongly recommend leaving the default alone and choosing other formats manually when needed using File → Save As. This helps ensure that all content and formatting are saved along with documents.

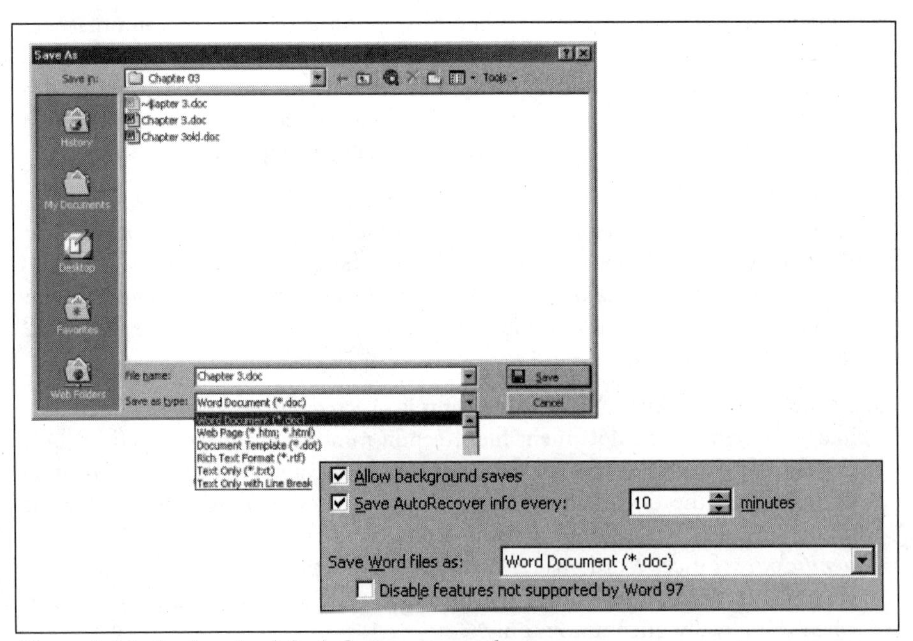

Figure 3-13: Setting the default format to save documents

10. *Disable features not supported by Word 97.* When sharing documents with people who use Word 97, consider turning this feature on. Even though Word 2000 and Word 97 use the same document format (meaning no converter is needed), Word 2000 does sport some features that Word 97 does not, such as new ways of laying out AutoShapes and footnotes.

11. *Password to open.* Enter a password of up to 15 characters in this box (Figure 3-14) to keep anyone without the password from opening the document at all. Unlike the rest of the options on this tab (save for embedding TrueType fonts), this and the other password options only apply to the current document.

Figure 3-14: Protecting a document with a password

WARNING

If you forget a password assigned to a document, there is no way provided within Word to recover it. While some third-party applications do exist (check out http://www.elcomsoft.com/ao97pr.html for an example), most of these programs work using what's called a "brute force" method. Provide certain parameters (such as minimum and maximum password length) and the program tries out every character combination that fits the criteria until it finds the password or has exhausted the search.

12. *Password to modify.* Enter a password to keep anyone from saving changes to the document. They can save changes to another filename using File → Save As. This password can be used in conjunction with the open password.

13. *Read-only recommended.* With this option selected, a dialog opens whenever the current document loads, suggesting that the user open the document in read-only mode so that changes to the document cannot be saved. This is only a suggestion; users can disregard it if they wish.

Tools → Options → Spelling & Grammar Tab

The Spelling & Grammar tab (Figure 3-15) controls the behavior of Word's spelling and grammar checkers (Tools → Spelling and Grammar). All of the options on this tab apply globally to Word and not just to the open document. Find detailed coverage of Word's Spelling and Grammar tool in Chapter 9.

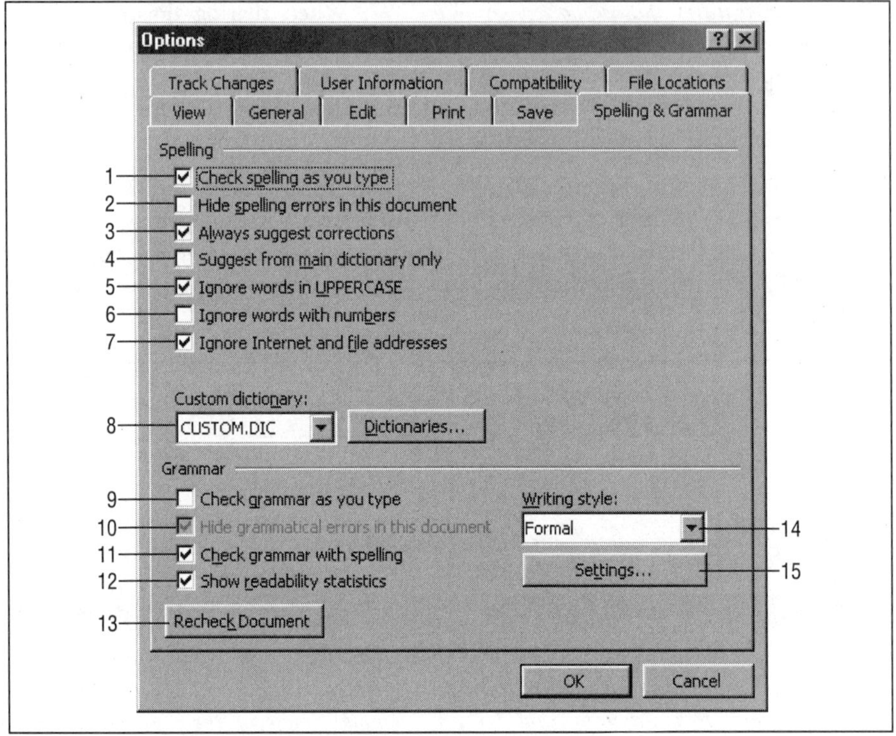

Figure 3-15: The Spelling & Grammar tab

1. *Check spelling as you type.* This is the option that puts those squiggly red lines underneath misspelled words in the document. Some people hate it; some love it. Disable this option to turn it off.

2. *Hide spelling errors in this document.* This option is only available if option #1 is turned on and simply keeps the squiggly lines from showing in a document, even though Word still checks spelling as you type. For an explanation of why this option is useful, see Tip # 31.

TIP # 31

Spelling and Grammar Status

Leave background spelling and grammar checking on, but hide the errors in the document to avoid those distracting squiggly lines. A book icon with an X on it appears in the Spelling and Grammar Status box on Word's status bar to indicate that the document contains errors. Right-click this icon to toggle the hide errors option and to open the Spelling & Grammar tab. Double-click the icon to jump to the next misspelled word after the insertion point. Word automatically highlights the error and opens a context menu with correction suggestions.

3. *Always suggest corrections.* When this option is enabled, Word offers alternative spellings to misspelled words during a manual spell-check using Tools → Spelling and Grammar. Unless your system is particularly slow, I can see no reason why you'd want to turn this off.

4. *Suggest from main dictionary only.* When this is selected, Word only offers spelling corrections from its main dictionary and not from any open custom dictionaries. Word's use of dictionaries is detailed in Chapter 9.

5. *Ignore words in UPPERCASE.* When this option is selected, words that are in all uppercase are not included in the spell-check.

6. *Ignore words with numbers.* When this is selected, words with numbers in them are not included in the spell-check.

7. *Ignore Internet and file addresses.* When this option is selected, Internet addresses (like *http://anything.com*) and file addresses (like *c:\windows*) are not included in the spell-check.

8. *Custom dictionary.* During a manual spell-check (or on the context menu for a misspelled word in a document), Word provides the option to add the word to a custom dictionary. This option specifies the default custom dictionary. See Chapter 9 for more on using dictionaries.

9. *Check grammar as you type.* Even those people who like the squiggly red spelling lines tend to find the green grammar lines annoying. Turn them off here.

10. *Hide grammatical errors in this document.* This option is only available if option #9 is turned on and simply keeps the squiggly lines from showing in a document, even though Word still checks grammar as you type.

11. *Check grammar with spelling.* When this option is enabled (the default), Word checks both grammar and spelling during a manual spell-check. Turn this option off to have Word check only spelling. After starting Tools → Spelling and Grammar, turn this option back on using the "Check Grammar" option. For more on this, see Chapter 9.

12. *Show readability statistics.* When enabled, Word displays a dialog showing various readability statistics after finishing a manual spelling and grammar check. A sample is shown in Figure 3-16. While this can be interesting, the only information I find useful on the page is in the Counts section and you can get that more easily using Tools → Word Count.

13. *Recheck Document.* This button is named Check Document if a spelling and grammar check has not yet been performed during the current session and Recheck Document if one has. Use this button to check the spelling and grammar after changing any spelling and grammar options. Recheck Document also resets the internal Ignore All list, meaning that during the next

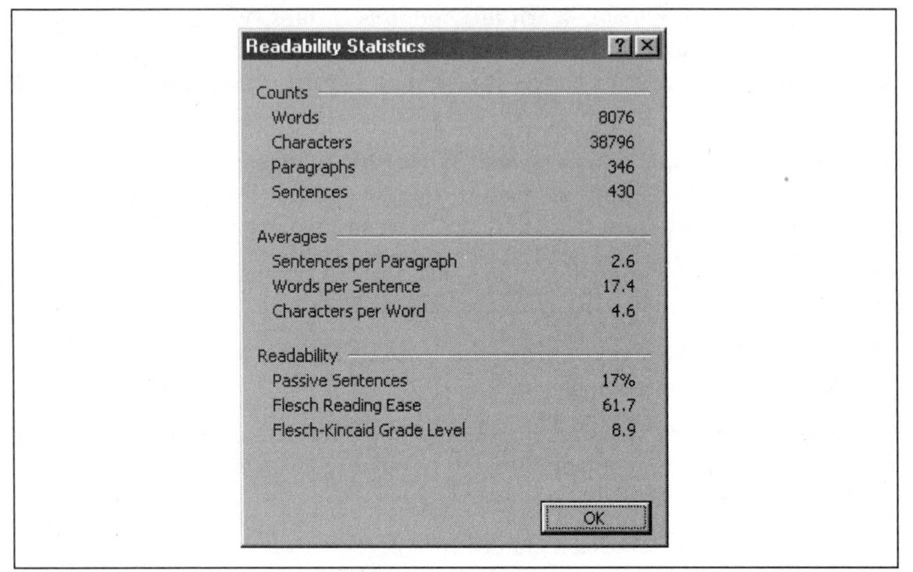

Figure 3-16: Readability statistics shown after a grammar check

spelling and grammar check, Word rechecks anything ignored during a previous check. For more on this, see Chapter 9.

14. *Writing style*. Choose from preset writing styles, including Standard, Casual, Formal, Technical, and Custom. Each of these is actually just a predefined set of the same options set using the Settings button, described next. Choose one of these styles to set a number of rules at once.

15. *Settings*. Use this button to adjust the specific rules Word uses when checking grammar for a document. Change settings for each of the five predefined writing styles, listed previously. Read more about changing these settings in Chapter 9.

Tools → Options → Track Changes Tab

Word includes a feature called revision marking (Tools → Track Changes → Highlight Changes) that keeps track of edits as multiple users work on a document. This feature and the Track Changes tab are covered in Chapter 13.

Tools → Options → User Information Tab

The User Information tab (Figure 3-17) changes basic information about the primary user of Word. Normally, your name and initials are entered when Word is installed, but they can be changed at any time.

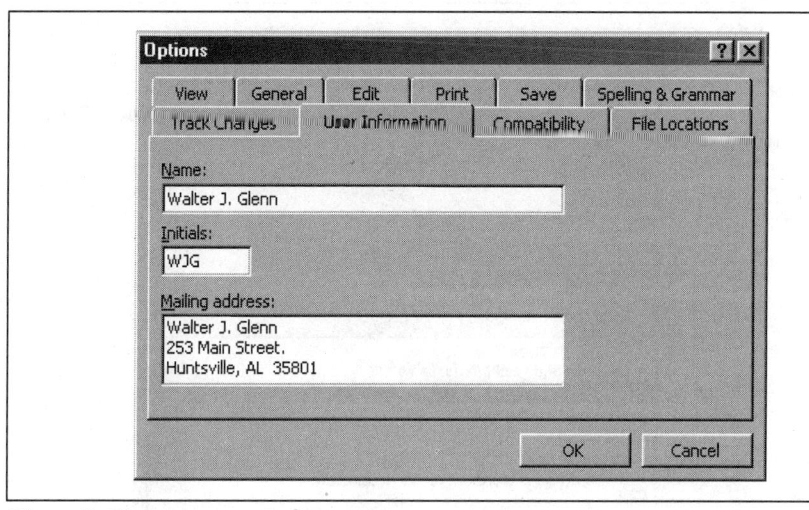

Figure 3-17: Setting user information

The information on the User Information tab is used in many places throughout Word:

- The Name and Mailing address are used to construct the return address when using Tools → Envelopes and Labels. If you change the return address on the Envelopes and Labels screen, Word asks whether it should make the change your permanent return address (unless you change it to blank). Select Yes and the information is changed on the User Information tab automatically. Read more about envelopes and labels in Chapter 9.
- The Name is also used in a document's properties (File → Properties) to fill in the last saved by field on the Statistics tab and the Author field on the Summary tab.
- Initials are used to identify comments inserted using Insert → Comments and the Name is used to identify changes when revision marking is turned on (holding the pointer over a change pops up a bubble with the name of the reviewer and date of the change).
- The Name and Initials are also used in various fields when creating letters and faxes from templates.

Tools → Options → Compatibility Tab

The Compatibility tab (Figure 3-18) controls display options regarding certain compatibility issues. View and modify the fonts substituted when actual fonts used in a document aren't available. This tab also specifies how Word should handle the display of various features in documents created with other applications.

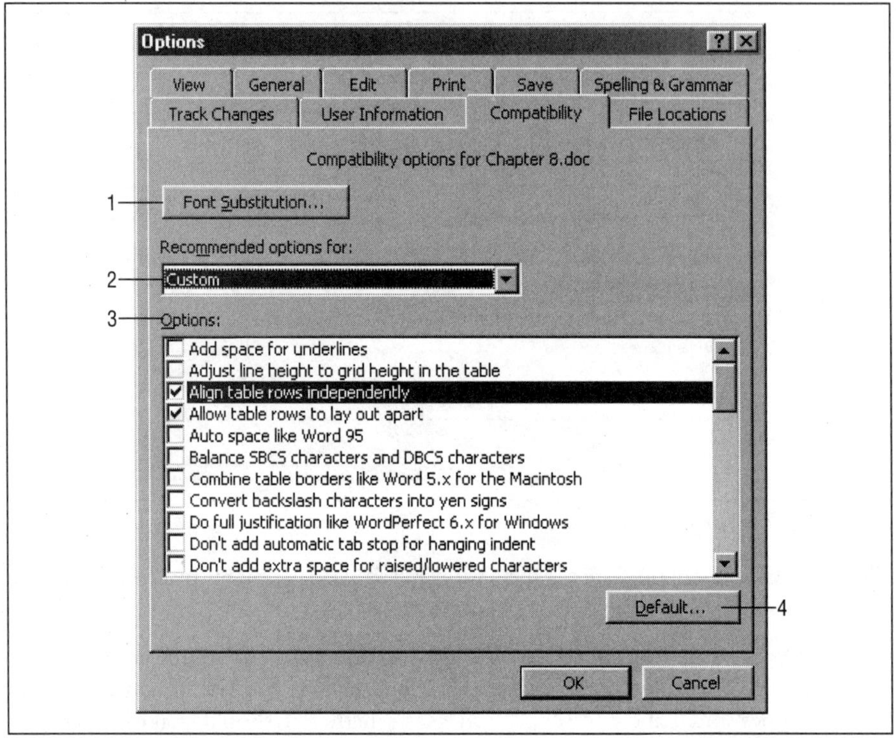

Figure 3-18: Setting compatibility options

1. *Font Substitution.* This button opens a dialog showing any fonts used in the current document that are not installed on your system. It also displays the fonts that Word has automatically selected to display in place of the missing fonts. For each missing font, choose the substitute font to display using the Substituted Font drop-down list. Use the Convert Permanently button in the substitution dialog to convert the missing fonts to those listed instead of just displaying them that way.

2. *Recommended options for.* This drop-down list and the Options window under it control how Word should display documents in different formats. Available formats include Microsoft Word 2000, 97, and 6.0/95; Word for Windows 1.0 and 2.0; Word for Macintosh 5.0; Word for MS-DOS; WordPerfect 5.x, 6.0 for Windows, and 6.x for DOS. Select a format and Word displays a preconfigured list of options for that format in the Options window. For each format, enable or disable any of the options in the list. Keep in mind that the options set for any document type only apply to the display of documents of that type and do not change document itself in any way.

3. *Options.* The list of display options that you can set is quite long and often esoteric, so we've decided not to include details of the options here. However, Microsoft Knowledge Base article #Q193266 covers these options well and is

available at *http://www.microsoft.com/technet/support/searchkb.asp.* Just search for the article ID number.

4. *Default.* Use this button to reset the display for all document types to the built-in Word default.

Tools → Options → File Locations Tab

The File Locations tab (Figure 3-19) is where Word saves and looks for certain types of files by default. Select any entry and use the Modify button to open a dialog for selecting a new drive and folder.

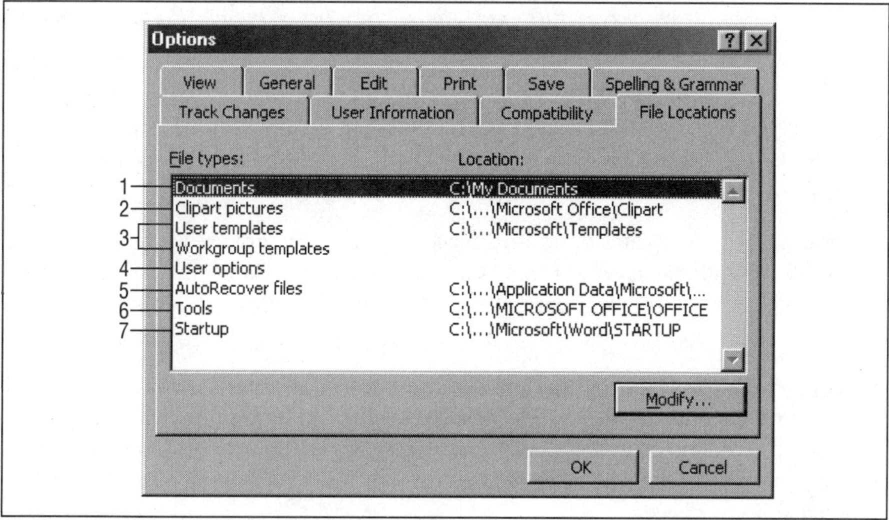

Figure 3-19: Setting default file locations

1. *Documents.* This is the folder location opened the first time a new document is saved or whenever the File → Open command is used. By default, this is set to *My Documents.* Unless you have a different location where you commonly store files, I recommend leaving this setting alone, mainly because all of the other Office applications and many non-Office applications use this default location too. Include shortcuts in the *My Documents* folder to other folders instead.

2. *Clipart pictures.* In previous versions of Word, clip art pictures were simply stored on file and Word itself was used to browse through those pictures. Now, Word uses a separate clip art program that manages file locations and this path is no longer used. It really doesn't matter what it is set to.

3. *User templates and Workgroup templates.* These locations hold templates that appear on the General tab along with Word's standard blank templates. These settings are covered in detail in Chapter 4.

4. *User options*. In previous versions of Word, most of the user options set using Tools → Options were stored in a binary file named *winword.opt*. In Word 2000, all user options are stored in the registry and the user options path is no longer used. You can enter a path here, but it won't do a thing.

5. *AutoRecover files*. Set the location that Word uses to save temporary AutoRecover files that are used to recover a document should Word crash.

On computers running Microsoft Windows 95 or Windows 98, automatically recovered files are stored in the Windows\Application Data\Microsoft\Word folder by default. In Microsoft Windows NT version 4.0 or later, or on a computer with more than one active user profile, automatically recovered files are stored in the Windows\Profiles\username\Application Data\Microsoft\Word folder.

6. *Tools*. This is where Word expects to find the executable files for the various tools that make up Word and Office 2000 (for example, the graphing program Word uses, *graph.exe*). Don't change this one without a really good reason—(I'm hard pressed to think of one).

7. *Startup*. Any templates or add-ins placed in this directory are loaded and added to Word's global layer during Word startup and before any documents are loaded. For more information on how Word builds its global layer, see Chapter 2.

Now that we've looked at all the options available in Word, it's time to delve into the realm of customizing Word. The options covered so far tend to deal mostly with how Word handles documents and how it displays certain items. The customization features we're going to cover next actually deal with changing Word's interface to better suit your needs.

Customizing the Word Interface

Browsing through Word's menus presents a superset of all of Word's functionality. While Word's new adaptive menus are designed to provide access to commonly used commands and suppress those used less frequently, these adaptive menus are really not a good solution, for a couple of reasons. First, different people have different ideas of what common commands are. Second, many people rely on scanning menus to find commands they use less frequently and may not remember where to find them. Some options selected here affect all Office programs; others—such as toolbar and menu customizations—remain local to the program they are used in.

Use the Tools → Customize command to perform four different types of customizations:

Tools → Customize → Options
: Set general customization options that govern how Word's personalized (adaptive) menus work and how icons appear on menus and toolbars.

Tools → Customize → Toolbars
Use this tab to create new toolbars, rename and delete existing toolbars, and reset default toolbars.

Tools → Customize → Commands
This tab lets you add, remove, and modify commands in Word's menus and toolbars. It's also used to create new menus.

Keyboard Customization
At the bottom of the Customize dialog that holds all three of these tabs, a Keyboard button opens a dialog for creating and modifying keyboard shortcuts for just about every command in Word.

TIP # 32

Access Tools → Customize More Quickly

Access the Customize dialog quickly by right-clicking on any toolbar and choosing Customize from the context menu or using View → Toolbars → Customize.

Setting Customization Options

By default, Word 2000 uses *adaptive* menus that display only certain basic commands (as decided by Microsoft) and your most frequently used commands. Some users find it helpful not to have to weed through the full menus; some find it disconcerting not to see all of the available commands immediately. Use Tools → Customize → Options (Figure 3-20) to adjust the behavior of adaptive menus and even turn them off. The tab is also used to customize other aspects of toolbar and menu behavior. The following list describes the customization options:

1. *Standard and Formatting toolbars share one row.* By default, Word displays the Standard and Formatting toolbars on a single row. Turn this option off to display each on its own row. Dragging one of the toolbars to a new row implicitly turns off this option. This option is dimmed if one or both of the toolbars are not turned on in Word. This option applies only to Word (i.e., turning it off in Word does not turn it off in Outlook).

2. *Menus show recently used commands first.* Turn this option off to disable adaptive menus so that Word shows all menu commands. If this option is disabled in one Office application, it is disabled in all Office applications.

TIP # 33

Disabling Adaptive Menus

Most advanced Word users can't stand adaptive menus. And I feel that they are also a hindrance to new users who need to become familiar with Word's menu structure and what commands are found there. Turn them off using Tools → Customize → Options → "Menus show recently used command first".

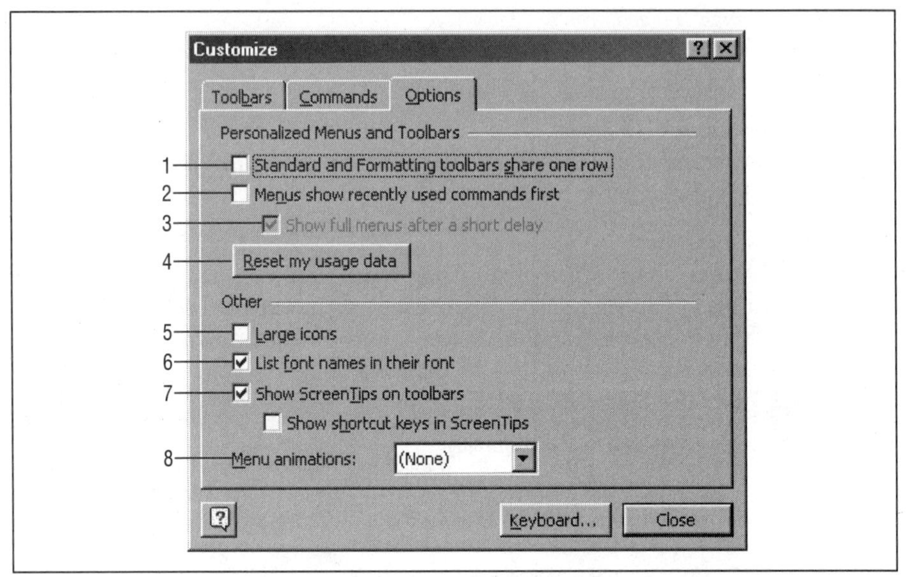

Figure 3-20: Changing command bar behavior with Tools → Customize → Options

3. *Show full menus after a short delay.* This option is only available if adaptive menus are turned on. When it is enabled, Word displays the full menu automatically if no command is chosen for about five seconds after opening a menu. With this option off, you must select the double-caret (>>) graphic at the bottom of a menu to display the full menu.

4. *Reset my usage data.* This button deletes the adaptive menu history stored in Word. After resetting your data, Word relearns your style and adapts the menus again. This action only applies to Word. Resetting data in Word does not also reset data in other applications.

5. *Large icons.* This option displays large icons on Word's toolbars and even displays toolbars on two or more rows to fit all the buttons in. Though most users won't find much use for it, it is handy for those who can't see small objects so well or those who work on particularly large monitors in high resolution.

6. *List font names in their font.* This option displays fonts from the font list on the formatting toolbar in their actual typefaces. If you don't use that many fonts or find it a bit slow to generate the displays, turn this option off.

7. *Show ScreenTips on toolbars.* ScreenTips are those little pop-up balloons that appear when the pointer is held over an interface item (Figure 3-21). On toolbars, ScreenTips show the names of the buttons. Turn this option off if this is annoying. If ScreenTips are turned on, they can also show keyboard shortcuts by turning on the "Show shortcut keys in ScreenTips" option.

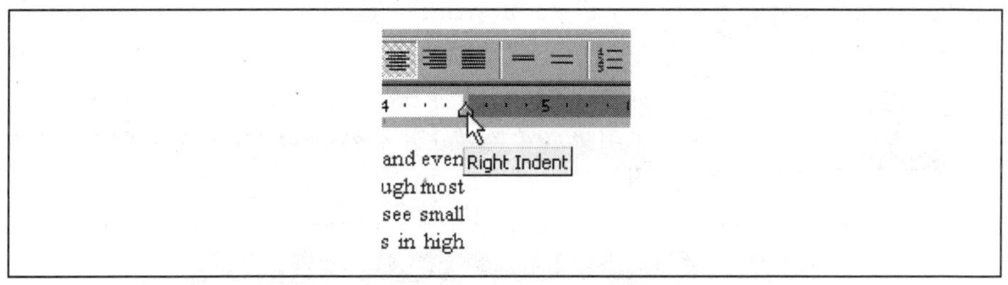

Figure 3-21: Viewing a ScreenTip

8. *Menu animations.* By default, no menu animations are used in Word. Two animations are available, though. Slide displays the menu as if it were sliding down from its top edge. Unfold makes it look as though the menu were unfolding from its top left corner. A third choice, Random, chooses randomly between Slide and Unfold each time a menu opens.

Creating and Modifying Toolbars

Word's toolbars were designed with two purposes in mind: to provide access to common commands in a context-sensitive fashion and also to provide some marketing of features. For example, do you think the typical Word user really uses columns and Excel spreadsheets so much that they need buttons on the toolbar for faster access? However, the buttons do look neat and show off some of the things Word can do.

Any customizations applied to toolbars and menus are program specific. For example, removing commands from the File menu in Word does nothing to the File menu in any other Office application.

Fortunately, Word provides a way to cut out all this fluff. This is where the Tools → Customize dialog seems to take an odd little turn. The Toolbars tab is used to create and modify toolbars. The Commands tab is used to add, remove, and modify commands on the toolbars and menus. So why isn't there a tab called Menus for adding new menus? The answer is that Word's menu bar is really just another toolbar.

To see what I mean, use the procedure I describe below in Customizing Commands to add a button to the menu bar. It sits there, fully functional, right alongside Word's menus. Also, a menu is really just a special type of command that holds other commands. Menus can be placed anywhere, including on a toolbar or inside another menu. Does this mean you can create your own custom menu bar and fill it with your own menus and commands? You bet it does. However, you are not allowed to close Word's built-in menu bar.

Tools → Customize → Toolbars (Figure 3-22) shows a list of all of Word's toolbars (including the Menu bar). More toolbars are listed here than in the View → Toolbars submenu or when right-clicking an open toolbar. Those two methods only show 16 of Word's toolbars—the 16 Microsoft thought were the most commonly needed. The Toolbars tab shows all 23 of Word's default toolbars and any custom toolbars created.

For the purposes of this discussion, a custom toolbar is a new toolbar that you create and a customized toolbar is a built-in Word toolbar that you change in some way.

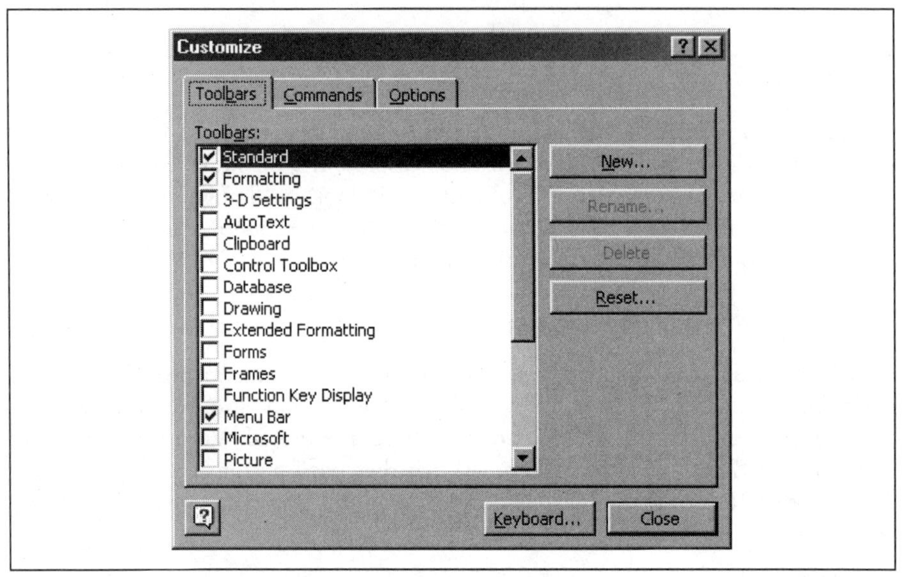

Figure 3-22: Modifying command bars with Tools → Customize → Toolbars

Use the Toolbars tab to toggle toolbars on and off, to rename and delete custom toolbars, and to create new ones. To create a new toolbar, click New, give the new toolbar a name, and a new toolbar is created. To do anything with that new toolbar (like add commands), use Tools → Customize → Commands, which is covered in the next section.

The Toolbars tab is also used to reset any of Word's built-in toolbars to their default state, which is great if you've been monkeying around and don't like the changes.

The Reset command can also be used on Word's Menu Bar, which is listed along with the toolbars on Tools → Customize → Toolbars. Resetting the Menu Bar resets all of Word's menus to their default state.

Customizing Commands

Customizing the commands on Word's menus is much better than relying on adaptive menus, or even on the full built-in menus. Customize the commands on any of Word's built-in command bars using Tools → Customize → Commands (Figure 3-23).

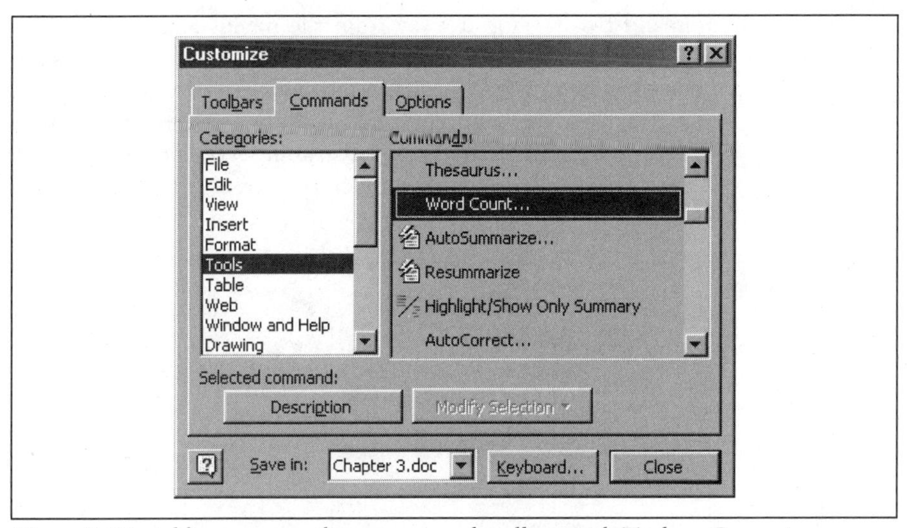

Figure 3-23: Adding commands to menus and toolbars with Tools → Customize → Commands

Opening Tools → Customize puts Word into an editing mode where, unlike with other Word dialogs, you can interact with Word's menus and toolbars. The commands themselves are not available in this editing mode, except for customization.

After adjusting the menu and toolbar commands, choose where to save your customization. By default, changes are only saved in the active document. If you allow this, be aware that any person opening the document after you (assuming you collaborate) may wonder just what happened to the usual menus. Warn people when you send them customized documents. Changes can also be saved in any template associated with the document (including normal.dot) by selecting it from the "Save in" list (see Figure 3-23). I recommend creating a separate global template (load it automatically with Word, as described in Chapter 2) used just to save customizations.

The Tools → Customize → Commands tab offers a number of actions:

- Move a command (on a menu or toolbar) simply by dragging it to a different location—a different place on the same menu or toolbar, a different menu or toolbar, and between menus and toolbars. A toolbar button can be moved to Word's menu bar or an entire menu can be moved to a toolbar.

TIP # 34

How to Copy Commands When Dragging

The default behavior when dragging commands is to move them. To copy them instead, hold down the Ctrl key while dragging.

- Remove a command by dragging it away from the menus and toolbars altogether. When dragging a command away, an "x" appears on the icon to show that the command will be removed (Figure 3-24). Don't worry. If you remove a built-in button that you later want back, add it using Tools → Customize → Commands or reset the toolbar with Tools → Customize → Toolbars → Reset. Use this method to remove commands from menus, buttons from toolbars, and even whole menus.

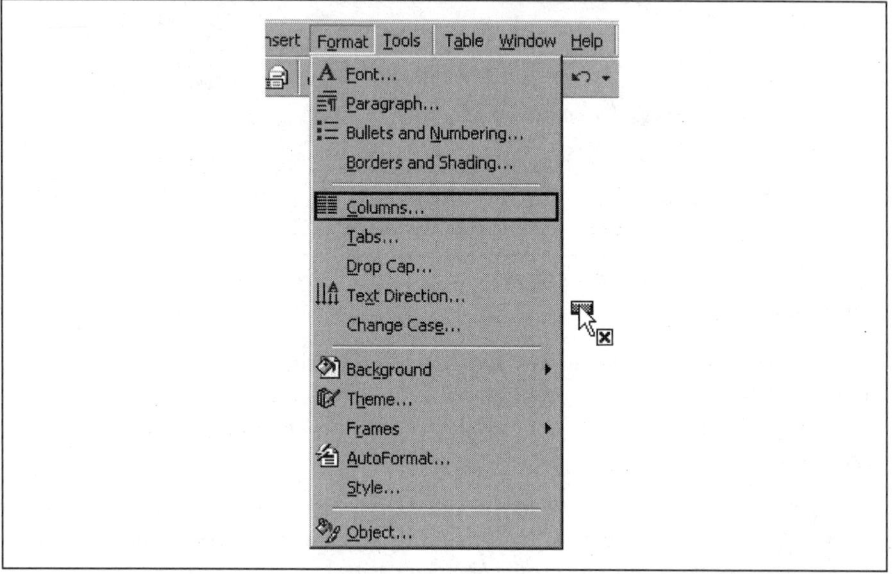

Figure 3-24: Moving a command away from a menu

TIP # 35

Move and Remove Commands Right from Word

Move and remove commands without going into Tools → Customize → Commands by holding the Alt key down and dragging the commands. The Customize dialog must be used to add new commands.

- Add a command to the toolbar by first selecting the category and then choosing the command. Drag it from the Commands list to any location on a toolbar or menu (see Figure 3-25). Commands can even be dragged right onto Word's menu bar. In fact, this is exactly how to go about creating a new menu. At the bottom of the Category list is a category named New Menu, inside which is a single command also named New Menu. Drag that command onto Word's menu bar to create a new menu. You can also create new menus on toolbars. Click the Description button to see a pop-up description of any selected command.

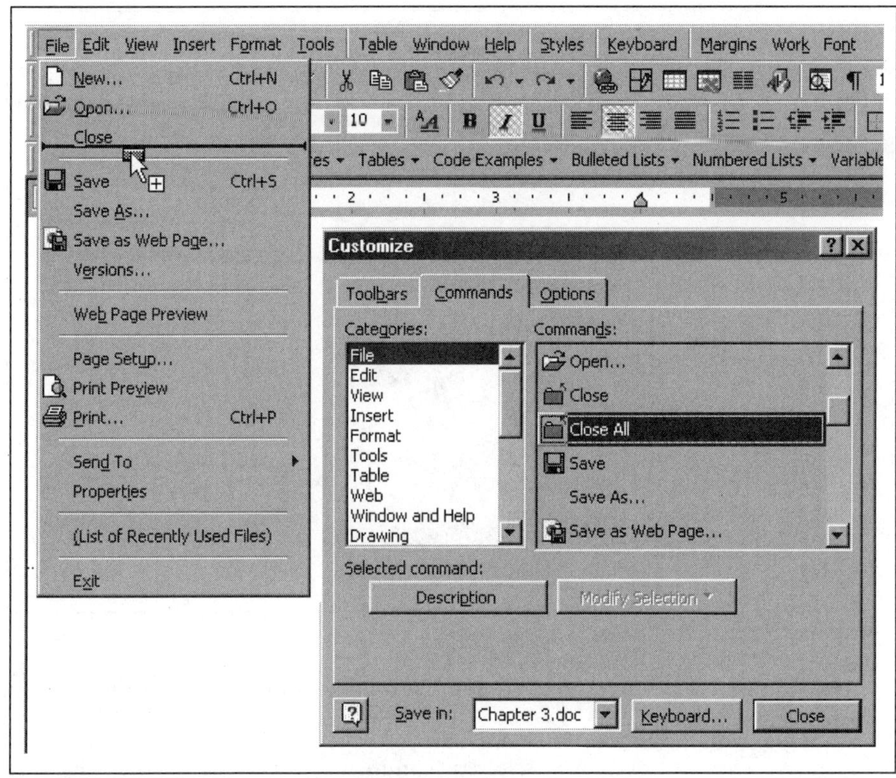

Figure 3-25: Adding the Close All command to the File menu

Take some time to browse through the categories and commands on these lists. Most of them are not found on Word's default menus or are buried deep in sub-menus. Make commonly used commands easier to get to by moving them to a better menu location or by creating a toolbar or menu.

TIP # 36

Two Built-in Menus You May Not Know About

There are two built-in menus available in Word that are not shown on Word's menu bar by default. The Work menu works something like a Favorites menu. Choose Work → Add to Work Menu to add the current document as a command on the Work menu. The other built-in menu is named Fonts and displays a list of fonts formatted in the font style.

- Modify the settings for an existing command by selecting it in the Word interface (click it once) and clicking the Modify Selection button on the Commands tab. Right-click any command to open the same pop-up menu (Figure 3-26). Most of these settings deal with how the command is displayed on the toolbar.

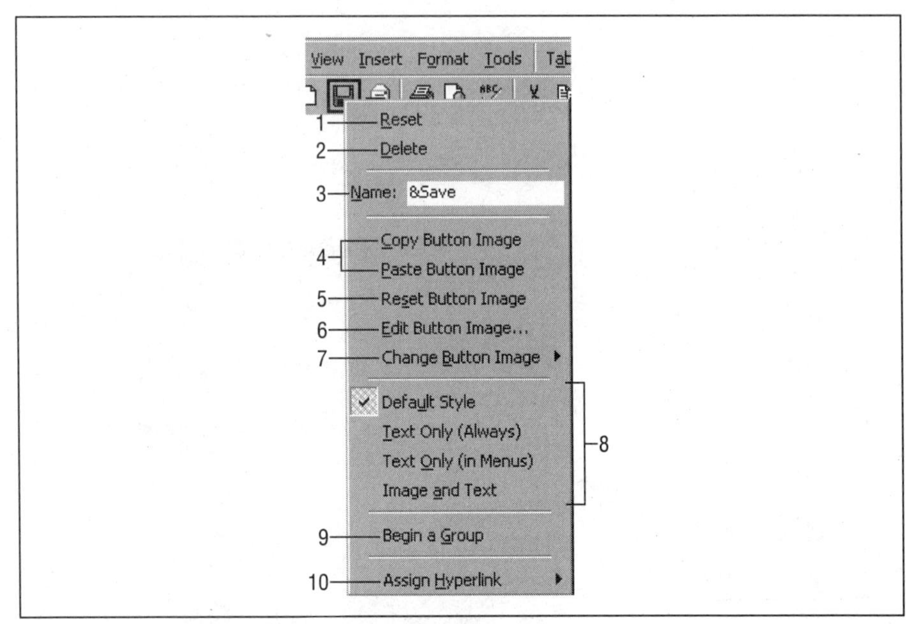

Figure 3-26: Modifying an existing command

1. *Reset.* This resets the command (or button or entire menu) to the built-in default.

2. *Delete.* This removes the selected command, identical to dragging the command away.

3. *Name.* For a menu or menu command, the name is what appears on the menu. For a button, the name is what appears in the ScreenTip. The ampersand (&) sets the keyboard accelerator for the menu. For example, the default name for the File menu is &File, and pressing Alt-F to access the menu. The default name for the Save command is &Save and once the File menu is open, pressing **s** issues the Save command. An underscore under the appropriate letter visually denotes it as an accelerator.

4. *Copy/Paste Button Image.* These commands are only available on buttons and menu commands and work pretty much like the copy and paste commands in Word. Copy Button Image places a picture of the button in the clipboard. Paste Button Image replaces a button's image with the one in the clipboard. The button image can even be pasted onto a button in another Office application or right into a document.

5. *Reset Button Image.* This command resets the button image to its default state. Note that if you crafted your own button with the Button Editor, it will be lost unless you cut and paste the image somewhere else before resetting the button. This option is not available for menus themselves, only for commands on the menus and on toolbars.

6. *Edit Button Image.* This command opens the Button Editor (Figure 3-27). Issue the Edit Button Image command on a button with an image and the image is loaded into the Button Editor, where it can be modified or replaced. Opening the Button Editor for a command that has no image starts with a blank canvas. This option is not available for menus themselves, only for commands on the menus and on toolbars.

Figure 3-27: The Button Editor

7. *Change Button Image.* Use this command to select from a number of built-in button images. Available images are displayed on a palette submenu (Figure 3-28). This option is not available for menus themselves, only for commands on the menus and on toolbars.

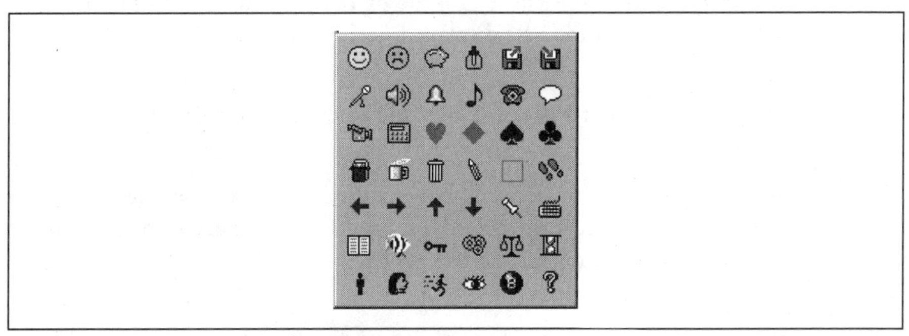

Figure 3-28: Choosing built-in button images

8. *Styles*. Choose from several different ways to display a button:

   Default
   : This option sets the command to its default display.

   Text Only (always)
   : This option makes commands display only as text in both menus and toolbars. Text Only (in Menus) displays menu commands as text only. This means the picture of the icon is not displayed in the menu, but remains unchanged on the toolbar.

   Image and Text
   : This option displays both the text and the associated image for menu and toolbar commands. Menu commands with an associated image use this by default.

9. *Begin a Group*. When this option is activated for an item, a divider is inserted *above* the selected item, helping to group like commands (Figure 3-29). For top-level menus and toolbars, above means "to the left of." When moving an existing menu or toolbar into another, this also creates a group around the moved item.

Figure 3-29: Separating commands into logical groups

10. *Assign Hyperlink*. This opens a separate dialog (Figure 3-30) for assigning a hyperlink to a command. This is the same hyperlink dialog opened by Insert → Hyperlink.

The "Link to" bar on the left presents several choices:

Existing File or Web Page
: Use this option to enter the name of a file or Internet address in the form of a URL. Select from one of the lists displayed:

  Recent Files
  : This is a list of recently accessed files stored by the operating system.

  Browsed Pages
  : This is a list of recently accessed pages stored by Internet Explorer or a list of Inserted Links recently pasted or otherwise inserted into documents. You can also browse for files or web pages.

Place in This Document
: Normally, this option creates a hyperlink to a bookmark in the current document. However, this option is not available to commands. When browsing though the list of recent files or browsed pages, a Bookmark button appears,

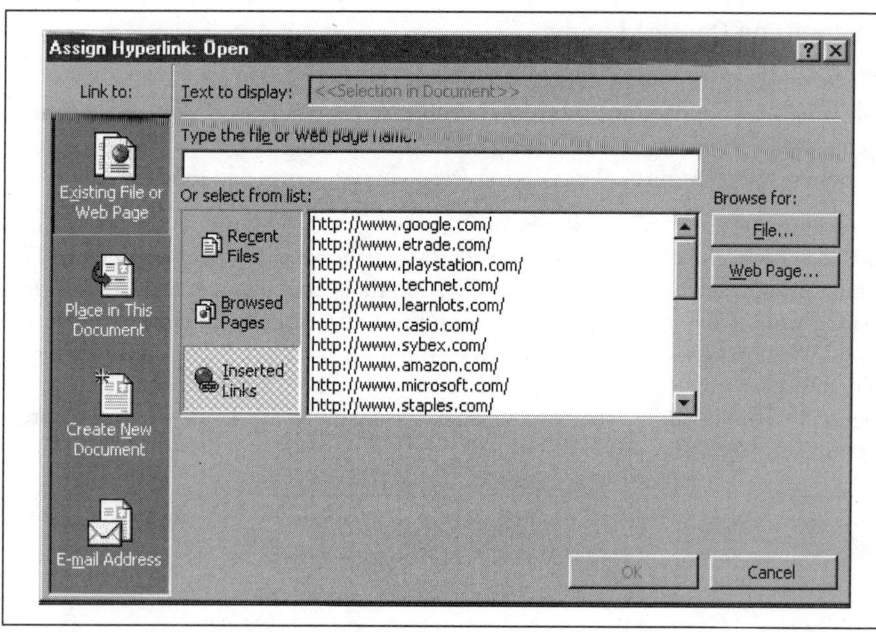

Figure 3-30: Assigning hyperlinks to a command

Customizing Word

but clicking it doesn't do anything. In the normal Insert Hyperlink dialog that you access straight from Word, this button does essentially the same thing as the Place in this Document selection.

Create New Document

This option creates a new document. Choose whether to edit the document now or later. Notice that choosing the "later" option places a hyperlink on a menu or toolbar. Issuing the command later actually creates that new document.

E-mail Address

This option creates a command that opens a new email message with the address and even subject line filled in as specified.

TIP # 37

Create a Menu of Email Contacts

First, create a new menu in Word and fill it with a number of commands. It doesn't matter which commands are used, because the next step is to rename the commands and assign a hyperlink to them. Name each command for an email contact and assign a hyperlink to the command with the person's email address. Choose any command on the menu and Word creates a new message addressed to that person.

Customizing Context Menus

While most of the other Office 2000 applications allow you to customize the command bars, only Word lets you customize context menus. Every single context menu available throughout the program can be customized using the same techniques we just went through for customizing normal menus and toolbars.

First, open the Customize dialog using Tools → Customize and switch to the Toolbars tab. From the list, select the Shortcut Menus toolbar to open it onscreen. This toolbar is only available while in customization mode and closes as soon as you close the Customize dialog. The three menus on this toolbar hold submenus representing all of Word's context menus. Use the Commands tab of the Customize dialog to add commands to a context menu the same way you would to a normal menu. In Figure 3-31, I am adding the Next Change command to the Track Changes context menu.

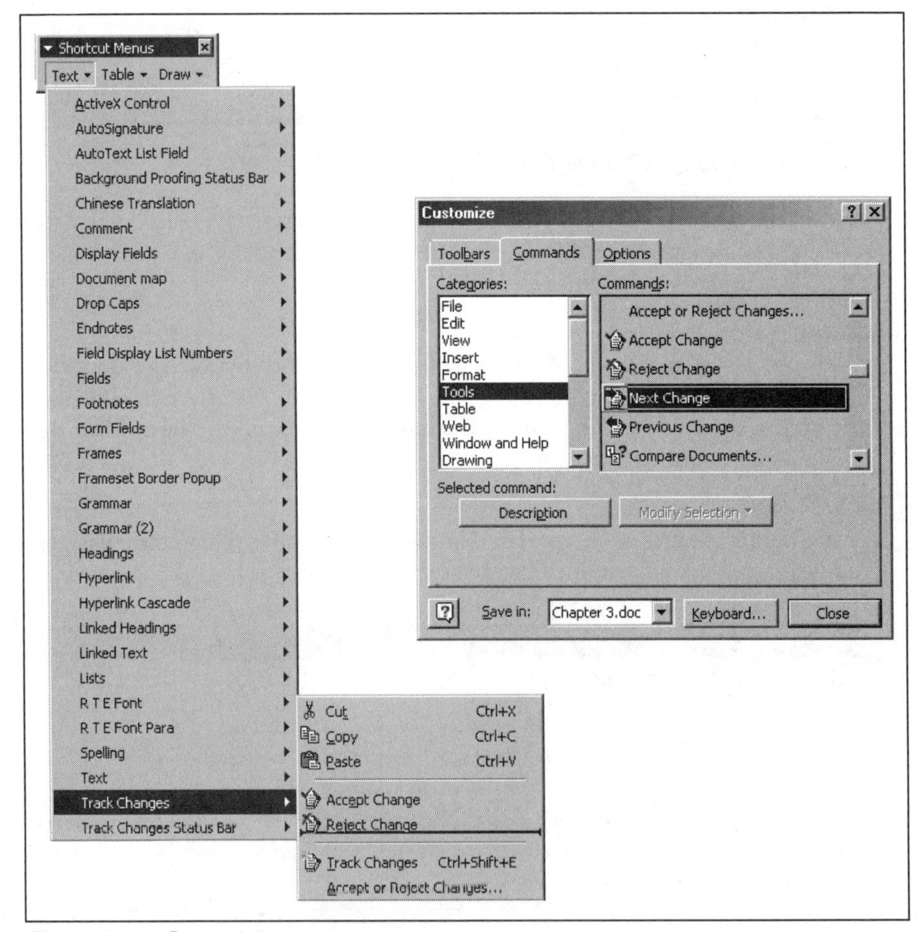

Figure 3-31: Customizing a context menu

I would also add the Previous Change command. That way, I could navigate through revisions using the context menu rather than the Reviewing toolbar. Throughout this book, I will try to point out useful additions you can make to Word's context menus with this powerful ability.

Customizing Keyboard Shortcuts

At the bottom of the Tools → Customize dialog on all three tabs, a button named Keyboard leads to one of Word's great customization tools. The button opens a dialog (Figure 3-32) for viewing, changing, and assigning keyboard shortcuts to every command in Word.

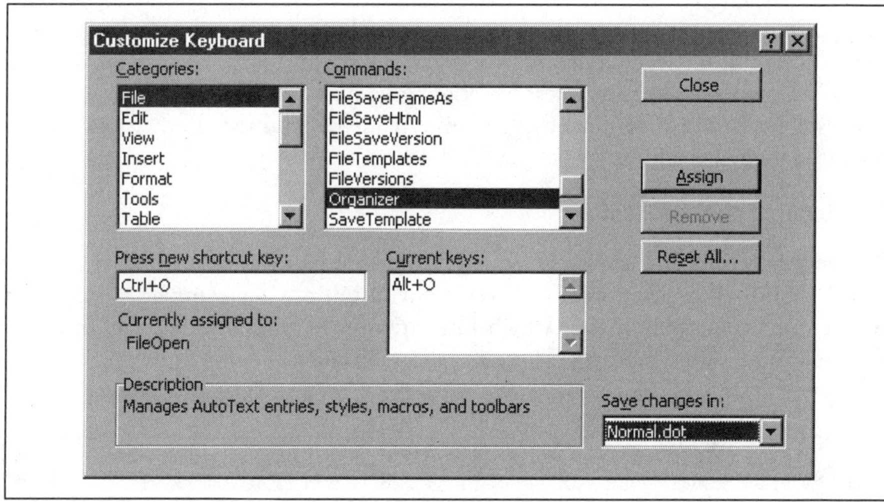

Figure 3-32: Assigning keyboard shortcuts to commands

The Categories list shows categories for all of Word's menus, complex commands such as tables and borders, and other things like macros, fonts, AutoText entries, styles, and common symbols. Select a category, then select a command or item in that category. The "Current keys" box shows all key combinations currently assigned to that command. The Description box shows what the command is used for.

To set a new keyboard shortcut for the selected command, place the cursor inside the "Press new shortcut key" box and press the keys to assign. The key combination appears in the box. If the combination is currently assigned to another command, a description is given underneath. To assign the new shortcut, click Assign. Note that, unlike command customizations, keyboard shortcuts are saved by default in *normal.dot,* not the active document.

When assigning a shortcut that is already assigned to another command, it is reassigned to the currently selected command. Since there is no way to cancel out of this dialog or undo changes, it is best to assign keys that do not already have assignments. For a list of common key assignments in Word, see Appendix A, Keyboard Shortcuts.

Our Favorite Customizations

I thought I'd end this chapter with a look at some of the customizations I enjoy using on my own system. Of course, all users are going to have different ideas of what is required and what is just taking up space, so by all means experiment. Browse through the command list and see what gems await.

This section shows two customized toolbars (Word's Standard and Formatting toolbars) and a customized File menu. For each, my overall goal was to remove items that I felt were just as easily accessible another way or were there just for marketing purposes. I also added commands that I use frequently and that I otherwise have to dig through menus and dialogs to get to.

A customized standard toolbar

The very first thing I customized on my Word interface was the Standard toolbar. The default toolbar (Figure 3-33) is replete with buttons for commands that most people don't use regularly, but which I'm sure offered Microsoft a great chance to market various Word features. There are also a number of commands that I use all the time that were left out.

Figure 3-33: Word's default Standard toolbar

Here is a rundown of the changes I made:

1. I started by going to Tools → Customize → Commands to enter editing mode and displaying the list of available commands. I chose to save my customizations in *normal.dot*. Some people warn against this, saying it's better to create a new global template that contains your customizations and loads each time Word starts. You can do that if you want, but I decided just to save it in *normal.dot*—it's easy enough to reset it to the default and save a backup copy.
2. For my first change, I replaced the standard New button with the New command that brings up the same dialog as File → New instead of just creating a blank document. I did this by deleting the old button and dragging the New command with the ellipses following it (...) up there instead.
3. Next, I added a Close All button so that I can quickly shut down all of my open documents.

4. I removed the Email button because I never used it.
5. I removed the Print Preview button because I don't really like the command and it's easy enough to get to on the File menu anyway.
6. I removed the Spell Check button because I don't use the command enough and it's too difficult to choose it from the Tools menu.
7. I added an Envelopes and Labels button because I print envelopes often.
8. I added a Find button and a Find Next button because I find it more convenient to have it on a toolbar than to dig through menus or use the browse buttons under the vertical scrollbar.
9. I removed the Format Painter button. Even though I use this command all the time, I felt it belonged on the Formatting toolbar instead.
10. I removed the Insert Hyperlink button because I use it rarely enough that getting it from the Insert menu isn't a big hassle.
11. I removed the Table Button because all it does is open the Tables and Borders toolbar for me, and that's easy enough to do by right-clicking any open toolbar.
12. I removed the Excel button because I don't use Excel much.
13. I removed the column button because I never use columns.
14. I added an Insert page break button because I use it frequently and it saves having to use Insert → Break and pick the page break off a separate dialog box.
15. I removed the Drawing button because it just opens a drawing toolbar, which is easy to get by right-clicking on any existing toolbar.
16. I removed the Document Map button because I don't use it for anything but very long documents that I have outlined using Word's built-in headings.

Figure 3-34 shows what the Standard toolbar looks like after my changes.

Figure 3-34: A customized Standard toolbar

A customized formatting toolbar

I didn't do nearly as much to the Formatting toolbar as I did to the Standard toolbar, but I did make a few changes:

1. I added the Format Painter button because I think it belongs here rather than on the Standard toolbar.
2. I added Double and Single Spacing buttons because I do documents that use both types.

3. I removed the Borders button because I don't use borders enough and I prefer the control I get with the Format → Borders and Shading dialog.
4. I removed the Indents buttons because I never used them.

Figure 3-35 shows the Formatting toolbar after my changes.

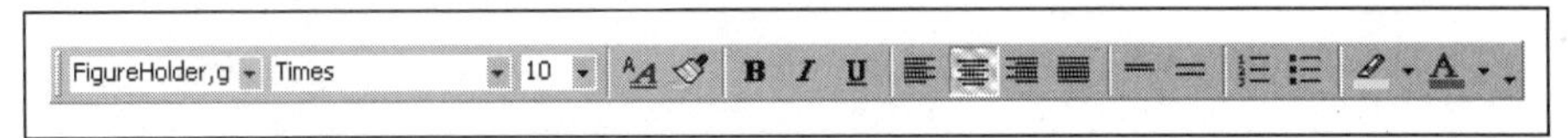

Figure 3-35: A customized Formatting toolbar

A customized file menu

For the File menu (Figure 3-36), I moved some of the more useless commands and added some that I thought were glaring omissions.

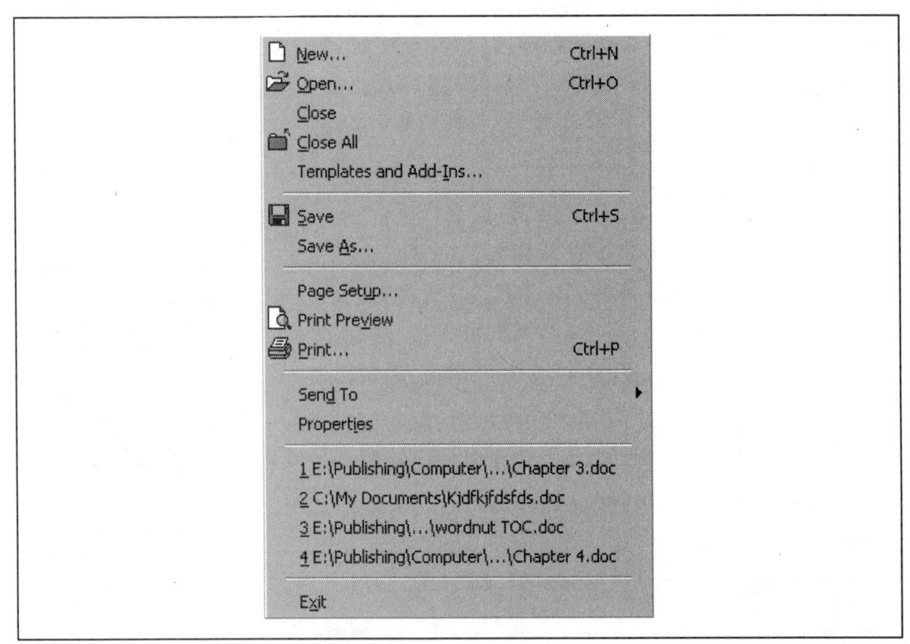

Figure 3-36: A customized File menu

Here are the changes I made:

1. I added a Close All command to quickly close all open documents.
2. I added a Templates and Add-Ins command because I associate them with files.
3. I removed Versions because I don't use it.

4. I removed the Save As Web Page command because it really just opens the Save As dialog and selects the *.htm* extension for you.

5. I removed the Web Page Preview command, because I kept looking for it on the View menu instead, so I moved it there.

I'd also like to take a moment to plug another book published by O'Reilly. Word 97 Annoyances, by Woody Leonhard, Lee Hudspeth, and T.J. Lee, is one of the best books I've read on using Microsoft Word. It is replete with good advice on how to customize Word to do what you want and how to live with what you can't customize.

Part 2

Menu Reference

Chapter 4

File

The File menu performs many common functions, such as creating, saving, and printing documents. Using this menu, it is possible to create multiple versions of a document within the same Word file using the Versions command. You can even save a document as a web page in HTML format or send documents to various types of recipients, such as mail and routing recipients, Exchange Server folders, and programs like Microsoft PowerPoint.

File → New

Whenever a new document is created in Word, it is based on one or more document templates (*.dot* files). Templates serve as boilerplates, containing settings, text, and formatting that is applied to a new document. Templates may also contain macros that can be used in a new document. The Normal document template (*normal.dot*) is automatically loaded with Word, making it *the* global template. For a complete discussion of how Word uses templates, refer to Chapter 2, *How Word Works*.

A generic blank document is created based on *normal.dot* (found in *\Program Files\Microsoft Office\Templates*) by using Ctrl-N, by selecting the New Blank Document toolbar button, or by simply starting Word.

File → New launches the New dialog box shown in Figure 4-1, containing templates and wizards to create other document types.

TIP # 38

Generating a Preview

No preview is available for some templates, especially those without text. If you create a template and wish a preview to be available, open the template in Word and select File → Properties → Summary → Save Preview Picture. The preview of the document is available in both Word and Windows Explorer. The preview area on the New dialog box is often too small to be of much use. Choose Format → Theme → Style Gallery for a better way of previewing templates without having to open each one in Word. For more on using the style gallery, see Chapter 8, Format.

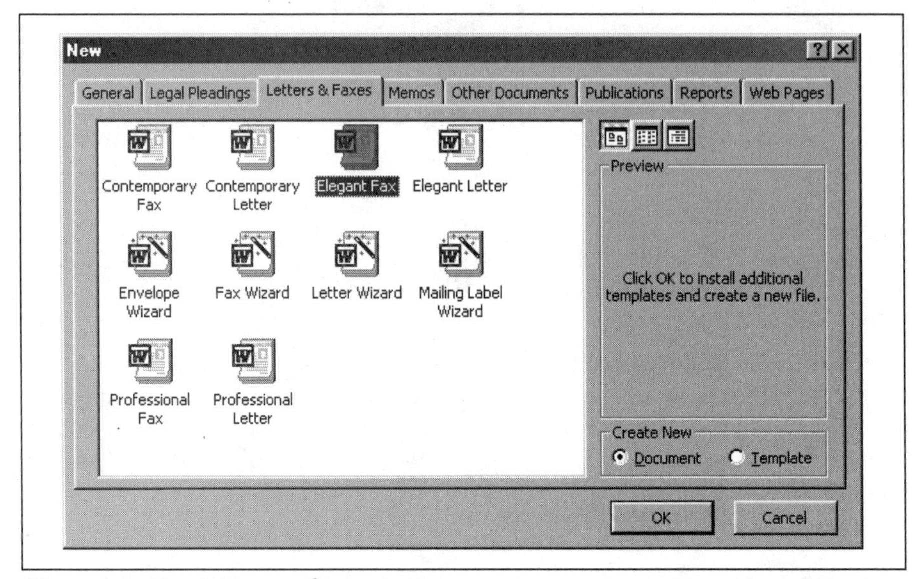

Figure 4-1: Creating a new document

The tabs across the top of the New dialog represent categories of templates and wizards. You may see fewer tabs and templates depending on the installation of Word. Select a template to create a document from, and a preview of the document is shown if one is available. By default, a new document (*.doc* file) is created based on the template selected. If a specific template was configured only to be installed on first use, a note to this effect is displayed in the preview area. Click OK to install the necessary template and create the new document. Creating a new template (*.dot* file) is also an option. Templates are discussed in detail in Chapter 2 and Chapter 14, *Creating a Template*.

Like most of Word, it's possible to customize the New dialog box if you are willing to dig beneath the surface a little. Unlike Word 97, it's not possible to alter the default category tabs. It is possible, however, to add templates to the standard tabs and to create new tabs of your own. Word 2000 constructs the category tabs from three sources:

The Registry
: The default tabs (General, Letters & Faxes, etc.) are coded in the Registry and cannot be changed. The tabs displayed depend upon the templates installed with Word, which reside in *C:\Program Files\Microsoft Office\Templates\1033*.

The User Templates directory
: The default directory for user templates is *C:\Windows\Application Data\Microsoft\Templates*, although this can be changed using Tools → Options → File Locations → User Templates → Modify. Any templates stored in this location appear on the General tab along with the standard blank templates. Any

folder (or shortcut to a folder) created in this directory that includes at least one template will become a tab in the New dialog box.

The Workgroup Templates directory
: This directory works the same as the user templates directory, but is meant for storing templates accessible by multiple users. There is no default directory, but a directory can be specified (even one on the network) using Tools → Options → File Locations → Workgroup Templates → Modify. Any templates stored in this directory will be available in the General tab on the New dialog. With more than one user accessing the template at a given time, no changes to the template can be made.

You'll notice the \1033 subdirectory a lot when working in Word. In fact, it's a subdirectory in most directories (and registry entries) related to Office 2000 because the software handles languages a bit differently than previous versions. The primary program files are now consistent, regardless of the language version of Office used since the same product is shipped all over the world. Language-specific files (such as templates) are included in subdirectories for each language (1033 is English).

It's possible to quickly add templates to any tabs (custom or standard) in the New dialog. Just drag a template file from any open window on the Windows desktop (or in Windows Explorer) to the file list on the appropriate tab. The New dialog box must be open and on the right tab before doing this. Be sure you can see the item you want to drag from the desktop before opening the New dialog.

File → Open

The Open dialog box (Figure 4-2) has changed from previous versions of Word. Most obvious is the addition of the Places bar (on the left), which allows quick access to the five places Microsoft thinks you'll need most. How to use and change this bar is covered later in this section. First, let's take a brief tour of the rest of the Open dialog.

The first time File → Open is launched in a new Word session, the folder shown is the one specified in Tools → Options → File Locations → Documents (*C:\My Documents* by default). For all subsequent times File → Open is launched during the Word session, the folder shown is the last folder a file was opened or saved in.

Only documents matching the type selected in the "Files of type" box are shown in the view. By default, only files that can be created by Word (*.doc*, *.dot*, *.htm*, *.html*, and *.url*) are shown, but the view can be changed by selecting a new file type from the drop-down list. Type the extension of the file you wish to open in the "File name" text box to instantly display all files of that type. For example, typing `*.doc` displays all files with the *.doc* extension in the current folder. It's also possible to filter the view by entering criteria into the "File name" box. When entering a letter, the name of the first file beginning with this letter is displayed. As more letters are

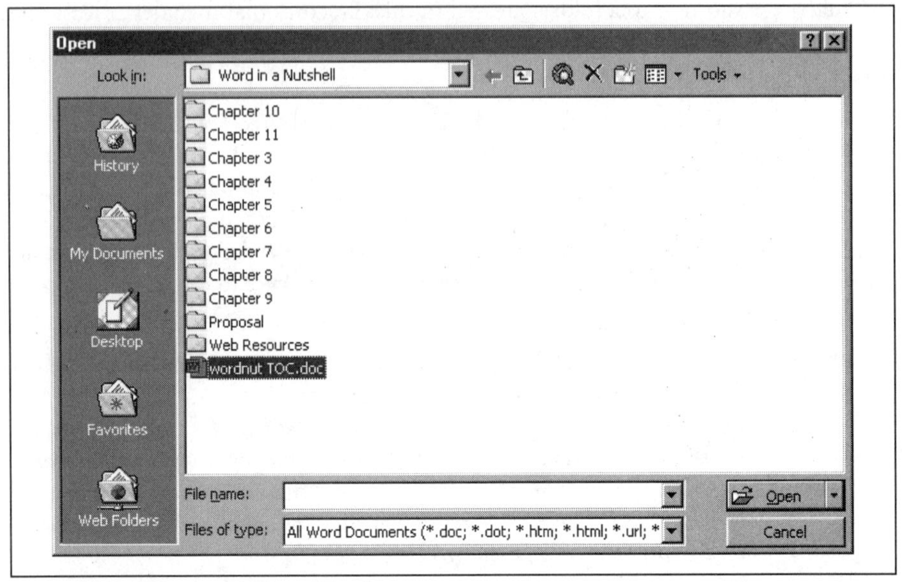

Figure 4-2: Opening a file in Word

entered, the filename fills in. Wildcards can also be used in the "File name" box. For example, entering `f*` will show all files of the selected type whose name begins with "f". You can even type a UNC address, such as *\\Server1\Documents* in the "File name" text box to display files on a network share. The wildcard "?" is also supported and stands for any single character. For example, typing `chapter?0` would display files named *chapter10*, *chapter20*, and so on.

TIP # 39

Reverting to Previous Versions of a File

If you try to open a file that is already open, Word will ask if you wish to revert to the saved version of the file. This is a handy way of getting rid of new changes and starting over.

Opening a File from a Web Location

Word treats the Web the way it does any other network, as if it were an extension of your own system. When you install Word 2000, a new folder named *Web Folders* is added to the *My Computer* folder in Word's Open dialog box. *Web Folders* is not visible from Windows Explorer. *Web Folders* simply holds a collection of shortcuts that point to folders on the Internet (or on a company's intranet). To create one of these shortcuts, go to My Computer → Web Folders and double-click Add Web Folder. A wizard will step you through the process, asking for the URL and a user name/password if the URL is secured. Start this same wizard from the Open dialog box by clicking the Create New Folder button.

Once web locations have been created, browse through them for files in the Open dialog just like you would browse through any other folder, as shown in Figure 4-3. Note, however, that connecting to a Web Folder often requires a username and password. As with most other password dialogs in Windows, you can elect to save the password to avoid entering it each time.

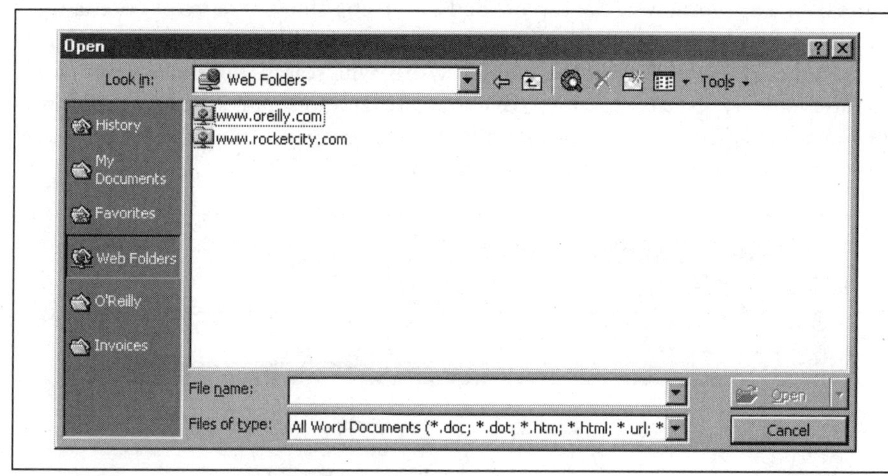

Figure 4-3: Opening files from a Web Folder

Opening a File from an FTP Location

File Transfer Protocol (FTP) has long been a favored method of transferring files over the Internet. FTP servers hold files that are accessible to anyone who can successfully log onto the server with an FTP client. Some FTP servers allow anonymous access, while others require a username and password.

Word can act as a limited FTP client, allowing the transfer of documents from the FTP server to a computer for editing and back to the server for saving. Once connected to an FTP server using the Open or Save As dialogs, browse for files on that server as if they are on a drive or directory on your own system.

To retrieve a file from an FTP server, open the "Look in" list in the Open dialog box (refer to Figure 4-2). At the bottom of the list, is a heading named FTP Locations. Select Add/Modify FTP Locations to create an entry for a new FTP Server. An entry holds the FTP URL, log on mode, and password. Double-click an FTP entry location to connect to the FTP server. Any entries created are saved for easy access in future Word sessions.

Using the Tools Menu

Most of the items on the Tools menu of the Open dialog are standard file and folder commands (Delete, Rename, Print, etc.). Two that deserve more explanation are Map Network Drive and Find.

Map Network Drive is used to add a shared directory on the network to the *My Computer* folder so it appears as another disk drive. This can be a real time saver if you frequently use files on the network. When mapping the network drive, be sure to select the option to have Windows reconnect the drive each time you log on.

The second important command is Find, which opens the dialog shown in Figure 4-4. The window at the top of the Find dialog shows a series of criteria used to search for a file. Any selected criteria are displayed in this window in the order of application. In Figure 4-4, for example, Word will search for documents of all supported file types created this week that are at most ten pages long. This is different than searching for files that are at most ten pages long and were created this week. The order of criteria in this window matters.

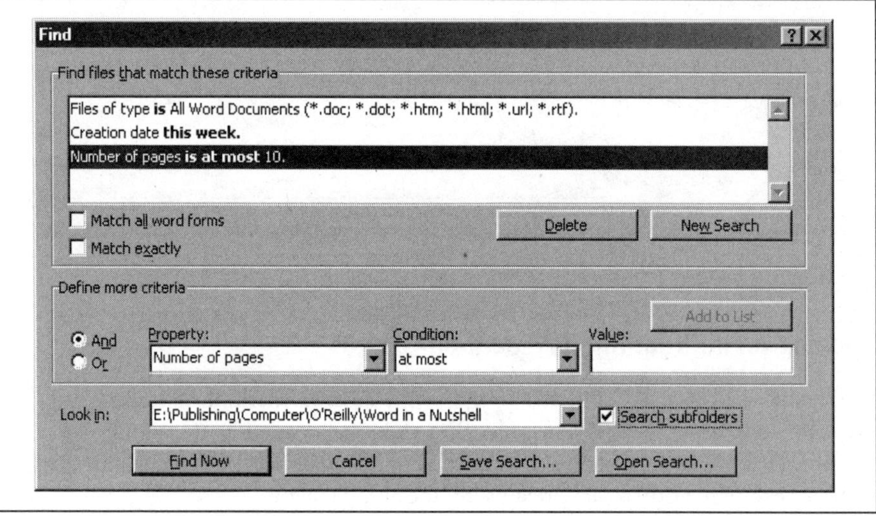

Figure 4-4: Using the Find tool

It is also possible to specify the exact combination of upper- and lowercase characters to match a given search using the "Match exactly" checkbox. For example, if you search for all files containing the name "Day," then files containing "day" or "DAY" are not returned in the search. This setting applies to all the criteria added to the search.

The "Look in" drop-down list is also crucial to a good search, since it limits the scope of the search. Searching the entire hard drive is necessary at times (when you don't know exactly where the file resides), but wastes a lot of time when you're sure a file is in a particular folder.

Find Fast is a utility that builds indexes to speed up finding documents from the Open dialog box. If Find Fast is not already installed on your system when you perform certain searches, installation may be required. Word will show a notification if this is the case and request the installation CD.

To add a criterion to the list of criteria, define it in the "Define more criteria" section. For each criterion, you must define four parameters:

- Whether the criterion should be combined with the existing criteria (And) or used independently of existing criteria (Or)
- A property, such as file contents or file type
- A condition, such as items that contain the words or a specific type of file
- A value, such as a text string or number

Once your criteria are defined, specify the folder to begin the search in and whether or not subfolders should be searched. Click Find Now to return the list of files.

Use the Save Search button to save a set of criteria for performing searches in the future. This saves the criteria in the Windows registry in the HKEY_CURRENT_USER\Software\Microsoft\Office\8.0\Common\Open Find\MicrosoftWord\Saved Searches subkey. If you don't save a set of criteria, you must reconstruct it the next time you want to perform the search. Open saved searches with the Open Search button.

The Places Bar

The Places bar is a handy feature of the Open and Save As dialog boxes that allows you to quickly jump to various places on your system. Unfortunately, Microsoft (displaying their usual logic) decided that there are only five locations in which Word users commonly look for files: *History*, *My Documents*, *Desktop*, *Favorites*, and *Web Folders*. There is no built-in way of changing those locations.

TIP # 40

Customizing the Places Bar

A utility named the WOPR Places Bar Customizer is a COM add-in that provides a handy interface for customizing the Places bar. It was created by Woody Leonhard and is available on the Office Update Site (choose Help → Office on the Web), or go directly to the site at: http://officeupdate.microsoft.com/downloadCatalog/dldWord.htm. Figure 4-5 shows a modified Places bar. The Places bar is common across all of the Office 2000 applications. Any customization performed shows up in the Open and Save As dialog boxes in Access, Excel, Power Point, Outlook, and Word.

File → Close

This command immediately closes the active document. If the document has been modified since being opened or saved, a dialog asks whether or not to save changes to the document.

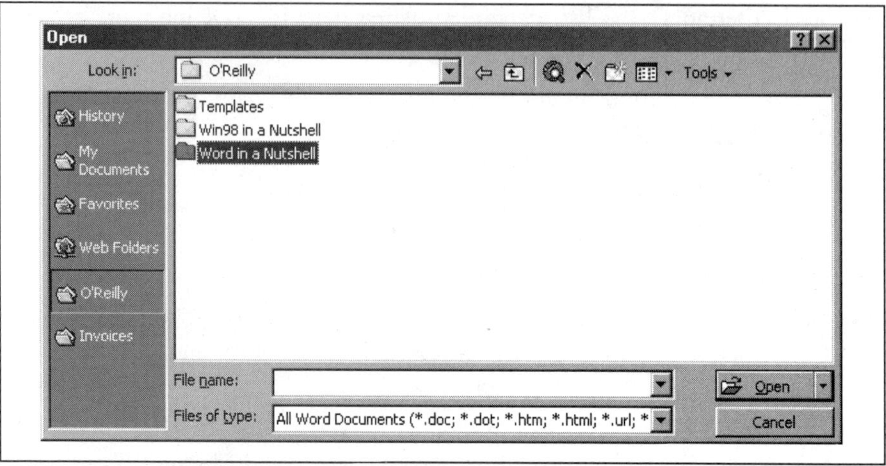

Figure 4-5: The Places bar

Like most programs in Windows, Word offers a Close button on the far right side of its title bar, as shown in Figure 4-6. With its new Single Document Interface, Word opens a new window for each open document. If multiple documents are open, clicking the Close button on any particular document closes that document. If only one document is open, clicking its Close button exits Word (the same as choosing File → Exit). In addition, if only one document is open, a Close Window button also becomes available on the far right side of the *menu* bar. Clicking this button closes the document, but does not exit Word.

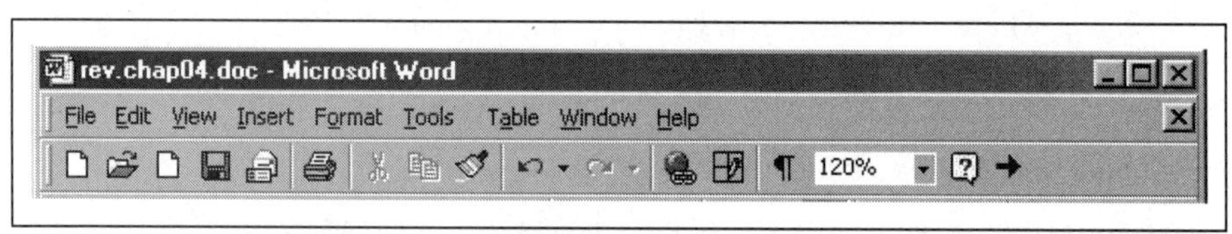

Figure 4-6: Closing Windows in Word

If you find it convenient to have a Close button on a toolbar, click the down arrow at the far right end of the Standard toolbar and choose Add or Remove Buttons → Close. The new button looks like a suitcase with an arrow above it. Like all toolbar buttons, it's possible to move the button to a different place on the toolbar by holding the Alt key down and dragging the button to the new toolbar location.

TIP # 41

Opening or Closing All Documents

Hold down the Shift key before opening the File menu to show two new commands: Save All and Close All. The former saves all open documents. If any document has not been saved before, the Save As dialog box opens. The latter closes all open documents, but leaves Word itself running.

File → Save

This command saves the active document. If the document has no name (if it has never been saved before) or if the original document is marked as read-only, the Save As dialog opens. See Chapter 3, *Customizing Word*, for details on configuring various save options.

File → Save As

This command opens the dialog shown in Figure 4-7, which is used to designate the filename and location for the saved file. This dialog also opens automatically the first time any document is saved, regardless of whether the Save As or Save command is used. This dialog is identical to the Open dialog, it even has a Places bar. Choose the location to save the document in, enter a filename, choose the format to save the document in, and you're finished. Unfortunately, Word gives no clear indication of the file path in this dialog. However, opening the "Look in" drop-down list reveals the location where the file is saved, making it easier to find later.

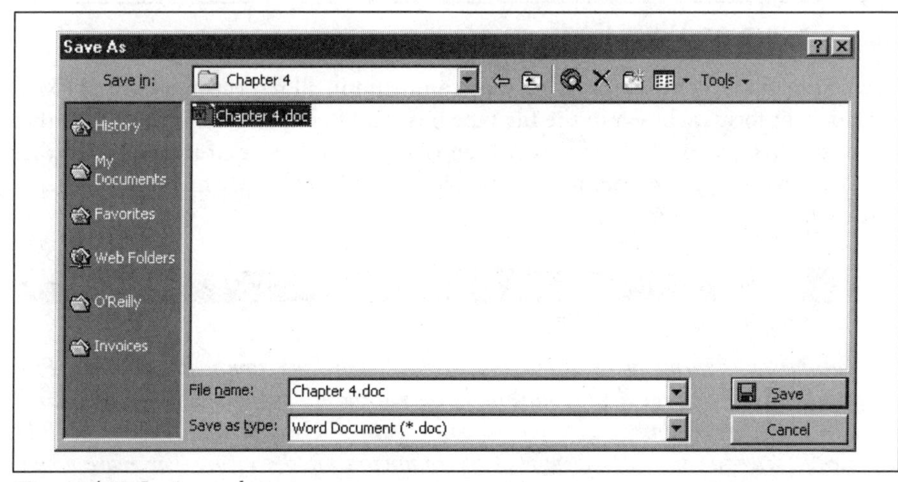

Figure 4-7: Saving a document

TIP # 42

Remove the MRU List of Files in Save As

It makes many users uncomfortable that Word maintains a list of the most recently used files opened with the Save As dialog (open the "File name" drop-down list to see them). Get rid of these using the following registry hack. Find and select the HKEY_CURRENT_USER\Software\Microsoft\Office\8.0\Common\OpenFind\MicrosoftWord\Settings\Save As\File Name MRU subkey. Right-click the Value entry and choose Modify from the context menu. Delete all the text and click OK. The list is gone.

Although the Save As and Open dialogs are very similar, there are three options that exist in the drop-down Tools menu on the Save As dialog that don't exist on the Open dialog:

Web Options
: Opens the same dialog shown by clicking Web Options on Tools → Options → General from Word's standard menu, which is covered in Chapter 8.

General Options
: Opens the Tools → Options → Save tab, which is covered in detail in Chapter 8.

Save Version
: Provides some of the functionality found in File → Versions, which is covered later in this chapter.

When saving a document as a web page, Word creates a folder with the same name as the document and in the same location. This folder holds supporting files, such as images, associated with the web page.

File → Save as Web Page

This command is identical to the Save As command in all respects but two: HTML is the default format chosen in the file type box, and there is a button to change the title of the web page. This is different than changing the name of the file itself: the title is the name that appears in the title bar of the browser when the web page is displayed.

TIP # 43

Removing the Save As Web Page Command

To save some menu space, delete the Save as Web Page command from the File menu. It doesn't provide any advantage over using the regular Save As command and choosing an .html extension. Choose Tools → Customize and open the File menu, dragging the Save as Web Page command off the menu. For more about customizing Word's menus, see Chapter 3.

File → Versions

Use this command to save and track multiple versions of a single document within one document file. While it is possible to track multiple versions of a document by repeatedly saving it with different filenames, the Versions command offers an easier way. The Versions command adds the ability to conveniently store all versions of a document in a single file and see information regarding all versions in one location (the Versions dialog shown in Figure 4-8) with comments added. It also saves you from having to create all those extra filenames and numbers. Keep in mind, however, that saving extra versions of a document *significantly* increases that document's size, since all previous formatting information must also be saved.

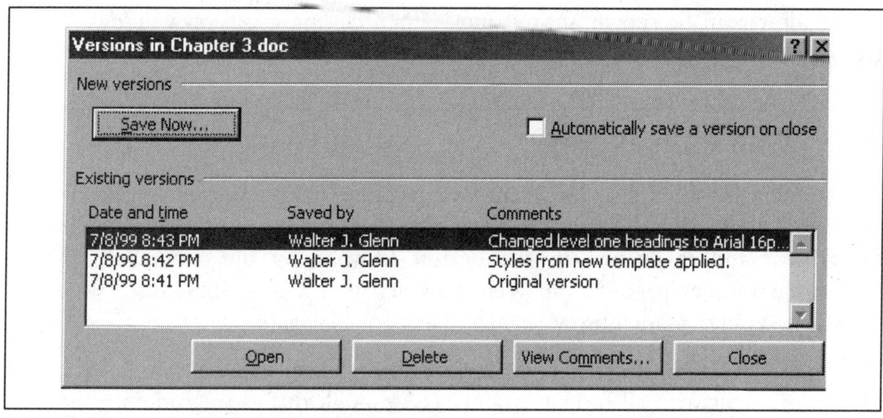

Figure 4-8: Saving multiple versions of a document

TIP # 44

Use Track Changes with Versions

When using versions to help track the work of multiple reviewers of a document, it is best to turn on Word's change tracking feature (Tools → Track Changes → Highlight Changes). This causes changes by different reviewers to show up in different colors, making it much easier to do side-by-side comparisons of versions. For more about tracking changes, see Chapter 13, Collaborating.

When saving a version of any document for the first time, a Versions icon is added to Word's status bar (Figure 4-9) to indicate the document contains more than one version. Double-clicking this icon at any time opens the Versions dialog box.

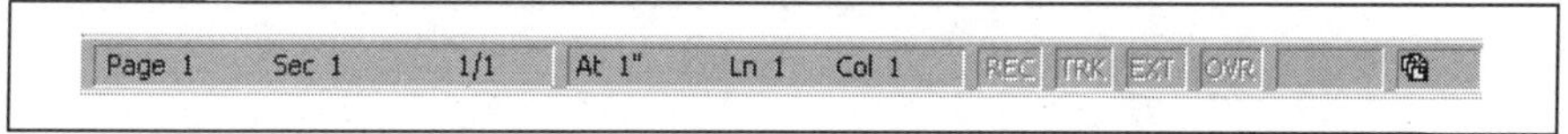

Figure 4-9: The Versions icon in the Word status bar

When choosing File → Save while working with a multiple version documents, the current document is saved in the normal manner. All saved versions remain unchanged. When choosing the Save command in a previous version of a document, the Save As dialog appears, allowing the document to be saved as a new file. You cannot modify an old version of a document and then save those modifications in that document. You must instead save it as an external file. When choosing File → Save As in a multiple versions document, be sure to save the document by another filename. The new document will be an exact copy of the current document and all versions of the document will also be transferred to the new file.

When opening one version of a document while another version is open, Word tiles both versions so they can be compared side-by-side. Opening more than two versions of a document pushes the oldest version into the background, since only two windows can be shown at any time. When closing a version window, Word does not resize the remaining window; that must be done manually.

File → Web Page Preview

This command displays a document as it would look if viewed in the default browser. Actually, the document is saved temporarily as an *.htm* file in *\Windows\Temp\Word* and is opened in the default browser by this command. When publishing complex pages to the Web, however, it is a good idea to see what the HTML looks like in other browsers (e.g., Netscape Navigator).

Word generates a lot of excess HTML code used to later convert the file back to a Word document with all formatting intact. Although this excess code may be fine for intranet purposes, we don't recommend using these HTML files on the Internet, since they can take longer to load in a browser. Try working in Word's Web Layout view (View → Web Layout), to get a good idea of how the page will look in Internet Explorer as you work. For more on Word's views, check out Chapter 6, *View*. For more on cleaning up Word's HTML, see Chapter 16, *Creating a Web Page*.

TIP # 45

Cleaning Up Your HTML

Microsoft has posted the Office HTML Filter utility on the Office Update web site (http://officeupdate.com) that removes Office-specific markup tags embedded in Office 2000 documents saved as HTML. Learn more about this tool in Chapter 16.

File → Page Setup

Use this command to configure settings that affect an entire document, or at least large parts of it. Open the Page Setup dialog with the menu command or by double-clicking in the dark gray (margin) areas of the ruler.

The Page Setup dialog box is divided into four tabs: Margins, Paper Size, Paper Source, and Layout. These tabs are covered later in this section. Here are a few items that apply to all tabs in the Page Setup dialog (see Figure 4-10):

- The Preview section changes to reflect all settings made between the time the Page Setup dialog is opened, and the time OK (or Cancel) is clicked. Thus, changes on every tab can be made to see what the collected changes look like at once.

- The "Apply to" setting affects the entire Page Setup dialog, not just the settings on the current tab. The "Apply to" list may contain the following choices:
  - "Whole document" applies settings to the whole document.
  - "This point forward" applies settings from the insertion point on.
  - "Selected text" applies settings only to selected paragraphs and only shows up in the list when a selection is made in the document prior to opening File → Page Setup.
  - "This section" applies settings to the document section that contains the insertion point and only shows up in the list if your document contains more than one section.
  - "Selected sections" applies settings to the section or sections with selected text. This only shows up in the list if your document contains more than one section and text is highlighted prior to opening File → Page Setup.
- The Default button applies the changes made in the Page Setup dialog to the document template. Those changes become the default page settings used when new documents are created from the template. See Chapter 2 for more information on using templates.

WARNING

Be careful when making any settings in Word the default settings, as they are usually applied to normal.dot and really do become the settings used on all new documents created.

Margins Tab

The Margins tab, shown in Figure 4-10, contains margin settings that apply to the part of the document selected in the "Apply to" list. The top, bottom, left, and right margins are exactly what you'd expect. You can also specify the space that should exist between the edge of the page and the top of the header or the bottom of the footer using the settings in the "From edge" section. Clicking the up or down arrow changes the margin value by tenth-of-an-inch increments. Enter text directly into the box to specify increments in hundredths of inches (it's possible to enter as many digits as you like after the decimal, but Word will round off to the nearest hundredth).

Use the "Mirror margins" checkbox to create facing-page layouts, where the left and right pages face one another. If the "Mirror margins" option is selected, the Margins tab changes to show the facing-page layout in the Preview section, as shown in Figure 4-11. Notice also that the left and right margin options change to inside and outside margins, and the "2 pages per sheet" option (which allows you to print 2 pages to a single sheet of paper) is unavailable when using mirrored margins.

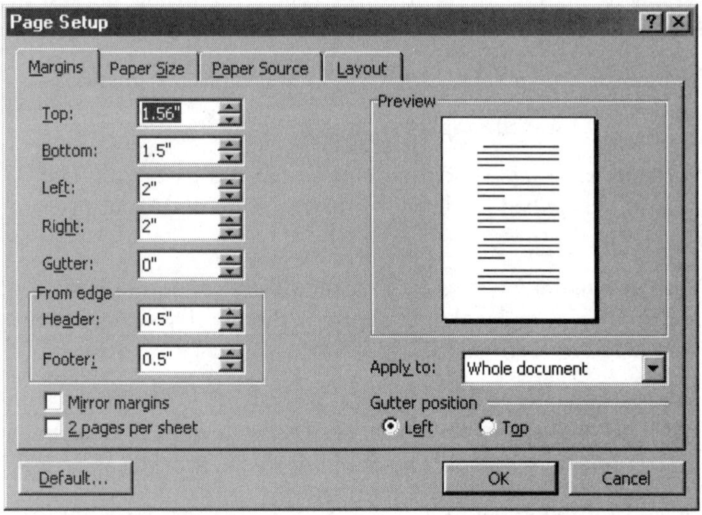

Figure 4-10: Changing margins

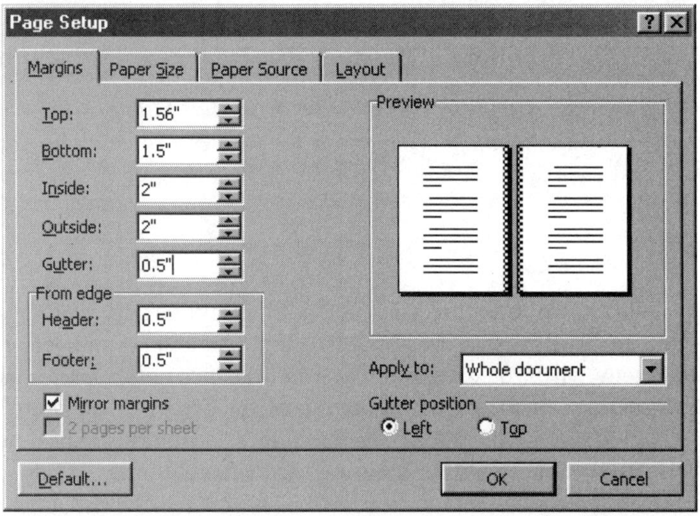

Figure 4-11: Using mirrored margins

A gutter is extra space left at the edge of a page to compensate for the portion of the page covered by binding. You can add a gutter to single-page or facing-page layouts. With single-page layouts, gutters can be placed at either the left or top of pages. With facing-page layouts, gutters can only be placed on the inside (even though the left-side option is selected on the Margins tab). Figure 4-11 shows a ½-inch gutter on the inside of facing pages.

Paper Size Tab

Use the Paper Size tab (Figure 4-12) to select the size of the paper to print to and the orientation of the text on the page.

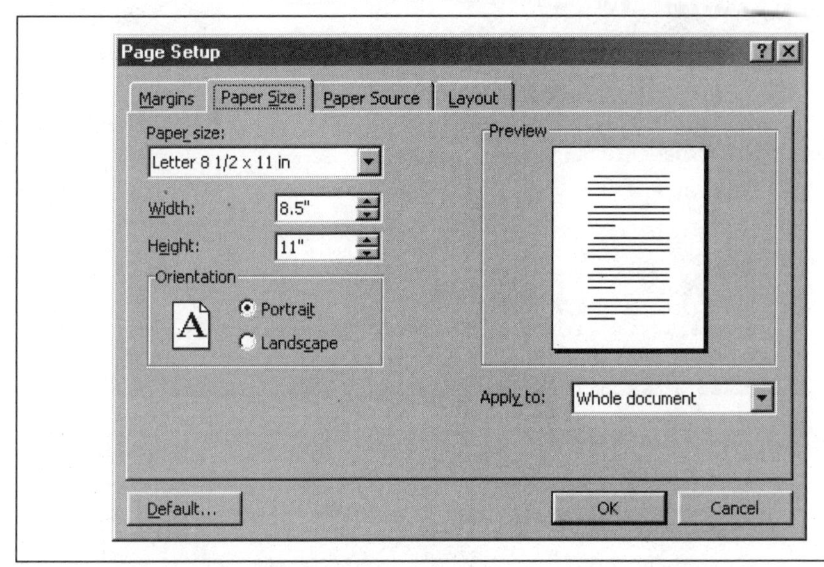

Figure 4-12: Choosing a paper size

Choose from among predefined paper sizes using the "Paper size" drop-down list. Be aware that some predefined sizes may not print to your printer. You can also type in your own paper dimensions using the Width and Height fields.

Use the Orientation section to select whether the document should be printed in normal portrait view, or horizontally on the page in landscape view.

Paper Source Tab

Choose a paper source for the first page of a document and a source for all other pages using the Paper Source tab (Figure 4-13). The selections available depend upon the printer Word is currently set to use. Using different paper sources might be useful, for instance, if you want to print the first page of a document on preprinted company letterhead and the rest of the pages on normal blank paper.

Layout Tab

Use the Layout tab, shown in Figure 4-14, to configure these page layout settings:

1. *Section start.* Once a section in a document is created (see Chapter 7, *Insert*), there are two ways to change it to another section type. You can simply delete the section (select it on the page and hit Delete) and create a new section in its

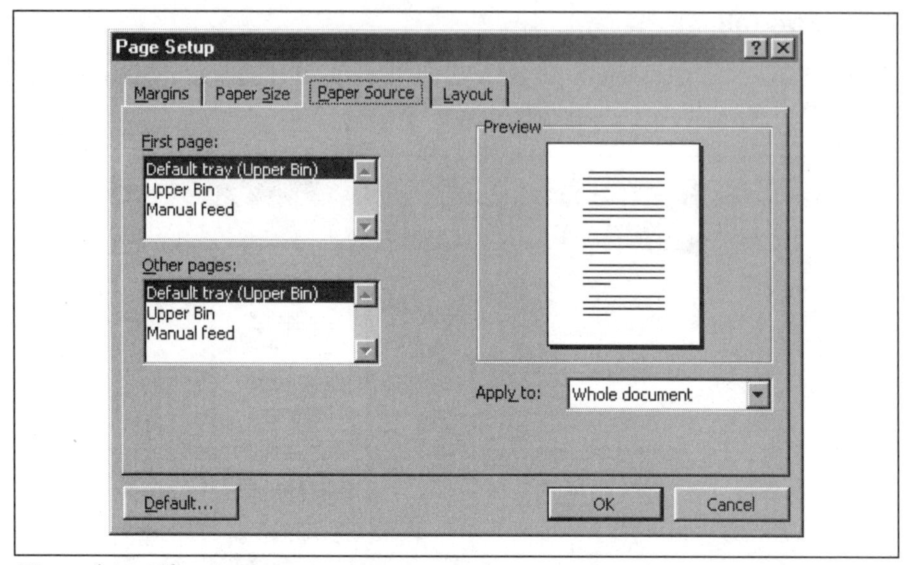

Figure 4-13: Choosing a paper source

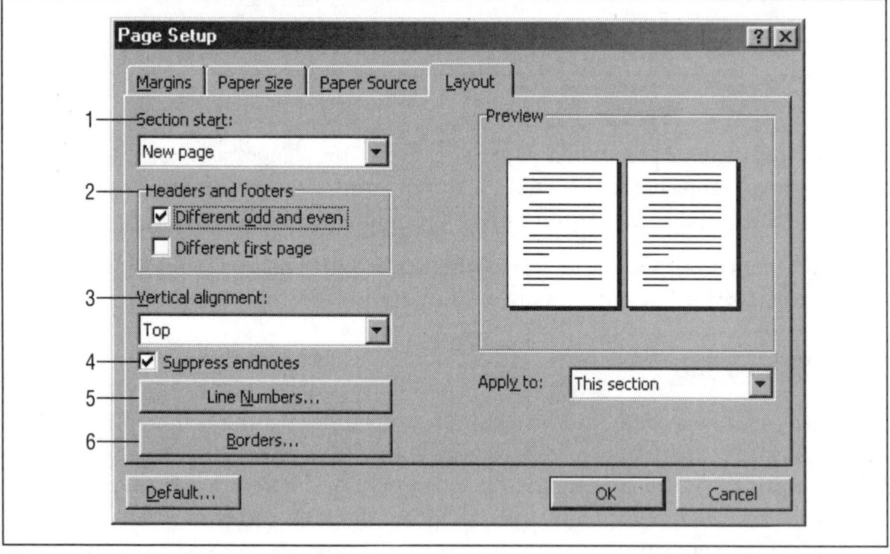

Figure 4-14: Configuring page layout

place. You can also place the insertion point on the section line and double-click on the gray area on the ruler. Choose the new section type from the "Section start" list and select the range from the "Apply to" list.

2. *Headers and footers.* This setting provides you with two simple choices: whether separate headers and footers should be used for even- and odd-numbered pages

and whether a separate header and footer should be used for the first page of the document. For more on working with headers and footers, see Chapter 6.

3. *Vertical alignment.* This setting defines whether text is aligned to the top, center, bottom, or both top and bottom (justified) of pages in a section. By default, Word aligns text to the top of a page. When you choose the justified setting, Word aligns the text to the top and bottom of the page *if* the page is full. For partial pages, Word aligns the text to the top of the page even if you choose justified.
4. *Suppress endnotes.* This checkbox prevents endnotes from being printed at the end of a section and instead prints those endnotes at the end of the next section, just before the footnotes for that next section. This option is only available if you have configured endnotes to be placed at the end of each section (Insert → Footnote → Options → All Endnotes → Place at → End of section). By default, Word places endnotes at the end of the document. For more on using footnotes and endnotes, see Chapter 7.
5. *Line Numbers.* This button pops up the Line Numbers dialog that prints line numbers at the left edge of all or part of a document (great for long poems and legal documents). Specify the starting number, the distance the numbers should be placed from the text, and the counting increments. With a counting increment greater than one, lines are still counted the normal way but only lines that match the increment will be numbered. For example, entering 2 in the Count by box causes only even numbered lines to show line numbers. Line numbering can restart on each page (the default), each section, or be continuous throughout the document.
6. *Borders.* The Borders button on the Layout tab brings up the same Borders and Shading dialog box that is available through Format → Borders and Shading. It is used to create borders and shading for pages, paragraphs, and text selections. You can learn more about it in Chapter 7.

File → Print Preview

File → Print Preview changes the document window, showing a document as it would look if printed (Figure 4-15). Although you can edit the document in the Print Preview window, this mode is best used for getting a visual feel for a document as a whole before sending it to the printer.

Alternately, Word's Print Layout view shows the printed look of the document and allows you to edit it at the same time. For more on using Print Layout View, see Chapter 6.

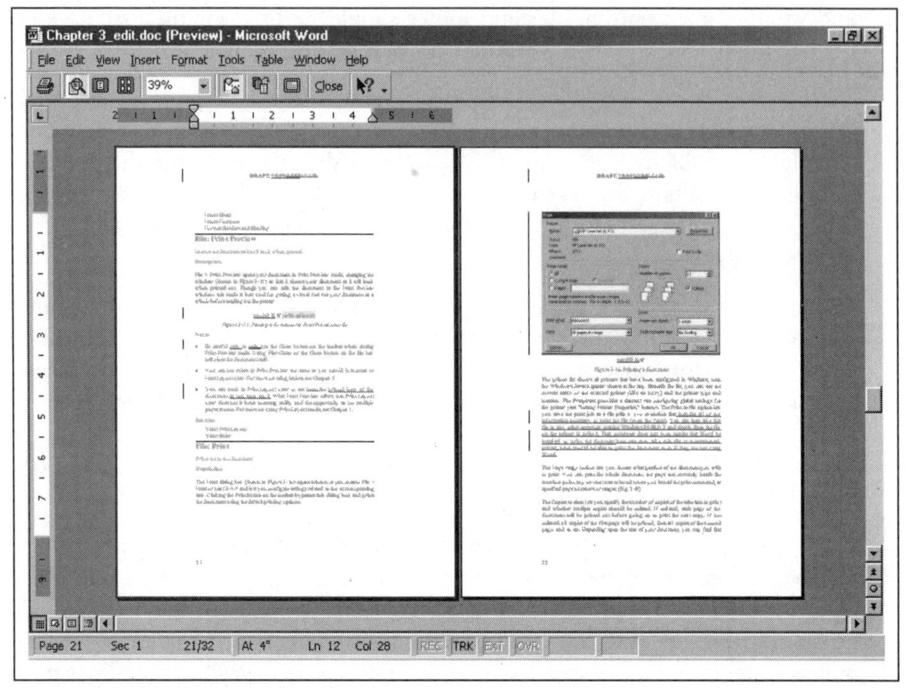

Figure 4-15: Viewing a document in Print Preview mode

WARNING

The Shrink to Fit button in the Print Preview window actually causes Word to reduce the size of the font throughout the document in order to reduce the size of the document by one page. Cancel this view by selecting any other view button. While Shrink to Fit is useful for previewing, and possibly printing a document, don't save a document while this view is turned on. If you do, all of the fonts in the document will remain at their reduced size. The document will need to be manually restored to normal.

Be careful only to use the Close button on the toolbar when closing Print Preview mode. Using File → Close or the Close button on the title bar will close the document itself. Changing to a different document view will also close the Print Preview window.

File → Print

The Print dialog box (Figure 4-16) opens whenever you choose File → Print or use Ctrl-P and is used to configure settings related to the current printing task. Clicking the Print button on the toolbar bypasses this dialog box and prints the document using the default printing options without further user intervention. It is always a good idea to save a document before you print it. Sometimes printing problems can lock up Word or even your computer, causing the loss of any unsaved changes.

When you are closing a document right after printing it, Word prompts you to save the document, even if no changes have been made. This is due to Word tracking the latest printing date of the document as part of its statistical summary, which can be viewed at File → Properties → Statistics.

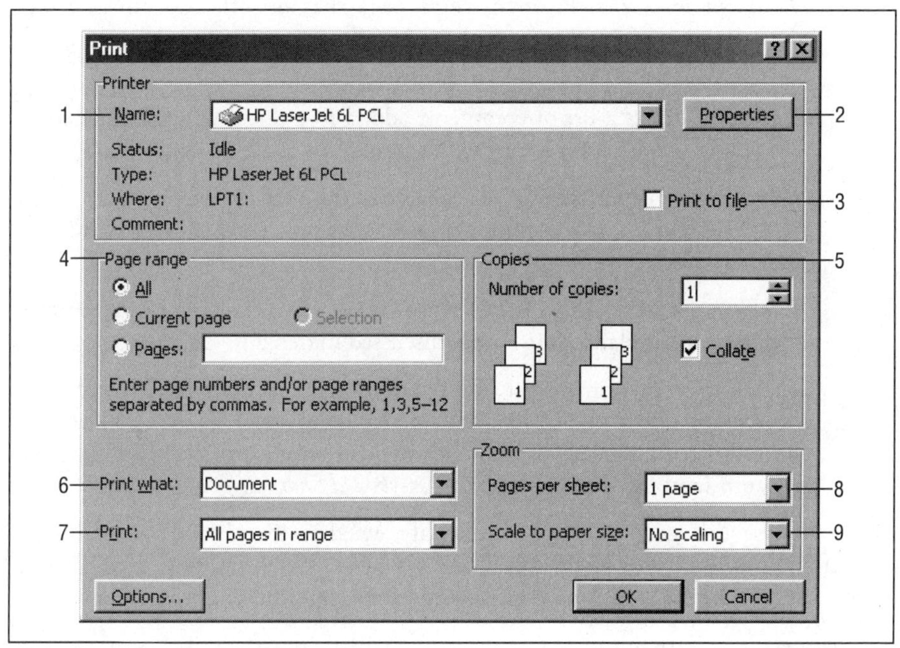

Figure 4-16: Printing a document

1. *Name.* Choose from Windows printers in this drop-down list. To change the default Windows printer, shown at the top of the list, use My Computer → Printers → any printer → right-click → Set as Default.

2. *Properties.* This button provides a shortcut for configuring global settings for the printer (see "Setting Printer Properties," below).

3. *Print to file.* This option saves the print job as a file with a *.prn* extension, including all information necessary to print the file (even the fonts). You can then take this file to any other computer running Windows 95/98/NT and drop the file on the printer icon to print it. The document will print without a Word installation.

4. *Page range.* This option prints the whole document, the page that currently holds the insertion point, text selected prior to using the print command, or specified page numbers or ranges (e.g., 2–9).

5. *Copies*. Use this to specify the number of printed copies and whether multiple copies should be collated. If copies are collated, each page of the document is printed out before printing the next copy. If not collated, all copies of the first page are printed, then all copies of the second page, and so on.
6. *Print what*. Use this drop-down list to choose what to print in the document by selecting one of the following settings:
   - *Document properties*. Prints a single page that lists the document's filename, directory, template, and all of the information included on the Summary and Statistics tabs of File → Properties.
   - *Comments*. Prints a list of comments added to a document using Insert → Comment. See Chapter 6 for more information on using comments.
   - *Styles*. Prints a list of every style available in the current document. For each style, a description of the components of that style (font, font size, etc.) are also included.
   - *AutoText entries*. Prints a list of AutoText entries available in the current document's template. AutoText is discussed in detail in Chapter 6.
   - *Key assignments*. Prints a list of any additional key assignments (keyboard shortcuts) made in the current document's template. This list includes only those shortcuts created and not the standard keyboard shortcuts available in Word (and listed in Appendix A, *Keyboard Shortcuts*).
7. *Print*. Use this drop-down list to specify whether to print all pages in the defined print range or just the odd or even pages. When creating a facing-page document, consider printing even and odd pages on different types of paper.
8. *Pages per sheet*. Use this option to decide how many document pages to print on a single sheet of paper. The default is one, but you can print as many as 16 pages per sheet. This can be great for saving paper when proofreading documents. You can also force the document to print to a different size paper than your page setup using File → Page Setup → Paper Source. It is also a handy way of printing documents formatted for very large paper sizes (such as 17") on regular letter-sized paper to get a feel for the layout.
9. *Scale to paper size*. This controls various advanced printing options that affect all documents printed in Word. See the section "Advanced Printing Options."

Setting Printer Properties

The Properties button on the Print dialog (see Figure 4-16 earlier in this chapter) is used to configure global printer settings for all documents printed in Word, and opens a separate dialog box like the one shown in Figure 4-17. This dialog varies depending upon the type of printer, but it usually has options for configuring paper size and orientation, paper source, and graphics.

The tabs on the Properties dialog duplicate some of the tabs found at My Computer → Printers → `any printer` *→ right-click → Properties (actually all tabs except General, Details, and Sharing should be in both places). These two dialogs are not the same, however. Settings made in Word using File → Print → Properties override the settings made in My Computer → Printers for Word documents only. Documents printed in other programs or documents still use settings configured in My Computer → Printers.*

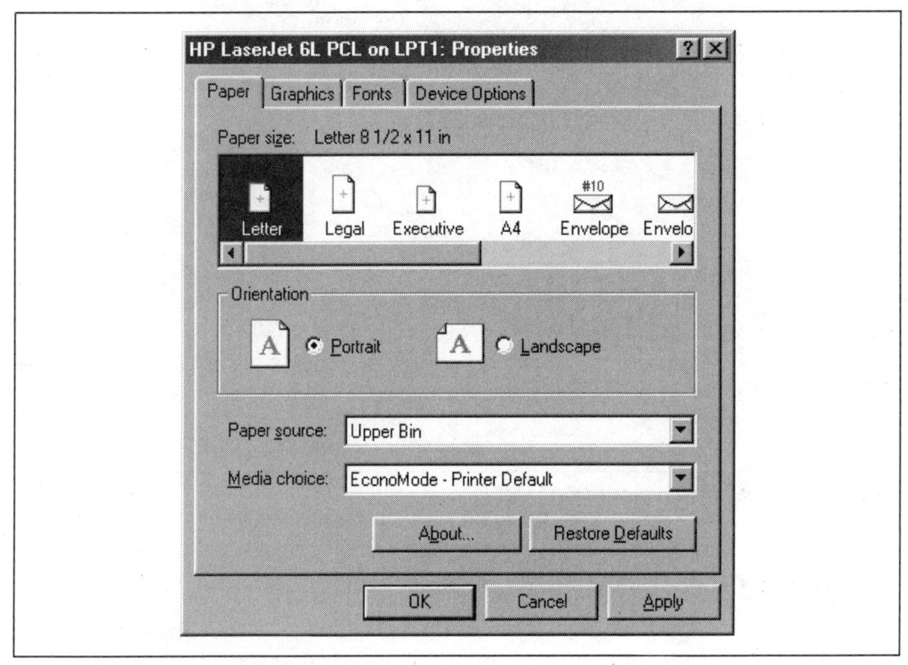

Figure 4-17: Setting global printer properties

Advanced Printing Options

The Options button on the Print dialog brings up a separate dialog, shown in Figure 4-18. This dialog controls various advanced printing options that also affect all documents printed in Word. The dialog is identical to the Tools → Options → Print tab.

The following list describes the advanced printing options:

1. *Draft output.* When this option is selected, Word does not print documents with formatting or graphics. This speeds up printing and uses less ink with ink jet printers. Only certain models of printers support draft mode printing. For those that do not, selecting this option has no effect.
2. *Update fields.* This option updates the contents of all fields in documents before printing. It is *not* set by default. This is something you might want to do if you

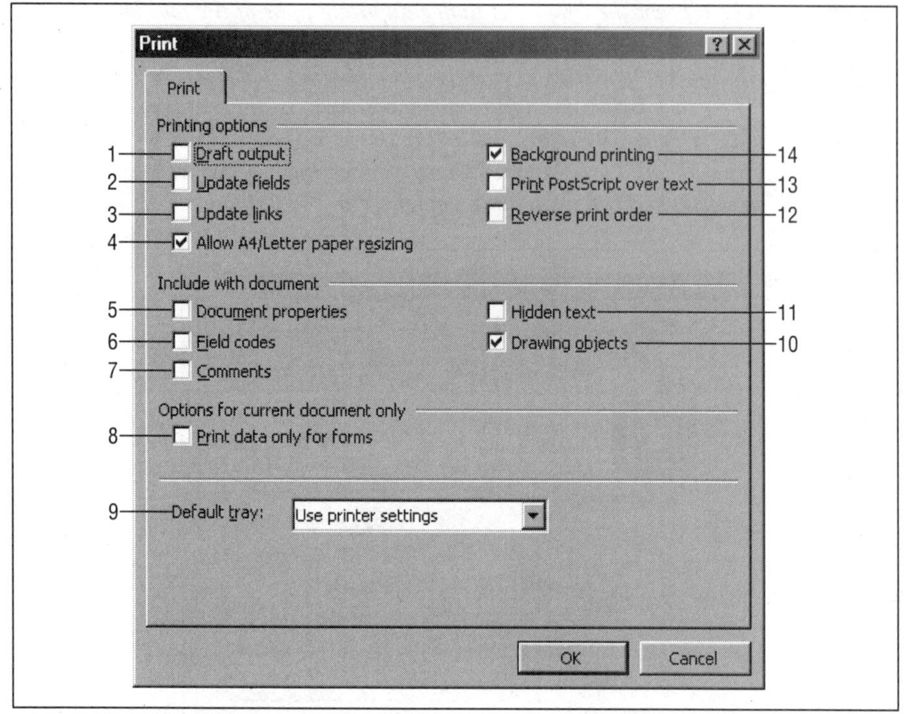

Figure 4-18: Setting advanced print options

have fields that often change, such as dates or information pulled from other programs. For more on using fields, see Chapter 6.

3. *Update links.* Updates contents of links (a linked Excel spreadsheet, for example) in documents before printing. For more on linking, see Chapter 6.

4. *Allow A4/Letter paper resizing.* Allows the resizing of documents formatted for the A4 paper size so they can print on Letter paper size. This setting affects printing only, not the document itself.

5. *Document properties.* Causes Word to print document properties on a separate page at the end of the document.

6. *Field codes.* Prints all field codes on a separate page at the end of the document if the document contains fields.

7. *Comments.* This causes Word to print all reviewer comments on a separate page at the end of the document if the document contains comments. The printed comments include page number headings indicating where each comment comes from. Reviewers' initials also appear in the printed document to indicate comment placement. Without this option selected, neither the comments nor the initials are printed.

8. *Print data only for forms*. This causes Word to print only the data entered into a form without printing the fields and borders of the form itself. For more on this, see Chapter 15, *Fields and Forms*.
9. *Default tray*. Selects the default paper source to use when printing documents from Word. This setting overrides the paper source set using the Properties button on the Print dialog.
10. *Drawing objects*. Prints drawing objects when printing a document. When this option is not selected, a blank box is printed to indicate the placement of the drawing. This option does not work with all printers.
11. *Hidden text*. Prints any hidden text, such as table of contents entries. For more on using hidden text, see Chapter 7.
12. *Reverse print order*. Prints the document from the last page to the first page. This is useful for older printers that may output pages face up.
13. *Print PostScript over text*. Prints any PostScript code in documents converted from Word for Macintosh on top of normal text instead of underneath.
14. *Background printing*. Using this option, it's possible to continue working while Word prints the document in the background. This option uses system memory and can cause Word to slow down while the document is printing. Of course, this may be better than not using Word at all while a document prints.

Controlling Printing in Windows

With background printing turned on (see #14 in the previous list), the document enters the Windows print queue, where it awaits its turn at the printer. When the print queue is active, a printer icon appears in the system tray near the clock. Check on the status of a print job at any time by double-clicking the print queue icon. This opens a print queue window similar to the one shown in Figure 4-19. If no other documents are waiting in the print queue, a print job may enter and leave the queue too fast for the print queue icon to appear. The print queue can also be opened using Start → Settings → Printers → Any Printer. If the queue is opened before printing, you might stand a chance of catching a fast-printing document in the queue.

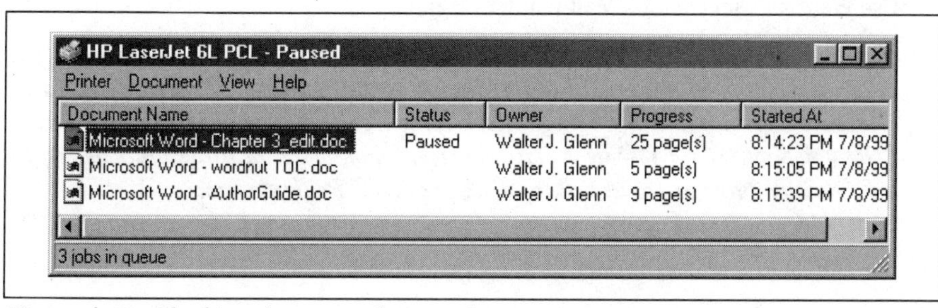

Figure 4-19: Checking the status of print jobs

Print jobs are listed in the order they will print. For each job, the document name, current status, owner of the document, print progress, and time and date of the printing are displayed. Rearrange jobs in the queue simply by dragging them around. For each document, pause or cancel printing using the Document menu or by right-clicking the document. You can also pause or purge the entire print queue from the Printer menu on the print queue window.

If working with a network printer shared by others, you can only manipulate your own documents using the Windows print queue.

File → Send To

Commands found on this submenu change depending on your installation of Microsoft Word or Microsoft Office, and depending on whether other programs on your system are designed to hook into Word. In the following sections, I describe the commands found in a default installation of Office 2000 on a Windows 98 system.

File → Send To → Mail Recipient

Word attaches an email header to the current document, as shown in Figure 4-20. Select message recipients, add a subject, attach files, and set the same kinds of options you would in any email message. By clicking Send a Copy, Word converts the document to HTML format and mails the message using the default email program on your system. Recipients actually view the Word document in the body of the message they receive, if they have a mail reader such as Outlook or Outlook Express that supports HTML. This can be great for sending documents to people who don't have a copy of Word on their system, but depending on the recipient's email program, the document may end up anywhere from perfect to perfectly scrambled in their message window. My advice is to send documents as attachments (described in the next section) whenever possible and use this method only when you know the recipient's email software supports HTML.

TIP # 46

Use Word as Your Outlook Mail Editor

You can use Word as the default email editor when using Microsoft Outlook instead of using the built-in editor. All of the formatting available in Word can be used in email messages. Enable this from Outlook using Tools → Options → Mail Format → "Use Microsoft Word to edit e-mail messages." For more on using Outlook, check out Outlook 2000 in a Nutshell, by Tom Syroid (O'Reilly & Associates).

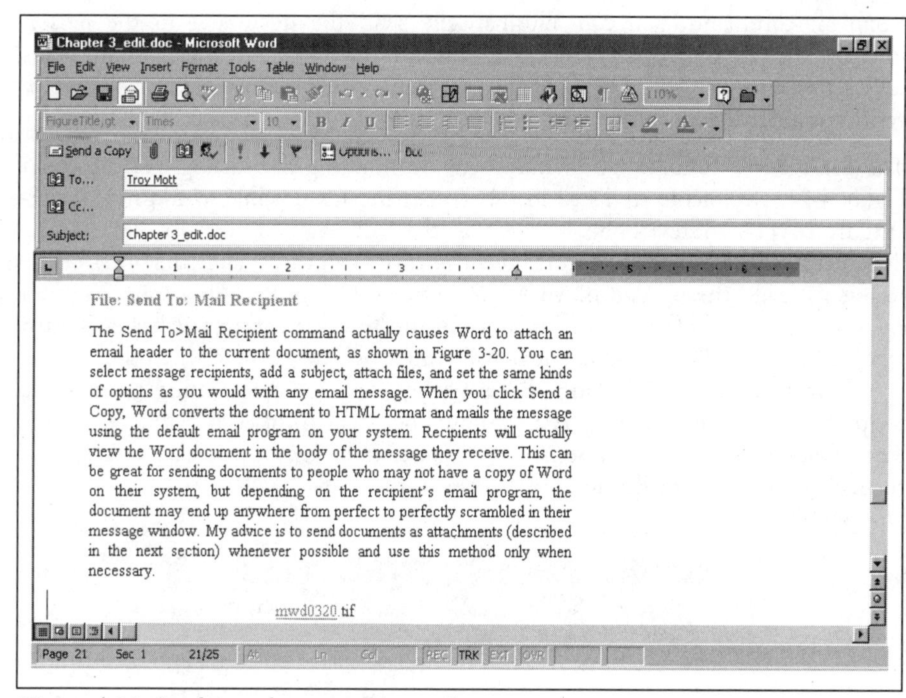

Figure 4-20: Sending a document via email

File → Send To → Mail Recipient (as Attachment)

This command works like the Send To → Mail Recipient command, except that it opens a new message form using the default email program. A copy of the active Word document is attached to the message in its native file format. Recipients must have Word 97 or Word 2000 installed in order to view files sent as attachments.

If you want to send a document to someone who does not have Word and whose email client does not support HTML format, your best bet is to save the file in a format that the recipient can access. For a list of supported formats and supplied converters, see Appendix C, Converters and Filters.

File → Send To → Routing Recipient

This command routes the document via email to one or more designated recipients (explained in detail later in this section). Word handles the details of routing a document and supports most popular email clients. When routing a document rather than sending it to someone, you can designate the entire route the document will take and track the document along the way. Suppose, for example, you are working on a sales report that eventually needs to be sent to your manager. First, however, you need to send the report to a person who will insert a chart before sending it to your assistant, who will print out several copies. Using the Routing

Recipient command, you can automatically send the document to the person inserting the chart via email. Once that person finishes, the document is automatically sent on to your assistant, then to your manager. At each step, you will receive verification that the document continued on its route.

The Send To → Routing command opens the Routing Slip dialog box shown in Figure 4-21. Recipients are listed in the To list and it's possible to add new recipients from your address book by clicking the Addresses button. By default, the document will be routed to each recipient in turn. You can change the order of the recipients using the up and down Move buttons. Using the "All at once" option causes the document to be routed to all recipients simultaneously. Click the "Return when done" option so the document will come back to you after the other recipients have reviewed it. Selecting "Return when done" when routing to multiple recipients simultaneously delivers a separate document from each of the recipients. The "Track status" option causes an email notice to be sent to you each time one of the recipients routes the document to the next recipient.

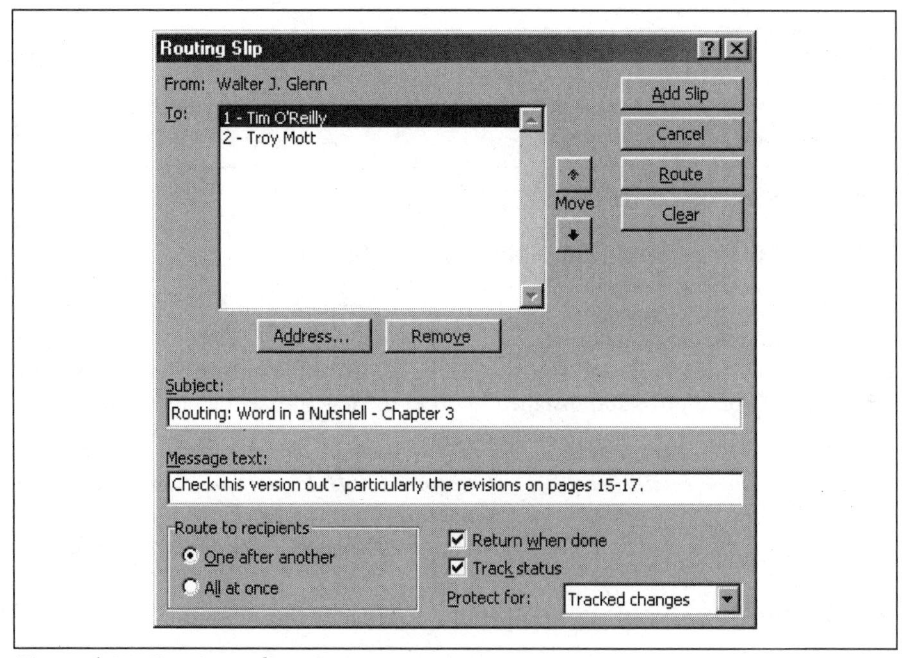

Figure 4-21: Routing a document

It's possible to protect a routed document in several ways. The default is to protect for tracked changes, which turns revision marking on for the document (see Chapter 13 for more on revision marking) and preserves all changes made by routing recipients. "Protect for comments" allows recipients to insert comments into the document (see Chapter 7 for more on this), but not make any actual changes. If the document you are routing contains fields, the "Protect for forms" option lets recipients enter information into the fields without changing any other part of the document. The final option is not to protect the document at all.

Each of the Send To recipients must be using Word 97 or Word 2000 to use the routing slip feature. Any email client is supported. Any recipient can receive the document copy, however, and send it to the next recipient on the routing list by attaching it to an email message manually. This method does not preserve the routing slip functionality beyond this recipient.

File → Send To → Exchange Folder

Microsoft Exchange Server is a groupware messaging system that makes public documents available via public folders. The Send To → Exchange Folder command sends the active document directly to an Exchange public folder. For this to work, of course, your network must be running Exchange server.

File → Send To → Online Meeting Participants

Sends a message directly to a participant in an online meeting using Microsoft NetMeeting or another online collaboration utility. The meeting must be in progress for this option to be available. When issuing the command, you can choose from a list of participants. The chosen participants receive a copy of the document transferred to their system, which can be saved or opened in Word.

File → Send To → Fax Recipient

Launches Word's Fax wizard, allowing you to choose a cover sheet template for the document and set up the document for faxing. This wizard contains two options: printing the document to send it via a fax machine or sending the document to a fax program installed on your system. The Fax wizard helps prepare a document for faxing by attaching a cover page and handing the files off to installed system fax software.

TIP # 47

Bypassing the Fax Wizard

Most fax programs integrate with Word by creating a printer in Windows (My Computer → Printers) that looks like a printer to most applications but actually relays documents to the fax software. To bypass Word's fax wizard (which doesn't add much value), choose File → Print and select the fax "printer" instead of your default printer using the printer's properties.

File → Send To → Microsoft PowerPoint

PowerPoint is a program used to create slide presentations. When working in outline view (View → Outline), you can convert a Word outline into a PowerPoint presentation simply by selecting File → Send To → Microsoft PowerPoint. Each "Heading 1" line in the outline is made into a separate slide with the heading as the title. Heading levels beneath the "Heading 1" line are constructed as an outline on the slide. For the conversion to PowerPoint to work, you must use Word's built-in heading styles.

> **TIP # 48**
>
> **Print Just a Heading Outline Using PowerPoint**
>
> *Word does not provide the ability to print just the outline of a document (the major headings of a document as viewed in Outline view, which is discussed in Chapter 6). You can, however, send a document to PowerPoint and then print the outline view in PowerPoint, as long as you haven't customized your own heading styles.*

File → Properties

This command opens a property sheet for the active document. This dialog is divided into five tabs: General, Summary, Statistics, Contents, Custom. These tabs are covered in detail in the following sections.

General Tab

This tab is the basic Windows property sheet for the document file and shows the basic attributes of the file for the document, such as the filename, type, location, and size. The Word properties for a document (those on the other tabs described below) are only available from Windows if the document is not open in Word. If a document is open, only the General tab is displayed in Windows.

Summary Tab

This tab shows the basic attributes of the document itself, which can be used as criteria when searching for the file. Attributes include title, subject, author, manager, company, category, keywords, and comments. Any of these fields can be specified as search criteria when using File → Open → Tools → Find, as described earlier in this chapter.

A hyperlink base can also be defined on this tab, which is the URL that serves as a base for all hyperlinks created in the document. The hyperlink base can be an Internet address, a file location on a local system, or a Universal Naming Convention (UNC) address pointing to a location on a local network. When creating a document that will reference a number of documents in a folder named *C:\My Documents\Brochures,* enter that path as the hyperlink base. When creating a hyperlink in the document, you can simply enter the name of the file to link to, instead of entering the entire path each time. For more information on using hyperlinks in documents, see Chapter 7.

The Summary tab also contains the option to save a preview picture with the document. This can be useful for three things. First, the picture shows up in the preview pane of the Open dialog if you are viewing files in preview mode. Second, the headings show up on the Contents tab of the Properties dialog box. Third, previews for templates show up in the New dialog box and in the Style Gallery. Keep in mind that saving the preview picture for a document does increase its file size a small amount.

Statistics Tab

Figure 4-22 shows the Statistics tab.

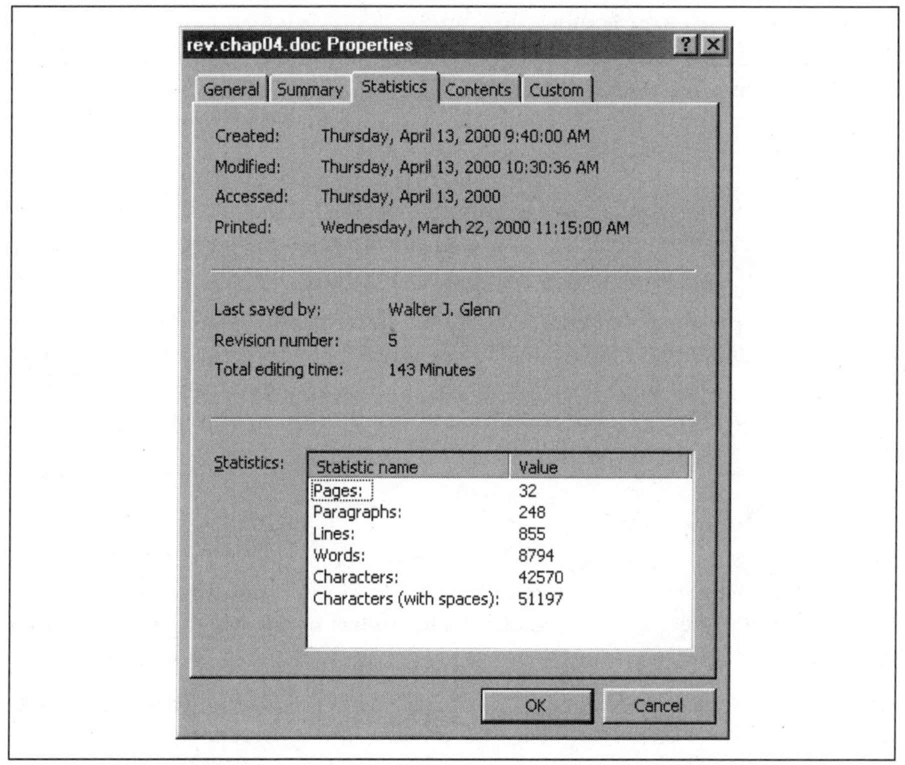

Figure 4-22: The Statistics tab

The Statistics tab lets you view a number of very useful statistics for a document, including:

- When the document was created, modified last, accessed last, and printed last
- Who saved the document last
- How many revisions have been made to the document (how many times it's been saved)
- The total number of minutes that have been spent editing the document (it doesn't count times when a file is opened but not edited)
- Common document statistics such as number of pages, paragraphs, lines, words, and characters

Contents Tab

This tab shows a quick preview of the contents of the document. By default, only the title of the document is shown here. When a preview picture is saved with the document using the Summary tab, as discussed earlier, the headings of the document are shown here as well.

Custom Tab

This tab provides the ability to add custom properties for the file. Either use the list of predefined variables or type your own variable name in the Name field. The most useful option is the ability to show a link to a named field in your document.

For example, if a document contains a form, create custom links to fields in that form so the values can be viewed by looking at the File Properties without opening the document. To do this, create a name on the Custom tab for the field, select the Link to Content checkbox, and select the name of the field in the Source field.

File → 1-4

By default, Word presents a list of the four most recently used (MRU) documents on the File menu for quick access. Just click the filename (or type the corresponding number key) to open the file. If a file shown on the MRU has been moved or deleted, you'll get an error stating that the document name or path is not valid.

Change the number of documents shown (or turn the feature off altogether) at Tools → Options → General. Change the number of most recently used documents displayed on the File menu to any number between 0 (no MRU list shown) and 9 using Tools → Options → General → Recently Used File List.

TIP # 49

The Work Menu

Word also provides a built-in menu named Work that is not displayed by default. Turn it on using Tools → Customize → Commands → Built In Menus and drag the Work command to the Word Menu bar. Add any open document to the Work menu by choosing Work → Add To Work Menu. Add any number of documents to the Work menu and open any document simply by selecting it. See Chapter 3 for details on customizing menus.

File → Exit

This command closes all open Word documents, offering to save those that have not yet been saved, and exits Word.

Chapter 5

Edit

As its name implies, Word's Edit menu is used to edit text and other objects in a Word document. Use it to undo and redo actions; cut, copy, and paste text and objects; insert objects such as pictures, hyperlinks, and fields; and search for elements within.

Central to these editing commands is the ability to cut, copy, and paste. Whenever you cut or copy selections in a document, Word uses a special area of memory named the Clipboard to store those selections. These selections could be text, tables, graphics, or anything else you can select. In previous versions of Word, the Clipboard stored only one item at a time. New cut or copied items replaced whatever was previously in the Clipboard. In Word 2000, a new and improved Clipboard can now hold up to twelve items.

When more than one item is added, a Clipboard toolbar opens that presents a button for each stored item (Figure 5-1). Hover the pointer over a button for a moment to see the actual contents of each item in a pop-up ScreenTip. Click any button to paste the contents of that item at the insertion point. The toolbar also has buttons for copying the current selection, for pasting all items in the clipboard at once, and for clearing all items from the clipboard.

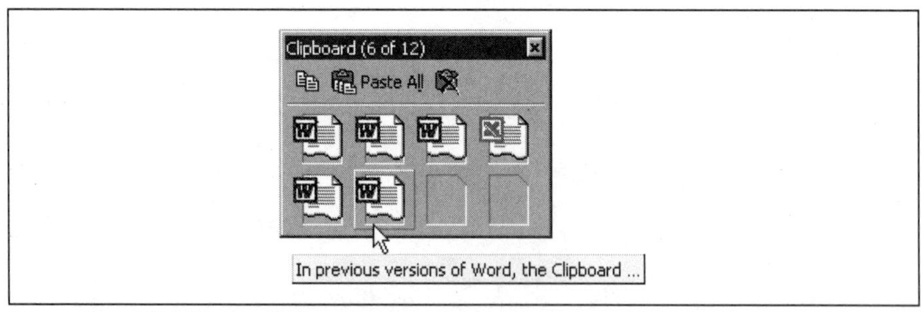

Figure 5-1: Word's new clipboard

Many new users aren't aware of the new Clipboard and simply close the toolbar whenever it appears. After a few times, Word assumes that you do not want the Clipboard toolbar to appear and does not open it in the future. Force it to appear again later by right-clicking on any toolbar and choosing Clipboard from the context menu.

Working with the extended Clipboard is fairly simple within Office 2000 applications. Each of the major applications (Word, Excel, Access, and PowerPoint) uses the same Clipboard and toolbar as Word. Place several items in the clipboard from a Word document and they are available when working on an Excel spreadsheet. However, neither Outlook 2000 nor FrontPage 2000 allows access to the Clipboard toolbar. Only the last selection copied to the Clipboard in any of the supporting Office applications is available when you use the standard paste command in Outlook or FrontPage.

Outside the realm of Office 2000, things work differently altogether:

- Copy or cut an item to the Clipboard and then switch to a different application (say, Notepad), and the item is pasted in the usual manner.
- Paste the most recently added item in the clipboard into a Word document and you can still go to Notepad and paste that item.
- Paste any item except for the most recent using the Clipboard toolbar in Word and nothing can be pasted in Notepad. The Windows clipboard cannot handle this action.

Edit → Undo

Most programs have an undo feature for reversing the most recent action, and Word is no exception, but Word does have a few interesting twists.

For starters, the name of the menu command (Edit → Undo) changes slightly to reflect the action that will be undone. If you have just typed some words, for example, the command becomes "Undo Typing." If you have just changed the formatting of a group of characters to boldface, the command becomes "Undo Bold." Most Word users just hit Ctrl-Z to perform an undo, but this subtle menu feature can help a great deal when you're not sure what the last action was.

The Undo button on the Standard toolbar is also used to undo an action. The floating tip that appears when the cursor hovers over the button changes in the same way the menu command does to reflect the actual change to be made. The Undo button also includes an Undo list (click the down-arrow by the button, as in Figure 5-2), which includes all actions taken since opening the current document.

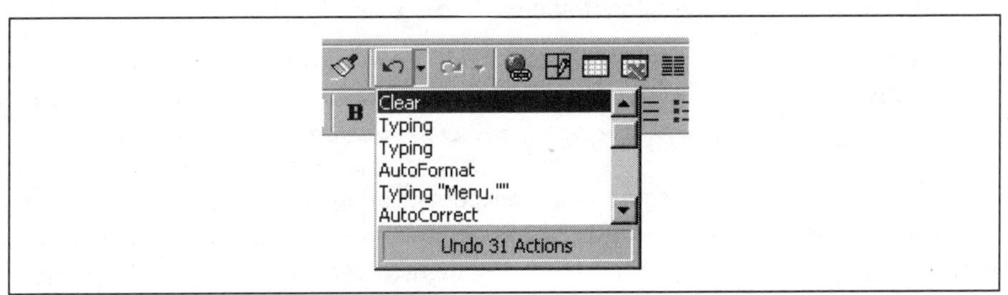

Figure 5-2: Undoing multiple actions

Drag the pointer over the list to select multiple actions to undo. This is a much more precise technique than just repeatedly using Edit → Undo or Ctrl-Z. The Undo list does not automatically scroll with the pointer. Use the scrollbar to see the whole list.

You cannot undo a single action on Word's Undo list without also undoing all of the actions that were performed after it.

Undo often does not work the way it seems it should. Continuous typing is considered a single action until it's interrupted by some other action, such as clicking a different point in the document, choosing a menu command, or making a Word AutoCorrect change.

Edit → Repeat (Redo)

By default, the command available directly below the Undo command on the Edit menu is Repeat, which repeats the last typing or formatting action performed in Word. The F4 key performs the same action, which is handy for adding text or applying a format in multiple places throughout a document. The command's name changes slightly to show the actual action performed ("Repeat Bold," for instance).

When the last action taken in Word was to undo something, the Repeat command is replaced by a Redo command, which reverses the last undo action performed. Redo multiple actions by repeatedly selecting the command or by using the Redo list on the Standard toolbar, which works the same way as the Undo list discussed previously.

Edit → Cut

It is easy enough to move text around in Word (even between different documents) by simply highlighting the text and dragging it to a new location. This method is fine for relocating small pieces of text short distances, but can quickly become tiresome for more sophisticated operations. This is where the clipboard and Word's cut, copy, and paste commands come in.

TIP # 50

Right-Drag Selections for More Options

Cutting and then pasting is the default action that occurs when you drag a selection to another location in the same document or a separate document. Drag with the right mouse button to open a pop-up menu with options for copying or moving.

The Cut command (Ctrl-X) removes a selection from a document and places it in the Word Clipboard. This selection can be text, a graphic, a table, or anything else selectable in Word. For example, cut a highlighted sentence and that sentence is deleted from the document and placed in the Clipboard.

Using the Spike

Another way to cut items from a Word document is by using Ctrl-F3. Selected items are removed from the document and placed into an area of memory named the *Spike*. There are a few differences between the Spike and the Clipboard. The first is that only text can be placed in the Spike (the Clipboard allows images, tables, etc.). The second difference is that the Spike can hold an unlimited number of items, whereas the Clipboard can hold only twelve. The final difference is that you can only paste the entire contents of the Spike, not individual items. The Spike is actually an AutoText entry that is pasted by using Ctrl-Shift-F3 or by using Insert → AutoText → AutoText and choosing the Spike. You can also just type "spike" and press Enter (for more on using AutoText, see Chapter 7, *Insert*). When pasting the contents of the Spike into a document, each item in the Spike is pasted onto a separate line. For example, you could go through your document and copy all proper names to the Spike. When you paste the Spike, each name would appear on its own line.

Edit → Copy

The Copy command works in much the same way as the Cut command (see the previous section), except that selections are not removed from their original location.

Copy a selection using drag-and-drop by holding down the Ctrl key while dragging the selection or by dragging with the right mouse button and selecting Copy Here from the context menu that appears when you release the button.

Edit Menu

TIP # 51

Using Document Scraps

Use document scraps to copy and paste information in documents. Create a document scrap by dragging a selection from a document and releasing it on the Windows desktop (or in a folder). A file with a .shs extension is created that contains the selection. Paste the contents of the document scrap into a document by simply dragging the icon for the scrap from the desktop to a location in the document. Edit a scrap directly in Word by double-clicking it. Document scraps are a useful way of inserting standard entries (such as an address or a disclaimer) used repeatedly in documents, and are often easier to organize than AutoText entries (see Chapter 7).

Edit → Paste

Edit → Paste inserts the item most recently added to the Clipboard at the insertion point. The item also remains in the Clipboard. Paste previous entries in the Clipboard by opening the Clipboard Toolbar (View → Toolbars → Clipboard) and clicking the button for the desired item.

Items assume the format of the location where they are pasted. Alter the format of an item while pasting it using Edit → Paste Special. This command is discussed in the next section.

The result from pasting a selection depends largely on how text is selected before cutting or copying it. For example, copy a paragraph by dragging the selection over all of the words in that paragraph and use the copy command. When the selection is pasted, it assumes the formatting dictated by the location in which you paste it. If you select the source paragraph by triple-clicking (this selects the whole paragraph, including the paragraph mark), the formatting of the original paragraph is also transferred to the new location. See Chapter 2, *How Word Works*, for details about how styles and other formats are saved in the paragraph mark.

Edit → Paste Special

The Paste command inserts a selection from the Clipboard at the insertion point. The selection takes on the formatting of the location where it is pasted unless an entire paragraph is pasted with formatting. The Paste Special command opens a separate dialog (Figure 5-3) that provides a little more formatting control when pasting a selection.

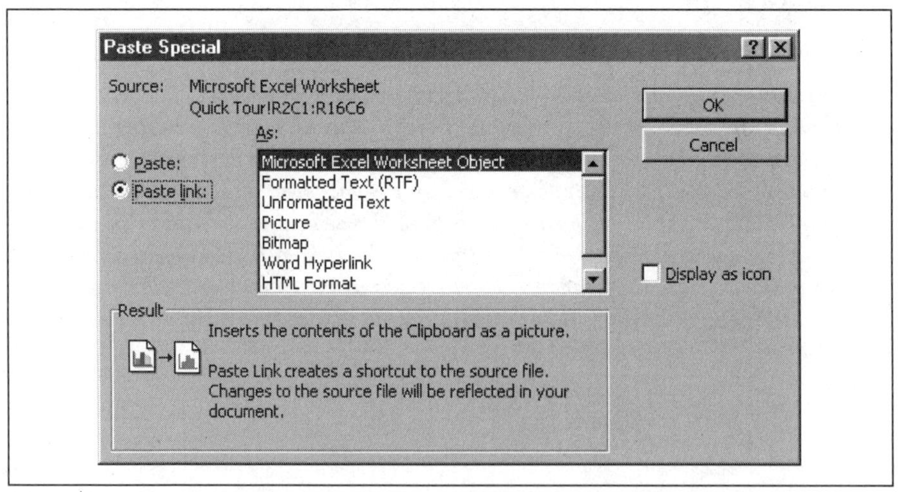

Figure 5-3: Choosing formatting with Paste Special

TIP # 52

Add Paste Special to the Context Menu

Use the techniques described in Chapter 3, Customizing Word, to add the Paste Special command (in the Edit category) to the Text context menu.

Available formats change slightly depending on the source of the selection. For example, if the selection was copied from Notepad, it can only be pasted as unformatted text. If the selection is from an Excel worksheet, many more format options await. The following list represents a superset of available formats:

Microsoft Office Document Object
: If the selection comes from any Microsoft Office application, including Word, the selection can be pasted as a document object. Though the selection is in no way linked to its original source, it can be edited using the application that created it. For example, assume that you copy a table from an Excel worksheet and paste that table into a Word document as a Microsoft Excel Document Object. In the Word document, the object looks exactly like an Excel table. Double-clicking the object actually opens Excel toolbars in Word for editing the object.

Formatted Text (RTF)
: Rich Text Format (RTF) is a fairly widely adopted standard developed by Microsoft for specifying the formatting of documents. Pasting a selection as formatted text retains font, margin, and table formatting information.

Unformatted text
: This option pastes the selection without retaining any formatting instructions. The selection will take on the formatting characteristics dictated by the target location.

Picture
: This option pastes the selection as a picture. Modify the picture after pasting using Word's Picture toolbar. For more on this, see Chapter 6, *View*.

Word Hyperlink
: This option is available only when pasting a link, which is described following this list. The pasted selection retains its original formatting, much as when using the Formatted Text option. However, the selection is also converted to a Word Hyperlink, which is colored as blue text and underlined. Clicking the selection links to the target. For more on using Word Hyperlinks, see Chapter 7.

HTML Format
: This option pastes the selection using HTML format, which retains the original formatting of the text. Use this format when pasting selections from an HTML document (such as a web page) to retain the formatting and any hyperlinks defined in the original selection.

Unformatted Unicode Text

Unicode is a formatting standard that allows for the representation of over 65,000 unique characters—far more than most other file formats. Unicode is generally used in foreign-language documents.

In addition to choosing the formatting for the selection, you can also choose whether to paste that selection as a link. A link is a selection from another document that is presented in a Word document. For example, you might be working on a report in which you want to include a passage from one of your coworker's documents. You could simply copy and paste that passage from her document to yours, but your document would become outdated if hers changed. If you instead paste the passage as a link, the text in your document would be automatically updated whenever the original document changes. Keep in mind that the original document must be kept in the same location for the link to continue to work. If you do not paste a selection into your document as a link, that selection is embedded in your document. For complete details on embedding and linking, see Chapter 7.

TIP # 53

Pasting from Another Application into Word

When copying selections from another application to paste into a Word document as an embedded or linked object, it is important to leave the source application open before selecting Edit → Paste Special in Word. If you close the source application first, you are only allowed to paste the selection into the Word document as text—not as an embedded or linked object. This is true even if you tell the source application to save the information in the Clipboard on closing the application.

Once a link is inserted, double-click it to edit the source data. If linking to a document created in another Office application, double-clicking opens the document in the Word window and replaces the Word menus with the menus of the other application. Otherwise, double-clicking opens the original document in a separate window.

Insert a linked object into a Word document using Insert → Object, which is covered in Chapter 7. The difference between using Insert → Object and Edit → Paste Special to insert a link is that Paste Special can link to only part of the data in the target file (i.e., a single paragraph in a Word document). Insert → Object is used to link to the entire target document. Insert → Object, on the other hand, allows you to create and link a new object without having to start the associated external application.

Linking information from other documents is a handy way to make sure documents stay up to date. There are potential problems, however, especially when sharing files with other users. If the original file is moved, for example, the link may be broken.

Once any links are inserted into a document, the Links command also becomes available on the Edit menu. This command, which is discussed later in this chapter, is used to change how and when links in a document are updated.

Edit → Paste as Hyperlink

Create a hyperlink in Word to any file, to a web resource, or even to part of another Office document. The hyperlink appears in the Word document the same as it would on a web page—blue and underlined. Clicking it opens the target item.

Paste as Hyperlink really only works when copying information between or within Office applications. For example, select a phrase in one Word (or Excel, PowerPoint, or Access) document, copy it, then paste it as a hyperlink into a Word document. Clicking the resulting link opens the target document and jumps to the target selection. Hyperlinks can also link to other locations in the same Word document. For more on using hyperlinks in Word, see Chapter 7.

Edit → Clear

The Clear command performs the same function as the Delete key. If any text is selected, Clear deletes that selection. If no text is selected, Clear deletes the character directly in front of the insertion point.

TIP # 54

Cut, Don't Delete

When you use Edit → Clear, Delete, or Backspace, the deleted information is permanently removed from a document. Develop the habit of cutting items instead of deleting them, ensuring that the items are still available if a mistake is made.

Edit → Select All

Select All (also Ctrl-A) selects everything in a document (text, graphics, headers, and everything else). It is useful, for example, for changing the font size of all of the text in a document.

Edit → Find

Word's Find command is useful for finding just about anything in a document. In its default state, the Find dialog (Figure 5-4) is fairly simple to use. Enter up to 255 characters in the "Find what" box, click Find Next, and Word jumps to the first instance of that text after the insertion point and selects the found text. Clicking

Find Next again jumps to the next occurrence. When Find reaches the end of the document, it offers to start over at the beginning. The Find and Replace dialog box remains visible and on top the whole time.

If any text is selected when the Find command is issued, Word only searches within that selection.

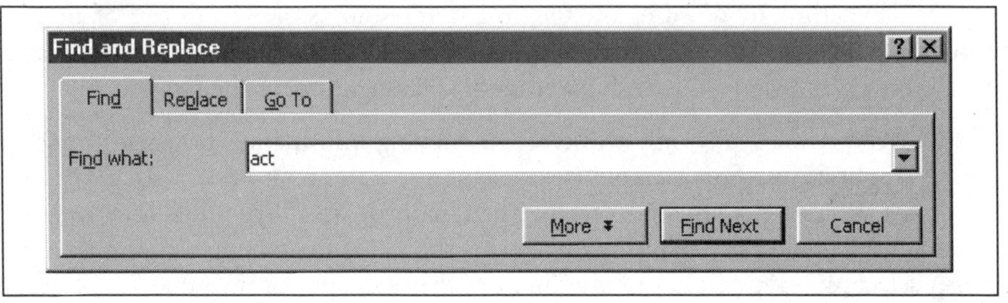

Figure 5-4: Finding text in Word

By default, Word finds all strings match the search criteria. For example, enter "act" and Word also finds "acting," "react," and "characters." Also by default, Word ignores case in all searches. Thus, a search for "act" also finds "Act" and "ACT."

Getting More Find Options

Access additional options for using the Find command by clicking More on the Find and Replace dialog (see Figure 5-4). This extends the dialog box so that it looks like the one shown in Figure 5-5.

The following list describes the additional Find options:

1. *Find what.* Word remembers searches during the active session. The drop-down list is reset as soon as Word closes. Use the "Find what" drop-down menu to access previous search phrases during a current session.
2. *Options.* Any special options chosen for the search are displayed right below the search entry.
3. *Search.* This drop-down list specifies the portion of the document to search. Search the whole document (all), from the insertion point onward (down), or from the insertion point backward (up).
4. *Match case.* This option causes Word to find only instances of the specified text that exactly match the case as entered. For example, "Act" will find only "Act" and not "act."
5. *Find whole words only.* This causes Word to ignore instances of the specified text if they are only part of a word. For example, "act" would find only "act" and not "react" or "action."

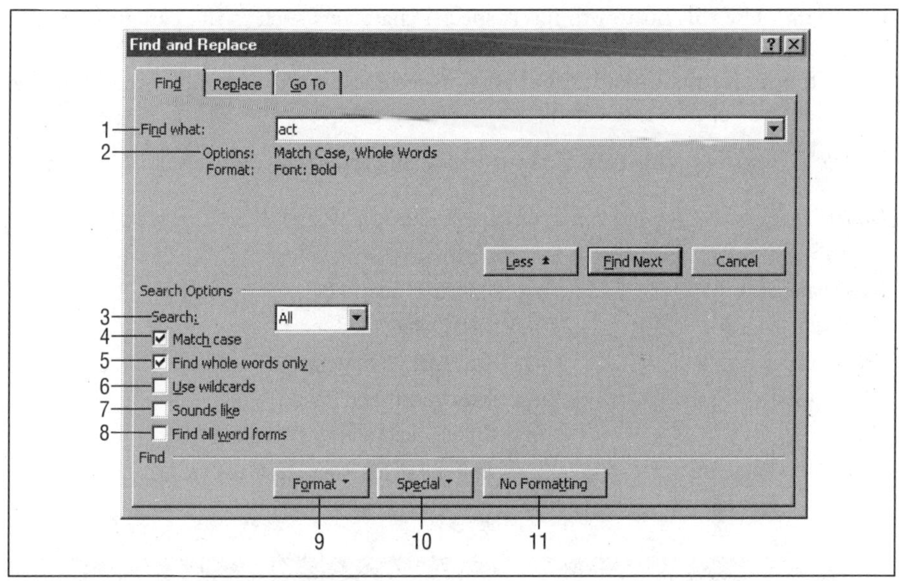

Figure 5-5: Finding items in a document

6. *Use wildcards.* Wildcards are characters that can substitute for other characters. For example, searching for "??act" would find all five-letter words in which the last three characters are "act," such as "react." The "Use wildcards" option causes Word to read certain symbols (i.e., *, ?, and !) as wildcards. The Special menu (discussed in item #10) changes to include all available wildcard characters.

7. *Sounds like.* This causes Word to find all words that sound like the entered text. For example, entering the text "scrole" causes Word to find instances of the word "scroll." This option is really pretty limited, but it can come in handy when you just don't know how to spell a word. Word will only find whole words when using this option.

8. *Find all word forms.* This causes Word to find all forms of the entered test. For example, searching for "hit" returns the words "hit," "hitter," and "hitting."

9. *Format.* This button leads to a series of other dialog boxes used to search for specific types of formatting in a document. You can even search for formatting without searching for any particular text. For example, Word could find all boldfaced text that was font size 12. Formatting options appear on the dialog under the "Find what" list. There are seven choices on the Format menu: Font, Paragraph, Tabs, Language, Frame, Style, and Highlight. All but Language and Highlight open dialogs that are nearly identical to the format dialogs shown when using Format → Paragraph. Find more information on these in Chapter 8, *Format*. Language finds occurrences of a selected language. Highlight finds text that has been highlighted with Word's highlight button.

10. *Special.* Use this button to insert special characters such as the paragraph mark, tab mark, or footnote mark into the "Find what" box. Table 5-1 provides a list of the more useful wildcard characters available on this menu when the "Use wildcards" option is selected.

11. *No Formatting.* This removes any formatting criteria already added to a search.

Table 5-1: Special Characters and Wildcards Used in Word's Find Command

Name	Symbol	Example
Any character	?	"a?t" finds "act" and "art".
Character in range	[ ]	"[fp]act" finds "fact" and "pact".
Beginning of word	<	"<act" finds "act" and "action".
End of word	>	">act" finds "react" and "fact".
Not	[!]	"[!p]act" finds "act" and "fact" but not "pact".
0 or more characters	*	"*act" finds all words where "act" are the last three letters.

TIP # 55

Use the Browse Buttons Instead of the Find Dialog

After performing a Find, quickly find the next or previous occurrence of that Find using the Next and Previous buttons at the bottom of the right-hand scroll bar. Even better, use the techniques described in Chapter 3 to add the Find command to the Text context menu.

Edit → Replace

The Replace command is very similar to the Find command except that, in addition to finding the next occurrence of a specified text, Word also replaces it with a new entry. The dialog box that opens (Figure 5-6) is actually the same Find and Replace dialog box used for the Find command, just a different tab. Enter the text to find in the "Find what" box and enter the text to replace it with in the "Replace with" box. The Replace button replaces the currently selected occurrence of the text and finds and selects the next one. Replace All replaces all found occurrences of the text throughout the document. Find Next jumps to the next occurrence and selects it without replacing the currently selected one. All of the advanced search options are identical to those used with the Find command.

TIP # 56

Use Special Characters in the Replace Dialog

Here's a great example of the usefulness of the Replace command. Say you open a file formatted as plain text (ASCII) with line breaks in Word and want to remove the line breaks. You can simply replace the line breaks with spaces by using Word's Replace command to replace all instances of ^p (the code for a line break) with spaces. If you have double line breaks, use ^p^p instead. Find a list of special characters used in Word in Appendix B, Registry Keys.

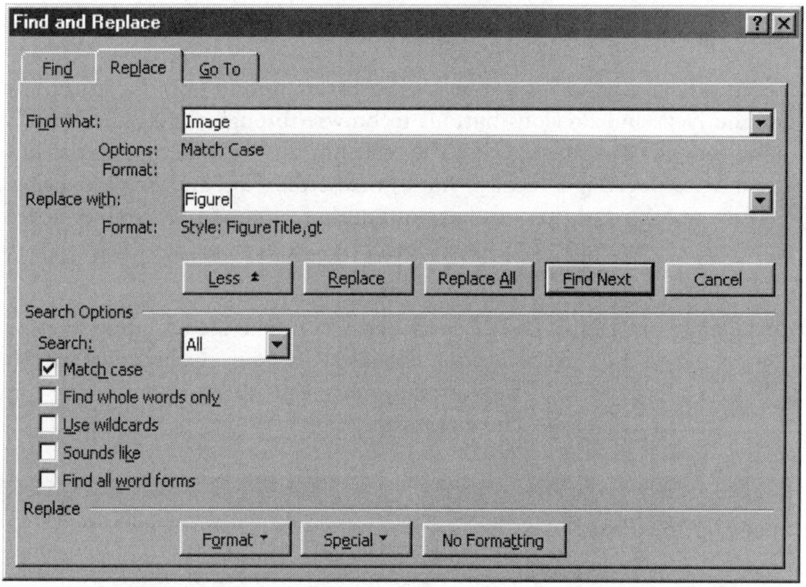

Figure 5-6: Replacing text in a document

WARNING

Be careful using Replace All. Remember that by default, Word finds all occurrences of a string of text, even if they are part of another word.

Edit → Go To

Go To is used to locate document features, such as pages, sections, comments, or graphics. Use Edit → Go To to open the Go To tab of the Find and Replace dialog box (Figure 5-7). You can also open the Go To tab using F5, Ctrl-G, or by double-clicking the page number display area of the status bar. This is also a quick way of getting to the Find and Replace tabs.

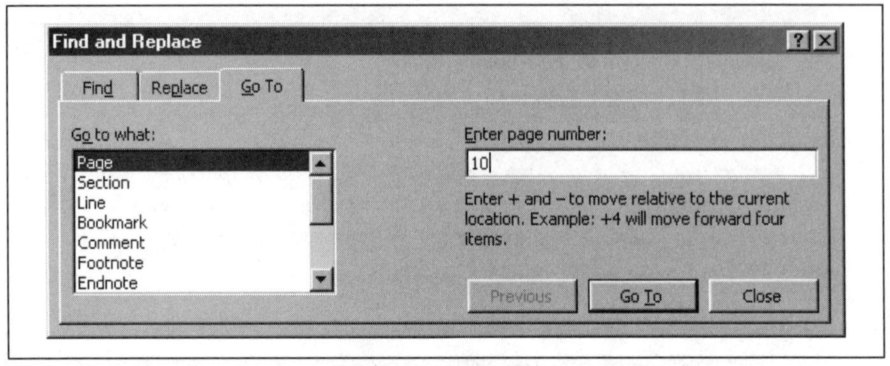

Figure 5-7: Browsing document features with Go To

The easiest way to use Go To is to select the feature to find from the list on the left and use the Next and Previous buttons to browse through the document. Choose Footnote, for example, and the Next button jumps to the next footnote in your document. After locating a feature, you can close the Find and Replace dialog and use the Browse Next and Previous buttons under the right-hand scrollbar to achieve the same effect (for more on using Word's browse feature, see Chapter 1, *Word Overview*).

For each feature on the Go To tab, special criteria can be used to jump to a specific location relative to the current location. Choose Page from the list and enter 10, for example, to go to page 10. Use plus and minus signs to jump that many features ahead: +3, for example, jumps three pages ahead.

TIP # 57

Speed Up Your Browsing

Type the first letter of the feature type plus the criteria itself in the text box rather than selecting the feature first and then entering the criteria. For example, instead of selecting Footnote and then entering "14" to go to footnote 14, simply enter "F14." Entering "P0" in the text box moves to the beginning of a document. Entering "P+x," where x is any number greater than the number of pages in a document, moves to the last page of a document. These will work no matter what feature is currently selected.

Some of the feature choices (namely Object, Field, Comment, and Bookmark) offer a drop-down menu. Bookmark, for example, has a drop-down menu with all bookmarks in your document.

Edit → Links

Objects are linked to a Word document using either Edit → Paste Special or Insert → Object. Linking itself is discussed in detail in Chapter 7. Edit → Links is used to change how links in a document are updated. By default, links within a document are automatically updated whenever the source object changes. For example, a chart from an Excel spreadsheet linked to your document is updated whenever the Excel spreadsheet changes. This default behavior is useful for objects that are in flux, like when charts and graphs are being finalized for a big report.

Sometimes, though, you may not want links to be updated automatically. Change the default behavior so that links are updated manually using the Edit → Links command, which brings up the Links dialog box (Figure 5-8). This dialog displays all of the links in a document. For each link, choose whether that link should be updated automatically or manually using the Update options at the bottom of the dialog. Thus, some links in a document could be updated automatically and others would have to be updated manually.

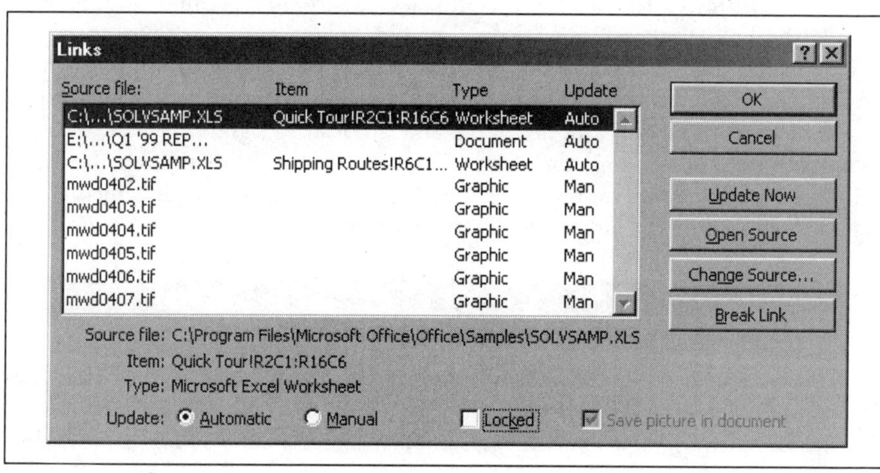

Figure 5-8: Choosing how links are updated in a document

To update a link manually (and you can do this even if the link is set to be updated automatically), select it from the list and click Update Now. Select and update multiple links simultaneously using the Shift and Ctrl keys.

The link information for a selected link is shown beneath the list. This information includes the source file for the linked object, the linked item (this is actually the name of the field that hold the link), and the type of object it is. Open the linked object in its source application by clicking Open Source. This is the same as double-clicking the object in the document itself.

When a source file is deleted, the link is broken. This becomes evident in Word when opening a document that contains a link for which the source file no longer exists. Word informs you on opening the document that the object cannot be edited if you try to open it. In the Links dialog box, an unavailable link is noted with a "N/A" in the Update column. If a link is unintentionally broken, reestablish the link using Change Source, which brings up a standard Open-style dialog for choosing a new file to serve as the source for the linked object.

Sever the connection to the source object yourself using Break Link. Once a link is broken, the object becomes fixed in the Word document as a picture and is no longer associated with the source object at all. The link is removed from the Document altogether and no longer appears in the Links dialog box.

To temporarily disable a link without breaking it, lock the link using the Locked option at the bottom of the Links dialog. Updates will not occur while a link is locked.

Normally, a linked object in a Word document is represented as a picture of the source object. Double-clicking the picture opens the source object. When a link is first inserted (using either Edit → Paste Special or Insert → Hyperlink), you can elect to have the link displayed as an icon. Double-clicking the icon then opens the source file and this saves the reader of a document from having to flip through all the graphics. However, the picture itself is still stored in a document even when it is viewed as an icon. Pictures are pretty big and can lead to significant increases in a document's size. Turning off the "Save picture in document" option on the Links dialog box causes Word not to save these graphics within the document. The picture is replaced by the link's name in the document.

TIP # 58

Keep Linked Objects in the Same Directory as a Document

If linked objects are in the same directory as the Word file itself, Word automatically reestablishes links when you open the document. This makes it easy to send documents with links to someone else; just make sure everything's in the same folder.

Edit → Object

Edit → Object is a submenu that becomes available only when a linked or embedded object is selected (for more on using linked and embedded objects, see Chapter 7). The submenu actually changes slightly depending upon the type of object selected. For a linked Excel chart, the submenu becomes Edit → Chart Object. The commands available on the Edit → Object submenu also change depending upon the type of object selected, but there are a few commands that are always present:

Open
: This opens a linked or embedded object along with the object's source application. This allows for editing the object using all the tools available in that application. For example, choosing Open on an Excel spreadsheet in a Word document launches Excel and opens the spreadsheet.

Edit

When working with a linked object, the Edit command works just like the Open command. Typically, this is also true when working with an embedded object created by an application that is not a part of Windows or Microsoft Office. When working with an embedded object from a supported application, the Edit command lets you edit the object directly from within Word. Toolbars for working with the object replace Word's own toolbars. For example, when editing an embedded PowerPoint slide, Word's toolbars are actually replaced with PowerPoint's toolbars. Clicking anywhere in a document outside the object reopens Word's toolbars and closes any extra toolbars.

Convert

This command only works with embedded objects. Linked objects must be converted using their source application. Embedded objects may often be converted to a different format from that of their source application. This is useful when viewing a document that contains objects for which an appropriate viewer or editor is not installed. For example, you could convert an image created in a third-party drawing application to Windows bitmap format so that it can be viewed and edited in Paint. You might also convert embedded items such as Excel charts into Microsoft Drawing objects so that they take up less space, often resulting in significantly lower file sizes.

In addition to these commands, some types of objects have additional commands available. For example, a linked PowerPoint presentation includes a Show command that launches the presentation in a full-screen window, just as it would from PowerPoint.

TIP # 59

Use Context Menus

The same editing commands found on the Edit → Object submenu are also available by right-clicking the object itself within the Word document and choosing the Object submenu from the context menu.

Chapter 6

View

The View menu contains commands for changing the visual perspective on the active document. The menu also contains tools for displaying parts of the document that are not always visible, such as comments, headers, and toolbars.

Word's four document views provide different ways of looking at a document for different needs. The four views include:

Normal
: Work in normal view for typing, editing, and formatting text. Normal view shows text formatting but simplifies the layout of the page so that you can type and edit quickly.

Web Layout
: Work in Web layout view when creating a web page or a document that is viewed on the screen.

Print Layout
: Work in print layout view to see how text, graphics, and other elements will be positioned on the printed page.

Outline
: Work in outline view to see the structure of a document and to move, copy, and reorganize text by dragging headings.

View → Normal

Access Word's Normal view using View → Normal or the Normal view button at the far left of the horizontal scroll bar. In Normal view, the document appears as if it were one, infinitely long, scrollable piece of paper (Figure 6-1). Normal is the default view and is the most useful during the course of document creation, as it shows text and formatting, but does not cloud the screen with headers, footers, footnotes, and precise page layout.

Normal is the default for new documents. However, Word remembers the view last used before exiting a document and opens the document again using that view.

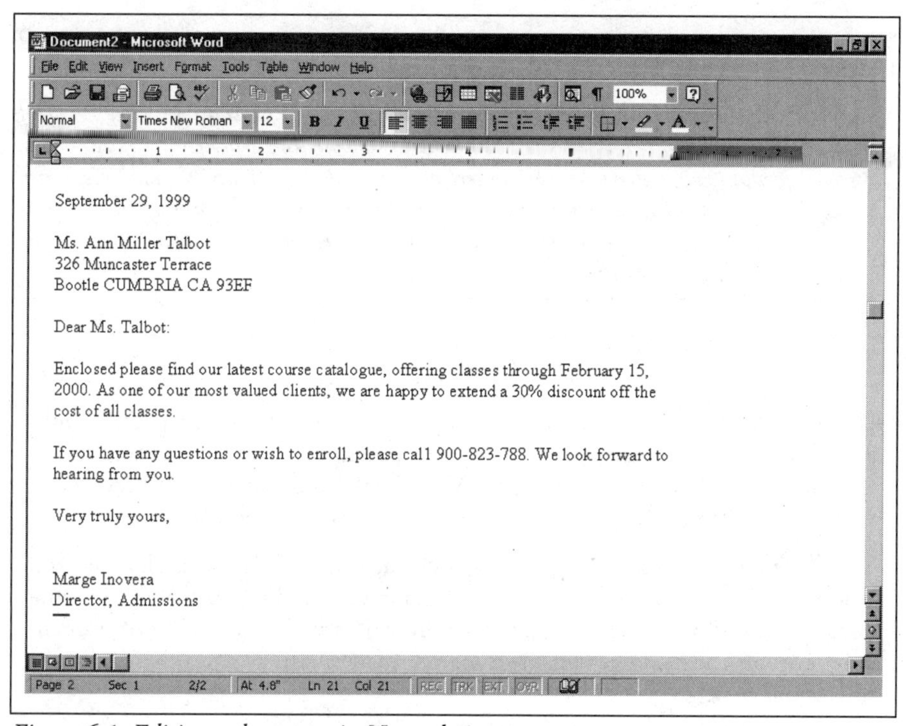
September 29, 1999

Ms. Ann Miller Talbot
326 Muncaster Terrace
Bootle CUMBRIA CA 93EF

Dear Ms. Talbot:

Enclosed please find our latest course catalogue, offering classes through February 15, 2000. As one of our most valued clients, we are happy to extend a 30% discount off the cost of all classes.

If you have any questions or wish to enroll, please call 900-823-788. We look forward to hearing from you.

Very truly yours,

Marge Inovera
Director, Admissions

Figure 6-1: Editing a document in Normal view

Here are a number of things to keep in mind when working in Normal view:

- Normal view does not show what text looks like in relationship to page margins.
- Multiple columns are not shown side by side, but in single columns, though the correct width of the columns is maintained.
- Graphics are shown where you insert them, which is not necessarily where they will print.
- Automatic page breaks are shown as single dotted lines. Manual page breaks (inserted using Insert → Break → Page Break are shown as thicker dotted lines with the words "Page Break" in them. Other section breaks are shown as double rows of dotted lines.
- Normal view is not great when a document contains a lot of graphical content—clip art, columns, drawn shapes and lines. Consider Print Layout view, which displays all graphical and text elements exactly as they'll print.

TIP # 60

Speed Up Normal View

Speed up working in Normal view by choosing Tools → Options → View → Draft Font. This causes all text in the document to appear as 12 pt. Courier. Any character formatting is displayed as underlined text. To speed up Normal view even more, select the Picture Placeholders option, which shows all graphics in the document as a simple outline the same size as the picture. This saves Word from having to redraw the screen as the document is scrolled.

Draft View

Word includes another view that is not shown on the View menu by default. Add Draft View to the View menu by going to Tools → Customize → Commands → View and dragging the View Draft command to the View menu (for more on customizing menus, see Chapter 3, *Customizing Word)*.

The View Draft command displays most character formatting as underlined and bold and displays placeholders instead of graphics, speeding up the viewing of a document. The View Draft command only works in Normal view. If a document is shown in another view, turning on View Draft switches the document to Normal view.

View → Web Layout

Web Layout view (Figure 6-2) displays a document as it would look in a typical web browser. It is also useful for viewing documents that have certain characteristics designed for web browsers, such as document backgrounds. Web Layout view wraps lines to fit the window and graphics are positioned as they would be in a web browser.

Here are a number of things to keep in mind when working in Web Layout view:

- Don't confuse Web Layout view with File → Web Page Preview, which actually opens an Internet Explorer window and displays the active document as a web page.
- While in Web Layout view, the New button on the Standard toolbar is replaced by a New Web Page button. To create a non-web document, choose File → New to open the New dialog box.
- While in Web Layout view, both the Standard and Formatting toolbars are onscreen, and all tools are available. Certain menu commands like Insert → Page Numbers and Insert → Comment are not available, though, because these elements are not usable parts of a web page.

Figure 6-2: Editing a web page in Web Layout view

TIP # 61

Don't Rely on Web Layout View Alone

Web Layout view doesn't really provide the same view of a web page as looking at it in a web browser. Web Layout view provides a Word environment in which to build a web page. Before posting it to a web site, always preview it in at least one browser, and preferably in all browsers that may be used to view the page.

View → Print Layout

Many users only switch to Print Layout view (Figure 6-3) to check out how a document looks just before printing it. However, this view is a useful tool throughout document development. In Print Layout view, the document resembles actual sheets of paper. This view provides a vertical ruler on the left side of the window and displays columns, headers and footers, and page numbers onscreen.

Page breaks are displayed graphically as a physical split between pages. This is helpful when creating a long document, as in longer documents the position of page breaks relative to text and headings is important.

Using the vertical ruler to adjust top and bottom margins is much faster than opening File → Page Setup, although dragging elements on the ruler is not quite as precise as entering exact numbers into the Page Setup dialog box. To adjust margins, point to the spot where the gray margin area and the white portion of the ruler meet. The pointer becomes a two-headed arrow and a ScreenTip appears, indicating which

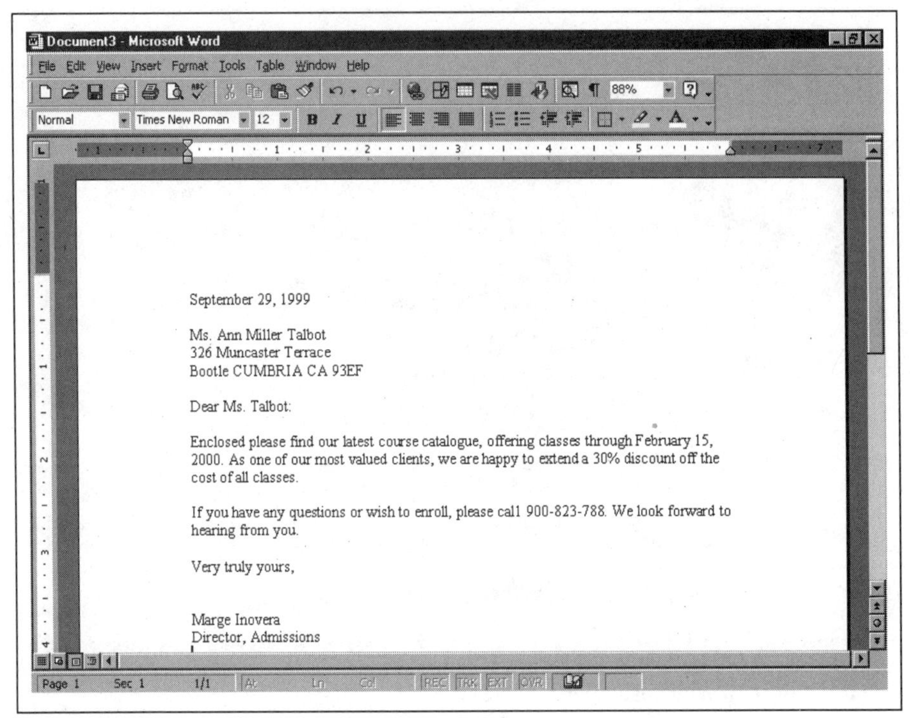

Figure 6-3: Editing a page in Print Layout view

margin is being adjusted. The ruler calibrations move as they're being dragged, helping achieve a particular measurement or adjustment. When adjusting margins from the ruler, it's helpful to set the Zoom to Whole Page, which is only available from Print Layout view.

TIP # 62

Shortcut to Page Setup

To open the Page Setup dialog box quickly, double-click any grey portion of the ruler or the grey space around the ruler. You can also double-click the upper portion of the white space, but double-clicking in most of the white area will insert a tab and open the Tab dialog box.

Print Layout view is also a useful alternative to Print Preview, as it can show a document in Full Page, Page Width, Two Pages, or any percentage of its actual size. Select View → Zoom to access these options, which are discussed in detail later in this chapter.

TIP # 63

Open the Header and Footer Toolbar Quickly

Double-click the dimmed header or footer text to move the insertion point into that area and display the Header and Footer toolbar. While the header or footer layer is active, the main document text is dimmed.

View → Outline

Outline view (Figure 6-4) shows a document as a hierarchy of headings and supporting text. Explorer-like plusses and minuses expand and collapse entire sections of a document for easy editing. Outline view is mostly used to set up the headings that will become the major sections of a long document, though many users enjoy working in Outline view as well.

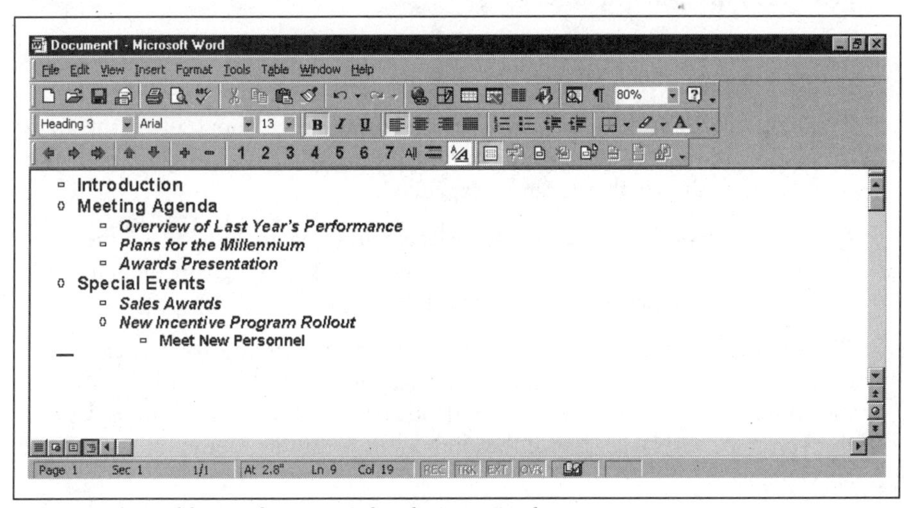

Figure 6-4: Building a document's headings in Outline view

Outline view works most effectively with Word's built-in heading styles (Heading 1–Heading 7), but any custom style will work if its name begins with *Heading*. Creating a document in Outline view is simple. Switch a new blank document to Outline view and the default style becomes Heading 1. In other views (Normal, Print Layout, and Web Layout), hitting Return after typing a heading switches you to the normal style. This is logical in those views because most users want to start typing text after a heading. In Outline view, however, hitting return does not cause a change of styles. The style for the next paragraph remains the same.

Switching to Outline view also opens the Outlining toolbar (Figure 6-5), a great tool for use in creating outlines.

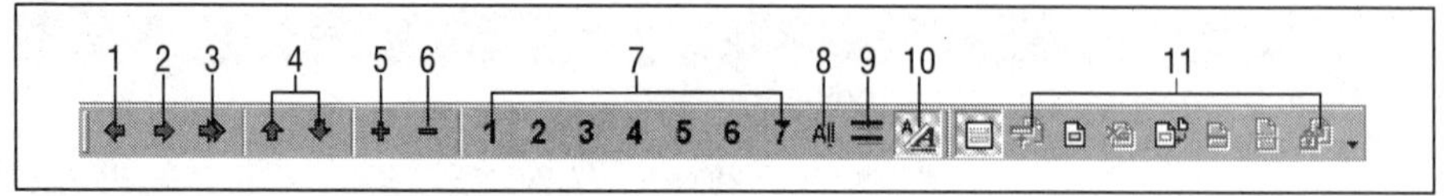

Figure 6-5: Using the Outlining toolbar

1. *Promote.* This option promotes the heading that contains the insertion point to the next higher heading level. For example, a paragraph styled with Heading 4 would become Heading 3. If a block of text is selected, such as a number of headings, the whole block is promoted.
2. *Demote.* This option demotes a heading or block of headings to the next lower level. Heading 4 would become Heading 5.
3. *Demote to body text.* This option demotes a heading to body text, applying the Normal style to it. The body text shows up under whatever heading was previous to the demoted heading.
4. *Move up and down.* These buttons move an entire heading or block of text up or down in the outline, *without* changing the heading's level.
5. *Expand.* This option expands the selected heading to show all of the items (headings and text) under it in the outline hierarchy. A minus sign to the left of the heading indicates that it can be expanded.
6. *Collapse.* This option collapses the selected heading to hide all of the items under it at the level the command was invoked. A plus sign to the left of the heading indicates that it can be collapsed.
7. *Show heading levels.* The seven numbers on the Outlining toolbar expand or collapse the entire outline to a certain level. For example, the 5 button causes the whole outline to be shown to a depth of Heading 5. All heading levels 1 through 5 are displayed, but all heading levels 6 through 7 and all normal text are collapsed.
8. *Show all.* This option expands the entire outline to show all headings and body text.
9. *Show first line only.* This option shows only the first line of any paragraph of body text in the outline. This option does not apply to headings that take up more than one line.
10. *Show formatting.* It is often visually distracting to see formatted text in Outline view. This option toggles text formatting on and off.
11. *Master documents.* Master documents are sort of a governing template used to bring multiple documents together for common formatting and page numbering and are covered in in Chapter 17, *Using Master Documents.*

The outlining toolbar offers the most precise way to promote and demote headings and to move them up and down, though dragging and dropping is an option. Drag an entire heading with all of the headings and text under it by clicking and dragging the graphic indicator (plus, minus, or whatever) next to it. Drag up or down to move the whole heading up or down, without changing its heading level. A horizontal line appears to indicate where the heading will be placed. Drag left or right to promote or demote a heading. A vertical line appears in this case. Once you begin dragging along one axis (say, up or down), it becomes impossible to drag the selection along the other axis. This means you cannot promote or demote a heading at the same time you move it up or down.

TIP # 64

Modify Tables in Outline View

The standard way to move rows around in a table is to select the row, cut it, and paste it somewhere else—often resulting in strange formatting and lost text. Instead, switch to Outline view. Since Word treats each row as a paragraph, it is easy to drag rows around by their "handles."

View → Toolbars

This command displays a list of the toolbars available within Word, including any custom toolbars created through the Tools → Customize command (covered in Chapter 3). Right-click any menu or toolbar area to quickly open the same menu. Specific toolbars are discussed throughout this book.

View → Ruler

View → Ruler toggles the display of the ruler. The ruler can be used to change the layout of a document by adjusting margins and setting indents. Double-click the ruler to open the Page Setup dialog box, which is used to set margins and change other page settings. See Chapter 4, *File*, for more on page setup.

To adjust margins with the ruler, point to the spot where the gray margin area meets the white portion of the ruler. When your mouse turns to a two-headed arrow, drag your mouse to change the margin setting—increasing the margin area reduces the amount of the page on which you can type, decreasing the margin gives you more room on the page. You can do this on both the left and right ends of the horizontal ruler, and at the top and bottom of the vertical ruler. Later, if you choose to view or edit your margins through the Page Setup dialog box (File → Page Setup), you'll see the measurements attained by your adjustment of the margins from the ruler.

Rulers work a bit differently in different views:

- In Print Layout view, turning the Ruler on displays both the horizontal and vertical rulers.

- In Outline view, the Ruler command is unavailable.
- To display the vertical ruler in Normal view, choose Tools → Options → View → "Vertical ruler." Use the same technique to turn off the vertical ruler in Print Layout view.

Indents control the horizontal position of paragraphs on the page. To set indents on the ruler, click inside a single paragraph to be adjusted, or select a series of contiguous paragraphs, and drag the indent triangles (Figure 6-6). The top triangle represents the first line of the paragraph, the bottom triangle represents the body of the paragraph. There's also a single triangle on the right side of the horizontal ruler that adjusts the right indent. For more on using these elements, see Chapter 1, *Word Overview*.

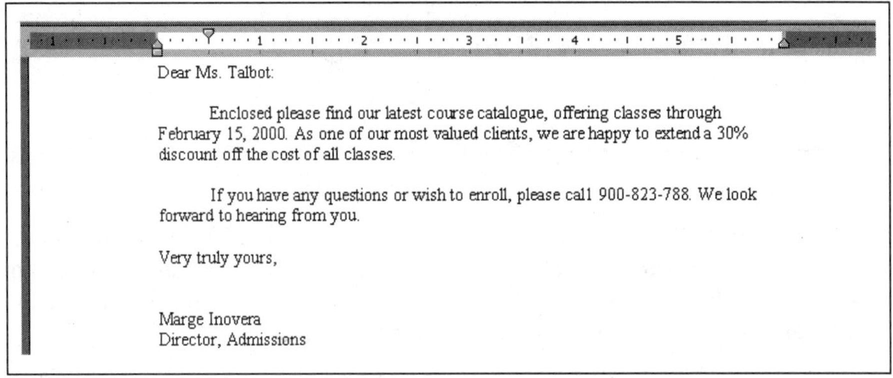

Dear Ms. Talbot:

Enclosed please find our latest course catalogue, offering classes through February 15, 2000. As one of our most valued clients, we are happy to extend a 30% discount off the cost of all classes.

If you have any questions or wish to enroll, please call 900-823-788. We look forward to hearing from you.

Very truly yours,

Marge Inovera
Director, Admissions

Figure 6-6: Dragging the indent triangles to adjust the position of selected paragraphs

TIP # 65

Set Indents with Keyboard Shortcuts

Some indents can also be set through the use of keyboard shortcuts. Press Ctrl-T to create a ½" hanging indent, Ctrl-M for a full ½" indent, and Ctrl-Q to remove all indents (and any other paragraph formatting). You can use the shortcuts on a single paragraph by positioning your cursor in the paragraph, or on several contiguous paragraphs by selecting them with your mouse prior to using the shortcut.

View → Document Map

View → Document Map displays the heading styles applied to major sections of a document in a navigation panel on the left side of the document window (Figure 6-7). If no heading styles are applied to document text, the panel is blank. Heading styles include the default heading styles (Heading1 and so on) or any new styles created that begin with the word "Heading." Clicking on the headings in this panel moves the display directly to that text in the document. This is an especially useful view for reading long documents and, like using Outline view, it displays a hierarchy of headings. Unlike in Outline view, Drag and Drop is not supported for rearranging headings. In addition, formatting cannot be applied to the headings listed in the Map panel. To adjust the hierarchy of your headings, you must work within the text panel of the document in this view.

Click the plus or minus signs to expand or collapse headings that have other headings under them. Right-click any of the displayed headings in the Document Map panel to display a context menu. The context menu offers commands to Expand or Collapse the heading, or to choose which levels (Heading 1 through Heading 7) to display.

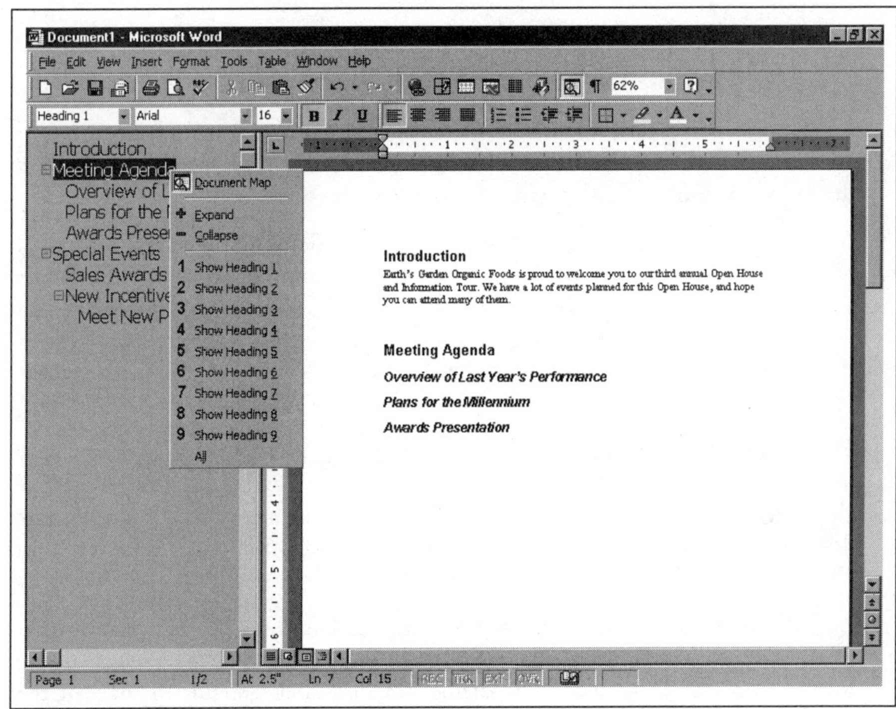

Figure 6-7: Viewing headings in Document Map view

View → Header and Footer

The header/footer layer contains any page numbers, text, or graphics that have been added to headers or footers in a document. Headers and footers are only visible in Print Layout view. Choosing View → Header and Footer in any other Word view changes the view to Print Layout. When headers and footers are displayed, a Header and Footer toolbar also opens (Figure 6-8). See Chapter 2, *How Word Works*, for details on all of Word's layers.

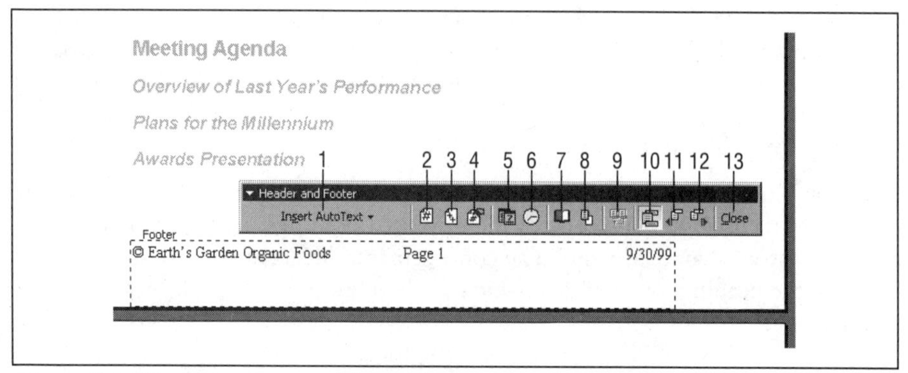

Figure 6-8: Viewing a footer and its toolbar

1. *Insert AutoText.* Insert a stored AutoText entry. This menu is the same as the Insert → AutoText → Header/Footer submenu.

2. *Insert Page Number.* This button inserts an automatic page numbering field in the header or footer of the document.

3. *Insert Number of Pages.* This button inserts a field that displays the total number of pages in the document. Use this in combination with the Insert Page Number button to display the current and total number of pages in a document. A better way to do this, however, is to use the Insert AutoText → Page X of Y option, which inserts these same two fields along with the words "Page" and "of" with one command.

4. *Format Page Number.* This button opens the Page Number dialog box. Use it to choose an alternate numbering format (roman numerals, letters of the alphabet) and to number chapters within a long document. This is the same dialog shown using Insert → Page Numbers → Format and is covered in Chapter 7, *Insert.*

5. *Insert Date.* This button inserts a field with the current date. The date format used is the default format set using Insert → Date and Time. Select a date format from the Date and Time dialog box and click Default to make it the default format.

6. *Insert Time.* This button inserts a field with the current date. The date format used is the default format set using Insert → Date and Time. Change the default time format the same way you change the date format.

7. *Page Setup.* This button opens the Page Setup dialog box, which contains settings for determining the distance between the header or footer and the edge of the paper, and for printing different headers on odd and even pages of your document (useful when a document will be bound and/or printed on both sides of the paper).

8. *Show/Hide Document Text.* This button toggles the display of the main document text when working in a header or footer. When displayed, the main document text appears dimmed and is uneditable.

9. *Same as Previous.* This option controls the flow of header/footer text across document section breaks. By default, the header and footer content you type in one section flows through the next and previous sections of the document. However, you can break the connection between sections' headers and footers by clicking the Same as Previous button. If there are section breaks within a document, the button appears depressed (on) by default. This assures the consistency of your headers and footers throughout the document, regardless of section breaks. Turn this option off to create different headers and footers for different sections.

10. *Switch Between Header and Footer.* Use this button to quickly move the insertion point between the header and footer.

11. *Show Previous.* Use this option to switch to the header or footer from the previous section of the document.

12. *Show Next.* Use this option to switch to the header or footer in the next document section.

13. *Close.* This button closes the Header and Footer toolbar, and returns the insertion point to the main document. The document returns to the view you were in when you opened headers and footers.

TIP # 66

Add Borders to Headers and Footers

It's a good idea to add a border above the footer and below the header, especially if a document's text runs right up to the top margin and down to the bottom margin on each page. The border helps visually separate the header and footer from the rest of the printed text. Click the header or footer text (while that layer is active) and choose Format → Borders and Shading, which is discussed in detail in Chapter 8, Format.

View → Footnotes

Footnotes are parenthetical or supporting information at the bottom of a page (not in the footer, but at the bottom of the document on the current page) or at the end of a document. Insert footnotes using the Insert → Footnote command (discussed in Chapter 7).

The View → Footnotes command displays footnotes and endnotes, referenced by numbers in superscript throughout the document text (Figure 6-9). If a document contains neither footnotes nor endnotes, the command is unavailable.

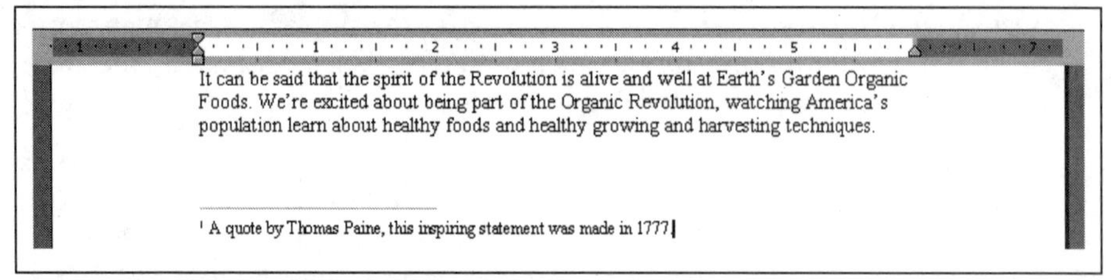

Figure 6-9: Viewing footnote or endnote text

Choosing View → Footnotes or double-clicking a footnote number in the main text switches to the footnotes or endnotes. If a document contains both footnotes and endnotes, a dialog box opens so that you can choose which to view. Footnotes are also displayed a bit differently depending on which view a document is currently displayed in:

- In Print Layout view, footnotes are always visible and are shown exactly as they will be printed. View → Footnotes simply moves you between the footnote and the footnote indicator (the superscript number in the main text). Double-clicking the footnote indicator or the footnote itself does the same thing.
- In Normal, Outline, and Web Layout views, footnote indicators are displayed in the main text, but the actual footnotes are not. View → Footnotes (or double-clicking a footnote indicator) opens a separate pane displaying the footnotes (Figure 6-10).

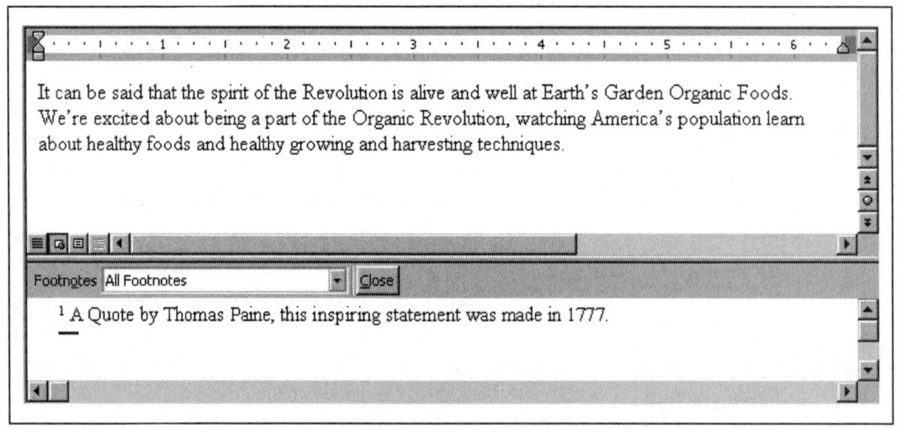

Figure 6-10: Footnotes in their own pane (Normal, Outline, and Web Layout views)

Word separates document text from footnotes and endnotes with a short horizontal line called a note separator. If a note overflows onto the next page, Word also prints a longer line called a note continuation separator. Word inserts note separators automatically and there's not much you can do to govern their placement aside from arranging page breaks to try to accommodate longer notes.

It is, however, fairly easy to customize separators by adding borders, text, or graphics, and to customize the notice Word prints after a note continuation separator. This notice is called a note continuation notice and the default text used is "This note continues on the next page."

To customize a note separator or notice, first switch to Normal view and choose View → Footnotes. In the footnotes pane, select the item to customize from the drop-down menu. Available items include Footnote Separator, Footnote Continuation Separator, and Footnote Continuation Notice. An Endnote version of these is also displayed if the document contains endnotes. Once the item to customize is selected, format it using any of Word's formatting tools. These items are paragraphs just like any other and accept formatting and inserted objects, such as graphics or fields.

Here are a few other things to think about as you explore footnotes and endnotes:

- Two predefined paragraph styles, Footnote Text and Endnote Text, govern the formatting of footnotes and endnotes. Change these styles to alter the default formatting.
- Word automatically renumbers all existing footnotes and endnotes in a document whenever a new note is inserted or one is deleted.
- Select any text in the main document and the footnote indicator that accompanies it. Copy or move that text to a new location and Word copies or moves the text, the indicator, and the note itself for you. When copying, Word actually renumbers the new note to fit in with the rest of the notes in the document.
- Word's find and replace features (Edit → Find and Edit → Replace) include all footnote and endnote text in their searches.
- Word ignores any index and table of contents entries in notes.

View → Comments

The View Comments command opens a separate comments pane (Figure 6-11) that shows the initials of the commenter, the comment number, and the text of any comments inserted using Word's Insert → Comment command. Comments are shown in the main text as yellow highlighting with the commenter's initials in brackets. Double-clicking on any comment also opens the comments pane.

Click the Comments From list box to view only comments from one reviewer. You can edit the displayed comments, but you cannot add new comments while in the Comments pane. To delete a comment, right-click the commented text in your document and choose Delete Comment from the context menu. This is the only way to delete comments. While you can delete the comment text through the Comments pane, you can't delete the comment code in the document.

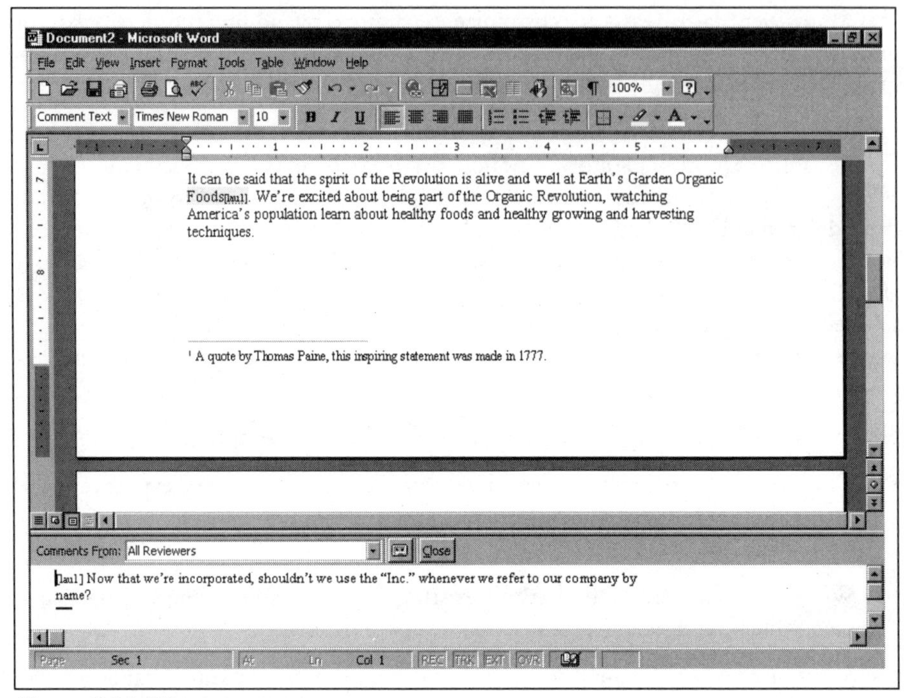

Figure 6-11: Viewing comments

Word's comment feature, along with other collaborative tools, is covered in detail in Chapter 13, *Collaborating*.

TIP # 67

Use Screentips Instead of the Comments Pane

Point to the top edge of the pane, and when the pointer turns to a two-headed arrow, resize the pane by dragging. If the Comments pane takes up too much room, view the comments in a document one at a time by pointing to the yellow comment marker within the text. A ScreenTip containing the comment text appears.

View → Full Screen

Full Screen view hides all screen elements other than the page itself (Figure 6-12), providing maximum room to read and edit a document. Full file, editing, and formatting capability is retained in Full Screen view as well. To see the menus again in order to perform a task unavailable with a keyboard shortcut, move the pointer to the top of the screen and the menus reappear. Pressing Esc also exits Full Screen view.

If a document has more than one page (or will have more than one page), click the Show/Hide button on the Standard toolbar prior to invoking Full Screen view. The

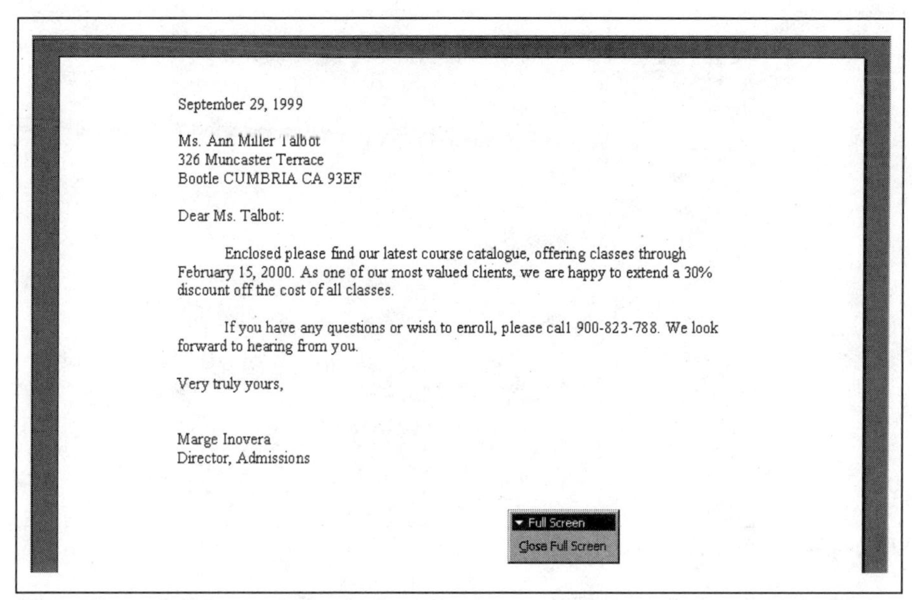

September 29, 1999

Ms. Ann Miller Talbot
326 Muncaster Terrace
Bootle CUMBRIA CA 93EF

Dear Ms. Talbot:

Enclosed please find our latest course catalogue, offering classes through February 15, 2000. As one of our most valued clients, we are happy to extend a 30% discount off the cost of all classes.

If you have any questions or wish to enroll, please call 900-823-788. We look forward to hearing from you.

Very truly yours,

Marge Inovera
Director, Admissions

Figure 6-12: Full Screen view

page break indicators that Show/Hide displays provide the only means of determing page numbers in Full Screen view. Word's scrollbars and Status bar are hidden in Full Screen view.

To access a toolbar button, click the Close Full Screen button in the floating Full Screen toolbar. The screen returns to the view it was in prior to opening Full Screen view. To get to a particular toolbar while in Full Screen view, right-click the Full Screen floating toolbar and choose the toolbar from the context menu that appears.

View → Zoom

View → Zoom (Figure 6-13) opens a dialog that can display a document at any magnification from 25% to 200%. For a larger or smaller magnification, or something in between the standard offerings, enter a specific percentage in the Percent box manually.

The document view in effect when opening the Zoom dialog box determines the available Zoom options. In Normal, Outline, and Web Layout views, only the numeric percentage views (200, 100, and 75%) and the "Page width" option are available. "Page width" reduces or enlarges the display of a document so that the right and left margins fit inside the window. The Percent box is also available in all of these views.

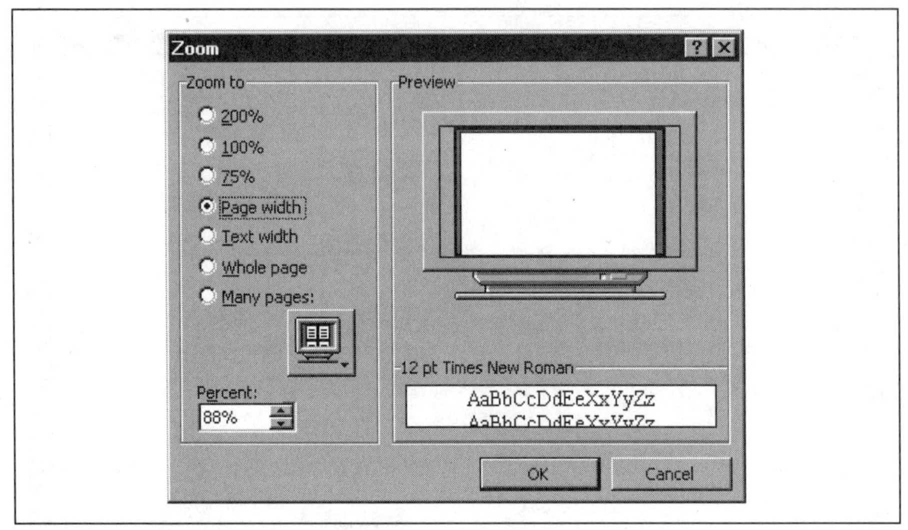

Figure 6-13: The Zoom dialog

TIP # 68

Add Zoom Tools to Context Menus

If you use the Zoom feature regularly, consider adding Zoom commands to the Text context menu using the techniques described in Chapter 3. I added commands for opening the Zoom dialog and for zooming to 100%, page width, and whole page to my Text context menu.

In Print Layout view, all of these options are available and a few more:

- "Text width" reduces or enlarges the display of a document to fit the width of the text on the page.
- "Whole page" reduces or enlarges a document's display so that one whole page fits inside the window.
- "Many pages" shows multiple pages of the document in the window at once. Clicking this option sets the view to the maximum value (24 pages in a single window) and the Zoom percentage changes to 10%. Click the button below the "Many pages" option to set the exact number of pages you want to see. After switching to "Many pages" view, change the Zoom percentage (via the dialog or the Standard toolbar) to anything up to around 40% and remain in "Many pages" zoom.

The Zoom tool on the Standard toolbar is also used to select a magnification setting for a document. When using the Zoom tool on the Standard toolbar, the drop list of Zoom options varies depending on the document view. Print Layout view offers the greatest number of Zoom options, including "Whole page" and "Two pages", neither of which is available in the other views. For more specific Zoom settings regardless of which view you're in, use View → Zoom.

Chapter 7

Insert

As word processing software evolves, documents consisting only of text are becoming rare. Word's Insert menu contains commands for adding the extra elements that make up many contemporary documents. The commands are primarily used to add special Word objects, such as page breaks, fields, comments, footnotes, and drawing objects. The menu also provides commands for adding content from other Word documents or even from other types of files, such as spreadsheets or databases.

Insert → Break

When typing a document that runs over the length of a page, Word inserts a page break and typing automatically continues on the next page. These breaks are referred to as *automatic breaks*, and cannot be changed or deleted.

In Normal view, page and section breaks show onscreen at all times as dashed horizontal lines. In Print Layout view, page breaks appear as physical splits in the paper, and no break codes appear. To see breaks onscreen in Print Layout view, use the Show/Hide button on the Standard toolbar. Working in Show/Hide mode also makes it easy to delete a page break by selecting the break and pressing Delete.

Forced breaks are manually inserted into a document to control where Word breaks a page, column, or text wrapping. Insert a forced break using the Insert → Break command, which opens the Break dialog box (Figure 7-1).

TIP # 69

Double-Click the Section Break Line

Double-click a section break line to quickly open the File → Page Setup → Layout dialog.

The following list describes the Break dialog options:

1. *Page break*. This is the default selection in the dialog box and forces the beginning of a new page. Pressing Ctrl-Enter while in the main document also inserts a page break.

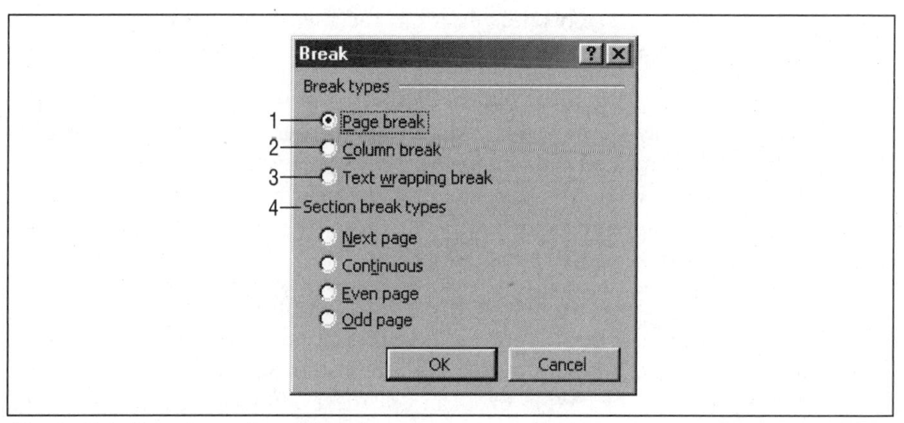

Figure 7-1: Inserting a forced break

2. *Column break.* This break forces text in a newspaper-style column to stop and continue in the next consecutive column, leaving white space at the bottom of the column where the break was inserted. This is useful for starting a new article at the top of the next column of a newsletter.

Column, Text wrapping, and Section breaks and their effect on a document are only visible in Print Layout view and upon inserting any of them, Word switches to that view.

3. *Text wrapping break.* Select this to have text break just above a picture or graphic and continue on the next blank line following the image. To use a Text wrapping break, place the cursor where the text should break before the image and insert the break. Next, insert the image. Turn on Show/Hide to see a soft return (Shift-Enter) symbol with vertical lines before and after it indicating the break. This break provides extra control over where text stops before a graphic, which can be very helpful in a newsletter where text may refer to a photograph or line drawing.

TIP # 70

Text-Wrapping Breaks Give Better Control

When you choose text wrapping for an object using Format → Object → Layout, the flow of text around a graphic depends on the exact positioning of the graphic and may require very small mouse maneuvers to achieve. Inserting a text wrapping break just before the object is often more effective.

4. *Section break types.* While section breaks do occur naturally (changing the margins or orientation of a single page in a document causes a natural section break), most are inserted by the user. Section breaks come in four varieties:

– *Next page.* This inserts not only a section break, but a page break as well. Text following the break is forced onto the next page of the document.

- *Continuous*. No page break is inserted, and the section break occurs at the cursor. This type of break can be inserted anywhere on the page.
- *Even page*. If a document will be bound or printed on both sides of the paper, you may want to treat odd and even pages differently—setting up different headers and footers, for example. An Even page break causes the text following it to start at the top of the next even page. If the break is inserted on an even page, a new blank odd page is added (through a forced page break) to accomplish the task.
- *Odd page*. The opposite of an Even page section break, this break forces text following the break onto the next odd-numbered page. If the break is inserted on an odd page, a new even-numbered page will be added (and left blank) between the section break and the next odd page. If the File → Page Setup → Layout → "Different odd and even" option is enabled, odd and even section breaks are automatically inserted throughout the document.

TIP # 71

Headers and Footers in Section Breaks

By default, header and footer content remains consistent throughout the sections in a document. If a different header or footer is needed for a particular section, go to the Header and Footer layer (double-click the header or footer text or choose View → Header and Footer) and click the Same as Previous button to break the connection between sections.

Insert → Page Numbers

The Page Numbers command (Figure 7-2) makes adding page numbers to a document easy. The default settings for the alignment and position of the page numbers work for most documents, requiring very little adjustment.

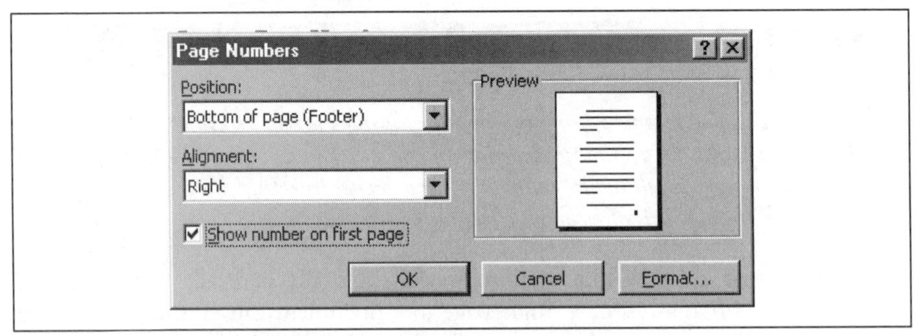

Figure 7-2: Adding page numbers to a document

Page numbers are added to the header or footer layer. The choice for the alignment depends largely on the intended print method:

- If printing will be only on one side of the paper, place the page numbers on the right or in the center.
- For printing on both sides of the paper, use inside or outside placement or use File → Page Setup to set up different odd and even settings for the document's pages.

By default, the "Show number on first page" option is enabled. Since no number is required on the first page of most documents, you'll probably want to turn this option off.

To change to a different numbering system or to pick a different starting number, click the Format button to open the Page Number Format dialog (Figure 7-3). You can apply format settings to the entire document or just to a specific section. To apply settings to a section, open the Page Number Format dialog from the Header and Footer toolbar. Opening it from the main document text applies changes to all sections of the document.

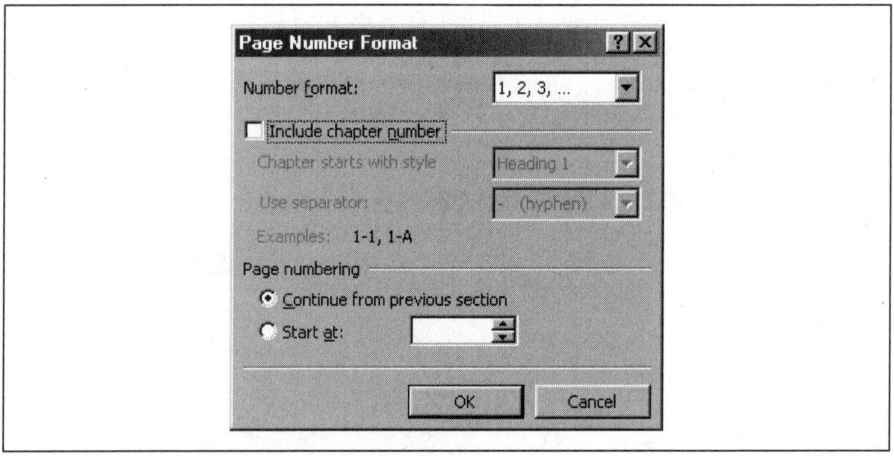

Figure 7-3: Customizing page number format

Formatting options include choosing a different type of number. Many people use lowercase Roman numerals for a document's table of contents or preface pages, switching to Arabic numbers for the body of the document. Indices are also numbered in lowercase Roman numerals. You can also number pages by chapters, in which case Word looks for Heading 1–styled text (or text formatted in another style you specify), and numbers the pages accordingly; for example, 1-1 for page 1 in Chapter 1.

TIP # 72

Removing Page Numbers

If an entire document contains page numbers and you later decide to break the document into sections (or just want to remove the numbers), delete the document-wide page numbers in the header or footer by highlighting them in the header or footer layer and pressing the Delete key. Do this before breaking the document into sections, however. Otherwise you'll have to delete the numbers in each of the new sections individually to get rid of them throughout the document.

The Page Number Format dialog is also used to change the starting number for a document. For example, choose "0" if there is a cover page and the second page should be page 1 or choose some other number if the document will be printed and bound as a continuation of another document. Be sure the "Show number on first page" option is disabled, or Word actually prints "0" on the first page.

Insert → Date and Time

This command inserts the system date or time (the current date or time according to your computer). Insert them as simple text or as a field by checking the "Update automatically" checkbox (Figure 7-4). When inserted as a field, the date or time will update to reflect the current system date or time each time the document is opened. For more on fields, see Chapter 15, *Fields and Forms*.

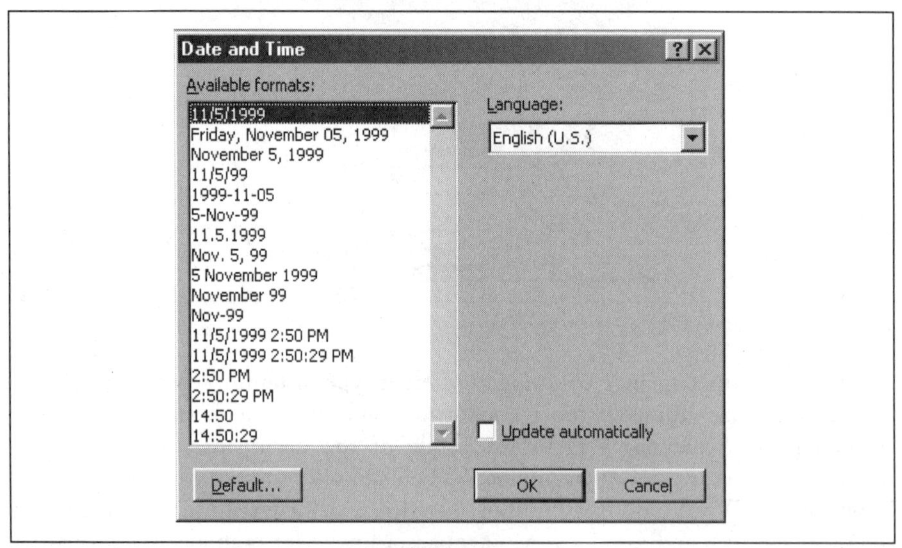

Figure 7-4: Inserting the system date and/or time

If the date or time is already inserted as a field, change it to non-updating text by selecting the field in the document and choosing Insert → Date and Time. Remove the "Update automatically" checkmark and click OK to close the dialog box. The date/time is converted to simple text and will not update the next time the document is opened.

Use the Date and Time dialog box to set the default date and/or time setting to use in future documents. For example, if you prefer the date to appear in mm/dd/yy format, select that format from the list of Available formats and click the Default button. You may have to close and reopen Word for this setting to take effect.

TIP # 73

International Date and Time

If the current document will be sent to or used by someone who speaks another language or lives in another country, use the Control Panel's Regional Settings to select another language and when prompted, restart the computer. When selecting the Default button on the Date and Time dialog, you'll now find the new language format set as the default language.

Insert → AutoText

AutoText is inserted through the use of a trigger, which could be making an AutoText selection from the AutoText submenu or typing text set to represent a longer AutoText entry. The AutoText submenu (Figure 7-5) contains a list of installed and user-created AutoText entries in categorized groups such as Closing (for common letter closings) and Header/Footer.

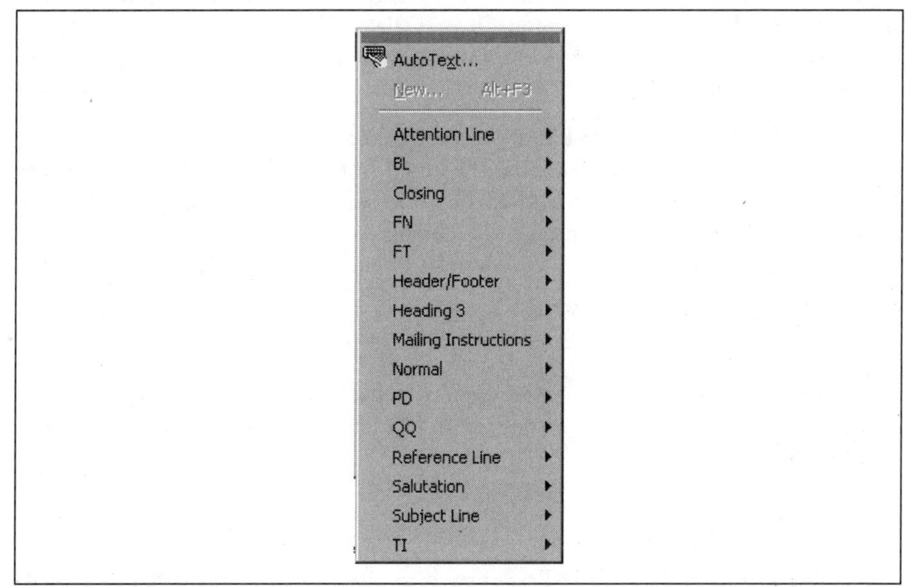

Figure 7-5: Using AutoText

It also contains the command that pops up the AutoText tab on the AutoCorrect dialog and the New command for creating new entries, covered later in this section.

Many people get AutoText and AutoCorrect confused. There are two differences. AutoCorrect entries are shorter and are automatically applied as you type. For example, one built-in AutoCorrect entry changes "teh" to "the" as soon as the former is typed. AutoText can hold longer, formatted entries and suggests text in a pop-up window based on what you're typing (see Figure 7-7, later). AutoCorrect is detailed in Chapter 9, Tools.

Default AutoText entries are part of the *normal.dot* template, on which all new, blank documents are based. As AutoText entries are created, these too become part of the template. AutoText entries can also be stored in a custom template and made available to multiple users using Word's Style Organizer, which is covered in Chapter 8, *Format*.

WARNING

Beware copying another user's Normal template to replace your own. You risk losing your AutoText entries, as well as AutoCorrect entries you've made (see Chapter 9 for more information on AutoCorrect).

Insert → AutoText → AutoText

Insert → AutoText → AutoText displays the AutoText tab in the AutoCorrect dialog box (Figure 7-6), which shows a list and preview of all AutoText entries (those installed with Word and those created by the user). Insert AutoText entries into a document by clicking the Insert button or Delete them with the Delete button. Note that if the deleted entry is the only one in a given category, the category submenu is removed as well.

Create a new AutoText entry based on selected text in your active document by typing the entry name (the text that will be used to trigger the entry) in the "Enter AutoText entries here" text box and clicking the Add button. Be sure to check the Preview box to verify that the content is accurate.

The "Show AutoComplete tip" option causes Word to suggest AutoText entries in a ScreenTip as you type (Figure 7-7). Press Enter or Tab to accept the suggestion and enter the AutoText.

The AutoText toolbar also offers toolbar buttons for inserting AutoText from a list of stored entries and for creating an AutoText entry from selected text.

Insert → AutoText → New

The fastest way to build an AutoText entry is to select existing formatted document text and then choose Insert → AutoText → New. The New button on the AutoText

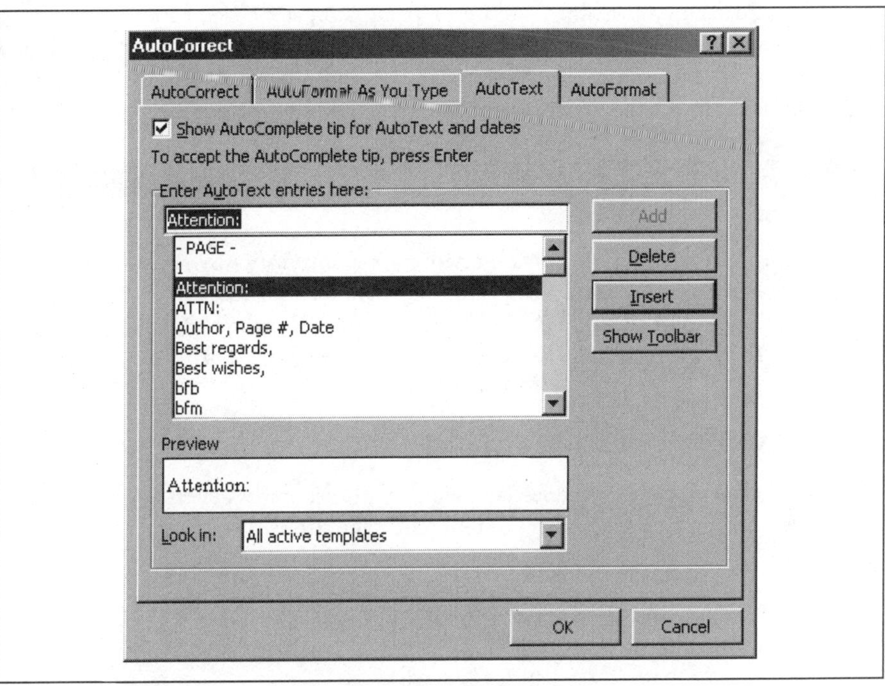

Figure 7-6: Previewing a complete list of AutoText entries

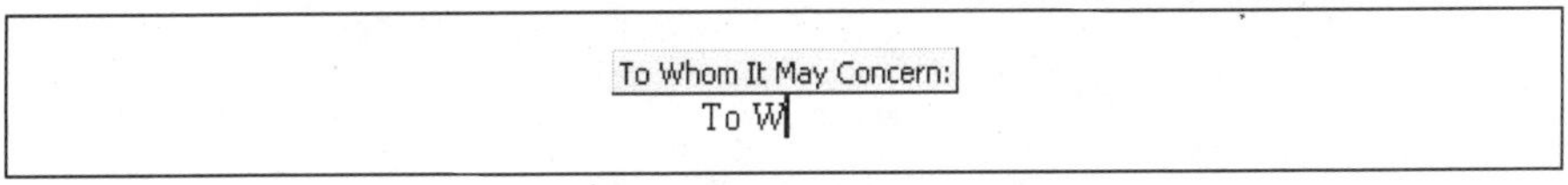

To Whom It May Concern:
To W

Figure 7-7: Using AutoComplete to suggest and insert AutoText entries

toolbar achieves the same effect. In either case, the Create AutoText dialog box opens (Figure 7-8), displaying a suggested entry name based on the first few words of the selected text.

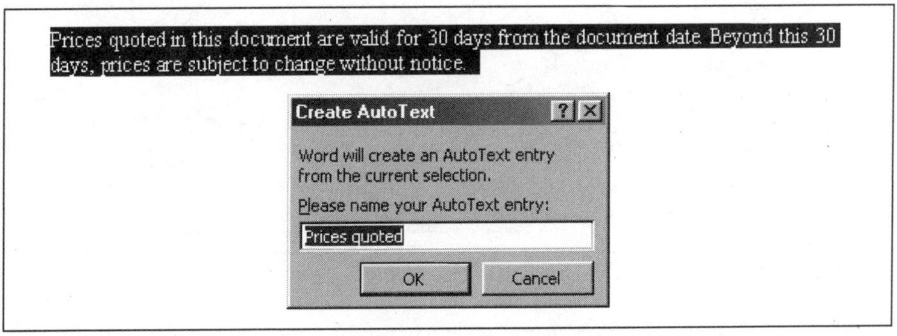

Prices quoted in this document are valid for 30 days from the document date. Beyond this 30 days, prices are subject to change without notice.

Create AutoText
Word will create an AutoText entry from the current selection.
Please name your AutoText entry:
Prices quoted
OK
Cancel

Figure 7-8: Creating a new AutoText entry from existing document text

If the AutoText entry is a short phrase or paragraph, it's a good idea to choose a short entry name for it. For example, an AutoText entry that creates the closing for a letter (closing text such as "Very truly yours," and a person's name separated by two blank lines) should be given a name such as "close" or the author's initials.

TIP # 74

Remembering Autotext Entries

Create a printed list of all AutoText entries (or just certain easy-to-forget entries) by inserting them into a single document, one after the other, down the page. Choose File → Print, and in the Print What section of the Print dialog box, choose AutoText entries. A list of the entries used in the document will be printed.

Insert → AutoText → Available Entries

Word's installed AutoText entries (see Figure 7-9) are fairly generic—simple letter closings, typical header and footer content, and salutations.

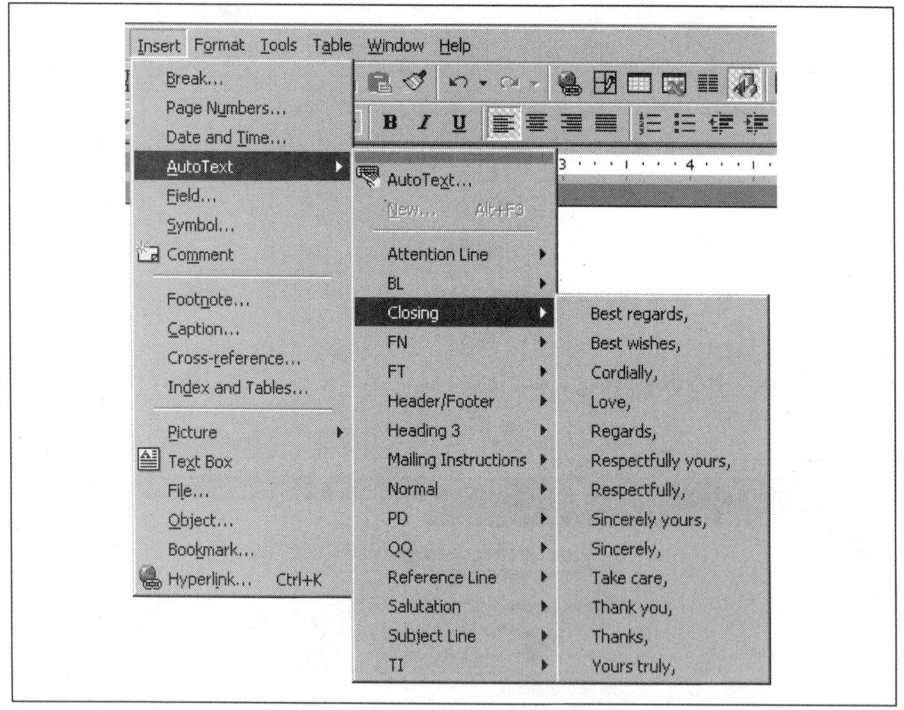

Figure 7-9: Word's installed AutoText entries

Using the available entries avoids typos and maintains consistency. In addition, the initials and name of the person established as the user appear in the Reference

Initials, Signature, and Signature Company categories, making it easy to insert one's name or company name into a document.

Insert → Field

The Insert → Field command provides nine different categories to choose from. Several of the categories include fields that can be inserted in other ways (such as through Insert → Date and Time or Insert → Index and Tables).

To insert a field, choose Insert → Field, select a category and a field, and click OK (Figure 7-10). The field data immediately appears in the document. Once a field is inserted, the field content appears highlighted in gray. This serves as a reminder that the content is field data not a typed entry. To delete field data from your document, double-click the data and press Delete.

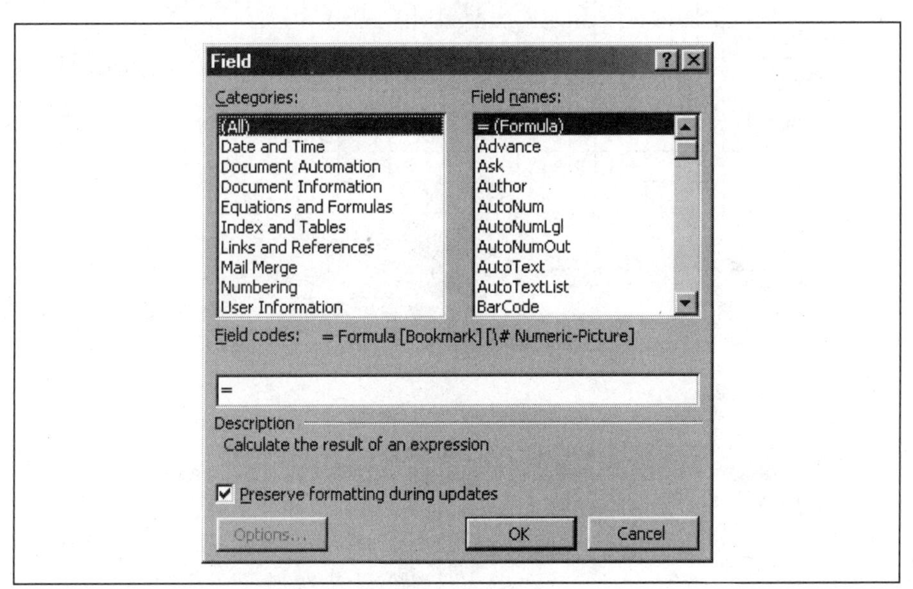

Figure 7-10: Inserting a data placeholder

To see the actual field codes in a document instead of the data in the fields, choose Tools → Options → View tab → Field codes. This causes field codes to appear in a set of curly brackets (a.k.a. French braces) in your document, followed by the data inserted through the field. If you want field data to be highlighted in gray at all times, choose Tools → Options, and on the View tab, choose Always from the Field shading drop list. For more information on using fields, see Chapter 15.

Insert → Symbol

There are several fonts, such as Symbol, Monotype Sorts, and Wingdings, that contain pictures and symbols instead of letters of the alphabet. Depending on the printer and other software loaded on your computer, there may be hundreds of images to add to a document. To insert a character from any character set, choose Insert → Symbol (Figure 7-11).

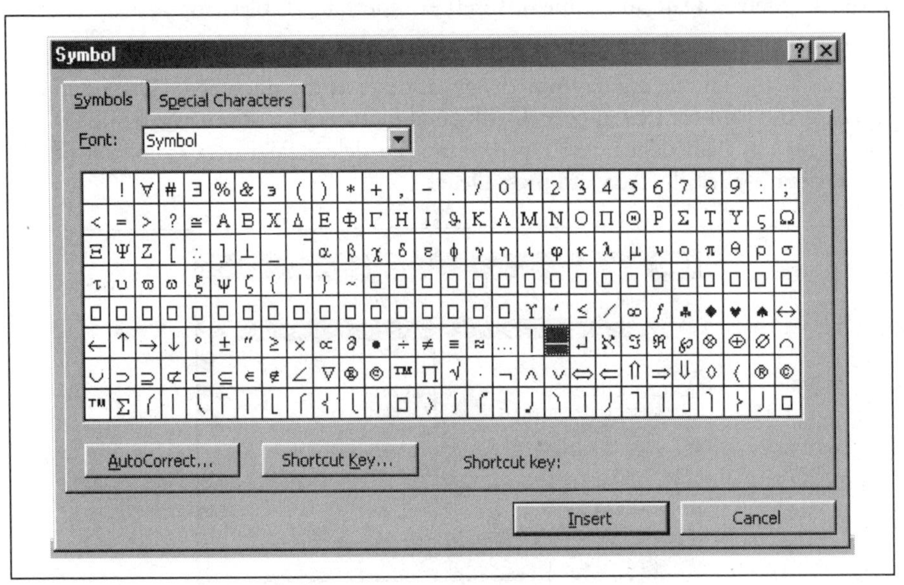

Figure 7-11: Inserting symbols

TIP # 75

See Symbols in Better Detail

The display of the various fonts is tiny. To see a bigger version of a symbol, click and hold on the symbol. Drag through the rows of symbols with the mouse button depressed to see enlarged versions of each symbol as you go by.

Symbols are inserted and formatted just like any other character. To speed future insertions of symbols, assign keyboard shortcuts. Click the symbol on the Symbol dialog and click the Shortcut key button to open the Customize Keyboard dialog box (Figure 7-12). Use this dialog to assign a key combination.

Symbols can also be assigned to AutoCorrect entries. Some already installed Auto-Correct entries include :-) , which turns into a graphical smiley face when typed. Create a custom AutoCorrect entry by selecting the symbol and then click the Auto-Correct button. The full use of the AutoCorrect dialog box is discussed in Chapter 9.

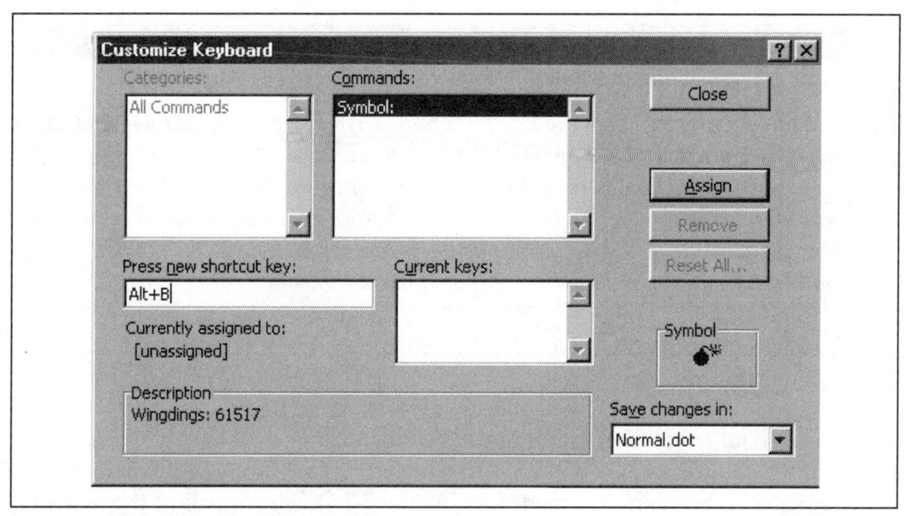

Figure 7-12: Assigning a keyboard shortcut

The Symbol dialog can also be used to insert Special Characters (Figure 7-13), such as section marks and em or en dashes. Preset keyboard shortcuts exist for most of these symbols.

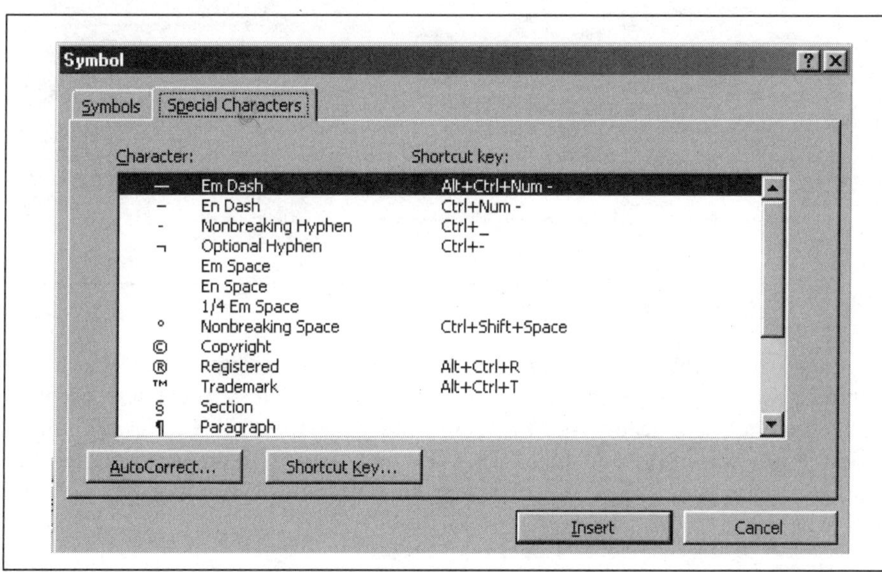

Figure 7-13: Choosing symbols on the Special Characters tab

TIP # 76

Create a Graphic from a Symbol

To create a freely moving graphic image from a symbol, draw a text box and insert the symbol into it. Enlarge the symbol as you would any text, and even apply a color to it. When the symbol is correctly formatted, adjust the text box settings for placement and text wrapping. Right-click the text box and choose Format Text Box from the context menu. If the text box has no border or fill color, this method will go undetected in any print or online version of the document.

Insert → Comment

A comment is an annotation that is not in the document's main text. Comments are visible in the comments pane (View → Comments) and by holding the pointer over the comment in the main document text (Figure 7-14). The initials of the user who inserted the comment appear at the end of the comment in the Comments pane, and their full name appears at the beginning of the comment as it is displayed in a ScreenTip.

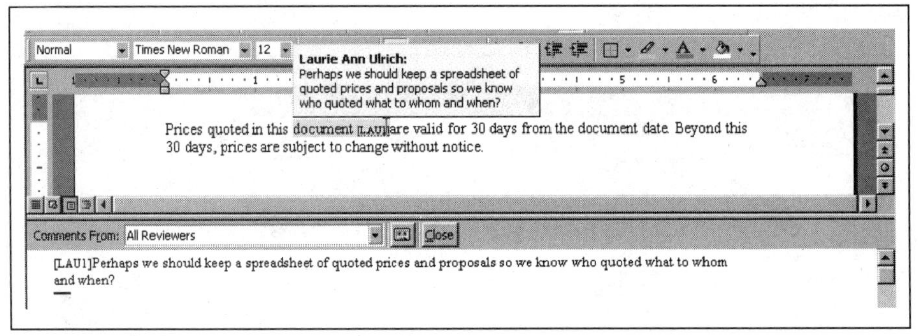

Figure 7-14: Commenting

To insert a comment, select the word, sentence, or paragraph to which the comment will refer, and choose Insert → Comment. The selected text becomes highlighted in bright yellow, and the Comments pane opens. The reviewer's initials appear in brackets next to the highlighted text and along with the insertion point in the Comments pane. Type the comment and click the Comment pane's Close button to return to the document.

For detailed information on using comments and other collaborative features in Word, see Chapter 13, Collaborating.

Insert → Footnote

Footnotes and endnotes typically contain supporting or explanatory information about text in a document. A superscript number appears next to the noted text, and that same number appears in front of the footnote or endnote. When noted text is deleted or moved and the new location changes the order of notes in the document, the numbers update automatically.

The only real difference between footnotes and endnotes is their location—footnotes appear at the foot of the page containing their relevant text, while endnotes are located at the end of the document. Use the Options dialog box to choose where endnotes appear. If a document is broken into sections, endnotes can appear at the end of the relevant section instead of at the end of the document.

Insert → Footnote opens the Footnote and Endnote dialog box (Figure 7-15), which is used to choose the type of note to insert, and whether or not Word should automatically number each note. In lieu of automatic numbering, a symbol, such as an asterisk, can appear on the noted text and before the footnote or endnote itself.

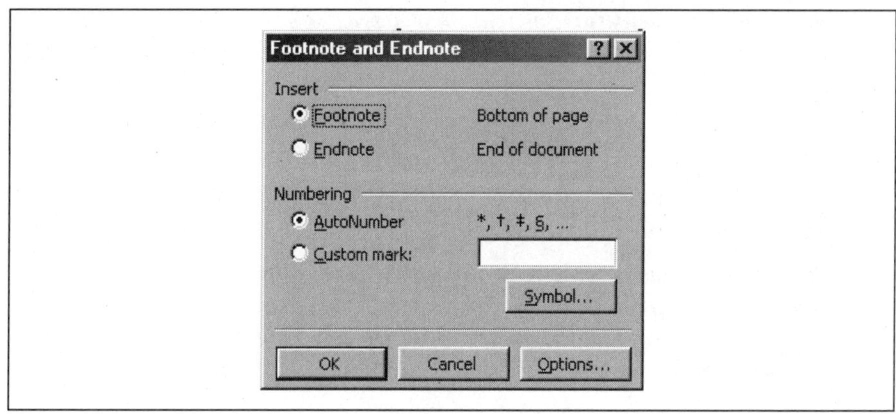

Figure 7-15: Inserting a footnote or endnote

It's a good idea to let Word apply automatic numbering to footnotes and endnotes for the simple reason that things change. Moving and deleting text often moves and deletes notes as well. Word handles this automatically, updating note numbers to reflect their new positions.

Customize footnotes and endnotes by clicking the Options button in the Footnote and Endnote dialog to open the Note Options dialog box (Figure 7-16). Customize notes by choosing an alternate location and selecting a different numbering format. Once notes are created, view and edit them using the View → Footnotes command, detailed in Chapter 6, *View*.

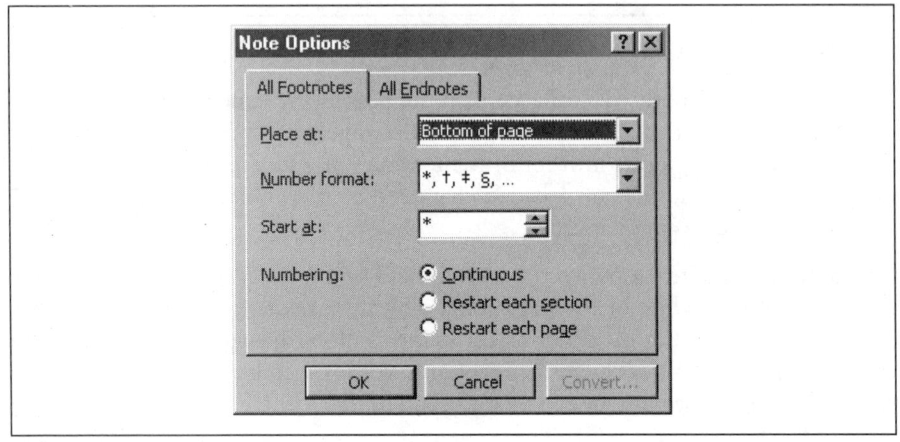

Figure 7-16: Customizing footnotes and endnotes

TIP # 77

Numbering Notes in Consecutive Documents

When using separate documents that must appear to be one long document when printed, set the Start at number for your notes in each document. If, for example, the previous document's last footnote was 14, choose to start numbering the footnotes in the next document with 15.

Insert → Caption

All of the figures in this book have captions that explain the content and relevance of graphic images. Captions are usually preceded by a label; for example, "Figure 5-2," denotes the second figure in the fifth chapter of a book. In addition to captions that identify graphics, captions can also supply labels for tables or equations.

Word creates captions using a field named SEQ, for "sequencing." Choose Tools → Options → View → Field Codes to view the actual field code for captions. Fields are detailed in Chapter 15.

Insert → Caption opens the Caption dialog box (Figure 7-17). Select the type of label (Figure, Table, or Equation) and select where the caption will appear in relation to the figure, table, or equation. Options are above or below the selected item. If the three built-in types of labels don't meet your needs, create a new one with the New Label button.

As captions are inserted, the label numbers increment. Edit these numbers after adding objects and creating captions for them if you haven't inserted your images in chronological order in the document. To choose a different number format, such as Roman numerals or letters of the alphabet, click the Numbering button to open the

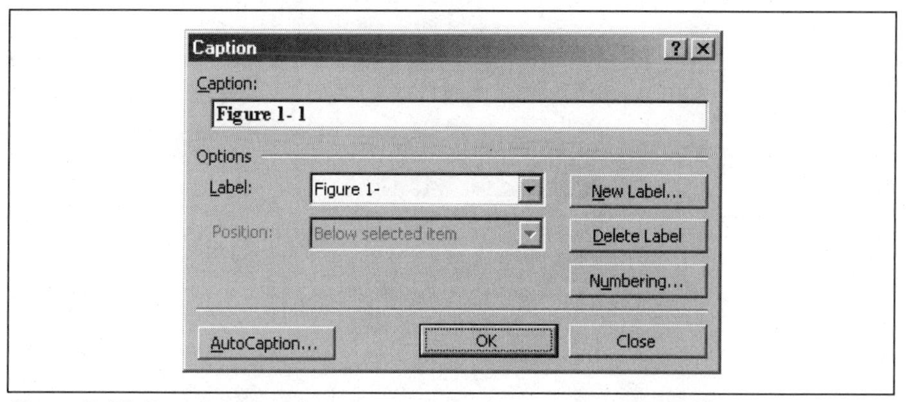

Figure 7-17: Inserting a caption

Caption Numbering dialog box (Figure 7-18). Also use the dialog to include chapter numbers in caption labels, if heading styles are used throughout a document for chapter titles.

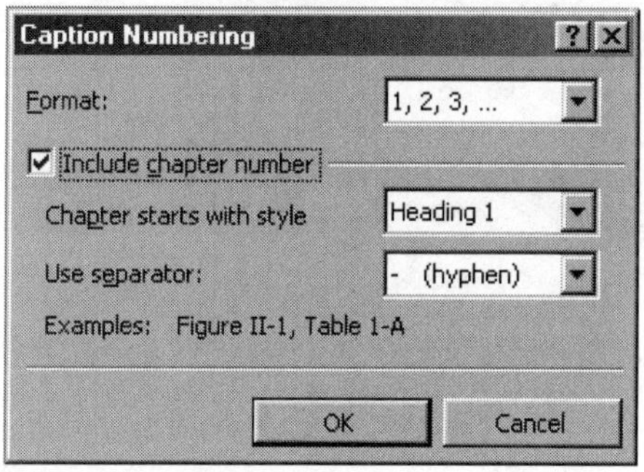

Figure 7-18: Changing a caption's number format

Click the AutoCaption button on the Caption dialog to choose from a long list of automatic captions, each one the name of a potential object in a document, such as Microsoft Map or Paintbrush Picture (Figure 7-19).

Insert → Cross-Reference

Like a "see also" in an index, a cross-reference points from one topic to another related topic in the same document. This pointer can take the form of hyperlink text or a page or paragraph number that points to another part of the document. The relationship between the reference and the cross-reference is established by the user through the Cross-reference dialog box (Figure 7-20).

To insert a cross-reference, position the insertion point at the place in the document where the reference should appear. Any selected text can also serve as the

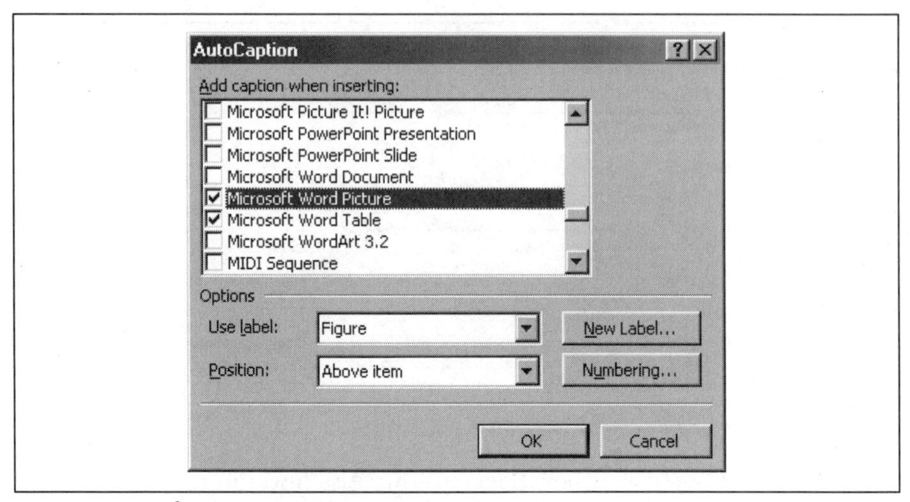

Figure 7-19: Selecting an automatic caption

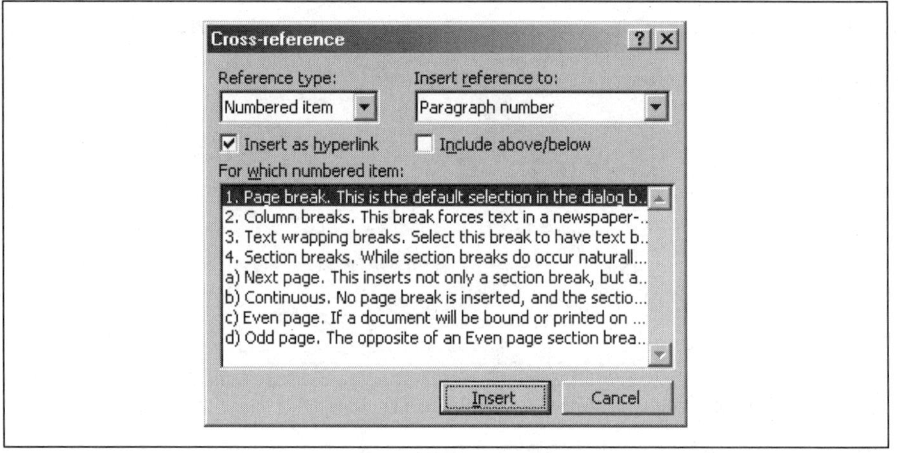

Figure 7-20: Connecting topics with a cross-reference

reference. Choose Insert → Cross-reference, which opens the Cross-reference dialog box. Choose the Reference type (a numbered paragraph, a heading, a footnote) and then select what type of content that reference will point to.

Don't confuse inserting a hyperlinked cross-reference with a hyperlink. A hyperlink points to another document, a file, a web address, or to a bookmark or text in Heading style within the same document. Hyperlinks are discussed later in this chapter. A hyperlink cross-reference is an actual cross-reference that acts like a hyperlink.

After selecting the type of content to which a reference will point, select the actual reference from the "For which..." box. The complete name of this box corresponds to the selection in the Reference type box, for example, "For which numbered item" or "For which heading." After establishing the nature and destination of the reference, click the Insert button. You can also click outside of the Cross-reference dialog box to create additional references. After completing all of the needed cross-references, click the Close button to close the Cross-reference dialog box.

As soon as a cross-reference is inserted into a document, the Web toolbar appears onscreen. Use the Back and Forward buttons on this toolbar to move from cross-reference back to reference point, and vice versa. To delete a cross-reference, highlight the link or reference number and press the Delete key.

TIP # 78

Test Cross-References Before Distributing Documents

It's a good idea to test cross-references before distributing the documents that contain them. Click the reference text to make sure the cross-reference links to or displays the appropriate content.

Insert → Index and Tables

While it is possible to create a table of contents or an index manually, it's often much easier to let Word do it. In addition, Word provides greater accuracy and can more efficiently update the table or index as a document changes over time.

The Index and Tables dialog box provides four tabs relating to the types of tables/indices: Index, Table of Contents, Table of Figures, and Table of Authorities.

Index

The Index tab (Figure 7-21) controls the layout of an index. It also provides tools for marking index entries within your document. The preview window shows a sample index that changes to reflect your format settings.

To create an index for a document, you first have to mark the entries (words or phrases) that should go into the document. There are two options for doing this. Mark entries in a document manually using the Mark Entry button on the Index and Tables dialog. Alternately, supply an AutoMark file (a separate Word document that lists words to index).

Clicking the Mark Entry button opens the Mark Index Entry dialog box (Figure 7-22). Alt-Shift-X also opens this dialog directly from within a document. The dialog stays open so you can quickly add more entries as you work. To mark an entry, select the word or phrase in the document and click the Mark button. Clicking Mark All marks all occurrences of the word or phrase. By default, the index entries created are "Current page" entries, which means the page number on which the entry is marked appears next to the entry in the index. Mark the entry as a subentry under another main entry by typing it in the subentry box. To include a

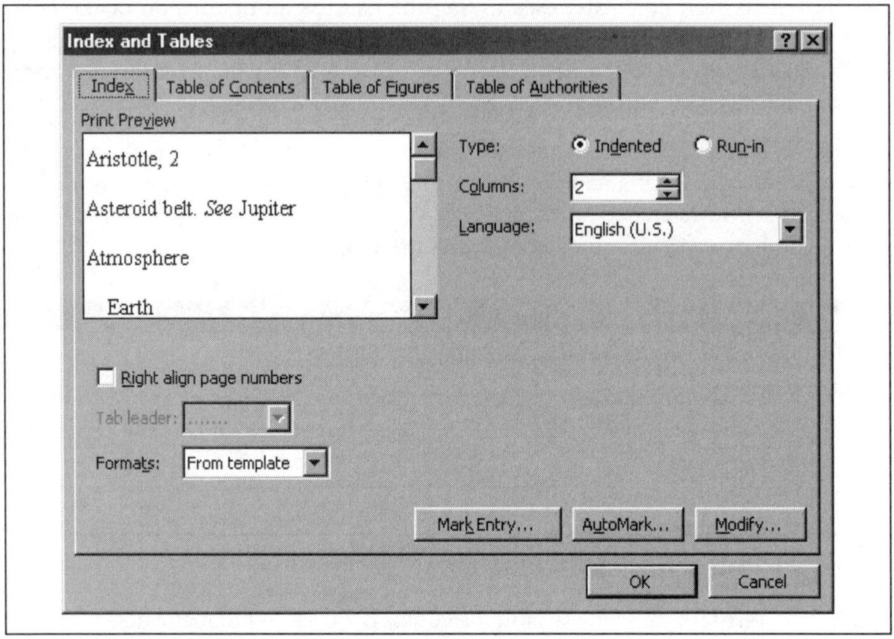

Figure 7-21: Creating an Index

third-level entry, type the subentry text followed by a colon (:) and the text of the third-level entry. Unfortunately, you must know the exact name of the main entry you want to add subentries to, as Word does not offer a way to view the current list while marking entries.

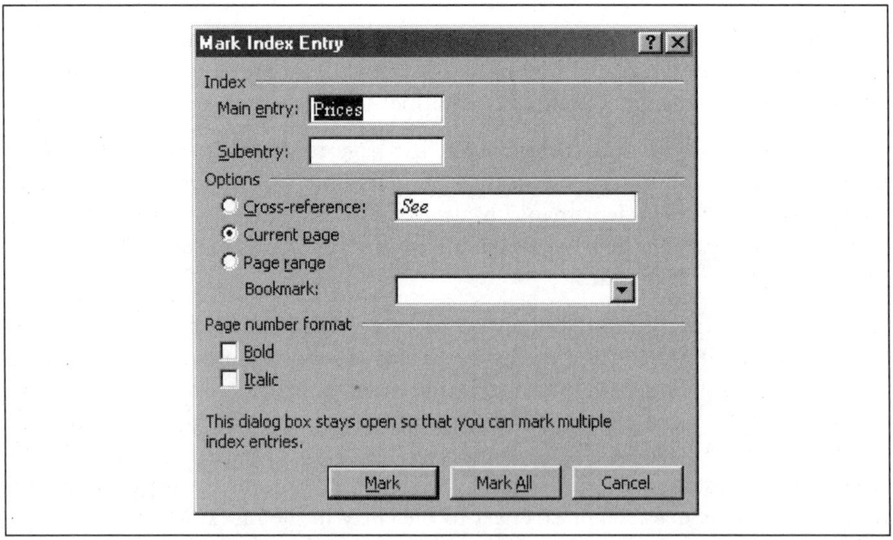

Figure 7-22: Marking index entries

TIP # 79

Add Mark Entry Commands to Context Menus

When marking entries for an index or table of contents, try adding the Mark Entry commands to the Text context menu using the techniques described in Chapter 3, Customizing Word.

There are also two other types of entries:

- Cross-references are terms or phrases that Word will use as See Also entries.
- Create a bookmark for a range of pages by selecting those pages and using Insert → Bookmark, and then reference that bookmark in the Page range Bookmark text box when completing the index entry.

When you first start marking entries, Word turns on the "Show hidden characters" feature. Turn this off using the Show/Hide button on the Standard toolbar.

When inserting an index entry, Word marks off the term or phrase in the document using brackets and some special characters. Figure 7-23 shows an example of all three types of entries:

- The first line shows a simple current page entry. The marked term is enclosed in quotes, the letters XE precede it, and the whole thing is enclosed in brackets.
- The second line shows an example of a cross-reference entry, which adds the \t switch and the wording chosen for your cross-references in italics (the default wording is *See*).
- The final line shows a page range entry, which adds the \r switch and the name of the bookmark set off in quotes.

```
Prices{·XE·"Prices"·}·quoted·in·this·document·are·valid{·XE·"valid"·\t·"See··Price·validation"·}·
for·30·days·from·the·document·date.·¶
¶
Beyond·this·30·days,·prices·are·subject·to·change{·XE·"change"·\r·"Proposal"·}·without·notice.·¶
```

Figure 7-23: Marked index entries

TIP # 80

Deleting an Index Entry

Deleting a index entry is easy. No matter what type of entry it is, select the letters XE and delete them. Word deletes the brackets, quotes, and switches and reverts the word to normal.

Create entries in a document automatically using a prepared list of words or phrases saved as a separate document. This can be used to create an index from scratch or to supplement an existing index. Though this sounds tempting, it can cause problems, since Word marks all occurrences of any word on the list in the document. Marking entries manually provides much finer control over the quality of the index.

To use this feature, you must first prepare a list. Create a new, blank document and insert a two-column table into it. In the left column, type a word or phrase that Word should find in the document. Enter it exactly as it will appear in the document, including capitalization. In the right-hand column, enter the index entry as it should appear in the index.

When the list is done, save it as a separate document and return to the document the index will be created for. Go to Insert → Indexes and Tables → Index. Click the AutoMark button and use the Open dialog to find the document that contains the list. Word locates and marks all of the entries in the list. When it's finished, go to Insert → Index and Tables → Index again and click OK to create the index.

Table of Contents

A table of contents is based on the use of Heading styles throughout a document. Word's Table of Contents feature creates a table that refers to the text formatted in Heading 1, Heading 2, or Heading 3 styles. It lists those headings along with the page numbers on which they can be found. Choose the Type, number of Columns, and Formats for the table of contents and also select the number of Heading levels (the default is 3) using the Table of Contents tab on the Index and Tables dialog (Figure 7-24).

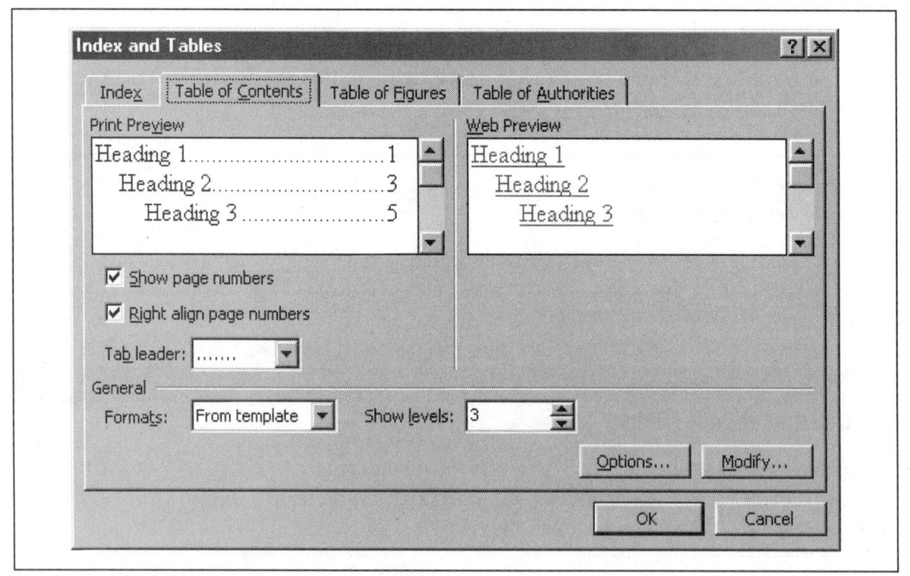

Figure 7-24: Creating a table of contents

TIP # 81

Create a Web Table of Contents Automatically

Create a table of contents for a web page and have headings listed in the table of contents serve as hyperlinks to the actual headings. Save a Word document as HTML and the table of contents becomes a web table of contents, and the hyperlinks are created automatically.

WARNING

When setting up a table of contents through the use of Heading styles, be sure NOT to apply a heading style to the table of contents heading "Table of Contents". If you do, the table of contents will be listed within itself!

If you don't want to use Word's heading styles as the triggers for your table of contents entries, assign different styles through the Table of Contents tab (Figure 7-24). Click the Options button to open the Table of Contents Options dialog (Figure 7-25) and choose which styles will be associated with which table of contents levels in a document.

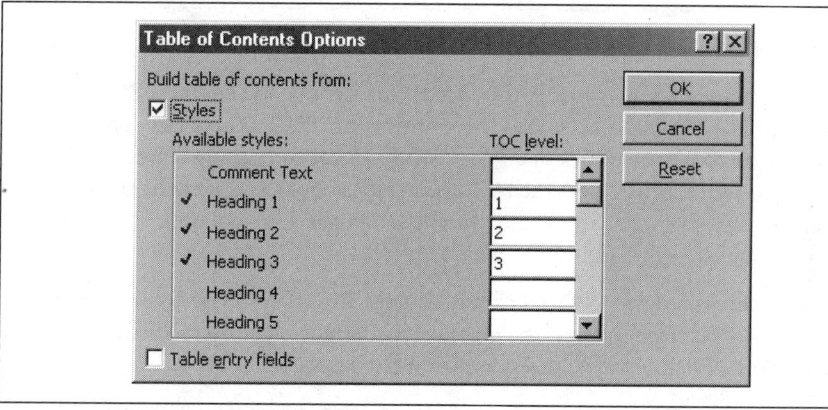

Figure 7-25: Choosing styles included in the table of contents

If a document is edited after creating a table of contents, select the table of contents text and press F9. The table of contents is updated to reflect any new, moved, or deleted headings (or text in whatever styles you've assigned when customizing your table of contents settings). Page numbers for all entries are updated accordingly.

Table of Figures

A table of figures lists all the figures in a document and indicates the pages (by number) on which they can be found. Figure captions (Insert → Caption) are used to designate figures when creating the table.

If any items are captioned as tables or equations in a document, list them along with their page locations by using the Table of Figures tab and switching to either Table or Equation in the Caption Label list. Unless a graphic image or other object has a true caption associated with it, it will not appear in the Table of Figures.

Table of Authorities

The Table of Authorities tab contains tools for selecting an authorities category, such as Cases, Statutes, or Rules, and for marking document text and page numbers for listing in the table. Select citations within text and mark them, adding short or long citations to each marked entry. If you click the Mark Citation button, you can click outside of the dialog box to continue selecting text and marking the selections as citations.

As a document changes over time, pages are added or deleted, and content is moved around in the document. To keep tables and indices up to date, select the table or index (drag through it with your mouse) and press the F9 key. Page number references are automatically updated, as are changes in heading text or changes in the content of indexed text.

Insert → Picture → ClipArt

Insert → Picture → ClipArt opens the Insert ClipArt dialog (Figure 7-26). The clip art images that were installed with Office appear on the Pictures tab. The Pictures tab displays up to 51 categories of clip art images, each containing a group of images that can be inserted into a document. To select a category and view its images, click once on the category icon. Once the category's images are displayed, scroll through the pictures and select to add to the document.

To insert a clip art image, right-click and choose Insert from the context menu (or double-click the image). After the image is inserted, the Insert Picture window remains open, allowing you to insert additional images.

Once clip art images have been inserted, resize them by dragging their handles or move them by clicking and dragging to a new location on the page. To control the way text flows around a clip art image, right-click the picture and choose Format Picture from the context menu. Click the Layout tab (Figure 7-27) and choose the Wrapping style to use. Wrapping styles are detailed in Chapter 8.

If you've downloaded additional clip art images from the Web or bought them on CD-ROM, add them to the Insert Picture window's clip art gallery by clicking the Import Clips button at the top of the Insert Picture window (see Figure 7-26). This opens a dialog box for selecting the image to add, naming it, and choosing the category to add it to.

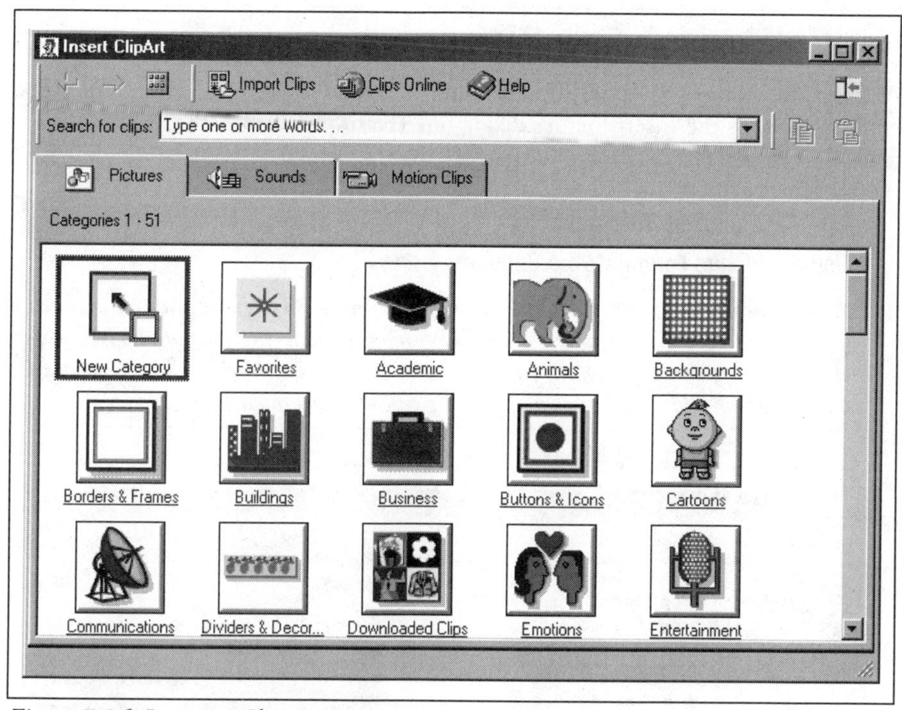

Figure 7-26: Inserting Clip Art

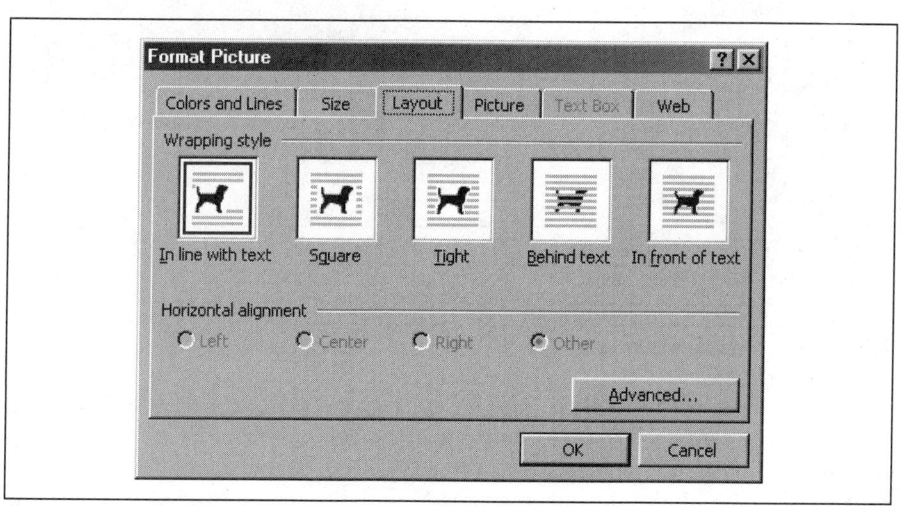

Figure 7-27: Choosing a wrapping style

Insert Menu

Insert → Picture → From File

Add graphic images to a document using Insert → Picture → From File. The command opens the Insert Picture dialog box (Figure 7-28), which is used to select any file in an acceptable graphic format (see the tip, below).

TIP # 82

Find the Picture Formats Word Supports

When downloading files from the Web or obtaining them from another source, be sure they're in an acceptable format. Common graphic file formats include .bmp (bitmap), .gif (graphic image file), and .tif (tagged image file). See Appendix C, Converters and Filters, for a list of graphic types Word supports.

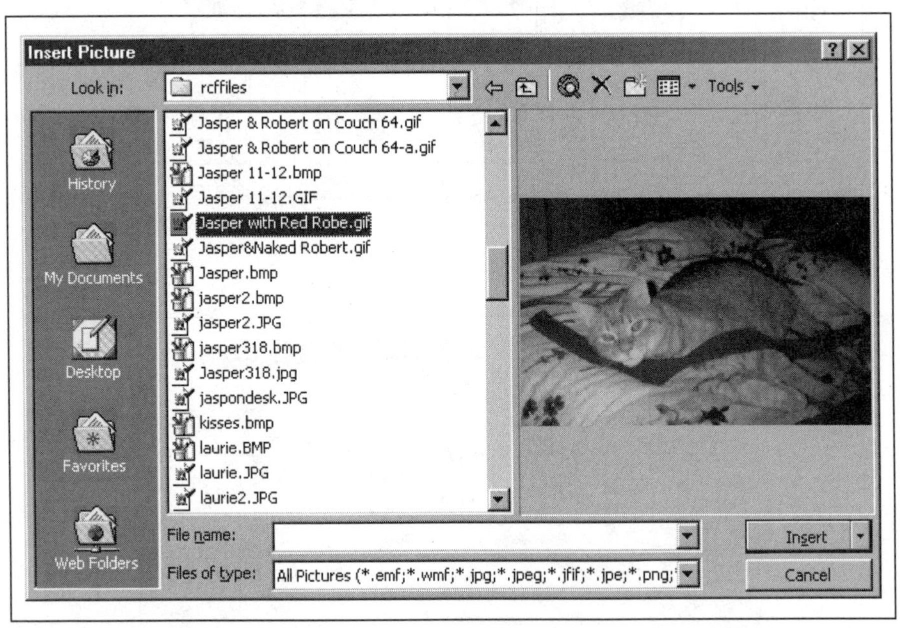

Figure 7-28: Inserting a picture

Double-click any file to insert it. The file appears in the document at the insertion point. After the image is inserted, resize it by dragging its handles and move it by clicking and dragging the image to a new location in the document. Once in place, control the flow of the document's text around the image by right-clicking the picture, choosing Format Picture from the context menu, and switching to the Layout tab.

To tinker with the appearance of the image, open the Picture toolbar by right-clicking the image and choosing Show Picture Toolbar from the context menu. Unfortunately, the Picture toolbar's tools are not terribly extensive or powerful, especially for photographs or highly detailed graphic images. Using a program designed for photo retouching and drawing may be a more effective approach.

Insert → Picture → AutoShapes

Choose Insert → Picture → AutoShapes to display the AutoShapes toolbar (Figure 7-29), which offers six different categories of geometric shapes, callouts, and lines.

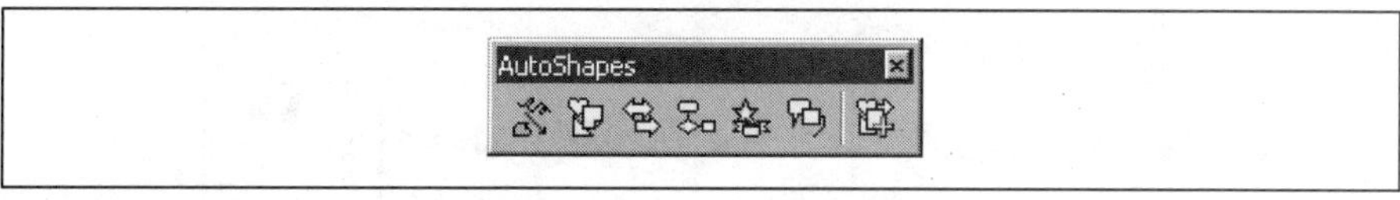

Figure 7-29: Choosing an AutoShape

To draw a shape, select one of the categories by clicking the Lines, Basic Shapes, Block Arrows, Flowchart, Stars and Banners, or Callouts button. From the resulting palette, click a line or shape and move the pointer onto the page. When your pointer turns into a cross, click and drag to draw the shape. Figure 7-30 shows an AutoShape in progress.

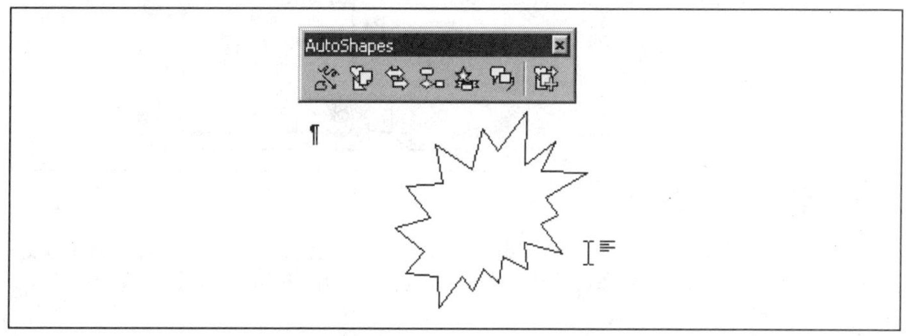

Figure 7-30: Drawing an AutoShape

Once the AutoShape is drawn, move it by dragging or resize it by selecting the object and dragging the handles that appear. Use the Drawing toolbar's buttons to change the rotation, fill color, outline color, and to apply shadows or 3D effects.

Access the same group of AutoShape palettes from the Drawing toolbar's AutoShapes menu. Click the menu and select a group, and from that group click a shape or line to draw. Once the shape is drawn, change its appearance, position, and relationship to surrounding text by right-clicking the shape or line and choosing Format AutoShape from the context menu.

Insert → Picture → WordArt

WordArt is a great tool for creating artistic text for signs, banners, cover pages, or to jazz up a simple section heading. Choose Insert → Picture → WordArt or click the WordArt button on the Drawing toolbar to open the WordArt Gallery (Figure 7-31).

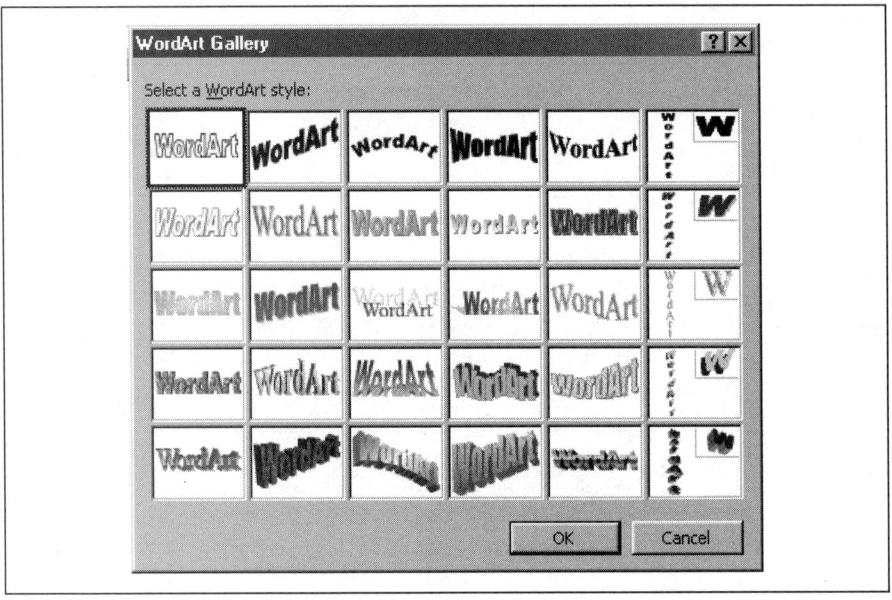

Figure 7-31: Choosing a WordArt style

To select one of the Gallery's styles, double-click it or click on the desired style once and click the OK button. Type the desired text in the Edit WordArt Text dialog box that opens (Figure 7-32).

Figure 7-32: Configuring WordArt

After typing WordArt text in the dialog box, use the Font and Size lists to change the formatting of the text. To create the WordArt object, click OK. As soon as the WordArt appears in the document, the WordArt toolbar appears onscreen as well (Figure 7-33). Use this toolbar to switch to a different WordArt style by reopening the Gallery.

Figure 7-33: Using the WordArt toolbar

Insert → Picture → From Scanner or Camera

Scan pictures from within Word and place them in a document or import an image from a digital camera using Word's Insert → Picture → From Scanner or Camera (Figure 7-34).

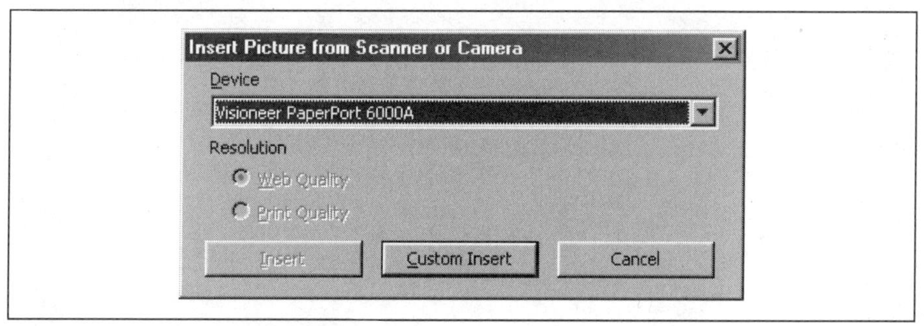

Figure 7-34: Selecting a scanner or camera

The content of the Device list depends on what scanners and/or cameras are installed on your computer. Select the device and click Custom Insert to connect to the device. At this point, the scanner or camera's software starts and scans the picture on the scanner's plate or downloads the picture on the digital camera and places the image in the document.

If no scanner or camera is attached to the computer, the Insert → Picture → From Scanner or Camera command results in a prompt indicating that no device can be found. If this prompt appears in error (you do have a scanner and/or camera attached to your computer), check the device through the Control Panel. Run the Add/Remove Hardware program there to detect and configure the device/s for proper functioning.

Regardless of the scanning software you use, the process generally consists of first running a preview scan, during which the image is viewed by the scanner and displayed in the scanning software window. Draw a selection rectangle around the portion of the plate to formally scan and issue the command to perform the actual scan. Once scanned, the image can be sent to a variety of other software programs for photo retouching or optical character recognition (converting scanned text into editable document text). These tools may also be part of a scanning software's arsenal—if not, save the scanned image in any graphic format and open the scanned file in other software.

Insert → Picture → Chart

There are few things as visually boring as long lists of numbers. To keep documents interesting and convert numeric information to an easily understood graphic, use Insert → Picture → Chart. This command invokes a separate program named Microsoft Graph 2000. It's the same software that generates charts in PowerPoint and Excel. Figure 7-35 shows the resulting charting toolbar, Datasheet window, and sample chart.

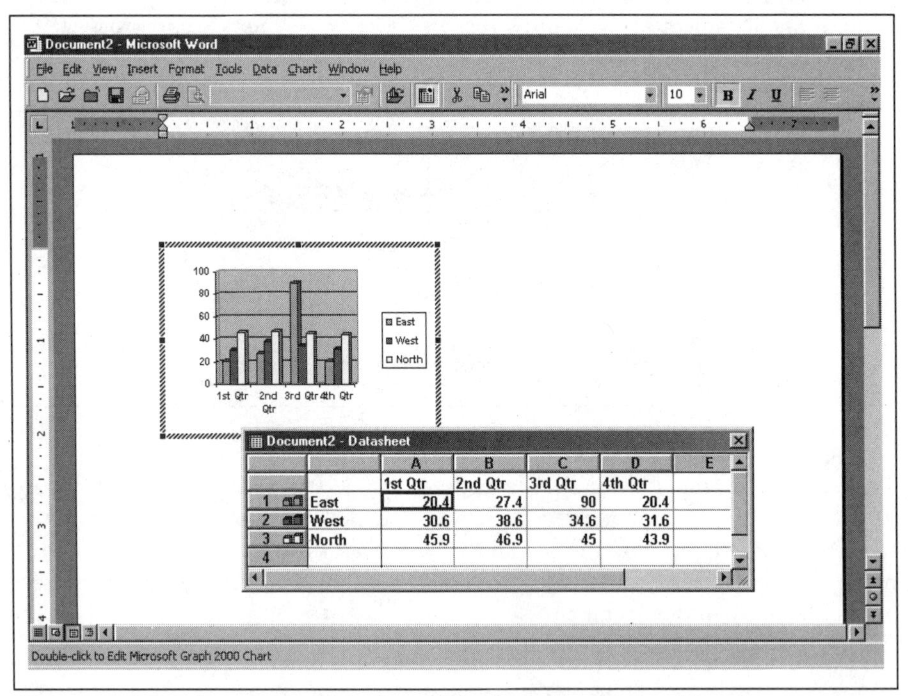

Figure 7-35: Display your numeric data in the form of an eye-catching chart.

When Word's charting tools appear onscreen, they consist of a charting toolbar, a Datasheet window for entering your numeric data, and a sample chart based on the sample data in the Datasheet. A column chart is the default chart type. Choose Chart → Chart Type to depict data as a different type of chart. Pie charts are good for comparing data, line charts show trends, and bar and column charts can do both, showing trends over time and comparing values.

Paste existing numeric data from an Excel worksheet into the Datasheet window or type the data in manually after removing the sample data. After pasting or entering your new data, the chart will reform, based on the new numbers. Each number in the datasheet becomes a plotted data *point* on the chart and each logical group of data points becomes a data *series*. Column headings become category axis labels; row headings end up in the legend.

TIP # 83

Link Content from Other Documents

If Datasheet content comes from an existing spreadsheet, consider linking the source data (in the spreadsheet) to the Datasheet by choosing Edit → Paste Link instead of doing a simple Paste. With a link established, if changes are made to the spreadsheet cells that were pasted into the Datasheet, the Datasheet and the associated chart will update as well.

Format just about any aspect of a chart using the charting toolbar and/or the Format menu. Click on the part of the chart to format and choose Format → Selected Element (where "element" is the selected part of the chart). A dialog box appears, offering tools appropriate for reformatting the selected portion of the chart.

To edit the Datasheet later, double-click the chart object in your document, and the Datasheet will reappear. Make your changes and see them reflected in the chart.

Insert → Text Box

Text boxes provide the freedom to place text where it can't easily be typed on the text layer of a document. Place a text box on top of or behind existing text, or place the text box alongside your paragraphs and force them to flow around it. Text boxes are always placed in the front drawing layer of a document by default, but can be rearranged by right-clicking the box and using the context menu displayed. See Chapter 2, *How Word Works*, for more information on the different layers of Word.

To create a text box, choose Insert → Text Box or click the Text Box button on the Drawing toolbar. The pointer turns to a cross. Drag it to draw a text box of any size. Don't worry about being exact when drawing a text box. It can always be resized later.

Once the text box is drawn (Figure 7-36), the insertion point appears inside it. Text typed inside wraps within the text box, adhering to preset text box margins. If typing exceeds the capacity of the box, the excess is hidden. To reveal it, resize the box by dragging its handles.

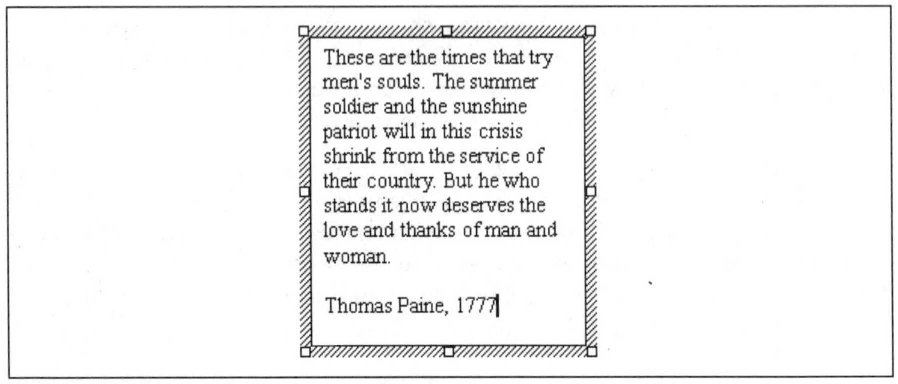

Figure 7-36: Using a text box

Select any existing text in a document before issuing the Text Box command to cut that text from the main document text and paste it into a new text box.

As soon as the text box is created, the Text Box toolbar appears onscreen (Figure 7-37). Use it to rotate the text so that it runs vertically instead of horizontally and to string text from one text box to another. Click in the starting box (where the text will flow from) and then click the Create Textbox Link button. The pointer turns to a pitcher, which is used to "pour" the overflow text from the starting box to another text box. Click the text box that will accept the chained content, and the link is created. Many people use linked text boxes in newsletters to continue stories on different pages throughout a document (as in "story continued on page C3").

Figure 7-37: Using the Text Box toolbar

To edit the content of a text box, click inside it to position the pointer and edit it the same way as text in the main document. Format the text in the box to be different from the surrounding text and really make the text box stand out. The text box operates like a small document—all the typing, editing, and formatting rules that apply to the main document apply in a text box.

To change text box settings, right-click the text box and choose Format Text Box from the context menu. Formatting objects is detailed in Chapter 8.

Text boxes also support colored backgrounds and outlines. Use the Drawing toolbar's Fill Color and Line Color tools. Turn the text box into a cube by applying a 3D effect to it (use the Drawing toolbar's 3D tool) or use the Shadow button to give the text box the appearance of floating above the page.

Insert → Object

An object, in Word-speak, is a document or part of a document created in another program and inserted into Word. An Excel spreadsheet, a paragraph from another Word document, and a PowerPoint slideshow are all examples of objects and each could be placed inside a Word document.

There are two ways to insert an object into Word:

Linking
: When an object is linked to a Word document, a field for that link is created in the document. The location of the object (say, a spreadsheet) and the object's source application (say, Excel) are stored in that field. The object itself remains separate from Word and is updated in the Word document when the original object is updated.

Embedding
: An embedded object actually becomes a physical part of the Word document and is stored in the document file. Updating the original file from which the object came does not update the object embedded in the Word document.

The choice between linking and embedding objects is not always a clear one. Most people link objects that they expect to change, especially if the object is used in multiple documents. That way, changing the original object updates the object linked to the various documents. When a document is ready for distribution, it is easy enough to break the link so that future changes to the original object are not updated. Once a link is broken, however, there is no way to reestablish it other than to create the link again from scratch.

Embedded objects are often used when there is no original object from which to draw, but you want to use the tools from another application to create and format something in Word. Updating and editing links is discussed in detail in Chapter 5, *Edit.*

Insert → Object opens the Object dialog box in Word (Figure 7-38).

The two tabs on this dialog represent two methods of inserting objects into a document:

Create New
: Used to build an object directly inside the Word document. Using this method always embeds an object into the document. Select the type of object to create from the Object type list and click OK to embed the object. The toolbars for the object's application actually replace Word's toolbars temporarily while building the new object. Clicking anywhere else in the document brings Word's toolbars back up. Choose the "Display as icon" option to display only an icon for the object in the document. Double-click the icon in the document to display it. This eliminates the time it takes to draw objects when scrolling through a document.

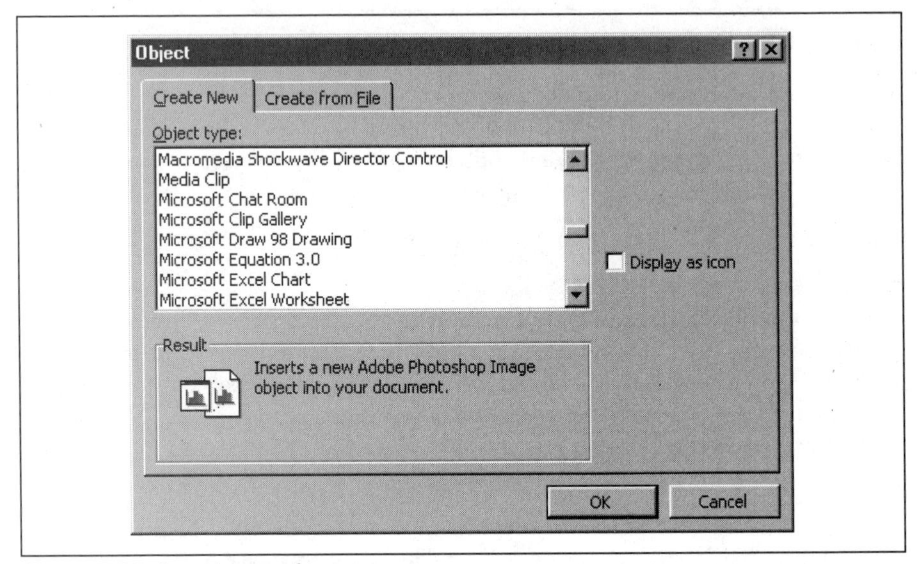

Figure 7-38: Inserting an object

Create from File

Used to link or embed an entire existing file as an object. Enter the name or browse for the file and click OK to insert the object. If you enter a filename that does not exist, a new file is created. Files are created in the *My Documents* folder unless another path is specified. By default, the file is embedded into the Word document. Select the Link to File option to link the file instead. This tab also contains an option for displaying the object as an icon.

Word's Edit → Paste Special command represents yet another way to insert an object into a document and even allows you to insert a specific selection from another file as an object. This command is covered in Chapter 5.

Insert → Bookmark

A bookmark is a selection of text that is given a name—a word, a paragraph, even a whole page. To create a bookmark, select the text and choose Insert → Bookmark. This opens the Bookmark dialog box (Figure 7-39). Type a name for the bookmark, and click the Add button. The Bookmark dialog box closes automatically.

To use bookmarks, open the Bookmark dialog box and select a bookmark from the list. Click the Go To button, and the dialog box closes, moving the insertion point to the bookmarked position in the document. Edit → Go To also provides a quick way to jump to bookmarks. Choose Bookmark from the "Go to what" list, select the bookmark, and click the Go To button. Press Ctrl-G or F5 to open the Go To tab even more quickly.

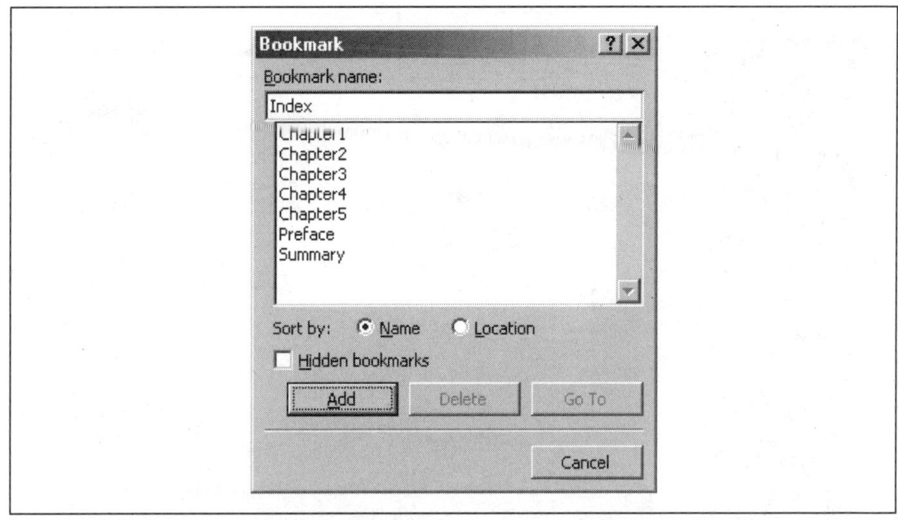

Figure 7-39: Creating a bookmark

TIP # 84

Use Bookmarks for Cross-References

Use bookmarks as the reference point for cross-references. Select Bookmark from the Reference list in the Cross-reference dialog box, and then continue the cross-reference process: select the text that the reference points to and click Insert. You can also create a hyperlink in a document that references a bookmark in that or another document.

Insert → Hyperlink

Anyone who has used the Web has used a hyperlink—a text or graphic that jumps to another location when clicked. A Word document can contain hyperlinks that link to another place in the same document, a different document (or a place in it), a file in another application, or a web site.

To insert a hyperlink, choose Insert → Hyperlink or click the Insert Hyperlink button on the Standard toolbar to open the Insert Hyperlink dialog box (Figure 7-40). To use existing content as a hyperlink, select it before choosing Insert → Hyperlink.

The Insert Hyperlink dialog box offers four types of hyperlinks:

Existing File or Web Page
: Click this button (shown in Figure 7-40) to insert a link to a web site or a file on the computer's local drive or the network to which the computer is attached. Type the URL or filename and pathname directly or Browse to find it. You can also specify a ScreenTip to display when the hyperlink is pointed to (but not

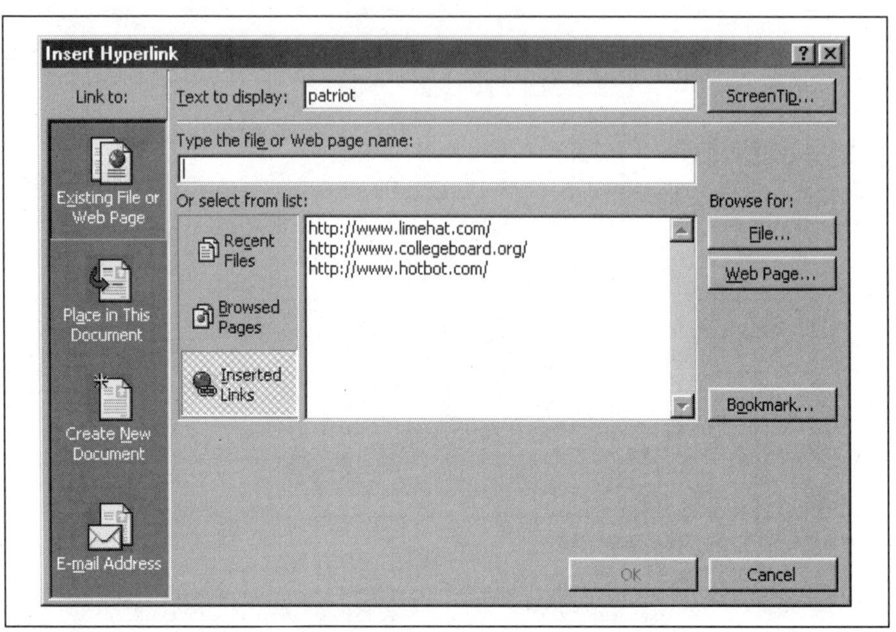

Figure 7-40: Using hyperlinks

clicked on). In addition, the Bookmark button creates a link to a bookmark in the current document, something you can also do using the "Place in this document" selection.

Place in This Document

Have the hyperlink point to a heading or bookmark in the current document (Figure 7-41). The heading must be one that uses a default heading style or a custom one that begins with "Heading".

Bookmarks must be defined before opening the Insert Hyperlink dialog.

Create New Document

Use this option (Figure 7-42) to have the hyperlink refer to a document that is not yet created. Enter a name for the document, specify the full path the document should be stored in, and specify whether to edit the document now or later, when the hyperlink is clicked.

The "Create New Document" feature works with both Office applications and other applications that have file types registered on your system. However, only Office documents support the ability to create the document later by clicking the hyperlink. Select this option for another document type and Word still forces you to create the document at that time.

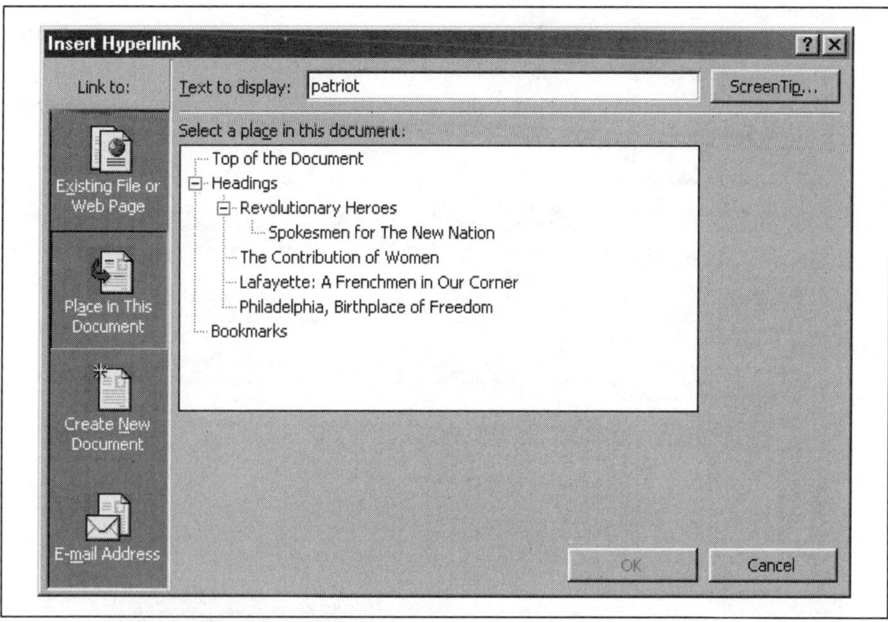

Figure 7-41: Selecting a place in the document

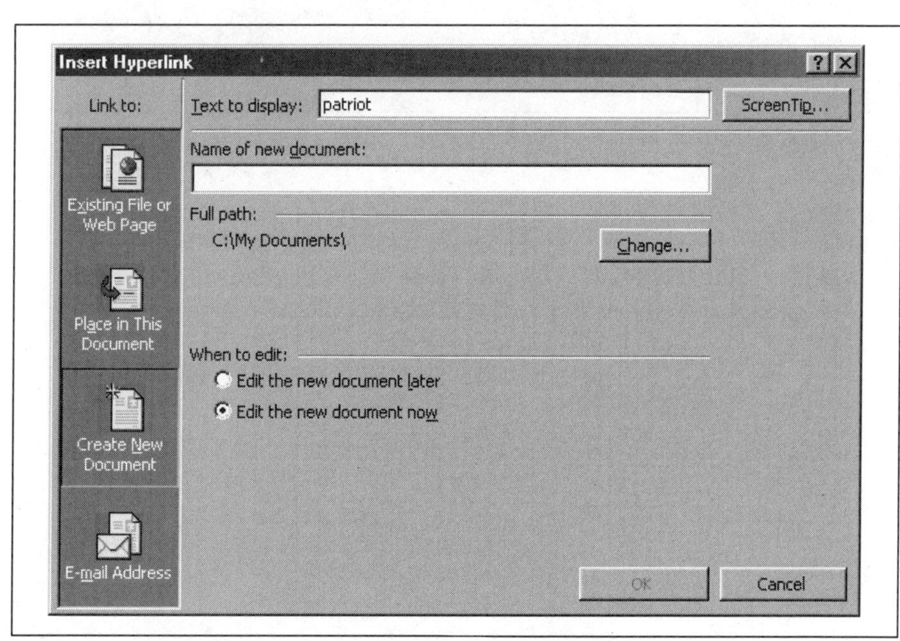

Figure 7-42: Setting up a hyperlink to open a new blank document

Insert Menu

Email Address

Add a hyperlink that opens a new message window, addressed to a specified email address. Click the Email Address button and enter the complete address of the email recipient (Figure 7-43). This can be useful when a document requires feedback from its users.

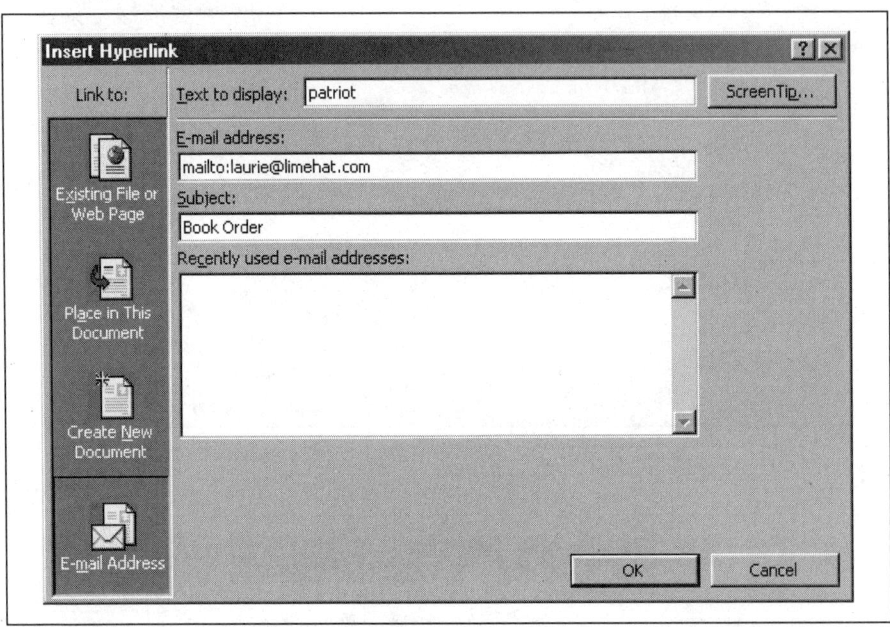

Figure 7-43: Inserting an email hyperlink

To delete a hyperlink, right-click it and choose Hyperlink → Remove Hyperlink from the context menu. To change a hyperlink's settings, right-click it and choose Hyperlink → Edit Hyperlink. The Edit Hyperlink dialog box opens, offering the same set of tools and options used in the Insert Hyperlink dialog box.

Chapter 8

Format

Word's Format menu helps make any document more visually compelling. The commands change the appearance of a document's text, paragraphs, and background and even create styles that allow numerous formatting settings to be applied at once. There are also commands for fixing capitalization mistakes, adding drop caps, converting text to columns, configuring tabs, and even forcing text to appear vertically instead of horizontally.

Format → Font

In Word, characters are the letters, numbers, and symbols typed on a keyboard. Every character typed in Word is actually represented by a numeric code. Hit Shift-Z to put in a capital letter Z, for example, and you're really inserting the keyboard code 90 into a document.

A font is a routine that tells Word how to draw each of the codes onscreen and how to print them. So a font is really just a facade applied to the numeric code. To see that this is true, type a capital Z into a document in the Arial font. Now, switch to the Wingdings 3 font. The Z you typed should now look like a left arrow. It's still the same keyboard code; it just has a different font applied to it.

Characters can have other formatting applied to them as well, specifying everything from italic to size to color. Though many of these formatting features are available on the Formatting toolbar, the Format → Font command offers greater variety and more precise control.

TIP # 85

Use Styles for Quicker Formatting

Unless you are only making simple, one-time changes to character formatting, it is probably better to create a style. Styles are collections of character or paragraph formats that you can apply all at once. For more on using styles, see the "Format → Style" section later in this chapter.

To apply formatting to existing text, be sure the text is selected and then use Format → Font to open the Font dialog box. Ctrl-D also opens the dialog. Opening the dialog without selecting text first causes any changes to apply to new text typed at the insertion point.

Why is the command called Format → Font instead of Format → Character? Beats me. Just keep in mind that you are applying formatting to characters and not to an actual font. In fact, the font is one of the types of character formatting you can apply.

The Font dialog box has three tabs: Font, Character Spacing, and Text Effects.

Font Tab

Use the Font tab (Figure 8-1) to change the basic font, size, and style of text and to apply special effects such as outlining, embossing, and text color.

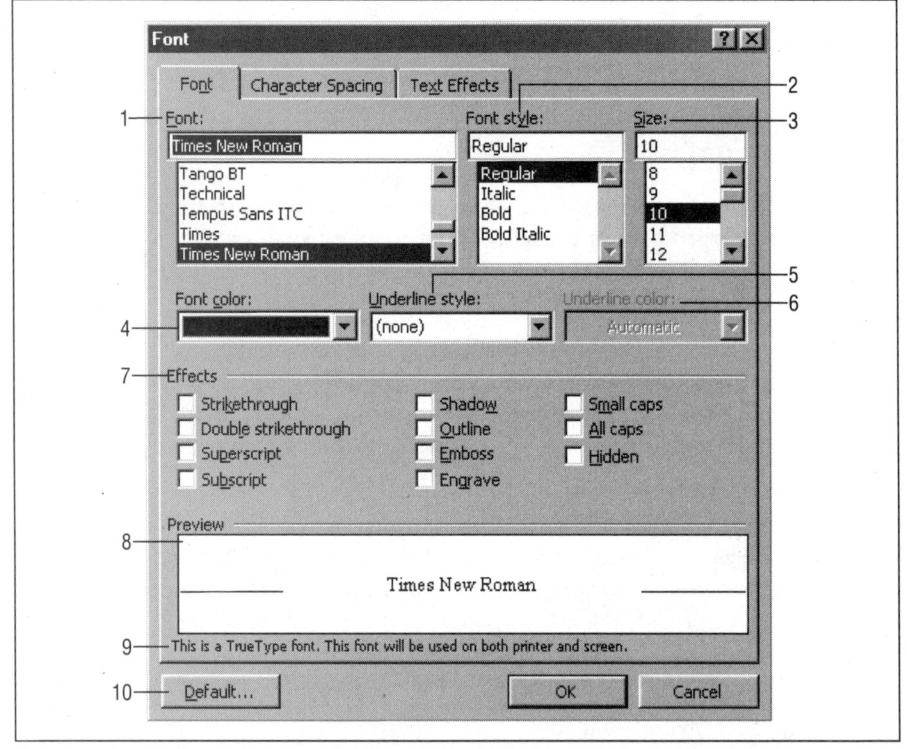

Figure 8-1: Applying character formatting with the Font dialog box

1. *Font.* All of the font families are listed here. A font family is a collection of fonts that are similar in appearance. For example, the Times New Roman family contains the fonts Times New Roman, Times New Roman Bold, Times New Roman Italic, and Times New Roman Bold Italic.

2. *Font style*. All of the members of any font family are listed here. Regular is the default selection and stands for the basic font of the family. Most families have regular, bold, italic, and bold italic styles. Some families have fewer styles.

In case you haven't guessed by now, when you choose bold or italic formatting (or both) you are actually choosing different fonts. Word hides this fact to make life a bit simpler for the average user.

3. *Size*. Change the character's display size. The list presents sizes ranging in various increments from 8 to 72. Type any number directly into the box for a custom size, including decimal fractions (e.g., 10.5).

4. *Font color*. The default color of a character is Automatic, though that default could be changed using character or paragraph styles. The automatic setting is whatever font color is specified on the Appearance tab of the Windows Display Control Panel. By default, this is black. In addition, the Automatic setting allows Word to change the color of the font to reflect changes in the document. For example, applying a dark shade of gray or black shading to a line or paragraph containing black text causes the text to turn white automatically so it can be read against the shading.

5. *Underline style*. By default, no underline style is set. Underlining options include Words Only (in which the words are underlined but not the spaces between them) and several different thicknesses and styles of single and double underlines.

6. *Underline color*. The default color of underlines is Automatic, which uses the same settings described for Font color.

7. *Effects*. The Effects section offers 11 different text effects, ranging from Strikethrough (to show an intended deletion without removing the text) to Hidden, which hides text onscreen and prevents it from printing. Apply a shadow, make text look raised with emboss, reduce it to a wire frame with Outline, give it a chiseled look with Engrave, or change the text size and distance from the baseline with Superscript or Subscript.

TIP # 86

Use Hidden Text

Use the Format → Font dialog to apply the "hidden" character format to text. By default, hidden text does not show up on screen or print. Display hidden text using Tools → Options → View → Hidden Text and it shows up in the document dimmed and underlined with dashes. Make it print using Tools → Options → Print → Hidden Text. Hidden text can be a great way of creating a document for which you want to print two versions, one with certain text and one without. For example, a quiz might use hidden text formatting on the answers. Print out a copy without hidden text showing for students and one with the answers revealed for the teacher.

8. *Preview.* The Preview window shows the cumulative effect of all formatting specified on the Font tab.

9. *Font description.* Fonts come in two types, as far as Word is concerned: TrueType and Printer Scalable. TrueType fonts are used both onscreen and for printing. Scalable fonts often do not match the font as shown onscreen.

10. *Default.* Apply the current format settings to the default font in whatever template is attached to the current document. The default button applies to settings made on all three tabs of the Font dialog box.

TIP # 87

Select Fonts Quickly by Typing the First Letter

To move to a particular font in the Font list, type the first letter of the font's name on your keyboard. The list will move to the first font beginning with that letter, and you can scroll from there.

Character Spacing Tab

The Character Spacing tab (Figure 8-2) provides tools for adjusting the spacing between letters, also known as kerning.

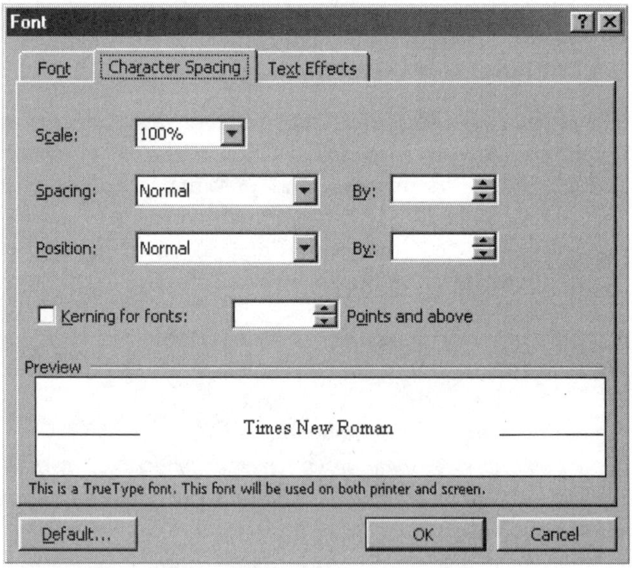

Figure 8-2: Modifying character spacing and position along the baseline

Expand or collapse the letters in a selected word, sentence, or paragraph, and control the amount of the compression or expansion by entering a point measurement into the Spacing item's By box. Adjust the vertical position of text, moving it above or below the invisible "baseline" on which normal text rests. By entering a point measurement in the Position item's By box. When adjusting horizontal spacing, the By spinner box increments or decrements in tenths of a point; the vertical spacing is in full point increments unless you enter a smaller increment manually, such as .25.

The "Kerning for fonts" option makes automatic adjustments to certain letter combinations in various fonts. For example, if not kerned properly, a lowercase "r" followed by a lowercase "n" can look like a lowercase "m," especially in sans-serif fonts such as Arial and AvantGarde. If the option is enabled, you can specify what size fonts (starting with a selected size) are kerned. Generally, the smaller the text, the more important kerning can be, as the text legibility is already compromised by small size.

Text Effects Tab

The Text Effects tab is used to apply animation to text meant for onscreen viewing. Animation effects don't show when printed, but they add movement to headlines, titles, and section headings.

Animated text does not translate if you save your document as HTML. A dialog box appears informing you that your animated text will be converted to italics, and that most browsers won't deal with the animation at all. If you open your file in Internet Explorer or Netscape, the previously animated text appears simply italicized, and retains whatever size or color was applied to it.

Format → Paragraph

Format → Paragraph is the least efficient way to do some things, and the most efficient (or only) way to do others. Setting indents, for example, is much easier to do from the ruler or with keyboard shortcuts. Setting an automatic space between paragraphs, on the other hand, can only be done through the Paragraph dialog box. For a complete discussion of character and paragraph formatting and styles, check out Chapter 2, *How Word Works*.

Choose Format → Paragraph to open the Paragraph dialog box. To apply paragraph formats to a single paragraph, the insertion point need only be in the paragraph; the paragraph itself doesn't have to be selected. If you wish to apply formats to a series of existing paragraphs, however, all of them must be selected before opening the Paragraph dialog box.

TIP # 88

Use Styles for Paragraph Formatting, Too

Unless making minor adjustments to an individual paragraph's formatting, it is almost always better to modify the paragraph formatting for style used by the paragraph instead. This changes all paragraphs using that style and helps maintain consistency. Read more about styles later in this chapter.

The Paragraph dialog is divided into two tabs: Indents and Spacing and Line and Page Breaks.

Indents and Spacing Tab

Use the Indentation section of the Indents and Spacing tab (Figure 8-3) to modify first line, left and right side, and hanging indents for a paragraph. Left and right indents control the spacing of the paragraph from the left and right margins. For a left indent, use a negative number to go outside the margin. First line indents and hanging indents are mutually exclusive; you can set only one or the other. A first line indent indents the first line of a paragraph in from the left indent setting. A hanging indent indents all lines but the first line in from the left indent setting.

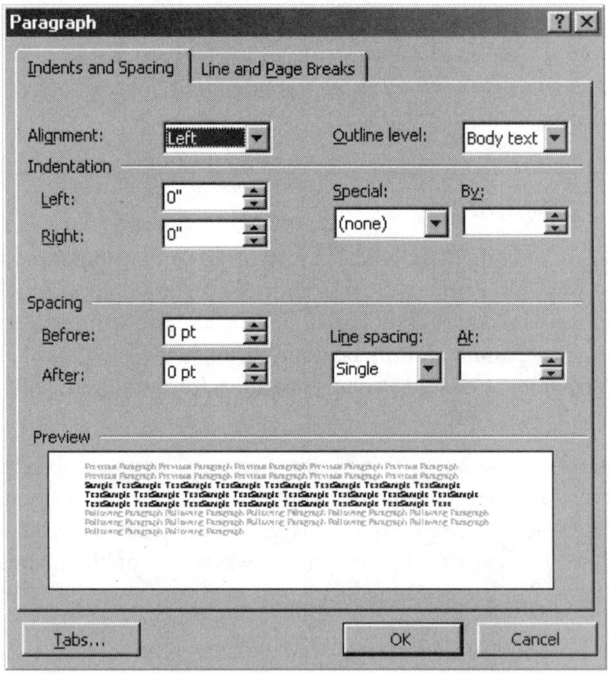

Figure 8-3: Changing the appearance and position of paragraphs

Enter inch measurements for each of the three portions of the paragraph, or use the Special drop list to create hanging indents or first-line indents that don't affect the right side of the paragraph.

Indents can also be set from the ruler or with keyboard shortcuts. Check out Chapter 1, Word Overview, for details on using Word's rulers and see Appendix A, Keyboard Shortcuts, for a complete list of key combinations.

The Spacing section of this tab creates added space before and after a paragraph. Many users choose to add vertical space equal to the default font size (12 pts, normally) after each paragraph, eliminating the need to press Enter twice at the end of a paragraph—the 12 points of vertical space after a paragraph creates the appearance of a blank line.

The Indents and Spacing tab can also be used to adjust Alignment (Left, Center, Right, Justified) and the outline level for the paragraph (from Body text to Level 9), although it is easier to do this from the Formatting and Outlining toolbars.

Line and Page Breaks Tab

The Line and Page Breaks (Figure 8-4) tab controls the flow of text throughout a document.

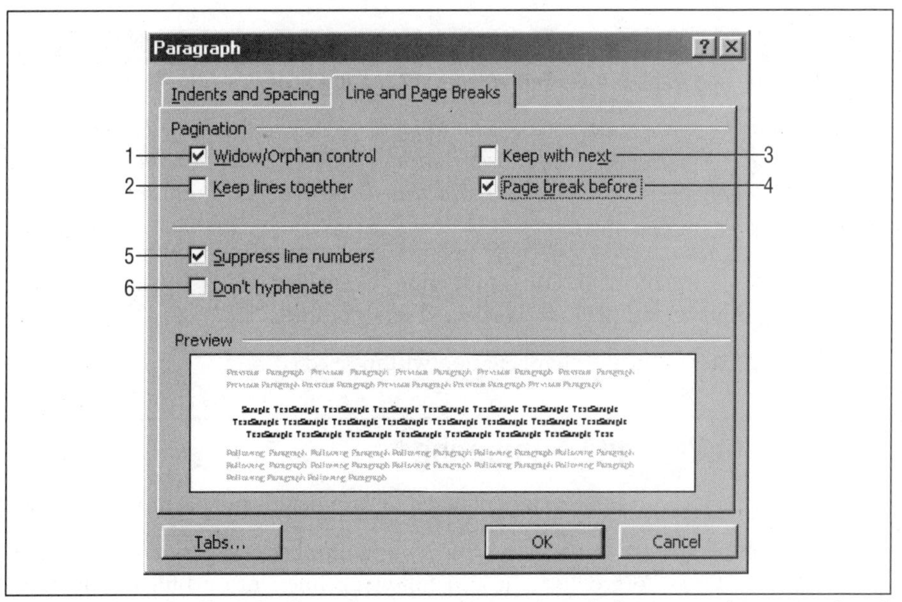

Figure 8-4: Controlling the flow of text in a paragraph with the Line and Page Breaks tab

1. *Widow/Orphan control.* A widow is the first line of a paragraph that gets left behind on the previous page when the rest of the paragraph moves to the next page. An orphan is the last line of a paragraph that strays onto the next page,

while the rest of the paragraph remains on the previous page. To prevent single sentences from paragraphs being left behind or moved ahead without the rest of the paragraph, turn this option on.

2. *Keep lines together.* If single lines (standing as distinct paragraphs) or entire paragraphs must remain on the same page, select them all and then choose Format → Paragraph and turn this option on. If a page break should occur naturally within this series of selected paragraphs, the entire group of paragraphs will be forced onto the next page so that they aren't broken up by the page break.
3. *Keep with next.* Useful for headings that have paragraph text following them, or higher-level headings followed by lower-level headings, this option keeps pairs of selected text items together. Select the item to be kept with whatever should follow it, and invoke this option. For example, you might have a legal disclaimer that includes a heading and text directly beneath. Select the "Keep with next" option for the heading paragraph and moving either paragraph automatically moves both.
4. *Page break before.* If a certain paragraph absolutely must be at the top of a page (whatever page it ends up on), select the paragraph and then turn on this option. Once this option is invoked, the text to which it applies will always follow a page break, and will always be the first text on the page it occupies.

TIP # 89

Check Line and Page Breaks Tab Whenever Creating Styles

When using a style to apply paragraph formats, be sure to check the Line and Page Breaks tab for settings that will help control the flow of text to which the style is applied. Apply the necessary control and then build the style based on the selected, formatted text.

5. *Suppress line numbers.* If line numbering is enabled (File → Page Setup → Layout), omit the numbers for a selected series of lines.
6. *Don't hyphenate.* Turn off hyphenation within selected text.

Format → Bullets and Numbering

There are several ways to create a list (bulleted or numbered) in Word:

- Type a line that starts with an asterisk (*) or a number and period (1.). As soon as you hit Enter, Word turns it and following lines into a bulleted or numbered list.
- Click the Numbering or Bullets buttons on the Formatting toolbar and start typing. Word formats the list automatically. Using the Format → Bullets and Numbering command works too.

- Select a range of paragraphs and click the Numbering or Bullets buttons. Word turns the selected text into a list. Using the Format → Bullets and Numbering command works too.

For most documents, the default round bullets or Arabic numbers that Word creates automatically are fine. When they're not, use Format → Bullets and Numbering to open the Bullets and Numbering dialog box and customize the list format.

The Bullets and Numbering dialog box offers three tabs: Bulleted, Numbered, and Outline Numbered.

The Bulleted Tab

Use the Bulleted tab (Figure 8-5) to choose from seven different bullet characters, plus a None option that turns off bulleting for the selected text. To choose fancy clip art bullets from the Office Clip Gallery, click the Picture button (for more on using the gallery, see Chapter 7, *Insert*). To choose an alternate font character (such as Wingdings or Monotype Sorts), bullet size, indent position, or distance between bullet and text, click the Customize button.

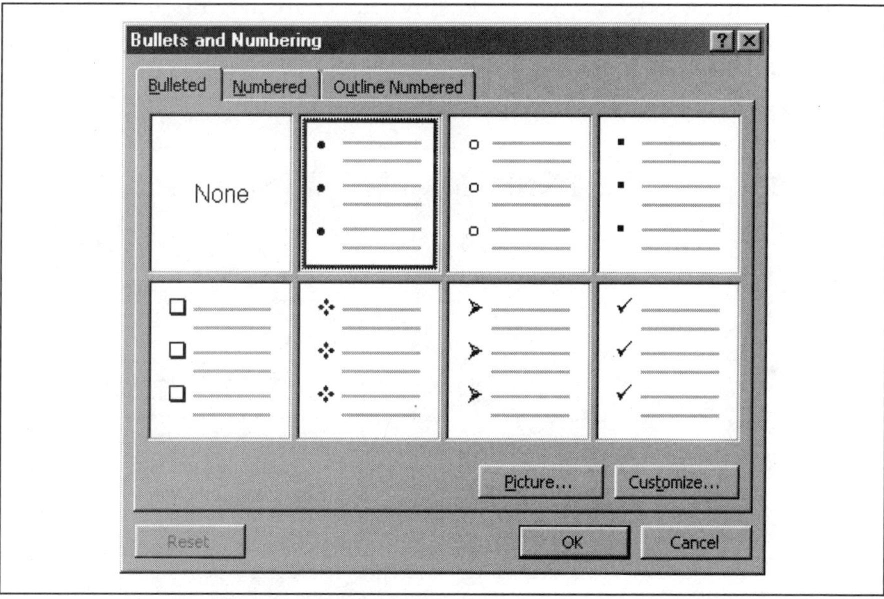

Figure 8-5: Choosing an alternate bullet

Choosing an alternate bullet for a list in a document sets it as the default for that document. Use the Bullets and Numbering dialog box to go back to the standard round bullet (or pick another bullet entirely) for other lists in the document. When you start a new document, the bullet default reverts to the Normal template's default bullet.

The Numbered Tab

The Numbered tab works just like the Bulleted tab and provides all of the same options, with a few exceptions:

Restart Numbering
: Choose this option to have numbering restart with the currently selected paragraph. This is useful with two consecutive lists that must be separately numbered. In addition, Word has a bug that sometimes continues numbering from a previous list even when the two lists are separated by non-list paragraphs. Use this option to fix that.

Continue Previous List
: Choose this option when numbering a series of lines or paragraphs that are separated by a non-numbered paragraph. Word usually restarts the numbering at this point.

Customize Numbered List
: This dialog (Figure 8-6) has settings for customizing numbers used in a list. Change the formatting of the numbers with the Font button. Choose a style of number (normal, roman, etc.) and the number to start the list with. The number position controls the alignment of the numbers themselves: choose Right to have numbers align on the right digit. The Preview area shows the effects of your choices.

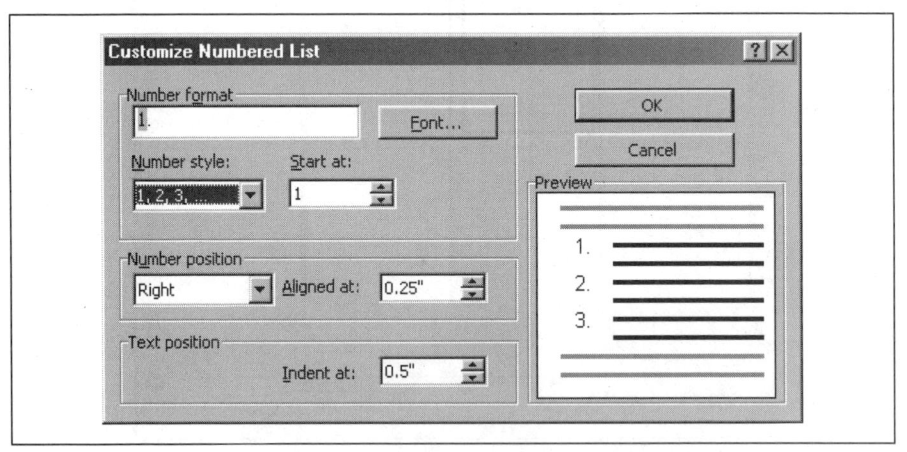

Figure 8-6: Changing the format and horizontal alignment of numbers

The Outline Numbered Tab

The Outline Numbered tab is used to turn a simple list into an elaborate outline with automatically numbered or lettered levels (Figure 8-7).

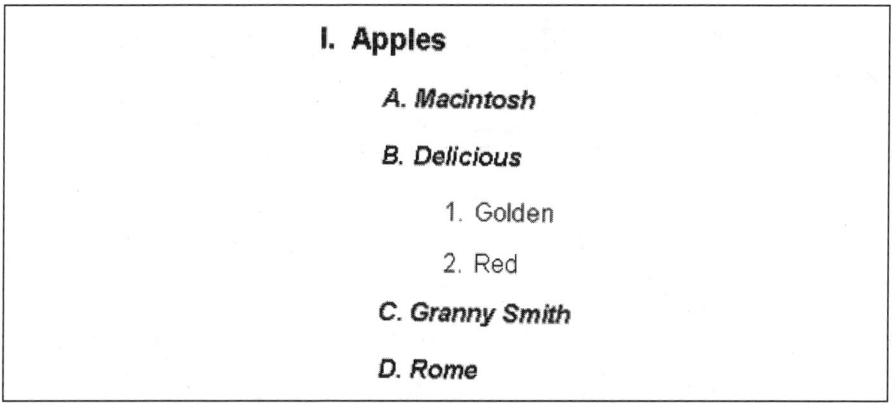

I. Apples

A. Macintosh

B. Delicious

1. Golden

2. Red

C. Granny Smith

D. Rome

Figure 8-7: Using the Tab key to indicate the rank of the items and subitems

Type a simple list of items, sentences, and/or paragraphs, using the Tab key to indent the lower-level items in the list. Select the list, and then choose Format → Bullets and Numbering → Outline Numbered tab. Choose an outline and click OK. Because the list was numbered or lettered automatically, modifications to the outline cause the remaining items to be updated automatically.

Outline numbered lists are not the same as documents built or edited in Outline view. Outline view relies on the use of heading styles to rank items in the outline, whereas an outline numbered list relies on the use of the Tab key to demote items in the list and Shift-Tab to promote items. The use of heading styles is not recommended for outline numbered lists.

Format → Borders and Shading

Borders and shading can give a document visual impact, setting apart important information from the rest of the document. Formatting applied using the Borders and Shading dialog box (or the toolbar equivalents) can also be made part of a style, and therefore becomes easier to apply repeatedly in your open document.

The Borders and Shading dialog is composed of three tabs: Borders, Page Border, and Shading.

The Borders Tab

Use the Borders tab (Figure 8-8) to add or change borders for a selection. The Borders tab settings are as follows:

1. *Setting*. Choose the type of border to apply. Select Custom to add borders only to specific sides of the selection using the border buttons in the Preview pane. Clicking any of the border buttons automatically selects the Custom setting. When formatting borders for a table, buttons for borders between cells and for diagonal borders are added to the Preview pane.

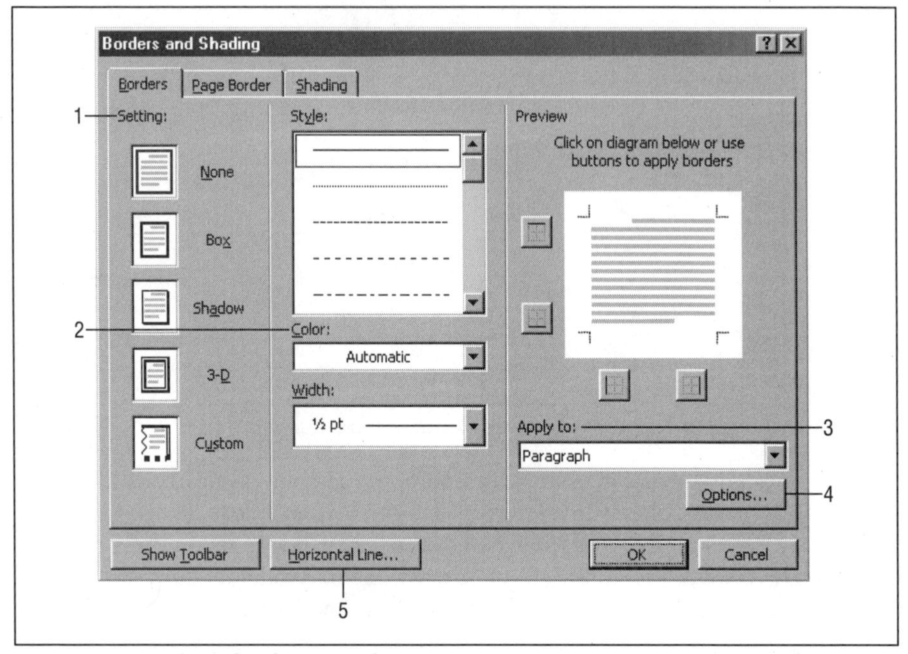

Figure 8-8: Applying borders to a selection

2. *Color*. Select the color for the border. The Automatic color setting applies the default window text color as specified in the Windows Control Panel. To change this default setting, go to Start → Settings → Control Panel → Display → Appearance → Item → Window and change the Font color. You can apply a different style, color, and width to each border. Choose a Custom setting. Select a style, color, and width and then click the border button

3. *Apply to*. Select the item to which the border should be applied. You can apply a border to the paragraph, table, or cell that holds the insertion point or to any specifically selected text.

4. *Options*. Specify the distance from each side of a selection to the border. By default, the border is placed 1 point from the top and bottom borders and 4 points from the sides. Valid values range from 0 to 31 points.

5. *Horizontal Line*. This button closes the Borders and Shading dialog and opens another dialog that lets you choose a graphic to insert as a horizontal line in the document. These lines are specially designed for use in web pages, but may be used in any document.

For a quick, black, hairline border around selected text or table cells, use the Border tool on the Formatting toolbar. A palette descends for choosing border sides to apply, including a full outside border (to put a box around selected text) and an inside Border (to place full borders around a block of selected table cells).

The Page Borders Tab

The Page Borders tab is functionally identical to the Borders tab. There are only three differences:

- An Art drop-down list selects a graphical page border to replace the current border style selection. Apply different art to each border by selecting the graphic and clicking a border button.
- Apply a page border to the whole document, the section of the document with the insertion point, the first page of that section, or all pages in that section except the first.
- In the Options dialog, borders are placed 24 points from the edge of the page by default. Set values from 0 to 31 points and specify whether to measure border placement from the edge of the page or the edge of the text.

The Shading Tab

This tab presents a simple palette used to fill a paragraph, table, cell, or selected text with a color and/or pattern. The "Apply to" selection changes depending upon the placement of the insertion point in Word:

- Within a normal paragraph, shading can only be applied to the paragraph.
- Within a table, shading can be applied to the whole table, the cell that contains the insertion point, or the paragraph within that cell.
- With text selected, shading can be applied to that text or to the paragraph containing the text.

Shading is especially useful in tables, where it can be applied to draw attention to a particular cell or to create a visual divider between sections of the table. To shade a single cell, click in the cell before applying the shading. To shade a block of cells (or a column or row), select the block and then open the Borders and Shading dialog box. The Tables and Borders toolbar can also be used to apply borders and shading to your text or pages. Click the Tables and Borders Toolbar button on the Standard toolbar, and use the floating toolbar's buttons to apply and customize your borders and shading effects.

TIP # 90

Avoid Shading in Documents to Be Copied or Faxed

If a document will be photocopied or faxed, avoid the use of shading—most photocopiers will not provide a clean, even image of the shaded area. In addition, using darker shades of gray or deep colors can compete with text, decreasing legibility. This applies to both printed and photocopied output.

Format → Columns

Columns are just like those found in most newspapers and can be applied to existing text or set up for new text. Most business documents, such as reports and newsletters, are formatted with no more than three columns, especially on Portrait-oriented paper. More than three columns can result in narrow columns of text that are very difficult to read.

To apply columns to existing text, select the text and choose Format → Columns to open the Columns dialog box (Figure 8-9).

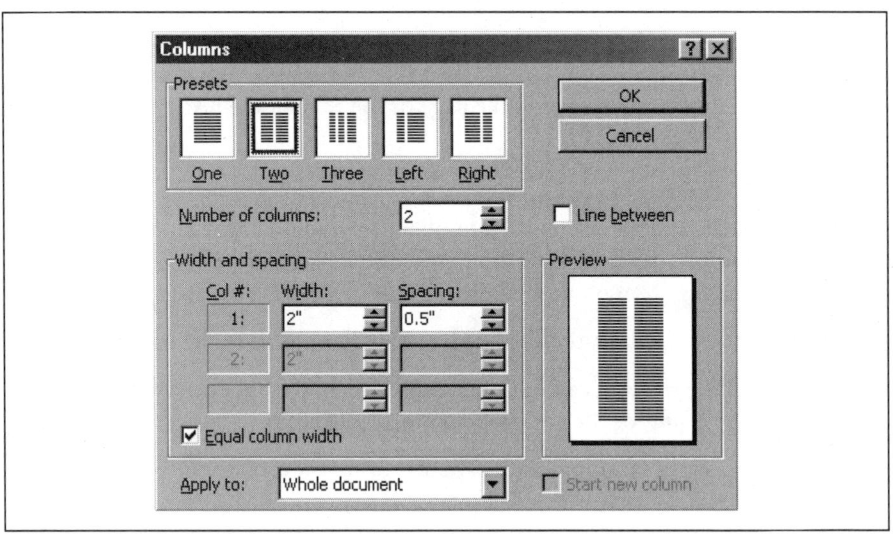

Figure 8-9: Converting paragraph text to newspaper columns

From this dialog box, choose the number of columns, set the column width, and establish the amount of space between columns. By default, all columns are of identical width, with identical spacing, although this can be turned off by deselecting the "Equal column width" option. Once this is off, adjust the width and spacing of each column individually.

TIP # 91

Use a Line Between Columns

If columns are very narrow, turn on the "Line between" option in the Columns dialog box. This places a vertical line in the space between the selected columns in your document, and makes it easier for the reader to focus on one column as they read down the page.

When the columns are applied, Word switches to Print Layout view. Columns are visible in Normal view, but you'll see one narrow column of text running down the left side of the page (though column width is preserved). For this reason, it's a good idea to work in Print Layout view while typing, editing, or formatting column text.

Column text flows down the page, and when it hits the bottom margin, it begins again at the top of the next column. Only when the entire page is filled will text flow onto the next page. Control this flow by inserting Column Breaks (Insert → Break), which force the text following the break to the top of the next column. This is useful for beginning a new article at the top of a column in a newsletter, even if the previous column isn't full of text.

There are alternatives to the Columns dialog box for working with columns. The Columns button on the Standard toolbar opens a palette for quickly formatting text in up to five columns. Though this method is great for quickly laying out columns, you still have to use the Columns dialog box to do any customization.

Another alternative to the Columns dialog box for adjusting column width is the ruler. With the insertion point in the column, drag the column control grid on your ruler (Figure 8-10). Adjust the space between columns by dragging the edges of the gray column space on the ruler. Use the Columns dialog box Presets to apply thinner right or left columns, or to quickly apply one, two, or three equal-width columns.

To remove columns, set the number of columns to one, either with the Columns dialog box or by using the Columns button on the Standard toolbar.

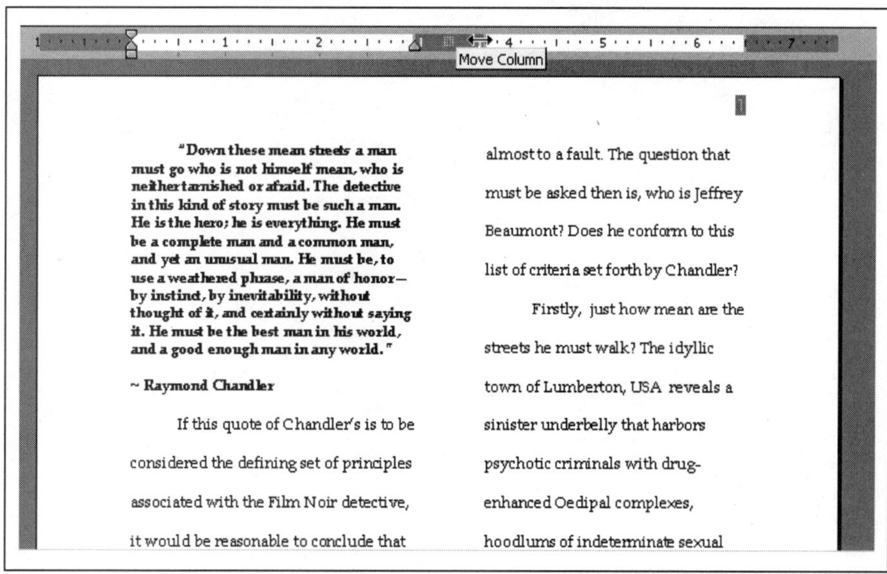

Figure 8-10: Using the ruler to adjust columns and the space between them

TIP # 92

Use Text Boxes Instead of Columns

Sometimes the use of actual columns is overkill from a creation, formatting, and maintenance standpoint. If all you need is the appearance of a narrow column of text alongside a paragraph or graphic, try creating a text box (turn its borders off if you want the fact that it's a text box to be invisible to the reader), and type the text in the box. You can easily resize or move the box and adjust the way surrounding paragraph text relates to it. See Chapter 7 for more on text boxes.

Format → Tabs

Normal.dot, the default template on which new documents are based, provides left-aligned tabs set at every half-inch across the width of a page. For most documents, these tabs are sufficient.

To set tabs at other ruler positions than the default half-inch increments or if the content at a tab stop must be centered or right-aligned, custom tabs are required. Choose Format → Tabs to open the Tabs dialog box (Figure 8-11).

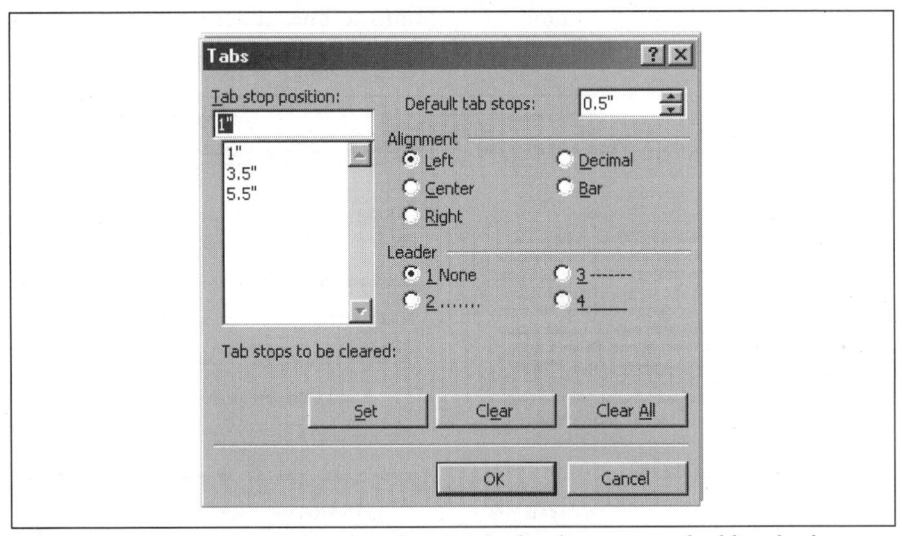

Figure 8-11: Customizing tab settings by varying the alignment and adding leader characters

Before setting tabs, position the insertion point where the new tab stops should go into effect, normally at the beginning of a line. A Word document can potentially have a new set of tab stops for every paragraph. Use the Show/Hide tool and the horizontal ruler to see which tab settings are in force at different points in a document.

TIP # 93

Don't Use Tabs to Indent

Many people use tabs at the beginning of a paragraph as a first-line indent. I don't recommend this. Not only will you have to press Tab at the beginning of every paragraph to indent, you will have to delete the tabs manually if you combine consecutive paragraphs. Instead, use Word's first-line indent feature (Format → Paragraph → Indents and Spacing), described earlier in this chapter.

When the Tabs dialog box opens, click the Clear All button to remove any previous custom tab settings. This doesn't clear the ½" default tabs. Setting the first custom tab stop removes all default tabs to the left of the custom stop automatically.

Click inside the Tab stop position box and type the ruler position for the first tab, for example, 1.25. Next, choose the Alignment for the tab stop. Five alignments are used for tab stops:

Left
: These tabs are Word's default and the type most users think of when they think of tabs. Text is aligned against the left edge of the tab stop.

Center
: These tabs align the text around the center of the tab stop.

Right
: These tabs align text against the tab stop's right edge and are a great way to align the rightmost digits of lengthy lists of numbers as you enter them.

Decimal
: These tabs align numbers (or text) based on decimal points. They are great for aligning currency figures. Be careful, though. Text is also aligned on decimals, so if you type a sentence with a period, the period will align on the tab stop.

Bar
: These tabs do not create an actual tab stop. Rather, they create a vertical line at the position where they are inserted. This is great for putting vertical lines between tabbed columns in instances where you would rather not use a table.

If the tab needs a leader (a character *leading* up to it), choose one—the second leader option (dots) is the most popular. The leader should be set for any text that needs something to draw the reader's eye in a straight line from text on the left to text on the right, such as topics and page numbers in a table of contents. The leader would be applied to the second of these two tabs, the text to which the reader's eye will be led by the dots. As you build tab stops, their positions are listed on the left side of the dialog box.

TIP # 94

Create Signature Lines with Tabs

Create underlines for a signature using the underscore leader (option 4). This way, underlines can be lined up with text underneath. For example, the word "signature" could be lined up with a line above it for a person to actually sign on. To have two underlines on the same page, set up three tabs, but use no underscore leader on the middle one. Note that this method doesn't work for text that will be typed into the document, because the typing will break up the underline rather than appearing on top of it.

As soon as all of your tabs are set, click the OK button. The dialog box closes, and the ruler displays tab stop markers for each of your tab positions. The markers themselves indicate the alignment set for each tab.

Adjust tab stop positions by dragging the markers on the ruler or by reopening the Tabs dialog box to clear unwanted tabs and replace them with new ones. To remove a tab by using the dialog box, select the position, and click the Clear button.

TIP # 95

Make Tabs Part of a Style

You probably saw this one coming. Like any other type of formatting, tabs can be made part of a paragraph style so that they can be easily applied. Styles are covered later in this chapter.

Format → Drop Cap

A drop cap (Figure 8-12) is used at the beginning the first line of a chapter or article. Use the Format → Drop Cap command to open the Drop Cap dialog box (Figure 8-13) and apply settings to whatever paragraph contains the insertion point. Issuing this command switches a document to Print Layout view. Drop caps are displayed properly only in Print Layout view. In other views, the drop cap appears above the first line of the paragraph.

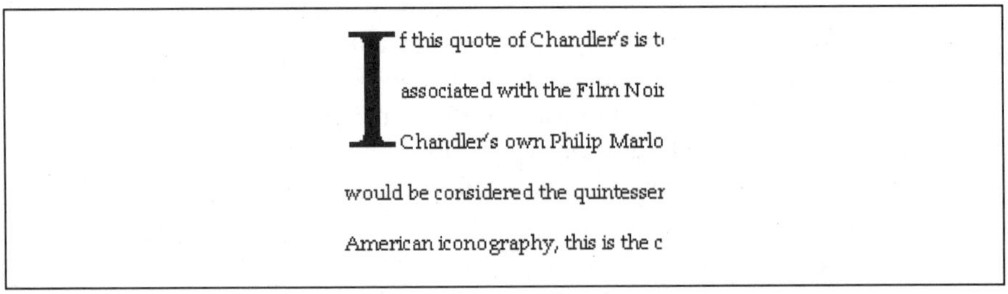

Figure 8-12: Making a paragraph stand out with a drop cap

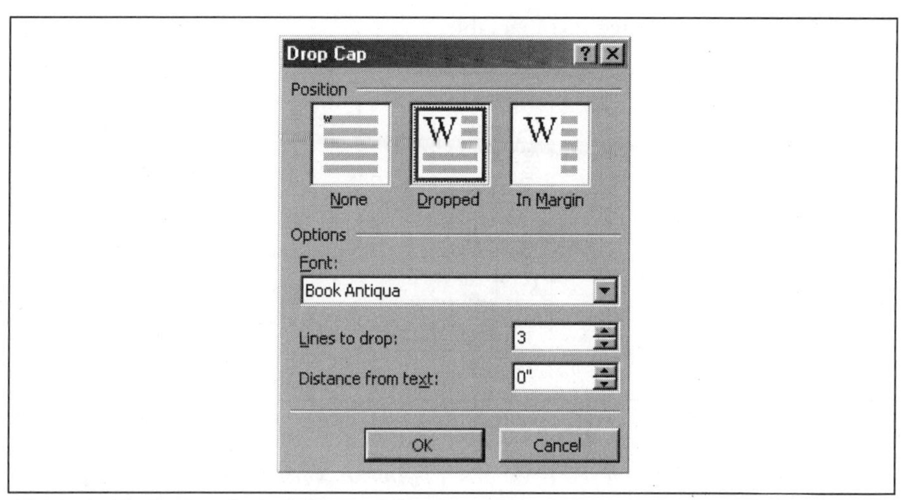

Figure 8-13: Setting the position and font for a drop cap

Drop caps exist in one of three states:

None
: Means no drop cap at all is used. Use it to remove an existing drop cap.

Dropped
: The most common setting; creates the drop cap within the left margin, moving text aside to accommodate and wrap it.

In Margin
: Puts the drop cap outside the left margin.

Customize both dropped and in-margin drop caps by setting the font, how many lines down it should be dropped (3 is the default), and the distance it should be from the text.

TIP # 96

Manipulate Drop Caps Right in the Document

Once a drop cap is created, manipulate it in much the same way as a text box. Click it once to display moving and resizing handles. This only works in Print Layout view.

Format → Text Direction

The first noticeable thing about the Format → Text Direction command is that it is rarely available from the menu. This is because only certain text—text in a table, or text in a text box—can be redirected.

Figure 8-14 shows redirected text in a table.

Product Number	Location	Warehouse Number
G15	2B	3
G16	2G	4
G25	3F	1

Figure 8-14: Changing the direction of text in a table cell or text box

Remember that text boxes aren't visible in Normal view. To add a text box or redirect the text in an existing text box, be sure you're in Print Layout view.

If the insertion point is in a table cell or text box, the command opens the Text Direction dialog box. Use it to choose from visual samples of different vertical text positions, and see a Preview of the selection.

After changing the text direction, the Alignment, Bullets, Numbering, and Indent buttons on the Formatting toolbar are displayed vertically as well. This change is only in effect when redirected text is selected.

Format → Change Case

It's easy to forget that the Caps Lock is on and to type an entire sentence in all caps or to leave the first character of your sentence in lowercase. Rather than retype the characters, though, select the text and choose Format → Change Case. The Change Case dialog box (Figure 8-15) provides several case options to choose from.

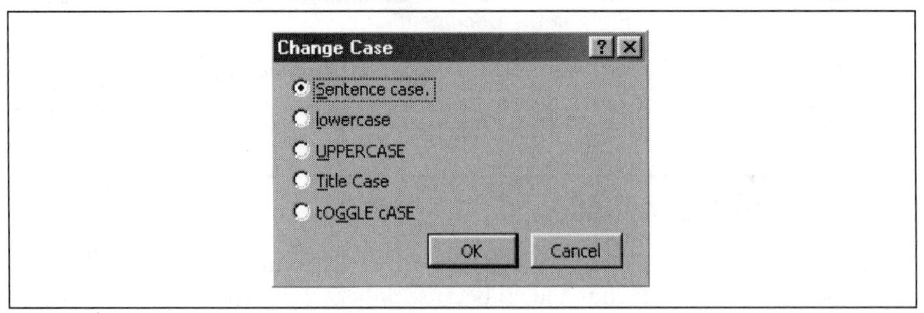

Figure 8-15: Changing the case of selected text

AutoCorrect has a feature (on by default) that corrects accidental use of the Caps Lock key. If you turn on Caps Lock and then type text, any time you press the Shift key, the case of the word you're typing will be reversed—lower to upper, upper to lower. To check that this feature is on, choose Tools → AutoCorrect.

TIP # 97

Use Shift-F3 to Switch Between Cases

Shift-F3 changes the case of selected text. Each tap of the F3 key changes the case between Sentence case, all lowercase, and all uppercase.

Format → Background

The Format → Background command is used to apply a background to the current document. This command automatically places you in Web Layout view, as the feature is mainly intended for use with web pages or documents that are only viewed onscreen. Backgrounds applied with this command are only visible in Web Layout view or when the saved document is viewed in a web browser.

Backgrounds can take one of three forms:

No fill
: Use this option to remove an existing background.

A color
: Use the color palette on the Format → Background submenu to choose from 64 colors for the background. Choose the "More colors" option to open a dialog boasting a more sophisticated, high-resolution palette.

  Choosing a dark background color requires use of light text colors. If a document already contains text, change its color by pressing Ctrl-A to select all document content, and then use the Text Color button's palette to choose a color for text that will show against the dark background.

Gradient
: Select the Fill Effect command on the Format → Background submenu to open a dialog with four tabs. The Gradient tab (Figure 8-16) creates a gradient between two colors (or different shades of a single color). Choose between several different ways the colors can blend.

Texture
: The Texture tab (Figure 8-17) creates a background from a picture that was designed to be tiled, giving the effect of a continuous texture. Choose from one of Word's textures or import a picture of your own in any popular picture format using the Other Texture button.

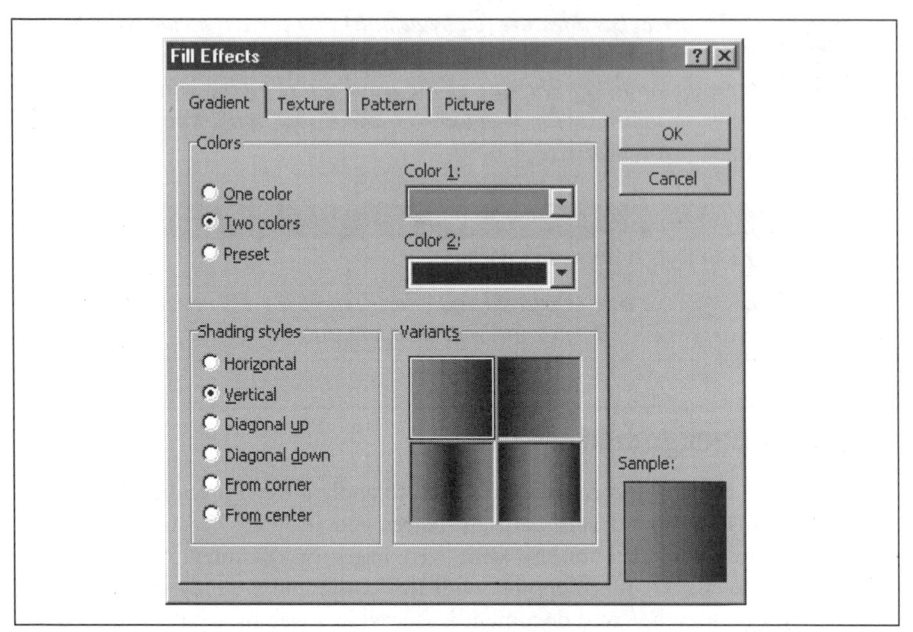

Figure 8-16: Making backgrounds eye-catching with gradients

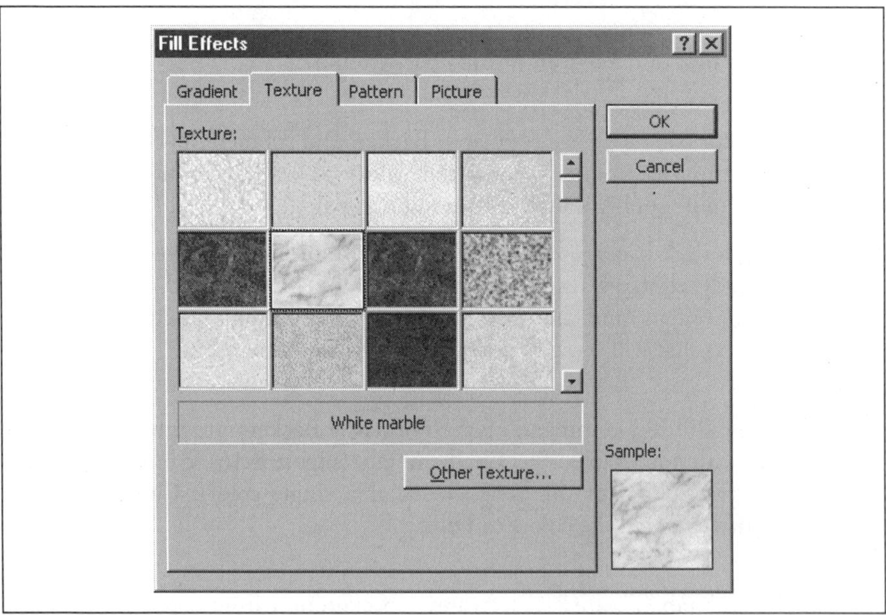

Figure 8-17: Creating a continuous effect with a tiled texture

Pattern

A pattern (Figure 8-18) is an effect created with two colors that is tiled to create a continuous pattern. All patterns have a foreground and a background. Colors for each are customizable, but it is often hard to tell what part of a pattern is the background and what part is the foreground. The only way to tell is to experiment.

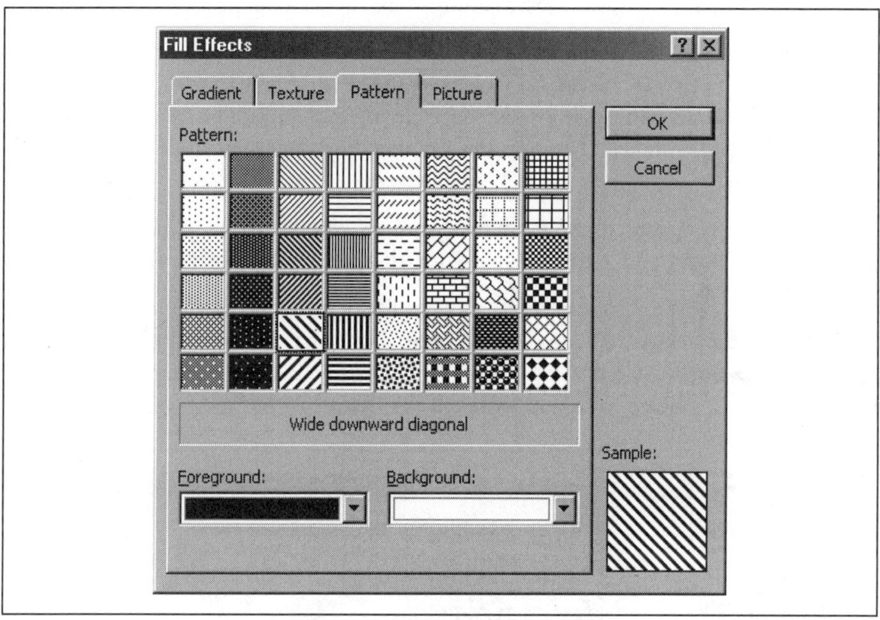

Figure 8-18: Creating a two-color tiled effect with a pattern

Picture

Any picture in a popular graphic format can also be used as the background for a document. The image is tiled, meaning it will be repeated as many times as needed to fill the document background. If this creates an undesirable effect, consider expanding the size of the image through an illustration or photo-retouching program (increase the image's pixel dimensions or canvas size) and then reapply it to the document.

TIP # 98

For the Most Part, Avoid Backgrounds

While backgrounds sound cool in theory, in practice they are usually irritating to those viewing a web page. Backgrounds make text difficult to read and make a page feel a bit claustrophobic. If you really want a background color, try choosing something very pale.

Format → Theme

Themes are mostly used for creating web pages, though they can also be used to jazz up a document that is viewed onscreen. A theme is a collection of formatting elements that defines the appearance of a web page. Elements included in a theme are backgrounds, styles, bullets, horizontal lines, hyperlink colors, and table border colors. A theme is really just a way to apply all of these elements at a stroke.

Themes are part of the Word application, and can be applied to any document, no matter which template the document is based on. Themes are not part of any particular template, although if you apply a theme and then save the file as a template, that theme will be in force on any document created based on that template.

Before you get too excited about themes, though, know that they have one serious drawback. You can't create new themes yourself and they are not very modifiable.

The Theme dialog box (Figure 8-19) shows a list of available themes on the left and a preview of the selected theme on the right. Note that all themes are listed, even those that are not installed. Choosing one that is not installed brings up a note in the preview dialog box asking you to install the theme.

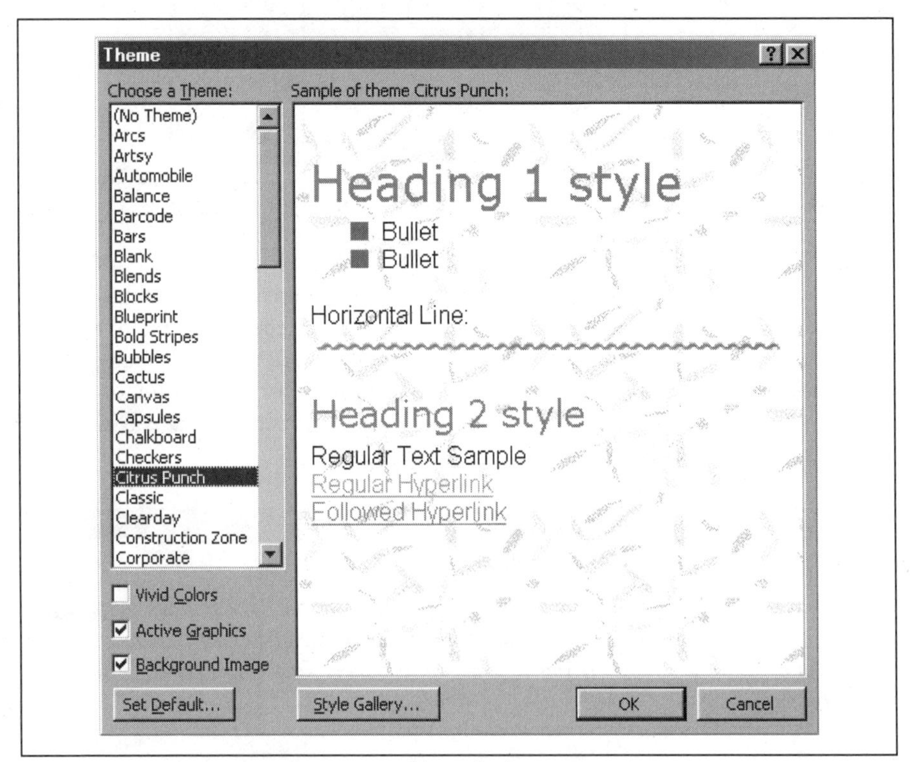

Figure 8-19: Designing web pages quickly with themes

For each theme, the following features can also be set:

Vivid Colors
: Off by default, this option increases the vibrancy of the colors in your selected theme.

Active Graphics
: If the selected theme contains any animated graphics, this option (on by default in most themes) includes them in the document. The animation is only visible if the document is viewed through a web browser such as Netscape or Internet Explorer. When viewed through Word, the animated graphic is visible but motionless.

Background Image
: Also on by default, this feature merely means that the background fill for the selected theme will be applied to the document. This is an option because you might not want a filled background, but would like the rest of the theme elements, such as font choices and graphic images.

As an alternate to using a theme, click the Style Gallery button to see a list of available templates (such as brochures, memos, and letters) that can also be used to format a document.

You can always tweak the fonts and colors in your document after you've applied a theme. You aren't stuck with any of the theme-induced elements, and you can use your normal formatting tools to change anything you want, including the use of styles, through the Style button on the Formatting toolbar or the Format → Style dialog box.

Format → Frames

Frames are mostly used in web pages and are separate documents viewed within the same browser window. Each document is a distinct web page. Frames can target one another so that clicking a link in one frame cause a page to display in another frame. For example, links on a navigation frame could open the various parts of a web site in another frame (Figure 8-20).

Creating a frame automatically switches the document to Web Layout view and opens the Web and Frames toolbars. The Web toolbar provides browser-like controls for navigating pages and the Frames toolbar provides a quick way to add frames to the left, right, above, or below the current page, add a table of contents frame, delete frames, and view frame properties.

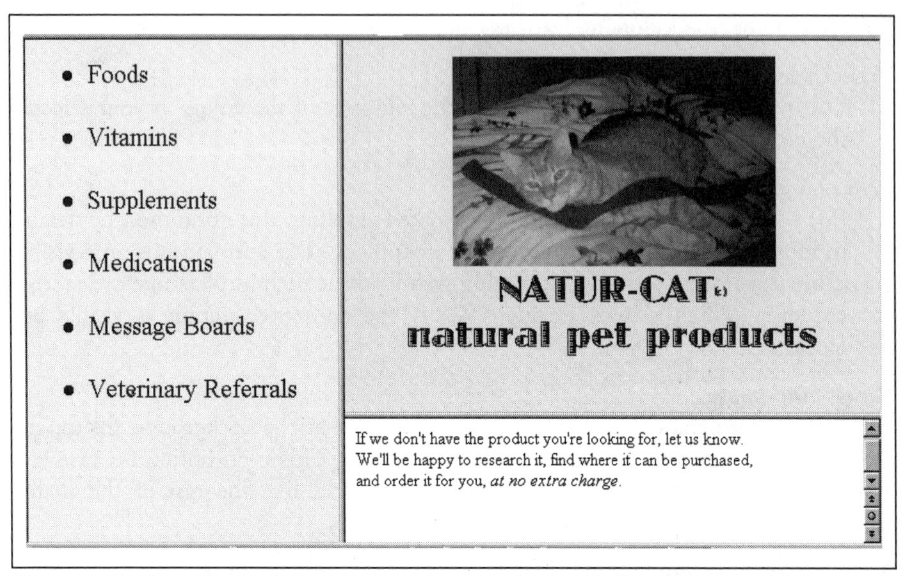

Figure 8-20: Breaking web pages into separate sections with frames

TIP # 99

Use Different Views for Different Frames

The default view when working with frames is Web Layout. Place the insertion point inside a particular frame to change the view for just that frame. A different view can be used for every frame.

The Format → Frames submenu offers only two choices (Table of Contents in a Frame and Add Frame Page) when the current document has no existing frames. When the current document does have frames, the menu expands to mirror the choices on the Frames toolbar.

Using a Table of Contents Frame

Normally, a document's table of contents is a static list of headings and the page numbers on which the headings can be found. By placing this table of contents in a frame, it turns into a series of hyperlinks, each pointing to the heading text in the main document. This creates an interactive table of contents that can be used to navigate the document (Figure 8-21).

To create a Table of Contents in a Frame, the headings in the document must first be formatted in default heading style (Heading 1, 2, and so on) or a style selected for the table of contents using Insert → Index and Tables → Table of Contents → Options. Once the headings are properly formatted, choose Format → Frames → Table of Contents in Frame.

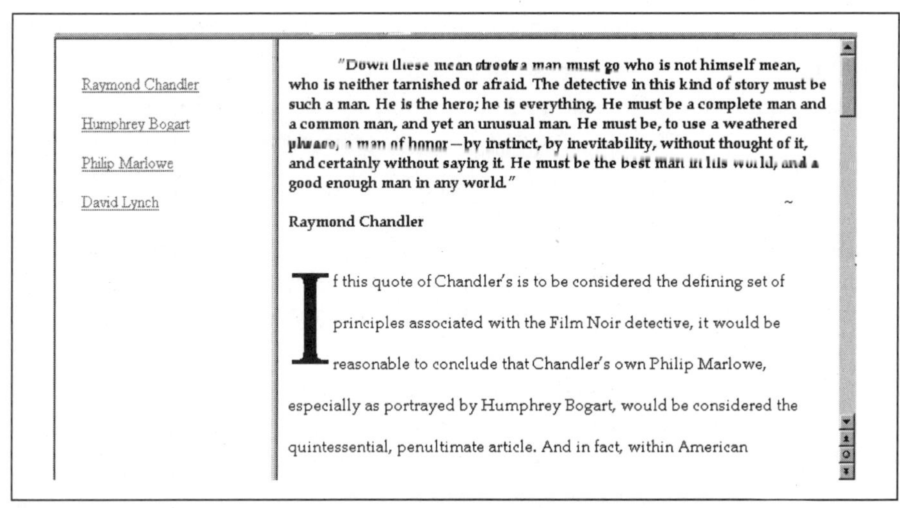

Figure 8-21: Using an interactive table of contents

When a document with a simple table of contents (not in a frame) is saved as HTML, the table of contents is converted to a series of hyperlinks right within the document page instead of in a frame.

TIP # 100

Updating a Table of Contents

If you add or format headings in a document after creating a Table of Contents frame, select the entire Table of Contents frame and press F9 to update it.

Using Other Frames

The Format → Frames → New Frames page switches Word to Web Layout view, opens the Frames toolbar, and adds a number of new commands to the Format → Frames submenu that mirror those found on the Frames toolbar. This command does not add a new frame to the document; to do that, choose one of the New Frame commands (Left, Right, Above, or Below) from the toolbar or menu.

When the first frame is added to a document, Word does several things:

1. First, it turns the document currently displayed into a frame document. If the document has already been saved, it keeps its original name. Otherwise, it is automatically named based on the first line of text in the document and saved in the same folder as the frames page (described next).

2. Next, Word creates a new document to act as a *frames page,* a sort of holder document for all of the frames. All frame documents are embedded into this frames page. When you save the document, Word opens the Save As dialog for naming the frames page. This is true even when adding frames to a document

that has been saved. Remember that the frames page is a new document; the original is now a frame document.

3. Any frames added from now on are automatically saved and named based on the first line of text in the document.

Using Word, it's easy to rename these files to something more suitable, but do not simply rename them in Windows Explorer, as this will break the links between the frames page and the frames. Also, when moving a frames page, be sure to move all the related frames pages with it. Otherwise, the hyperlinks may not work and any graphical elements, such as backgrounds and clip art, won't appear in the frames that are moved.

Each frame on a page is a completely separate document and can be treated as such. Each frame can be displayed in a different view, formatted with a different theme, or can even be based on a different template. Resize frames by dragging the frame borders. To adjust the properties for any frame, right-click anywhere in the frame and choose Properties from the context menu. The Frame Properties dialog has two tabs: Frame and Borders.

The Frame tab

Use the Frame tab (Figure 8-22) to set general options relating to the current frame.

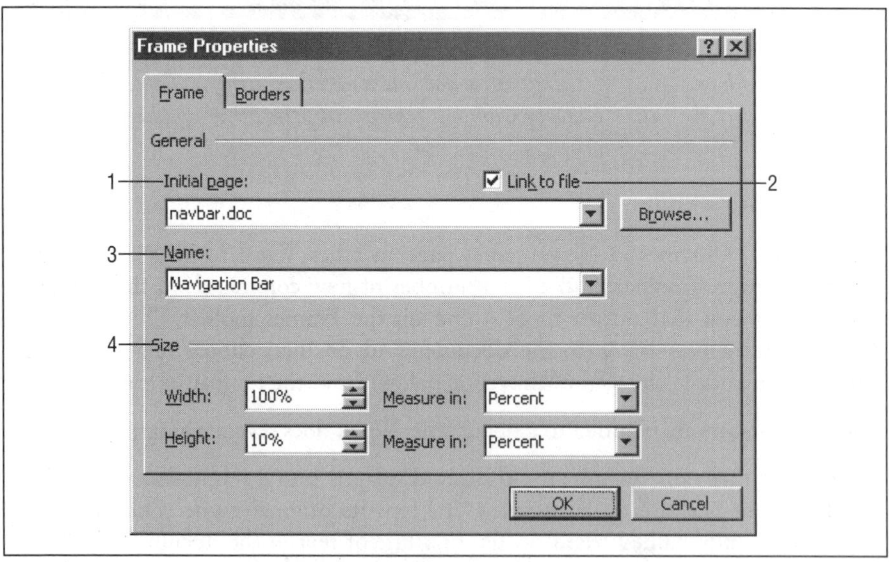

Figure 8-22: Adjusting a frame's properties

1. *Initial page.* This is the page that the frame should display whenever the frames page is opened. Click Browse to select a new document. To rename a document, first rename it in Windows Explorer and then set the new filename as the initial page here.

2. *Link to file*. With this option enabled, changes made to the document specified as the initial page are automatically updated in the frame.
3. *Name*. This is the name of the frame itself. When viewed as a separate page, the name is displayed on the title bar of the browser. When viewed as part of a frameset, only the name of the frames page is displayed.
4. *Size*. Specify the height and width of the frame as a fixed measurement (like inches) or as a percentage of the screen.

The Borders tab

Use the Borders tab (Figure 8-23) to set options that control the entire frames page and border settings for the current frame.

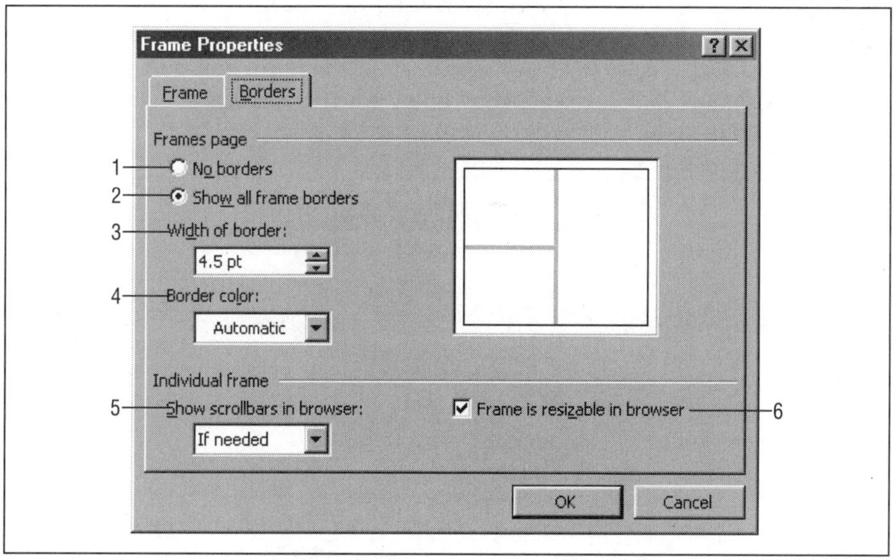

Figure 8-23: Setting options for a frames page

1. *No borders*. Select this option to makes all borders on a frames page invisible. This can provide a more streamlined look to a web page, but it looks a bit strange if any of the frames have scrollbars.
2. *Show all frame borders*. Select this option to make the borders on a frames page visible. There is no way to make some borders visible and others invisible.
3. *Width of border*. Select a width for the borders between .5 and 1584 points (pixels). I usually find the default setting (4.5) appropriate when I want borders shown.
4. *Border color*. Choose a color for the border from a palette.

5. *Show scrollbars in browser.* This setting applies only to the current frame. Options include showing scrollbars only when needed (if the page is longer than can be shown in the frame), always, and never. If you choose never and the page does not fit entirely into a frame, the excess content is not accessible.

6. *Frame is resizable in browser.* When enabled, users can drag the border in their browser window to resize the frame.

Format → AutoFormat

The AutoFormat command scans the document and suggests formatting changes that you accept or reject. It applies automatic heading styles to text that is placed in typical heading positions or that uses typical heading formats; it turns any series of paragraphs or items preceded by an asterisk (*) or a dash (-) to a bulleted list; it changes straight quotes to smart quotes, and so on. Issuing the command opens the AutoFormat dialog (Figure 8-24). Choose to apply the AutoFormat all at once or to review each change as it is made. Also choose whether settings should be applied based on templates for a general document, letter, or email.

Figure 8-24: AutoFormatting a document

To see each intended change before it is made, choose the "AutoFormat and review each change" option. Each intended change is highlighted in the document, and you choose whether or not to apply it (Figure 8-25).

To customize how AutoFormat is applied, click the Options button to display the AutoFormat tab in the AutoCorrect dialog box. This dialog is covered in detail in Chapter 9, *Tools*.

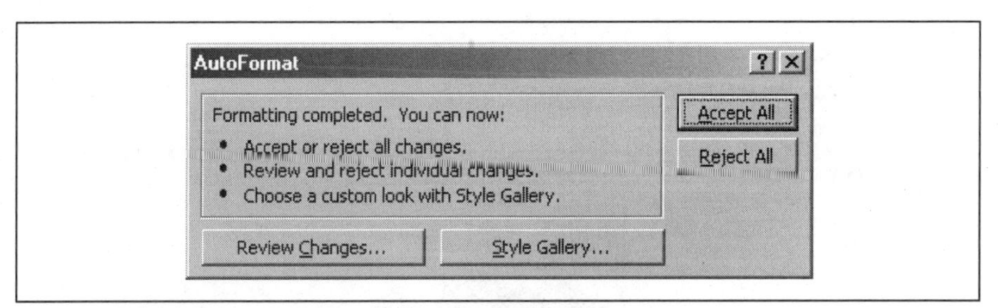

Figure 8-25: Reviewing changes before they're applied

Format → Style

Styles are collections of formats, and come in two flavors:

Character styles
: These contain formatting that is applied only to selected characters within a paragraph. Characters within a paragraph can have their own style even if a paragraph style is applied to the paragraph as a whole. Character styles can include only character formatting.

Paragraph styles
: These contain formatting that is applied to an entire paragraph. Paragraph styles can include paragraph formatting (such as tabs, line spacing, and indenting), character formatting (such as font, size, and color), and formatting that applies to either characters or paragraphs (such as borders or languages).

This section is intended to provide a description of the tools used in managing styles. For a look at how styles fit into Word's big picture, check out Chapter 2. For a look at creating styles as part of a template, see Chapter 14, Creating a Template.

The easiest way to view styles in Word is using the Style drop-down list on the Formatting toolbar. It shows whether a style is character or paragraph and gives some basic formatting information about the style, such as font color and size.

TIP # 101

View Paragraph Styles in a Document's Style Area

Set the Tools → Options → View → Style Area Width option to anything greater than zero to display a pane to the left of the document that shows the names of paragraph styles used. Find out more about this tool in Chapter 3, Customizing Word.

Word also offers a Style dialog box (Figure 8-26) that provides a comprehensive way to look at styles. Open the dialog using Format → Style. Choose any paragraph or character style from the list to see a preview of both paragraph and character settings, and a description of the formatting applied. This dialog also provides buttons for creating a new style from scratch or modifying an existing style.

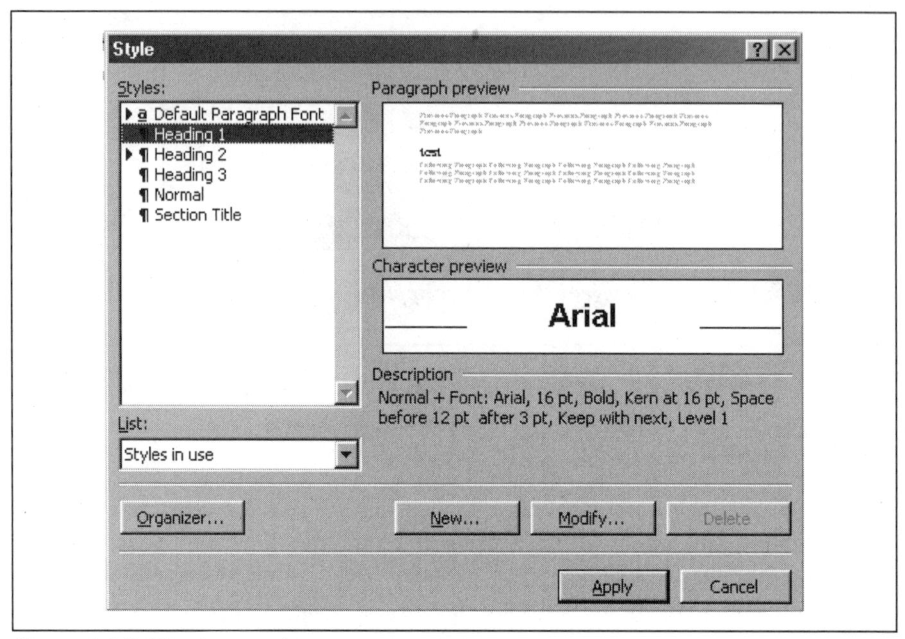

Figure 8-26: Viewing a style

TIP # 102

Print a List of Styles

To print a list of the styles in a document, choose File → Print → Print What → Styles.

Creating and Modifying Styles

Create a new style or modify an existing style from the Style dialog box (Figure 8-26) using the New and Modify buttons. The New Style and Modify Style (Figure 8-27) dialogs are essentially the same, except that the Modify Style box does not let you change the style type (character or paragraph).

The following list describes the options for creating and modifying styles:

1. *Based on*. The original style that a new style is based on becomes the beginning of a potential chain of formatting changes. Suppose, for example, that your style is based on Normal. If you change anything about the Normal style later on, that change will apply to your new style as well. If you build a third style based on your own style (which was based on Normal), any change to Normal will affect that style, too. This can be powerful if set up properly, enabling you to change several styles by merely editing the original style on which they're all ultimately based. It can also be a problem, if you aren't aware of your style's ancestry: unexpected changes can occur if you edit a style and don't remember or didn't bother to control which other styles it is based on.

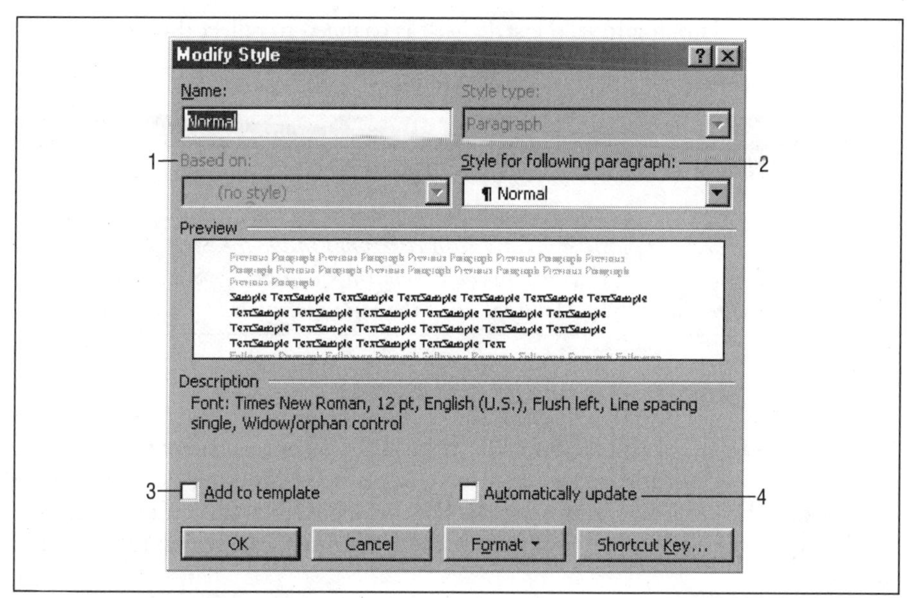

Figure 8-27: Modifying a style

2. *Style for following paragraph.* Every time you hit the Enter key, Word starts a new paragraph. If you are in the middle of one paragraph and hit Enter, both the old and new paragraphs are formatted using the old paragraph's style.

   If you are at the end of a paragraph (i.e., your insertion point is directly in front of the paragraph mark for that paragraph), Word looks up the entry defined in the Style for following paragraph option to determine what the style for the new paragraph will be.

   This powerful feature lets you define styles applied while you type a document without having to define them manually. For example, you might find that you always follow a style you use for numbering a figure with a style you use for creating a figure caption. You can use this feature to let Word automatically select the caption style as soon as you finish the figure number and hit Enter.

   There is one thing to be aware of when using the "Style for following paragraph" feature. If the option is set to the same style as the previous paragraph, Word retains all of the manual formatting you may have applied while typing the previous paragraph. If it is a different style, Word does not retain manual formatting.

3. *Add to template.* Add the style to the current document template.

4. *Automatically update.* When this box is checked, Word automatically updates the style whenever you manually change any paragraph within your document that uses the style. Read that again. This means that if you are typing along using your newly formatted double-indented paragraph style and decide to

apply double-spacing to it, the style itself is changed to reflect this and all paragraphs (old and new) created using that style are also double-spaced.

TIP # 103

Create a New Style Based on Existing Formatting

You can quickly create a new paragraph style based on formatting applied in your document. Select the paragraph, and then click once inside the Style drop-down list (not the arrow, the actual word) on the Formatting toolbar. Type a name and click Enter to create a new style. Modify it using the Style dialog box.

Using the Organizer

Use Word's Organizer (Figure 8-28) to make styles in one document or template available in other documents or templates. Access it by choosing Format → Style and clicking the Organizer button on the Style dialog. Other tabs on the Organizer window work the same as the Styles tab for copying AutoText entries, toolbars, and macros.

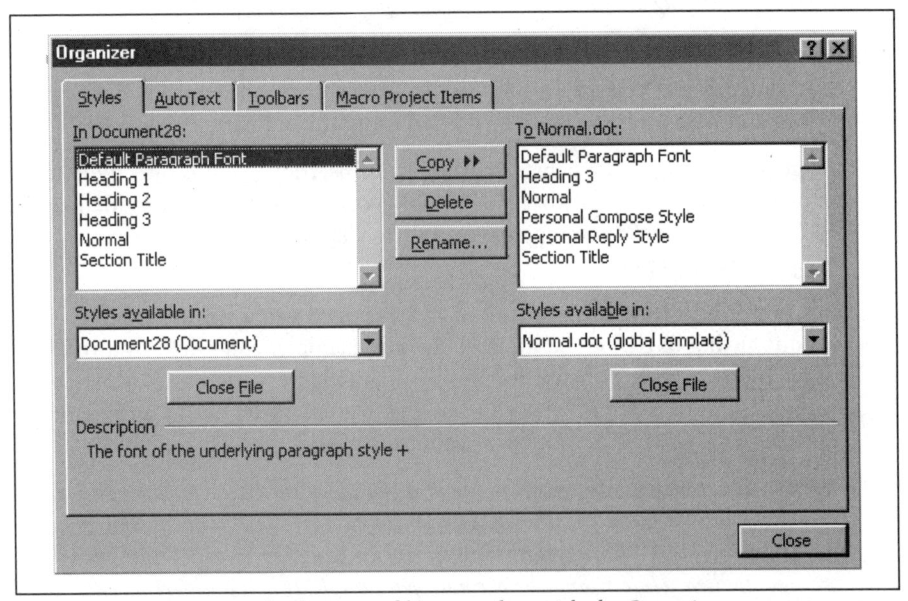

Figure 8-28: Copying styles from one file to another with the Organizer

The Organizer lists the styles from one document on the left and from another document on the right. By default, the current document is loaded on the left and *normal.dot* is loaded on the right. Use the Close File button on either side to remove that file from the Organizer window (note that this action does *not* actually close the file if it is open in Word). The Close File button turns into an Open File button. Click it to browse for a different file and load it into the Organizer. The drop-down lists on either side show all files that are currently open in Word. Switch between files with the list or click the Close button to close a file. The Close button turns into an Open button that, when clicked, brings up a dialog to browse for a different file.

Once the two files you want to copy items between are displayed in the Organizer window, select an item from one file and click the Copy button to copy it to the other file (arrows on the Copy button change direction to indicate which way the file will be copied). Select an item and click Delete to remove it from the file altogether.

WARNING

If you use the Organizer to copy a style from one file to another file that has a style with the same name, the style in the target document is replaced with no warning from Word. Deleting and renaming items also does not offer any warning. If you make a mistake, there is no way to undo it.

Format → Object

Object is a broad term that can include drawn shapes, clip art, text boxes, and even documents from other applications. The Format → Object menu command is only available when an object is selected in a Word document, and the command itself sometimes changes to reflect the object. For example, select a text box and the Format → Object command becomes Format → Text Box.

The command opens a dialog box with options for how the object appears on the page and how it relates to nearby text. This dialog can also be opened by right-clicking any object and choosing Format Object from the context menu. The dialog has the same tabs no matter what type of object is being formatted: Colors and Lines, Size, Layout, Picture, Text Box, and Web. Note however, that some tabs are unavailable for certain object types.

The Colors and Lines Tab

The Colors and Lines tab (Figure 8-29) is available for all objects, though many of the settings on the tab are only available for some objects.

The following list describes the Colors and Lines tab settings:

1. *Color (Fill)*. Change the fill color of the object. This works well for shapes like circles and WordArt, or to add color behind certain types of embedded objects like Excel graphs. The command is not available for drawn lines.

2. *Semitransparent*. This option makes the selected fill color partially transparent so that items on the layer behind the object show through. It is unavailable if

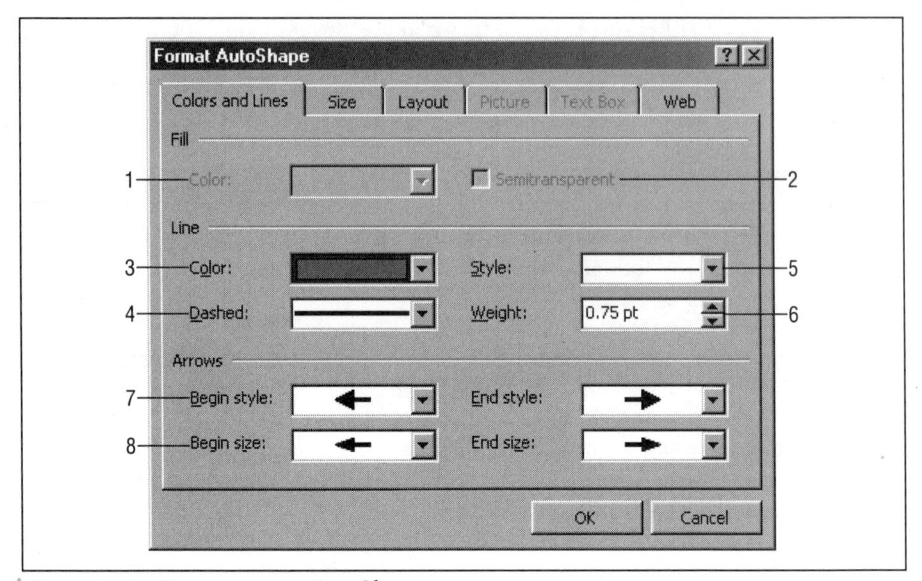

Figure 8-29: Formatting an AutoShape

the selected object contains a gradient, texture, pattern, or picture fill effect. It is also unavailable for drawn lines.

3. *Color (Line)*. Change the color for the outline of an object. This command is only available for text boxes and AutoShapes.
4. *Dashed*. Choose from several styles of dashed lines for the outline of an object. This command is also only available for text boxes and AutoShapes.
5. *Style*. Choose a preset line thickness or from a number of double-line styles. This command is only available for text boxes and AutoShapes.
6. *Weight*. Choose a specific thickness for a line. Choose preset line weights up to a 6-point thickness using the Style option. Use the Weight option for thicker lines or for finer control. This command is only available for text boxes and AutoShapes.
7. *Begin and End style*. These options are only available for lines drawn with AutoShape and specify the type of arrowhead used.
8. *Begin and End size*. These options are available only if a beginning or end style is chosen and specify the arrowhead size to use.

The Size Tab

The Size tab (Figure 8-30) is available for all object types, though some of the settings on the tab are not available for some objects.

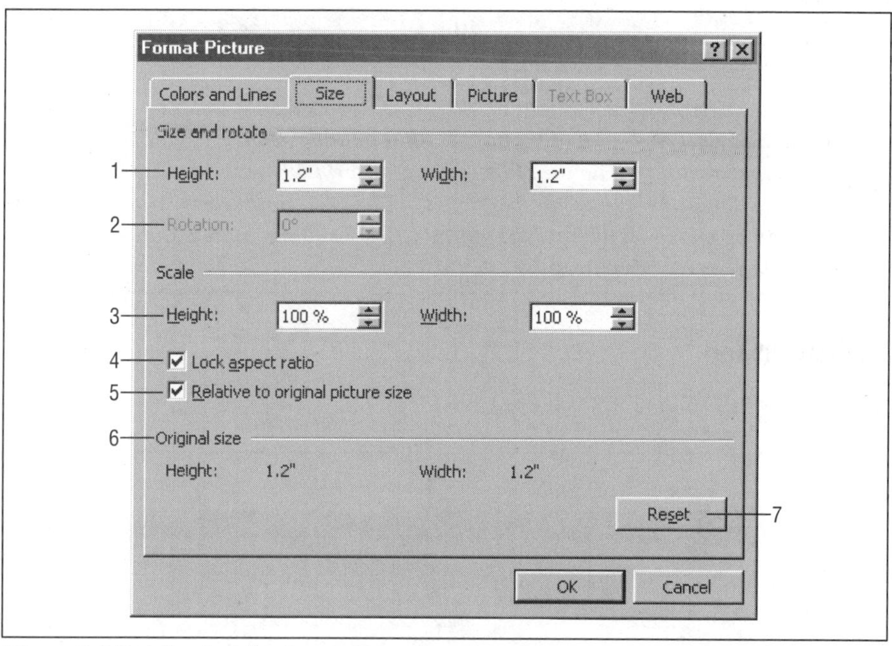

Figure 8-30: Adjusting the size and rotation of an object

1. *Height and Width (Size).* Adjust the height and width of the object in inches. Spinner controls adjust by tenths of an inch and you can enter specific values directly in the fields.
2. *Rotation.* Enter an setting from 0 to 359 degrees to rotate the object clockwise. Height and weight settings are always calculated for an unrotated object.
3. *Height and Width (Scale).* Adjust the height and width of the object as a percentage of its original size. Spinner controls adjust by one percent and you can enter specific values in fractions of a percent. The Scale and Size settings work together. Changing the scale of an object changes the values in the size fields and vice versa.
4. *Lock aspect ratio.* When this option is enabled, the original height to width ratio of an object is maintained. Adjusting either the height or width automatically adjusts the other value as well.
5. *Relative to original picture size.* This option is only available for picture objects. When enabled, this option causes the scale to be presented relative to the original size of the picture. When disabled, the scale is presented relative to the current size of the picture.
6. *Original size.* This option is only available for picture objects. This area displays the original size of a picture.
7. *Reset.* This option is only available for picture objects. Click this button to make the current size of the picture the original size.

TIP # 104

Size Several Objects at Once

To move or resize several objects at once, click the Drawing toolbar's Select Objects button and then click each of the objects while holding down the Shift key. When all objects are selected, release the Shift key and perform whatever moving or resizing is required. Once the objects are positioned and sized, group them so that no single item can be moved away from the others. Click the Draw button and choose Group while the items to be grouped are selected.

The Layout Tab

The Layout Tab (Figure 8-31) is available for all object types.

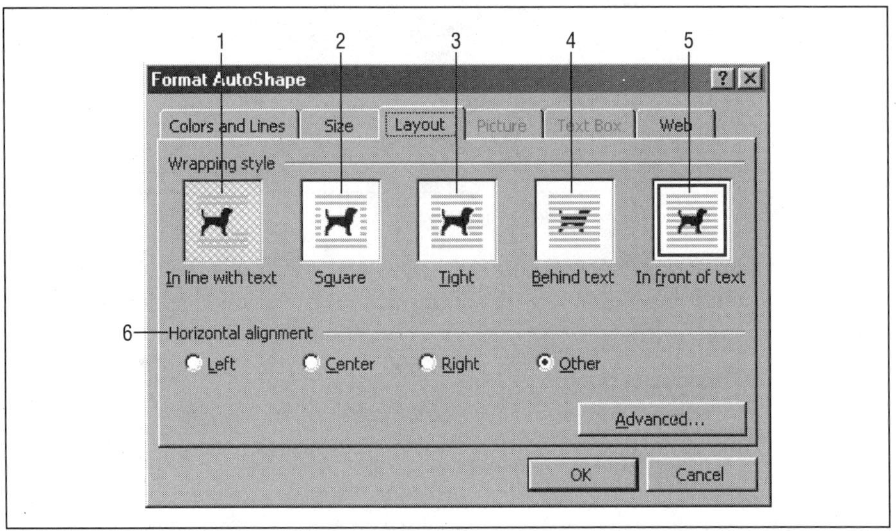

Figure 8-31: Using the Layout tab to control how an object interacts with surrounding text

1. *In line with text.* This text wrapping option places the object in the main text layer at the insertion point in a line of text. This makes the object stand by itself, with text above and below it. This option is not available for AutoShapes and text boxes. For details on the different layers Word uses, see Chapter 2.
2. *Square.* Also a text wrapping option, this causes surrounding text to create a square boundary around any object.
3. *Tight.* Another text wrapping option, this causes the surrounding text to wrap close to the object itself instead of to the square boundary.
4. *Behind text.* This option turns off text wrapping for the object and places the object on the back drawing layer behind the text layer.

5. *In front of text.* This option turns off text wrapping for the object and turns it into a floating object, placing it on the front drawing layer. The object appears in front of anything in the main text layer.

6. *Horizontal alignment.* These options are available for all wrapping styles except for the "In line with text" style. Choose left, center, or right to align the object horizontally within a document in much the same way text alignment works. The Other option applies any options specified using the Advanced button, described below.

The Layout tab provides basic text wrapping and alignment options. For more detailed control over the layout of an object, click the Advanced button to open the Advanced Layout dialog. This dialog consists of two tabs: Picture Position and Text Wrapping.

The Picture Position tab

The Picture Position tab (Figure 8-32) is used to control the exact placement of an object in a document. It provides much finer control than the simple alignment settings on the Layout tab of Format → Object.

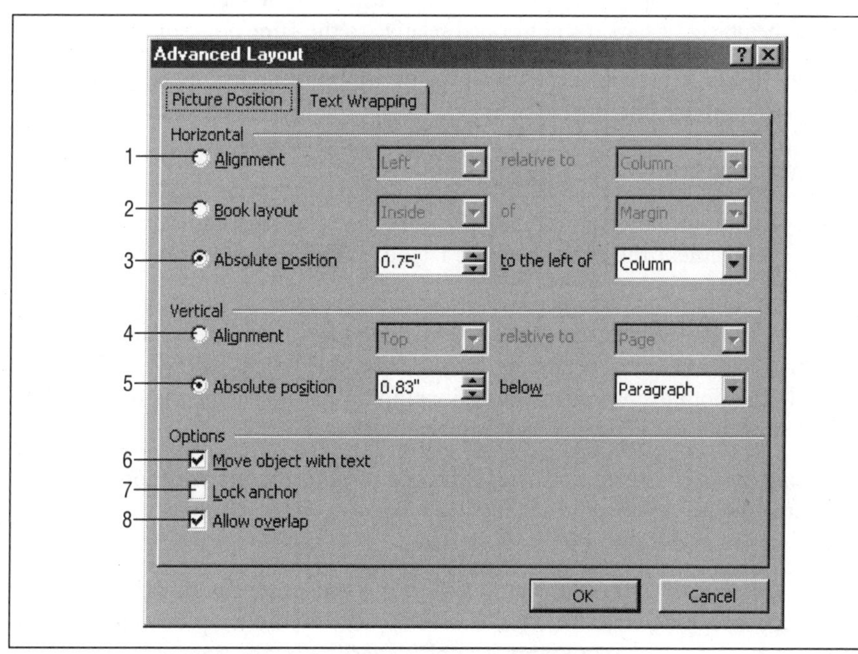

Figure 8-32: Setting advanced position options for an object

1. *Alignment (Horizontal).* This option is used to align an object horizontally relative to a specific element in a document. Objects can be left, right, or center aligned relative to a column, page, margin, or character.

2. *Book layout.* This option aligns an object with the inside or outside margin or the inside or outside of the page itself. For example, if the object appears on an odd page number in the document, aligning it to the inside of the margin aligns the object on the left, inside the margin of the page.
3. *Absolute position (Horizontal).* This option aligns the object a precise distance in inches from a specified element. The left edge of an object is aligned the specified distance from the left edge of a page or column, the left margin, or a character.
4. *Alignment (Vertical).* This option is used to align an object vertically relative to a specific element in a document. Objects can be top, bottom, inside, or center aligned relative to a page, margin, or line.
5. *Absolute position (Vertical).* This option aligns the object vertically using the specified distance between the top edge of the object and the page, margin, paragraph, or line.
6. *Move object with text.* This option causes the selected object to move along with the paragraph the object is anchored to.
7. *Lock anchor.* This option keeps the object's anchor in the same place. When you move the object, it remains positioned relative to the same point on the page.
8. *Allow overlap.* If two objects have the same wrapping style applied, this option allows them to overlap one another.

The Text Wrapping tab

The Text Wrapping tab (Figure 8-33) provides the following additional wrapping options to supplement the options on the Layout tab of Format → Object:

1. *Through.* This is similar to the tight wrapping option, but wraps inside any parts of the object that are open. After applying this style, open the Picture toolbar, click the Text Wrapping button, and then click Edit Wrap Points to display the dotted line indicating the wrapping perimeter for the object. Drag the line or the sizing handles to adjust the perimeter.
2. *Top and bottom.* This option wraps the text around the top and bottom of the objects, but not to the sides. This is similar to placing an object in line with text, but forces the object onto its own line.
3. *Wrap text.* These options are only available when using the Square, Tight, or Through wrapping styles. Click the sides the text should wrap on. The "Largest only" option causes text to wrap around either the left or right side, whichever is widest.
4. *Distance from text.* Control the distance between the text and the various edges of the object. The top and bottom distances cannot be set when using Tight or Through wrapping styles. The left and right distances cannot be set when using

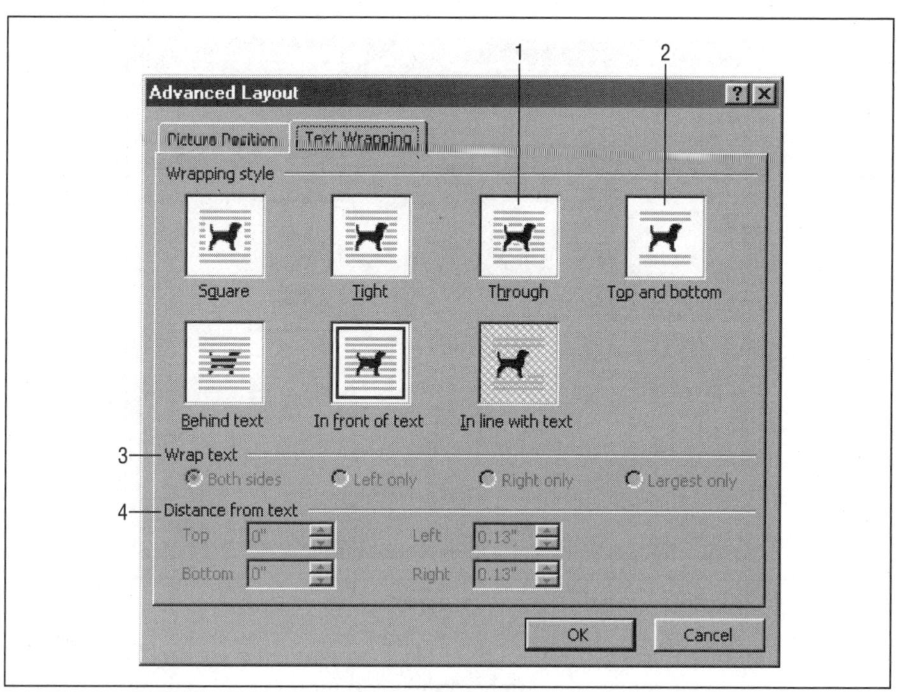

Figure 8-33: Setting advanced text wrapping options

the Top and Bottom style. None of these options is available when using the Behind Text, In front of text, or In line with text styles.

The Picture Tab

The Picture tab (Figure 8-34) is available only when formatting pictures or objects inserted from other applications. The Picture tab settings are:

1. *Crop from*. Crop a picture (remove part of it) at any of its four edges by entering a value in inches in the appropriate field. Entering 1 inch in the Left field, for example, removes 1" from the left side of the picture. Enter a negative number to add whitespace to the outside of the picture.

2. *Color*. The Automatic setting presents a picture in its original color format. Choose Grayscale to convert the picture to use 256 shades of gray. This setting is what you'd typically think of as a black-and-white picture. Choose Black and White to convert the color to pure black and white—useful for line art. Choose Watermark to convert the picture to use preset brightness and contrast settings that work well for watermarks.

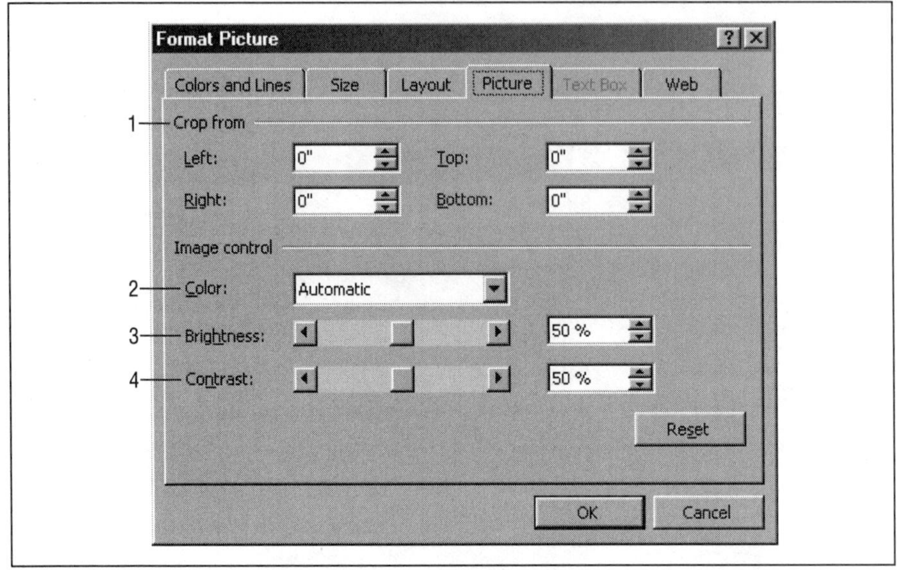

Figure 8-34: Adjusting settings for a picture object

3. *Brightness*. Brightness is the amount of black or white in a picture. Slide the dial or enter an exact percentage. Higher values add more white, making the picture brighter. Lower values darken the picture.

4. *Contrast*. Contrast is the saturation or intensity of color in a picture. Higher values make the color more intense. Lower values make the color more gray.

The Text Box Tab

This tab provides controls for setting the internal margin of a text box, or the distance from each edge to the text inside the box. Other options are provided for specifying a callout leader (if the text box is to be used as a callout linked to a figure) and for converting the text box to a frame. Text boxes exist only on Word's front or back drawing layers. Frames exist in the main text layer. For more information on Word's layers, see Chapter 2.

The Web Tab

The Web tab is available for all objects and is used to enter alternate text that is displayed in a web browser when the object itself is not available (for example, if a file becomes orphaned from its link). If the document is destined for the Web, insert some descriptive or instructional text in the Web tab's Alternative Text box. This text can be useful in the event that the object won't load in the user's browser or takes a long time to load—the text provides some indication of what the image should be.

Chapter 9

Tools

The Tools menu contains commands that customize the Word interface, automate tasks, proof a document's spelling and grammar, and collaborate with other Word users in several ways. This chapter examines commands in the first and third command groups of the menu—commands that concern spelling and language, AutoCorrect, AutoSummarize, Mail Merge, envelopes, and letters.

Commands in the second group, those that deal with collaboration, are detailed in Chapter 13, *Collaborating*. The Tools → Macro submenu is covered in Chapter 18, *Working with VBA*. The Tools → Customize and Tools → Options commands are covered in Chapter 3, *Customizing Word*.

Tools → Spelling and Grammar

The Tools → Spelling and Grammar command (Figure 9-1) shows errors in context along with suggested corrections. It presents choices for handling an error, including ways to show Word that the error isn't actually an error.

TIP # 105

Use Context Menus to Correct Spelling and Grammar Errors

Right-click any errors in the document to open a context menu with correction suggestions. Text underlined with squiggly red or green lines indicates spelling or grammar errors, respectively. Errors are only shown in the document if both the Tools → Options → Spelling and Grammar → "Check Spelling as you type" and "Check Grammar as you type" options are enabled (the default option).

The following list describes the options for spelling and grammar checking:

1. *Not in Dictionary*. The name of this window changes based on the error found. "Not in Dictionary" is displayed for spelling errors. For grammatical errors, Word displays the type of error found, such as "Passive voice" or "Repeated space." Spelling errors are indicated in red text, grammatical errors in green. Use the buttons on the right to act on the error. Type a change directly in this window and click the Change button to apply custom corrections.

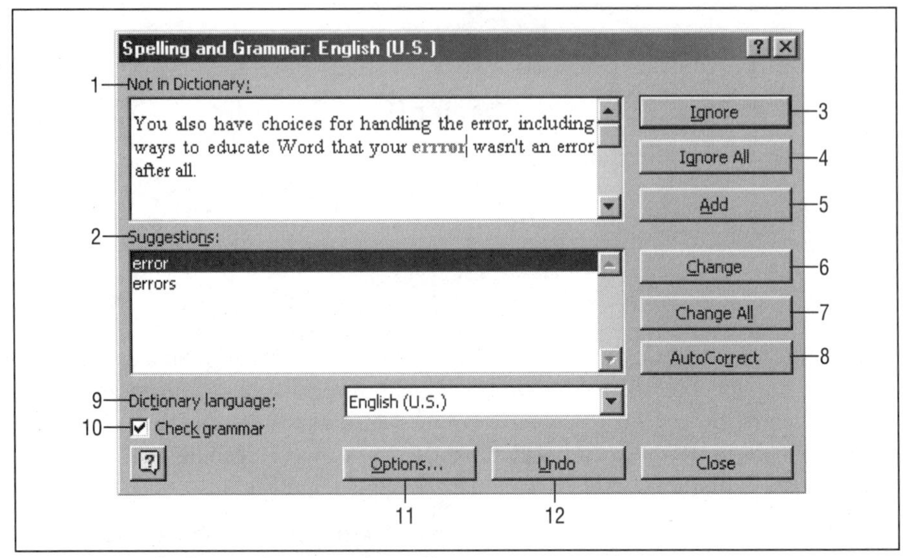

Figure 9-1: Checking a document for spelling errors

2. *Suggestions*. This window holds Word's suggested corrections for the error. For spelling errors, alternate spellings from Word's dictionary and any custom dictionaries are shown. For grammatical errors, Word only sometimes displays suggestions. Select a suggestion and click the Change or Change All buttons (see #6 and 7 in this list).

3. *Ignore*. Use this button to ignore the current instance of the error. The next time the document is checked, the error is displayed again.

4. *Ignore All (Ignore Rule)*. This command becomes Ignore Rule when a grammatical error is displayed. With spelling errors, this button causes Word to ignore *all* instances of the error in the document. The next time the document is checked, the errors are displayed again.

   The Ignore Rule button causes Word to ignore the grammatical rule (such as passive voice) throughout the document. Ignored rules are ignored in all *future* checks of the document, as well. Use Tools → Options → Spelling and Grammar → Recheck Document to reset the rules for a document so that ignored rules are checked again.

5. *Add (Next Sentence)*. For spelling errors, the Add button adds the spelling of the word displayed in the Not in Dictionary window to a custom dictionary. This dictionary is named *custom.dic* by default. The custom dictionary is used in combination with Word's main dictionary when spell-checking. Use the Tools → Options → Spelling and Grammar tab to modify the custom dictionary or to add other dictionaries, as detailed in Chapter 3.

   When a grammatical error is displayed, this command is replaced with the Next sentence command, which causes Word to skip the current error and resume checking with the next sentence. Use this button or the Change button to enter a custom correction in the error window.

6. *Change*. Select an correction in the Suggestions window or enter a custom correction in the error window and then click the Change button to effect that change.
7. *Change All*. Available only with spelling errors, this button changes all instances of the error in the document to the selected suggestion.
8. *AutoCorrect*. This button adds the misspelled word and the selected correction to the AutoCorrect list. The next time the same error is encountered in a document, Word corrects the error as soon as it's typed in the document. Read more about Word's AutoCorrect feature later in this chapter.
9. *Dictionary language*. Select a dictionary from any installed language.
10. *Check grammar*. This option is selected by default. Disable it to have Word check only spelling errors. This option remains disabled until you enable it again.
11. *Options*. This opens the Spelling and Grammar tab of Tools → Options, which is covered in detail in Chapter 3.
12. *Undo*. Reverse the last correction made.

TIP # 106

Use the Status Bar to Find Spelling Errors Quickly

If Word is set to check spelling as you type, a small book icon appears on the status bar, bearing either a red checkmark or a red X. The red X indicates that there are spelling errors in a document. Double-click the icon to jump to the first error after the insertion point. Word highlights the error and opens the context menu for you.

Tools → Language

Tools → Language is a submenu with commands for selecting the default language used in Word, opening a thesaurus, and controlling hyphenation. These commands are covered in the next few sections.

TIP # 107

Add a Dictionary Command to the Language Menu

To make the Tools → Language submenu complete, add the Dictionary command to it. Choose Tools → Customize → Commands and select the Tools category. Drag the Dictionary command to the Tools → Language submenu. Use this command to open and edit custom dictionaries defined using Tools → Options → Spelling&Grammar → Custom Dictionary.

Tools → Language → Set Language

A default language is selected when Word is installed, along with dictionaries and grammar-checking rules for that language. To change to a different language for selected text within a document, choose Tools → Language → Set Language (Figure 9-2).

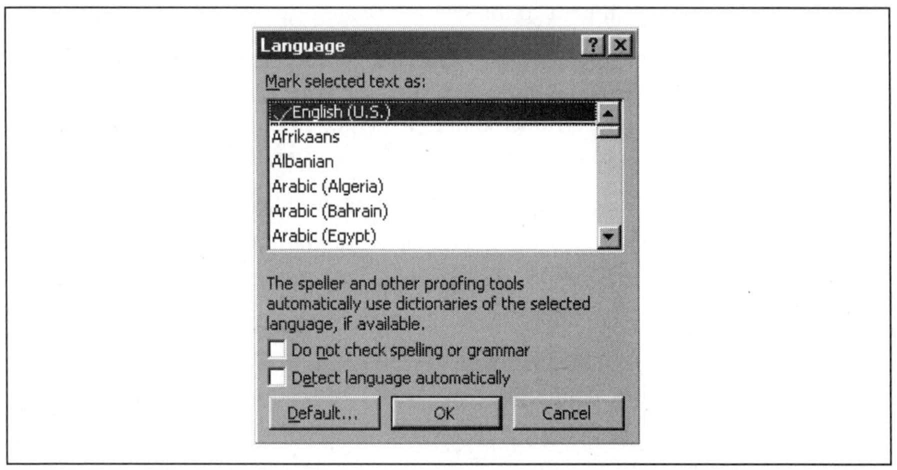

Figure 9-2: Picking a language and its accompanying formats for selected text

A checkmark next to a language in the "Mark selected text as" list means that a dictionary and set of grammatical rules are installed for that language. If a checkmark does not appear, only the document formatting for that language is installed. This feature makes it possible to check the spelling of a foreign word or phrase used in a document crafted in your native language. For example, to use a French figure of speech such as *c'est la vie* (such is life) in an English-based document, select the phrase and choose French as the language for that selected text. "C'est" will be underlined in red until you make this choice.

If you don't want Word to check spelling and grammar in the new language, check the "Do not check spelling or grammar" option in the Language dialog box.

Turn on the "Detect language automatically" option to have Word try to determine the language being typed in based on content. This option can produce undesired results if you tend to use foreign words or phrases mingled with a primary language—using phrases like *de rigueur* in a document otherwise typed in English, for example.

Click the Default button to make a different language the default language for all new documents. A prompt appears, confirming whether to update *normal.dot* with this change. From that point on, the selected language will be the default.

Depending on the country in which you purchased Office 2000, your version may only support a small group of languages for spelling and grammar checking. For example, the U.S. version only supports English, French, and Spanish (and several country-based variations on each one). Obtain additional language dictionaries by purchasing the Microsoft Office 2000 Proofing Tools Kit.

Tools → Language → Thesaurus

Word provides its own thesaurus for looking up alternatives to commonly used words. Choose Tools → Language → Thesaurus (or press Shift-F7) to open the Thesaurus dialog box (Figure 9-3).

Word's Thesaurus is not installed by default. If you did not make it part of the installation, be ready with the CD the first time you use the command.

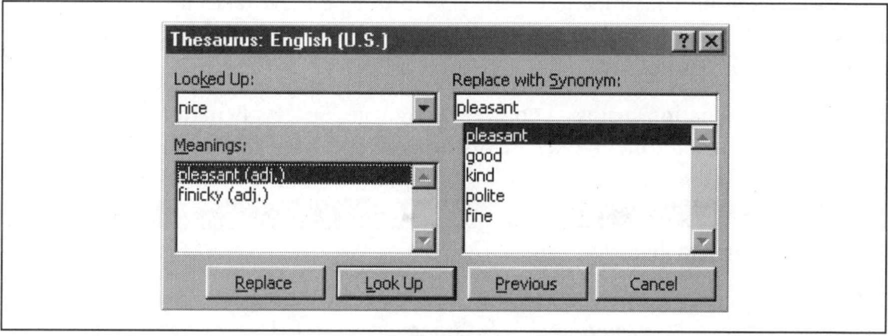

Figure 9-3: Finding an alternative word or phrase in Word's thesaurus

If the selected word can be used in different parts of speech (such as "grace," which can be a noun or a verb), choose the appropriate part of speech from those displayed in the Meanings list box and view the matching synonyms in the Replace with Synonym box. To replace the selected word with one of the synonyms listed, select it, and click the Replace button. A list of antonyms is often displayed at the bottom of the synonyms list.

If the selection is misspelled (or there's just no match for it in Word's dictionary), the Meanings box in the Thesaurus dialog changes to an Alphabetical List box and displays a list of alternative words. These are generated by Word's Spell Checker.

To find the meaning for a word that's not already in the document, open the Thesaurus and type the word in the Replace with Synonym text box. Click the Look Up button to see a list of synonyms for the word.

TIP # 108

Access Thesaurus Suggestions on a Context Menu

Right-click any word in a document and choose Synonyms from the context menu to view a list of synonyms for the selected word. However, if Track Changes is turned on and the word is in an edited portion of the document, the context menu that appears will not contain the Synonyms command.

Tools → Language → Hyphenation

By default, if the word being typed at the right margin of a document doesn't fit entirely on the line, the whole word is wrapped to the next line. This is normally acceptable, especially in single-column documents with left or full justification.

Word can hyphenate words that don't fit entirely at the end of a line when typing in newspaper columns, using narrow margins or creating a document whose layout calls for strict double justification. This is helpful when text takes up a narrow horizontal space, because moving entire words down a line leaves unattractive whitespace at the end of lines.

Turn on hyphenation using Tools → Language → Hyphenation (Figure 9-4). Enable the "Automatically hyphenate document" option to turn on hyphenation.

TIP # 109

Don't Hyphenate Acronyms

If you type many acronyms (such as ACLU or ASPCA), make sure that the Tools → Language → Hyphenation → "Hyphenate words in CAPS" option is turned off. If it is on, you risk breaking these acronyms at the margin with a hyphen, which can be confusing to the reader.

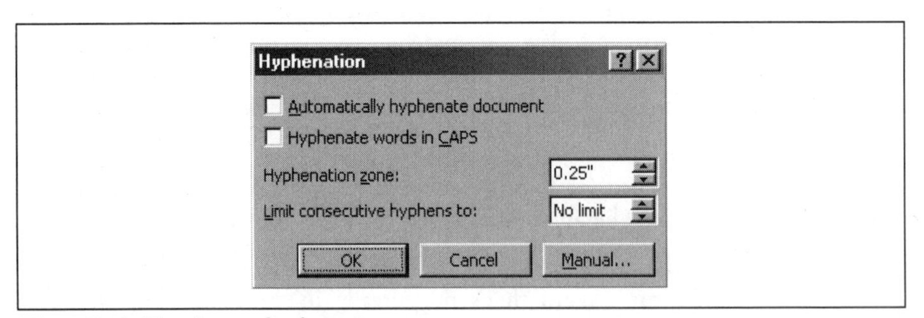

Figure 9-4: Turning on hyphenation

Specify the Hyphenation zone—the space between the text and the right margin that the word must enter and not fit before it is hyphenated. The default setting is

.25 inches. If there is less than .25" between the end of a word and the right margin, the word is hyphenated.

Enter a number into the "Limit consecutive hyphenations to" box to control the number of consecutive lines that can end in a hyphenated word. The default setting is "No limit", but in very narrow columns, this can result in several hyphens in a row, creating a fringed look to the right margin. Setting a limit of one or two is a good idea—you can always increase it if you find that too many words are still being forced down to the next line.

Use the Manual button to hyphenate existing text in a document. Select the text or click at the end of the section you want to hyphenate, and click the Manual button. Each word that is found within the default hyphenation zone is presented in a dialog box (Figure 9-5) and you can choose whether or not to hyphenate each. This is much safer than just letting Word do it all for you.

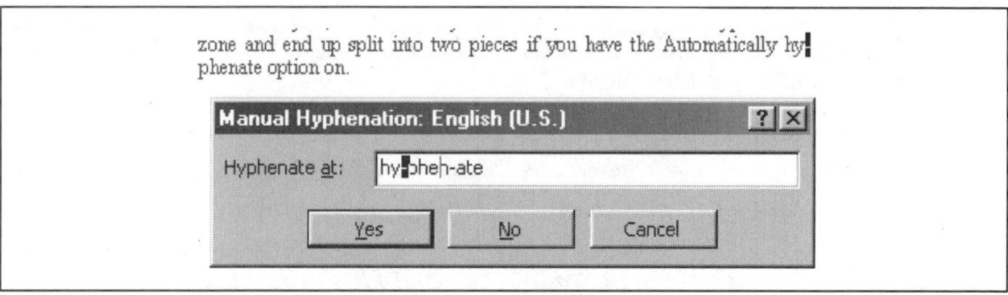

Figure 9-5: Hyphenate your document one word at a time

TIP # 110

Control Hyphens While Typing

Hyphens can be inserted manually in three ways—type a hyphen to separate words not at the right edge of a page (such as "up-to-date"), press Ctrl-hyphen to insert an Optional hyphen (so that the word breaks where indicated should the word get too close to the margin), or press Ctrl-Shift-hyphen to create a non-breaking hyphen (a hyphen that keeps a word or hyphenated phrase from being split at the margin).

Tools → Word Count

The Tools → Word Count command (Figure 9-6) displays statistics for the current document. These statistics are also available using File → Properties → Statistics. To include text in footnotes and endnotes, click the "Include footnotes and endnotes" checkbox. These are covered in Chapter 7, *Insert*. Close the Word Count dialog and open it again to reflect these changes.

Comments inserted with the Insert → Comments command and any header or footer content are not included in the Word Count tally.

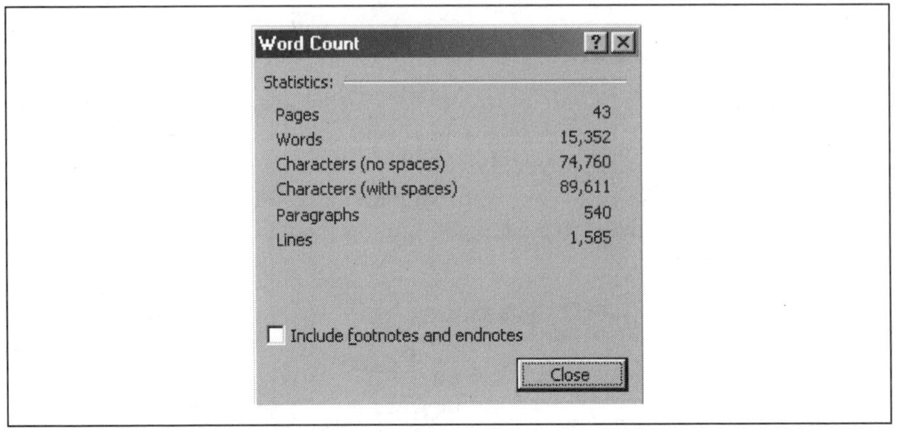

Figure 9-6: Checking statistics for a document

TIP # 111

Check Readability of a Document

To check statistics on writing style in terms of its readability to those of varying educational levels or ages, select the "Show readability statistics" option in the Spelling and Grammar tab (Tools → Options). After running the Spelling and Grammar check, the document's readability rating is generated based on a variety of established scales, such as Flesch Reading Ease and Flesch-Kincaid Reading Level.

Tools → AutoSummarize

Based on a document's content, Word can create a summary of the most significant points and display them in any one of the four following ways:

Highlight key points
: This option adds highlighting to the sentences within a document that Word's AutoSummarize tool deems to be important.

Insert an executive summary or abstract at the top of the document
: Creating an introduction of sorts, this option takes the content that is most important and turns it into a summary at the beginning of a document.

Create a new document and put summary there
: This option's description is self-explanatory. The executive summary/abstract is placed in a separate document (created through the AutoSummarize process).

Hide everything but the summary, without leaving the original document
: This command temporarily hides the parts of a document that are not in the summary. It also displays a toolbar for toggling non-summary parts display on and off and for highlighting the summary parts. Click the close button on the toolbar to return the document to its original state.

Set the length of the summary by entering a "Percent of original number." The default is 25%, meaning that the summary is ignoring roughly 75% of your text.

Use the "Update document statistics" option (on by default) to put the AutoSummarize information in the document's Properties. Keywords are listed and the Document Contents box is filled in with the summary content. Choose File → Properties to see this information.

Overall, I find Word's AutoSummarize pretty weak and would never trust it to summarize an important document. Though more time consuming, creating a summary by hand is much more effective.

Tools → AutoCorrect

AutoCorrect is used almost every time you enter text in a Word document. Character transpositions, forgotten capitalization, extra capitalization, and common misspellings are fixed by AutoCorrect. In addition, Word 2000 now uses suggestions from the spelling checker to correct commonly misspelled words as you type.

The AutoCorrect dialog box contains four tabs used to customize the way Word corrects and reformats document text: AutoCorrect, AutoFormat As You Type, AutoText, and AutoFormat.

The AutoCorrect Tab

The AutoCorrect tab (Figure 9-7) lists actions Word makes automatically as you type. The following list describes the AutoCorrect options:

1. *Correct TWo INitial CApitals.* This option causes Word to change words starting with two capital letters to start with only one capital letter.
2. *Capitalize first letter of sentences.* This option capitalizes the first letter of a sentence. Word usually decides that any string of text ending in a period is a sentence.
3. *Capitalize names of days.* This option automatically capitalizes the first letter in the days of the week (Monday, Tuesday, etc.).
4. *Correct accidental usage of cAPS LOCK key.* With this option, if the Caps Lock key is on and you type in normal title case (first letter capitalized, all others lowercase), Word automatically formats the sentence in normal title case. Word continues to use lowercase even if the Caps Lock key stays on. Press the Shift or Caps Lock key to turn Caps Lock off and then turn Caps Lock on to return it to typing all caps.
5. *Replace text as you type.* This option turns on all of the AutoCorrect entries listed in the table below the option. Word comes with hundreds of AutoCorrect

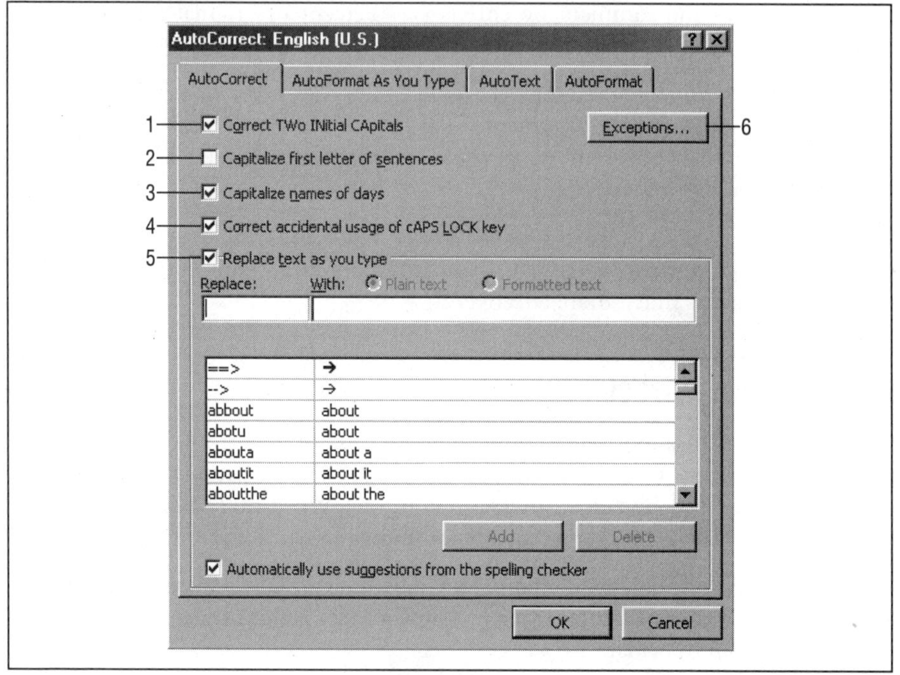

Figure 9-7: Setting AutoCorrect options

entries already installed, offering everything from smiley faces and arrows to the correct way to type and format the term vis-à-vis (with the accent over the a).

To add an AutoCorrect entry to the list, type the misspelled word or abbreviation that should trigger the correction in the Replace text box. If text is selected in the document when the dialog opens, that text is automatically placed in this box. Type the text Word should insert as a correction in the With box. Also choose whether the text should be plain or formatted.

6. *Exceptions*. Use the Exceptions button to choose or enter text that should be ignored by AutoCorrect, such as abbreviations ending in a period (like "acctg.") or words that should have two initial caps. The Exceptions dialog offers a powerful way to adjust your working environment to many annoyances that AutoCorrect causes.

TIP # 112

Use Autocorrect for Quicker Typing

AutoCorrect isn't just for corrections. If you'd rather not spell out a long name, create an abbreviation for it and type that in the Replace box. Then type the phrase or long name that should replace it in the With box.

The AutoFormat As You Type Tab

The first thing most people notice when they start typing in Word is that it does a lot of formatting for them automatically. For example, a list beginning with an asterisk is automatically converted to a standard bulleted list. Use the AutoFormat As You Type tab (Figure 9-8) to change the automatic formatting Word applies.

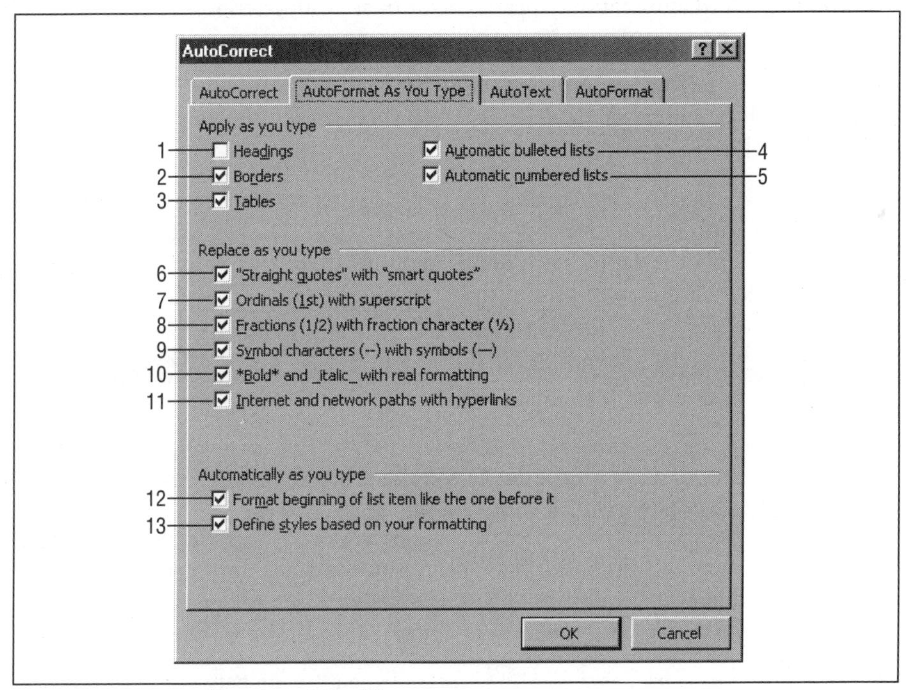

Figure 9-8: Controlling how Word formats items as you type

1. *Headings*. This automatically applies heading styles (Heading1 – Heading9, or any custom style that starts with "heading") to headings typed in Outline view.

2. *Borders*. This applies character and paragraph border style. Type more than three hyphens (-), underscores (_), or equal signs (=) on a line and press enter to have Word apply a thin, thick, or double-line border style, respectively.

3. *Tables*. Create the top border for a table by typing a series of hyphens and plus signs, such as +------+------+------+, on a blank line and pressing Enter. Word creates a table with one row and a column for each pair of plus signs. The number of hyphens used controls the initial width of the columns, but not very precisely. The example shown would have three columns.

4. *Automatic bulleted lists*. Apply bulleted list formatting by typing an asterisk (*), hyphen (-), or right arrow (>) followed by a space or tab at the beginning of a paragraph. For example, typing "* This is the first item in a list" and pressing Enter would begin a bulleted list.

5. *Automatic numbered lists.* Start a numbered list by typing a number or letter followed by a period and a space (or tab) at the beginning of a paragraph.

6. *"Straight quotes" with "smart quotes".* Changes straight quotations (") to smart (curly) quotations that surround the quoted material.

7. *Ordinals (1st) with superscript.* Type a number followed by an ordinal such as *st* or *rd* and Word automatically places the ordinal in superscript, such as in "1st."

8. *Fractions (1/2) with fraction character (½).* Type a fraction using the forward slash (1/2) and Word automatically applies fraction formatting ($^1/_2$). This only works with common single digit fractions such as $^1/4$, $^1/2$, and $^3/4$. For some reason, it does not work with $^1/3$.

9. *Symbol characters (--) with symbols (–).* This option replaces two hyphens with an en dash and three hyphens (---) with an em dash. Have Word replace other common symbol notation with actual symbols (like (tm) with ™) using the AutoCorrect tab discussed previously.

TIP # 113

Em and En Dashes with No Spaces

Typing two or three hyphens does not convert the text into an en or em dash symbol until you enter a space. To put a em dash between two words with no space, type the three hyphens and a space, then backspace once to close the gap.

---

10. **Bold* and _italic_ with real formatting.* Surround any text with asterisks to have word automatically boldface the text. Use underscores to apply underlining.

11. *Internet and network paths with hyperlinks.* Type a file or network path (like *c:\windows\temp*) or a URL (like *http://www.oreilly.com*) and Word creates a hyperlink for that text using the typed path.

12. *Format beginning of list item like the one before it.* Have Word repeat any formatting applied to the beginning of a list item. For example, create the first entry of a list so that the first two words are bold and Word automatically formats other entries in like fashion as you type.

13. *Define styles based on your formatting.* Have Word create new paragraph styles based on the manual formatting applied in documents. This applies only to certain paragraph styles, such as the built-in heading styles. Try this to see how it works:

    a. In a blank document, type a few words of text and hit Enter.

    b. Use F4 to repeat the action a few times.

    c. Apply Heading 1 to the first paragraph

d. Select one of the other paragraphs and apply some character or paragraph formatting manually.

e. Click another paragraph and then click back on the one you just modified.

In the style drop-down menu on the Formatting toolbar, the text is now defined as the Heading 2 style. The new formatting actually replaces the existing Heading 2 style, as Word assumed you were formatting a subheading under the Heading 1 you created.

I don't like this option, as I use styles often and prefer to control them myself rather than let Word do it for me.

TIP # 114

Don't Turn Autoformat Off; Just Undo It

Many users get frustrated with Word's attempts to format their documents for them and simply turn off AutoFormatting (or certain AutoFormat As You Type options). However, AutoFormatting can be a real timesaver. Instead of turning it off, undo AutoFormatting as soon as it happens using Ctrl -Z.

The AutoText Tab

Use the AutoText tab to set up AutoText entries. This tab is covered in Chapter 7.

The AutoFormat Tab

Use the AutoFormat tab to control the settings Word uses in conjunction with the Format → AutoFormat command, which formats an entire document at once. The options on this tab are nearly identical to the options available on the AutoFormat As You Type tab discussed previously. The AutoFormat command itself is covered in Chapter 8, *Format*.

Tools → Track Changes

The Track Changes feature helps track revisions made when multiple people edit a single document. Without Track Changes, it can be difficult to see who made changes and when they were made. Moreover, it can be difficult for one person to take charge of finishing the document and choose which changes to keep and which ones to delete without making many tedious visual comparisons between the original and the edited version.

The commands found in the Track Changes submenu toggle Track Changes on and off, accept or reject changes, and provide tools to compare two versions of the same document. The commands, along with other collaboration tools, are discussed in Chapter 13.

Tools → Merge Documents

Use Tools → Merge Documents to bring together the changes tracked in two separate versions of a document. This command is covered in detail in Chapter 13.

Tools → Protect Document

The most common use of this command is to turn on a fill-in form. If you've added checkboxes, text boxes, drop lists, or other form fields to a document (via the Forms toolbar or the Insert → Field command), it's best to protect the document before those form features are used for entering data. Without protection applied, any user of the form could potentially move, edit, or delete the form's actual fields and structural elements. With protection applied, users can enter data only into the form's fields; they cannot change anything else.

Another reason to use the Tools → Protect Document command is to prevent the editing of a document. This can be an added step taken to keep the original version of a document intact while copies of it are used for editing.

The Protect Document dialog box (Figure 9-9) is used to set the level of protection and to specify the portions of the document to protect.

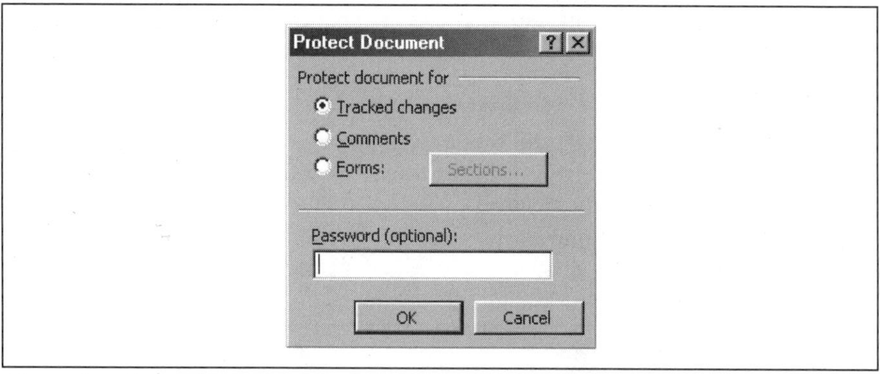

Figure 9-9: Protecting a document

By default, protection places a document in Track Changes mode. Track Changes cannot be turned off while a document is protected with the Tracked changes option. Turn off protection to exit Track Changes. In addition, the Accept or Reject Changes dialog box can be opened while a document is protected, but the Accept, Reject, Accept All, and Reject All buttons are not available. In short, no changes can be resolved until protection is turned off.

Protection can also be used to prevent the insertion of Comments (or the editing of comments that already exist) or to protect Forms only.

The use of the Tools → Protect Document feature shouldn't instill a great sense of security. Any user can turn protection off the same way you turned it on. To really protect a document, employ the password feature in the Protect Document dialog. Be sure to remember the password, however, because if it is lost, there is no way to recover it and get into the document.

Tools → Online Collaboration

Just as Track Changes makes it possible for two or more people to work on a document and mark their contributions to the process, Word 2000's Online Collaboration tools enable two or more people to talk online in real time about a project and to access an Office discussion server. The Online Collaboration submenu contains the Meet Now, Schedule Meeting, and Web Discussion subcommands. These commands are discussed in Chapter 13.

Tools → Mail Merge

Use the Mail Merge command to automatically combine a document's text with names, addresses, and just about any other information to create form letters, mailing labels, and other mass-produced documents. Mail Merge works by reading information from a data source and placing that data into fields in the Word document.

The Tools → Mail Merge command opens the Mail Merge Helper dialog (Figure 9-10), which outlines three of the four steps involved in using Mail Merge.

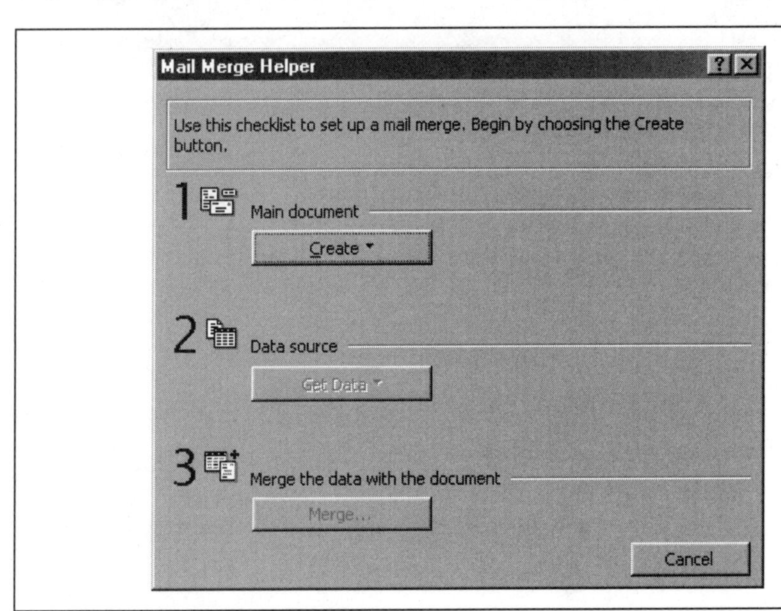

Figure 9-10: Using the Mail Merge Helper

The four steps for using Mail Merge are listed here and described in the following sections:

1. Create a main document.
2. Select a data source.
3. The next step (not present on the dialog) is to use the Mail Merge Toolbar to insert fields into the main document.
4. Merge the documents.

Creating a Main Document

Only the feature for creating a main document is available when the Mail Merge Helper first opens. The Create drop-down menu lists several types of document to create, including form letters, mailing labels, envelopes, and catalogs. A fifth choice, "Restore to normal document," restores a document that is targeted for a mail merge to normal. This last command is available only after a main document has been specified. No matter which option is chosen, Word presents a dialog (Figure 9-11) with two options: Active Window, used to turn the current document into a mail merge document, and New Main Document, used to create a new document as the mail merge document. Note that there is no Cancel button. Use the Close button to cancel out of the window.

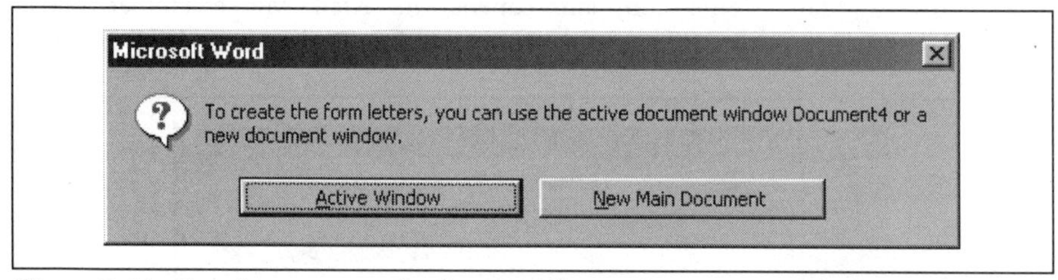

Figure 9-11: Creating a new main document for mail merge

After selecting an option, Word returns to the Mail Merge Helper dialog, which now boasts an Edit button next to the Create button. The Edit button closes the Mail Merge Helper dialog and switches to the document in Word. Create and edit the document using normal Word tools and the Mail Merge toolbar (discussed in its own section later).

When the document looks the way you want, use Tools → Mail Merge to open the Mail Merge Helper dialog again. Use the Create button on the Mail Merge Helper dialog at any time to create a new main document or to return the existing main document to normal. Once the main document is created, the next step is choosing a data source.

NOTE *Do not add the fields for the merged data to the document at this time. Fields are created when selecting a data source.*

Selecting a Data Source

Once the main document is squared away, use the Get Data button on the Mail Merge Helper dialog to select a data source. There are a few options:

Create data source
: This option brings up a separate dialog (Figure 9-12) used to create the fields that are inserted into the main document. Commonly used fields (like name, address, phone, and so on) are displayed. Clicking OK at this point inserts all of those fields into the main mail merge document. Select any field and click Remove Field Name to take it off the list. Type a name into the Field name box and click Add Field Name to add custom fields to the list. Use the up and down arrows to adjust the order of the fields in the list. Use the MS Query button to select source records from an existing database. MS Query is useful for selecting only specified records from a database that is too large to import in its entirety. Databases that support Dynamic Document Exchange (DDE) and have an Open Database Connectivity (ODBC) driver installed can be used in conjunction with MS Query.

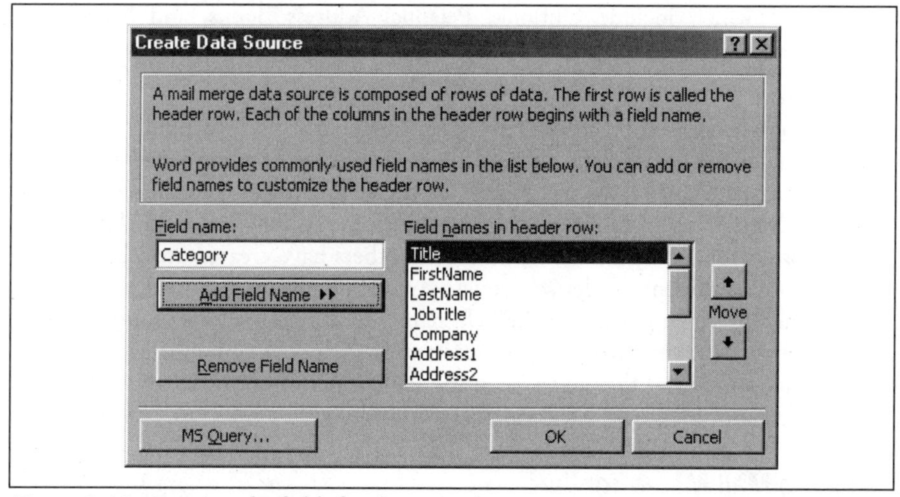

Figure 9-12: Creating the fields for the main document

When the fields look the way you want, click OK. Word opens a Save dialog box at this point. The data source is saved as a separate Word document. Once the file is saved, an Edit button is added to the data source section of the Mail Merge Helper dialog. This button closes the helper dialog, opens the data source document, and displays a Data Form dialog (Figure 9-13), used to enter the data for the fields.

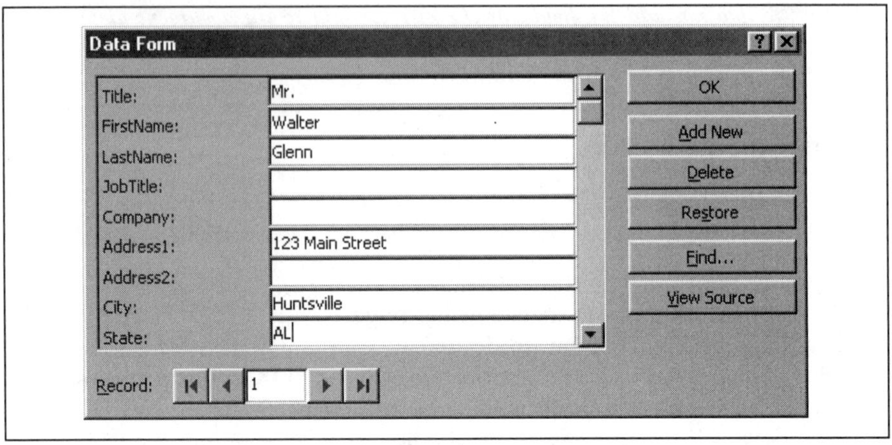

Figure 9-13: Entering data into a data source

Open data source

This option brings up a standard open dialog used to browse for an existing data source. Valid file formats include Word (*.doc*, *.dot*, *.html*), Access (*.mdb*, *.mde*), FoxPro (*.dbf*), Excel (*.xls*), text (*.txt*), MS Query (*.qry*), and dBase (*.dbf*).

Use address book

This option brings up a dialog used to select from supported address book formats, which include Outlook, Personal Address Books, and Schedule + contacts.

Header options

This option is used to create a separate data source used to hold the headers (names) of the fields in the actual data source. When creating a new source file from scratch, you create the names for the fields in the data source yourself. When importing from an existing data source, you may not have that option and often you'll find that the field names others have created are a bit cryptic. Creating a different header source lets you create meaningful field names for a data source, while preserving the field names in the original data source as well. Note that the alternative header source must include a name for every field in the data source and they must be in the same order in both sources. Otherwise, Word cannot merge the file properly.

Using the Mail Merge Toolbar

The Mail Merge toolbar (Figure 9-14) is displayed while editing a main document and offers commands for inserting merge fields (discussed in the previous section, "Selecting a Data Source") and standard Word fields, and for viewing and editing the merged data and data source. After selecting a main document and a data source, edit the main document again (select Edit on the Mail Merge Helper dialog) and use the toolbar to insert fields into the document.

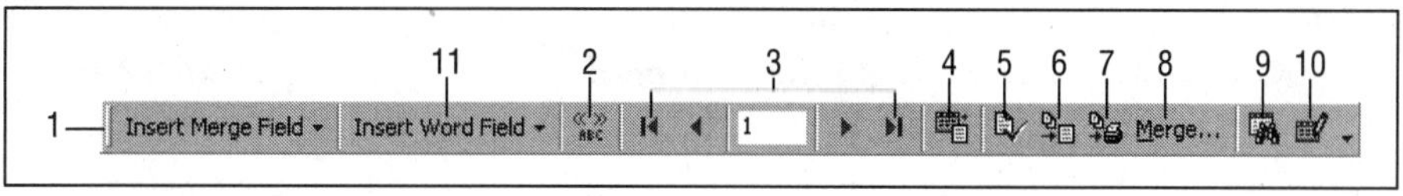

Figure 9-14: Using the Mail Merge toolbar

1. *Insert Merge Field.* Use this drop-down list to insert any of the merge fields defined by the data source. Data in the fields takes on the formatting of the surrounding text by default. Change it using standard character formatting (discussed in Chapter 8).

2. *View Merged Data.* This option displays the main document as it will look when the data source is merged into it. Use this option in conjunction with the record controls to select the actual record viewed.

3. *Record controls.* These controls work only if the View Merged Data option is on. Use the controls to move to the previous or next record, to the first or last record, to a specific record number.

4. *Mail Merge Helper.* This command opens the Mail Merge Helper dialog, the same as choosing Tools → Mail Merge.

5. *Check for Errors.* This option only checks for basic errors such as when fields in the main document don't actually exist in the data source. It cannot check for formatting errors like merged data not fitting into a field properly. The command can be helpful for making sure your data source is properly structured, but don't rely on it for much else. This command opens a dialog with three options for checking for merge errors:

   - *Simulate the merge and report errors in a new document.* I always recommend using this option when creating a new mail merge document.
   - *Perform an actual merge and pause to report errors as they occur.* I use this one for long mail merges that I have already used at least once. I don't want to go through an entire long merge only to find out there were errors at the end, especially if I'm merging directly to the printer.
   - *Perform an actual merge without pausing and report any errors in a new document afterward.* This is fine for short merges.

6. *Merge to new document.* This command performs a merge, combining the data source and main document and presenting the results in a new document. This command skips the Merge dialog box and goes straight to the actual merge. The Merge dialog and merge targets are discussed in the next section, "Merging Data With a Document."

7. *Merge to printer.* This command skips the Merge dialog and merges the data source and main document to a printout.

8. *Merge.* This command opens the Merge dialog.

9. *Find Record.* This command opens a simple dialog used to search a specific field for a text string. Pick the field from a drop-down list, type in the search criteria, and matching records are displayed. This is useful for finding, editing, or merging records that all match a certain criteria (maybe all people from the same state).
10. *Edit Data Source.* This opens the Data Form dialog (Figure 9-13), used to enter records.
11. *Insert Word Field.* Use this drop-down list to insert special Word fields to help control the merge process. Available fields include:
    - *Ask.* This field causes a dialog to open during the merge process asking for further input. For example, you might want to add a personal comment to a form letter. During the merge process, a dialog opens for each record asking for that comment.

Ask fields rely on bookmarks as data locations when merging. Since the same bookmark can be added to multiple places in a document, a single Ask field can insert text in multiple locations. For more on using bookmarks, see Chapter 7.

Use the Insert Word Field: Ask dialog (Figure 9-15) to set up the Ask field. Enter instructions to the user for entering text into the Prompt box. Enter suggested text (such as a sample comment) into the "Default bookmark text" field. Select the "Ask once" option to have Word ask for input only once at the beginning of the merge process; the same input is used for all records created. Choose a bookmark from the list of available bookmarks or type a name in the Bookmark field to create a new one.

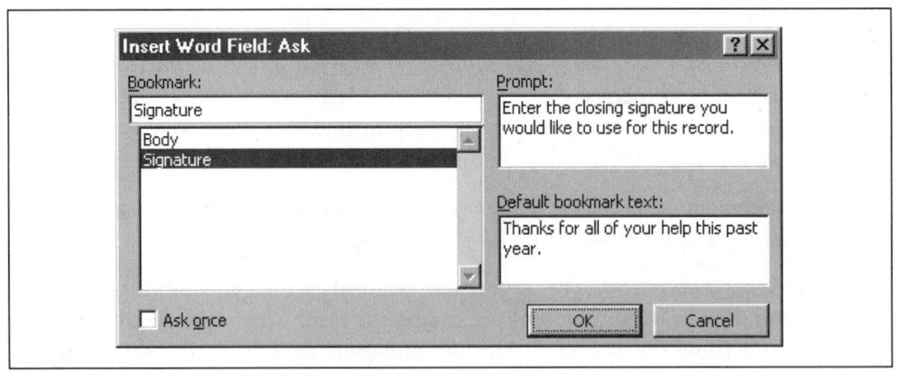

Figure 9-15: Using an Ask field to prompt for input

- *Fill-in.* This field opens a dialog during the merge process asking for further input. Unlike the Ask field, the Fill-in field inserts text in only one location—wherever the field is inserted. Options when creating the field include the options already discussed: Prompt text for the user, Default text, and "Ask once."

- *If...Then...Else.* This field causes Word to enter one of two text strings based on an evaluation of another field in the data source. For example, suppose you are sending invitations to an event and want to vary the text of the letter based on whether the recipients are friends or business contacts. The Insert Word Field: IF dialog (Figure 9-16) is used to build the IF statement and set the results. Choose from available fields in the data source, choose a comparison (equal to, etc.), and enter the text to be used for the comparison. An example would be "If company equal to friend." Enter the text that should be inserted if the statement is true in the top window and text to be used if the statement is false in the second window.

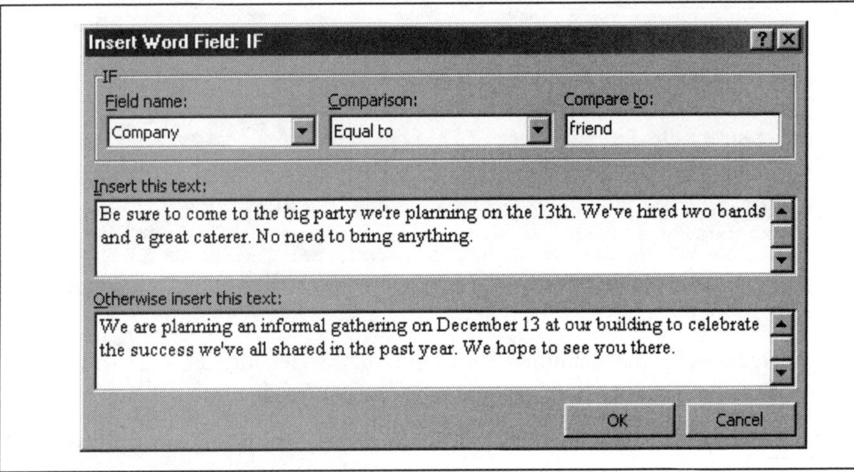

Figure 9-16: Building an If...Then...Else field

- *Merge Record #.* This field inserts the number of the current record being merged from the data source.
- *Merge Sequence #.* This field inserts the number of each particular merge document. For example, the fifth form letter created during a merge would have the number 5 added to it.
- *Next Record.* This field causes Word to insert data from the following record in the data source to the same merge document.
- *Next Record If.* Use this field to insert data from the following record if a certain condition is met. Conditions are defined in much the same way as with the If...Then...Else field.
- *Set Bookmark.* Use this field to insert the data associated with a bookmark into every merge document. Unlike the Ask field, the data never changes from one document to the next.

– *Skip Record If.* Use this field to skip a record in the data source when a condition is met. Conditions are defined the same way as in the If...Then...Else field.

Merging Data with a Document

After the main document is formatted and the data source is complete, the merge is ready to perform. Click the Merge command on the Mail Merge Helper dialog (Figure 9-10) or on the Mail Merge toolbar to open the Merge dialog (Figure 9-17).

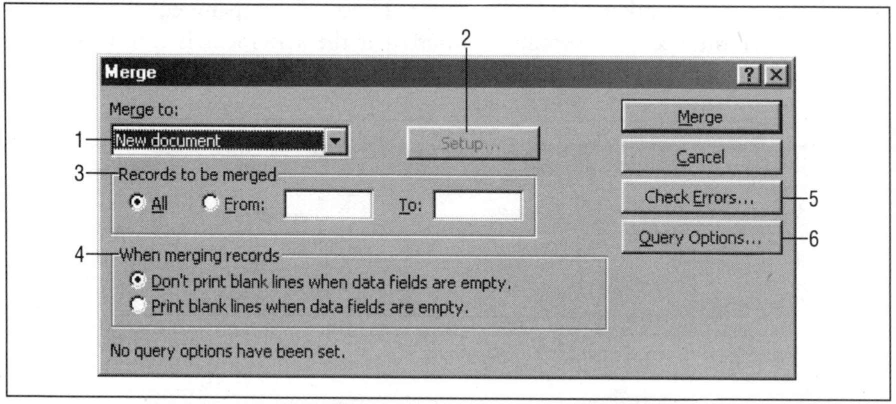

Figure 9-17: Merging a data source with a main document

1. *Merge to.* Specify the document to merge to. By default, the data source and main document are merged into a new document (or documents).

   Choose Printer to have the merge sent directly to the printer instead of being displayed on the screen. This option opens the Print dialog so that you can specify print options. These options are covered in Chapter 4, *File*.

   Choose Electronic Mail to send the merge to a new email message. When this option is selected, the Setup button becomes available for setting options.

2. *Setup.* Only available when merging to electronic mail, this button is used to select the field in the data source that contains the email address or fax number to be used when creating the messages. You can also enter a subject line for the messages and specify whether to send the message as an attachment instead of embedded in the message text.

3. *Records to be merged.* Merge all records or only a certain range of records identified by record number.

4. *When merging records.* Missing data in fields often occurs when using a preexisting data source. Use this section to specify whether Word should add a simple blank line in the merged document to indicate missing data or whether to simply ignore it.

5. *Check Errors.* This button opens a dialog with several error checking options, which were discussed previously in the section "Using the Mail Merge toolbar."

6. *Query Options.* This button opens a dialog with tabs for sorting and filtering the merge records before merging. When you want to merge only certain records from the data source, filter the records by adding conditions based on the fields in the records. For example, you could filter the records so that only those with a particular company name are merged. Set up to five conditions at once and use standard And or OR operators to control them.

   You might sort records before they are merged so that, for example, all form letters sent to particular zip codes are printed together. Sort by up to three fields and, for each field, choose whether to use an ascending or descending search.

Tools → Envelopes and Labels

Use the Envelopes and Labels command to format and print a variety of predefined envelope and label sizes. When issuing the command with a letter open (a document created using the Letter Wizard described later in this chapter or one of Word's letter templates), Word automatically fills in the recipient information. Issue the command from a blank document to start from scratch.

The Envelopes and Labels dialog consists of two tabs: Envelopes and Labels.

The Envelopes Tab

Use the Envelopes tab (Figure 9-18) to format and print an envelope. The Envelopes tab settings are:

1. *Delivery address.* Type an address in the box or click the Address Book button to choose one. When creating a envelope from a letter using one of Word's letter templates, this box is filled in automatically.

2. *Address Book.* This button opens whatever is the default address book for your system as defined in *Control Panel → Internet Options → Programs → Contact List.* Supported address books include Microsoft Outlook, the Windows Address Book (used by Outlook Express), or Schedule +. The Address Book functions only if one of these programs is installed. Click the down arrow next to the Address Book button to choose from a list of recently used addresses.

3. *Add to Document.* This button adds the envelope to the front of the existing document so that they may be saved together and printed at the same time.

4. *Return address.* The default return address is defined in Tools → Options → User Information. Type a new address in this box and Word offers to replace the address on the User Information tab with the address typed when you close the Envelopes and Labels dialog. This does not hold true if you make the return address blank.

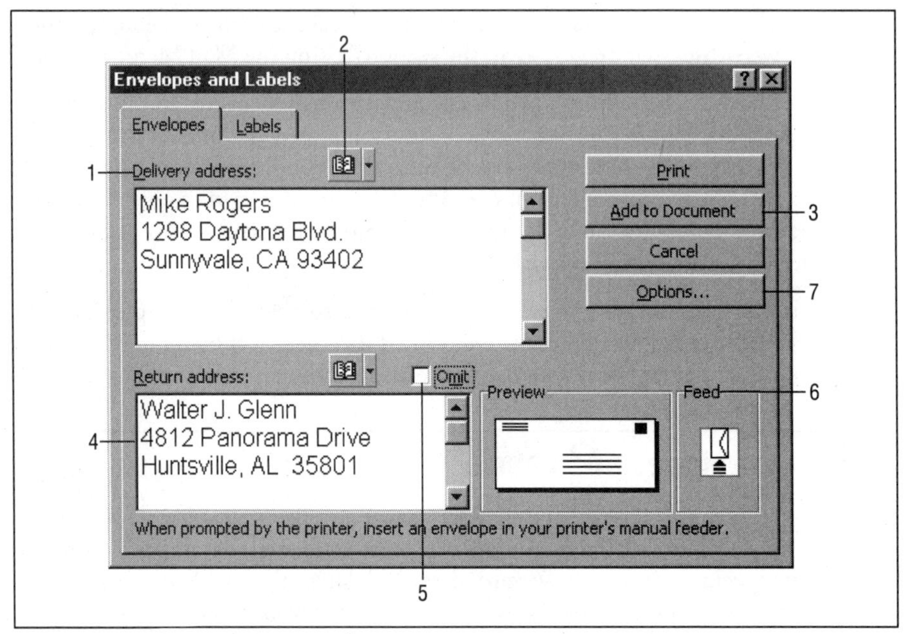

Figure 9-18: Formatting an envelope

5. *Omit.* Select this option to omit the return address when printing the envelope. This is effectively the same as deleting the return address.

6. *Feed.* This graphic shows the suggested way to feed an envelope into the printer and is based on the options set using the Options button, described next. This graphic is only a suggestion based on the type of printer used and is often incorrect. I recommend printing to scratch paper the first time you try printing envelopes with a new printer to make sure you know how to feed the envelope.

7. *Options.* This button opens a separate Envelope Options dialog box (Figure 9-19). Clicking the Preview graphic also opens the Options dialog. Settings for Envelope Options are:

    a. *Envelope size.* Select from numerous industry standard envelope sizes. Size 10 is a typical business-sized envelope. Size 6 is typical for greeting cards. Choose the Custom Size option to enter exact horizontal and vertical measurements in inches.

    b. *Delivery point barcode.* This options prints a POSTNET (Postal Numeric Encoding Technique) bar code on the envelope. This is a machine-readable representation of the address and zip code. Sometimes you can get a better price on metered mail when including this bar code. This option is not available when using daisy-wheel printers.

    c. *FIM-A courtesy reply mail.* This option prints a Facing Identification Mark (FIM), used in the United States on courtesy reply mail. A courtesy reply is

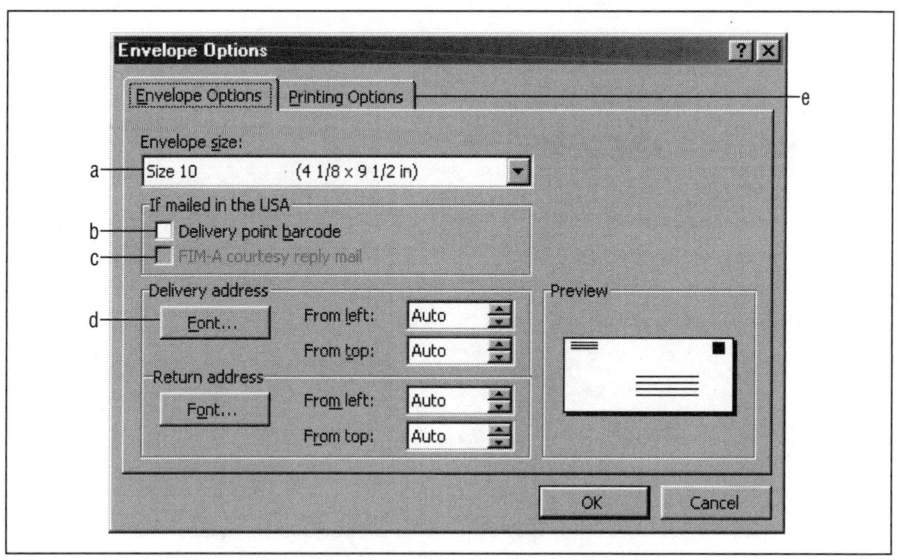

Figure 9-19: Setting envelope options

used on preprinted envelopes sent to customers so that they can easily reply. This option is not available when using daisy-wheel printers.

d. *Delivery and Return Address*. Apply character formatting of any sort that you can use in a typical document (see Chapter 8 for details on formatting available) using the Font button. Set the exact distance in inches from the top and left edges of the page for either address.

e. *Printing Options*. Use this tab to specify the direction in which envelopes should be fed into the printer and the printer tray that contains envelopes on printers with multiple trays.

The Labels Tab

Printing a label (Figure 9-20) works much the same way as printing an envelope, except that Word can print an entire sheet of labels at once. The address can be drawn from the open document, entered manually, or chosen from an address book. Most of the options on this tab are the same as those on the Envelopes tab. Select the "Use return address" option to use the address configured in Tools → Options → User Information as the label address. Use the Print section to specify whether to print a full page of the label or to print a single label at a specified location on a label sheet. The label sheet used is defined with the Options button. When possible, I recommend printing an entire page at a time. Feeding a label sheet through a printer more than once can cause the labels to start peeling off, and is an easy way to jam a printer.

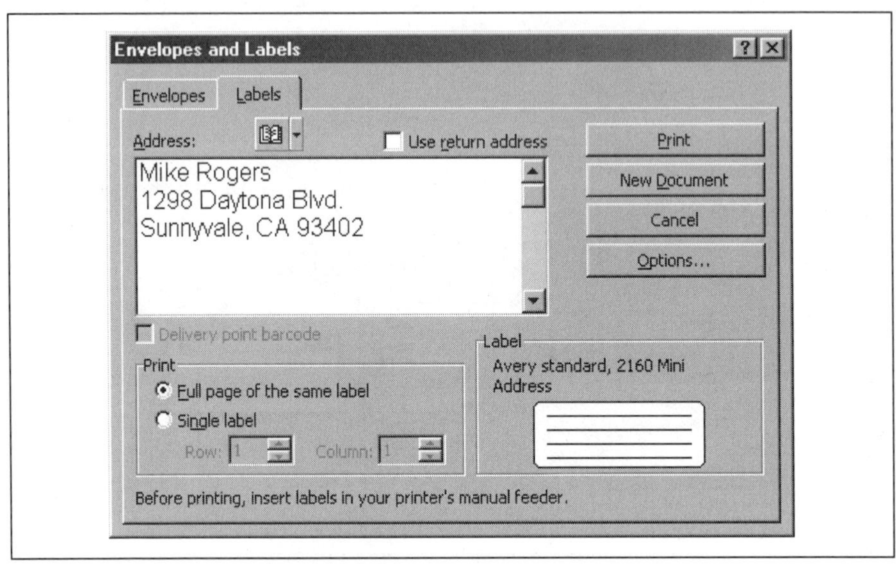

Figure 9-20: Printing a sheet of labels

Rather than going directly to the printer with your sheet of labels, click the New Document button to create a document that consists of a large table with cells sized to match the dimensions of the selected label type. Format the label text, and even insert symbols or graphics to dress up the labels.

The Options button (or clicking the preview graphic) opens a separate dialog (Figure 9-21) used to configure labeling options.

Label Options
Printer information
Dot matrix
Laser and ink jet
Tray: Manual feed
Label products: Avery standard
Product number:
2160 Mini - Address
2162 Mini - Address
2163 Mini - Shipping
2164 - Shipping
2180 Mini - File Folder
2181 Mini - File Folder
2186 Mini - Diskette
Label information
Type: Address
Height: 1"
Width: 2.63"
Page size: Mini (4 ¼ x 5 in)
OK
Cancel
Details...
New Label...
Delete

Figure 9-21: Setting options for labels

Select the type of printer and print feed used and choose from hundreds of different label sheets from several manufacturers. Just about every type of label sheet you can buy is listed here. For those not listed, use the Details button to customize an existing sheet style or the New Label button to create a new label sheet style from scratch. These tools are very similar and let you choose exact dimensions and page placement for labels.

The list of label styles also includes tent cards, business cards, and a variety of non-label items. These, too, are selected by the Avery (or other selected manufacturer) number on the product's box.

Tools → Letter Wizard

The Letter Wizard provides tools for everything from inserting the date in a document to choosing a letter closing. Select a letter format, insert elements like reference lines and carbon copy recipients, and even allow space on the page for preprinted letterhead. The Letter Wizard's four-tab dialog box appears in Figure 9-22.

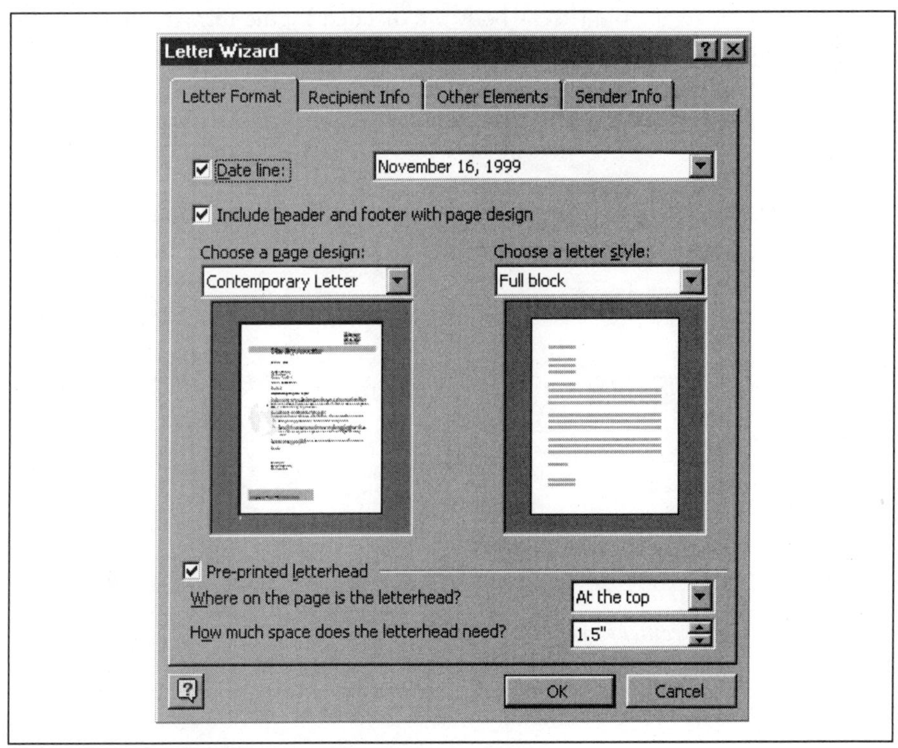

Figure 9-22: Using the Letter Wizard to build a letter

The Wizard creates a letter based on one of Word's built-in letter templates. When making a selection from the "Choose a page design" list, the names of the templates are available—Elegant, Contemporary, Normal, and Professional. Open and edit these templates directly in Word to customize the wizard's output. Typically, templates are stored in the *C:\Program Files\Microsoft Office\Templates\1033* folder.

Be sure to save them with the same name and in the same location after editing so that they'll be available to the Letter Wizard.

Generally, I find it easier to use the templates directly from the File → New dialog to create a letter instead of using a wizard.

The Recipient Info, Other Elements, and Sender Info tabs all utilize Word's AutoText entries, offering them as choices for the salutation, closing text, reference lines, and other letter elements. View Word's installed AutoText entries using Insert → AutoText → AutoText to open the AutoText dialog box. The installed AutoText entries are broken into categories such as Attention line and Closing, and these (among others) are the entries offered through the Letter Wizard's tabs.

After entering the requested information into the four tabs in the dialog box, create the letter by clicking OK. After that, type the body of the letter. The alignment, spacing, and indents for the letter's body are dictated by the format chosen in the Wizard (Figure 9-23).

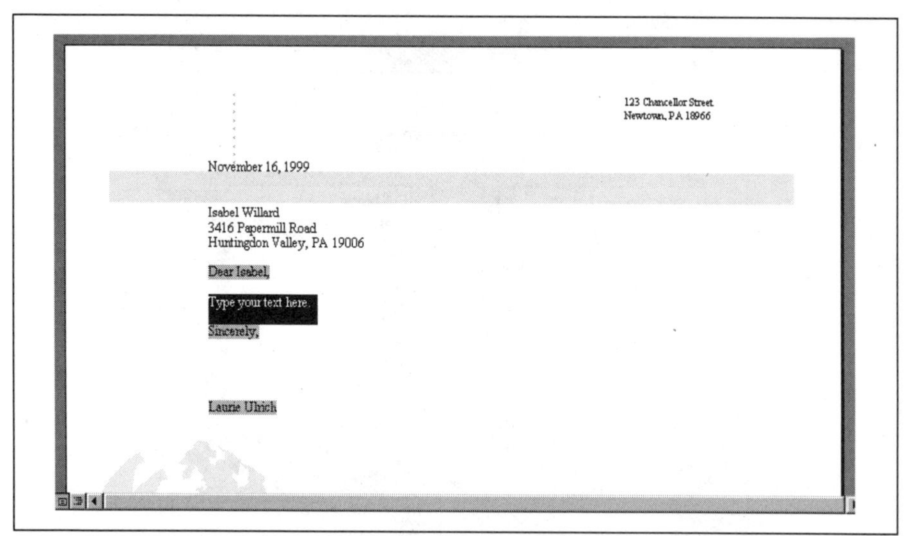

Figure 9-23: Adding content to a letter

Tools → Macro

A macro is a series of Word commands and instructions grouped together as a single command to accomplish a task automatically. The Macro Recorder records steps you take in Word and converts that recording to Visual Basic for Applications (VBA) code. Macros can also be built manually using the Visual Basic Editor. Macros, VBA, and the commands on this menu are covered in Chapter 18.

Tools → Templates and Add-Ins

Use the Templates and Add-ins dialog (Figure 9-24) to change the template attached to the current document and to manage any global templates loaded other than *normal.dot*. You can find a complete discussion of how Word uses templates in Chapter 2, *How Word Works*.

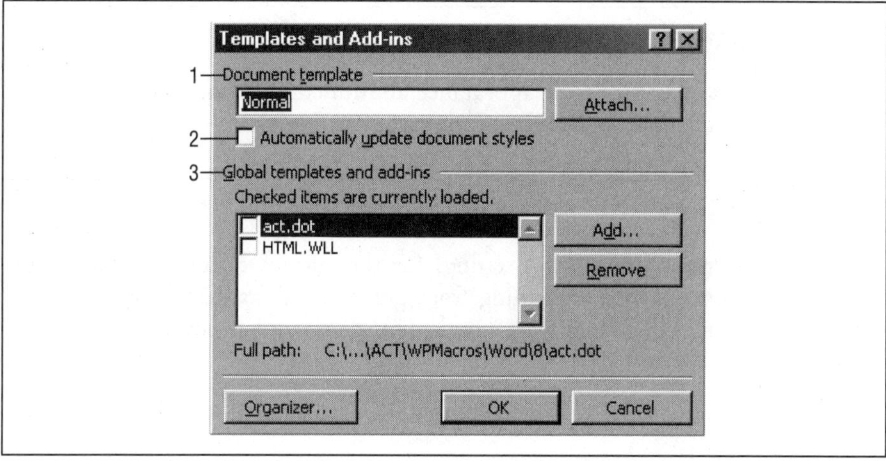

Figure 9-24: Managing global templates and the template attached to a document

1. *Document template.* This box shows the template attached to the current document. Use the Attach button to browse for a new template to attach.

2. *Automatically update document styles.* This option causes Word to automatically update any styles in the document whenever the styles in the template attached to the document are updated. This option is disabled by default.

   When a template is first attached to a document, the styles in the document are updated to reflect those in the template. With the "Automatically update document styles" option disabled, this is the only time styles are updated.

3. *Global templates and add-ins.* This box shows the global templates Word currently has loaded. Clear the checkbox next to a template to temporarily disable that template. The disabled template remains on the list so that you can enable it again later. Click the Add button to browse for a new global template to load. Click the Remove button to remove the selected template from the list. Note that templates can be set to load automatically when Word starts, so removing a template from the list may not prevent it from loading in the future. Learn more about this in Chapter 2.

TIP # 115

Check Out a Template Before Attaching It

To find out what's included in a template before attaching it to a document, try attaching it to a blank document first and then using the Style Organizer (covered in Chapter 8) to browse the templates features.

Tools → Customize

Tools → Customize controls the appearance and functions of menus and toolbars. This command is covered in detail in Chapter 3.

Tools → Options

Use Tools → Options to control settings for the current document and for the Word application. Change everything from grammatical standards for proofing a document to where documents are saved. This command is covered in detail in Chapter 3.

Chapter 10

Table

Tables are one of Word's most powerful features, used both to organize information and to lay out documents. A table is a container holding any number of cells arranged in rows and columns (Figure 10-1). Tables get special treatment from Word. They can be created or resized like graphics, but the cells in the table can hold text, graphics, fields, and other types of objects—even other tables.

Composer¤	Title¤	Year·Published¤	Notes¤	¤
Beethoven¤	Beethoven:·5·Piano·Concertos¤	1963¤	scratchy¤	¤
Beethoven¤	Beethoven:·Violin·Concerto¤	1988¤	Missing·insert¤	¤
Mozart¤	Mozart:·Symphonies·#·35-41·¤	1997¤	¤	¤

Figure 10-1: Viewing the special formatting marks in a table

Word uses a number of special formatting marks to identify a table and its parts:

- *Move handle*. Hold the pointer over the table for about two seconds to make the move and resize handles appear (shown in the top left corner of Figure 10-1). Click and drag the move handle to move the table around in the document (this works for all Word views except for Normal view).
- *Resize handle*. Click this handle to turn the pointer into a double-headed arrow. Drag the handle to resize the table.
- *End of cell mark*. Turn on the Show/Hide feature on the Standard toolbar to show end of cell and row marks on a table. End of cell marks are nonprinting characters that denote the end of a cell and are shown only by using the Show/Hide command.
- *End of row mark*. End of row marks are nonprinting characters that denote the end of a row and are shown only by using the Show/Hide command.

Several other marks exist, depending on the view that's used. Another common one is a black arrow that when clicked will select an entire row or column.

Many people think of tables only as a means to organize numbers and text in a quasi-spreadsheet, like the example in Figure 10-1. However, tables are also used as layout tools in all kinds of different documents. A table does not have to be as strictly defined in rows and columns as you might think. Cells can be merged or divided and can even hold other tables. Figure 10-2 shows a document created using a table to lay out the various elements.

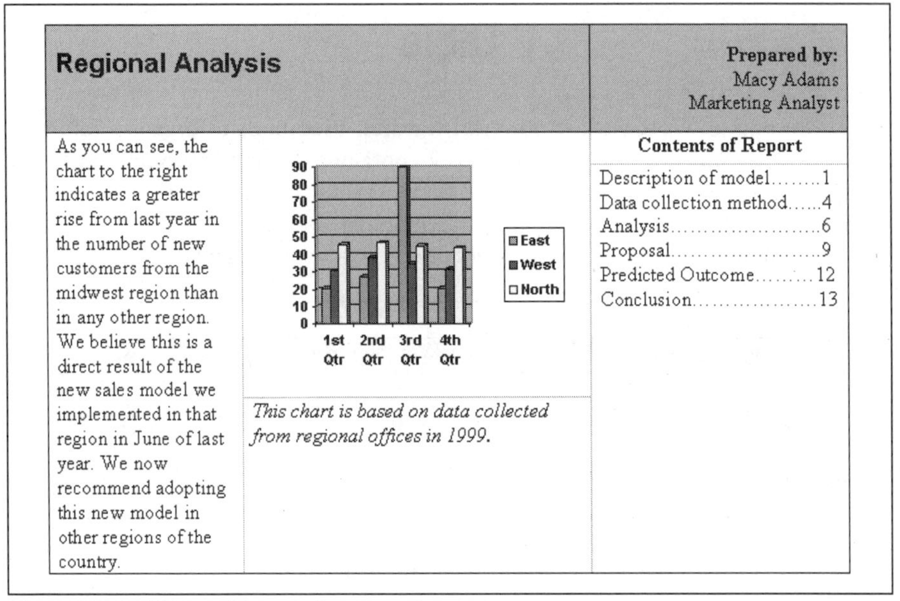

Regional Analysis

Prepared by:
Macy Adams
Marketing Analyst

As you can see, the chart to the right indicates a greater rise from last year in the number of new customers from the midwest region than in any other region. We believe this is a direct result of the new sales model we implemented in that region in June of last year. We now recommend adopting this new model in other regions of the country.

This chart is based on data collected from regional offices in 1999.

Contents of Report

Figure 10-2: Using tables as a layout tool

Using tables in a document can replace the need for custom tabs, columns, and even paragraph formats such as left and right indents. Tables give a document structure, whether used for a short multicolumn list beside standard paragraph text or for an entire document's layout, such as in a newsletter or resume.

Word's Table menu provides commands for creating and formatting tables, rows, columns, and cells, as well as sorting and calculation tools. Format the text in a table the same way you would format non-tabular text.

There are three basic ways to create a table in Word:

- Use Table → Draw Table to create a free-form table by drawing cells with the mouse.
- Use Table → Insert → Table to create a table by specifying its exact dimensions in a dialog box.
- Convert normal text to a table using Table → Convert → Text to Table.

All of these methods are detailed later in this chapter. No matter which creation method is used, though, Word opens the Tables and Borders toolbar (Figure 10-3), which contains most of the tools used to create and manipulate tables. These tools are described here briefly for reference. Details on the tools can be found throughout the chapter, as the commands on the toolbar duplicate many of those found on the Table menu.

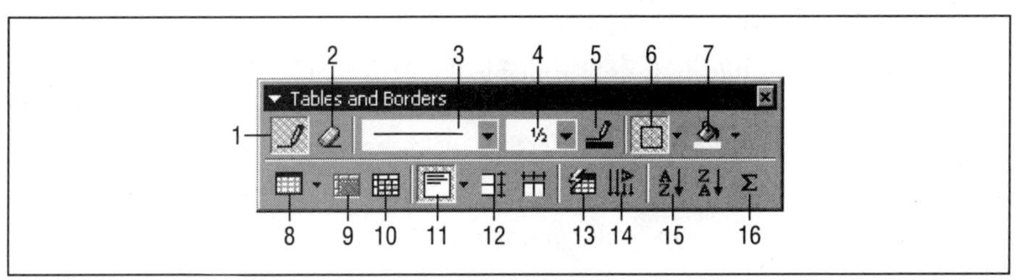

Figure 10-3: Using the Tables and Borders toolbar

1. *Draw Table*. This button turns the pointer into a pencil used to draw a table in freehand. It performs the same action as the Table → Draw Table command.
2. *Eraser*. This button turns the pointer into an eraser. Click any line in the table to remove it. This is mainly used to merge cells by removing the dividers between them, an action also performed by the Table → Merge Cells command, covered later in this chapter. Clicking the outside borders of a table makes them invisible in Print and Web Layout views and when the document is printed. In Normal view, "erased" outside borders appear as dim gray lines.
3. *Line Style*. Select one of many line styles to turn the pointer into a pencil. Click on any line in the table to convert the line to the selected line style. This can also be done for larger portions of a table at once by selecting a portion of the table and using the Format → Borders and Shading command, discussed in Chapter 8, *Format*.
4. *Line Weight*. This button works much like the line style command described in #3. Use it to apply different line weights (thickness) to borders in a table.
5. *Border Color*. Use this command to apply colors to table borders. The command works the same way as the Line Weight and Line Style commands.

> **NOTE** *The Line Style, Line Weight, and Border Color commands on the Tables and Borders toolbar work in conjunction. Make a selection for all three, and then apply them at once with the pencil pointer.*

6. *Outside Border*. Use this button to quickly apply Line Style, Line Weight, and Border Color settings to the outside border of the cell with the insertion point or to any selected part of the table. Use the arrow beside the button to drop down a menu used to apply the settings to different sets of borders in the table.

7. *Shading Color*. This button opens a palette of colors. Select a color to apply it as a background shading to the cell containing the insertion point or to any selected part of the table.

8. *Insert Table*. This button opens the Insert Table dialog box; it performs the same action as the Table → Insert Table command. Click the arrow beside the button to open a menu with commands from Word's Table → Insert and Table → AutoFit submenus.

9. *Merge Cells*. This button is only available if two or more cells are selected. Use it to remove the dividing borders of the cells and merge them into a single cell. This is the same as the Table → Merge Cells command.

10. *Split Cells*. Use this to split a cell into more than one cell. The command is the same as the Table → Split Cells command.

11. *Align Top Left*. Use the arrow beside this button to open a menu with several selections for aligning text horizontally and vertically within a cell. Use the button itself to apply whatever setting is made using the drop-down menu.

12. *Distribute Rows (Columns) Evenly*. Use these commands for the table or any selected cells to make the rows or columns in the selection the same size. These are the same as the commands found on the Table → AutoFit submenu.

13. *Table AutoFormat*. This is the same as the Table → AutoFormat command and opens a separate dialog used to choose from predetermined table styles.

14. *Change Text Direction*. Toggle the direction of text in a cell between vertical and horizontal. This is useful in heading cells where the text is too long to be used horizontally (Figure 10-4).

	January	February	March	April	May	June	July	August	September	October	November	December
Sales	97	104	98	79	115	109	120	119	132	139	141	117

Figure 10-4: Using vertical text in a cell

15. *Sort Ascending (Descending)*. Use the commands to sort the rows in a table in ascending or descending order. This is the same as the Table → Sort command.

16. *AutoSum*. Use this to sum the content of a range of cells. Unlike the AutoSum tool in Excel, this tool cannot be redirected—it always sums the cells above the active cell. It will not sum numbers to the left or right of the active cell, or specific cell addresses.

TIP # 116

Summing Cells to the Left or Right of an Active Cell

To sum the cells to the left or right of the active cell, use the Table → Formula command, and change =SUM(ABOVE) to =SUM(LEFT) or =SUM(RIGHT).

Table → Draw Table

The Draw Table command can only be used in Print or Web Layout views. Starting the command in Normal or Outline view changes the document to Print Layout view.

This command turns the pointer into a pencil, used to draw the box outlines of cells. Start by drawing a rectangle that becomes a table with a single cell. Once the table is drawn, split cells vertically or horizontally by drawing a line that bisects the cell (Figure 10-5). This does not require perfect accuracy. Word second-guesses you by extending drawn lines to the nearest perpendicular line. This sort of table construction lends itself well to the creation of elaborate forms and layout tables, as it provides the freedom to place cells and blocks of cells anywhere on the page.

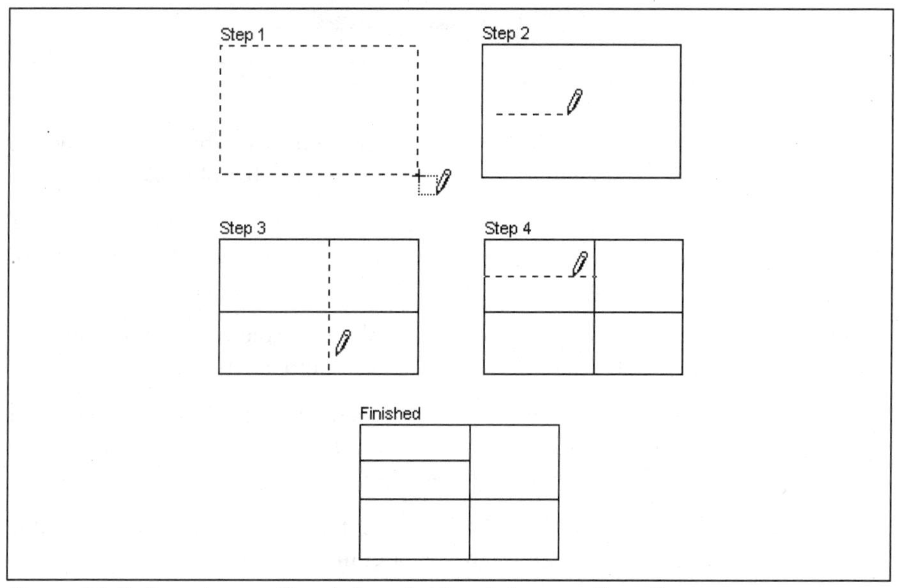

Figure 10-5: Drawing a cell and then dividing it into smaller cells

Table → Insert Table

Use the Insert Table command to create a table by specifying the exact number of columns and rows a table should start with and how the cells in the table should be sized (Figure 10-6).

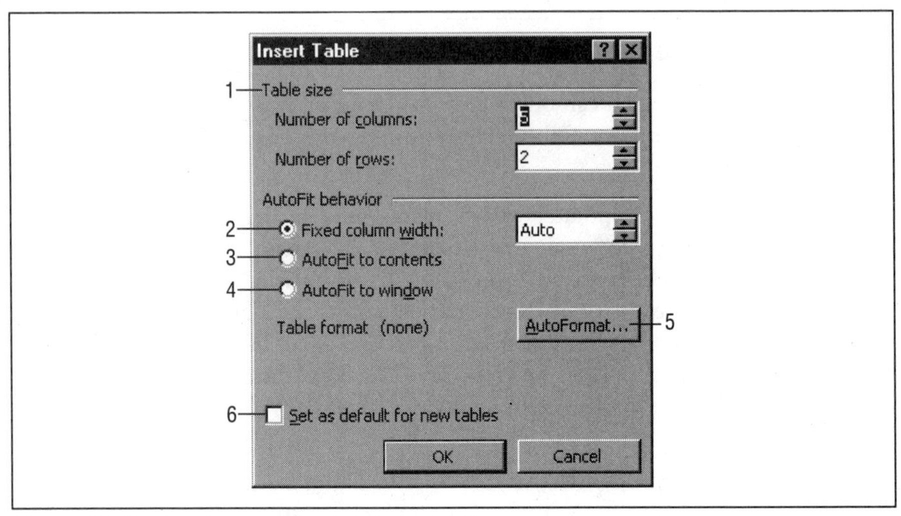

Figure 10-6: Creating a table with Insert Table

1. *Table Size.* Enter the number of rows and columns the table should have. A table can have up to 63 columns, but can have any number of rows.
2. *Fixed column width.* Each column in the table will have the same width. Use the Auto setting to create a table that fits just within the document's margins. Use the up and down arrows to set a specific size for the columns.
3. *AutoFit to contents.* This option creates a table with columns that are small to start, but automatically resize themselves to accommodate typed text.
4. *AutoFit to window.* This option is used for documents that will be viewed in a web browser. It creates a table that automatically resizes itself to fit within the browser window when the window itself is resized.
5. *AutoFormat.* This button performs the same function as the Table → Table AutoFormat command, which is covered later in this chapter.
6. *Set as default for new tables.* Any options set on the Insert Table dialog are preserved and used as the default choices each time a new table is created.

TIP # 117

Create a Small Uniform Table Quickly

Insert a table with fixed-width rows and columns quickly using the Insert Table button on the Standard toolbar (Figure 10-7). This button opens a palette used to create tables up to four rows by five columns.

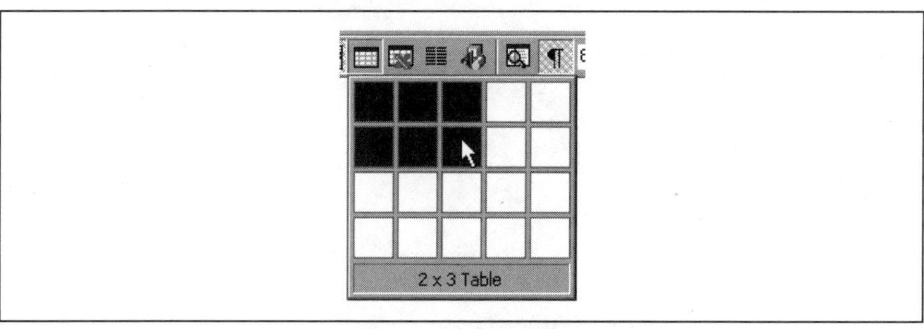

Figure 10-7: Using the Insert Table button to create a uniform table

Table → Insert → Columns to the Left

Use the Columns to the Left command to add columns to an existing table. Select the column in a table that the new column should appear to the left of. To insert more than one column, select an equal number of existing columns before executing the command (Figure 10-8). If a table has uniform column width before inserting extra columns, any additional columns cause the original columns to shrink so that all the columns, new and original, have the same width.

TIP # 118

Select a Column by Dragging or Pointing

To select a column, drag through it with the pointer or point just above the column and, when the pointer turns to a small arrow, click. To select multiple columns, drag this arrow to the left or right to select the additional columns. Both of these selection techniques work with rows, too.

Table → Insert → Columns to the Right

Use the Columns to the Right command to add columns on the right side of any selected columns. This command works identically to the Columns to the Left command described previously. To insert several columns at once, select the desired number of existing columns and then issue the command.

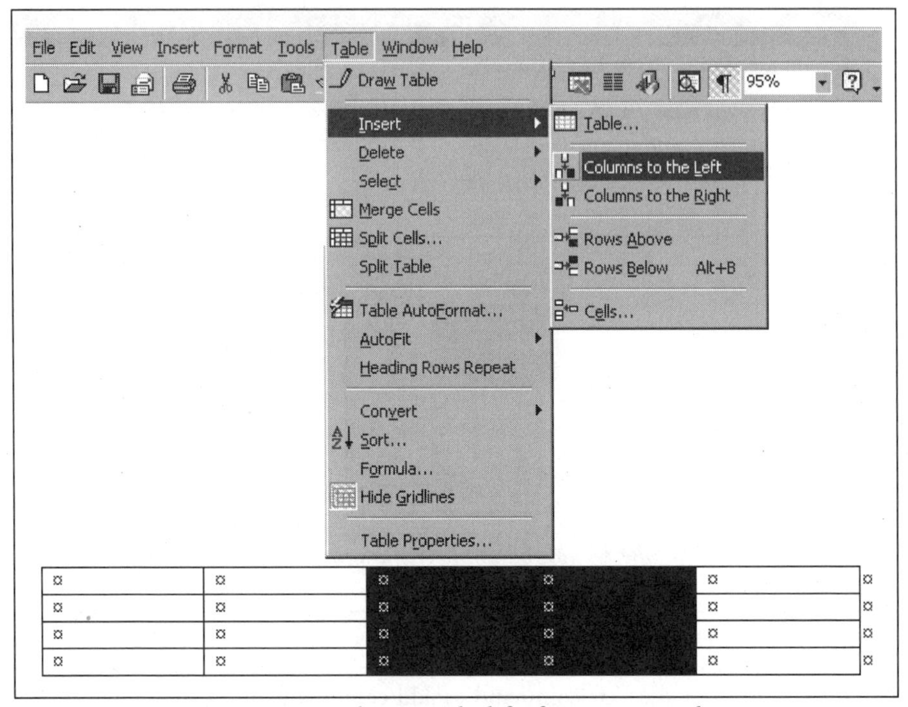

Figure 10-8: Inserting two new columns to the left of two existing columns

Table → Insert → Rows Above

Use the Rows Above command to insert a new row above an existing row that holds the insertion point. To insert several rows at once, select that number of rows from the existing rows before issuing the command.

TIP # 119

Insert New Rows at the End of a Table by Tabbing

Put the insertion point in the last row of the table and press Tab to quickly insert new rows at the end of a table. New rows take on any formatting applied to the existing last row.

Table → Insert → Rows Below

Use the Rows Below command to insert a new row below an existing row that holds the insertion point. To insert several rows at once, select that number of rows from the existing rows before issuing the command.

Table → Insert → Cells

The Table → Insert → Cells command inserts a single cell into an existing table. The command works differently depending on what is selected in the existing table and offers several options for handling existing cells (Figure 10-9).

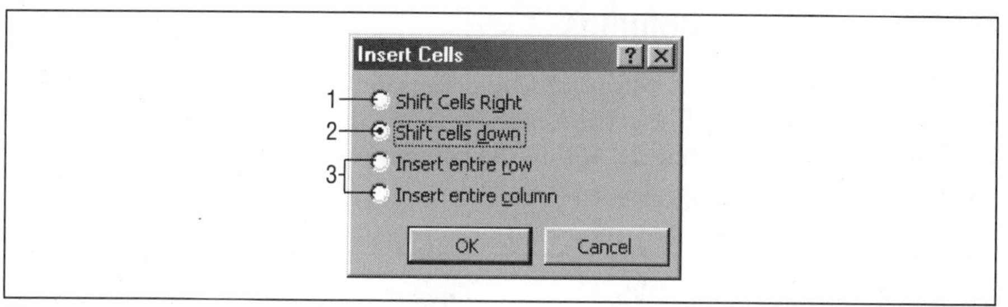

Figure 10-9: Inserting a cell into a table

1. *Shift Cells Right.* This option inserts a new cell to the left of whatever cell holds the insertion point or whatever range of cells is selected when the Insert Cells command is issued. Existing cells are moved to the right to accommodate the new cell. Figure 10-10 shows a table in which cells shifting to the right caused a cell to move outside the boundary of the table. Selecting a block of cells in a column would move cells in that many columns to the right. Selecting a block of cells in a row would insert the same number of cells and move existing cells to the right.

Figure 10-10: Shifting cells to the right when inserting a cell

If an entire column is selected, this command works the same as the Table → Insert → Columns to the Left command.

2. *Shift cells down.* This is the default option. It inserts a new cell above whatever cell holds the insertion point or whatever range of cells is selected when the Insert Cells command is issued. Unlike the Shift Cells Right option, cells shifted downwards cannot extend past the lower boundary of the table. Word fills out any new rows that would be created.

3. *Insert entire row (or column).* These options work the same as the Columns to the Right and Columns to the Left commands available on the Table menu, covered previously.

Table → Delete → Table

Delete an active table using the Table → Delete → Table command. The deletion applies to the entire table, including any tables nested inside the table.

Table → Delete → Columns

The Table → Delete → Columns command deletes the column containing the insertion point or a range of selected columns. The command deletes all columns containing selected cells. If a cell within the column to be deleted contains a nested table, the nested table is also deleted.

Table → Delete → Rows

This command deletes the row containing the insertion point or a range of selected rows. The command deletes all rows containing selected cells. If a cell within the row to be deleted contains a nested table, the nested table is also deleted.

TIP # 120

Rearrange Table Rows in Outline View

Most people rearrange rows in a table by selecting the row, cutting it, and then pasting it where they want it to go. A much easier way is to switch to Outline view (View → Outline). Each row of the table is displayed as a separate paragraph in the outline, complete with the outline bullet to the left of the margin. Drag the bullet to move the row around. A horizontal line indicates exactly where the row will be placed.

Table → Delete → Cells

Use the Delete Cells command to delete the cell that contains the insertion point or any range of selected cells. This command opens the Delete Cells dialog box (Figure 10-11), which presents several options for deleting the cell.

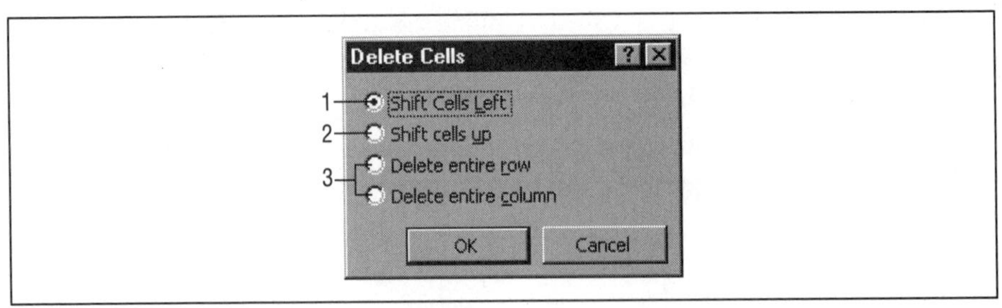

Figure 10-11: Choosing how to delete cells

The options for deleting cells are as follows:

1. *Shift Cells Left*. This option deletes the cell and shifts all cells to the right of the deleted cell in the same row to the left. This often causes a "hole" in a table (Figure 10-12) at the end of the row.

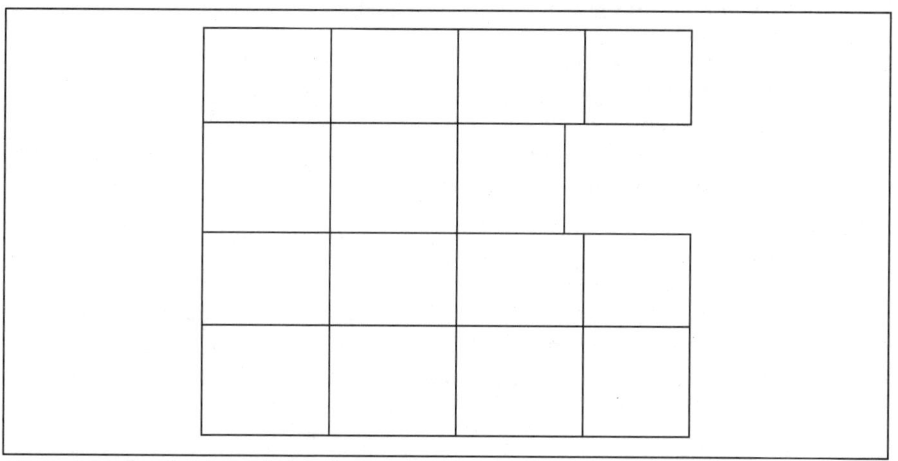

Figure 10-12: Shifting cells left, leaving a hole at the end of the row

TIP # 121

Delete the Contents of a Cell Instead of the Cell Itself

The Table → Delete → Cells command is used to delete all selected cells from the table. You can also do this by selecting the cells and pressing Backspace. This shifts remaining cells around, often causing unpredictable results. To delete just the contents of selected cells, use the Delete key instead.

2. *Shift cells up*. This option deletes the cell and shifts up all cells below the deleted cell in the same column. Unlike the "Shift cells left" option, this option does not leave a hole in the table at the bottom of the column. Instead, Word, fills in the hole with a blank cell.

3. *Delete entire row (or column)*. Use these commands to delete the cell and the entire row or column it is in. Using these commands on a range of cells delete all of the columns or rows affected by those cells. Using this command is the same as using the Table → Delete → Columns or Table → Delete → Rows commands.

WARNING

Be careful when deleting cells in a table that is not uniform. If you delete a cell that has two cells below it and use the "Shift cells up" option, only one of the cells below is shifted up and the other is deleted. It is difficult to predict which cell is shifted and which is deleted.

Table → Select

Table → Select opens a submenu with commands for selecting a table, column, row, or individual cell based on the position of the insertion point.

Here are a few useful tips for selecting parts of a table:

- For small tables, it is often easier to use the pointer to select table elements. Select a row by clicking the left border when the pointer turns to a small black arrow. Select columns at the top border in the same way. Drag the pointer to select multiple rows or columns. For larger tables, it is usually easier to use the selection commands from the Table menu.
- To select multiple columns or rows with the selection commands, select a block of cells, one cell in each column or row.
- In a freeform table created with the Draw Table tool, a column is defined as any vertical series of stacked cells, even if the cells are not all the same width. A row is defined as any horizontal grouping of cells sharing common left and/or right sides.

TIP # 122

Add Selection Controls to Table Context Menus

I've always found it infuriating that the context menus for table elements do not hold commands for selecting parts of the table. Fortunately, you can change this using the techniques for customizing context menus discussed in Chapter 3, Customizing Word. Just add the TableSelectCell, TableSelectColumn, TableSelectRow, and TableSelectTable commands (from the All Commands category) to the Cell, Tables, and Whole Tables context menus. While you're at it, add the commands for inserting rows and columns, as well.

Table → Merge Cells

Use the Merge Cells command to turn one or more selected cells into a single cell (Figure 10-13). This command is not available unless more than one cell is selected. It is also not available when two cells of different sizes are selected in a freeform table. The content in any merged cells is stacked in separate paragraphs in the resulting merged cell.

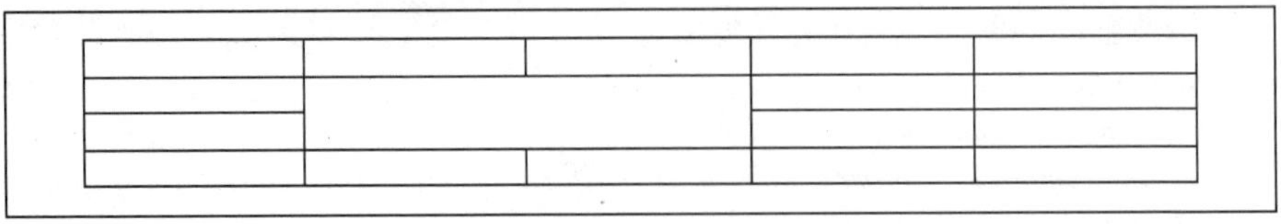

Figure 10-13: Merging four identical cells into one large cell

Cells can also be merged by removing the border between the cells with the Eraser tool on the Tables and Borders toolbar. Be sure only to erase one border at a time, though, as dragging through multiple borders may also delete the content of some cells.

Table → Split Cells

The Table → Split Cells command (Figure 10-14) is used to split a cell or selected range of cells into a specified number of rows and columns. When using the command on multiple cells, the "Merge cells before split" option becomes available. This turns several cells into one large cell before subdividing that larger cell. The data is dispersed throughout the cells into only the first row of new cells created in the split instead of throughout all cells on all rows. This is a problem that Microsoft has acknowledged in Word, but has not yet fixed.

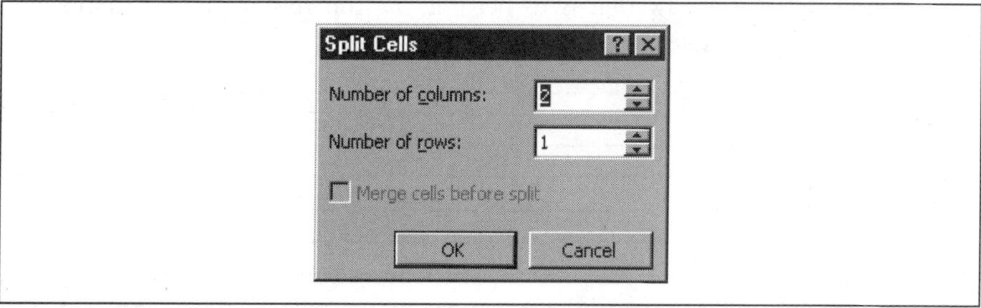

Figure 10-14: Splitting cells into additional cells of uniform width and height

When working with freehand tables and attempting to split a range of cells, the "Number of columns" or "Number of rows" options are sometimes not available, as Word has trouble splitting cells that are not of the same size. Even when the commands are available, they sometimes do not work at all or produce strange effects. When working with freehand tables, it is usually better to split any cells manually using the table drawing tool.

Table → Split Table

The Table → Split Table command separates a single table into two tables along a row. Tables cannot be split along a column. Splitting a table also inserts a blank line above the selected row (or row containing the active cell).

For tables created with the table drawing tool, results vary depending on the construction of the drawn table. Figure 10-15 shows the results of splitting a freehand table—the table on the left is the "before" table, the table on the right is the "after" version.

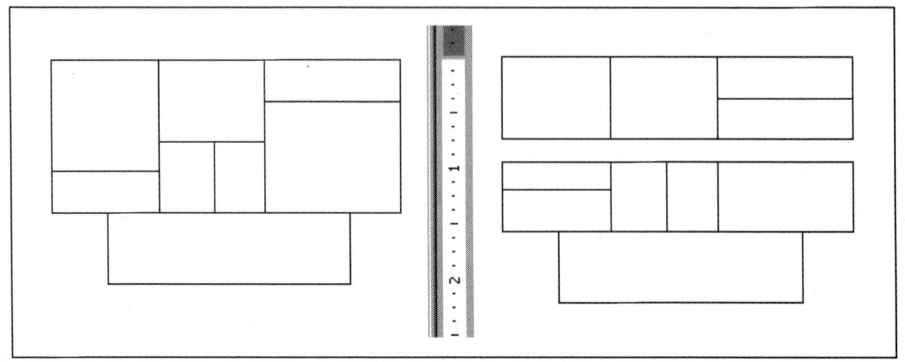

Figure 10-15: Splitting a drawn table can have unpredictable results

On the other hand, tables created with the Table → Insert → Table command or the Insert Table button can be predictably split into two uniform tables (Figure 10-16). Click in any cell in the row that is to become the top row in the new table and choose Table → Split Table.

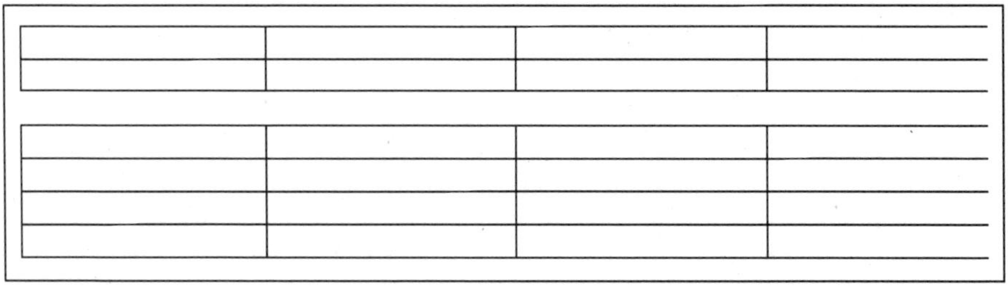

Figure 10-16: Splitting a table created with Insert Table into two sections

Table → Table AutoFormat

Use the Table → Table AutoFormat command to choose from a series of 42 different table formats (Figure 10-17). A preview is shown for any selected format in the Formats list. Specify which formats to apply and the parts of the table the formats should be applied to. In many table formats, the heading row (the first row in the table) and the first column receive a different format from the other parts of the table. Some table formats also apply special formatting to the last row or column. Uncheck any elements that should not be formatted.

Turn off the AutoFit option unless all table columns should be resized to fit the widest entry in the column. This is especially important when applying a format to an existing table that has already been sized correctly.

Use the "Apply special formats to" section of the Table AutoFormat dialog box to choose where any extra formatting such as bolding, double borders, or different colored shading is applied. Most formats apply this extra or "special" formatting to

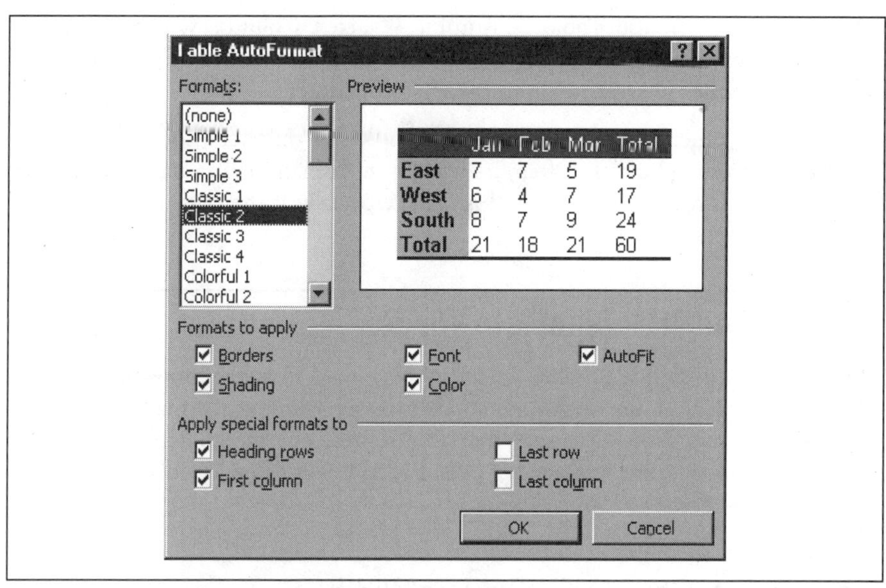

Figure 10-17: Applying an AutoFormat to a table

the column headings and/or the first row of the table, and these two options are checked by default in this section of the dialog box. If the last row or last column also needs special treatment, turn those options on as well.

WARNING

If you've applied any formatting to formulas in a table (like formatting numbers as currency), the AutoFormats may remove that formatting unless the Table → AutoFormat → Font option is disabled.

Table → AutoFit → AutoFit to Contents

The AutoFit to Contents command automatically resizes all of the rows and columns in an entire table to fit the table cells' content (Figure 10-18).

Invoice	Amount	Date Invoiced	Date Due
A35891	$542.35	6/22/99	7/22/99
A32190	$350.00	6/26/99	7/26/99
TOTAL	$892.35		

Figure 10-18: Automatically adjusting table cells to fit content

No matter what is selected when the command is issued, the entire table is resized. This command has more than a one-time effect: after you AutoFit a table, typing text or adding objects to a cell will adjust the size of the columns as you work. To turn the feature off, use Table → AutoFit → Fixed Column Width. Once the AutoFit command has been applied to a table, it does not need to be reapplied. Any new columns added are resized automatically to fit content.

As with many other table formatting commands, this one does not work particularly well on freehand tables. Often, many cells in freehand tables are not resized to fit content at all when this command is used, especially if the cells do not fall into uniform columns.

Table → AutoFit → AutoFit to Window

This command is used with tables meant to be viewed in a web browser. It keeps a table sized so that it fits within the web browser window no matter how that window is resized. Note that only the table resizes, not the content of the cells. Content is wrapped to fit into smaller cells. For more on using Word's web features, see Chapter 16, *Creating a Web Page*.

Table → AutoFit → Fixed Column Width

Normally, cells widen automatically to accommodate new text or content. In many cases, this is an undesirable effect, especially if columns are already sized to meet specific requirements. To keep columns at their current width, no matter how much text is typed into (or removed from) the cells, use Table → AutoFit → Fixed Column Width.

This command does not prevent the manual resizing of columns or the application of AutoFit from the Table AutoFormat dialog box. Any commands that typically result in changes in column width (other than typing into the cells) continue to work on columns to which the Fixed Column Width command has been applied.

Table → AutoFit → Distribute Rows Evenly

The Table → AutoFit → Distribute Rows Evenly command converts all rows in an active table (or all selected rows) to a consistent height. This can be very useful in giving a uniform look to a freehand table.

If this command is applied to a freehand table that does not have an equal number of cells in each row, some cells become taller or shorter than others as they are stretched to accommodate adjoining cells.

Typing content into cells after issuing the Distribute Rows Evenly command usually increases cell dimensions. You must reissue the command to keep rows evenly spaced.

Table → AutoFit → Distribute Columns Evenly

Create equally spaced columns across the width of a entire table (or any selected columns) with the Table → AutoFit → Distribute Columns Evenly command. Like the Distribute Rows Evenly command, this command does not work well on free-hand tables. If not all of columns have an equal number of cells in them, some cells may become wider or narrower than others as Word attempts to make all of the columns equal.

Typing content into cells after issuing the Distribute Columns Evenly command usually increases cell dimensions. You must reissue the command to keep columns evenly spaced.

Table → Heading Rows Repeat

If a table spans more than one page, it may be useful to repeat column headings at the top of each page of the table. To do this, select the heading row and choose Table → Heading Rows Repeat. Figure 10-19 shows a table's headings repeated at the top of the second page of a table. As a table grows to span more pages, the heading rows continue to appear at the top of any new pages exactly as they do in the designated header row.

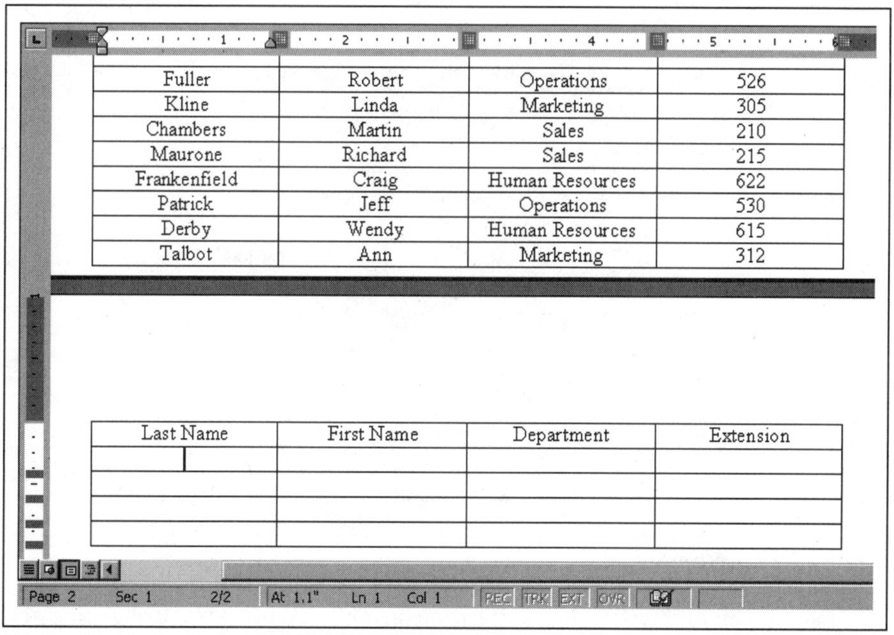

Fuller	Robert	Operations	526
Kline	Linda	Marketing	305
Chambers	Martin	Sales	210
Maurone	Richard	Sales	215
Frankenfield	Craig	Human Resources	622
Patrick	Jeff	Operations	530
Derby	Wendy	Human Resources	615
Talbot	Ann	Marketing	312

Last Name	First Name	Department	Extension

Page 2 Sec 1 2/2 At 1.1" Ln 1 Col 1 REC TRK EXT OVR

Figure 10-19: Repeating a table's headings at the top of each page

You cannot edit the repeated header rows. To format them or change their content, change the original designated header row content and the repeated headers will follow suit.

Choose Table → Heading Rows Repeat again to turn the feature off. As soon as you click back inside the table, the heading rows will disappear from second and subsequent pages.

Table → Convert → Text to Table

The Text to Table command converts virtually any text to a table. Anything from a tabbed list to a series of paragraphs can be turned into a table by determining the number of columns and rows, applying an AutoFormat (if desired), and selecting the *delimiter* (a character or code that tells Word where to break the text to place it in individual cells).

The Convert Text to Table dialog (Figure 10-20) works pretty much like the Insert Table dialog used to create a new table. First, choose the number of columns and rows for the new table. Next, specify how the columns should be sized. These options are covered earlier in the chapter. Finally, choose the type of character that delimits, or separates, the items in the text that should be placed in individual cells. For example, select commas and a new cell is created for each comma in the original text. Use the Other option to enter a custom delimiter.

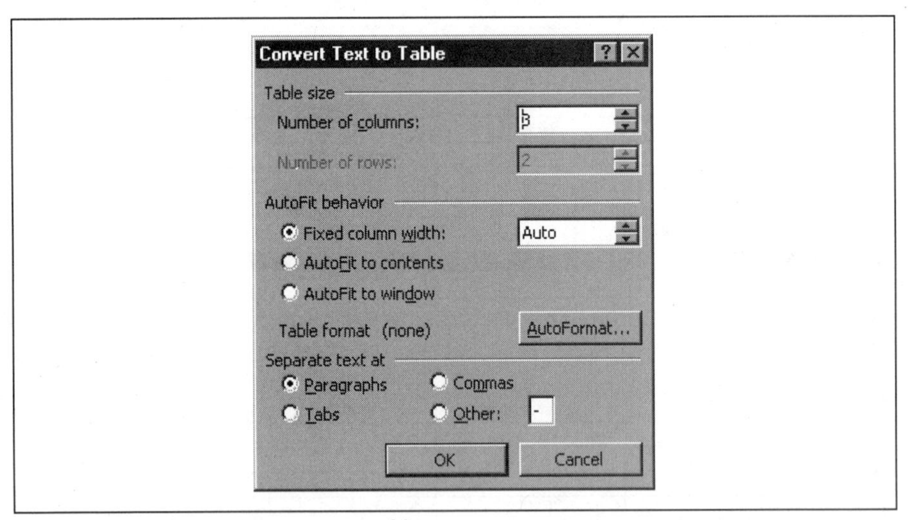

Figure 10-20: Converting text to a table

The most common text-to-table conversion involves tabbed text. Converting the tabbed list in Figure 10-21 creates a three-column, four-row table.

Invoice	Amount	Date
1234	$350.00	10/5/99
2468	$500.00	10/6/99
3579	$750.00	10/11/99

Figure 10-21: Tabbed lists are easily converted to tables

TIP # 123

Show Hidden Formatting Before Converting Text to a Table

Before using either of the Convert submenu's commands, it is a good idea to use the Show/Hide button on the Standard toolbar to display hard returns, tabs, spaces, and page break codes. This helps you select the text to convert more precisely and choose the best delimiter for the job.

Table → Convert → Table to Text

The Table to Text command (Figure 10-22) converts an existing table to text, using a delimiter character to separate the content of individual cells. For example, delimiting the content with tabs usually creates a list with tabbed columns.

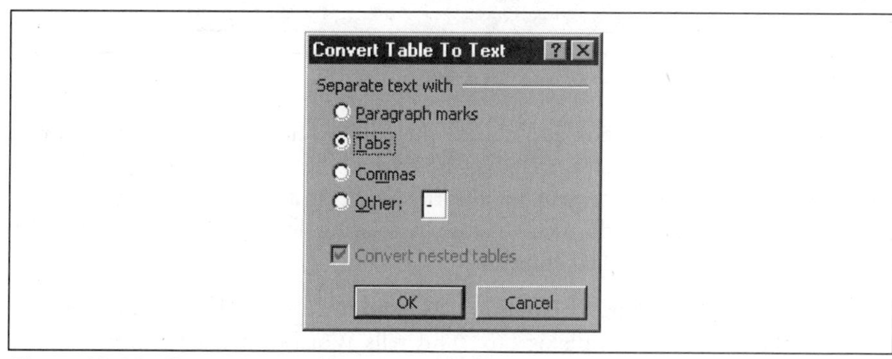

Figure 10-22: Converting a table to non-tabular text

If the table contains a nested table, the "Convert nested tables" option becomes available in the Convert Table to Text dialog box and is enabled by default. If the chosen delimiter is a paragraph mark, the "Convert nested tables" option can be disabled. With commas, tabs, and custom delimiters, it cannot be disabled.

When nested table is converted, the contents of the cells in the nested table are placed right along with the contents of cells in the main table. When nested tables are not converted, they appear as standalone tables within the text from the main table. Nested tables are delimited just like the contents of any other cells in the main table.

Table → Sort

Many tables are designed to look (and perhaps operate) like mini-databases. A list of records, one in each row, topped by a row of column headings that identify the components of each row (functioning as database fields) is a typical arrangement. The Table → Sort command (Figure 10-23) sorts rows by up to three column headings within a table.

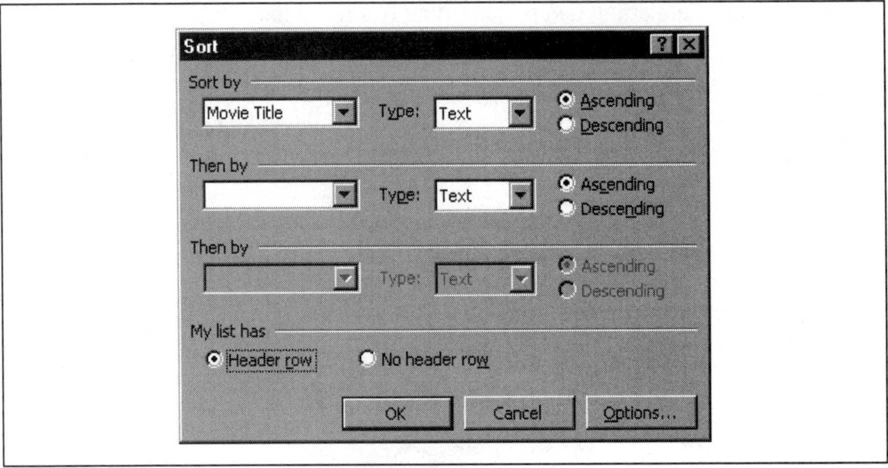

Figure 10-23: Sorting the rows of data in a table

Click the first Sort by list box and choose the column heading on which to sort a table's rows. Once the first Sort by box is set, use the others to apply additional levels of sorting. For example, you could sort a list of contacts first by state and then by city. For each sort performed, choose Ascending for an alphabetical sort or Descending for a reverse alphabetical sort.

If the lists display columns as Column 1, Column 2, etc., click the Header row option at the bottom of the dialog box. This tells Word to use the contents of the cells on the top row of the table for sorting. This also tells Word not to include the header row in the actual sort.

The Options button on the Sort dialog opens a separate dialog with additional options. Use it to:

- Set delimiters when sorting non-tabular text (see Tip # 124)
- Set a language for the sort
- Make capitalized words come before lowercased words in a sort
- Sort only a selected column instead of the whole table

TIP # 124

Use Table → Sort on Non-Tabular Text

The Table → Sort command can sort tabbed columns of text and lists of items as well as tables. For tabbed columns, the first line in the text is interpreted as the header row. To further define the sort's parameters for non-table text, click the Options button in the Sort dialog box to choose the delimiter that separates non-table text.

Table → Formula

Use the Formula command to perform calculations on cells with numbers. For example, a column of numbers can be summed and the total presented at the bottom of the table. Place the insertion point in the cell that should contain the results of the formula and choose Table → Formula (Figure 10-24).

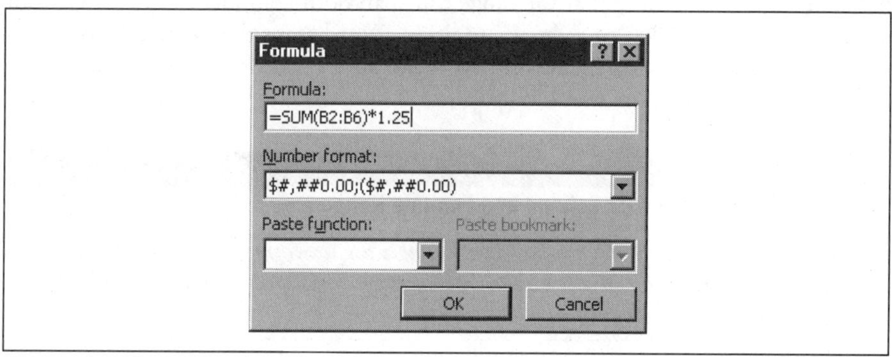

Figure 10-24: Constructing formulas that reference cells in a table

Word always suggests a formula based on the position of the active cell when the command is issued. This formula is rarely what is really needed. Just erase it to build your own. All formulas must start with an equals sign. After this, formulas are composed of three parts:

Operators
: Common mathematical operators such as +, -, *, and /.

Functions
: Special procedures provided by Word. Functions always appear outside parentheses. Examples of common functions are SUM, which is used to add specified values together, AVERAGE, which calculates the average of specified values, and MIN, which calculates the smallest of any specified values. Enter the name of a function directly into the Formula box or choose a function from the Paste Function list. Choosing from the list enters the value in the Formula box at the insertion point.

Values

Simple numbers or the data in specific cells in a table. Values that are acted on by functions appear inside parentheses to the right of the function. For example, in the formula =SUM(5,8,9), the numbers five, eight, and nine are the values acted on by the SUM function.

A value can be more than just a number. It can also reference a specific cell in the active table or in any table in the document. Cells are typically referred to by their column and row position. Columns are lettered from left to right and rows are numbered from top to bottom. Thus, the cell in the third row of the third column would be C3. Note that cell references like this are always absolute. Inserting rows or columns later would mess up an existing formula.

Cells can be referenced by themselves or as part of a range. The formula =SUM(B2,C3,C8) would calculate the sum of the three cells listed inside the parentheses. Reference a range of cells by separating the first and last cell with a colon. For example, the formula =SUM(B2:C8) would calculate the sum of all of the cells between B2 and C8. Note that the range can span both columns and rows. Cells in a range are read from left to right. In addition, Word stops the range calculation as soon as it encounters any blank cell, so make sure no cells in a range are blank before performing a calculation.

TIP # 125

Specify a Whole Row or Column in a Formula Range

To specify an entire row or column in a range, use the same row or column name on both sides of the colon in a formula. For example, C:C specifies the entire C column. 5:5 specifies the whole fifth row.

Mark frequently used ranges with a bookmark by selecting the group of cells in the table and using the Insert → Bookmark command. The name that you give the bookmark appears in the Paste Bookmark list on the Formula dialog for easy reference.

Formulas can also include references to other tables in the same Word document. First, bookmark the table to reference by selecting the entire table and using the Insert → Bookmark command. When creating the formula in a cell in another table, reference the bookmarked table and the cells in the formula. For example, the formula =SUM(Table1 C4:E4) would calculate the sum of the cells between C4 and E4 in the table bookmarked "Table 1."

Table → Hide/Show Gridlines

Table gridlines are thin gray lines displayed by default so that it is easier to see where rows and columns are in tables where borders are not displayed. When gridlines are hidden, the menu command changes to Show Gridlines. Many users find gridlines distracting while working with tables where borders will not be shown in the final product. Note that the Hide/Show Gridlines command affects an entire document, not just a single table, so a table need not be selected to use the command.

Table → Table Properties

The Table Properties dialog box shows the current settings for the selected table. These settings appear as options in four different tabs: Table, Row, Column, and Cell. Note that many of the properties found on the four tabs can also be accessed on a context menu by right-clicking the appropriate table element in the document.

The Table Tab

Use the Table tab (Figure 10-25) to select a preferred width for the table and a measurement method (inches or a percentage of the window size). Set the alignment for a table (left, center, or right), and choose how or if non-table text flows around the table.

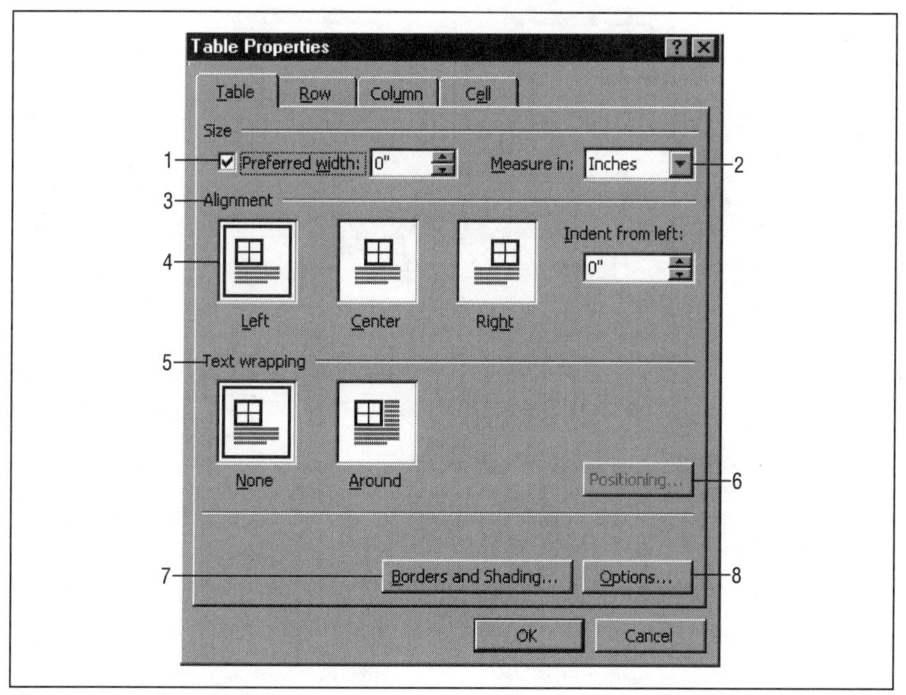

Figure 10-25: Setting table properties

1. *Preferred width*. Enter the width the table should be on the page. By default, this option is disabled and the table extends from margin to margin. Set a value in the box to alter the table's width. Entering a zero value disables the option.

2. *Measure in.* By default, table widths are expressed in inches. Alternately, tables can be measured as a percentage of the entire page width.
3. *Alignment.* Align the table to the left, center, or right of the page relative to the page margins.
4. *Indent from left.* If the table is left aligned, use the "Indent from left" to set the distance the table should be from the left margin. This option is not available when center or right alignment is selected.
5. *Text wrapping.* Specify whether a table should use text wrapping or not. When not wrapped, text resumes on the line below the table. When the Around option is set, the text wraps around tables that are less than a full-page width.
6. *Positioning.* The Positioning button becomes available only when the Around text wrapping style is selected and opens a separate dialog used to configure wrapping (Figure 10-26).

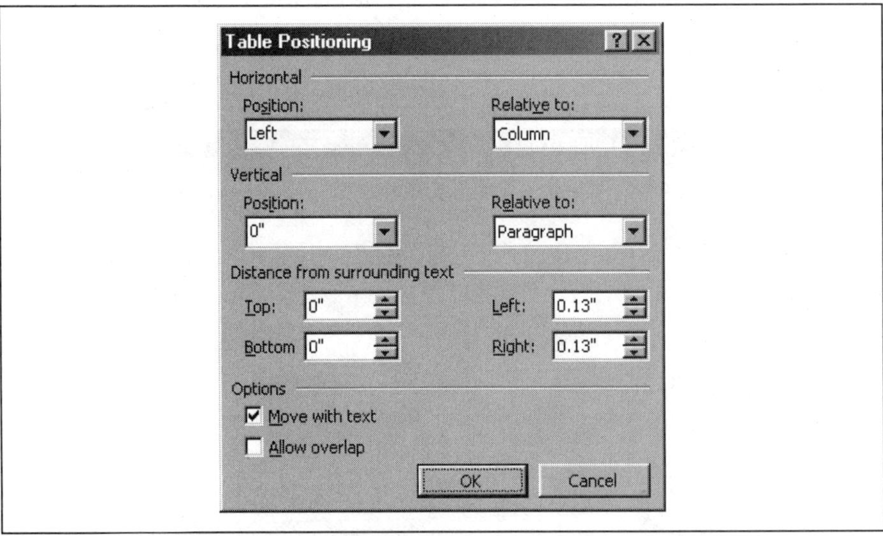

Figure 10-26: Setting wrapping options for a table

- *Horizontal.* Set the horizontal position of the table (left, right, center, inside, or outside) relative to the nearest page, margin, or column.
- *Vertical.* Set the vertical position of the table (top, center, bottom, inside, or outside) relative to the nearest page, margin, or paragraph.
- *Distance from surrounding text.* Set the distance between the outside of the table and the text on all four sides of the table.

- *Move with text*. With this option enabled, moving the text surrounding the table in the document moves the table as well.
- *Allow overlap*. This option is used mainly for web documents and allows the table to overlap with text or pictures when viewed in a web browser.

7. *Borders and Shading*. This button on the Table tab opens the same Borders and Shading dialog available through Format → Borders and Shading. This command is covered in Chapter 8.
8. *Options*. This button opens a separate dialog (Figure 10-27) used to set optional table parameters.

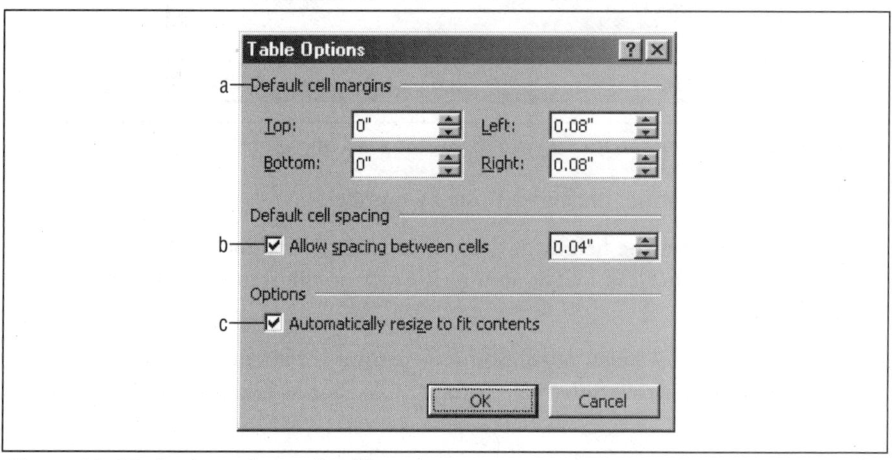

Figure 10-27: Setting advanced table options

a. *Default cell margins*. Set the margins used by default inside the cells of the table. The margin specifies the distance used between the cell wall and the contents of the cell. This is also sometimes referred to as cell padding.

b. *Allow spacing between cells*. Set the distance used between cells in a table. By default, no spacing is used. Cell spacing is especially useful when creating a table for layout that does not use interior borders. Often the contents of different cells can appear too close together using the default settings.

c. *Automatically resize to fit contents*. Set this option to have Word automatically resize columns to accommodate text and objects. This is the same setting made using Table → AutoFit → Fit to Contents.

The Row Tab

Use the Row tab (Figure 10-28) to set the height of selected rows, and choose whether rows can break across pages.

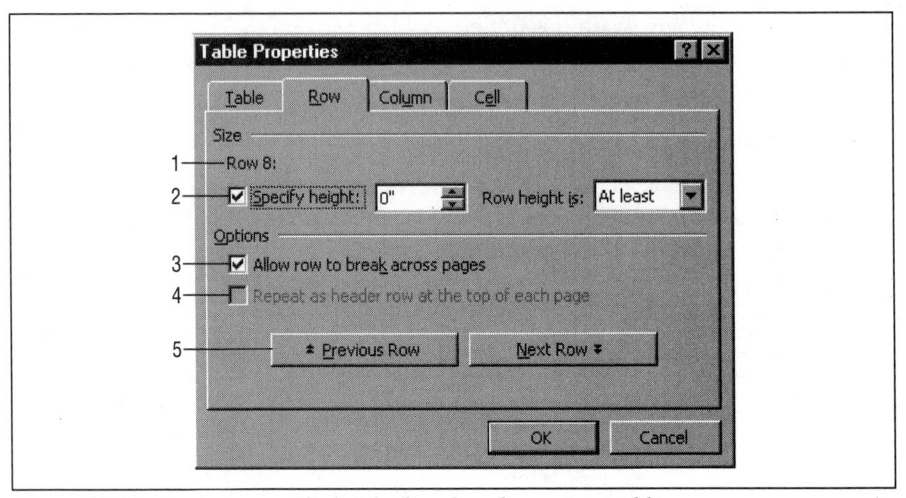

Figure 10-28: Setting a specific height for selected rows in a table

1. *Row x.* This identifies the current row by number.
2. *Specify height.* Set the height of the row in inches. Use the "Row height is" list to specify whether the height setting is exact or the minimum height the row should be.
3. *Allow row to break across pages.* Sometimes rows are long. Enable this option to allow a particular row to have an internal page break. Disable it if the row must be on one page.
4. *Repeat as header row at the top of each page.* This option designates the selected rows to be a table heading that is repeated on subsequent pages. This option is only available if the selected rows include the top row of a table. This is the same option set using the Table → Heading Rows Repeat command.
5. *Previous (Next) Row.* Use these buttons to move between rows in a table without having to close and reopen the Table Properties dialog.

The Column Tab

Use the Column tab (Figure 10-29) to set the width of selected columns in inches or as percentage of the total page width. Use the Previous Column and Next Column buttons to move between columns without closing the dialog.

The Cell Tab

Use the Cell tab (Figure 10-30) to set the width for selected cells in inches or as a percentage of the total page width. In addition, choose how text is aligned vertically within the cells: top, center, and bottom. These alignment settings duplicate those found on the Tables and Borders toolbar.

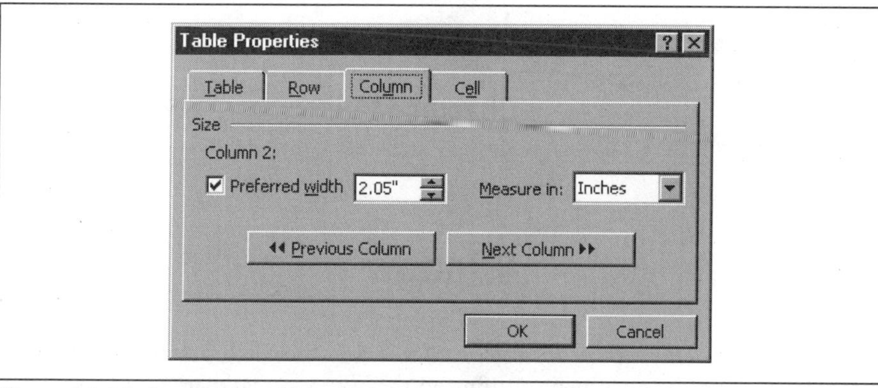

Figure 10-29: Setting the width of selected columns

The Options button opens a separate dialog used to adjust the interior margins of the selected cells in inches. These margins override the default cell margins for the table set on the Table tab of the Table Properties dialog. There are also two other settings on the Options dialog:

- Set the text wrapping in a cell so that cells lengthen with new text but the cell width remains the same.
- Make text fit into a cell of fixed size regardless of how much text is entered (text just gets smaller as it's typed to fit).

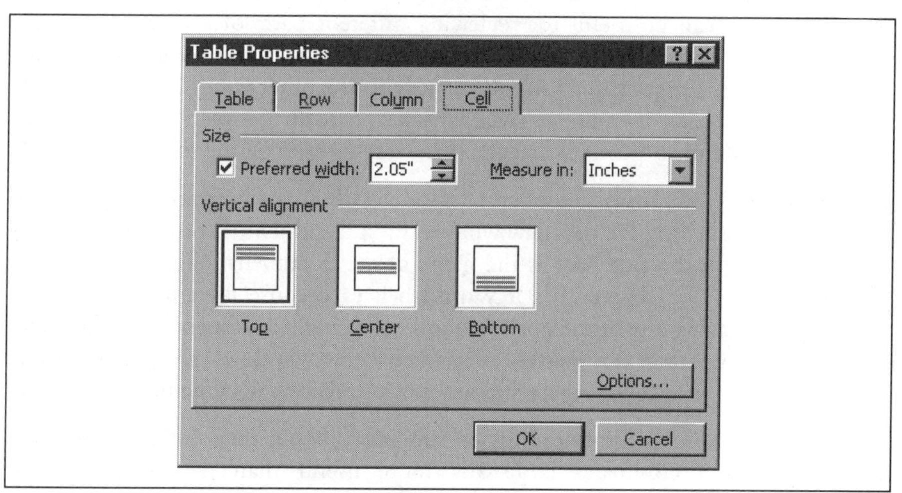

Figure 10-30: Setting the width and alignment of a cell

Chapter 11

Window

Word's new *Single Document Interface* makes it easy to switch between open documents by clicking the document buttons on the Windows taskbar. Word also offers another convenient way to switch between documents: the Window menu. The Window menu offers users the advantage of quickly switching between documents using the keyboard, something more difficult to do with taskbar buttons.

In addition, the Window menu offers three commands for viewing multiple instances of a single document and arranging documents that are already open: New Window, Arrange All, and Split.

Window → New Window

The Window → New Window command opens a duplicate of the currently active document. This can be useful for reviewing different parts of a document at the same time. The contents of the two windows are identical: make an edit in one window and the changes appear simultaneously in the other window. Each window behaves like a regular document; switch back and forth between them using the taskbar or the Window menu or arrange them side-by-side on the screen.

There's no real limit to the number of windows that can be opened for a given document. On opening the first new window for a document, Word labels the original document (in the title bar) as the name of the document followed by a colon followed by a 1 (i.e., Chapter 10:1). Word labels each consecutive new window :2, :3, and so on. Saving any of the open windows of a single document saves the document. Remember that no matter how many new windows are created using Window → New Window, you are still looking at only one document.

When running your monitor at a higher resolution (better than 800x600, say), the Window → Split command is usually more useful than the New Window command. The Split command is discussed later in this chapter.

TIP # 126

Different Views for Different Windows

One great advantage to using more than one window for a document is being able to look at the document in different views. For example, you could view a document in Normal view in one window and in Web view in another. Edits made in either window are automatically reflected in the other window.

Window → Arrange All

The Window → Arrange All command attempts to tile all of the currently open documents to fit on the screen at the same time. In theory, this sounds nice. In practice, I've found it to be a pretty useless command. When working with more than two documents, even at a high screen resolution, viewing all the documents on the screen at once makes each of the windows too small to do any real work (see Figure 11-1 for an example of what I'm talking about), even at a high monitor resolution. In addition, Word's tiling of windows is usually not as effective as the tiling you can do yourself by manually resizing and moving document windows.

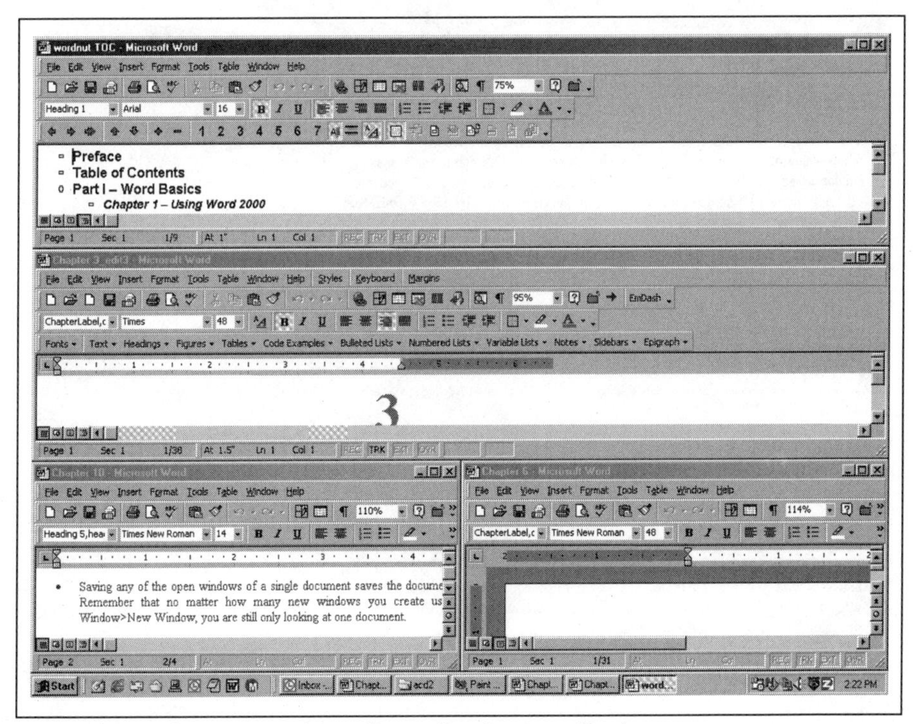

Figure 11-1: The more windows, the smaller the view of each

When working with two document windows, the Arrange All command does do a good job of tiling windows vertically, placing one document above the other on the screen. Word does not sport a command for tiling windows horizontally; you have to do it yourself.

When using multiple monitors on the same computer (Windows 98 and Windows 2000 allow this), Word's Arrange All command still takes all open documents and arranges them only on the primary monitor.

Window → Split

The Window → Split command splits the view of an open document into two panes, one above the other (Figure 11-2). The pointer changes to a split indicator for placing the split. Adjust the split any time by dragging the bar between the two panes.

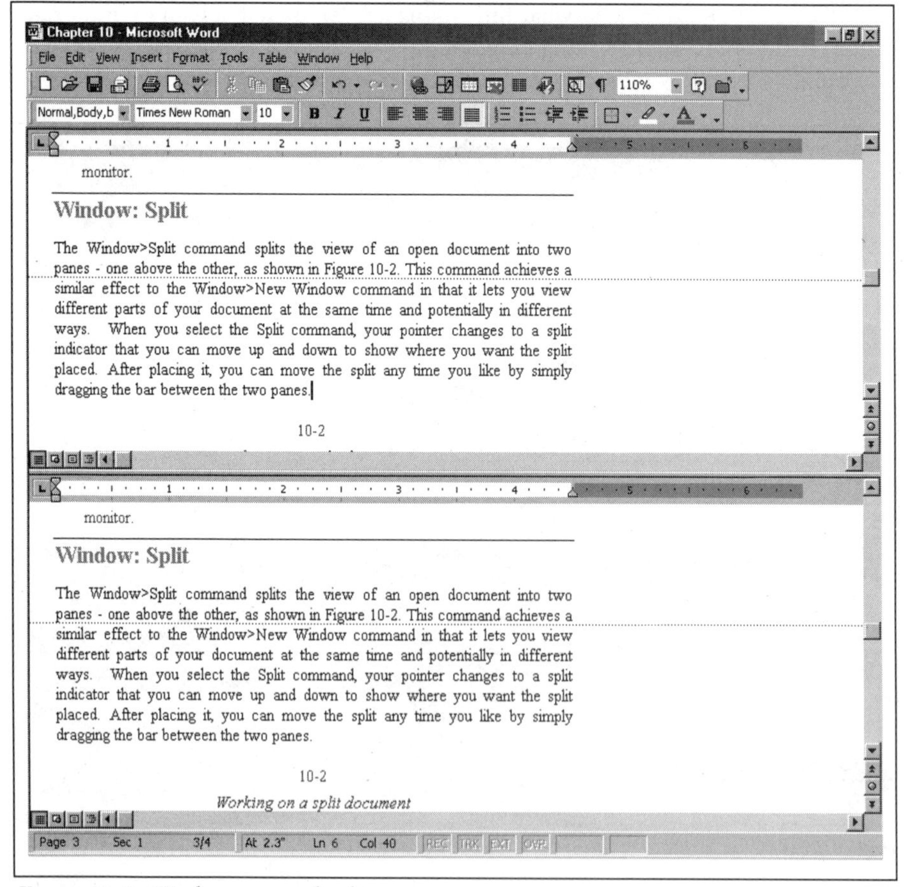

Figure 11-2: Working on a split document

This command achieves a similar effect to the Window → New Window command in that different parts of your document can be displayed at the same time and potentially in different ways. After splitting a window, the Window → Split command changes into Window → Remove Split. Once a split is removed, whatever window contains the insertion point becomes the working view.

After splitting a window, modifications in either of the two panes are automatically reflected in the other pane. Many of Word's View menu commands apply to whatever window the insertion point is in when the command is selected. For example, place the insertion point in the top pane and select View → Normal. Then place the insertion point in the bottom pane and select View → Outline. As shown in Figure 11-3, this displays the document in Normal view in one pane while keeping tabs on the outline in another.

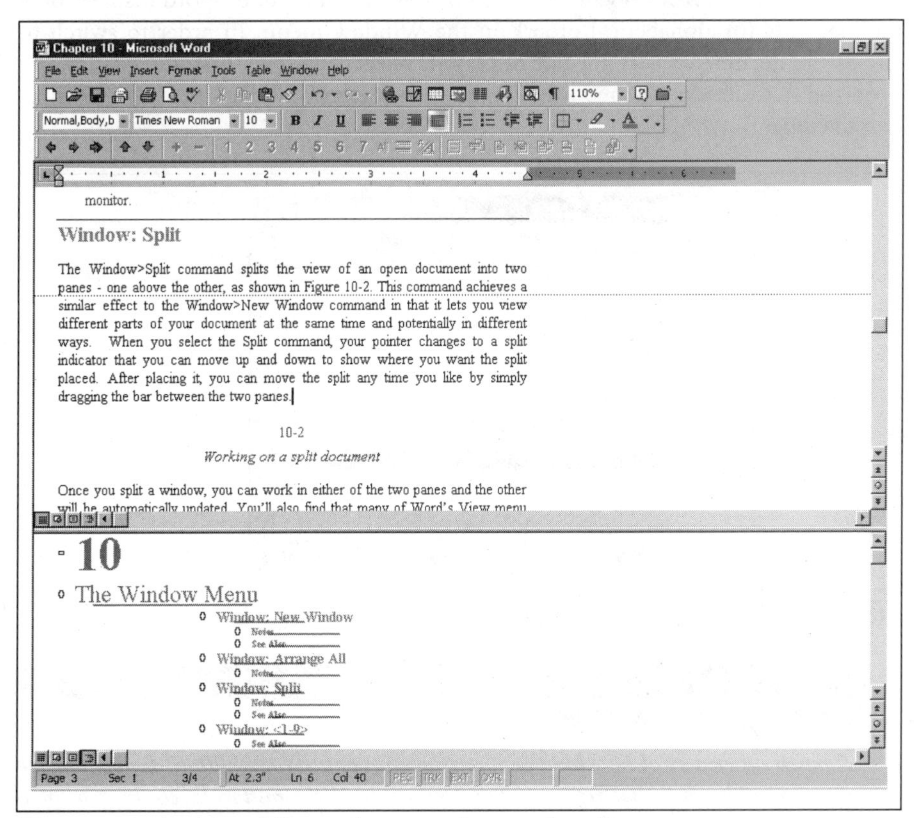

Figure 11-3: Applying different views to each pane of a split

Window → <1-9>

A list of currently open Word documents follows the Window → Split command. Select any of these documents (or type the number of the document on the keyboard) to switch to that document.

Word displays only nine documents on the Window menu at any time, and these are arranged in alphabetical order. If more than nine documents are open, the More Windows command is added to the Window menu to manage the extra documents.

Window → More Windows

If more than nine Word documents are open at the same time, Word displays only the first nine (in alphabetical order) on the Window menu. In order to switch to any of the documents that are not displayed, select Window → More Windows to open the Activate dialog shown in Figure 11-4. Select any document to switch to that document.

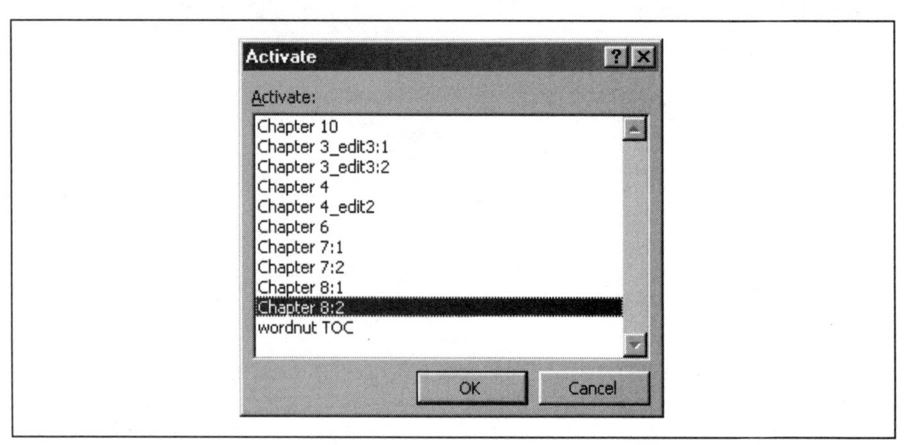

Figure 11-4: Work with more documents

TIP # 127

Use the Taskbar to Switch Between Documents

A much easier way of switching between documents in Word 2000 is simply to click the taskbar buttons that represent the documents. If the button labels are too small to read, hover the pointer over a button for a moment to display a pop-up tip. You might also want to increase the size of your taskbar.

Chapter 12

Help

Let's face it—Word is a big program, and all the users I know find themselves needing help sometimes. Word's online help system is a pretty useful tool, though most users find themselves wanting to turn off the Office Assistant the first chance they get. In addition to providing access to Word's standard help system, the Help menu offers a few other tools as well. The What's This command is a handy way to see what a particular item in Word's interface does or what the formatting is for a character or paragraph. Office on the Web links to Microsoft's web site, which provides information on Word and even a few handy downloads. WordPerfect Help leads to a complete command reference (and even demos) for WordPerfect users. Finally, Detect and Repair scans all of the Word program files to detect corrupt or missing files and replace them from the Office CD.

Help → Microsoft Word Help

Word offers two basic interfaces to the help system: the traditional help window and the disreputable Office Assistant. Both offer access to all of the same help files.

The Office Assistant

Unless you performed a custom installation of Word and specifically chose not to install the Office Assistant, that little animated paper clip (see Figure 12-1) was likely your first introduction to Word's online help.

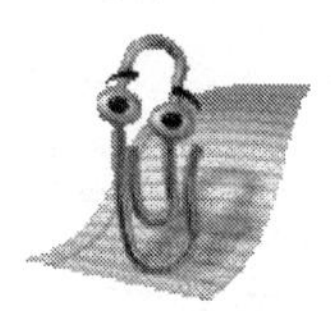

Figure 12-1: Clippit, looking innocuous, but he's annoyed more people than Word itself

TIP # 128

Turn the Office Assistant Off

Some people love it and some people hate it, but the one thing about the Office Assistant Microsoft did right was to give users a way to turn it off. Right-click the Office Assistant and choose Options from the shortcut menu. Remove the check next to "Use Office Assistant" and you'll be bothered no more. To use the assistant but not have to look at it all the time, choose Hide from the same shortcut menu. The assistant reappears when it has something to say.

Help → Microsoft Word Help opens the Office Assistant, which promptly asks what you would like to do (Figure 12-2). If the Office Assistant is already displayed, click it once to get the same effect. Enter a topic, some keywords, or even a complete question, click Search and the Office Assistant shows you up to twelve topics that match the query (click See More to view the second screen of topics). Click on any topic to jump to that page in the help window. The help window is the same as the one used in the traditional help interface, which is described in the next section.

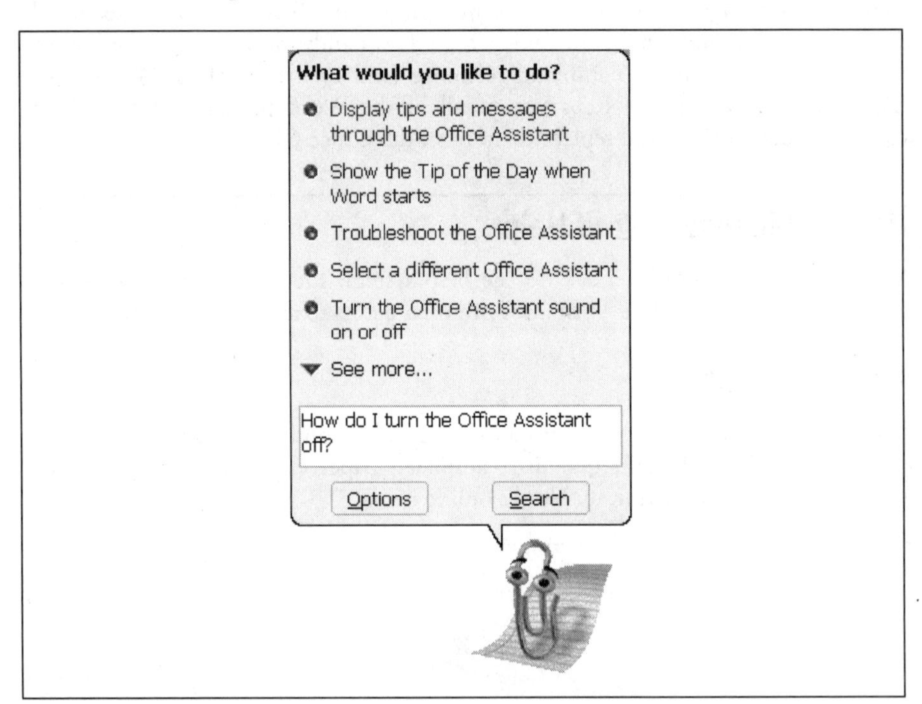

Figure 12-2: Using the Office Assistant

The Microsoft Word Help button on the Standard toolbar displays the Office Assistant if it is not showing. If it is showing, the button displays the search box (which is also shown when you click the assistant itself). If the assistant is turned off, the button starts up the traditional help window.

In addition to providing a way to search for help topics, the Office Assistant does a few other things. Perhaps the best way to see some of these things is to look at the Office Assistant configuration options. While the Office Assistant is showing, right-click it and choose Options from the shortcut menu. This opens up the dialog box shown in Figure 12-3 and provides access to the options detailed in the following list.

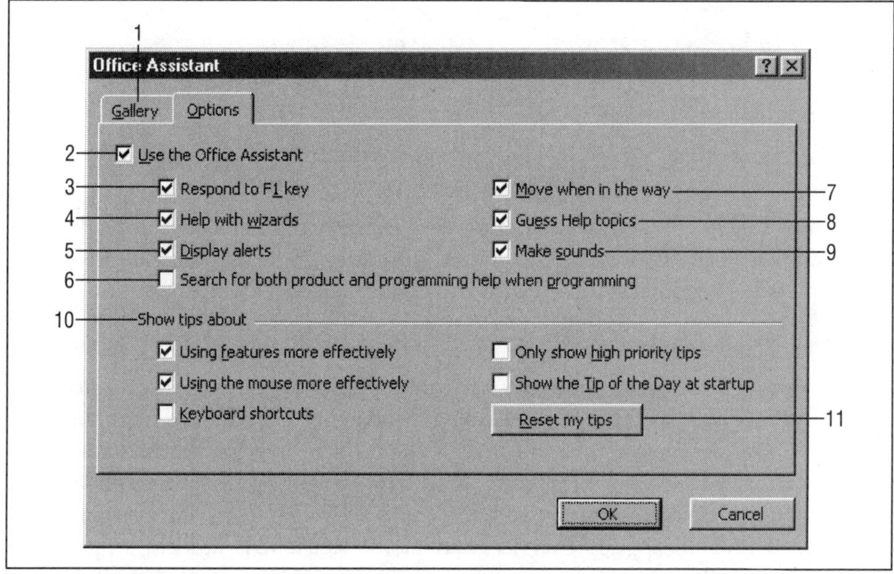

Figure 12-3: Configuring (or disabling) the Office Assistant

1. *Gallery*. Choose from a number of different Office Assistants. Click the Gallery tab and scroll through the characters displayed. Select one and he'll be your pal from then on. The least annoying assistant? Probably Einstein. You'll likely need to install additional assistants from your CD, so make sure to have it handy. Other assistants are also available from the Office web site.

2. *Use the Office Assistant*. Remove the check next to "Use the Office Assistant" to turn it off completely. From then on, Word only displays the traditional help window, regular dialog boxes, and none of the Office Assistant's tips.

3. *Respond to F1 key*. You can also leave the assistant running, but control what types of things it responds to. The "Respond to F1 key" option makes the assistant respond to the context-sensitive help invoked using the F1 key.

4. *Help with wizards*. This option causes the assistant to pop-up additional "helpful" text during Word's many wizards. Since the wizards themselves usually include most of the necessary information, this one is pretty useless.

5. *Display alerts*. Alerts are the dialog boxes that pop up asking things like "Do you want to save changes made to *xyz.doc*?" This option makes it appear as if the assistant is asking those questions instead of them appearing in a traditional

dialog box. This option can be particularly dangerous, as many people tend to automatically answer No or Cancel when the assistant asks them a question.

6. *Search for both product and programming help when programming.* When using VBA to program Word, the help system can display help both on Word itself and on the VBA language. This option makes the wizard search help topics for both categories.
7. *Move when in the way.* When using the Office Assistant, make sure this option is turned on. It makes the assistant automatically jump out of the focus of your work (dialog boxes, selected words, etc.).
8. *Guess Help topics.* This option causes the assistant to display help topics based on the work you are doing when you first open the search box (see Figure 12-2). For example, suppose you are copying text between documents and then click the assistant to ask it a question. The assistant automatically displays help topics associated with copying text between documents.
9. *Make sounds.* Just turn it off.
10. *Show tips about.* Word watches what you do. Each of the tip options causes the assistant to display advice about doing a job more effectively. For example, if the "Using the mouse more effectively" option is turned on, the assistant might notice that you usually select paragraphs by highlighting the paragraph yourself and suggest doing it more quickly by triple-clicking. When the assistant has a tip, a light bulb appears over its head. If the assistant is hidden, a light bulb appears on the Microsoft Word Help button on the Standard toolbar. The assistant can also show you a tip each time you start Word.
11. *Reset my tips.* Click this button to reset all of the tips that the Office Assistant has shown in the past. All of the tips are displayed again.

The Traditional Help Window

If the Office Assistant is disabled, Help → Microsoft Word Help shrinks the document and brings up a more traditional, and more useful, help window right beside it (Figure 12-4). This window works in much the same way as Windows help and provides the same functionality as the Office Assistant except for tips. It also lets you browse through the contents of the help files and search an index of terms.

The following list describes the Help window options:

1. *Hide/Show Tabs.* Click this button to toggle the display of the Contents, Answer Wizard, and Index tabs on and off. When off, only the right pane (the help file itself) shows.
2. *Options.* This button opens a menu with several options on it. These options duplicate the functions provided by the buttons on the toolbar and also add

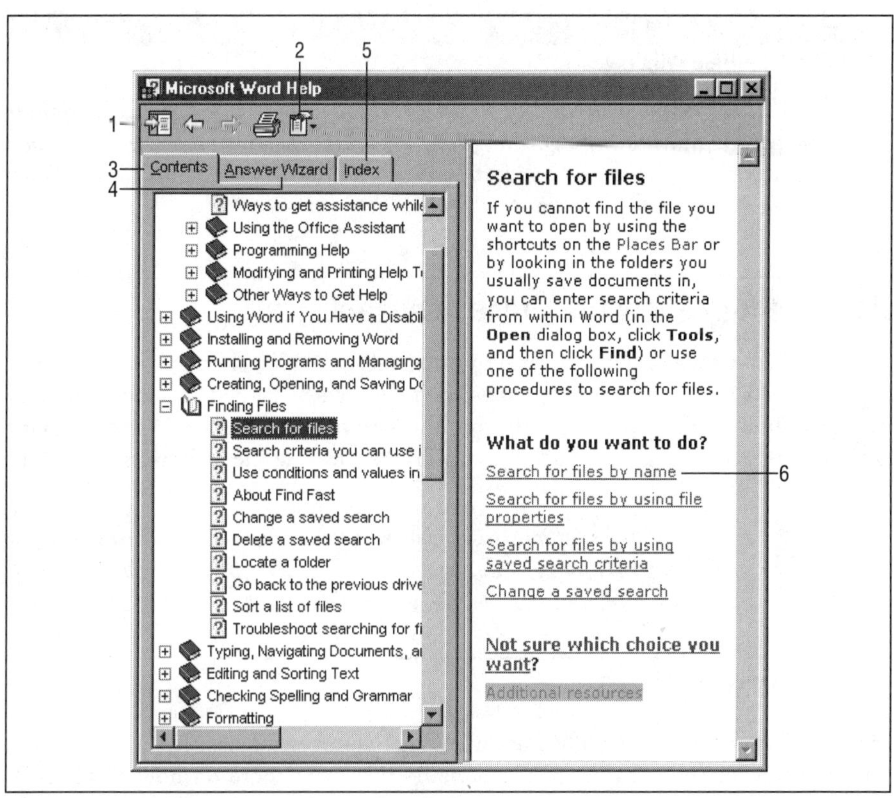

Figure 12-4: A better approach to getting help

Stop and Refresh commands, as well as a shortcut to the Windows Internet Settings dialog box (Windows Control Panel → Internet Settings).

3. *Contents*. Use this tab to browse through the contents of Word help. The standard Windows plusses and minuses expand and collapse entries. Click any help topic to display that help page in the right-hand pane.

4. *Answer Wizard*. This tab provides access to the same search functionality as is provided by the Office Assistant. Enter a topic, some keywords, or even a complete question, click Search and help will show you topics that match the query. Pick one to display it in the right-hand pane.

5. *Index*. Use this tab to search an index of the help files for keywords. This option is great for finding information on specific features that may not have their own associated category or help page. I use this help feature more than any other.

6. *Links*. Many help pages contain hyperlinks that lead to other pages in the help system, web sites, or even to dialog boxes within Word.

TIP # 129

Resize the Help Window

Drag the Help window around by clicking and dragging its title bar (unlike regular windows, the title bar is gray). After dragging a bit, the window changes to a more manageable size. Resize and put it anywhere. The next time Help is opened, Word remembers the previous size and position.

Help → Hide/Show the Office Assistant

This command toggles between Hide Office Assistant and Show Office Assistant, depending on the situation. If the assistant is hidden or turned off, the command becomes Show Office Assistant. Selecting this command while the Office Assistant is turned off actually turns it back on and displays it. Use the assistant's options to turn it off again.

After hiding the Office Assistant several times, the assistant learns that you don't like it and opens a dialog asking whether to just hide it or turn it off altogether. Almost makes you feel guilty, doesn't it?

Help → What's This?

Help → What's This? is actually a useful enough command that it has found its way onto my toolbar (see Chapter 3, *Customizing Word*, for more on how to do this). After selecting the command, the pointer turns into an arrow and question mark. Click anything on the screen to get information. For example, click on a toolbar button to see the name of the button and a brief description of what it does.

While this alone may not seem very useful, What's This also does something else that's pretty cool. After selecting the command (or pressing Shift-F1), click on any character in a document to pop up a ScreenTip showing that text's character and paragraph formatting properties (Figure 12-5). Though much of this information is available by selecting the text and looking at the formatting toolbar and the status bar, the What's This pop-ups also provide additional information on style settings. Notice that a box is drawn around the character in the document to indicate the selection.

Click an interface element, such as a button, after viewing the pop-up tip and the pointer returns to normal. Click another character, however, and the pointer remains the What's This pointer, letting you click other characters to display their properties. Turn this off by selecting Help → What's This? again or by clicking an interface element.

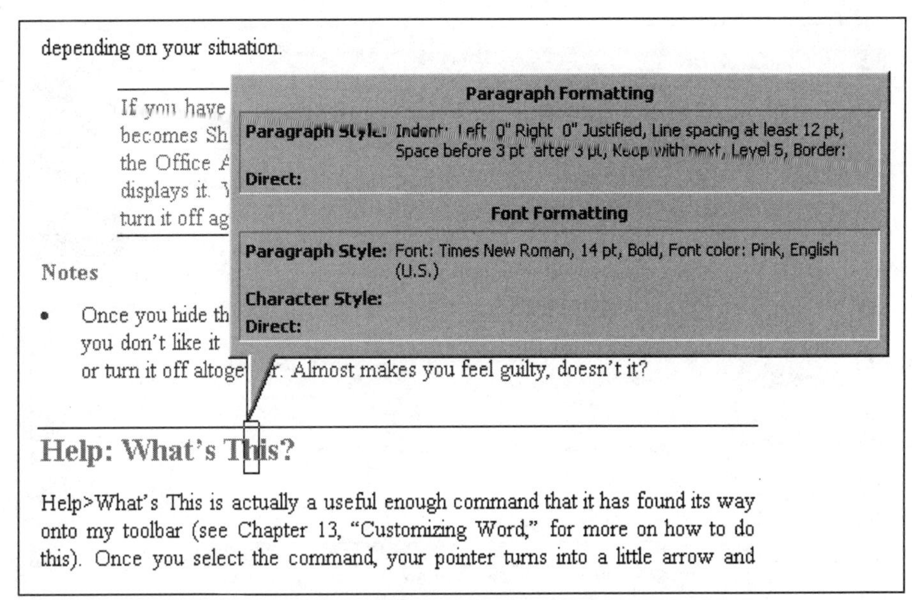

Figure 12-5: Using Help → What's This? to display formatting properties

TIP # 130

Other Pop-up Tips

Dialog boxes usually offer their own What's This tips accessed by right-clicking any element of the dialog and choosing What's This from the shortcut menu that appears. Point to many interface elements without using the What's This command to pop-up a screen tip that shows the name of the element.

Help → Office on the Web

If your computer has an Internet connection, Help → Office on the Web opens the default browser and links to the Word section of the Microsoft Office Update site (Figure 12-6). This site offers the latest official word on Word, useful utilities to download, and online assistance.

My favorite downloads are:

WOPR 2000 PlaceBar Customizer
: A utility for customizing the places in the Open and Save As dialogs. For more about these dialogs, check out Chapter 4, *File*.

Microsoft Office 2000 Customizable Alerts
: This one adds a Web Info button to many of the most frequently occurring Office alert dialogs. Clicking the button links to a web page with more information.

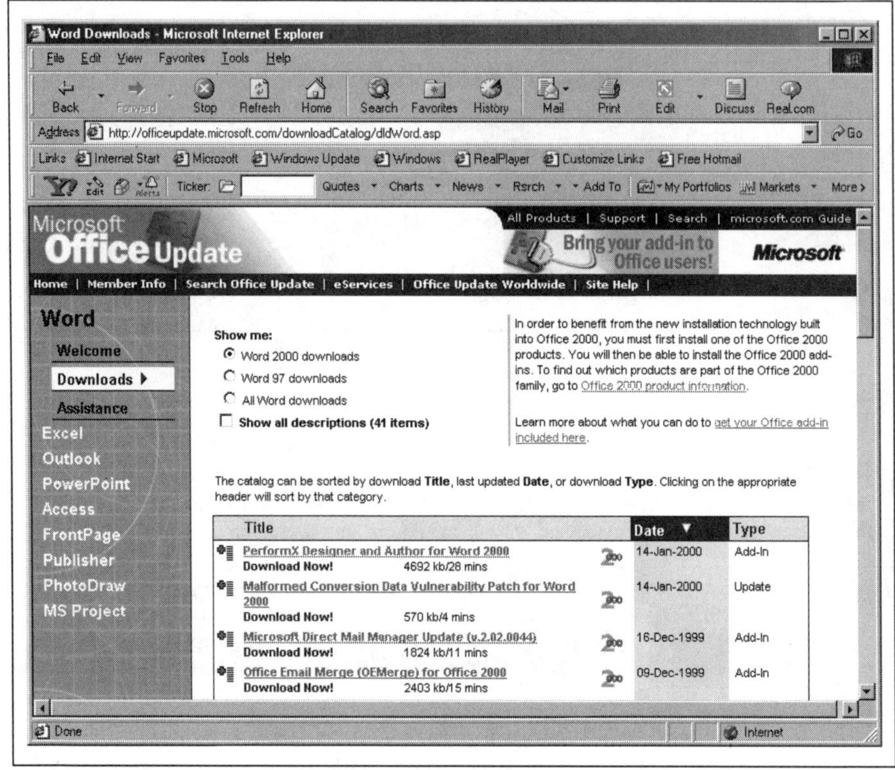

Figure 12-6: Downloading from the Office Update site

PRIME Bookmark Popup
: This utility creates an alphabetical list of all the bookmarks in a Word 2000 document and provides navigation between them via a pop-up menu.

Office HTML Filter 2.0
: This is a tool for removing Office-specific markup tags embedded in Office 2000 documents saved as HTML. This is discussed further in Chapter 16, *Creating a Web Page*.

Help → WordPerfect Help

For users switching from WordPerfect to Word (or those of you who must use both), Word provides a nice, if sometimes finicky, tool to help ease the transition. Help → WordPerfect Help opens the Help for WordPerfect Users dialog (Figure 12-7). A list of commands is shown in the Command keys box. Select any command and text to the right shows information about using the command in both Word and WordPerfect. If applicable, it also shows the command keys used in each application.

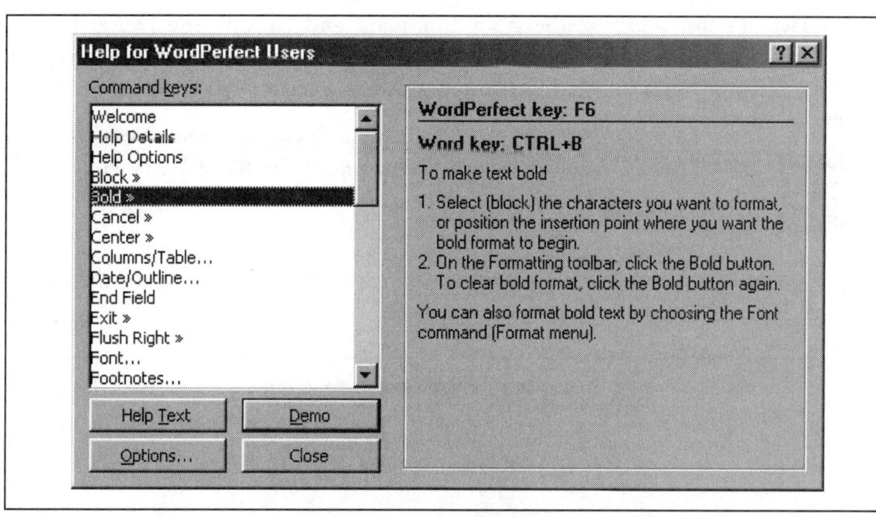

Figure 12-7: Getting help with WordPerfect commands

For each command listed, the following characters (shown to the right of the command in the dialog) tell something about the kind of help available:

- A double caret (>>), as shown beside the Block command in Figure 12-7, means that a demo is available. Double-click the command (or select the command and press Alt-D) to launch the demo. In a demo, Word opens a dialog that provides text instructions on using the command. The dialog remains open while you perform the instructions. On closing the demo dialog, WordPerfect Help also closes and you must reopen it from the Help menu.
- An ellipse (...), as shown beside the Font command, indicates that the command has a submenu. Double-click the command (or select the command and press Enter) to open the submenu. The submenu for the font command, for example, shows associated commands for changing the size, appearance, and other font formatting. Interestingly, once you view a submenu, there is no way to get back to the parent menu. You must close WordPerfect Help and reopen it.

The Help Text and Demo buttons on the WordPerfect Help dialog can be a little difficult to get the hang of. First off, clicking either button after opening the Help dialog (while the command selected is Welcome, Help Details, or Help Options) makes the dialog just go away. If any other command is selected, WordPerfect Help attempts to display the help text or a demo (depending on the button you press) for the command.

Help Text displays a dialog that provides text instructions on using the command and even lets you perform the steps while the dialog is open. If this sounds like the description of the demo in the first bullet above, that's because it's exactly the same. The Demo button, on the other hand, actually attempts to perform the action for you so that you can see the effects. For example, if text is selected when Word

Perfect Help opens, selecting the Bold command and clicking the Demo button makes that text bold. This action also closes WordPerfect Help. If no text was selected, clicking Demo for the bold command would just close the dialog (no error message or anything).

The default action of the Help Text button in WordPerfect Help is the same as double-clicking to launch a demo of a command. It performs the action.

Set options in WordPerfect Help using the Options button, which opens the dialog shown in Figure 12-8.

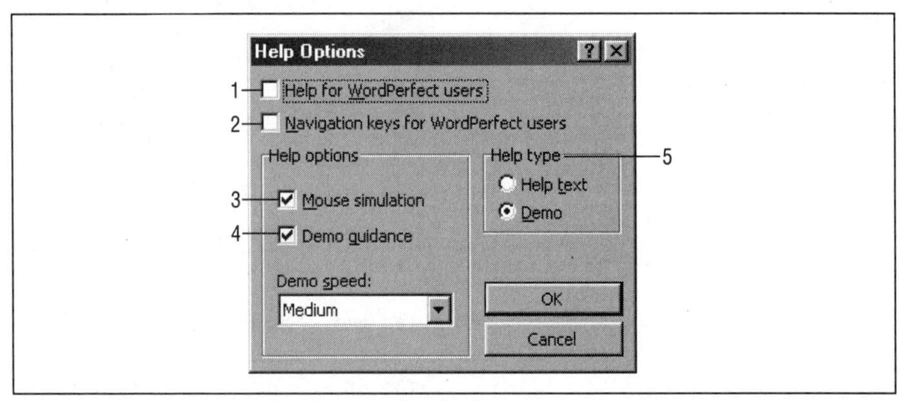

Figure 12-8: Setting Options for WordPerfect help

1. *Help for WordPerfect users.* This option could be labeled better. When it is enabled, WordPerfect keyboard commands work in Word. What happens when using them depends on what Help Type is set (see #5). If this option is set to Help text, Word pops up the text instructions on using the command just like the Help Text button on the main WordPerfect Help dialog. If it is set to Demo, Word performs the command for you, just like the Demo button on the WordPerfect Help dialog. This is the functional equivalent to using Word-Perfect commands in Word.
2. *Navigation keys for WordPerfect users.* In WordPerfect, certain navigation keys perform different functions than in Word. Select this option to make these keys work in Word as they would in WordPerfect.
3. *Mouse simulation.* This option causes Word to display the pointer during demos that include simulations of mouse activities.
4. *Demo guidance.* This option causes Word to display additional help using screen tips during simulations.
5. *Help type.* Specifies whether Word should display help text or perform demos when the Help for WordPerfect users (see #1) is turned on.

Word Perfect Help is not part of the standard installation of Word. Unless it is specifically installed during setup, Word must install this feature from the CD the first time you use it.

Help → Detect and Repair

Word's new Detect and Repair feature actually scans the Office (or Word) installation and offers to replace any missing or corrupted program files from the original Office 2000 CD-ROM. Start Detect and Repair in one of two ways:

- Use Help → Detect and Repair.
- Insert the installation CD, run Setup, and choose the Detect and Repair option.

When using Help → Detect and Repair, specify whether or not Word should replace any missing default shortcuts during the process, something that is done automatically when running Detect and Repair directly from the CD. I recommend using the Detect and Repair command from within Word for more control.

Detect and Repair may find files that it thinks are corrupt but that may have just been replaced by custom utilities or add-ins installed since the initial Word installation. Using Detect and Repair should not cause you to lose any customized settings made in Word, but it may screw up custom add-ons, forcing you to reinstall them.

Although you can run Detect and Repair manually, Word takes care of it automatically most of the time. If you attempt to launch a program or use a feature for which files are corrupted or missing, Word offers to replace them for you. Test it out if you're feeling brave. Go into your Office program folder (C:\Program Files\Microsoft Office\Office) and delete the file winword.exe. No kidding; delete it! Next, try to run Word from your Start menu. Word should detect that the file is missing and ask you for the CD so that it can reinstall the file.

Help → About Microsoft Word

The Help → About Microsoft Word command opens a splash screen that shows various items of legal information about Word. The only interesting things about this screen are the following:

- The version (and build number) of Word at the top, which is often required when making a technical support request of Microsoft.
- The product code in the middle, also a requested item from Microsoft tech support.
- The link to the Windows System Information Utility (*msinfo32.exe*) at the bottom, which is used in Windows troubleshooting. For more on using this handy utility, check out *Windows 98 in Nutshell,* by Tim O'Reilly, Troy Mott, and Walter Glenn (O'Reilly & Associates).

Part 3

Beyond the Basics

Chapter 13

Collaborating

It is unusual never to show a Word document to anyone else. Many of us pass Word documents around so that others can collaborate on and review them. This chapter covers the major Word tools for collaborating with multiple users on a document. These include:

Track Changes
: This feature allows you to visibly keep track of each author's revisions within a document. Word automatically marks each author's edits with colored text. In addition, whenever you point to a marked change, a ScreenTip pops up to let you know the author and date.

Comments
: These annotate a document with notes that don't really belong in the document text itself.

NetMeeting
: This is a separate program that lets users collaborate in real time using tools such as chat, voice, video, and a shared whiteboard.

Web Discussions
: This is a new tool that lets users who have access to a central discussion server create threaded discussions within and about a document and subscribe to documents so that they are emailed when the document changes.

Tracking Changes

Word's Track Changes feature is one that many people find confusing. In truth, I find the feature itself pretty straightforward. Part of what makes it seem complicated is that there are several different ways to get at it in the Word interface.

Here is what Track Changes basically does:

1. When Track Changes is turned on, Word marks any changes made to the document in a different color for each author that makes changes.

2. You can then review the document, see what changes each author made and when, and accept or reject each of the changes.

Sound pretty simple? It is. Let's see how it works.

Turning Track Changes On

As with most things in Word, there are several ways to turn on Track Changes. The first is to choose Tools → Track Changes → Highlight Changes. This opens the dialog shown in Figure 13-1. Choose the "Track changes while editing" option and click OK to turn on Track Changes. The other two options on the dialog specify whether changes are visible on the screen and whether they are printed along with the document. The Options button on this dialog opens the Track Changes tab of the Tools → Options dialog, which is covered a bit later in the "Setting Change Options" section.

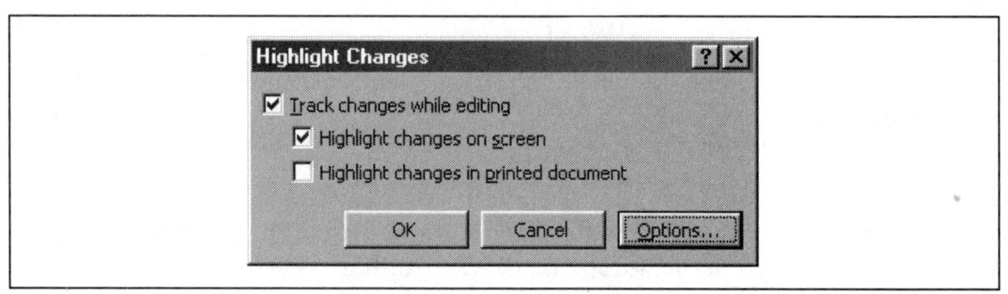

Figure 13-1: Turning on Track Changes using Tools → Track Changes → Highlight Changes

The "Highlight Changes in printed document" option prints all of the changes and change marking in the document. When this option is disabled, Word prints the document as it would look were you to accept all of the changes in the document. Printing a document with changes can sometimes be useful, but keep in mind that without a color printer it can be pretty hard to tell between different authors' changes.

TIP # 131

Turn the Track Changes Display Off

When working with documents that have a lot of changes in them, it is often helpful to turn off the "Highlight changes on screen" option. Word still tracks any changes made, but you can read the document without weeding through all the deleted text and different colors. If you receive a document that you expect to see changes in but don't see the changes, be sure to check this setting.

Now that you've seen the formal way of turning on Track Changes, there are several easier ways to do it. The first is by double-clicking the TRK button in the status bar at the bottom of Word's window. Double-click to turn it off again. Another easy way to toggle Track Changes on and off is with Ctrl-Shift-E. Yet another way to toggle the feature is with the Track Changes button on the Reviewing toolbar (which you'll see more of in the "Reviewing toolbar" section). Note that all these methods only turn the whole Track Changes feature on and off. The display and printing settings made on Tools → Track Changes → Highlight Changes still hold.

Making and Viewing Changes

Once you turn Track Changes on, Word automatically marks all of the changes made to the document using an assigned color (different authors get different colors). By default, any additions made are underlined and anything deleted is marked with a strikethrough (see Figure 13-2). Also by default, formatting changes are not marked. When multiple people work on a document with Track Changes turned on, different authors' changes are marked in different colors so it's easier to tell who did what. To find out which author made the change, just hold the pointer above a change for a moment to display a ScreenTip showing the author, date, and type of the change.

All changes in the document (including formatting changes) are also marked with a vertical bar outside the left margin, by default.

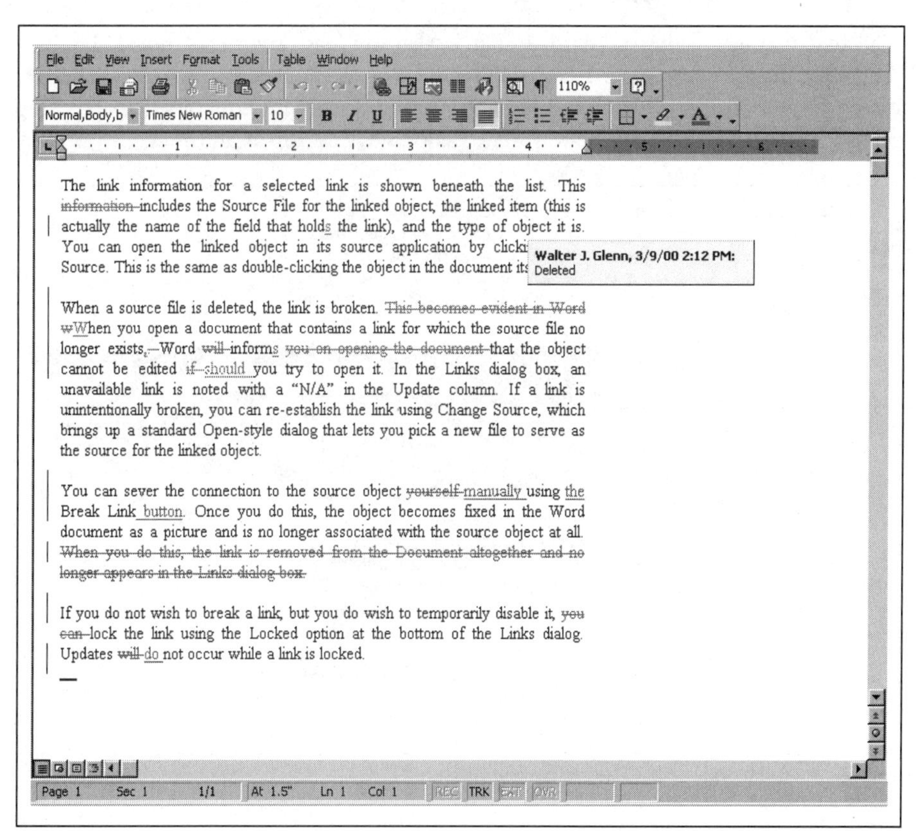

Figure 13-2: Tracking changes in a document

TIP # 132

Make Sure Your Name Is Right

The name that Word displays in a ScreenTip for tracked changes or comments and the initials used with comments (covered later in this chapter) are defined using Tools → Options → User Information.

Accepting and Rejecting Changes

Tracking changes to a document is only the first step. At some point, you'll need to review those changes and decide whether to accept or reject them. Word provides a few ways to do this.

Accept or Reject Changes dialog box

The first method is the standard, but it is also my least favorite. Choose Tools → Track Changes → Accept or Reject Changes to open the Accept or Reject Changes dialog (Figure 13-3). This dialog steps through a document edit by edit, accepting or rejecting each edit along the way. The dialog stays on top at all times.

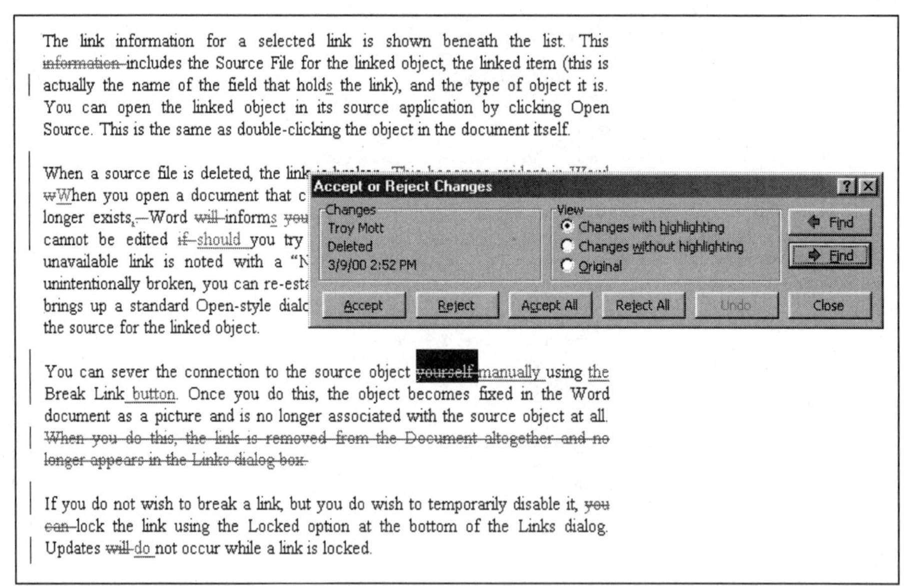

Figure 13-3: Accepting and rejecting changes

Changes

Information about any change selected in a document is shown in the Changes section. This is the same information shown in the pop-up ScreenTip when the pointer is held over a change in the main document window.

View

This section alters the way changes are shown in the document, but does not affect any permanent changes. "Changes with highlighting" displays the document with all of the edits shown in their various colors. "Changes without highlighting" shows what the document would look like if all of the changes were accepted. "Original" shows what the document would look like if all the changes were rejected.

Find buttons

Click either of the two Find buttons (back arrow goes to the first change previous to the insertion point, forward arrow to the next) to move the insertion point to the next change in the document and highlight the change.

Accept

Click Accept to make the change a permanent part of the document. This converts the marked change into standard document text (using whatever formatting is applied in the document) and deletes any old version of the text.

Reject

Click Reject to delete the marked change and revert to the original text.

Accept All

This button accepts all of the changes in the document in one fell swoop.

TIP # 133

Use Accept All (Changes) with Caution

Word records the Accept All action as one event. This means that the Undo button (or Word's main Undo feature) reverses only the whole acceptance. All of the changes are undone. When accepting and rejecting individual changes, you can step back through each change with Undo.

Undo

This button undoes the last change made (Accept, Reject, or Reject All). Close the dialog and you can still undo changes made using Edit → Undo.

Reviewing toolbar

The Reviewing toolbar (Figure 13-4) is also used for reviewing changes. Display it using View → Toolbars → Reviewing or by right-clicking any open toolbar and clicking Reviewing. I find the Reviewing toolbar a bit handier for everyday use than the Accept or Reject Changes dialog. It does, however, lack two good features from the dialog: the ability to accept all changes and the ability to quickly change the view. Of course, you could always customize the toolbar to include these commands using the techniques in Chapter 3, *Customizing Word*.

TIP # 134

Put the Reviewing Toolbar Where the Work Is

If you find it inconvenient to move the pointer back and forth between the Reviewing toolbar and your document, drag it away from the toolbar and put it wherever it feels comfortable. I recommend putting it outside the document margin if possible, so that it doesn't obscure any changes.

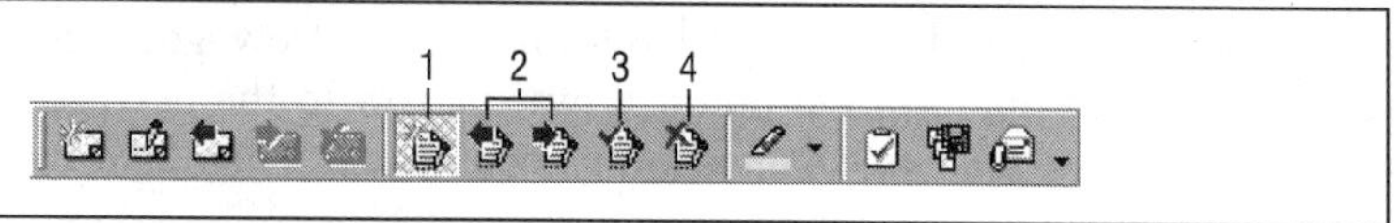

Figure 13-4: Using the Reviewing toolbar

1. *Track Changes.* This button toggles the Track Changes feature on and off.
2. *Previous and Next Change.* These buttons move the insertion point to and select the previous or next marked change. You can also use the browse buttons below the vertical scrollbar (first use the browse object button to browse by edits) to jump to previous and next changes.
3. *Accept Change.* Click to accept the selected change. One great advantage this button provides that isn't found anywhere else is the ability to accept all of the changes in any selected block of text, such as an entire paragraph.
4. *Reject Change.* Reject the selected change and revert to the original text.

Context menus

My favorite method for working with changes is using context menus. Right-click any change in a document, and the menu that opens (Figure 13-5) provides the ability to accept or reject the change, toggle track changes on and off, and open the Accept or Reject Changes dialog.

TIP # 135

Put Next and Previous Change on Context Menus

For handy access, add the Next and Previous Change commands to the Track Changes context menu using the techniques described in Chapter 3.

The reason I like the context menus is that I rarely find myself just searching through changes and deciding to accept or reject them, which is what the previous two methods are really good for. Instead, I find myself wanting to read the document itself (sometimes for the fifteenth time) and decide on changes as I come across them. Context menus are great for that and interrupt my reading the least.

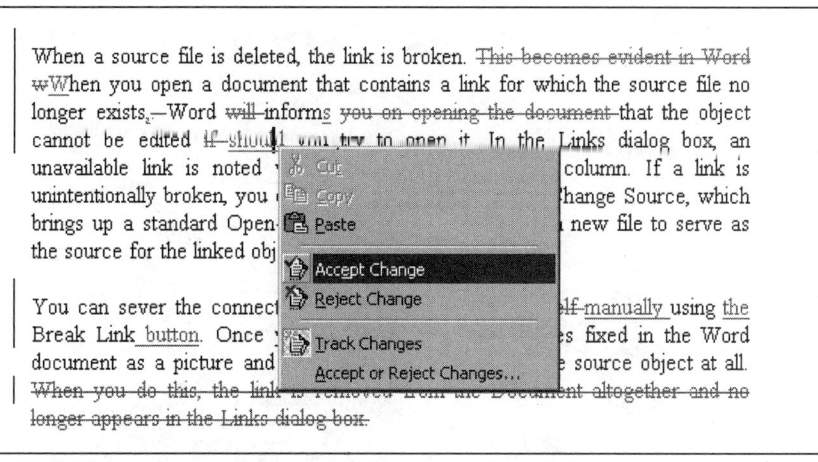

Figure 13-5: Using context menus

Collaborating

TIP # 136

Accepting or Rejecting Scattered Changes

One thing I often find myself doing is reading a paragraph that has several changes scattered throughout and then deciding to accept (or reject) all the changes in the paragraph. This can only be done with the Reviewing toolbar. Select the paragraph (or any block of text containing scattered changes) and click the Accept or Reject button on the toolbar. Context menus can't be used for this because, for some reason, the reviewing options do not appear if any part of the selected text is not a marked change.

Setting Change Options

By default, Word assigns a single color automatically to each author who edits a document, strikes through deleted text, and underlines added text. Specify the colors and marks used to track different types of edits using the Track Changes tab shown in Figure 13-6. Open this tab using Tools → Options → Track Changes or the Options button on Tools → Track Changes → Highlight Changes, or by right-clicking the TRK button on the status bar.

The following list describes the Track Changes settings:

1. *Inserted text.* By default, any text added to the document while revision marking is on is marked with a single underling and assigned a color based on the author of the addition. Other markings options include none, bold, italic, and double underline. Specific colors can be assigned to individual authors.

2. *Deleted text.* By default, any text deleted while revision marking is on is marked with a strikethrough and assigned a color based on the author. Other markings options include hidden, ^, and #. Using the ^ or # symbols replaces any deleted

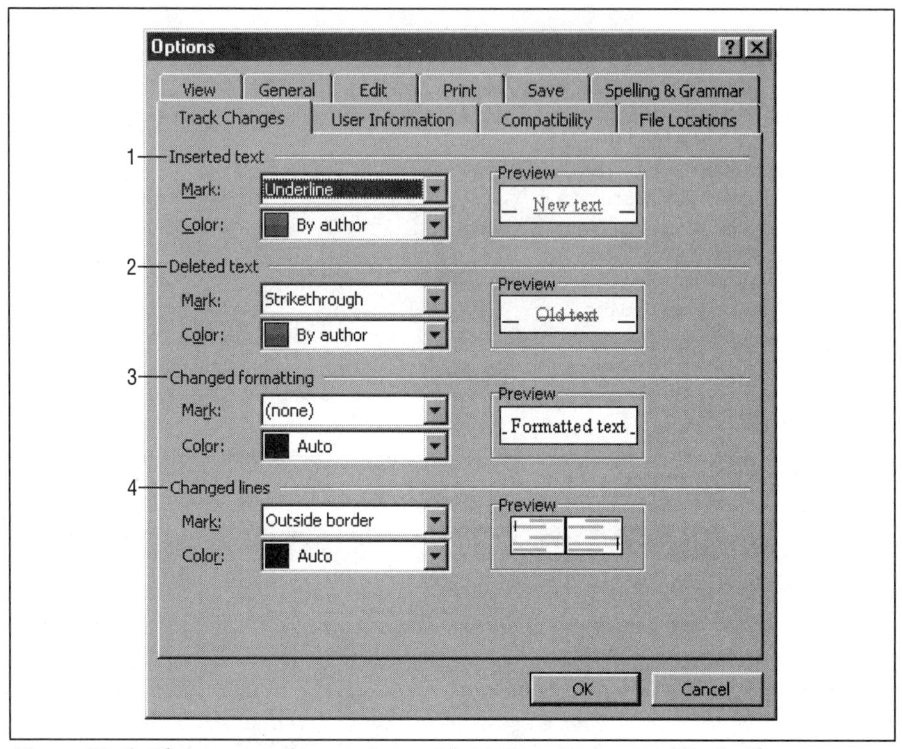

Figure 13-6: Changing tracking options with Tools → Options → Track Changes

selection of text with the chosen symbol, meant simply to indicate that text has been deleted. Specific colors can also be assigned.

3. *Changed formatting*. By default, changed formatting is not marked in any special way and text coloring is set to Auto, meaning that the text coloring is changed only based on the new format. Change the marking option to none, bold, italic, underline, and double underline. Change the color to "By author" or to any specific color.

Unfortunately, Word simply cannot track certain formatting changes. These include manually changing text color, size, and font style, as well as applying any formatting using a style. There is no workaround for this that I have found other than to include a comment or inline reference indicating the change.

4. *Changed lines*. By default, whenever any kind of change is made, a vertical line is placed outside the border on the left margin of the page. This lets readers quickly scan the pages for edits. Disable this function by choosing none, or set the marks to appear on the left or right border. Normally, the change lines are automatically colored (here Auto refers to the standard text color defined in Windows

Control Panel → Display → Appearance → Item → Window → Font Color, usually black). You can also change this to "By author" or any specific color.

TIP # 137

Don't Customize Revision Marking Too Much

Don't get carried away changing marking options and colors for revision marking. Many Word users are familiar with the standard markings and may get confused if you change them. One change that may be useful, though, is changing the color of Changed lines to "By author," which lets you quickly scan for a particular person's changes.

Using Comments

After Track Changes, Comments are the most widely used collaborative tool in Word. Use comments to make notes and suggestions anywhere in a document's text.

Comments can be a little quirky, as you'll find out, but once you're used to those quirks, comments are invaluable. Comments were first added to Word when Word's designers noticed something: being able to track changes was great, but there was no good way to make side notations within a document. Many people were (and still are) making these notations right in the document (with Track Changes on) and then just rejecting the changes later to get rid of them. The problem with this method is that between actual changes to the document and the notations, the document can get pretty messy. Enter the comment.

Comments are really just notes attached at a selected point or to a selected piece of text in Word's text layer. They are not shown within the main document window, but text is highlighted with a dull yellow to indicate that a comment exists. The comments themselves are viewed in a pop-up window by holding the pointer over the highlighted comment or in a separate pane at the bottom of the document window by using View → Comments. Comments are initialed (using the initials in Tools → Options → User Information) so you can tell who said what.

Inserting a Comment

Inserting a comment is easy. Move the insertion point to where the comment should appear or select a block of text to comment on. Choose Insert → Comment. Word adds a yellow highlight to the word to the left of the insertion point (or to the block of selected text), inserts a comment marker with initials and a comment number on it, opens the Comments pane, and moves the insertion point to the Comments pane so that you can immediately begin typing the comment (see Figure 13-7). After typing the comment, close the Comments pane using the Close button or leave the pane open and just click somewhere in the document pane to begin working on the document again.

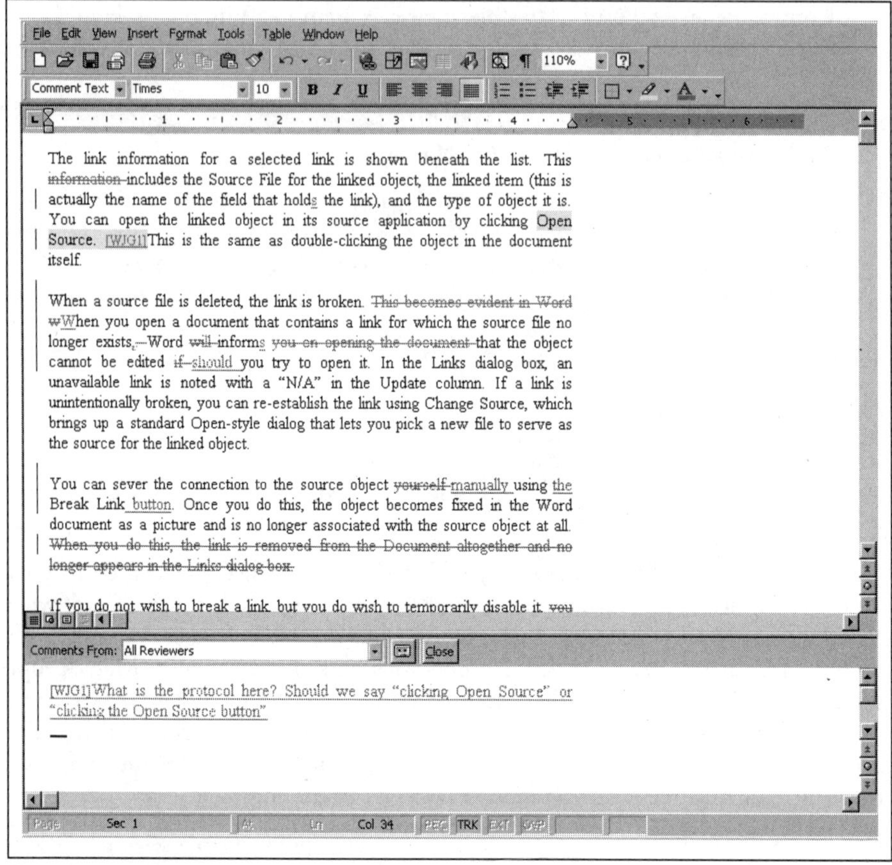

Figure 13-7: Insert a Comment using Insert → Comment

TIP # 138

Don't Refer to Comments by Number

When you add comments to a document that already has comments, it is tempting to refer to other comments by number. For example, "In comment #23, Mary says . . ." Don't do this! When a comment is inserted between two existing comments, all comments after the new comment are renumbered.

Click the Insert Sound Object button (looks like a cassette tape) within the comments pane to open the Windows Sound Recorder. If a microphone and sound card are present, record a spoken comment as a *.wav* file that is attached to the Word comment. A speaker icon appears that anyone can double-click on to open the associated media player and hear the audio comment. Click the speaker icon and press Delete to remove it from the comment.

Viewing and Editing Comments

Whenever a document with comments is opened, highlight marks in the text indicate the location of comments. To the right of the comment are the initials of the author who made the comment and the comment number. Hold the pointer over a comment for a moment to display a pop-up window with the comment's text and the full name of the person who inserted it (Figure 13-8).

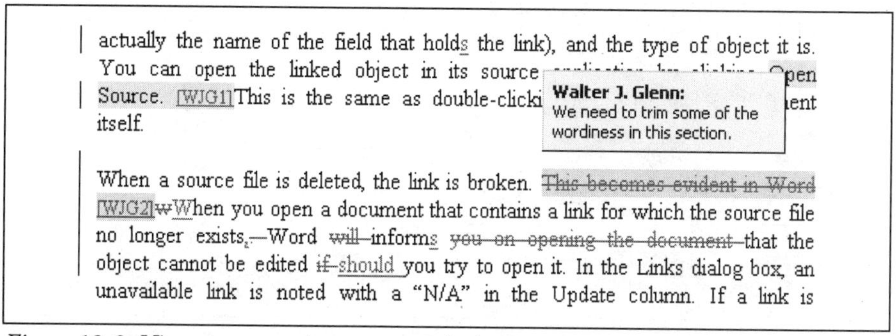

actually the name of the field that holds the link), and the type of object it is. You can open the linked object in its source ... Open Source. [WJG1]This is the same as double-clicki... ...ent itself.

Walter J. Glenn:
We need to trim some of the wordiness in this section.

When a source file is deleted, the link is broken. ~~This becomes evident in Word~~ [WJG2]~~w~~When you open a document that contains a link for which the source file no longer exists, ~~—~~Word ~~will~~ informs ~~you on opening the document~~ that the object cannot be edited ~~if~~ should you try to open it. In the Links dialog box, an unavailable link is noted with a "N/A" in the Update column. If a link is

Figure 13-8: View comments in a pop-up window

Move through the comments in a document easily using the Reviewing toolbar. The toolbar has buttons for inserting and editing comments, moving to the previous or next comment in the document, and deleting the selected comment.

View all of the comments in a document in the Comments Pane (see Figure 13-9) using View → Comments or by right-clicking a comment and choosing Edit Comment from the context menu.

The following list describes the Comments Pane contents:

1. *Comments From.* Use this drop-down list to view comments from all reviewers (default) or the only the comments of any particular reviewer. If viewing comments from a particular reviewer (say [WJG] in Figure 13-9), the whole comment is shown, including text other reviewers may have added to that comment.

2. *Comment.* Comments are preceded by the initials of the reviewer who inserted the comment and a comment number. These numbers change when new comments are inserted before them. Edit a comment the same way you edit normal text in a document. If Track Changes is turned on, changes are marked just as they are in a document.

3. *Insert Sound Object.* Open the Windows Sound Recorder to record a sound clip and attach it to a comment.

4. *Close.* Close the Comments pane and return the insertion point to the main document window.

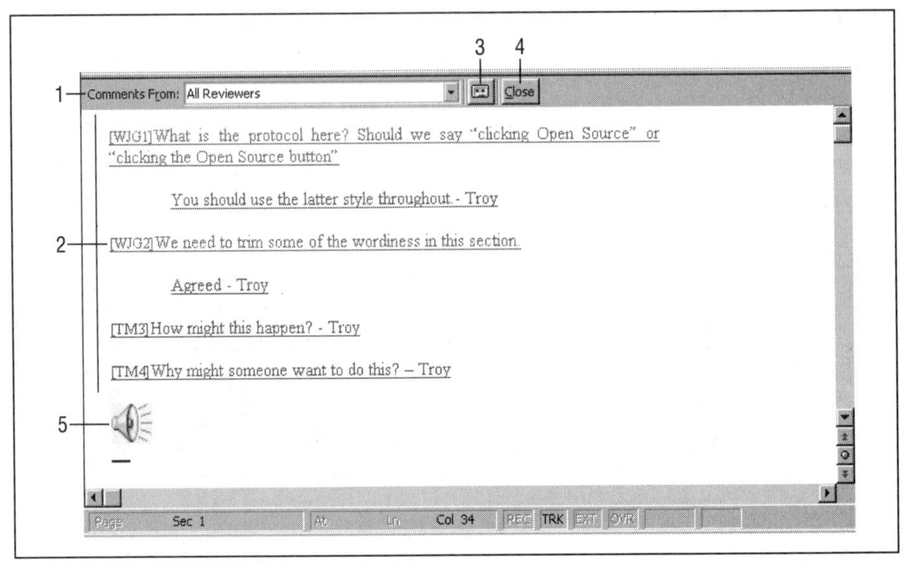

Figure 13-9: Using the Comments pane

5. *Sound Object.* Sound objects in the Comments pane work just like any other objects inserted into a Word document. Double-click to play the sound file. Right-click to open a context menu with options for editing the sound and configuring other object properties. For more on using Objects, check out Chapter 7, *Insert.*

TIP # 139

Double-Click a Comment to Jump There

If you double-click anywhere in a comment's text in the Comments pane, the main document window jumps to the location of the comment. Also, if you double-click a comment in the main document window while the Comments pane is closed, the pane opens and jumps to that comment.

Delete as much of the text for a comment as you want. However, the comment itself cannot be deleted from within the Comments pane. Try it and Word hands you an error. Comments can only be deleted within the main document. To do this, first highlight the comment by double-clicking it (or by backspacing over it) and then delete it like any normal character. The Delete Comment button on the Reviewing toolbar also deletes a highlighted comment. The easiest way to get rid of a comment, though, is to right-click anywhere in the comment highlight and choose Delete Comment from the context menu.

If you inserted the comment while Track Changes was turned on, you may have to accept the change before deleting the comment. Of course, you can also reject the change to delete it, as well.

You can move comments in the main document Window by cutting and pasting them or by dragging them to new locations. However, this removes the highlighting for the comment and makes it harder to find and select. Instead, cut the text for a comment in the Comment pane, create a new comment where you want to move it, and paste the comment text into the new comment. Then delete the old comment from the main text by right-clicking and choosing Delete Comment.

Word won't let you drag, cut, or paste comments in the Comments pane.

Replying to Comments

Replies to comments aren't really part of the Word interface; they're just a way I like to handle discussions. Instead of inserting a new comment to reply to an existing comment, place the insertion point at the end of the comment text in the comment pane and hit Enter. Tab to indent the reply and start typing. This is a very handy way of keeping discussions on a single topic all together. In addition, you may want to add your name after replies to make it easy to see who is commenting. I know you can just hold the pointer over text to see who inserted it, but why bother? If the names are there, it's much easier to scroll through comments.

TIP # 140

Print Your Comments

By default, comments are not printed along with the document. To print only the comments in a separate document, choose File → Print → Print What → Comments. To print comments at the end of the document, choose Tools → Options → Print → Comments. Note that the latter method affects all documents printed while the former method prints just the comments for one document once.

Merging Changes and Comments

For the most part, I recommend keeping only one copy of a document, letting each reviewer make his or her changes in turn, and then reviewing those changes at the end. Sometimes, however, it is necessary to let a document go to two or more reviewers at the same time.

Word provides two features for consolidating the changes in multiple copies of a document: Merge Documents and Compare Documents. Both work only on changes that have been tracked. Changes made when Track Changes is turned off cannot be merged or compared.

If a copy of a document contains changes that were made while Track Changes was not turned on, Word warns you before merging them into the master document with an option to cancel the operation or to merge changes up to the first unmarked change.

For both the merge and compare features, Word brings changes from a document that is not open into a document that is open (let's call the open document the *master copy*):

- Merge the changes from one copy into the master copy using Tools → Merge Documents. The changes and comments from both copies are shown in the merged document, just as if each author had edited the same document. If there are more than two copies of a document to merge, you must merge changes from one document at a time into the master copy.
- Compare one copy of a document with another using Tools → Track Changes → Compare Documents. Word inserts the changes and comments from one copy into the master copy, but marks them as deleted. Reject individual changes (deletions) to make them permanent.

TIP # 141

Merge or Compare Only Two Documents at a Time

If you ignore my advice to keep only one copy of a document floating around, then please heed this advice. If there are more than two copies of a document, merge one copy into the master copy and then review the changes. After accepting or rejecting all changes, bring in the changes from the next copy, and so on.

Working with Network Documents

Whether you are on a large company network or just have a few computers hooked together, Word makes it pretty easy to share files with others over a network. I don't plan to get into a discussion on networking or security here, as there would be just too much to cover. Also, since the Word interface makes opening and saving documents on a network almost identical to opening and saving on a local system, I'm not going to go over those procedures in detail either. Rather, I will offer a brief rundown on some of the useful things to be aware of when working on a network with Word:

- If you frequently use a particular shared folder on a network, map that folder as a network drive. Browse to the folder using Network Neighborhood either in Word's Open and Save dialogs or in Windows Explorer. Right-click the folder and choose Map Network Drive from the context menu. In the dialog that opens, assign a drive letter to the new mapped drive. The folder appears in Windows Explorer, My Computer, and the Word Open and Save dialogs as if it were a drive on your system, which is great for quick access.

- If you are working with files on an FTP server, Word provides an FTP client built in to its Open and Save dialog boxes. Work with files on an FTP server in much the same way as with local files. Learn more about doing this in Chapter 4, *File*.
- Web Folders are new to Word 2000 and Windows 98/2000. Basically, they let you assign a URL (an Internet web address) to a folder that acts much like a regular Windows folder. Use files in the folder the same way as local files. You can think of Web Folders as sort of the Internet equivalent to the Map Network Drive function.
- Share a folder or document on your own system with others on the network by opening the document file's properties in Windows (this assumes the system is correctly configured on the network). How to do this depends on the version of Windows being used, but you can normally assign permissions on the file in one of two ways:

  Share-level access
  This is probably the method to use if you have a simple peer-to-peer network (one without a server). Using this method, assign a single password to a folder or file. Anyone who knows this password can use the file.

  User-level access
  This is probably the method to use on larger networks with servers. Pick from a list of users on the network and assign each of them different permissions to access the file depending on what you want them to be able to do.
- There are also two other ways to protect a file that apply regardless of whether the file is accessed over a network, with your own system, or even if that file is copied to someone else's computer:

  Locking the file from certain types of revisions with a password
  Choose Tools → Protect Document and assign a password based on the desired level of protection. This is covered in detail in Chapter 9, *Tools*.

  Protecting the file from being opened or saved using a password
  To do this, select Tools → Options → Save and enter options at the bottom of the tab. These options are detailed in Chapter 3.

NetMeeting

Microsoft NetMeeting comes with Windows 98, Windows Millennium, and Windows 2000 and is used to participate in online meetings. In order to use NetMeeting, you will have to have the MSN Messenger (Microsoft's instant messaging application). You must also have a HotMail or Microsoft PassPort account (both free email services from Microsoft). You'll be prompted to download and install these the first time NetMeeting is run if they're not already configured. Together, these services let you maintain a list of contacts and invite those contacts into meetings using NetMeeting.

Launch NetMeeting from within Word using the Tools → Online Collaboration → Meet Now command. This opens a dialog used for browsing through MSN Messenger Contacts. Select contacts to invite them to participate in a meeting. Schedule a meeting from within Word using the Tools → Online Collaboration → Schedule Meeting command, which opens up a new calendar appointment in Microsoft Outlook.

Obviously, there's a lot more to NetMeeting and MSN Messenger than we can detail here. Check out the product documentation for more information on both products.

Starting a meeting in Word also opens the Online Meeting toolbar (Figure 13-10).

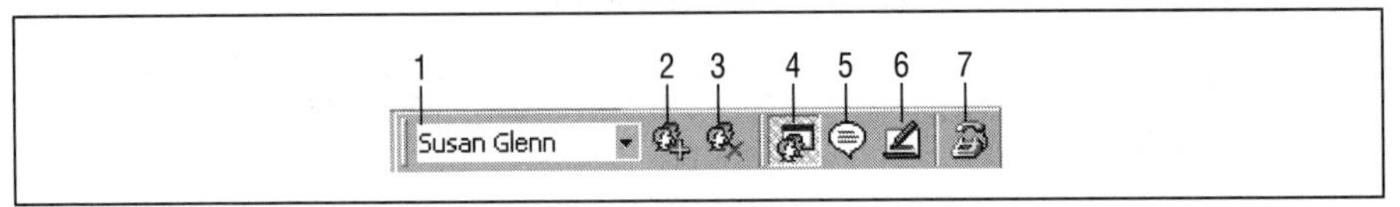

Figure 13-10: Using the Online Meeting toolbar

1. *Participants.* Use this drop-down list to view and select participants of the meeting.
2. *Call Participant.* If you are the host of a meeting, use this button to invite other contacts from your MSN Messenger list to join the meeting. Other participants can invite people to join using their NetMeeting applications.
3. *Remove Participant.* Remove the participant selected in the Participants drop-down list from the meeting.
4. *Allow others to edit.* In a whiteboard or shared application, this button allows other users to edit or control the window.
5. *Display chat window.* This button opens a chat window where users can type text messages to one another.
6. *Display whiteboard.* This button opens a shared whiteboard, covered in the following list of actions.
7. *End meeting.* Close the toolbar and end the meeting.

During a meeting, participants can perform several actions:

- Communicate with other participants by typing messages in a traditional chat window using Tools → Chat. Messages entered into the chat window are viewed by all meeting participants. At the end of the meeting, the chat log can be saved as a text file and makes a handy record of the meeting.
- Send files to other participants using Tools → File Transfer → Send File. Use the dialog that opens to browse for the file and to specify the meeting participants that should receive the file. Each participant can choose to accept or reject the transfer.

- Collaborate in real time on a Word document (Figure 13-11). Starting NetMeeting from a Word document automatically opens that Word document in the meeting for collaboration. The host controls the document when the meeting starts. Allow collaboration by the participants by clicking the "Allow others to edit" button on the Online Meeting toolbar. Turn off collaboration at any time by clicking the button again.

  When collaboration is turned on, any participant can control the document, but only one person at a time can have control. Take control of the document during collaboration by clicking on it. Any user with control of the document can edit it using the standard Word tools. Participants other than the host do not have to have Word installed on their computers or a copy of the document. They actually control the host's Word application remotely.

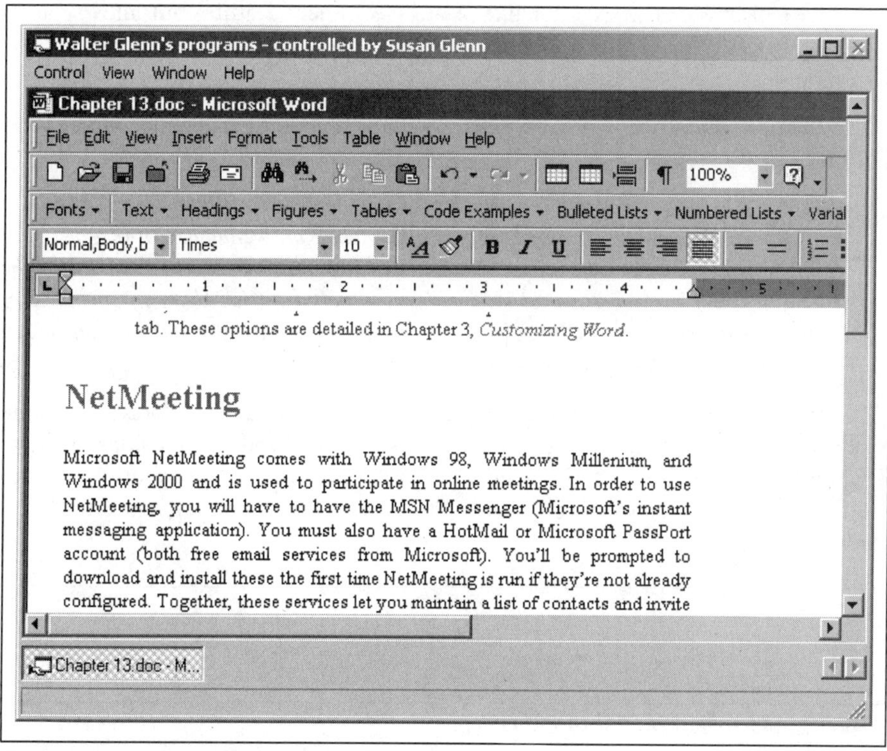

Figure 13-11: Controlling a Word document in NetMeeting

- Collaborate on a central whiteboard where participants can paste images, draw, and type. A whiteboard is a blank page on which all users can participate simultaneously. At first, only the host can manipulate the whiteboard. Allow collaboration by other participants by clicking the "Allow others to edit" button on the Online Meeting toolbar.

NetMeeting offers Word users with Internet access (or access to a corporate discussion server) a pretty cool way to talk about and even mark on a Word document in real time. Unfortunately, we don't have room here for a full discussion of NetMeeting. You can find out more about NetMeeting from its program documentation.

Web Discussions

Web Discussions are a collaboration element new to Word 2000. They are a heavily marketed new feature, but I've found that they are really only useful to a select handful of users—and even then, only marginally useful. Web Discussions allow users to:

Start a threaded discussion at a particular point within a Word document
: These discussions work a lot like Word's comment feature, but allow you to keep better track of who said what in a long, threaded discussion.

Subscribe to a document
: When you subscribe to a document, you basically ask to be emailed whenever a document changes.

To even use Web Discussions in the first place, you must have access to a discussion server, which is a Windows NT or Windows 2000 server that has the new Office Extensions installed on it. These extensions allow the server to keep track of certain types of collaborative elements included in the new Office 2000 suite. If you are not connected to a network with such a server, forget it.

To start a discussion or view existing discussions, first choose Tools → Online Collaboration → Web Discussions to open the Web Discussions toolbar (Figure 13-12). Designate a discussion server if you have not previously done so. Fortunately, Word automatically finds discussion servers if they are on a local network.

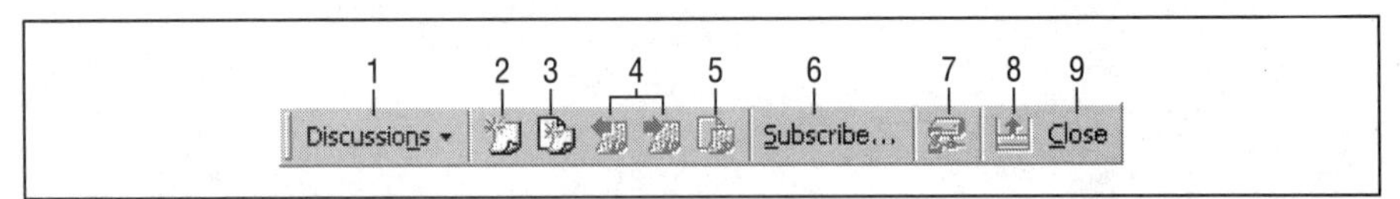

Figure 13-12: The Web Discussions toolbar

1. *Discussions.* The Discussions button opens a menu that provides commands for inserting discussions (same as on the toolbar) and also for doing four things you can't do with the toolbar:

   – *Refresh.* This command updates the discussion list to include any new entries that may have been made since the program was started.

   – *Filter.* Use this command to view only discussion entries from a selected person or only entries within a specified time frame (such as the last hour or last 24 hours). This filter applies to any discussion opened until you change the filter back.

- *Print.* This command prints all of the entries in the discussion currently being viewed.
- *Discussion options.* Use this to connect to a different discussion server and choose the specific discussion elements in the discussion pane, including display name, user name, subject, text, and time.

2. *Insert discussion in the document.* This option inserts a new threaded discussion at a particular point within the document (wherever the insertion point is or to the right of any selected text). A discussion is marked in the document using a small notepad icon (Figure 13-13). Whenever you select a discussion (by clicking it or by using the Previous and Next buttons described later in this list) the entire threaded discussion is displayed in the discussion pane

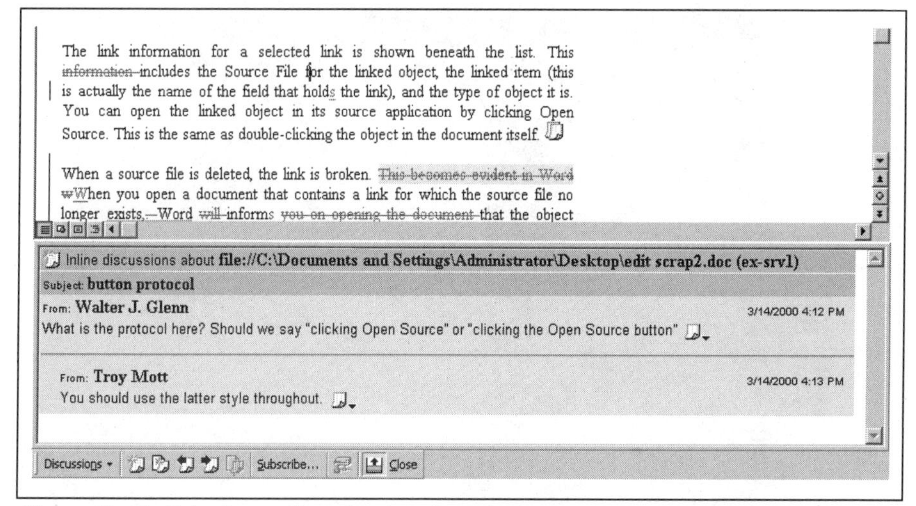

Figure 13-13: Selecting a discussion icon in a document

There is no real limit to how many discussions can be contained in a single document. Adding new discussions doesn't even increase the size of the document that much, since most of the information is actually stored on the discussion server. Of course, this also means that if a document is removed from the discussion server, the discussion text is lost.

3. *Insert discussion about the document.* Start general discussions about the document that don't really correspond to any discussion icon anywhere. To view them, click the Show General Discussions button. Otherwise, these discussions work exactly like discussions inserted into a document and are also stored on the discussion server.

4. *Previous and Next.* Quickly jump to and select the previous or next discussion in a document.

5. *Show General Discussions.* Show any general discussions inserted using the "Insert discussion about the document" button.

6. *Subscribe.* This button opens a separate dialog (Figure 13-14) that lets you specify that you should be notified by email whenever a document or any document in a folder changes. Simply specify the document (the default is the current document) or a folder (the default is the folder the current document is in). Next, choose when to be notified. Choices include: when anything changes, a new document is created, a document is modified, deleted, or moved, or a discussion item is inserted or deleted. Finally, enter an email address you would like the notification sent to and specify the interval at which the server should check for changes.

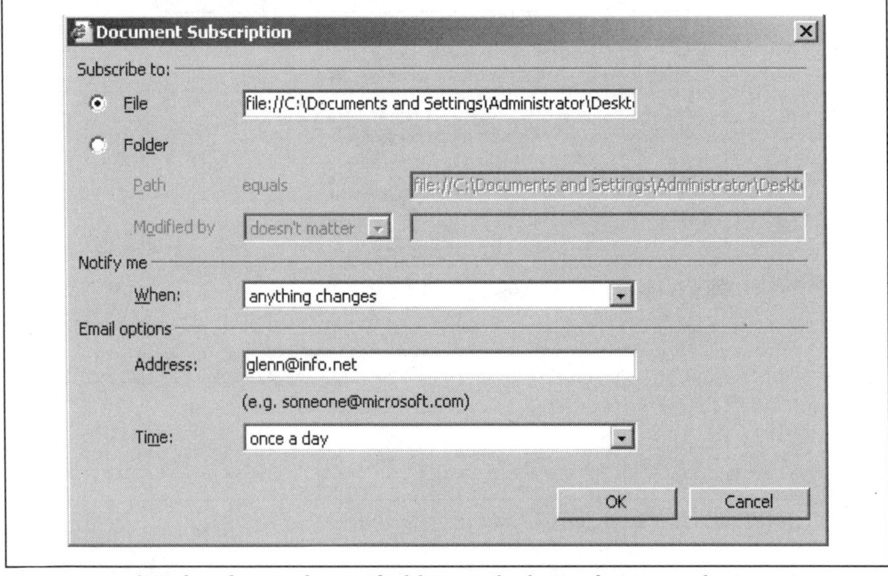

Figure 13-14: Subscribing to be notified by email when a document changes

7. *Stop communication with discussion server.* If the discussion server is on a local network, this button really doesn't do anything. If the server is on the Internet or you must access it over a dial-up connection, this button toggles that connection on and off.

8. *Show/Hide Discussion pane.* Use this button to toggle the discussion pane on and off. When hidden, you can still see discussion icons within the document. Double-click one (or select one and toggle the pane back on) to open the pane.

9. *Close*. This button closes the Web Discussions toolbar and the discussion pane and hides any discussion icons in the document. In order to see them again, choose Tools → Online Collaboration → Web Discussions.

I find three significant problems with Web Discussions. First, you have to have access to a discussion server, meaning that you can't just wrap the file up, email it to someone, and let them participate. Second, the pretty interface that the discussion pane uses takes up a lot of room, even though you can select the elements shown. Third, you must use a separate dialog to add or edit a comment. Wouldn't it be nice, instead, if Microsoft just gave us a way to easily thread regular comments?

Chapter 14

Creating a Template

As you learned in Chapter 2, *How Word Works*, all Word documents are based on templates, *.dot* files that contain styles, macros, customizations, and often boilerplate text. In Word, we say that a template is *attached* to a document.

Check out Chapter 2 for all the gory details on how Word handles templates. Here's a brief recap, though. Some templates are loaded globally during the Word startup process. The items in these templates (styles, etc.) are available in all documents opened in Word. Word's own *normal.dot* is the master global template and is loaded every time Word starts. Other global templates can be loaded automatically or manually, and unloaded at will using the Tools → Templates and Add-Ins command.

Every Word document is created using a template and, afterward, that template remains attached to the document unless you attach another one, again using the Templates and Add-Ins command. When a template is first attached to a document (either during the document's creation or later), all of the styles, macros, toolbars, etc. are copied to that document. After this, the document pretty much stands on its own and you can add new components to it without affecting the template. Similarly, modifying the template does not affect the document further, by default. Word does provide ways to alter this behavior so that documents and templates continues to affect each other, but once more, I'm going to refer you to Chapter 2 for details.

In this chapter, I walk you through the process of creating a template used to write a college term paper. This template has the following goals:

- It must use the official Modern Language Association (MLA) layout guidelines, including margins, indents, spacing, character size, and so on.
- It must prevent the use of any styles or features in Word that are not acceptable according to the MLA guidelines.
- It must make put the necessary tools within easy reach of the user.

Creating the Template File

The very first thing to do is create a new document to work with. Choose File → New to open the New dialog box (Figure 14-1). I'm going to base my template on *normal.dot* (the Blank Document template in the Figure) because it is pretty simple and I like starting from scratch—there are fewer surprises that way. If there's another document or template that comes pretty close to what you want in your new template, base it on that.

Since I know I'm creating a template, I've selected that option in the Create New section of the File → New dialog. This causes Word to save the new file as a template (a *.dot* file) by default. Any existing document can also be turned into a template by saving it with the *.dot* extension using File → Save As.

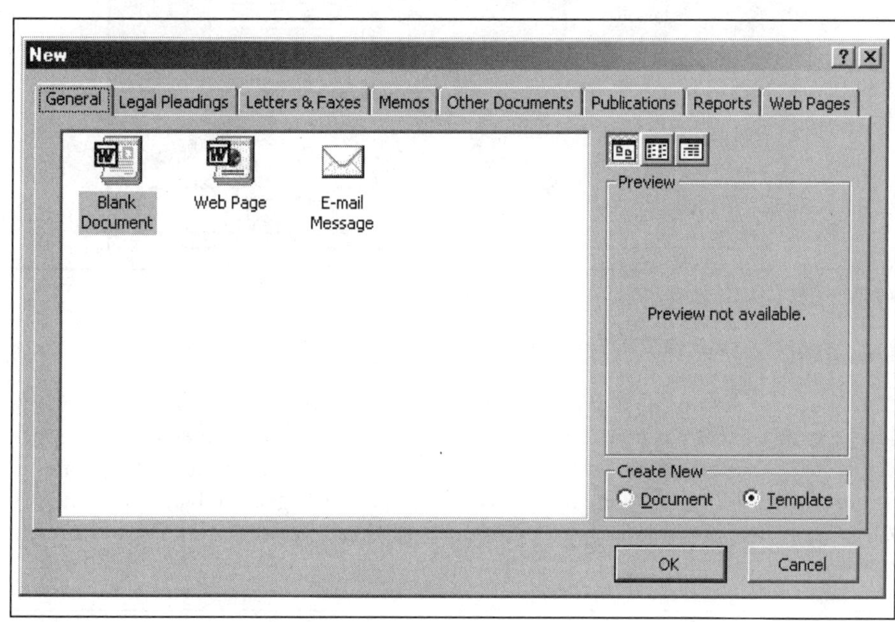

Figure 14-1: Creating a new template file

Creating the Page Layout

Once I've created the new file, I have a blank page awaiting me. I always like to start the creation of a template by setting up the overall dimensions of the page. For this template, I'm going to start by opening the Page Setup dialog (Figure 14-2). Use File → Page Setup to do this or double-click the gray area of Word's horizontal ruler. Figure 14-2 shows the default margins dictated by *normal.dot* when the new file was created. According to the MLA style, margins on all four sides must be one inch, so I'm going to make that change first. Headers and footers, mirror margins, and gutters are not allowed in the MLA style, so I'm just going to leave those items alone.

The paper size required by MLA is a standard 8.5" by 11". This is also the default Word setting, so I can leave the Paper Size tab alone. The default settings on the Layout tab (for vertical alignment, line numbering, and so on) are also correct.

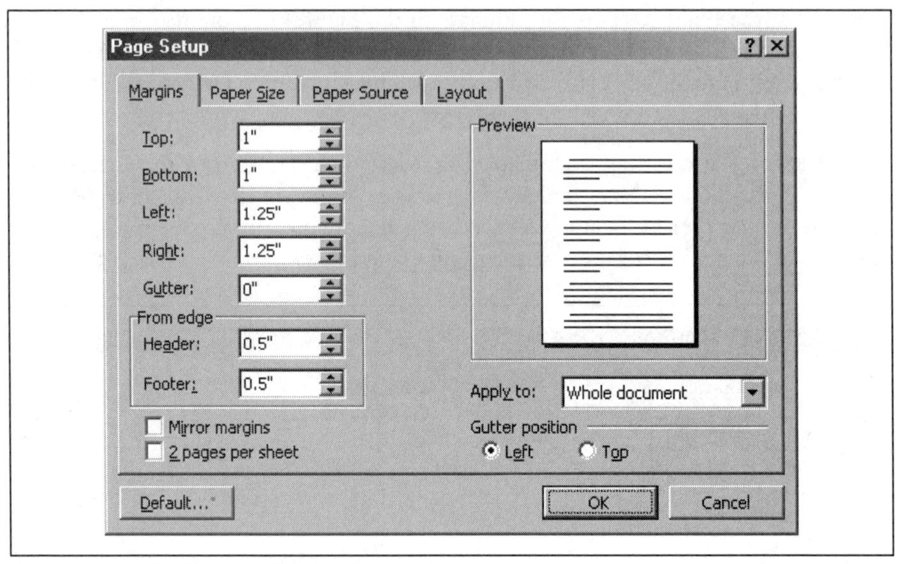

Figure 14-2: Setting margins for the template

Document-Level Settings

Now that I've set up the document layout, I turn my attention to other document-level settings. MLA requires that the pages of a document be numbered in the upper right corner, omitting the number on the first page. The number stands alone, without a "P." or anything next to it. Use the Insert → Page Numbers command for this. Figure 14-3 shows the appropriate settings already made in the Page Numbers dialog.

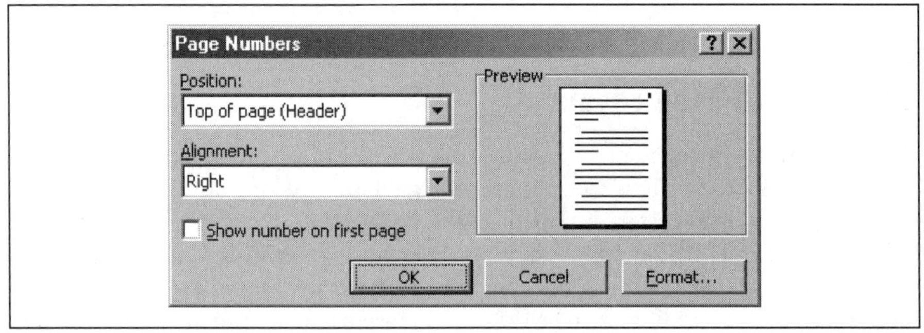

Figure 14-3: Setting page numbers

For this template, page numbering is the only document-level setting I'm going to use. When designing your own templates, here are a few ideas to consider:

- If headers and footers are to be used in the document, consider whether they will be the same throughout the document. If not, you may need to break the document up into sections to control the headers and footers. For more on this, see Chapter 7, *Insert*.
- If footnotes are to be used, you'll want to make sure the options for them are correctly set. It might even be a good idea to include a sample footnote in the boilerplate text for the template to show how they should be used. Footnotes are covered in Chapter 7.
- Will the document use a table of contents or index? If so, setting it up in the template can save a lot of time later. Go ahead and create the table of contents or index and include instructions in the template boilerplate text for how to mark entries, configure headings properly, and update the index or table of contents. This information is also covered in Chapter 7.
- If the template has any document-level formatting (like borders and shading), set it up now. This makes it easier to see what character and paragraph formatting looks like later.

Setting Options

The next thing to think about when creating a template is how the options for the document are set on Word's Tools → Options dialog. Chapter 3, *Customizing Word*, covered the options on all of the tabs on this dialog in detail, so I'm not going to rehash that here. Instead, I'll give you a few things to think about when designing your template:

- Decide how the document should be viewed by the people who will be using the template. Tools → Options → View offers a number of options for displaying hidden formatting marks, field codes, scrollbars, status bar, and more. If you think any of these are useful, turn them on. If you think they'll get in the way, disable them.
- The Tools → Options → Print tab holds many settings controlling how a document is printed. Make sure these settings are correctly set.
- Tools → Options → Spelling & Grammar controls Word's spellchecker. For my template, I'm turning off the squiggly lines that appear under spelling and grammar errors by disabling the "Check spelling (grammar) as you type" options. I usually find it much better to run a check after the document is complete, so as not to interrupt my train of thought while writing. If I wanted to get really fancy, I could also create a customized writing style based on the MLA style guide that Word used while checking grammar. To do this, open Tools → Options → Spelling & Grammar. Select a writing style from the drop-down list and click Settings to open a dialog that lets you modify the actual grammar settings. I won't subject you to all the details of the MLA style guidelines here, though.

It's probably best to scan through the options on all of these tabs whenever you create a new template. Although many of the options can be set later, the whole idea of templates is to make the documents created with them faster, easier, and more consistent.

Creating Styles

One of the most important aspects of creating any template is controlling the formatting of the text in the documents created from that template. No other Word feature is more useful for creating consistent, easy-to-apply formatting than styles.

Styles are really just collections of formats that have been given a name and can be applied all at once. There are two types of styles in Word:

Paragraph styles
: These contain formatting that is applied to an entire paragraph. Paragraph styles can include paragraph formatting (such as tabs, line spacing, and indenting), character formatting (such as font, size, and color), and formatting that applies to either characters or paragraphs (such as borders or languages).

Character styles
: These contain formatting that is applied only to selected characters within a paragraph. Characters within a paragraph can have their own style even if a paragraph style is applied to the paragraph as a whole. Character styles can only include character formatting.

Character styles overlay paragraph styles. For example, if a paragraph style uses a bold font, all of the text typed in a paragraph using that style is boldfaced. If a character style that uses normal text is applied to any text in that paragraph, the text turns out normal. Remove the character style (or any manual formatting) and the text reverts to that defined by the paragraph style. You can do this by applying the "Default Paragraph Font" character style, which reverts any selected text to use the character formatting defined by the underlying paragraph style. The keyboard shortcut for this is Ctrl-Space.

For the MLA template I've been creating, I'm going to create three paragraph styles:

- According to MLA style, normal body text is double-spaced and uses a 10-point font size. I'll create a new style named MLA Body for this.
- Headings use a 10-point font size and are boldfaced. I'll create a style for this named MLA Heading.
- Quotations longer than four lines are set apart from the body text, indented one inch from the left margin, and double-spaced. I'll create a new style named MLA Quotation for this.

I'm also going to create one character style named MLA Emphasis, which is used to emphasize words. Really, it will be the same as the body text, just italicized. The reason I'm creating a style instead of just letting the user italicize the text via a toolbar or format command is that MLA allows either italics or underlining to be used. The catch is that only one form must be used throughout the document. A character style helps maintain consistency and makes it easier to apply global changes.

TIP # 142

Make the Template Function Part of a Style's Name

When naming styles, it's tempting to just give them a name based on their function. This is okay, but I recommend prefixing that with a brief description of the template the style is part of. For example, instead of naming a style "Body," I chose to name it "MLA Body." This makes it obvious at a glance where the style comes from.

The first style I want to create is MLA Body. Choose Format → Style to open the Style dialog box (Figure 14-4), which lists all of the styles currently available. This list is based on styles in the active document and in any global templates currently loaded. A preview and description of any selected style are shown on the right.

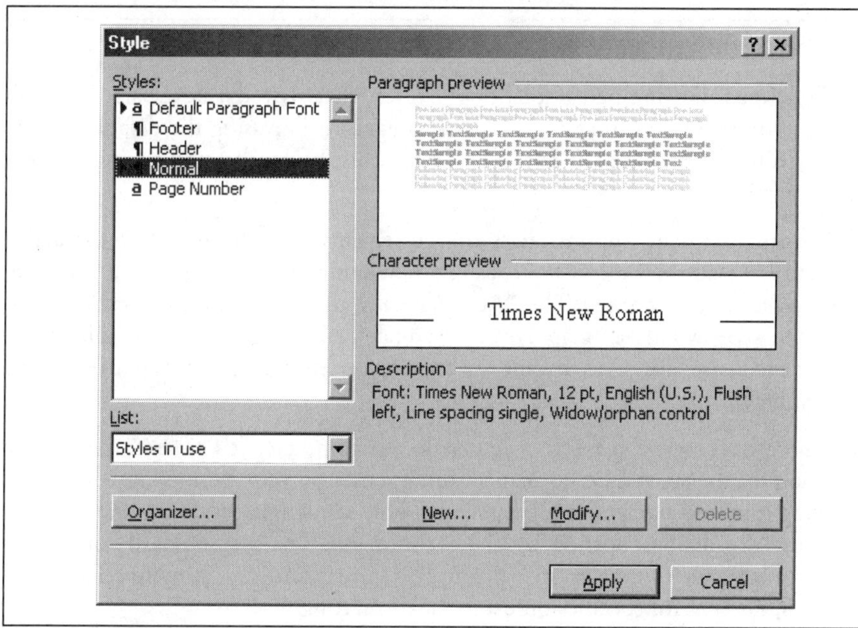

Figure 14-4: Viewing available styles

Click the New button to open the New Style dialog (Figure 14-5). As you can see from the figure, I've already given the style its name and specified that it is to be a paragraph style. All new styles must be based on an existing style: in this case, I used the default option and based my new style on Word's Normal style, as it already closely suits my needs.

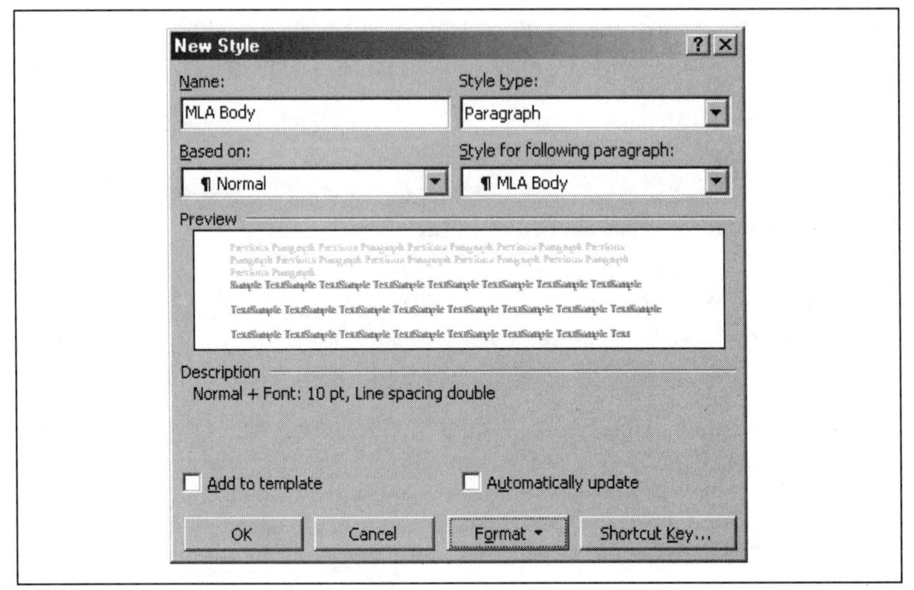

Figure 14-5: Creating a new style

The "Style for following paragraph" box defines what style the next paragraph will use when you press Return at the end of a paragraph. I'm using the default option, which is to keep using the current style. I expect most users to start typing another body paragraph.

The "Add to template" option adds the current style to the template the active document is based on. Since I'm creating a new template based on Word's *normal.dot*, I won't use this option. The "Automatically update" option causes Word to update the style whenever I apply any manual formatting to a paragraph in the document that uses the style. I want my style to be left alone, so I'm not using this option either.

Once these basic settings for the new style are complete, it's time to define the formatting for the style. The Format button opens a pop-up menu with commands for setting font and paragraph formats, tabs, borders, languages, and more. For the most part, the dialogs opened by these commands are the standard formatting dialogs available on Word's Format menu. For this reason, I'm going to refer you to Chapter 8, *Format*, for specifics on using the formatting tools.

As you can see from the description area in Figure 14-5, I've already applied the necessary formatting to the MLA Body style. The description means that I used the Normal style and added the 10-point font size formatting and double line spacing. Click OK once the style is defined and Word adds it to the document.

Next, I created the other styles I need using the same basic procedure. Here's a quick synopsis of the creation:

1. I based the new MLA Heading style on Word's Normal style. I reduced the font to 10-point, added bold facing, and set the line spacing to double. I also set it so that the style for the following paragraph would always be MLA Body, reasoning that after typing a heading, the user would start in on the body text.
2. I based the MLA Quotation style on the MLA Body style, reasoning that most of the formatting was the same and all I'd have to do was set the indents to 1 inch. I set the style for the following paragraph to MLA Body, since this is the most likely thing to follow a quotation.
3. I created the MLA Emphasis character style based on Word's built-in emphasis style, which is really the same thing. Why not just have users select Word's emphasis style instead? As noted above, the simple reason is convenience. By creating a new style that starts with the prefix "MLA," all of the styles that are used in an MLA document are grouped together on the Style drop-down list on the Standard toolbar (Figure 14-6). This makes it easier to find a style, especially if the user has other global templates open that have their own styles. This list can grow quite long. It is often easier to use the Format → Style command or to assign keyboard shortcuts to commonly used styles (see Chapter 3).

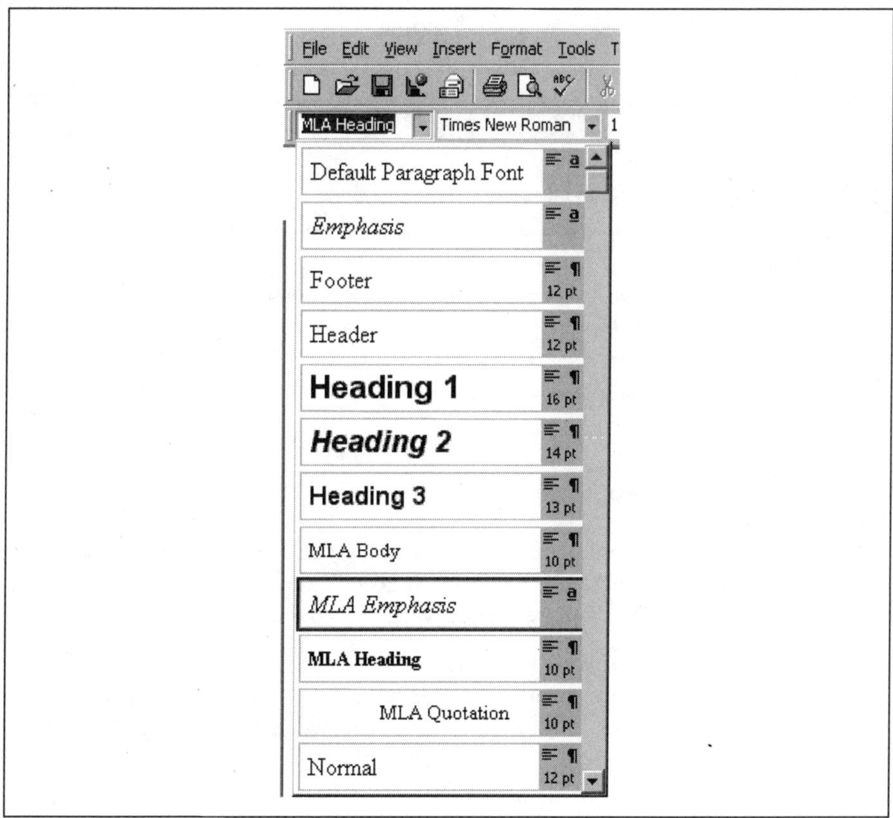

Figure 14-6: Viewing the new styles

Creating Boilerplate Text

Boilerplate text is text typed into a template that appears in all new documents created from that template. It serves two purposes. First, it allows the option of adding consistently formatted text to all documents created from the template. Examples might be disclaimers, addresses, and that sort of thing. Second, it is a great way of providing text that is already formatted the way it should be and just needs to be filled in. This is also a great method of providing instruction for using the template.

Figure 14-7 shows the boilerplate text I have created for the MLA template.

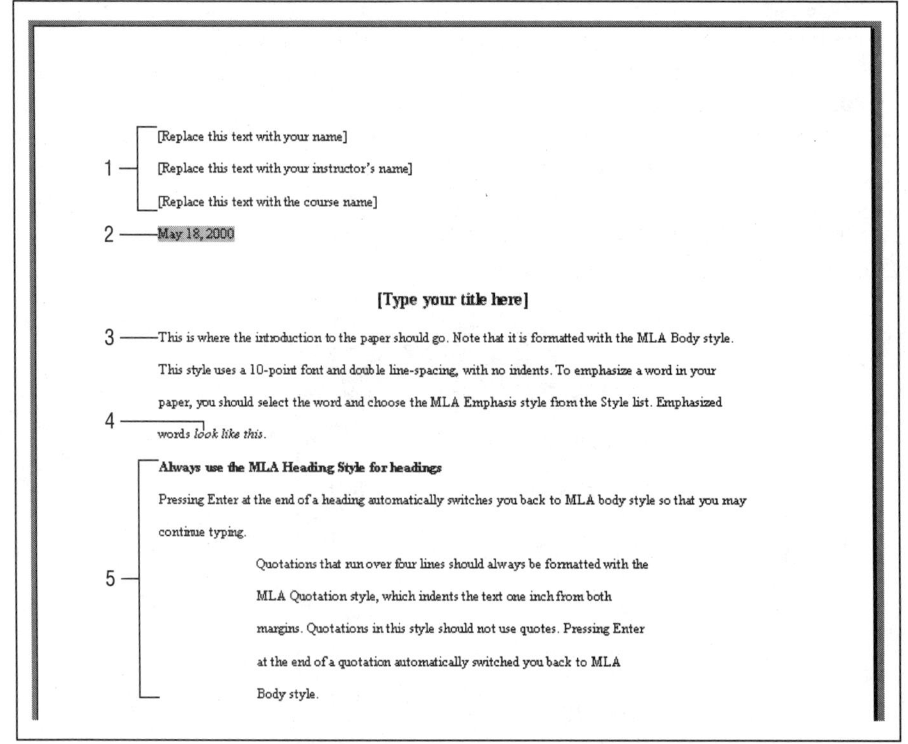

Figure 14-7: Boilerplate text in a template

1. These entries are simple text formatted with the MLA Body style and are already positioned where the first page heading should go. Instructions in the text ask the students to replace the text with their own.

2. I used a field here to provide the current date in the correct format. This field is updated every time the document is opened. Later in the boilerplate text, I might give instructions for unlinking this field when the paper is finished so that the date becomes fixed.

3. Here, I've used the MLA Body style to create instructional text that describes the style and its use.
4. I also included an example of the MLA Emphasis character style.
5. By putting an actual heading, quotation, and body text in the boilerplate, users will be able to see exactly how the paper should look when correctly formatted.

Customizing the Word Interface

At this point, I have a functional template. It conforms to the MLA page setup guidelines, has styles for applying the correct formatting, and even includes some boilerplate text to help the user get started. I could stop here, but there are a few more possible tweaks that might help users.

Customizing the Word interface can often help accomplish two goals related to working with templates:

- It can make it easier for people to access the features they ought to be using.
- It can make it more difficult for people to access the features they shouldn't be using.

Chapter 3 covers how to customize existing menus and toolbars and how to create new ones, so look there for the procedural details. Here, I want to show you some of the things I would do with my MLA template. Hopefully, seeing some of my decisions will point you in the right direction when you're thinking about how to design a template of your own.

The first thing I want to do is trim down Word's menus and toolbars. They have functions all over them that will never be used in an MLA-based paper, so why let them clutter things up? Here's a list of the changes I made to my template's menus:

- On the File menu, I removed the web commands (Preview Web Page and Save As Web Page) because they're not required in the context in which the template will be used. I also removed the Page Setup command because I don't want people tweaking the page layout settings. Users can change their paper source from the Print dialog instead of from the Paper Source tab of Page Setup.
- On the Insert menu, I removed most of the commands that let users insert special objects, such as fields, graphics, and files. They don't have any business in an MLA paper and removing them shortens the menu considerably.
- For the most part, I also don't want people monkeying around with the formatting for the paper. I want to force them to use the pre-created styles. For this reason, I did away with the Format menu altogether. I know it sounds a little heavy-handed, but I could only think of one reason to use it during the creation of an MLA-format paper where the styles were already defined: the users

might want to tweak the font size and paragraph spacing to make the paper seem longer than it really was. I didn't want them doing this.

- I removed the Table menu, as well. Tables are not allowed in an MLA paper.
- Finally, I removed many of the same commands from the toolbars as I did from the menus.

The next thing I wanted to do was centralize the commands that users would use most frequently on a single menu named MLA. Since there are so few styles, I also decided to include them there. Of course, I also left these commands and styles in their original locations for users who were more familiar with Word. Figure 14-8 shows my custom MLA menu.

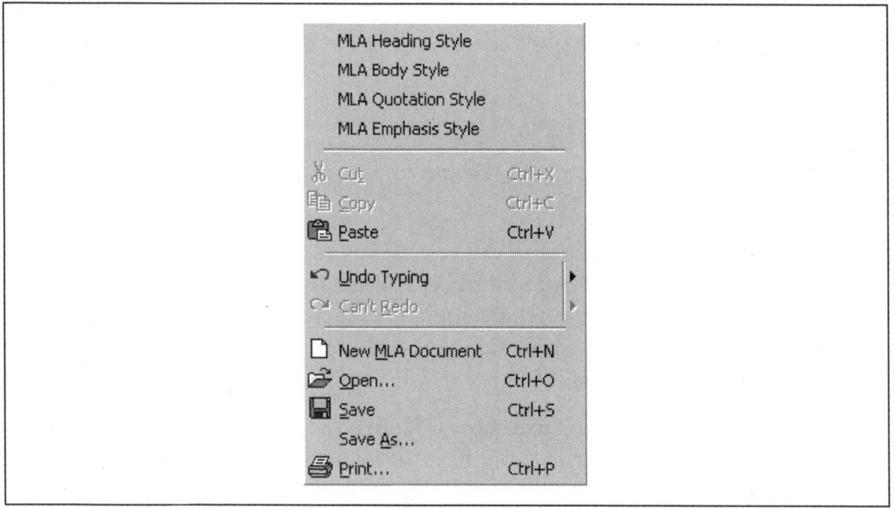

Figure 14-8: A custom menu for the MLA template

Saving the Template

If the Template option was selected on the File → New dialog, Word saves the new file as a *.dot* file. If the template was created based on a document, you must specify that Word save it as a *.dot* file using File → Save As (Figure 14-9).

The location where the template is saved (and where users put it when you send it to them) is very important:

- *\Windows\Application Data\Microsoft\Templates* is the default location set for user templates. When you save a template, Word opens this folder automatically in the Save As dialog. Change the default using Tools → Options → File Locations → User Templates → Modify (Figure 14-10). Templates stored here appear on the General tab of the File → New dialog.

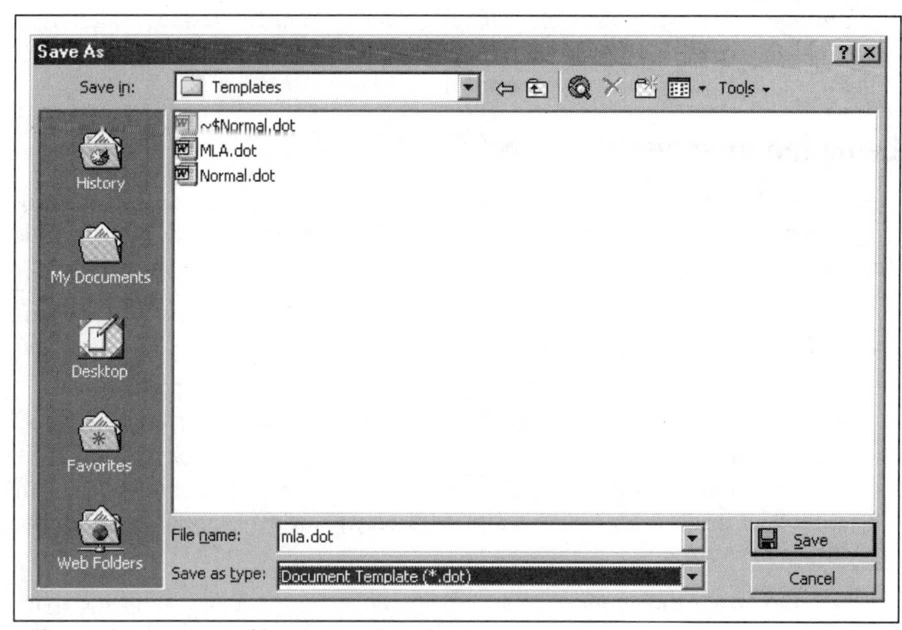

Figure 14-9: *Saving a file as a template*

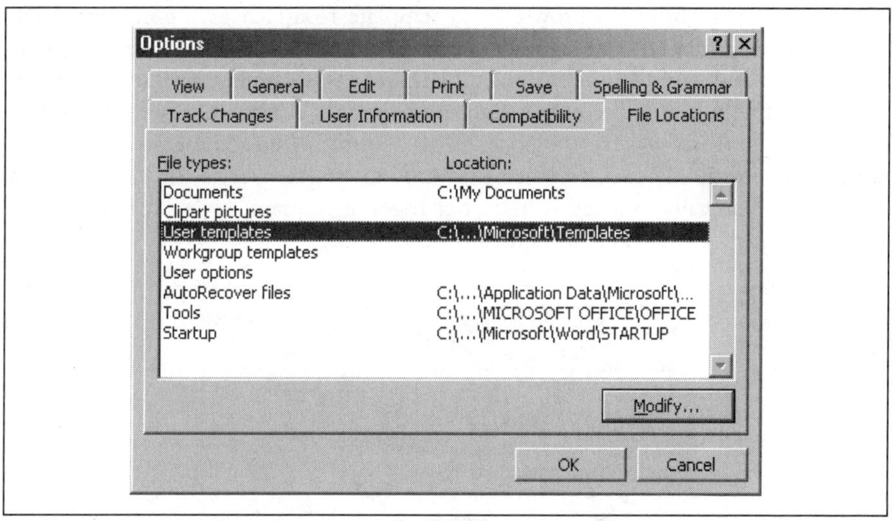

Figure 14-10: *Modifying default template locations*

- The workgroup templates directory works just like the user templates directory, but is used to store templates that multiple users on a network share. There is no default location, but you can set one using Tools → Options → File Locations → Workgroup Templates → Modify. Using these locations is covered in more detail in Chapter 4, *File*.

- *\Program Files\Microsoft Office\Office\Startup* is Word's startup folder. Any template saved in it is loaded as a global template every time Word starts. Components of global templates are available to all open documents.

Using the Template

Once a template is saved, it is pretty easy to use. From a simple document template like the one I created in this chapter, users will want to create a new document. This can be done in a couple of ways:

- In Windows Explorer, double-clicking a template actually starts a new document based on the template rather than opening it. To open the template, you must right-click the template and choose Open from the context menu.
- If the template is saved in one of the template directories mentioned previously, use it to create a new document by choosing File → New in Word. The template should appear on the General tab of the New dialog. If it was saved in a subfolder inside one of those template directories, it may appear on one of the other tabs instead.

You can also attach the template to an existing document, copying all of the styles and other components from the template into that document. To do this, open the document and use the Tools → Templates and Add-Ins command (Figure 14-11). Click the Attach button to browse for a template to attach to the current document. As soon as the template is attached, all of the styles and other components are copied into the document unless the template and the document have styles that use the same name but are different. In this case, use the "Automatically update document styles" option to have the styles in the template replace the styles with the same names in the document. When this option is selected, styles in the document are also automatically updated to reflect changes in the same styles in the attached template. For more detail on all of this, see Chapter 2.

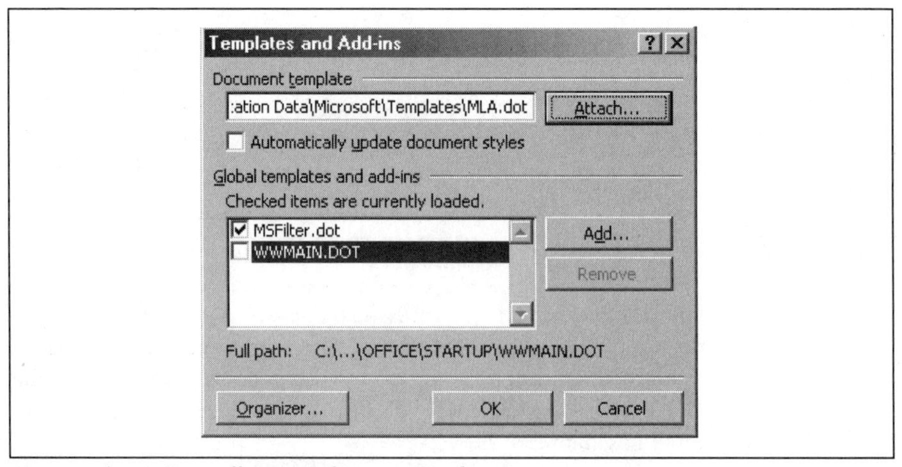

Figure 14-11: Controlling templates in Word

The Templates and Add-ins dialog is also used to control global templates. The list at the bottom of the dialog shows all global templates currently loaded except for *normal.dot*. Use the Add and Remove buttons to load and unload global templates. Remove the check next to any global template to temporarily disable it without actually unloading it.

Chapter 15

Fields and Forms

Word uses fields to perform all kinds of built-in functions, such as inserting automatic dates into headers, making calculations in tables, and creating indexes or tables of contents. Chapter 2, *How Word Works*, covers how fields fit into the overall Word document. This chapter details how to insert, edit, format, and manipulate fields.

There are dozens of fields in Word, and I'm not going to cover specific fields in much detail in this chapter. Rather, this chapter examines what a field is, what it does, and how it is constructed. With this foundation, it should be easy to browse through the available fields and put them to good use. Word's help file details every field in Word, lists the switches used with the field, and even gives examples.

This chapter also covers forms, documents created using collections of certain types of fields. Though form fields differ in structure and use from regular Word fields, the two are conceptually similar. Forms provide a structured way to collect user input (users enter data into the form fields) and then do something with that input —calculate it, format it, or just save it.

What Is a Field?

A field is a set of instructions that draws information from somewhere, formats and manipulates that information, and inserts the results into a document. This information might be drawn from another field, a file, the system clock on your computer, or from input requested when the field is activated.

The set of instructions is called a field code, but inserting a field into a document normally displays the results of a field rather than the field code itself. For example, insert a date field into a document and Word displays the date and time with the same character and paragraph formatting used by the surrounding text (Figure 15-1).

Today's date is Tuesday, May 16, 2000

Figure 15-1: Viewing the results of a field

Select the field by clicking anywhere in it, or just by moving the insertion point over it with the keyboard, and Word shades the field in gray. This shading is used onscreen to help identify fields. The field results are printed as normal, unshaded text.

TIP # 143

Change the Shading of Fields

By default, Word shades a field only when it is selected. Use Tools → Options → View → Field Shading to change this behavior. Set shading to Never and Word doesn't shade the field even when it's selected. Set shading to Always to have Word shade all fields whether they are selected or not.

Right-click the field result and use the Toggle Field Codes option on the context menu to view the field code instead of the results for that field. Figure 15-2 shows the field code for the results shown in previous figure. Move the insertion point into the field and use Shift-F9 to toggle the field code view with the keyboard. Toggle field codes for all of the fields in the document at once using the Tools → Options → View → Field Codes option.

Today's date is { DATE \@ "dddd, MMMM dd, yyyy" * MERGEFORMAT }

Figure 15-2: Viewing field codes

Viewing field codes in a document does not cause them to print. To print codes instead of results, you must turn on the Tools → Options → Print → Field Codes option. This option, along with other information on printing and fields, is covered later in this chapter.

A field code is made up of normal text enclosed in special curly brackets that look like the ones you can type, but really aren't the same. In other words, you can't insert a field code by just by typing the brackets.

Field codes are made up of three parts:

Field markers
: The curly brackets that let Word know where a field begins and ends. Word creates them during the insertion of a field.

Field name
: Simply the name of the field. Every different field type in Word has a unique name.

Field instructions
: These tell Word what information to use and what to do with that information to get the results for the field.

There are several different types of field instructions:

Bookmark instructions
: These refer to selections in the same document or in a separate document. Fields with bookmark instructions can use the contents of the bookmark as well as the page number on which the bookmark is found.

Expressions
: These are used in calculations and can be made up of mathematical or logical operations, numbers, or references to numbers in the document.

Text
: This is normally marked with quotation marks and represents content Word should display as part of the field results. Single words do not require quotation marks.

Switches
: These are optional instructions that tell Word how to format and display the results of the field. A switch is preceded by a backslash (\). General switches can be used with any field. Most fields also have field-specific switches. A field can have up to ten general switches and ten field-specific switches at one time.

Types of Fields

Although there are dozens of different fields available in Word and they are often grouped by category (document automation fields, calculations, numbering fields, etc.), there are really only three basic types of fields:

Result fields
: Calculate or retrieve information. Information may be retrieved from somewhere in the document (perhaps using a bookmark) or from Word itself (user information stored in Tools → Options → User Information and document information stored in File → Properties). The results of a result field are displayed immediately upon the creation of the field. Formula, date and time, and hyperlink fields are all examples of result fields.

Action fields
: Require further input from the document's user before displaying a result. For example, an Ask field opens a dialog asking the user for to enter text to be used in the result and the MacroButton field runs a macro when double-clicked.

Marker fields
: Identify text for use in indexes, tables of contents, footnotes, and the like. These fields don't really display or do anything besides marking the text.

So Why Use Fields?

There's actually little need to insert most of the fields in Word manually. For example, marker fields are used to identify text in a document that should be part of an index. You could create the marker field yourself (in which case you'd need to know the exact syntax to use). It's much easier, though, to select the words and use the Insert → Index and Tables command or just press Ctrl-Shift-X. Likewise, you could manually insert fields that displayed the author of a document and when that document was created, but it's easier to insert them automatically using the Insert → AutoText → Header/Footer commands. These are just a couple of examples, but there are more:

- Most of the action fields can only be used during the mail merge process and are much easier to use with the mail merge tools. Mail merge is covered in Chapter 9, *Tools*.
- Most of the user information, document information, and date/time result fields can be inserted easily using AutoText commands.
- All of the fields that control links and references can be accessed using the commands on Word's Insert menu.
- The equation and formula fields are easier to insert using the Table → Formula command.

So, again, why bother with fields? The short answer is control. Word uses fields in most of its advanced functions. Once you understand fields, it's easier to see just what Word is doing and to modify the results to better suit your needs. Also, manually inserting some types of fields can produce better results than using Word's automatic tools.

Inserting Fields

Fields can be inserted anywhere in a document's main text layer or header/footer text layer. In addition, some field types can be inserted into text boxes, which exist in the main drawing layer of a document.

TIP # 144

Fields in the Same Layer Can Communicate

Fields can draw on information provided by other fields, but only if they are in the same layer. Therefore, fields in text boxes cannot communicate with fields in the main text layer. Fields in the header/footer text layer cannot communicate with fields in the main text layer.

There are lots of different ways to insert a field into a document:

- Use the Table → Formula command to insert a calculation field into a table. See Chapter 10, *Table*, for more on this command.
- Use AutoText to insert document information such as the author's name or title of the document, covered in Chapter 7, *Insert*.
- Use Tools → Mail Merge to create a form letter using fields to fill in information from other sources automatically, covered in Chapter 9.
- Type a field code directly into the document. If you know the precise field name and instructions, press Ctrl-F9 to insert a pair of field markers into a document and move the insertion point inside those markers. Type the field name, instructions, and any switches. Click anywhere outside the field markers to complete the process.
- Use the Insert → Field command to choose a field and specify any field instructions.

All fields you can insert are listed in the Field dialog that opens after choosing Insert → Field (Figure 15-3). There are nine categories of fields and selecting any category displays a number of actual fields in the Field names box. Selecting any field displays a description of the field near the bottom of the Field dialog. To insert a field using its default instructions, just select the field and click OK.

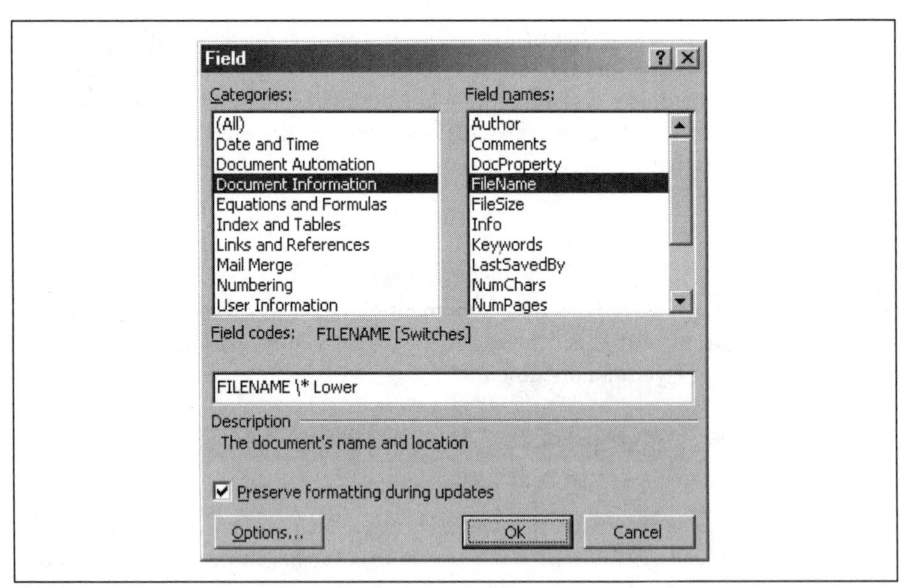

Figure 15-3: Inserting a field

TIP # 145

Access Word Help from the Field Dialog Box

Normally, right-clicking on an element in a dialog box and choosing What's This pops up a ScreenTip with a brief description of the element. In the Field dialog, though, choosing the What's This command for any field name launches Word Help and links you right to the help page for that field.

Selecting any field automatically enters the field code into the Field codes text box. You can type directly into this text box to create the field, but as with typing field codes into a document using Ctrl-F9, you must know the exact syntax.

The "Preserve formatting during updates" option adds a * MERGEFORMAT switch to the field (although it is not shown in the Field codes text box like other switches are). This switch forces the field to keep any manual formatting applied directly to the field during the updating of a field. Normally, any formatting applied by the field instructions, such as upper or lower case, overrides manual formatting. This option prevents that.

The Options button opens a separate dialog used to construct the switches, operators, bookmarks, and other instructions for a field. This button is not available for all fields. For the fields where options are available, the Options dialog is constructed from a number of different tabs. The most common tabs are General Switches and Field-Specific Switches, though you will often see tabs named Options, Bookmarks, etc.

The General Switches tab

The General Switches tab (Figure 15-4) is available for most fields. General switches are typically used to apply formatting to fields. Select a general switch from the list and click Add to Field to add the switch and display it in the Field codes box. Click Undo Add to remove the most-recently added switch.

TIP # 146

Format Fields with Character Formats When Possible

Format switches are useful for changing a field's number, date, or time format and sometimes for capitalization. Whenever possible, though, it's better to format fields using Word's standard formatting and styles.

There are four basic sets of general switches and different sets are available for different fields. Right-click any switch and choose What's This to pop-up a ScreenTip with better information than the description at the bottom of the dialog. Unfortunately, the Field Options screen does not link to the Word Help system the same way the fields themselves do on the Insert Field dialog. You'll just have to look them up in Help yourself.

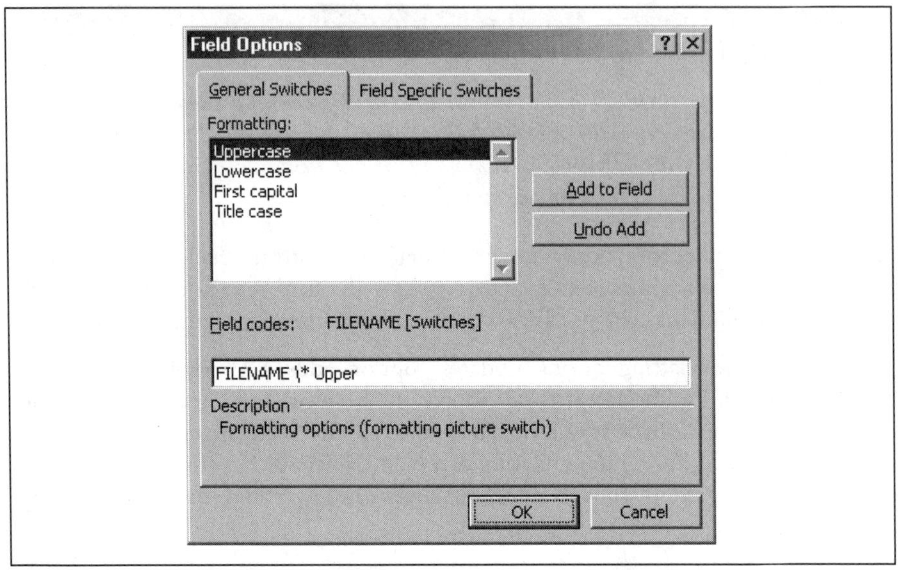

Figure 15-4: Applying general switches to a field

The four sets of general switches are:

Format switches (*)
: Apply capitalization and number formats and specify how character formatting should be handled. For example, * upper displays the fields result in uppercase.

Numeric Picture switches (\#)
: Control the display of numbers, including the number of decimal places and the use of currency symbols.

Date-Time Picture switches (\@)
: Control the format for fields with date or time results. For example, a date could be displayed as 05/05/00 (MM/dd/yy) or as May 6, 2000 (MMMM/d/yyyy).

Lock Result switch (\!)
: Prevents a field from being updated. Updating fields is covered later in this chapter.

There are a host of specific switches within each set of general switches. I couldn't do a better job of detailing these switches than the Word Help files, so I'm going to refer you there for details on using the specific switches.

The Field-Specific Switches tab

Use the Field-Specific Switches tab (Figure 15-5) to construct switches that are only available for the current field.

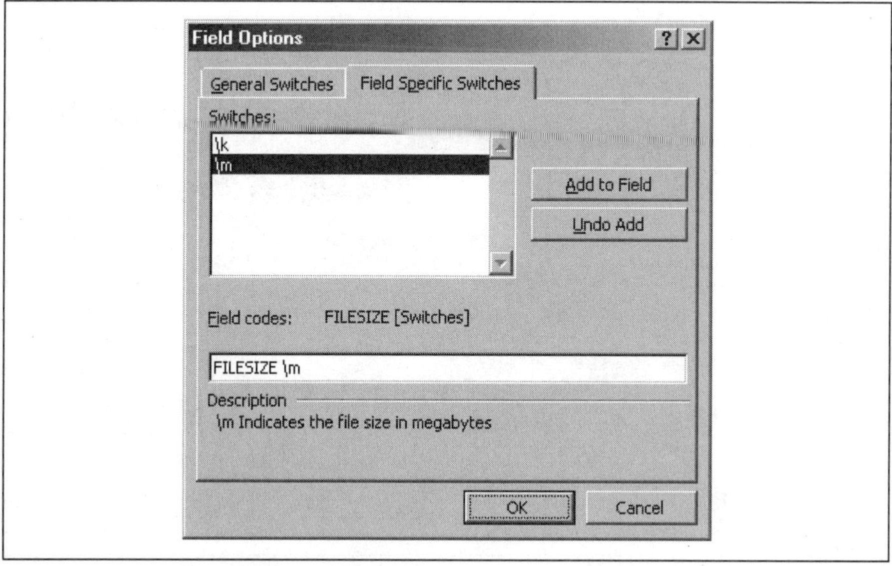

Figure 15-5: Applying field-specific switches

Not every field has field-specific switches. This tab works in the same way as the General Switches tab. Select a switch, click Add to Field, and the Field codes box is updated with the new switch. Again, there are so many switches for specific fields that I'm going to refer you to Windows Help for details.

The Options tab

Many fields boast Options tabs instead of General Switches and Field-Specific Switches tabs. However, all the Options tabs I've seen are just used to set switches and work the same as the two switches tabs. In fact, when you come across an Options tab, you'll probably notice that all of the switches available on it are the same general switches available for other fields or specific switches to that field.

Why did Word's designers decide to use Options tabs for some fields instead of the other two switches tabs? The only answer I can think of is that sometimes the Options tab is used to hold items that aren't really switches, but provide the field with some information it needs. Take, for example, the Options tab for the MacroButton field (Figure 15-6). The options listed on this Options tab are not switches. Instead, all of the macros available in Word are listed.

The MacroButton field runs a specified macro whenever the user clicks on designated text. For example, the field code in the figure runs a macro that opens the Print dialog (same as File → Print) whenever the user double-clicks on the word "here." You could stick this code at the end of a sentence that reads, "To print this document, double-click here".

You may run across a number of other tabs as well; for example, the Bookmarks tab. These tabs work the same way as the tabs we've already explored. They list a

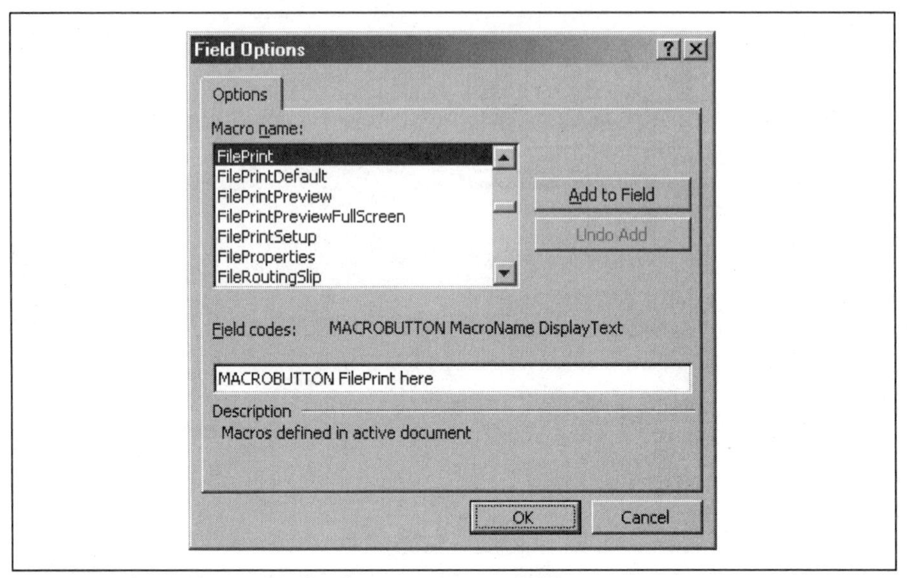

Figure 15-6: Setting options for the MacroButton field

number of options (or bookmarks or whatever) and let you add those options to the field. The use of these tabs in Word is a bit confusing, to put it kindly. Sometimes, you'll see bookmarks presented on a Bookmarks tab and sometimes on an Options tab. Just keep in mind that all of the tabs work pretty much the same way.

Selecting and Editing Fields

Once a field is inserted, it can be treated much like any other text in the document. Select an entire field by dragging the pointer across it. Once selected, apply any character styles or formatting, move, cut, or paste the field as normal.

TIP # 147

Jump Between Fields with F11

Press the F11 key to jump to the next field in a document after the insertion point and highlight that field. Press Shift-F11 to jump to and highlight the field prior to the insertion point.

Select any text inside the field by double-clicking or dragging. Whenever any text inside a field is selected, Word adds a normal selection highlight on top of any field shading (Figure 15-7). Apply the same character styles or formatting to text in the field that you would apply to non-field text.

Created on 5/16/2000 5:00 PM

Figure 15-7: Selecting text inside a field

You can also manipulate selected text inside a field in other ways. In fact, once a field is constructed, the only way to edit it is by manually typing the changes to the switches and field instructions. There is no way to return to the Insert Field dialog box. You'll have to know the exact syntax to use when making the change. Of course, you could always delete and recreate the field instead. Here are a few caveats to keep in mind when editing a field:

- If you delete part of the field results (say, the year from a date), the deleted text will return the next time the field is updated. Stop this by locking or breaking the field, discussed a bit later in the chapter.
- If you delete a part of the field code, the deleted text will not return.
- Word doesn't protest if you move vital pieces of a field (such as the field name) out of a field code, rendering the field useless.

Updating and Locking Fields

Result fields, which retrieve or calculate information, display their results based on information contained in the field. This information may point to a source outside the field (for example, a bookmark, the system clock, or a picture). If that information changes, the field must be updated to show current information.

Word automatically updates all fields whenever it opens a document. After that, no more updates occur automatically until the next time Word opens the document. There are, however, two ways to force an update:

- Select any field and press F9 to update it. Alternately, right-click the field and choose Update Field from the context menu. Select the whole document (Ctrl-A) and press F9 to update all the fields in a document at once.
- Turn on Tools → Options → Print → Update Fields to force Word to update all of the fields in the document before printing.

Fields and Forms

There are also a couple of ways to keep a field from updating, whether the update occurs automatically or manually:

- Lock a field by selecting it and pressing Ctrl-3 or Ctrl-F11. You can also do this by adding the Lock switch (\!) to the field. Locking a field prevents updates from occurring until the field is unlocked. Unlock a field by selecting it and pressing Ctrl-Shift-11.

TIP # 148

Use the Context Menu to See If a Field Is Locked

Right-click a field to quickly find out whether it is locked. If the Update Field command on the context menu is dimmed, the field is locked.

- Break a field by converting it to text. Select the field and press Ctrl-6 or Ctrl-Shift-F9. Once a field is broken, the process is irreversible.

Printing Fields

By default, Word prints only the results of fields. The Tools → Options → Print tab offers two options governing printing and fields:

Update Fields
: Use this option to have Word update all of the fields in a document just before printing. Locked fields are not updated.

Field Codes
: Use this option to have Word print the field codes instead of the field results.

Using Forms

Forms can be defined as a structured arrangement of data fields used to collect information and store it in an organized way. Many people use both paper and electronic forms to collect different types of information. Forms can be used for expense reports, invoices, contact information, and much more. Word is a useful tool for creating forms to print or use electronically.

In this section, I step through the creation of an electronic form. This form is an invoice that lets users fill in labeled fields for addresses, items, quantities sold, and prices. The form takes the quantities and prices, calculates line-item totals for the user, and calculates a final total for the invoice, including tax. The form also saves the data in the fields to a comma-delimited text file so that it can be imported into a database later.

Creating a Form

Unless you are creating a very simple form, it's a good idea to use a table to provide structure to the labels and fields. Figure 15-8 shows the table we will use to create a basic invoice. This is essentially a four-column table, but I have merged some cells, used some background shading, and made some of the cell borders invisible to make the form look nice (see Chapter 10 for more on creating tables). I've also filled in the title and the column headings.

My goal is to use this table as the basis for new invoices I create for my customers. For this reason, I'm going to save it as a template. I'll name it *invoice.dot*. Each time I want to create a new invoice, I'll start a new document based on this template.

Now, I could just stop with this nice-looking table and fill in all of the information as text within the table cells for each new invoice. However, I've decided to go ahead and create a form for three reasons:

- Other people within my company need to use this invoice and I want to make it as simple as possible for them to do so. I also want to make sure that they can only enter data into the invoice and not change its structure or content. A form will let me do this.

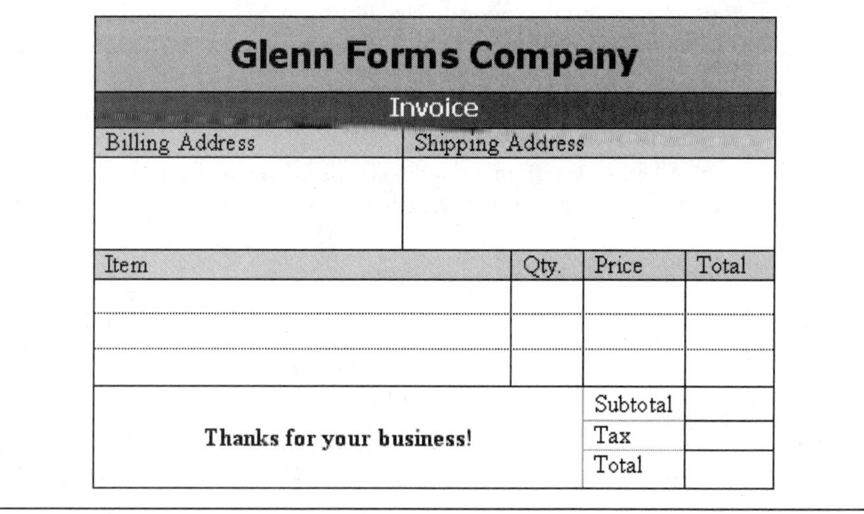

Glenn Forms Company

Invoice

Billing Address	Shipping Address

Item	Qty.	Price	Total
Thanks for your business!		Subtotal	
		Tax	
		Total	

Figure 15-8: *Using a table to provide structure to a form*

- I need to be able to save the data in each invoice in a text file so that I can later pull that information easily into a database. A form will also let me do this.
- People should be able to use a drop-down list to pick items on the invoice so that there are no mistakes.

Now that I've decided to create a form, the first step is to open the Forms toolbar (Figure 15-9). Right-click on any toolbar and click Forms to do this.

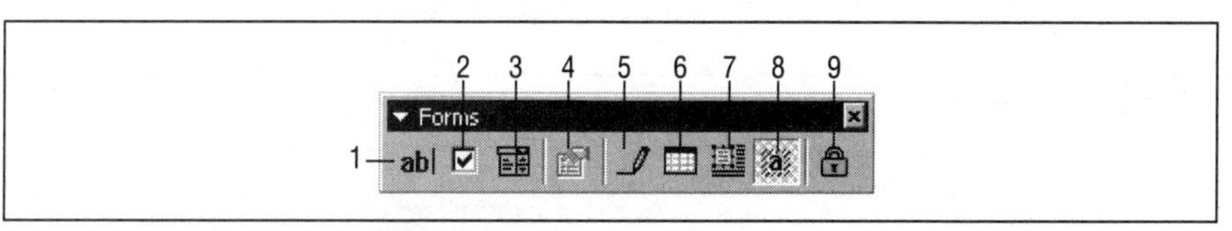

Figure 15-9: The Forms toolbar

Here's a brief rundown on the Forms toolbar:

1. *Text Form Field.* Insert a standard text box field where users can enter text.
2. *Checkbox Form Field.* Insert a checkbox that users can select or clear.
3. *Drop-down Form Field.* Insert a drop-down list that users can choose elements from.
4. *Form Field Options.* Open the Properties dialog for a selected field.
5. *Draw Table.* Use the table drawing tool as described in Chapter 10.
6. *Insert Table.* Insert a table with regular columns and rows as described in Chapter 10.

7. *Insert Frame*. Insert a frame around a selection so that you can position it more precisely on the page. See Chapter 7 for the lowdown on using framed objects.
8. *Form Field Shading*. This option toggles the field shading for all of the fields in a form.
9. *Protect Form*. When selected, only the data fields in a form can be modified. No other element of the document may be edited.

Using Form Fields

Now that you've seen the table, heard the reasons for making a form, and looked at the Forms toolbar, it's time to create the form.

First, I'm going to insert a number of fields into the form.

It is important to remember that form fields are not the same as the regular fields used in Word. Form fields are available only within the context of a form.

Insert a text field by placing the insertion point and clicking the Text Form Field button on the Forms toolbar. I'm putting text fields in all of the areas except for the Item column.

Next, I'm going to put one drop-down field in the first cell of the Item column with the Drop-Down Form Field button. After I've created the items to appear in the drop-down list, I'll copy that field to the other Item cells to save time.

When I'm done inserting fields, the form looks something like the one in Figure 15-10. Each of the gray boxes is a field waiting for someone to type data.

Glenn Forms Company			
Invoice			
Billing Address	Shipping Address		
Item	Qty.	Price	Total
Thanks for your business!		Subtotal	
		Tax	
		Total	

Figure 15-10: Inserting text fields in a form

Now that I've inserted my fields, the next step is configuring them. Open the properties for a field by selecting the field and clicking the Form Field Options button on the Forms toolbar or by right-clicking the field and choosing Properties from the context menu. Figure 15-11 shows the properties for a text field, in this case the text field for the billing address.

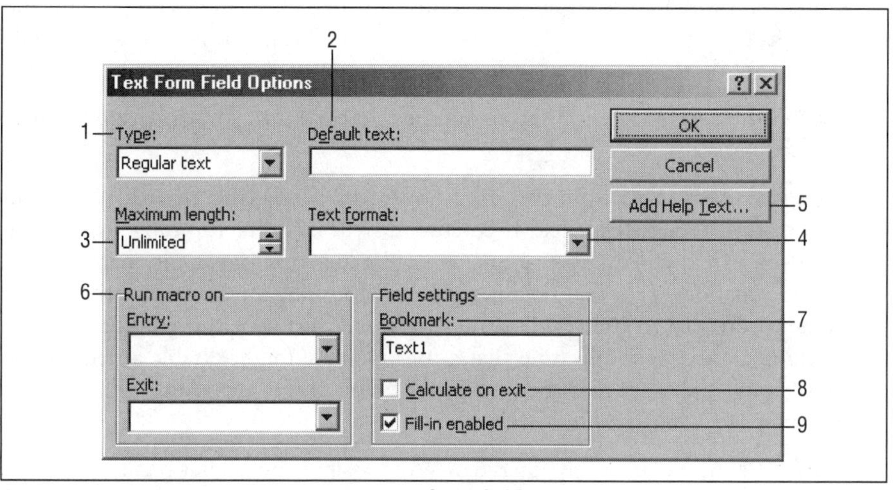

Figure 15-11: Setting properties on a text form field

1. *Type*. The type of text selected governs other options in the dialog. For example, choosing the Number type changes the Text format field to a Number format field. For this reason, it's important to choose the type before setting any other options.
   - *Regular text*. This is the default text type. Users can enter characters, numbers, or symbols.
   - *Number*. Only numbers are allowed in the field.
   - *Date*. Only dates can be entered. Selecting this field changes the Text format field to a Date format field for controlling the way that dates are entered.
   - *Current Date (Time)*. These options always display the current system date or time in the field. Users cannot enter data into these field types.
   - *Calculation*. Use this field type to calculate values from other fields using a formula. This is covered a bit later.
2. *Default text*. Enter any text that should appear in the field to start with. Users can enter different text, unless the "Fill-in enabled" option is disabled, in which case the text cannot be changed. This field changes to "Default number," "Default date," etc. to reflect the type of field selected in the Type box.

3. *Maximum length.* Enter the maximum number of characters a field may contain.
4. *Text format.* Choose the required format for the text from a drop-down list. By default, no format is required. This field changes to reflect the type of field selected in the Type box. For regular text, format options deal with capitalization. For dates and times, format options include all of the standard date and time format pictures. For calculations and numbers, format options include number of decimal places and use of currency symbols.
5. *Add Help Text.* Use this button to add help to the form. This is covered later in the chapter.
6. *Run macro on.* Select from two drop-down lists of available macros. Word can run macros as soon as a field is entered, exited, or both. Running a macro on entering a field could, for example, create default text (say, a city name) based on information in another field (a zip code). Running a macro on exiting might disable other fields based on information in the field being exited. For example, clicking a checkbox indicating that a user is single might disable a field asking how long the user has been married. For more on using Macros, see Chapter 18, *Working with VBA*.
7. *Bookmark.* All fields are bookmarked. Word assigns the default bookmark name based on the type of field. Enter any name to change it.
8. *Calculate on exit.* This option causes Word to update and recalculate every field in the form when this field is exited. This updating occurs after any exit macro is run.
9. *Fill-in enabled.* Disable this option to lock the field so that no new data can be entered. Use this in combination with the Default text box to create a field with preset data that cannot be altered.

So, back to the invoice form. I'm going to make a few quick changes to some of the fields in the form:

1. First, I'm changing the bookmark names of all of the fields to something more logical. For example, I'll change the bookmark name for the first field to "Billing" instead of "Text1."
2. Next, I'm entering default text in the Shipping Address field to read "Same as billing address." Users can enter a different address if they want.
3. I'm changing the fields in the Qty. column to number type.
4. Finally, I'm changing the fields in the Price column to number type and selecting the standard U.S. currency format ($x,xx0.00)

The next step in creating the invoice form is to modify the drop-down field I put into the Item column. The properties for the field look much like the properties for a text field (Figure 15-12).

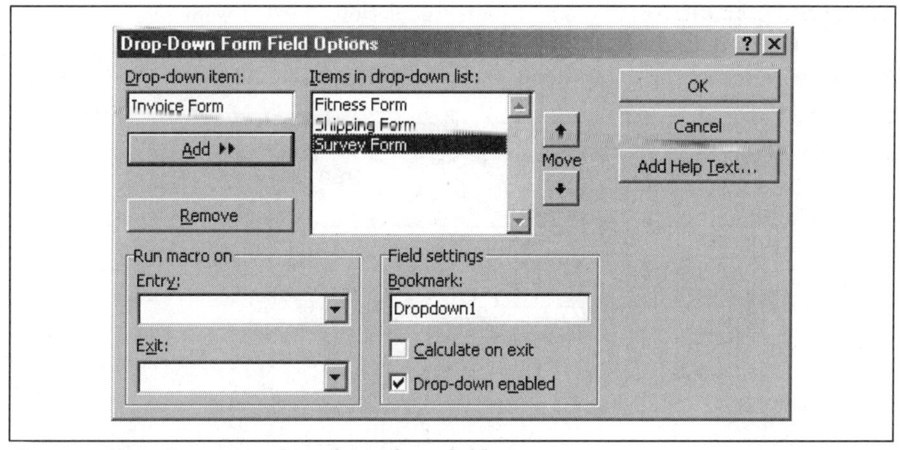

Figure 15-12: Creating a drop-down form field

Enter a list item in the "Drop-down item" field and click Add to add it to the list. Select an item in the list and click Remove to take it out. Use the Move buttons to arrange the order of items in the list. The rest of the dialog is exactly the same as for the text field.

After creating the drop-down field, I'm going to copy it to all of the other cells in the Item column. That way, I don't have to reconstruct the list for each field. After copying them, I'll go back and change the bookmark name and any options I want. At this point, the form looks something like the one shown in Figure 15-13. As you can see, the first item listed in the drop-down list is always used as the default text. Selecting a drop-down field opens a menu with the other selections.

Glenn Forms Company

Invoice

Billing Address	Shipping Address
	Same as billing address.

Item	Qty.	Price	Total
Fitness Form			
Fitness Form			
Fitness Form			
		Subtotal	
...nks for your business!		Tax	
		Total	

Fitness Form
Shipping Form
Survey Form
Invoice Form

Figure 15-13: Selecting an item from a drop-down form field

The final step in this form is to add some calculations. First, I want the fields in the Total column to multiply the quantity by the price to get a total cost for each item. Figure 15-14 shows the properties of the first field in that column.

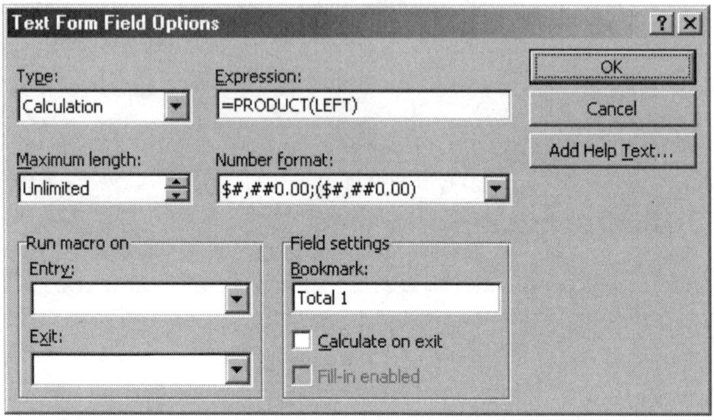

Figure 15-14: Creating a calculation field

I've made it a Calculation type using a number format. For the expression, I used a little trick. PRODUCT tells Word to multiply numbers. LEFT tells word to use the numbers in all of the fields to the left. Since the Item fields aren't numbers, Word ignores them and I get the result I'm after. This is much easier than referring to specific fields by row and column or even by their bookmark names. (For more information on constructing formulas, see Chapter 10.) I'll use the same properties for the other fields in the total column. Now, the form looks like Figure 15-15.

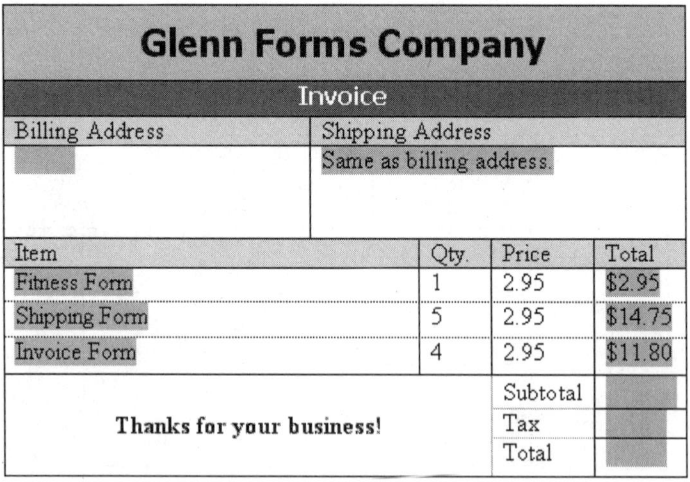

Figure 15-15: Viewing the results of a calculation.

I entered the quantity and price myself and Word calculated the item line totals for me. There are only three things left to do:

1. I want the Subtotal field to add up the fields in the Total column. To do this, I am going to make the field a calculation field and select the standard currency format. I'm going to use the formula =SUM(ABOVE) to add up all of the numbers above the cell in the column. This should give me the total I want.
2. My local sales tax is 8%, so I'm going to make the Tax field a calculation field that multiplies the Subtotal field by 8%, giving me the total tax. The formula I'll use is =(subtotal*.08). Notice that I refer to the Subtotal field by its bookmark name.
3. I want the Total field to multiply the Subtotal by the Tax number to get the total price of items on the invoice. Here, I'll have to construct a formula that refers to specific cells, since using the ABOVE value would grab the line-item totals—something I don't want. I've given the Subtotal field the bookmark name "subtotal" and the Tax field the bookmark name "tax," so it's not hard to refer to the fields. The formula I'm going to use is =(subtotal tax).

After all of this, the final form looks like the one in Figure 15-16.

Glenn Forms Company

Invoice

Billing Address	Shipping Address
	Same as billing address.

Item	Qty.	Price	Total
Fitness Form	1	2.95	$2.95
Shipping Form	5	2.95	$14.75
Invoice Form	4	2.95	$11.80
		Subtotal	$29.50
Thanks for your business!		Tax	$4.72
		Total	$34.22

Figure 15-16: Viewing the final form template

Adding Help to a Form

You can add your own help text to each field in a form. On the Properties dialog for each type of form field, you probably noticed a button named Add Help text. This button opens a separate dialog (Figure 15-17), used to create help text associated with the field. Use an AutoText entry to supply the help text or type your own text right into the dialog box.

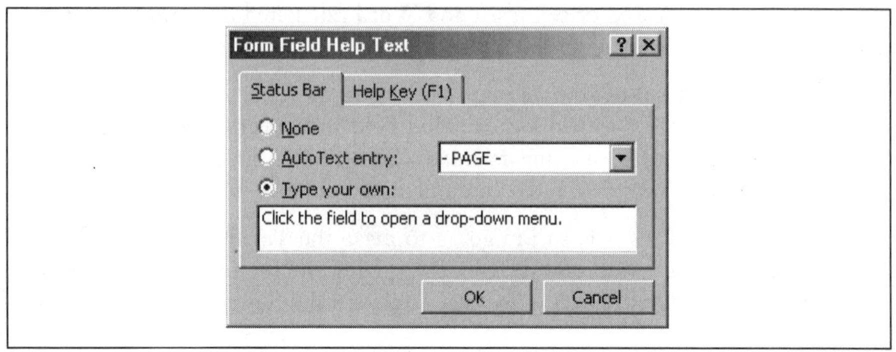

Figure 15-17: Adding help text to a field

There are two ways to display help text, which can be used simultaneously:

Status Bar help text
: Appears on Word's status bar whenever the field is selected. This type of help text is good for brief messages that give the user a simple instruction.

Help Key (F1) text
: Appears whenever the user presses F1 while in a field. This opens a separate dialog box with the help text, making this method better for providing longer descriptions of a field.

The tabs for creating the help text for each display type are identical. Both types are illustrated in Figure 15-18.

TIP # 149

Protect a Form to Test It

Many features of a form, such as help text, drop-down menus, and checkboxes, are not available while constructing a form. To access them, you must first protect the form using the Protect Form button on the Forms toolbar.

Protecting a Form

Once a form is created, it has to be protected from unwanted modification. Do this by selecting the Protect Form button on the Forms toolbar. Protecting a form locks its fields and text. Users can enter only data into the fields. They cannot modify (or even select) the fields' properties or change any of the other text in the document.

However, even when a form is protected, any user that knows something about Word can unprotect the form using the Forms toolbar. For this reason, consider also using a password to protect the document from modification. Do this using the Tools → Protect Document command, selecting the Forms option (using the Protect Forms button on the Forms toolbar also sets this option), and assigning a password. All the usual caveats about using passwords apply. If lost or forgotten, the

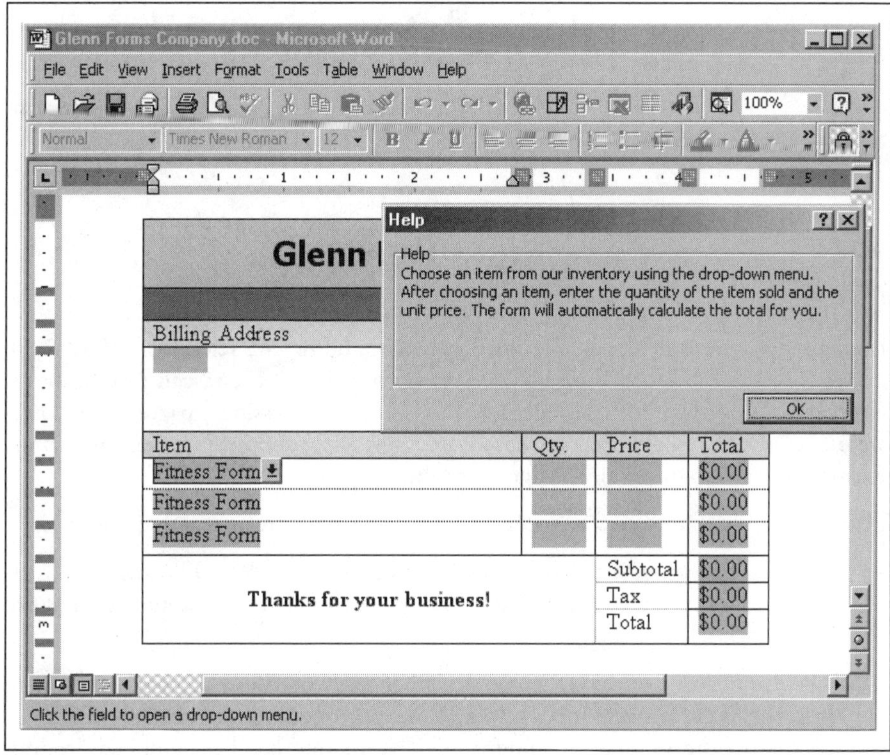

Figure 15-18: Viewing status bar and help key text for a field

password is unrecoverable from within Word, although many third-party tools exist that can help recover passwords.

Finishing the Form

Now that the form is exactly the way I want it and I have protected the form with a password, I'm almost ready to save it as a template. Before doing this, however, there are a couple of last-minute things to check:

- Make sure that all of the fields in the form are blank and don't contain any practice data you've entered.
- Close any toolbars (such as the Forms or Tables and Borders toolbar) that the user won't need. If you leave the toolbar open when you save the form, they will appear when a document is created.
- Change to the document view (Normal, Print, etc.) you want users to view the form in.

Save the form as a template and distribute the template however you want (see Chapter 14, *Creating a Template*, for information on distributing templates).

Chapter 16

Creating a Web Page

Even though much of the marketing hype surrounding the release of Word 2000 makes it seem that Word is highly integrated with the Web and can produce great web pages, Word was not really designed to produce professional pages at all. There are other tools for this, if that's what you're after. Microsoft even makes one named FrontPage that is part of select Microsoft Office packages.

Instead, Word was designed to accomplish two somewhat related web design tasks:

- It is meant to provide users a quick, easy way to put a Word document on the Web or on a company intranet as a web page and have it look just like a Word document.
- It is also meant to provide a way for other users of Word to take a document from the Web, convert it back to a Word document, and retain all of the formatting of the original document. This technique has been dubbed "round-tripping"—to the Web and back.

Word does both of these things very well. In order to do them, though, the HTML that Word produces even when you mean to create a simple web page contains tons of formatting code that isn't necessary for a traditional web page. This is why you'll often hear web designers poke fun at Word, saying that it produces terrible or bloated HTML.

At the end of this chapter, I talk about some ways to clean up the HTML that Word produces if you insist on using Word as a web design tool. Before that, however, I'm going to cover some of the web tools Word provides for creating a page.

Creating a New Web Page

Word offers a few different ways to create web pages. Perhaps the easiest is to open an existing Word document and save it as a web page using File → Save As Web Page. Using File → Save As and specifying an *.html* extension does the same thing. This procedure, detailed in Chapter 4, *File*, offers a quick way to publish an existing document to the Web that retains nearly all of the formatting of the original document.

Word also provides a few ways to create a new web page:

- Create a new document, add text and graphics to it, and save it as a web page.
- Use one of Word's web page templates to provide a starting layout and formatting.
- Use the Web Page Wizard to create a new page based on preferences you select.

Creating a Page from Scratch

Create a new web page from scratch by Selecting File → New and choosing the Web Page template on the General tab of the New dialog (Figure 16-1). This template is installed by default. If you configured it to be installed on first use, have the CD handy when you select it the first time.

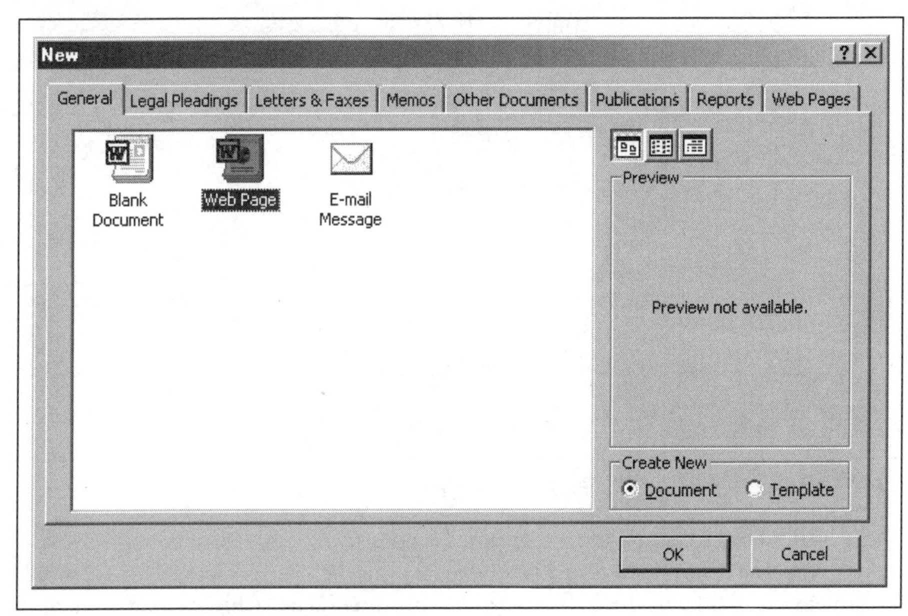

Figure 16-1: Creating a blank web page

The blank page created looks pretty much the same as a normal blank Word document, but there are a few subtle differences:

- Word sets the default file type in the Save dialog as HTML. For more information about saving documents, see Chapter 4.
- The default view for the document is Web Layout, which shows the page much as it will look when viewed in a generic web browser. Chapter 6, *View*, discusses the different views Word offers; we'll be looking at the Web Layout view in more detail throughout this chapter.

- Word adds the HTML Source command to the View menu. This command opens a separate window for viewing and editing the actual source code for the page. We'll also look at this later in the chapter.

Using a Template

Word also offers a number of web page templates on the Web Pages tab of the New dialog for creating specific types of pages (Figure 16-2). Select any of the templates and choose OK to create a new page.

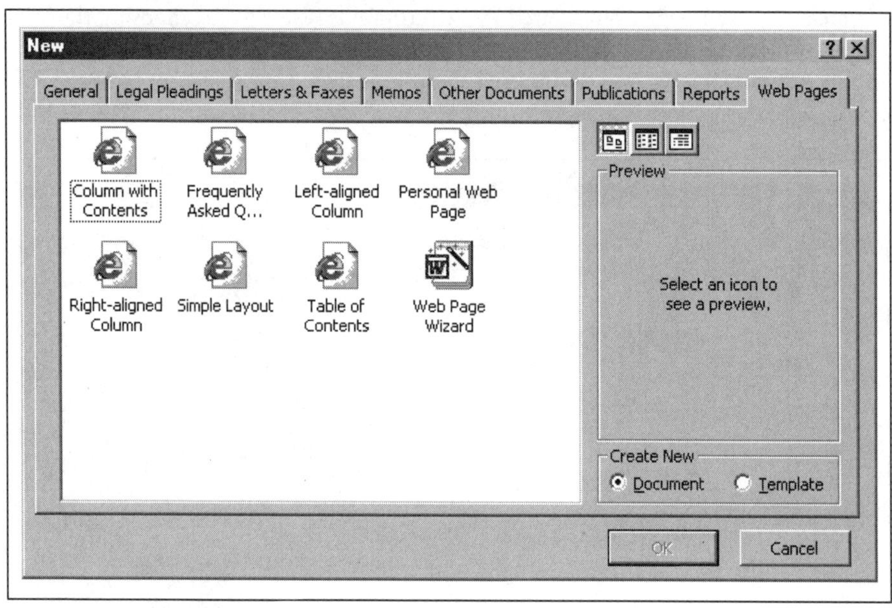

Figure 16-2: Creating a web page from a template

Most of the templates provide a structured layout using tables and contain instructional text and placeholders to help you fill in the page. Figure 16-3 shows a document created from the Left-aligned Column template, which uses a table with left-aligned columns for structure. Just replace the boilerplate text with your own text, insert a new picture, and you've got a web page.

Using the Web Page Wizard

Word also offers a Web Page Wizard that steps through the process of creating a web site with multiple pages, asking for preferences along the way. Choose File → New → Web Pages → Web Page Wizard to get started. The process goes something like this:

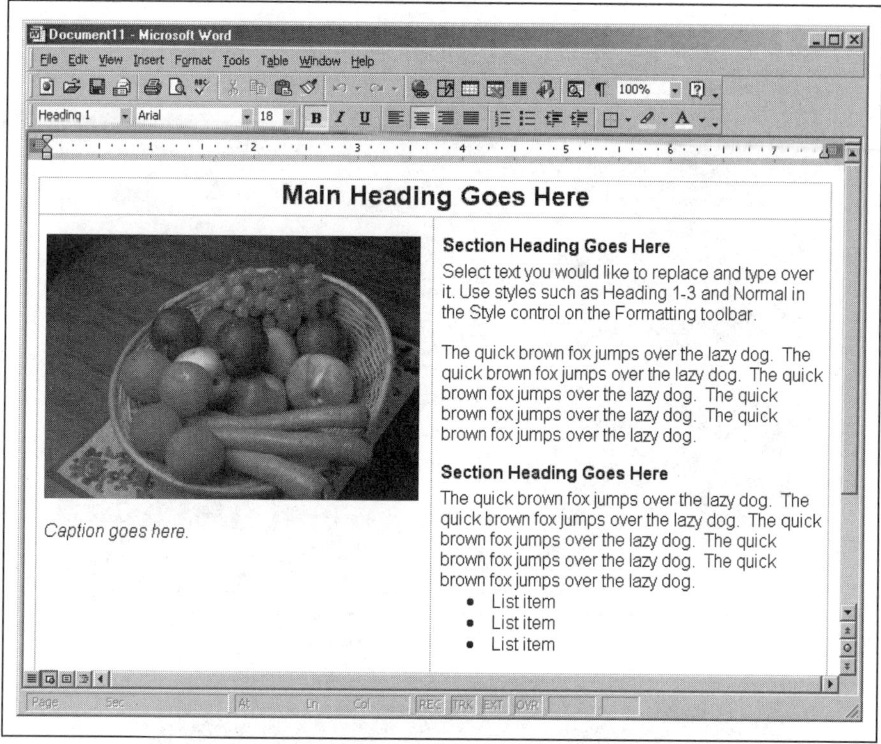

Figure 16-3: Using the template to build a page

1. *Enter a name for the site and the location the site is to be stored* (Figure 16-4). The site name is displayed on the title bar of the web browser when the site is viewed. For the location, enter a local folder or an Internet address.

2. *Choose the type of navigation the site should have* (Figure 16-5). If the navigational elements should appear in the same window as the web pages those elements point to, use one of the frame selections. Vertical frames are the most popular. Frames are discussed in detail in Chapter 8, *Format*, so I'm going to point you there for more on how to use them. If you'd rather not use frames (some older browsers don't support them), choose "Separate page."

3. *Add pages to the site* (Figure 16-6). Word starts the site off with three pages, a personal web page (created using one of the Web Page templates) and two blank pages. Remove these if you want, and add others. In Figure 16-6, I've created four pages that form a personal web site. You can add a new blank page, add a page based on one of Word's templates, or browse for an existing file to add.

4. *Organize the pages* (Figure 16-7). Select any page and use the buttons to move it up and down. Click Rename to change the name of the page. The order of pages in this list defines how the navigational element (whether on a separate

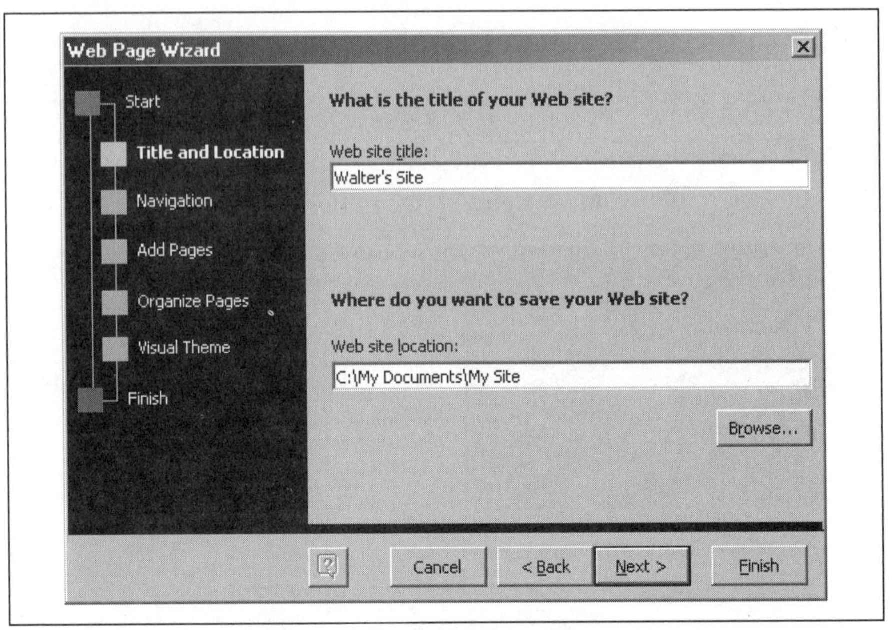

Figure 16-4: Setting the name and location for the site

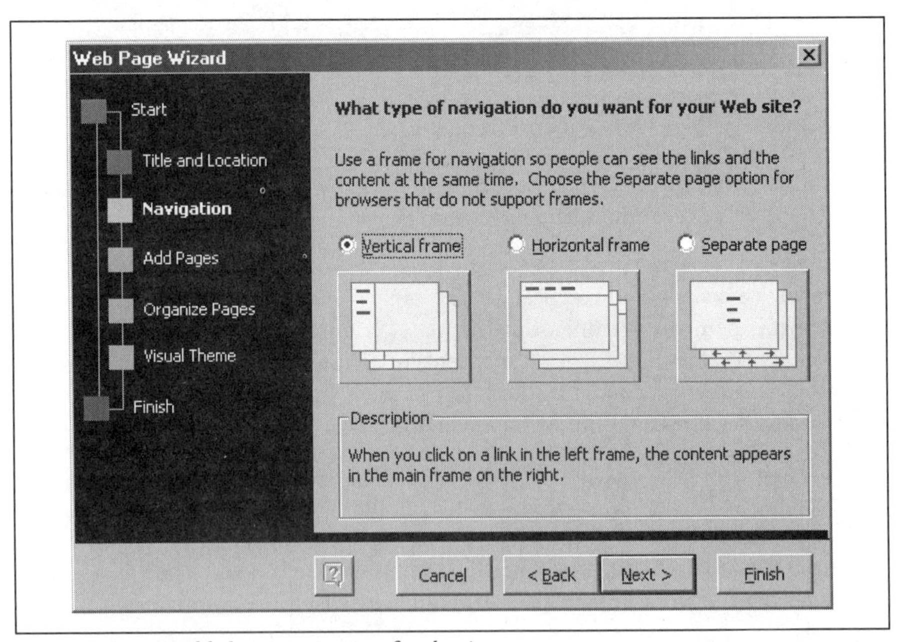

Figure 16-5: Establishing navigation for the site

page or in a frame) is built. Use the Rename button provided to change the page names to better describe the content of your site.

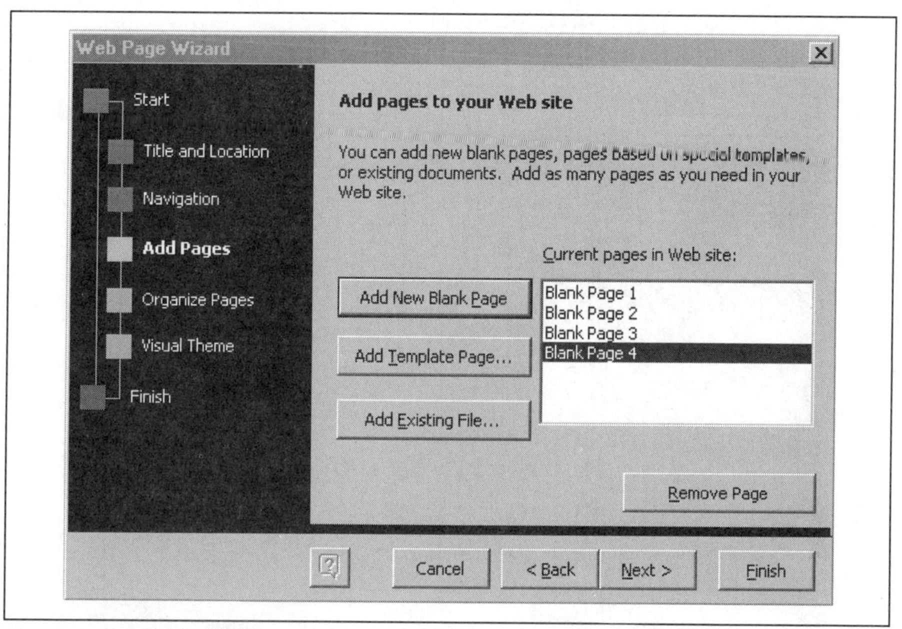

Figure 16-6: Adding pages to the site

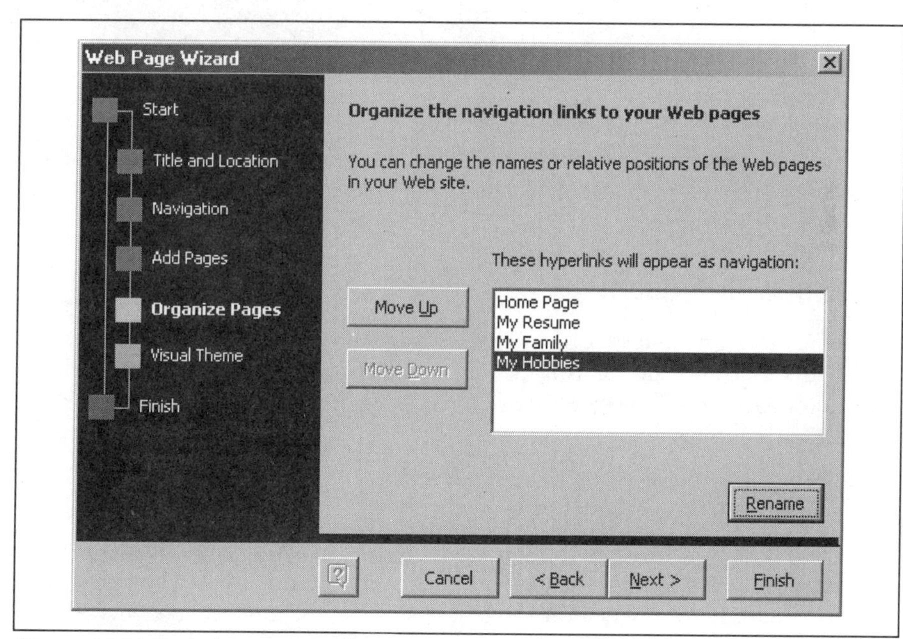

Figure 16-7: Ordering pages in the site

5. *Add a theme* (Figure 16-8). Word includes a host of themes that provide predefined formatting and graphic elements to a site. We'll talk about themes later in the chapter.

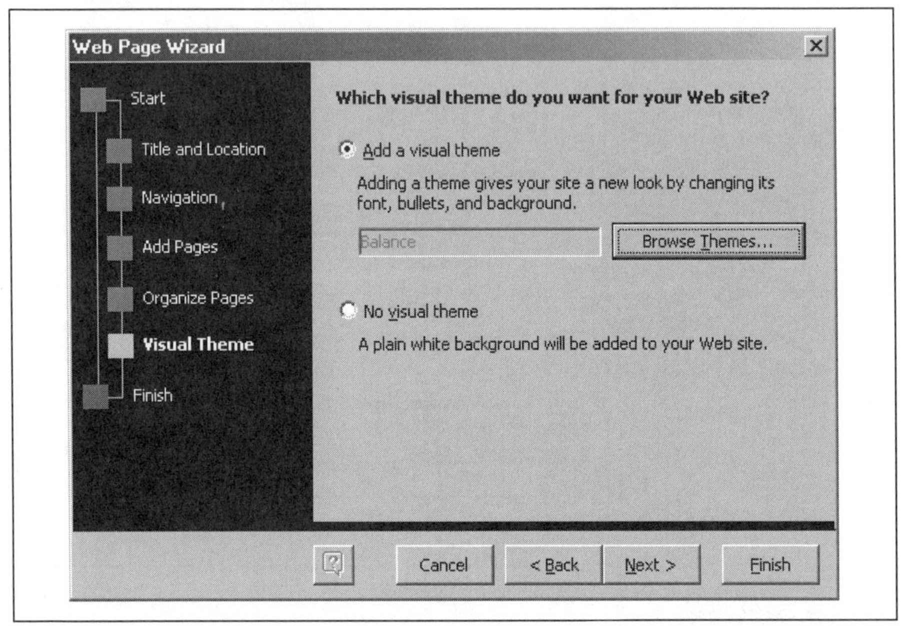

Figure 16-8: Adding a theme to the site

That's it. Once the wizard is done, Word creates each of the pages specified in the Wizard and creates a navigational element with links to those pages. It is then up to you to modify the pages.

Working with a Page

No matter what method is used to create a page, the same techniques are used to modify the page and add items to it. For the most part, Word's standard tools are used to format text and insert objects. However, there are some differences in using the tools on a web page.

Web Layout View

Word automatically switches the document to Web Layout view after creating a document from a web page template or the Web Wizard. Even when creating a page from scratch, Web Layout is the best view to use because it represents text the way it will appear in a web browser—not exactly the same, but close enough. In Web Layout, Word ignores formatting that doesn't apply to web pages, such as page breaks, margins, and tab stops. Web Layout view is also covered in Chapter 6.

TIP # 150

Preview Web Pages in a Browser

Use File → Web Page Preview to save the current document as a temporary file and open it in the default browser on your system. This gives a good idea of what the page will actually look like. For an even better idea, save the page and open it in different browsers.

Formatting Text

Word provides a number of good ways to format text on a web page:

Use Word's standard formatting commands
: Use Format → Font and Format → Paragraph to apply formatting the same way as in a normal Word document. These commands are detailed in Chapter 8.

Apply paragraph and character styles
: Styles are collections of formats that are applied all together and help keep the formatting of a document consistent and organized. Styles are covered in Chapter 2, *How Word Works*, and Chapter 8.

Apply themes
: Themes are collections of formatting elements built into Word that define the appearance of a web page. Elements included in a theme are backgrounds, styles, bullets, horizontal lines, hyperlink colors, and table border colors. A theme is really just a way to apply all of these elements at one stroke. Themes are also covered in Chapter 8.

Themes increase the size of web pages tremendously, more than any other Word feature. Using themes also makes it very difficult to convert pages to other programs for manipulation. If you decide later that you want to maintain your site with another program, you'll be faced with the huge task of stripping out all references to themes, rebuilding navigation bars, etc.

When formatting the text on a page, it is handy to know a couple of things about how HTML displays text on a page:

- HTML ignores more than one space between any two words, so you can't use spaces to position text on a web page. Instead, use Word's ruler or the Format → Paragraph command to set indents. Word translates these indents into HTML position tags.
- Use the built-in heading styles to format a page's title and headings. Word converts these headings into HTML heading tags for display on the page. This helps the heading come across accurately on whatever browser the page may be viewed in. In addition, Word uses paragraphs formatted with the heading styles to construct hyperlinks when you create a table of contents for a page using Insert → Index and Tables or Format → Frames → Table of Contents in Frame.

Adding Graphics

Add graphics to a web page using any of the standard commands from Word's Insert → Picture submenu. This includes pictures from files, Word Art, drawings, and charts. Keep in mind, however, that it's best to keep the size of the graphics files small if the page is to be downloaded from the Web. This helps make the page load faster.

TIP # 151

Measure Items in Pixels for Web Pages

On web pages, objects are normally measured in pixels rather than inches or centimeters. Use the Tools → Options → General → Show Pixels for HTML Features option to have Word show object sizes in pixels in its dialog boxes.

When a web page is saved, Word creates a new folder in the same save location and gives it the same name as the web page. If you insert graphics into a page in a format not supported by web browsers (anything other than *.gif* or *.jpg*), Word converts the graphic into two different formats and saves both in that folder:

.jpg (Joint Professional Graphics format)
: A standard format used in web browsers.

.png (Portable Network Graphics)
: A format that retains a higher resolution and color depth than *.jpg* and is used if the page is converted back into a standard Word document

Right-click any graphic and choose the Format command from the context menu to open the Format dialog for that graphic (Figure 16-9). The details of all the settings on these tabs are covered in Chapter 8 and are basically the same as formatting a picture for a normal Word document. The Web tab is used to enter alternate text for the graphics displayed while the graphic is loading or if the browser opening the page is set to not display graphics.

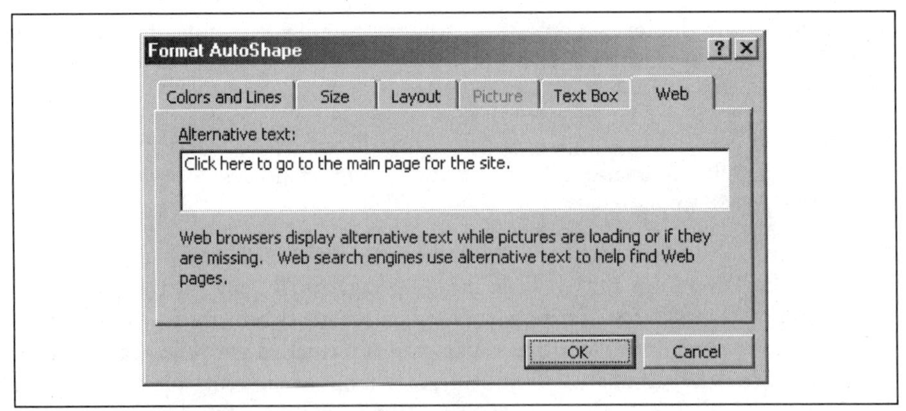

Figure 16-9: Entering alternate text for a graphic

TIP # 152

Use Alternate Text for Graphics on Web Pages

Get into the habit of entering alternate text for graphics used on web pages, especially if those graphics are to be used as hyperlinks on the page. Without the text, people who can't see the graphics won't know what's going on.

Adding Hyperlinks

Hyperlinks are a staple of web pages and can also be used in other types of Word documents. The use of hyperlinks is detailed in Chapter 7, *Insert*.

Saving Pages

Whenever a document is saved as a web page, Word saves the document file itself and creates a folder with the same name as the document (minus the extension). In this folder, Word saves all of the related components that go with the page as separate files. These components include any graphics or special objects inserted into the page. This is necessary because the protocol used to retrieve files from the Web (HTTP) is only capable of retrieving one file at a time. When a web page is requested, the browser first downloads the page itself. This page contains all of the HTML used to create the page and display the text on that page. This HTML also contains references to any additional components that then must be downloaded one at a time and displayed in the browser window.

Web pages can be saved anywhere. If saved on the local computer, they can only be accessed from that local computer or from computers on a network with that computer. If saved on a web server (whether on the Internet or on a local intranet), those pages can be viewed by anyone with access and even linked to from other web pages.

This chapter is really meant to be an overview of the kinds of tools Word provides to create web pages and doesn't pretend to cover them all in detail. If you're really interested in creating web pages, I'd like to offer two suggestions. First, don't use Word. It's fine for cranking out the occasional web page, but there are much better tools out there for the job. Second, get a good book. I recommend starting with something like O'Reilly's own Web Design in a Nutshell, by Jennifer Niederst.

Word's HTML

I said earlier that many web designers consider Word's HTML messy, to put it kindly. Now it's time to see what that means. Consider the rather simple web page shown in Figure 16-10. Not much to it, right? In this section, you're going to get a close look at the HTML code Word creates.

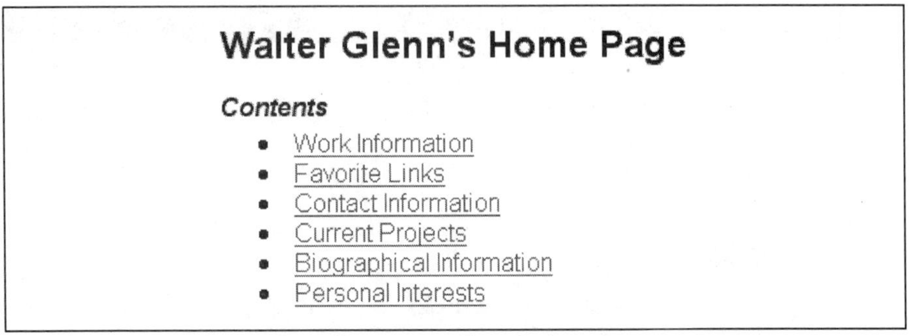

Walter Glenn's Home Page

Contents

- Work Information
- Favorite Links
- Contact Information
- Current Projects
- Biographical Information
- Personal Interests

Figure 16-10: Getting ready to dissect a simple web page

Web Folders

Word 2000 provides a new feature called Web Folders that is installed if the Web Publishing component is selected during the setup of Office 2000. If this component is installed, a Web Folders item is created in the *My Computer* folder available on the Windows desktop. If the component is set to be installed on first use, the Web Folders item is only available on the Save As and Open dialogs in Word. Have your CD handy the first time you use the feature. After installing it, the item is made available in Windows.

Inside Web Folders, you can create shortcuts to locations on the Internet using a simple URL. Web Folders functionality is contained in Office 2000 and does not require that any special extensions be installed on the web server.

To create a Web Folder, follow these steps:

1. Choose File → Open in Word.
2. Click the Web Folder icon in the Places Bar on the left of the Open dialog box. Word navigates to the Web Folders location on your hard drive.
3. Click the Create New Folder button on the Open dialog toolbar.
4. In the dialog that opens, type the URL of the web server on which to save pages. Click the Browse button to open the default web browser and browse to a page that way.
5. Click Next and Word will attempt to verify that the location is valid. If it does, you're asked to enter a name for the Web Folder.
6. Once a Web Folder is set up, open and save files in it the same way you would use any folder on your own computer. If the web server requires a username and password to connect, Word prompts you for it before opening the folder.

Working with HTML in Word

To start, let's look at the tool Word offers for working with HTML, the HTML Source Viewer (Figure 16-11). Access it by selecting View → HTML Source when viewing a web page. As HTML editors go, this is actually a good one. It lays out the code well and color codes the text by function. A Project Explorer on the right is used to switch between open pages.

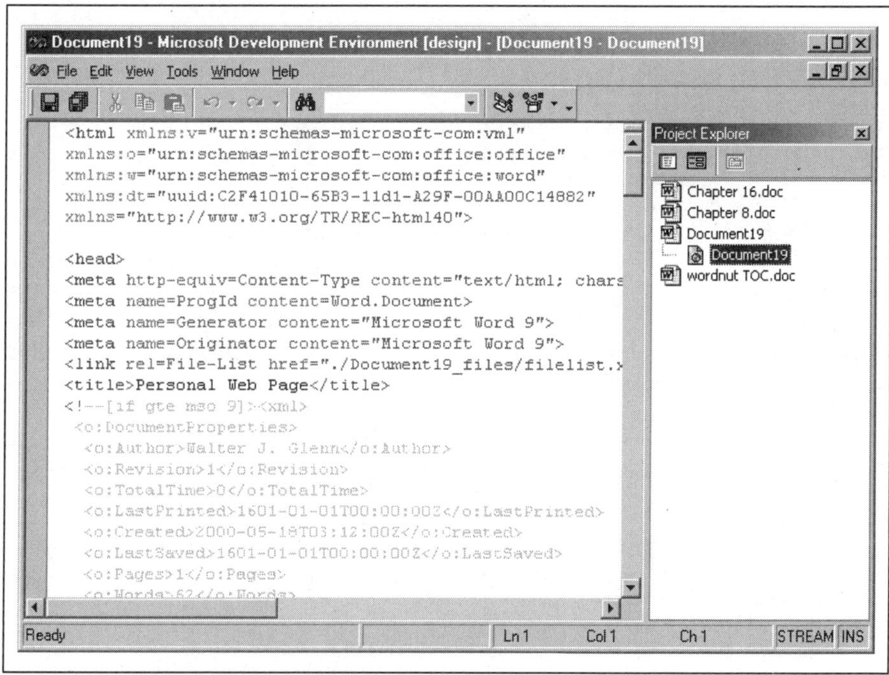

Figure 16-11: Using Word's HTML Source Viewer

TIP # 153

Use the HTML Source Viewer to Code by Hand

If you like to create HTML by hand, give this tool a chance. Since the source code is opened in a separate document, I like to keep the page itself up on one monitor and the HTML Source Viewer up on another. I can see and edit the HTML as I insert objects using Word's tools. I can also type code right into the editor and see what happens in the page at the same time.

Cleaning Up Word's HTML

Let's start our look at Word's HTML code by doing a quick comparison. Word created this web page for me by generating a whopping 214 lines of HTML code using 5844 characters. The file size was 6.5 kilobytes. I opened Notepad and created a page that looked the same and provided the same title, headings, and links by coding the HTML myself. My code was 19 lines using 469 characters. The file size was 514 bytes. All in all, my code was around 6–8% the size of Word's.

If this is true, then what is Word doing with all that extra code? The answer is "a few things." Let's break it down. The first bit of code that didn't look useful to me is shown in Example 16-1. This type of standard header information is used in many web pages, but Word uses it to insert product and content information that is not strictly necessary.

Example 16-1: Header Information

```
<meta http-equiv=Content-Type content="text/html; charset=windows-1252">
<meta name=ProgId content=Word.Document>
<meta name=Generator content="Microsoft Word 9">
<meta name=Originator content="Microsoft Word 9">
<link rel=File-List href="./Document19_files/filelist.xml">
```

Example 16-2 shows the first several lines of code that appear dimmed in the HTML Source Viewer in Figure 16-11. This code contains various document information, such as the author, revision times, and document statistics, that is pulled from Word's document properties (File → Properties). I'll bet you didn't know all of this stuff was going onto the Web when you saved a document.

Example 16-2: Document Property Information

```
<!--[if gte mso 9]><xml>
 <o:DocumentProperties>
  <o:Author>Walter J. Glenn</o:Author>
  <o:Revision>1</o:Revision>
  <o:TotalTime>0</o:TotalTime>
  <o:LastPrinted>1601-01-01T00:00:00Z</o:LastPrinted>
  <o:Created>2000-05-18T03:12:00Z</o:Created>
  <o:LastSaved>1601-01-01T00:00:00Z</o:LastSaved>
  <o:Pages>1</o:Pages>
  <o:Words>62</o:Words>
  <o:Characters>323</o:Characters>
  <o:Company>Microsoft</o:Company>
```

Example 16-3 shows the first part of a huge amount of code that makes up an internal cascading style sheet, which contains paragraph, section, and character formatting information for the entire document, as well as information on heading styles. This is information that must remain if the web page needs to retain the exact Word formatting, but for a simple web page it's mostly unnecessary. If you want to create a cascading style sheet, copy this information, use it to create another web page that is meant to be a external cascading style sheet, and refer to that page from your original web page.

Example 16-3: The Cascading Style Sheet (CSS)

```
<style>
<!--
 /* Style Definitions */
p.MsoNormal, li.MsoNormal, div.MsoNormal
    {mso-style-parent:"";
    margin:0in;
    margin-bottom:.0001pt;
    mso-pagination:widow-orphan;
    font-size:12.0pt;
    font-family:Arial;
    mso-fareast-font-family:"Times New Roman";
    mso-bidi-font-family:"Times New Roman";}
h1
    {mso-style-next:Normal;
    margin-top:12.0pt;
    margin-right:0in;
    margin-bottom:3.0pt;
    margin-left:0in;
    mso-pagination:widow-orphan;
    page-break-after:avoid;
    mso-outline-level:1;
    font-size:18.0pt;
    mso-bidi-font-size:16.0pt;
    font-family:Arial;
    mso-bidi-font-family:"Times New Roman";
    mso-font-kerning:16.0pt;}
h2
    {mso-style-next:Normal;
    margin-top:12.0pt;
    margin-right:0in;
```

Example 16-4 shows the bulleted list that contains the hyperlinks in the document. While some of the information in this code is necessary, much of it has to with Word's paragraph formatting. With the help of a good HTML reference, I extracted the extra Word formatting.

Example 16-4: Word HTML Hyperlinks Containing Formatting Information

```
<ul style='margin-top:0in' type=disc>
 <li class=MsoNormal style='mso-list:l2 level1 lfo3;tab-stops:list .5in'>
     <a href="#_Work_Information">Work Information</a></li>
 <li class=MsoNormal style='mso-list:l2 level1 lfo3;tab-stops:list .5in'>
    <a href="#_Favorite_Links">Favorite Links</a></li>
 <li class=MsoNormal style='mso-list:l2 level1 lfo3;tab-stops:list .5in'>
     <a href="#_Contact_Information">Contact Information</a></li>
 <li class=MsoNormal style='mso-list:l2 level1 lfo3;tab-stops:list .5in'>
     <a href="#_Current_Projects">Current Projects</a></li>
 <li class=MsoNormal style='mso-list:l2 level1 lfo3;tab-stops:list .5in'>
     <a href="#_Biographical_Information">Biographical Information</a></li>
 <li class=MsoNormal style='mso-list:l2 level1 lfo3;tab-stops:list .5in'>
     <a href="#_Personal_Interests">Personal Interests</a></li>
```

As you can see, it's not too hard to examine the HTML that Word generates and weed out the fluff, especially if you know your HTML or are willing to do some digging. For those of us who don't want to bother, though, Microsoft has created a tool to help.

Using the Office HTML Filter Tool

The Office HTML Filter is used to remove the Office-specific markup tags embedded in the Word's web pages. It is available for download on the Office Update web site at *http://www.officeupdate.com*. You can also get there by choosing Help → Office on the Web. I'd give a more exact URL, but Microsoft tends to change things enough that it's probably more useful this way. Browse to the Word section on the site and look at the available downloads. Find the Office HTML Filter, download it, and install it on your system.

Installing the filter builds three new tools into the Word interface. Two of these, the ability to filter a Word document and the ability to create a cascading style sheet from a document, are placed in a new submenu named Export that is created on Word's File menu. The third tool, which copies selected text from a Word document as compact HTML, is placed on the Edit menu.

Filtering a document

To filter a Word document, choose File → Export to → Compact HTML. This tool is designed to rip all Office-specific markup tags from an HTML document, and it actually does a pretty good job. It took out much of the code I complained about in my simple web page. One thing it left was the cascading style sheet information. Unfortunately, it also left all the document information and much of the formatting information as well. Just running this tool managed to trim the code down to a little more than half what it was before.

WARNING

A word to the wise: The Export to Compact HTML command doesn't really export. Instead, it converts the current document. Be sure to make a backup of the original document before using the command in case you don't like what it does.

Creating a cascading style sheet

To create a cascading style sheet from a Word document, choose File → Export to → CSS Style Sheet. This command creates a new document that contains all the CSS code from the original document. It names the new document with the same name as the original document, but uses a *.css* extension. The tool does not remove the CSS code from the original document, but that is easy enough to do by hand. I did this after compacting the HTML and ended up with around 70 lines of code.

Sure, this is still a lot more than the 19 lines of code I used to create the page myself, but it's also a lot less than the Word-generated page started with and it was a lot easier than digging through the code myself. So while this tool still does not make Word the optimum tool for creating a small, well-coded web page, it's not bad either.

Copying a selection as HTML

The final tool offered by the Office HTML Filter is accessed by a new command on the Edit menu named "Copy as HTML." Make a selection in a Word document and issue the command. Word translates the selection into its somewhat compacted HTML and copies the code to the clipboard. Paste it as HTML code into another document or into another program, such as Notepad.

Chapter 17

Using Master Documents

A master document contains links to other documents and makes it easy to apply formatting, check spelling, create indexes, and number pages throughout those other documents all at once. Think of a master document as a container that lets you view, edit, and perform other tasks on all of the subdocuments it links to. For example, you might organize the chapters of a book as separate subdocuments linked to from a single master document. You could then use the master document to apply formatting changes globally across the book, number all of the pages in the book, and print the pages all at once.

Creating a Master Document

There are a couple of basic strategies for creating a master document. The first is to create a master document and then create subdocuments from within it. The second is to create a master document that groups other documents that already exist. Either way, you will create the master document in the same way.

TIP # 154

Create a Folder for the Master Document First

Before you get started creating a master document and subdocuments, create a folder for them all. Moving master and subdocuments around after creating them breaks the link between the master document and the subdocument.

Start a new blank document with File → New or a new document based on any other template. In the new document, switch to Outline view. Word displays the Outlining toolbar. The tools used to create and control a master document are grouped at the right end (Figure 17-1) of the toolbar. These tools are covered in detail throughout the chapter, but are provided here for reference.

Although it's not required, I always find it best to create an outline for the project before messing with subdocuments. This holds true both when creating new subdocuments and when inserting existing documents as subdocuments.

Figure 17-2 shows the simple outline of a book with six chapters. The book is divided into two parts. Based on this outline, I will create eight subdocuments—one for each of the chapters, and one that contains the title page for each part.

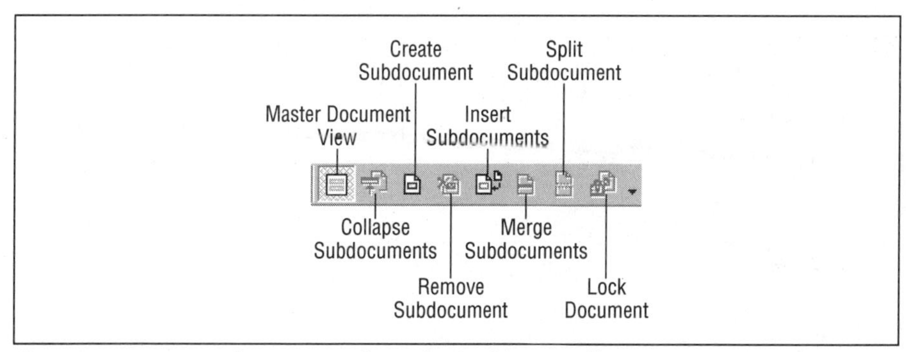

Figure 17-1: Master document tools on the Outlining toolbar

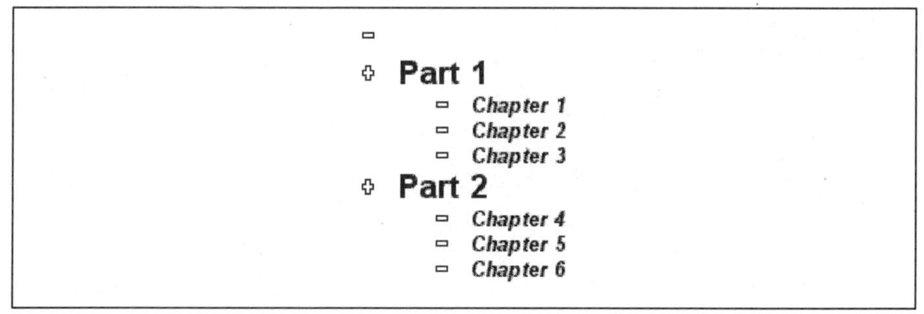

Figure 17-2: A simple book outline

Next, move the insertion point to where the first subdocument should appear and create or insert a subdocument (described next). That's it. Once a subdocument is inserted, the main document becomes a master document.

Creating a New Subdocument

Create a new subdocument using the Create Subdocument tool on the Outlining toolbar. The document is created just below the insertion point or so that it encompasses any selected text. Be sure to select all of the text that should become part of the new subdocument, because it can be tricky to move it there later. Figure 17-3 shows a new subdocument created for Part 1 of my outline. I selected the heading that reads "Part 1" and used the Create Subdocument button on the Outlining toolbar.

The Heading1 paragraph at the top of the subdocument box is used as the name of the new subdocument file. The document icon at the top of the subdocument box is used both to move the subdocument around in the master document (by dragging it) and to open the actual subdocument (by double-clicking it). Both of these procedures are covered later in the chapter.

Figure 17-3: Creating a subdocument

Using an Existing File as a Subdocument

If some parts of the master document already exist as Word files, you can insert them into the document instead of creating new subdocuments. To do this, place the insertion point where the subdocument should go or select the text as if you were creating a new subdocument. Then, click the Insert Subdocument button on the Outlining toolbar. This action opens a browse dialog for choosing the file to use as a subdocument. It is best to move any files that are to be used as subdocuments into the same folder as the master document before turning them into subdocuments.

Saving Documents

Since subdocuments are individual documents, they can be opened, edited, and saved on their own. The only restriction is that if a subdocument is locked within its master document, the subdocument is marked as read-only. It can be opened, but it cannot be saved over the original if any modifications are made. Of course, it's easy enough to right-click the file in Windows Explorer, open the properties for the file, and turn off the read-only option, but I don't recommend it. Usually, subdocuments are locked for a reason. See the section titled "Working in the Master Document" for more on locking subdocuments.

If subdocuments are edited from inside the master document (either by typing directly into the master document or by opening the subdocuments from the master), they are automatically saved when you issue the Save command from the master document.

If the master document contains any newly created subdocuments that have not yet been edited, the files for them are created the first time the master document is saved after their creation. Word creates a separate document for each of the subdocuments in the same location as the master document.

The subdocuments are named based on the heading paragraphs at the top of the subdocument. If the folder already contains files by that name, Word appends the new subdocument file with a numeric extension. For this reason, it's best to create the initial outline for the master with different heading names. This sounds obvious, but I've found that many people create outlines using text like "heading" that they plan to change later. Creating the subdocuments based on these headings results in a bunch of poorly named files.

Working in the Master Document

As you can see, it's pretty easy to create a master document and to create or insert subdocuments within it. I've taken the master document for the book that I started earlier in the chapter and created subdocuments for each of the chapters and part pages (Figure 17-4). This results in a master document with eight subdocuments.

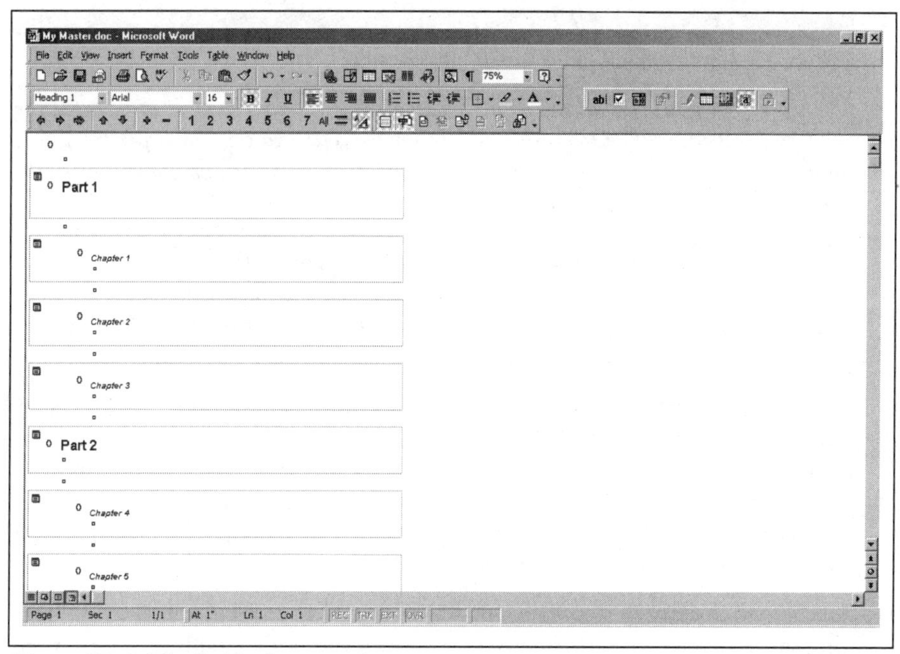

Figure 17-4: The finished master document

From within the master document, there are a number of different actions you can take:

- Edit the subdocument by typing directly into the subdocument box in the master document. Alternately, open the subdocument itself in a separate window by double-clicking the document icon in the upper left corner of the subdocument box or by clicking the hyperlink for a document shown in collapsed view (see the next bullet). Subdocuments can also be opened and edited directly from Windows by double-clicking the subdocument file.

- Collapse the view of all of the subdocuments by clicking the Collapse Subdocuments button on the Outlining toolbar. The collapsed view (Figure 17-5) shows the subdocument icon, a lock icon indicating that the subdocument is locked and cannot be edited from within the Master document, and a hyperlink for opening the subdocument itself. Once collapsed, the button on the toolbar becomes Expand Subdocuments for restoring the view. In expanded view, the subdocuments can be opened by double-clicking the document icon and edited right in the master document.

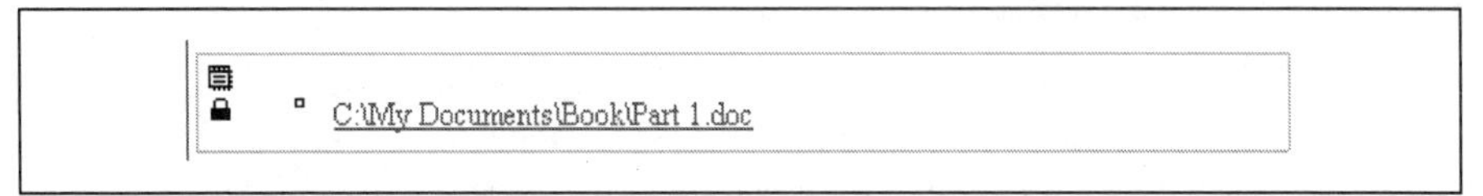

Figure 17-5: A collapsed subdocument

TIP # 155

Collapse a Subdocument to Determine Its Location

The easiest way to determine the file location of a subdocument is to collapse the subdocuments using the Outlining toolbar. In the collapsed view, a hyperlink to the subdocument provides an easy way to open the document file and shows where the file is located on your system.

- Delete a subdocument by clicking the document icon at the top of the subdocument box and then pressing the Delete key. This removes the subdocument from the master document entirely. Note that you cannot delete a locked document. Locking is discussed later in this list.
- Remove a subdocument from the master document and merge all of the subdocument's contents into the master document by placing the insertion point anywhere in the subdocument and clicking the Remove Subdocument button on the Outlining toolbar. If the subdocument and master document contain different styles that use the same name, the style in the master document is used and the style in the subdocument is discarded.
- Move a subdocument to a different position in the master document by dragging the document icon. While you are dragging, a horizontal line indicates the new position of the subdocument (Figure 17-6). A collapsed or locked document cannot be moved in this manner.
- Lock a subdocument by placing the insertion point in it and click the Lock Document button on the Outlining toolbar. Repeat the process to unlock a document. A subdocument that is locked in this manner cannot be edited or deleted until unlocked. The subdocument file is marked as read-only in Windows so that it can be opened, but any changes made cannot be saved.

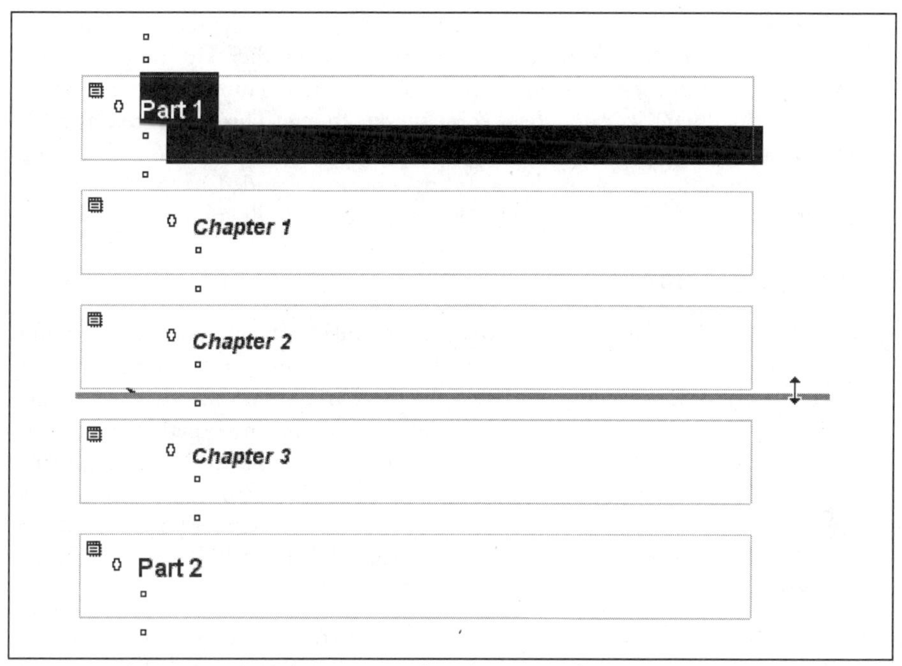

Figure 17-6: Moving a subdocument within the master document

Documents also become locked when the subdocuments are collapsed, as described previously, and when the actual subdocument file is open in another window. However, this type of locking works differently from locking with the Outlining toolbar. Subdocuments that are locked due to collapsing cannot be edited or deleted within the master document, but they *can* be edited when opened.

- Rename subdocuments by opening them from within the master document and using Word's Save As feature in the subdocument window. This causes Word to register the new name of the subdocument in the master document. You cannot change the name of a subdocument by altering the Heading1 paragraph in the master view. You can change the name of a document file directly from Windows, but Word will not register the name change in the master document if the change is made this way.
- Split a subdocument from within the master document by placing the insertion point where the split should occur in the subdocument box and clicking the Split Subdocument button on the Outlining toolbar. For this to work, the insertion point must be placed on a line that is formatted with the Heading1 style. Everything below the Heading1 style (including the heading itself) becomes a new subdocument below the original. A new file is created for the new subdocument based on the text in the Heading1 paragraph.

- Merge any two consecutive subdocuments in the master document. To do this, the subdocuments must be directly adjacent to one another with no paragraphs in between. Click the document icon for the first subdocument and then Shift-click the document icon for the second subdocument. This action selects both subdocuments. Next, click the Merge Subdocuments button on the Outlining toolbar. The contents of the lower subdocument are added to the upper subdocument and the lower subdocument is removed from the master document.

Formatting Documents

All of Word's standard formatting options are available in the master document and in all of the subdocuments. If you create new subdocuments from within the master document, those subdocuments are based on the template that is attached to the master document. Creating a blank, new document like the one I used earlier in this chapter attaches Word's *normal.dot* to the master template and to all subdocuments created from it, but it's easy enough to create a master document based on any template using the techniques discussed throughout this book. All subdocuments created from that master will use the same template and thus will have access to the same styles, macros, etc.

It gets a bit trickier when inserting existing documents into a master document, particularly if those existing documents have a different template attached to them than the master document has. This is allowed, by the way: master documents and subdocuments do not have to use the same template. It's just that a little extra handling is required if they use different templates.

When a document with different styles is inserted into a master document, all of those styles are added to the master document. Note that they are not added to the template attached to the master document.

If Word finds the same style in both the subdocument being added and the master document, it issues a warning (Figure 17-7). Choose Yes to have Word rename the style in the incoming document automatically.

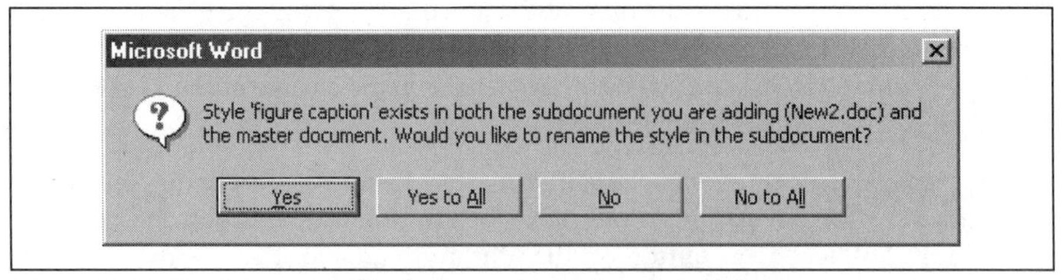

Figure 17-7: Resolving a conflict between the master and subdocument

Word renames styles by appending a number at the end. For example, the style "figure caption" becomes "figure caption1." Choose Yes to All to have Word go ahead and rename all of the duplicate styles it finds. Choose No and Word keeps all the styles in both documents and tries to display the documents based on that. For example, choosing No when a duplicate style is found means that both the subdocument and master document keep their own versions of the style. When the subdocument is viewed in the master document, the master document's version of the style is used. When the subdocument is viewed as a separate document, its native version of the style is used.

Ideally, you should plan the styles and templates used in the master documents and subdocuments so that this doesn't happen. Unfortunately, this is not always possible. I find that it is usually best to rename styles and add them to the master document, ensuring that I can view the subdocuments accurately. This also lets me have a complete set of styles in the master document that I can print out for reference.

Printing Master Documents

One of the best things about master documents is that you can print the whole thing, including all of the subdocuments, at once. The master document prints differently, however, depending on which Word view it is in when printed:

- Switch to Normal view and print the master document to print the master document and all of the subdocuments as consecutive pages at once.
- Switch to Outline view and turn off the Master Document view using the Outlining toolbar to print just the outline of the master document.
- Open a subdocument from within a master document to print out just that subdocument. The document prints out using the global pagination, cross-referencing, print options, and other features expected of a subdocument.
- Open the subdocument directly from Windows and *not* from within the master document to print the document on its own, separately from the master document. In this case, the document is printed using its own template and other attributes without using the global pagination, print options, and other features.

Chapter 18

Working with VBA

In previous chapters, you've seen how Word's look, feel, and general operations can be customized to suit your own style. This capability is a powerful aspect of using Word, but you're not limited to tweaking menus and toolbars.

This chapter provides an overview of using macros and Visual Basic for Applications (VBA) to push Word beyond its normal boundaries. It starts with a quick introduction to recording and running macros, then moves into a discussion of the VBA environment. The chapter includes:

- A language primer that examines the basic syntax and structure of VBA, including various constructs like statements, comments, variables, and constants.
- An overview of the Word object model, the hierarchy of related objects that represent almost all of the components of the Word interface. Word objects are used to retrieve information, create new items, and cause Word to perform actions.
- A look at Word's VBA Editor, the development environment used to write, test, and organize code.
- An examination of user forms, which are used to gather input from a user at runtime.

If what you see in this chapter whets your appetite, you can find a more complete treatment of Word programming in Writing Word Macros, by Steven Roman (O'Reilly & Associates). For more on general VBA programming, take a look at VB & VBA in a Nutshell, by Paul Lomax (O'Reilly & Associates).

Extending Word

There are several ways to enhance and *extend* the capabilities of Word:

Record a macro (Tools → Macro → Record New Macro)
Word watches your every step in the Word interface and actually records your actions as a Visual Basic for Applications (VBA) script. Useful as this is, recording macros doesn't give you the power you can get by writing your own VBA code. Recorded macros tend to be verbose, with lots of unnecessary code.

Write your own VBA code (Tools → Macro → Visual Basic Editor)
Create code from scratch with the Visual Basic Editor or record a macro and use its code as a basis. It's often easier to trim out the excess code than to write the code you need from scratch. Using macros is also a quick way to find out the correct syntax for a particular Word operation.

Write COM Add-ins
The Microsoft Office Developer (MOD) edition of Office 2000 provides developers with tools to write COM (Component Object Model) Add-ins, which are DLLs (Dynamically Linked Libraries) that extend Word even further than VBA does. Writing COM Add-ins is beyond the scope of this book. Most Word users will find VBA code to have an excellent balance of robustness, power and ease of use.

WordBasic and VBA—A Brief History

Word pioneered the customizable interface, allowing users to modify toolbars and menus to suit their needs. It also pioneered the use of a dialect of Basic (WordBasic) to allow users even greater control of the Word environment. Word versions up to Word 95 used the WordBasic dialect of Visual Basic (VB). It had a radically simple object model, consisting of one object, WordBasic.

With Word 97, WordBasic was replaced by the Office-standard Visual Basic for Applications (VBA), a dialect of Visual Basic, and was given a greatly expanded object model. VBA and the expanded object model allowed much greater control of Word, both from within Word, and from other Office applications (such as Access and Outlook) using Automation code.

The current version of VBA (in Word 2000) is VBA 6.0.

Word Macros

Macros are routines that you create to perform a task or set of tasks. They are not reactive like event handlers. You purposely execute a macro because you want Word to do something for you.

Recording Macros

The easiest way to create a macro (although not always the most efficient way) is to let Word record a series of actions you perform right in the interface. To do this, choose Tools → Macro → Record New Macro. This opens the Record Macro dialog (Figure 18-1).

Give the macro a name and click OK to start recording. While the macro is being recorded, a toolbar pops up with controls to stop the recording. If you want, you can use the Record Macro dialog to quickly assign the new macro to a toolbar

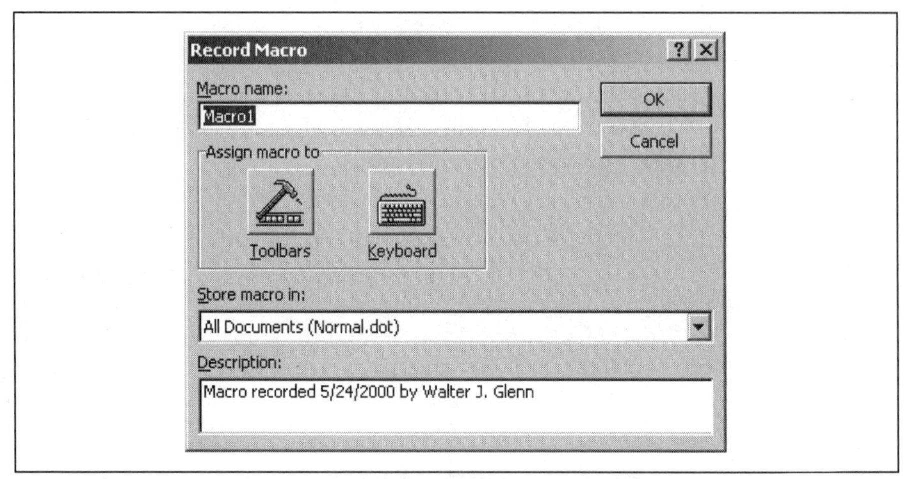

Figure 18-1: Setting up to record a new macro

button (this opens the Tools → Customize dialog, which is covered in Chapter 3, *Customizing Word*) or to a keyboard shortcut. You can also control where the macro is saved (the default is *normal.dot*) and give it a description.

Using Macros

You can view and manage macros you've created (either by recording or writing the code yourself) by selecting Tools → Macro → Macros from the Word window (not the editor), or by hitting Alt-F8. This brings up the Macros dialog in Figure 18-2. Use the dialog to run a macro, open a macro in the VBA Editor, create a new macro, or delete an existing one.

TIP # 156

Put Macros on Your Toolbars

To get easy access to often-used macros, assign macros to toolbar buttons using Tools → Customize → Commands. Select the Macros category to view all available macros. Drag a macro to one of your toolbars. You can now execute your macro with the click of a button.

Word had recordable macros long before it acquired VBA. With Office 2000, all Office applications use the same VB editor, and since all Word macros are actually subprocedures in a module, you can access them either from the Macros Dialog (select Tools → Macro → Macros), or by opening the VBA Editor (Tools → Macro → Visual Basic Editor) and selecting and opening the module containing the macros.

To create a standard module manually, launch the VB editor and select Insert → Module from the menu or right-click the project node in the Project Explorer to get a context menu and choose Insert → Module from there. This will add a code

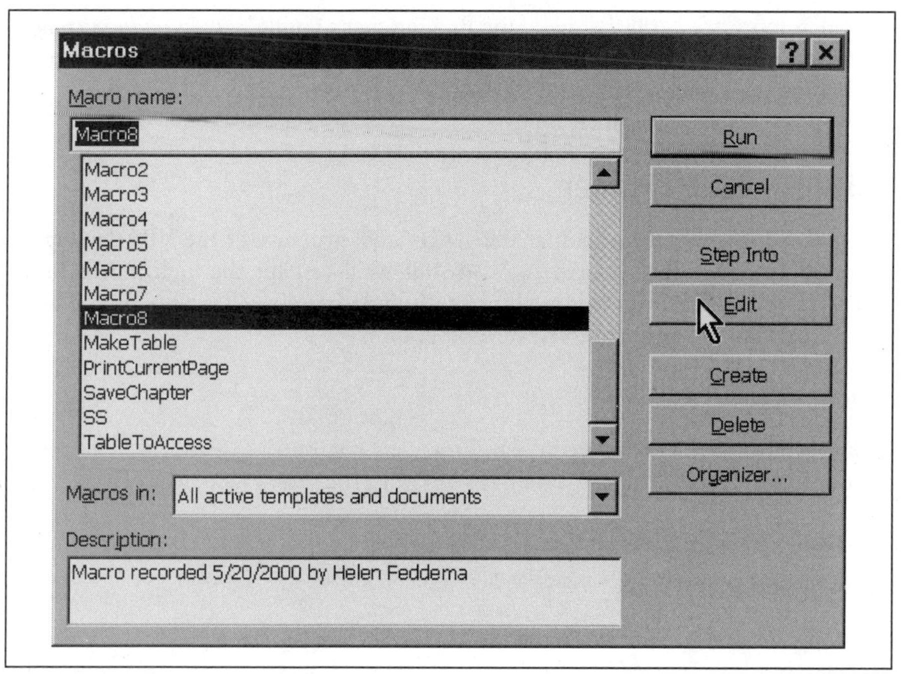

Figure 18-2: The Macros dialog

module called Module1 (which you may rename) to your VBA project and open that module for you.

What Is VBA?

VBA is a subset of the Visual Basic programming language. It is a hosted language component, meaning that an application provides the environment in which VBA code is written and executed. Word 2000 is one such application.

Each Office application has a slightly different flavor of VBA. The basic language is the same, but is extended with extra components through the host application's *object model.* An object model is a hierarchy of logical entities (objects) representing components of the application, such as a document in Word or a worksheet in Excel. By using an application's object model (explained later in this chapter), you can programmatically perform standard application functions, like text formatting, as well as more complex tasks, some of which may require interaction with the user.

You can even use VBA in one Office application to control another Office application using Automation code. This allows you to write programs that integrate the capabilities of several Office components. Some of the code samples in this chapter illustrate working with another application (Access or Outlook) from Word VBA code, though a full discussion of inter-Office Automation programming is beyond the scope of this book.

See "Microsoft Office 2000/Visual Basic Programmer's Guide" (*http://msdn.microsoft.com/library/officedev/odeopg/deovroffice2000visualbasicprogrammersguide.htm*) for more information on Visual Basic and Office 2000. This document is included in printed form in some editions of Office 2000.

A VBA Language Primer

In this section, we'll take a look at the syntax and structure of the VBA language. Entire books have been devoted to VBA, but we'll just hit the high points here. When you're through with this section, you'll understand the basic building blocks of VBA and how to use them to create a program.

Statements

A *statement* in VBA code is a command for your computer to perform. The statement in Example 18-1 displays a message box with the text "Hello, world!":

Example 18-1: Hello World

```
MsgBox "Hello, world!"
```

Very long statements may be broken into several lines by using the line continuation character "_" (Example 18-2). You can also use indentation to make your code more readable. Indentation does not affect the way the code is executed.

Example 18-2: Using the Line Continuation Character

```
.ParagraphFormat.TabStops.Add Position:=InchesToPoints(1.15), _
   Alignment:=wdAlignTabLeft, Leader:=wdTabLeaderSpaces
```

Comments

Comments are documentation in your code. The more you comment, the better you—and anybody else—will understand your code later. Add a comment by prefacing a line of text with a single quote, or by typing a single quote and additional text after a statement, but on the same line. Anything following the quote is considered a comment and will not be executed (Example 18-3).

Example 18-3: Commenting Your Code

```
' This is a comment that takes up an entire line.
i = 3 ' This is a comment after a statement
```

Variables

A *variable* is a name that you define to hold a value. Variables can hold basic types of data like numbers, text values, or dates, as well as more complex, structured data. In order to use a variable, it must first be *declared*; this associates a variable name with the chunk of memory that holds the variable's value. You usually declare a variable yourself, although VBA may declare a variable for you, as you'll see. Once declared, a variable's value can be changed; this is called *assignment*.

You can give a variable any name you wish, using any combination of letters and numbers. It's best to use descriptive variable names like `thisDoc` or `firstParagraph` to make your code more readable. You may also find it useful to prefix each variable name with a few characters describing the type of data the variable is holding. For example, you might use `doc` for a document, `n` for a number, and `str` for a string. However, if you intend to do serious programming, and in particular to exchange code with other developers, it is best to use one of the established naming conventions for VBA code, such as the Leszynski or Reddick naming conventions.* If you make up your own prefixes, they will be helpful to you, but other programmers may not understand them. The three-letter prefixes for the most commonly used variables are listed in Table 18-1.

Table 18-1: Standard Variable Prefixes

Prefix	Variable
int	Integer
lng	Long
sng	Single
dbl	Double
cur	Currency
dtm	Date
obj	Object
str	String
var	Variant

Use the `Dim` keyword (short for "dimension") to declare a variable. Example 18-4 shows two statements you can use to declare integer and string variables.

Example 18-4: Declaring a Variable with Dim

```
Dim intVariable As Integer
Dim strString As String
```

You can also declare a variable without specifying its data type (Example 18-5).

Example 18-5: Declaring a Variable Without a Data Type

```
Dim variable
```

* See the following for more information on these conventions: *http://msdn.microsoft.com/LIBRARY/BACKGRND/HTML/MSDN.20NAMING.HTM.*

Variables declared in this fashion have a default data type; they're called *variants*. A variant is a chameleon data type that can mimic any built-in VBA data type. So, one variant might contain an integer, while another contains a string.

Variables are also implicitly declared as variants when you assign a value to a variable that you haven't declared with `Dim` (Example 18-6).

Example 18-6: Implicitly Declaring a Variable as a Variant

```
' intVariable has not been declared
intVariable = 10
```

While variants are flexible, their use is discouraged except when you must store two different data types in the same variable. Your code runs slower when using variants, since variant values need to be interpreted as a specific data type before they can be used. It is best to declare your variables explicitly with `Dim`. *You can get some help from the VBA environment in this regard. Simply include the* `Option Explicit` *statement at the top of your VBA code. When this statement is present, the environment pops up an error message if you try to use a variable before declaring it.*

Assigning a value to a variable overwrites any previously stored data. An assignment statement consists of the variable name, an equals sign, and the data you want to assign. This can be a value, a calculated value, or another variable (Example 18-7).

Example 18-7: Overwriting a Previously Assigned Variable

```
intInteger = 2000 ' assigning an integer value of 2000
intInteger = 5 * 10 ' assigning the result of a multiplication
intThis = intThat ' assigning the contents of another variable
```

You can see that assigning numeric values is fairly intuitive. Text and date variables require a bit more explanation. Text values are called *strings,* and are surrounded by double quotes (Example 18-8).

Example 18-8: Assigning a String

```
strVar = "remember this" ' assigning a string to a variable
```

Create a string from smaller strings, or even different data types, by using an ampersand between each piece of data (Example 18-9).

Example 18-9: Concatenating Strings

```
' concatenating strings
strMessage = "The color is " & strColor

' concatenating strings and numeric data
strMessage = "The price of " & strItem & " is " curPrice
```

The ampersand (&) is the string concatenation operator in VBA, a fancy term for a character that splices together parts of a string. Don't confuse it with the plus sign (+), which is used to add numbers.

A date is written as text surrounded by pound signs (#), and can take one of several standard forms. The interpretation of some dates, such as 9/7/99, depends on your system's locale settings. Either of the following statements will assign September 7, 1999 to the variable `dtmSomeday` (Example 18-10).

Example 18-10: Assigning a Date

```
dtmSomeday = #7-September-1999#
dtmSomeday = #Sept 7, 1999#
```

Constants

Constants are essentially variables whose values cannot change. They have names like variables, and can contain any data type you'd use for a variable. However, you must assign a value to a constant when you declare it, and that value will remain static throughout the course of your program. Constants help document a program by replacing often-used values with a more meaningful label. Constants are also very useful for defining values that are used in more than one location in your VBA code, enabling easier code modification later. In Word VBA, you'll probably end up using Word's predefined constants more often than defining your own.

Declare a constant using the `Const` keyword, as shown in Example 18-11.

Example 18-11: Declaring a Constant

```
Const WordProcessor = "Word"
Const NumFingers = 10
```

TIP # 157

Declare All Constants at the Beginning of Code

It's best to declare all constants that you'll use in your VBA code in one spot (usually at the beginning), so you'll always know where to find them.

Use a constant just as you would use a variable, except that you can't assign a value (Example 18-12).

Example 18-12: Using a Constant

```
MsgBox "I have " & NumFingers & " fingers."
```

Conditional Statements

Conditional statements contain the logic of a program. The `If Then Else` construct makes decisions on which code to execute next, based on the truth of a condition or combination of conditions, as shown in Example 18-13.

Example 18-13: Using If...Then

```
If curPrice > 3.99 Then
    MsgBox "The price is too high!"
End If
```

In this case, if the variable `curPrice` contains a value greater than 3.99 (in other words, the condition is true), a message box is displayed. If the condition is false, the statement that displays the message box is not executed. We can also use the optional `Else` clause to execute code in this case (Example 18-14).

Example 18-14: Using If...Then...Else

```
If curPrice > 3.99 Then
    MsgBox "The price is too high!"
Else
    MsgBox "The price is right!"
End If
```

Note that the `If Then` portion of the code is paired with an `End If` statement to block off the conditional code.

Test multiple conditions using the `And` and/or `Or` keywords. For multiple conditions involving both `And` and `Or` operations, you may need to group conditions together with parentheses so that the compound condition is evaluated correctly. For example, the following test for a suitable car will be true if the car is a red V6, or if it's just a sports car (Example 18-15).

Example 18-15: Using And and OR operations

```
strEngine = "V6" and strColor = "red" or strStyle = "sports car"
```

The `And` operator has precedence over the `Or` operator. This means that `And` operations are evaluated first, just as in math, where multiplication has precedence over addition. In our example, this groups the "red" and "V6" conditions. We could force a different precedence and look for a car that's a V6 and is either red or sporty by adding parentheses (again like in math), which explicitly group conditions (Example 18-16).

Example 18-16: Grouping Conditions

```
strEngine = "V6" and (strColor = "red" or strStyle = "sports car")
```

Functions and Subprocedures

If statements are like sentences, then *functions* and *subprocedures* (usually abbreviated "subs") are like paragraphs. These are groups of statements that you can call (execute) by name to accomplish a task. For example, you might have a function that performs a math calculation and gives back the result. Or you might have a sub (macro) that extracts the current Outlook contact's data to address a Word letter. Note that functions return values back to your program, while subs do not.

The terms routine, subroutine, function, procedure, and subprocedure are sometimes interchanged loosely (as they are in the rest of this chapter). Functions and subprocedures are routines, but only functions return values.

In order for a function to do some useful work, you may have to give it some information (this is called *passing* information). For instance, a routine that adds two numbers needs the numbers passed to it. In this case, the two numbers are called *parameters*. Taken as a unit, the numbers are the routine's *parameter list*. Parameters appear as declared variables, surrounded by parentheses and separated by commas, after the name of the function or subprocedure. Note that a parameter list may be empty if the routine doesn't need information sent to it in order to do its job.

Some parameters are passed with the intent that their values won't be changed (i.e., they're read-only inside a function). This is called *passing by value*, and such parameters are preceded by the `ByVal` keyword. You may also pass parameters to receive values back from the function or subprocedure call. These parameters are preceded by the `ByRef` keyword and are *passed by reference*.

Functions and subprocedures are denoted by the `Function` and `Sub` keywords, respectively. To begin the body of a function or subprocedure, use one of these keywords in conjunction with the routine's name and parameter list. End the routine with the `End` keyword followed by `Function` or `Sub`. For example, suppose you have a subprocedure that displays a message. Pass it the message as a string and the procedure formats it and displays it in a message box (Example 18-17).

Example 18-17: Passing a Subroutine's Message as a String

```
Public Sub DisplayMsg(ByVal strMsg As String)
    MsgBox "Important message: " & strMsg
End Sub
```

Notice that the subprocedure begins with the `Public` keyword. This determines the *scope* of the procedure (more on this in the "Scope" section). The routine's name is `DisplayMsg`, and it is being passed a string in the variable called `strMsg`. Since `strMsg` is passed by value, we cannot modify its value in our subprocedure's body. Like all subprocedures, ours ends with `End Sub`.

To call a subprocedure, type its name followed by its parameters (separated by commas if there is more than one), as shown in Example 18-18.

Example 18-18: Calling a Subprocedure

```
DisplayMsg "This is a string to display."
```

As I mentioned earlier, a function returns a value (called, strangely enough, the *return value*) to the part of the program that calls it. Declare the data type of a function's return value after the function's parameter list, and assign its value to the function's name. Take a look at a function that calculates a circle's area in Example 18-19.

Example 18-19: Building a Function

```
Const PI = 3.14

Public Function CalcCircleArea(ByVal dblRadius As Double) _
            As Double
    CalcCircleArea = PI * (dblRadius^2)
End Function
```

The function `CalcCircleArea` takes a decimal number (denoted by Double) as a circle radius, squares it and multiplies it by the pi constant, and returns the result (by assigning it to the function name). Use the `Function` keyword in the first and last lines of the function body.

Call a function just as you would a subprocedure, except that you need a variable to hold the value that the function passes back (Example 18-20).

Example 18-20: Calling a Function

```
Dim dblThisArea As Double

dblThisArea = CalcCircleArea(2.5) ' dblThisArea = PI * (2.5^2)
```

You can choose to ignore a function's return value. In this case, you don't need to surround its parameter list with parentheses. Any time you want to assign the return value to a variable, parentheses are required around the function's parameter list.

The return values of one or more function calls can be used in place of variables in calculations, or as parameters to other function or subprocedure calls (Example 18-21).

Example 18-21: Using Return Values from Function Calls

```
dblCylinderVolume = CalcCircleArea(2.5) * dblLength

dblCylinderVolume = CalcCylinderVolume(CalcCircleArea(2.5), dblLength)
```

Scope

The *scope* of a variable, function, or subprocedure determines when—and from where—you can use it. In VBA, scope is determined by where a variable or routine resides and how you declare it.

Each Word template has its own VBA code, which is stored in *code modules*. In the case of Word VBA, there may be one or more modules under the template's *Modules* folder in the Project Explorer, and there is also a special module called *ThisDocument* under the template's *Microsoft Word Objects* folder. Code modules are files containing related variables, constants, functions, and subprocedures. A variable that you declare outside of a function or subroutine (in the module's Declarations section) has *global scope* within its code module. This means that any routine within the variable's module can access it. When you declare a variable in the body of a routine, it has *procedure scope*. The variable is not accessible from other functions in the same—or other any other—module. Put another way, you give the variable life when you declare it in a routine, but it dies when the routine is exited.

Use the `Public` and `Private` keywords to indicate if a routine or global variable can be accessed across its module's boundary (Example 18-22). Global variables declared as `Public` can be accessed from other modules in your project, as can public functions and subprocedures. (The prefix "g" is often used to indicate a global variable.) Variables and routines declared as `Private` can be used only within the code module in which they reside. In Word VBA, since modules are attached to templates, there is another consideration: which project (template) the module belongs to. To call a procedure in another project, you must set a reference to that project in the calling project. This is done using the References dialog accessible from the Tools menu in the VBA window.

Example 18-22: Using Public and Private Keywords

```
Public gintLookAtMe As Integer      ' visible outside this code module
Private strShyVar As String         ' visible in this module only
Dim dtmVar As Date                  ' visible in this module only

Public Sub DoThis()                 ' callable from other code modules
Private Sub SecretFunc()            ' callable only from this module
```

You'll notice that `Public` *and* `Private` *can be used in place of* `Dim` *to explicitly define a variable's module scope. Declaring a variable with the* `Dim` *keyword is the same as declaring it* `Private`.

Objects

In VBA programming, *objects* are logical abstractions that represent components of the host application (in this case, Word). Objects have *properties* (attributes) and can be acted upon through object *methods* (behavior). Additionally, some objects have *events* (actions). So a car modeled in software might have `Color` and `Horsepower` properties, and a `Brake` event. And we could use methods like `Accelerate` and `Slow` to control the speed of the "software car." Properties and methods are used in functions or subs; an event is a particular type of sub associated with an object.

Technically, objects are class instances. Classes are named templates from which you create objects. For example, we may have two objects of the `Car` *class. Each of these objects may contain different* `Color` *property values (one may be* `Red`*, the other* `Blue`*). Despite the differences in their* `Color` *values, they're of the same class. Classes are contained in their own code modules, called class modules.*

The way you assign (set) object variables differs slightly from the way you assign integers or strings—you must use the word `Set` in assigning an object variable. There are several ways to create objects. One way is to use the `New` keyword in an object variable declaration or assignment. Some objects can be created using the `CreateObject` function, and others are created by using methods.

However you create an object, you can then call the object's methods and access its properties by typing the object variable followed by a dot and a method or property name (this is called *dot notation*). When you're done using an object, you need to get rid of it. You do this by setting your variable to the special object value `Nothing`. This will delete the object's memory, and keep it from consuming resources on your machine unnecessarily. Example 18-23 illustrates these concepts.

Example 18-23: Creating, Calling, and Destroying an Object

```
' One line object creation
Dim objWidget As New Widget

' Object variable declaration, followed by assignment of a
' new object
Dim objThing As Thingamabob
Set objThing = New Thingamabob

Dim nResult As Integer
Dim nPropVal As Integer

' Calling an object method (subprocedure)
objWidget.DoSomething
' Calling an object method (function)
nResult = objThing.Calculate(5,3)

' Setting a property
objThing.Size = 5

' Examining a property's value
intPropVal = objWidget.Color

' Release the objects' memory
Set objWidget = Nothing
Set objThing = Nothing
```

Code samples later in this chapter illustrate the use of various Word objects.

TIP # 158

Delete an Object After Creating It

It's easy to forget to delete an object once you're done with it. One way to make sure you don't forget to release object memory is to type the statement that destroys an object as soon as you've typed in the statement that creates it.

Collections

A *collection* is a container object for a group of other objects. For example, in Word VBA, the Documents collection (a global collection in Word) contains the group of open Document objects:

Collections have a couple of useful read-only properties that help you iterate (loop) through the list of objects:

- The Count property returns the number of objects in the collection.
- The Item property returns a specified object from the collection.

These properties can be used in a For Next loop, a construct that traverses the objects in a collection over a range that you specify. In older versions of VBA, the only way to iterate through a collection was by using the For Next construct with a *counter*—a variable used to keep track of where you are in the collection—and a variable to hold the object reference returned by Item. The code in Example 18-24 illustrates this technique.

Example 18-24: Using a Counter to Track Collection Position

```
Dim objDoc As Document

For intCounter = 1 To Documents.Count
     Set objDoc = Documents.Item(intCounter)

     ' Display the document's filename
     MsgBox objDoc.Name
Next
```

Some things to note about this code:

- The For...To statement defines the range over which you want to iterate. In this case, we want to go from the first object (at index 1) to the last object.
- We use the Set keyword to fill our object variable with a value from the collection. We need to tell the collection *which* item we'd like back. We use the loop counter for this.
- Once we've filled our object variable, we can use it. In this case, we just display a recipient's name.
- We don't set the object variable to Nothing after using it. This is because the object is part of the collection, and we don't want to delete it.
- We end the body of the loop with a Next statement.

In more recent versions of VBA, there is another, easier way to loop through an entire collection. The For Each...Next construct does a lot of the legwork of looping for you. You don't need to declare a counter, and the Set operation is done under the covers for you. We could rewrite the previously example to the one shown in Example 18-25.

Example 18-25: Using For Each...Next to Loop Through Collections

```
For Each objDoc In Documents
    MsgBox objDoc.Name
Next
```

Through each iteration of the loop, subsequent `Document` objects are assigned to the `objDoc` loop variable, which does your work.

In our first looping example, we used the `Item` property and an index (the loop counter in this case) to indicate which recipient to grab from the collection. For collections in Word VBA, the `Item` property is the *default property*. This means that we can forgo querying the `Item` property and just type in an index after the collection variable (Example 18-26).

Example 18-26: Using an Index Instead of the Item Property

```
Set objDoc = Documents(intCounter)
```

Some collections (like the `Documents` collection) also support using a "key" string to reference an object in a collection. For instance, you can fetch a particular document by name (Example 18-27).

Example 18-27: Using a Key String to Reference an Object

```
Set objDoc = Documents("C:\MyDoc.doc")
```

Error Handling

Ideally, your code would run without any problems. But errors happen. Normally, a VBA program stops running and a message box is displayed when an error occurs. By using the `On Error` statement, you can replace this default error message with your own, which is probably more useful. You can react to otherwise fatal errors and take corrective action, or you can choose to ignore the error and continue executing —at your own risk, of course. You can even use an error handler as a way to branch to a different statement in case of a specific error, as in the second `Document_New` event procedure in a later section of this chapter.

The `On Error` statement has several forms, but the two of most interest are `On Error Resume Next` and `On Error Goto`. You use these statements before the piece of code in which you want to catch errors (Example 18-28).

Example 18-28: Using the On Error Statement

```
Private Sub DoLoop()
    On Error Resume Next
    For Each objDoc in Documents
        MsgBox objDoc.BuiltInDocumentProperties(wdPropertyKeywords)
    Next
End Sub
```

The DoLoop procedure (Example 18-29) uses the "Resume Next" form. If an error occurs in the loop, it is ignored, and execution continues (we keep on looping). This is the "so what?" form of error handling.

Example 18-29: Using the DoLoop procedure

```
Private Sub DoLoopCarefully()
     On Error Goto Loop_Err

     For Each objDoc in Documents
          MsgBox objDoc.BuiltInDocumentProperties(wdPropertyKeywords)
     Next

     Exit Sub

Loop_Err:
     MsgBox "Error " & Err.Number & ": " & Err.Description

End Sub
```

If we encounter an error in the DoLoopCarefully procedure, execution will continue at the Loop_Err label at the end of the procedure body. This part of the procedure is called an *error handler*. The error handler in this example is retrieving properties from an object called Err. This is VBA's built-in error object. Here, we're using it to display an error number and a description of the error.

You should also note the Exit Sub statement after the loop. At this point, the code is done, and you need to exit. If you don't, you fall into the error handler and get a bogus error message.

The Word Object Model

To accomplish a task in Word VBA, or to work with Word using Automation code from other applications, you use the Word object model, a hierarchy of related objects that represent almost all of the components of Word that you use in the interface. Word objects are used to retrieve information, create new items, and cause Word to perform actions. Figure 18-3 shows the top-level objects in the Word object model.

To open the object model diagram in Help, select the Programming Information book in the Help Contents tab, then the Getting Started with Microsoft Word Visual Basic subbook, and select the Understanding Objects, Properties and Methods Help topic. Near the end of this Help topic there is a Microsoft Word Objects hyperlink that opens to the Word object model diagram when clicked. When you have the diagram open in Help, you can click on its component objects to open related Help topics.

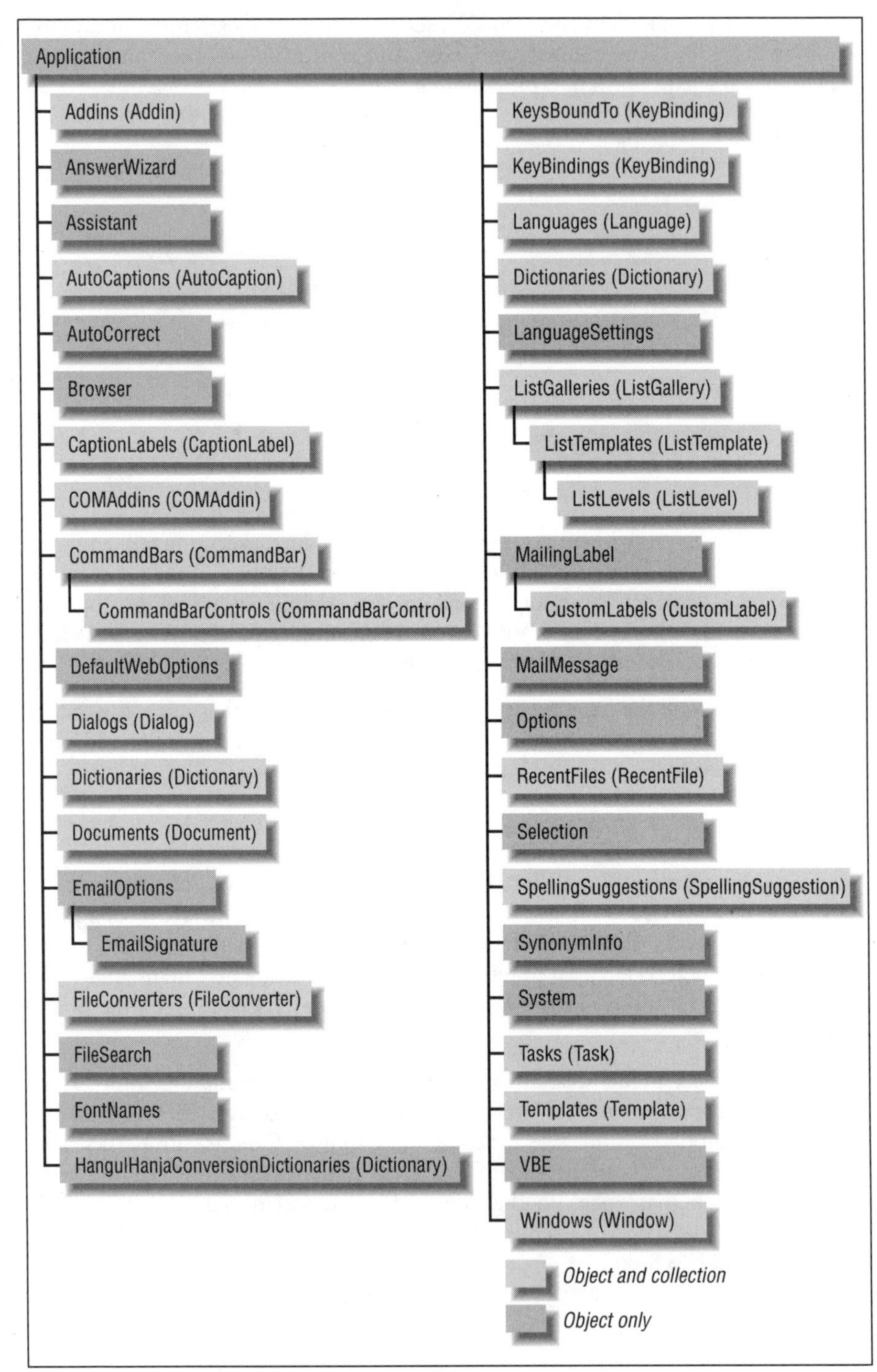

Figure 18-3: Part of the Word Object Model

The Application Object

The Application object is the root object of the Word object model, and represents the entire application. There is one—and only one—Application object available for use in Word-hosted VBA. When you are working in Word VBA, the Application object is always available, and can be referenced simply as Application. When you are working with Word objects from VBA hosted by other applications, you need to explicitly create the Word Application object using CreateObject or GetObject (Example 18-30).

Example 18-30: Using CreateObject

```
Set appWord = CreateObject("Word.Application")
```

The first code fragment in Example 18-31 uses one of the methods of the Application object to maximize the Word window, while the second restores the Word window, then moves and resizes it to a specific size and position.

Example 18-31: Controlling the Application Window

```
Application.WindowState = wdWindowStateMaximize

With Application
    .WindowState = wdWindowStateNormal
    .Move Left:=0, Top:=97
    .Resize Width:=473, Height:=489
    .Move Left:=135, Top:=51
End With
```

The Document Object

The Document object is used to work with Word documents in VBA code. To work with the currently open document, use the ActiveDocument property of the Application object, as in the code fragment in Example 18-32.

Example 18-32: Using the Document Object

```
Set doc = Application.ActiveDocument
```

Events are external actions on an object to which the object can react. The Document object has three events, for which you can write event procedures. The code in an event procedure runs when the event occurs. The Open event fires when a document is opened, the Close event when a document is closed, and the New event fires when a new document is created from a template.

To create an event procedure for a document, open the document, then open the VBA window (Figure 18-4). Select the document's project in the Project Explorer. Open the *Microsoft Word Objects* folder for the document, and double-click the ThisDocument object to open its module. Drop down the Objects box (the one at the top left of the Code window) and select the Document object. Drop down the

Events/Procedures box (the one at the top right of the Code window) to see the three document events. Selecting an event creates a code stub for that event.

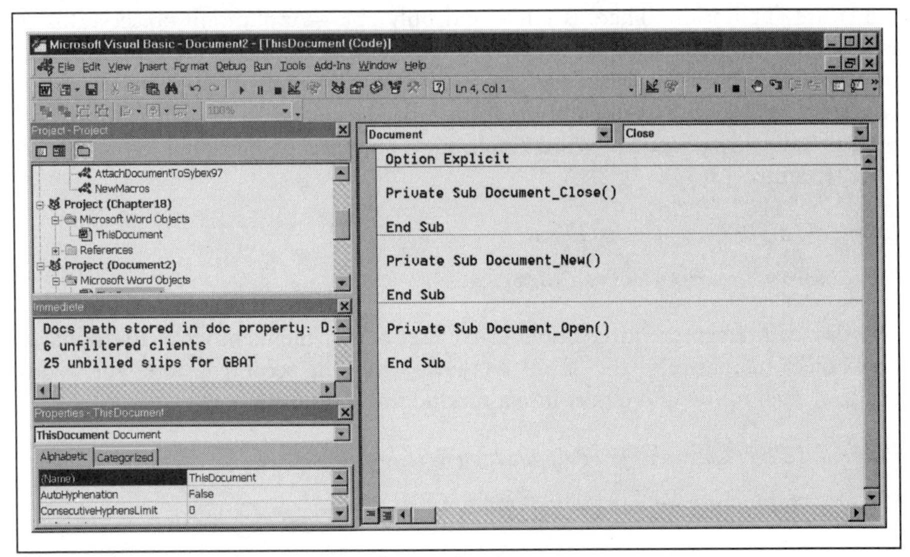

Figure 18-4: Document event procedure stubs

Next, type the code to be run when the event occurs in its event procedure. The `Document_New` event procedure in Example 18-33 hides the Word window and pops up a UserForm where the user can make selections before the document is made visible again. You will need to create the `frmChooseClient` UserForm with an OK button for this example to work. See the "UserForms" section later in this chapter for details on creating UserForms.

Example 18-33: Using an Event Procedure

```
Private Sub Document_New()

On Error GoTo ErrorHandler

   'Hide Word document until OK button on UserForm is pressed
   Application.Visible = False
   Load frmChooseClient
   frmChooseClient.Show

ErrorHandlerExit:
   Exit Sub

ErrorHandler:
   MsgBox "Error No: " & Err.Number & "; Description: " & Err.Description
   Resume ErrorHandlerExit

End Sub
```

The Document_New procedure shown in Example 18-34 might be stored in a template (for example, one that created a letter to a contact) and would run as soon as a new document was created from that template. The procedure pulls contact data from a contact item currently open in Outlook, writing the name and address data to the new blank letter. Note that this procedure hands back an error if Outlook is not open, or a contact is not open in Outlook.

Example 18-34: Running a Procedure when Creating a New Document

```
Private Sub Document_New()

On Error GoTo ErrorHandler

   Dim appOutlook As Outlook.Application
   Dim ins As Outlook.Inspector
   'Dim exp As Outlook.Explorer
   Dim nms As Outlook.NameSpace
   Dim itm As Object
   Dim strFullName As String
   Dim strAddress As String
   Dim strSalutation As String
   Dim strDocName As String

   'Set reference to Outlook item
   Set appOutlook = CreateObject("Outlook.Application")
   Set nms = appOutlook.GetNamespace("MAPI")
   Set ins = appOutlook.ActiveInspector
   'Set exp = appOutlook.ActiveExplorer

   Set itm = ins.CurrentItem
   If itm.Class <> olcontact Then
      'No contact item opened
      MsgBox "No contact item selected; cancelling merge from Outlook"
      Exit Sub
   End If

   'Create variables from Outlook item
   strFullName = itm.FullName
   If itm.JobTitle <> "" Then
      strAddress = itm.JobTitle & vbCrLf & itm.CompanyName & vbCrLf & itm.
MailingAddress
   ElseIf itm.CompanyName <> "" Then
      strAddress = itm.CompanyName & vbCrLf & itm.MailingAddress
   Else
      strAddress = itm.MailingAddress
   End If

   If itm.Title <> "" Then
      strSalutation = itm.Title & " " & itm.LastName
   Else
      strSalutation = "Mr. " & itm.LastName
   End If
```

Example 18-34: Running a Procedure when Creating a New Document (continued)

```
   'Paste Outlook data to document
   With Selection
      .ParagraphFormat.Alignment = wdAlignParagraphRight
      .InsertDateTime DateTimeFormat:="dddd, MMMM dd, yyyy", _
         InsertAsField:=False, DateLanguage:=wdEnglishUS, _
         CalendarType:=wdCalendarWestern, InsertAsFullWidth:=False
      .TypeParagraph
      .ParagraphFormat.Alignment = wdAlignParagraphLeft
      .TypeParagraph
      .TypeParagraph
      .TypeText Text:=strFullName
      .TypeParagraph
      .TypeText Text:=strAddress
      .TypeParagraph
      .TypeParagraph
      .TypeText Text:=strSalutation
      .TypeParagraph
      .TypeParagraph
   End With

ErrorHandlerExit:
   Exit Sub

ErrorHandler:
   If Err.Number = 91 Then
      MsgBox "No contact item open in Outlook; canceling merge"
      Application.ActiveDocument.Close
      Exit Sub
   Else
      MsgBox "Error No: " & Err.Number & "; Description: " & Err.Description
      Resume ErrorHandlerExit
   End If

End Sub
```

A more ambitious Document_New event procedure is shown in Example 18-35. It fills a table formatted for Avery #5160 labels (see Chapter 9, *Tools*, for more on doing this) with data from contacts in the default local Outlook *Contacts* folder.

Example 18-35: Pulling Contact Information from Outlook

```
Private Sub Document_New()

On Error GoTo ErrorHandler

   Dim appOutlook As New Outlook.Application
   Dim nms As Outlook.NameSpace
   Dim fld As Outlook.MAPIFolder
   Dim itms As Outlook.Items
   Dim itm As Object

   'Open Contacts folder
```

Example 18-35: Pulling Contact Information from Outlook (continued)

```
   Set nms = appOutlook.GetNamespace("MAPI")
   Set fld = nms.GetDefaultFolder(olFolderContacts)
   Set itms = fld.Items

      For Each itm In itms
         If itm.Class = olContact Then
            If itm.FullName <> "" _
               And itm.CompanyName <> "" And itm.BusinessAddress <> "" Then
               Debug.Print "Processing " & itm.FullName & " label"
               With Selection
                  .TypeText Text:=itm.FullName
                  .TypeParagraph
                  .TypeText Text:=itm.CompanyName
                  .TypeParagraph
                  .TypeText Text:=itm.BusinessAddress
                  .TypeParagraph
                  .MoveRight Unit:=wdCell
                  .MoveRight Unit:=wdCell
               End With
            End If
         End If
      Next itm

ErrorHandlerExit:
   Exit Sub

ErrorHandler:
   MsgBox "Error No: " & Err.Number & "; Description: " & Err.Description
   Resume ErrorHandlerExit

End Sub
```

Example 18-36 shows the use of the `Document_Close` event, which runs whenever a document is closed. This example increments the value of a document property named `InvoiceNumber` by 1.

Example 18-36: Using a Document_Close Event

```
Private Sub Document_Close()
'Written by Helen Feddema 9/30/99
'Last modified 3-26-2000

On Error GoTo ErrorHandler

   Dim prps As DocumentProperties
   Dim lngInvoiceNumber As Long

   'Store incremented invoice number in template doc property
   If ActiveDocument.Type = wdTypeDocument Then
         Set prps = ActiveDocument.AttachedTemplate.CustomDocumentProperties
         lngInvoiceNumber = prps.Item("InvoiceNumber") + 1
         prps.Item("InvoiceNumber") = lngInvoiceNumber
```

Example 18-36: Using a Document_Close Event (continued)

```
        ActiveDocument.AttachedTemplate.Save
    End If

ErrorHandlerExit:
    Exit Sub

ErrorHandler:
    MsgBox "Error No: " & Err.Number & "; Description: " & Err.Description
    Resume ErrorHandlerExit

End Sub
```

The Selection Object

When you record a macro, and open it for editing, you will probably find that the code makes extensive use of the Selection object, which represents the text currently selected in the Word document (or the position of the cursor, if no text is selected). While you can work with paragraphs, sentences, words, and characters via their respective collections under the Document object, it is more common to work with these collections under the Selection object.

The procedure in Example 18-37 selects the entire document and converts field codes into text, then places the cursor at the top of the document, using the `WholeStory` method of the Selection object (WholeStory means the entire document).

Example 18-37: Working with Selections

```
Sub CodeToText()

    Selection.WholeStory
    Selection.Fields.Unlink
    Selection.HomeKey Unit:=wdStory

End Sub
```

Note that the Selection object appears on each line of code; this is often true of recorded code. The above procedure can be made more efficient by using the `With...End With` structure, as shown in Example 18-38.

Example 18-38: Using the With...End With Structure

```
Sub CodeToText()

    With Selection
        .WholeStory
        .Fields.Unlink
        .HomeKey Unit:=wdStory
    End With

End Sub
```

The Range Object

The Range object represents a contiguous area in a document, which may or may not be selected. You can use this object to perform actions on a portion of a document, without having to select it. While there can be only one Selection object in a Word document, there can be multiple Range objects, which makes them more flexible. Other than that, Range and Selection objects share a great many properties and methods, and can be used in a similar manner.

For a detailed discussion of the Range and Selection objects and their use in VBA code, see *Writing Word Macros*, by Steven Roman (O'Reilly & Associates).

The entire object model is far too large to cover here. But you can get a good feeling for how to control Word by examining some of its major objects: Application, Document, Range, and Selection. (For full details on all objects and their methods and properties, consult the Word VBA help available through the VBA editor or the object model diagram.)

The VBA Editor in Word

We've seen some of the syntax and structure of the VBA language. Next we need to examine the Word VBA developer's environment, the window where you create and modify code. Like the other Office applications, Word uses the Visual Basic Editor as its development environment.

To launch the editor, select Tools → Macro → Visual Basic Editor in a Word window, or hit Alt-F11. The Microsoft Visual Basic window opens, looking something like Figure 18-5.

The major components of the VBA window are:

1. *Project Explorer.* Lists the open projects (templates and documents), with folders for their objects, references, forms and modules.
2. *Immediate Window.* Lists statements printed from code using the `Debug.Print` method.
3. *Properties Sheet.* Lists the properties of the selected object (in this case, a UserForm).
4. *Code Window.* Shows the code in a module.
5. *UserForm.* Shows a UserForm in design view.
6. *Object Browser.* Shows the components of the selected object library.

The Project Explorer and Properties Window

The Project Explorer window (the Project–TemplateProject window in Figure 18-5) contains open projects, displayed in a tree structure. To the Word VBA editor, a

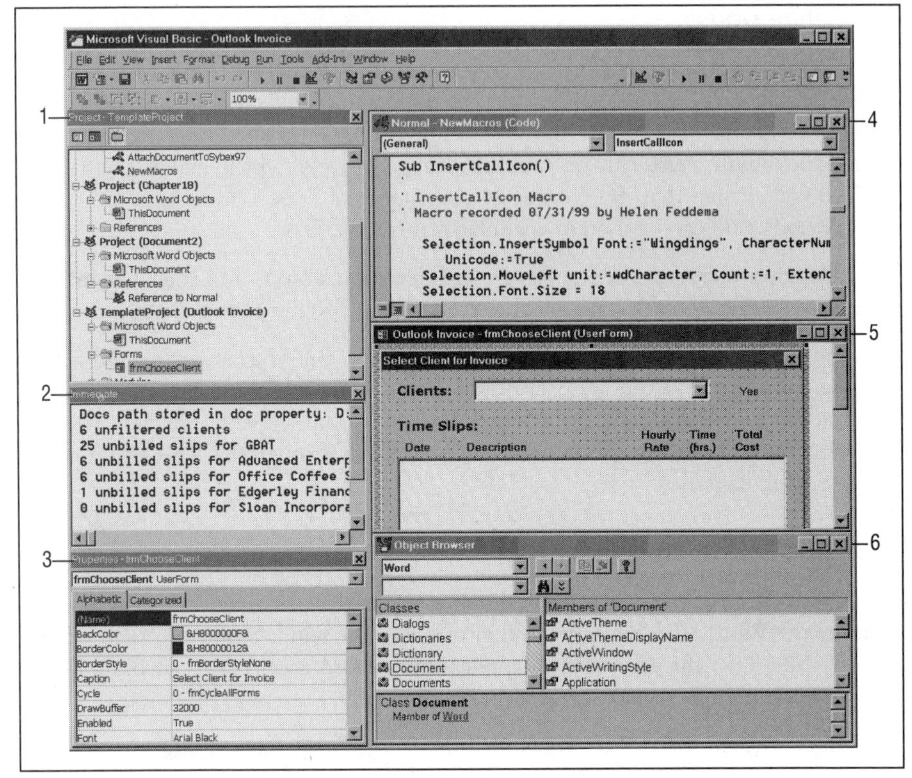

Figure 18-5: The Visual Basic Editor in Word

"project" is any open document (including templates). In Figure 18-3, *normal.dot* (which doesn't show in the figure), a document named *Chapter 18*, another document named *Document2*, and a template named *Outlook Invoice* are open. Each project is a node in the Project Explorer's tree, and has the form *ProjectName (DocumentName)*. Note that I've left the project names for both the document and its template as the defaults, *Project* and *TemplateProject*, respectively.

There is a project entry in the Project Explorer for each open document and template. Each global template also has a project entry (although global templates must be opened as documents in Word in order for you to edit their VBA code).

Below the project node in the Project Explorer are nodes for standard code modules, class modules, and UserForms, organized by module types into corresponding folders. In Word VBA, each project has a *Microsoft Word Objects* folder with a single class module called *ThisDocument*. The *ThisDocument* module contains event handlers for the Document object's events.

The *Modules* folder holds standard (non-class) code modules. Typically, your macro code will reside here. The *Class Modules* folder holds code modules containing user-defined classes, which we do not cover here. The *References* folder (found only in document projects) contains a reference to the template on which the document is based.

The Properties sheet shows the properties of various objects and allows you to modify them. You can use this window to can change the name of your VBA project by clicking on the project node in the Project Explorer, clicking the column next to `(Name)`, typing in a new value, and hitting `Enter`. The Properties sheet is especially useful for working with UserForms.

The Code Window, and Object and Procedure List Boxes

The Code window is used to create and modify VBA code. It has two drop-down lists, the one on the left used to select objects, and the one on the right to select procedures or events. As you type code in the code window, the editor formats it for you. Keywords are colored in blue, comments in green. When you hit Enter or move off a freshly typed statement, the editor capitalizes keywords for you. When you enter a statement with an error in it, the editor displays a message box telling you what's wrong, and colors the statement red until you fix it.

As you type, you'll also notice that the editor will try to help you out. After you type the name of a defined function or subprocedure, it will show the parameters in a tool tip, bolding the one you should currently be entering. It will show a list of data types as you type your `Dim` statement, and a list of methods and properties after you type an object variable and a period. If you select an item from the list and hit Tab, the editor will complete the code entry for you. This feature is called IntelliSense. You can type part of a variable name or constant and have the editor take its best guess at the full name by hitting Ctrl-Space. If the editor can't complete the name for you, it will display the closest matches to the name in a list box. Figures 18-6 and 18-7 show some of these features in action.

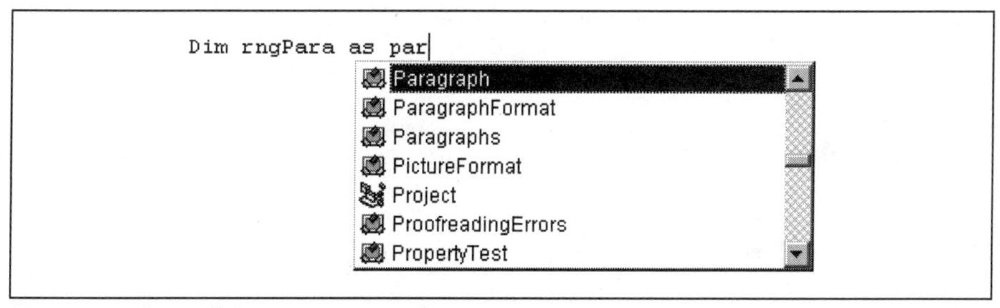

Figure 18-6: IntelliSense suggesting data types

As I mentioned earlier, the object and procedure drop-down boxes help you code more quickly. The object drop-down box is the leftmost of the two and contains a (General) entry and objects. The (General) entry is shown when the code window's cursor is in the module's global code, where you'd type `Option Explicit` or your global module variables for event handlers. When the cursor is in procedure code

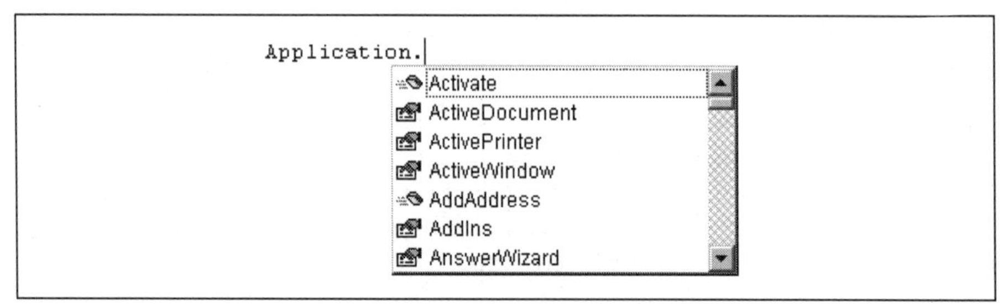

Figure 18-7: IntelliSense listing object properties and methods

for an object, the object is shown in the object drop-down box, and the procedure (which could be an event handler) in the procedure drop-down box. You can have the editor fill in the beginning and end of a particular procedure by selecting the object and procedure of interest in the drop-down boxes.

I'll guide you through an example to demonstrate some of the editor's features. Create a new template in Word and save it with the name *Test.dot*. With the template open, hit Alt-F11 to open the VBA editor. Double-click the Test project's ThisDocument node in the Project Explorer. This will open the code module for the project's associated Document object. From the object drop-down box, select Document. The editor will create a skeleton for the New procedure, since it's the first event handler in the procedure drop-down box. Now select Open from the procedure drop-down box. Your screen should now look like Figure 18-8, with two event handlers ready for the filling.

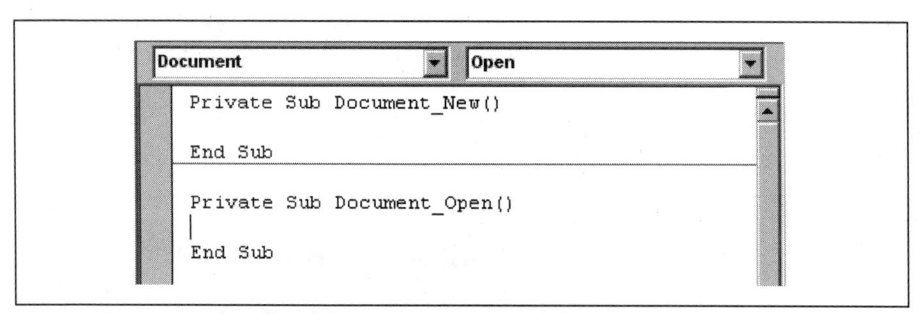

Figure 18-8: Event handler skeletons created via the object and procedure drop-down boxes

Now let's write a little code. Let's make a message box pop up whenever you create a new document based on the *Test.dot* template. Type the code in Example 18-39 into the New handler:

Example 18-39: Opening a Message Box for a New Document

```
Private Sub Document_New
     MsgBox "This document is based on the Test template."
End Sub
```

You can run this code by placing the cursor in the procedure's body and hitting F5, the Run Sub/UserForm toolbar button, or—for this particular example—by creating a new document and choosing *Test.dot* as its template. You should see a message box pop up and display the message text.

That's really all there is to writing code in the VBA editor, though procedures are usually considerably more complex than this example (see the UserForm code at the end of this chapter for some more complex examples of Word VBA code). If you want to get serious about VBA customizations to Word, you'll want to explore debugging and other helpful features of the editor.

The Object Browser

While you can certainly use the online help (accessed by the Help menu or F1) provided in the VBA editor to explore Word's object model, there is an alternative. The editor has a built-in tool called the Object Browser that lets you see the Word VBA objects and their methods, properties, and events. To access the object browser, select Tools → Object Browser, hit F2, or click the Object Browser button on the toolbar. The screen in Figure 18-9 overlays the code window (though it can be docked if you wish, by checking Immediate Window on the Docking page of the Options dialog opened from the VBA window).

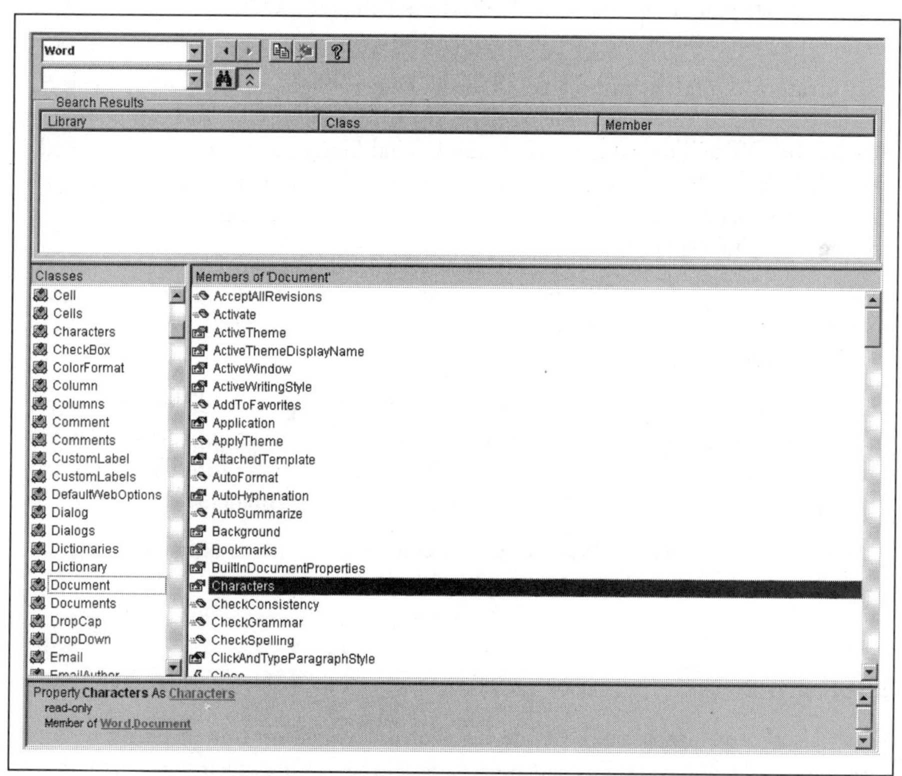

Figure 18-9: The Object Browser

Choose which library of objects is displayed in the browser by selecting one from the Libraries drop-down box at the top of the window. Here, I've chosen the Word object library.

View object properties, methods, and events in the Members pane by clicking on an object's class in the Classes pane. When you click on an entry in the Members pane, information about that entry will appear in the text area at the bottom of the browser screen. You can also bring up the help screen for a class or one of its members by hitting F1 when you have an entry in either pane highlighted.

Macro Security and Digital Signatures

After you've written some macros or event handlers in your VBA project, you'll get a macro security warning when you start Word. This happens with other Office applications, and is a good safeguard. But sometimes being safe can be a bit annoying.

You could just set your macro security level to Low in the Tools → Macro → Security → Security Level tab, but this would open an undesirable security hole. Fortunately, there's a better way: a personal digital signature. A digital signature allows you to sign your VBA code so that only you can run it. Having a digital signature lets you crank that macro security setting all way up to High, at which level only your macros can be run in your Word session.

To create a digital signature, you'll need Digital Signature for VBA Projects installed. This component is included on the Office 2000 CD, and can be found under the Office Tools folder. With the Digital Signature component installed, run the file `selfcert.exe` from your Office program folder (*C:\Program Files\Microsoft Office\Office* by default), put in your name, and click OK. You've just created a digital signature.

Now you can sign your VBA project. In the VBA editor, select Tools → Digital Signature, click the Choose button, and select your signature. Your VBA project is now signed.

Close and restart Word. You'll be presented with a portentous dialog telling you that you can't trust your own macros. Clicking the checkbox labeled "Always trust macros from this source" and then the Enable Macros button will dispatch this message—and that old macro security warning—permanently.

Office 2000 security patches (a response to several macro viruses in Spring 2000) may affect the information in this sidebar.

UserForms

Word UserForms are actually Office UserForms, which are hosted by most Office applications. They have a different object model than Word, so if you start working with them extensively, you will need to familiarize yourself with the Forms object library (MSForms in the Libraries drop-down box in the VBA window). But you can create and work with UserForms in the VBA window without using the Forms object model in code, and these forms are very useful for intermediate and advanced Word programming. UserForms allow you to go beyond a simple message box or input box and present users with a more extensive dialog box with (for example) combo boxes or list boxes where items can be selected, and text boxes for entering values.

To create a UserForm, open the VBA window, select the appropriate document or template in the Project Explorer, and click the Insert UserForm button on the toolbar. A new form opens (Figure 18-10), called UserForm1 (or a higher number, if there already are some forms for this template). When the UserForm has the focus, a Toolbox appears, with a selection of controls you can place on the form.

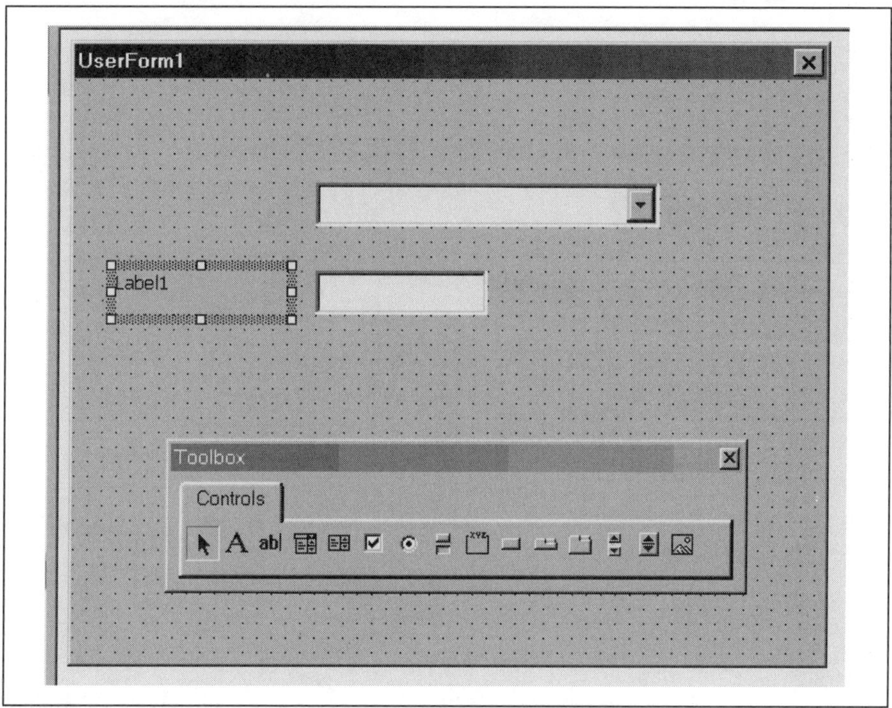

Figure 18-10: A newly created UserForm with several controls

UserForms (and controls placed on them) have several useful events:

Initialize
: The Initialize event of the form, which fires when the form is opened, is useful for filling in default values for controls on the form.

Click
: The Click event of many controls (most commonly used with a command button), which fires when the user clicks the control, can be used to run code.

Typically UserForms have an OK button with code that performs an action, often using values set from other controls on the form.

Change

The Change event of a text box control, which fires when the text in the control is changed, can be used to respond to a change made by a user.

A UserForm is often popped up from code on the `Document_New` or `Document_Open` event of a template, so that the user will be presented with the form when a document is opened, or a new document is created from a template. The UserForms could also be popped up from Word macros (event procedures) placed as buttons on the toolbar.

The code in Example 18-40 uses the `Document_New` event to give the user a choice of working with data from Access or Outlook.

Example 18-40: Opening a User Form with a New Document

```
Private Sub Document_New()

On Error GoTo ErrorHandler

   Dim strChoice As String

   strChoice = InputBox("Enter data source (Outlook or Access)", _
      "Choose data source", "Access")

   If strChoice = "Access" Then
      Load frmAccessData
      frmAccessData.Show
   ElseIf strChoice = "Outlook" Then
      Load frmOutlookData
      frmOutlookData.Show
   Else
      MsgBox "Please enter Outlook or Access as the data source"
   End If

ErrorHandlerExit:
   Exit Sub

ErrorHandler:
   MsgBox "Error No: " & Err.Number & "; Description: " & Err.Description
   Resume ErrorHandlerExit

End Sub
```

The template has two UserForms, frmAccessData and frmOutlookData. frmOutlookData is shown in design view in Figure 18-11.

frmAccessData's `Initialize` event (Example 18-41) fills a multi-select list box on the UserForm with employees from the Employees table in the sample Northwind database (included with Office 2000), and the `cmdMerge_Click` event creates letters to the

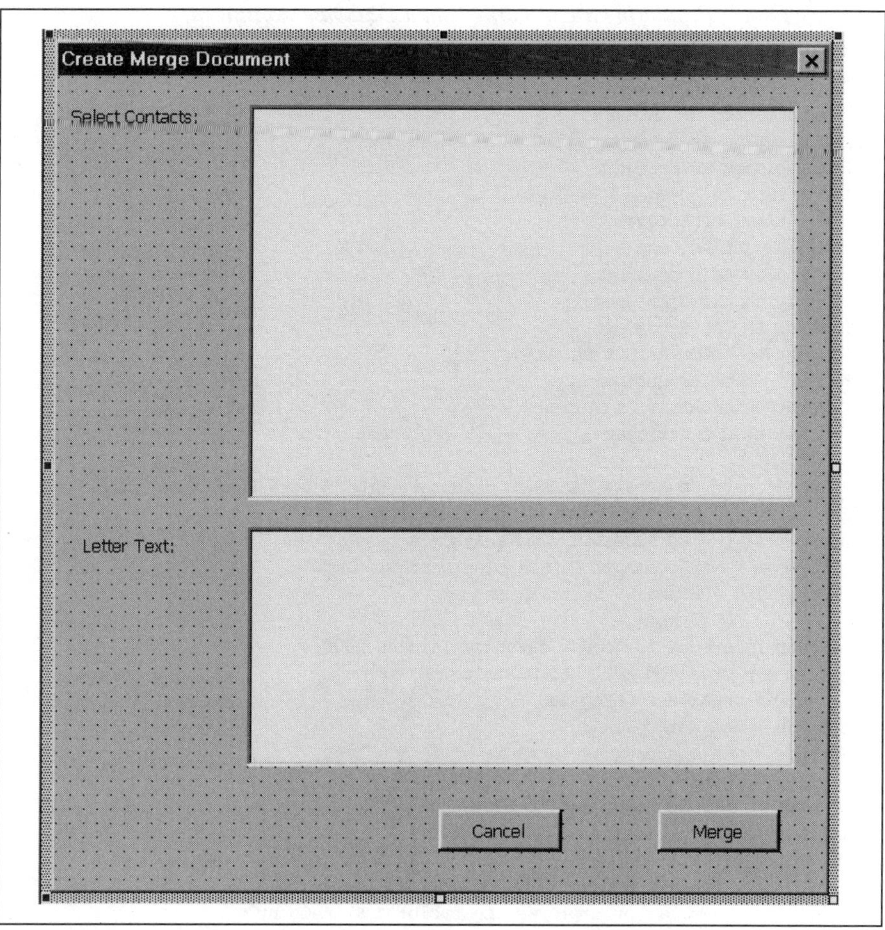

Figure 18-11: The frmOutlookData UserForm in design view.

selected contacts, with name and address data from the Northwind Employees table and letter text from the Letter Text text box `txtLetterText` on the form.

Example 18-41: Populating a UserForm from a Database

```
Option Explicit

Dim lst As MSForms.ListBox

Private Sub UserForm_Initialize()
'Written by Helen Feddema 5-21-2000
'Last modified 5-21-2000

On Error GoTo ErrorHandler

   Dim appAccess As Access.Application
   Dim dbe As DAO.DBEngine
```

Example 18-41: Populating a UserForm from a Database (continued)

```
    Dim dbs As DAO.Database
    Dim intItem As Integer
    Dim intColumn As Integer
    Dim intCount As Integer
    Dim intIndex As Integer
    Dim intRow As Integer
    Dim intRows As Integer
    Dim lngCount As Long
    Dim lngRow As Long
    Dim lngTableRows As Long
    Dim rst As DAO.Recordset
    Dim strAccessDir As String
    Dim strDBName As String
    Dim varContactArray As Variant
    Dim wks As DAO.Workspace

    'Pick up path to Access database directory from Access SysCmd function
    Set appAccess = CreateObject("Access.Application")
    strAccessDir = appAccess.SysCmd(acSysCmdAccessDir)
    strDBName = strAccessDir & "\Samples\Northwind.mdb"
    Debug.Print "DBName: " & strDBName

    'Set up reference to Access database (Access 2000)
    'Set dbe = CreateObject("DAO.DBEngine.36")
    Set dbe = appAccess.DBEngine
    Set wks = dbe.Workspaces(0)
    Set dbs = wks.OpenDatabase(strDBName)

    Set rst = dbs.OpenRecordset("Employees")
    rst.MoveLast
    rst.MoveFirst
    lngCount = rst.RecordCount
    Debug.Print "Number of employees in table: " & lngCount
    lngCount = rst.RecordCount - 1
    varContactArray = rst.GetRows(lngCount)
    rst.Close
    dbs.Close
    wks.Close

    Set lst = lstContacts
    lst.Column() = varContactArray
    Me![txtLetterText].Value = "Type letter text here"

ErrorHandlerExit:
    Exit Sub

ErrorHandler:
    MsgBox "Error No: " & Err.Number & "; Description: " & Err.Description
    Resume ErrorHandlerExit

End Sub
```

Example 18-41: Populating a UserForm from a Database (continued)

```
Private Sub cmdCancel_Click()

   Unload frmAccessData

End Sub


Private Sub cmdMerge_Click()

On Error GoTo ErrorHandler

   Dim intItem As Integer
   Dim intIndex As Integer
   Dim intRow As Integer
   Dim intRows As Integer
   Dim intColumn As Integer
   Dim intColumns As Integer
   Dim strLetterText As String

   Set lst = lstContacts
   strLetterText = Me![txtLetterText]
   intRows = lst.ListCount - 1

   For intItem = 1 To intRows
      If lst.Selected(intItem) = True Then
         'Open a new letter based on the Normal template
         'Debug.Print "Creating a letter to : " & Nz(lst.Column(3, intItem))
         Application.Documents.Add

         'Paste Outlook data to letter for each selected contact
         With Selection
            .ParagraphFormat.Alignment = wdAlignParagraphRight
            .InsertDateTime DateTimeFormat:="dddd, MMMM dd, yyyy", _
               InsertAsField:=False, DateLanguage:=wdEnglishUS, _
               CalendarType:=wdCalendarWestern, InsertAsFullWidth:=False
            .TypeParagraph
            .ParagraphFormat.Alignment = wdAlignParagraphLeft
            .TypeParagraph
            .TypeParagraph
            .TypeText Text:=Nz(lst.Column(4, intItem)) & " " & _
               Nz(lst.Column(2, intItem)) & " " & Nz(lst.Column(1, intItem))
            .TypeParagraph
            .TypeText Text:=Nz(lst.Column(3, intItem))
            .TypeParagraph
            .TypeText Text:="Northwind Traders"
            .TypeParagraph
            .TypeText Text:=Nz(lst.Column(7, intItem))
            .TypeParagraph
            .TypeText Text:=Nz(lst.Column(8, intItem)) & ", " & _
               Nz(lst.Column(9, intItem)) & "  " & Nz(lst.Column(10, intItem))
            .TypeParagraph
            .TypeText Text:=Nz(lst.Column(11, intItem))
```

Example 18-41: Populating a UserForm from a Database (continued)

```
            .TypeParagraph
            .TypeParagraph
            .TypeText Text:="Dear " & Nz(lst.Column(2, intItem)) & ":"
            .TypeParagraph
            .TypeParagraph
            .TypeText Text:=strLetterText
            .TypeParagraph
            .TypeParagraph
            .TypeText Text:="Yours sincerely"
            .TypeParagraph
            .TypeParagraph
            .TypeParagraph
            .TypeParagraph
            .TypeText Application.ActiveDocument.
BuiltInDocumentProperties(wdPropertyAuthor)
         End With
      End If

   Next intItem

   Unload frmAccessData

ErrorHandlerExit:
   Exit Sub

ErrorHandler:
   MsgBox "Error No: " & Err.Number & "; Description: " & Err.Description
   Resume ErrorHandlerExit

End Sub
```

The frmOutlookData UserForm (which is similar in appearance) fills its list box with Outlook contacts (from the default local *Contacts* folder), and merges data from the selected contacts to new letters. The code is shown in Example 18-42.

Example 18-42: Populating a User Form from Outlook Contact Information

```
Option Explicit

Dim lst As MSForms.ListBox

Private Sub UserForm_Initialize()
'Fill listbox with contact names from Outlook
'Created by Helen Feddema 5-20-2000
'Last modified 5-21-2000

On Error GoTo ErrorHandler

   Dim appOutlook As New Outlook.Application
   Dim nms As Outlook.NameSpace
   Dim fld As Outlook.MAPIFolder
   Dim itms As Outlook.Items
```

Example 18-42: Populating a User Form from Outlook Contact Information (continued)

```
   Dim strContactArray() As String
   Dim lngContactCount As Long
   Dim itm As Object
   Dim lngRow As Long

   Me![txtLetterText].Value = "Type letter text here"
   Set nms = appOutlook.GetNamespace("MAPI")
   Set fld = nms.GetDefaultFolder(olFolderContacts)
   Set itms = fld.Items
   lngContactCount = itms.Count
   itms.Sort "[LastName]", False
   Set lst = lstContacts

   lngContactCount = itms.Count
   If lngContactCount = 0 Then
      MsgBox "No contacts found in Contacts folder"
      Exit Sub
   Else
      Debug.Print lngContactCount & " unfiltered contacts"
   End If

   'Count number of contacts with basic name and address data
   lngRow = 0

   For Each itm In itms
      If itm.Class = 40 Then
         If itm.FullName <> "" And itm.CompanyName <> "" _
            And itm.BusinessAddress <> "" Then
            lngRow = lngRow + 1
         End If
      End If
   Next

   'Fill Contacts listbox with data from each contact in folder
   'that has basic name and address data
   ReDim strContactArray(lngRow - 1, 3)
   lngRow = 0

   For Each itm In itms
      If itm.Class = 40 Then
         If itm.FullName <> "" And itm.CompanyName <> "" _
            And itm.BusinessAddress <> "" Then
            'Debug.Print "Adding " & itm.LastNameAndFirstName & " to array"
            strContactArray(lngRow, 0) = itm.LastNameAndFirstName
            strContactArray(lngRow, 1) = itm.CompanyName
            strContactArray(lngRow, 2) = itm.BusinessAddress
            strContactArray(lngRow, 3) = itm.FullName
            lngRow = lngRow + 1
         End If
      End If
   Next
```

Example 18-42: Populating a User Form from Outlook Contact Information (continued)

```
   Debug.Print lngRow & " filtered contacts"
   lst.List() = strContactArray

ErrorHandlerExit:
   Exit Sub

ErrorHandler:
   MsgBox "Error No: " & Err.Number & "; Description: " & Err.Description
   Resume ErrorHandlerExit

End Sub

Private Sub cmdMerge_Click()
'Written by Helen Feddema 5-21-2000
'Last modified 5-21-2000

On Error GoTo ErrorHandler

   Dim intItem As Integer
   Dim intIndex As Integer
   Dim intRow As Integer
   Dim intRows As Integer
   Dim intColumn As Integer
   Dim intColumns As Integer
   Dim strLetterText As String

   Set lst = Me![lstContacts]
   strLetterText = Me![txtLetterText]

   intColumns = lst.ColumnCount
   intRows = lst.ListCount - 1

   For intItem = 1 To intRows
      If lst.Selected(intItem) = True Then
         'Open a new letter based on the Normal template
         'Debug.Print "Creating a letter to : " & Nz(lst.Column(3, intItem))
         Application.Documents.Add

         'Paste Outlook data to letter for each selected contact
         With Selection
            .ParagraphFormat.Alignment = wdAlignParagraphRight
            .InsertDateTime DateTimeFormat:="dddd, MMMM dd, yyyy", _
               InsertAsField:=False, DateLanguage:=wdEnglishUS, _
               CalendarType:=wdCalendarWestern, InsertAsFullWidth:=False
            .TypeParagraph
            .ParagraphFormat.Alignment = wdAlignParagraphLeft
            .TypeParagraph
            .TypeParagraph
            .TypeText Text:=Nz(lst.Column(3, intItem))
            .TypeParagraph
            .TypeText Text:=Nz(lst.Column(1, intItem))
            .TypeParagraph
```

Example 18-42: Populating a User Form from Outlook Contact Information (continued)

```
            .TypeText Text:=Nz(lst.Column(2, intItem))
            .TypeParagraph
            .TypeParagraph
            .TypeText "Dear Sir:"
            .TypeParagraph
            .TypeParagraph
            .TypeText strLetterText
            .TypeParagraph
            .TypeParagraph
            .TypeText "Yours sincerely"
            .TypeParagraph
            .TypeParagraph
            .TypeParagraph
            .TypeParagraph
            .TypeText Application.ActiveDocument.
BuiltInDocumentProperties(wdPropertyAuthor)
         End With
      End If

   Next intItem
   'Windows.Arrange

ErrorHandlerExit:
   Exit Sub

ErrorHandler:
   MsgBox "Error No: " & Err.Number & "; Description: " & Err.Description
   Resume ErrorHandlerExit

End Sub

Private Sub cmdCancel_Click()
'Written by Helen Feddema 1-15-2000
'Last modified 1-15-2000

On Error GoTo ErrorHandler

   Unload frmOutlookData

ErrorHandlerExit:
   Exit Sub

ErrorHandler:
   MsgBox "Error No: " & Err.Number & "; Description: " & Err.Description
   Resume ErrorHandlerExit

End Sub
```

Appendixes

Appendix A

Keyboard Shortcuts

As in most programs, many of Word's functions can be accessed with key combinations. In fact, Word supports more built-in key combinations than just about any other program I've used. Don't be overwhelmed by the large number of combinations, though. Find the few that represent frequent tasks and start with those.

Word also allows you to assign your own key combinations, as described in Chapter 3, Customizing Word. Key combinations you assign override any built-in combinations they may conflict with.

The tables in this chapter list all of the documented key combinations in Word and many undocumented ones as well. The tables are grouped by function. Each table focuses on a certain topic in Word, such as selecting text, applying character formatting, or working with tables.

TIP # 159

Turn on the Function Key Display Toolbar

Word includes a toolbar named Function Key Display (Figure A-1) that shows the action associated with pressing each function key (F1, etc.). Press Ctrl, Alt, or Ctrl-Shift and the display changes to show what the function keys will do in combination with the keys being pressed.

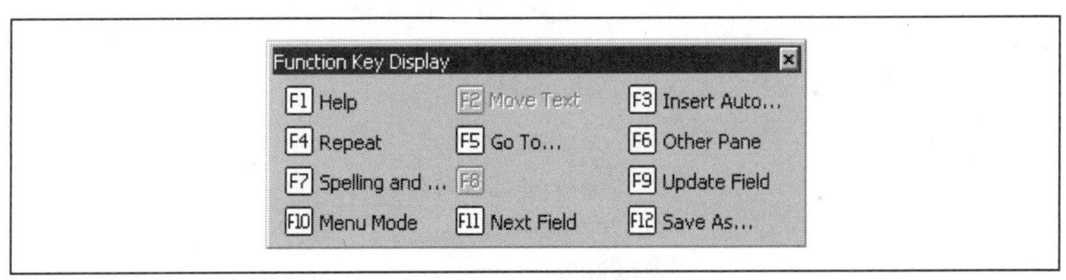

Figure A-1: Using the Function Key Display toolbar

Table A-1: General Program Keys

Key	Action
Ctrl-N	Create a new document.
Ctrl-O or F3 or Ctrl-F12	Open a document.

Table A-1: General Program Keys (continued)

Key	Action
Ctrl-S or F2 or Shift-F12	Save a document.
F12	Open the Save As dialog.
Ctrl-W or Alt-F4	Close a document. If it is the only document open, this action exits Word.
Ctrl-Z	Undo an action.
Ctrl-Y or F4	Redo or repeat an action.
Alt-Ctrl-S	Split a document.
Alt-Ctrl-P	Switch to page layout view.
Alt-Ctrl-O	Switch to outline view.
Alt-Ctrl-N	Switch to normal view.
Ctrl-\	Move between a master document and its subdocuments.
F1	Open Help or Office Assistant.
Shift-F1	Context-sensitive help or reveal formatting (as with Help → What's This?).
Ctrl-F6	Go to the next Window.
Ctrl-Shift-F6	Go to the previous window.
F7	Run the Spelling and Grammar checker.
Shift-F7	Open the thesaurus.
F10	Activate the Menu bar.
Shift-F10	Open a context menu.

Table A-2: Movement Keys

Key	Action
Left	Move the insertion point one character to the left.
Right	Move one character to the right.
Ctrl-Left	Move one word to the left.
Ctrl-Right	Move one word to the right.
Ctrl-Up	Move one paragraph up.
Ctrl-Down	Move one paragraph down.
Up	Move up one line.
Down	Move down one line.
End	Move to the end of a line.
Home	Move to the beginning of a line.
Alt-Ctrl-Page Up	Move to the top of the window.
Alt-Ctrl-Page Down	Move to the end of the window.
Page Up	Move up one screen.

Table A-2: Movement Keys (continued)

Key	Action
Page Down	Move down one screen.
Ctrl-Page Up	Move to the top of the previous page.
Ctrl-Page Down	Move to the top of the next page.
Ctrl-Home	Move to the beginning of a document.
Ctrl-End	Move to the end of a document.
Shift-F5	Move back up to three previous revisions or to the location of the insertion point when the document was last closed.

Table A-3: Selection Keys

Key	Action
Shift-Right	Select one character to the right.
Shift-Left	Select one character to the left.
Ctrl-Shift-Right	Select from the insertion point to the end of a word.
Ctrl-Shift-Left	Select to the beginning of a word.
Shift-End	Select to the end of a line.
Shift-Home	Select to the beginning of a line.
Shift-Down	Select one line down.
Shift-Up	Select one line up.
Ctrl-Shift-Down	Select to the end of a paragraph.
Ctrl-Shift-Up	Select to the beginning of a paragraph.
Shift-Page Down	Select one screen down.
Shift-Page Up	Select one screen up.
Alt-Ctrl-Page Down	Select to the end of a window.
Ctrl-Shift-Home	Select to the beginning of a document.
Ctrl-A	Select the entire document.
F8	Enter extend selection mode. Press repeatedly to extend a selection. First press enters mode, second selects word to right, third selects all characters in paragraph, fourth adds the paragraph mark, fifth adds the whole document. Use ESC to exit extend mode.
Shift-F8	Reduce the size of a selection while in extend selection mode.
Ctrl-Shift-F8-arrow keys	Select to a vertical block of text.
F8-arrow keys	Select to a specific location in a document.

Table A-4: Character Formatting Keys

Key	Action
Ctrl-Shift-F	Change the font.
Ctrl-Shift-P	Activate the Font drop-down menu on the Formatting toolbar.

Table A-4: Character Formatting Keys (continued)

Key	Action
Ctrl-Shift->	Increase the font size according to the preset sizes.
Ctrl-Shift-<	Decrease the font size according to the preset sizes.
Ctrl-]	Increase the font size by 1 point.
Ctrl-[	Decrease the font size by 1 point.
Ctrl-D	Open the Format → Font dialog.
Shift-F3	Cycle through the available case formats for letters.
Ctrl-Shift-A	Format letters as all capitals.
Ctrl-Shift-K	Format letters as small capitals.
Ctrl-B	Apply bold formatting.
Ctrl-I	Apply italic formatting.
Ctrl-U	Apply underline formatting.
Ctrl-Shift-W	Underline words but not spaces.
Ctrl-Shift-D	Double-underline text.
Ctrl-Shift-H	Apply hidden text formatting.
Ctrl-= (equal)	Apply subscript formatting (automatic spacing).
Ctrl-Shift-Plus	Apply superscript formatting (automatic spacing).
Ctrl-Shift-Q	Change the selection to Symbol font.
Ctrl-Shift-*	Display nonprinting characters.
Ctrl-Shift-C	Copy formats.
Ctrl-Shift-V	Paste formats.
Shift-F1-any text	Review text formatting (same as Help → What's This?).
Ctrl-Space	Remove manual character formatting.

Table A-5: Paragraph Formatting Keys

Key	Action
Ctrl-1	Single-space lines.
Ctrl-2	Double-space lines.
Ctrl-5	Set 1.5-line spacing.
Ctrl-0 (zero)	Add/Remove one-line spacing preceding a paragraph.
Ctrl-E	Center a paragraph.
Ctrl-J	Justify a paragraph.
Ctrl-L	Left-align a paragraph.
Ctrl-R	Right-align a paragraph.
Ctrl-M	Indent a paragraph from the left.
Ctrl-Shift-M	Remove a paragraph indent from the left.
Ctrl-T	Create a hanging indent.

Table A-5: Paragraph Formatting Keys (continued)

Key	Action
Ctrl-Shift-T	Reduce a hanging indent.
Ctrl-Shift-S	Activate the Style drop-down list on the Formatting toolbar.
Alt-Ctrl-K	Start AutoFormat.
Ctrl-Shift-N	Apply the Normal style.
Alt-Ctrl-1	Apply the Heading 1 style.
Alt-Ctrl-2	Apply the Heading 2 style.
Alt-Ctrl-3	Apply the Heading 3 style.
Ctrl-Shift-L	Apply the List style.
Ctrl-Q	Remove paragraph formatting.

Table A-6: Editing Keys

Key	Action
Backspace	Delete one character to the left.
Ctrl-Backspace	Delete one word to the left.
Delete	Delete one character to the right.
Ctrl-Delete	Delete one word to the right.
Ctrl-X	Cut selected text or graphics to the Clipboard.
Ctrl-F3	Cut selected text to the Spike.
Ctrl-C	Copy text or graphics to the Clipboard.
Ctrl-V	Paste the Clipboard contents.
Ctrl-Shift-F3	Paste the Spike contents.
Ctrl-C, Ctrl-C	Display the Clipboard.
F2	Move text or graphics (move insertion point after pressing F2 and press Enter to place selection).
Alt-F3	Create AutoText.
Alt-Shift-R	Copy the header or footer used in the previous section of the document.

Table A-7: Insertion Keys

Key	Action
Ctrl-F9	Insert a field.
Shift-Enter	Insert a line break.
Ctrl-Enter	Insert a page break.
Ctrl-Shift-Enter	Insert a column break.
Ctrl-Hyphen	Insert an optional hyphen.
Ctrl-Shift-Hyphen	Insert a nonbreaking hyphen.
Ctrl-Shift-Space	Insert a nonbreaking space.
Alt-Ctrl-C	Insert a copyright symbol.
Alt-Ctrl-R	Insert a registered trademark symbol.

Table A-7: Insertion Keys (continued)

Key	Action
Alt-Ctrl-T	Insert a trademark symbol.
Alt-Ctrl-Period	Insert an ellipsis.
Alt-Ctrl-E	Insert a euro symbol.

Table A-8: Table Keys

Key	Action
Tab	Move to the next cell in a row.
Shift-Tab	Move to and select the previous cell in a row.
Alt-Home	Move to the first cell in a row.
Alt-End	Move to the last cell in a row.
Alt-Page Up	Move to the first cell in a column.
Alt-Page Down	Move to the last cell in a column.
Up	Move to the previous row.
Down	Move to the next row.
Shift-Up	Select the cell in the previous row. Continue pressing the arrow key while the Shift key is depressed to add more rows to the selection.
Alt-5 (with Num Lock off)	Select an entire table.

Table A-9: Reviewing Keys

Key	Action
Alt-Ctrl-M	Insert a comment.
Ctrl-Shift-E	Turn revision marks on or off.
Ctrl-Home	Go to the beginning of a comment.
Ctrl-End	Go to the end of a comment.

Table A-10: Mail Merge Keys

Key	Action
Alt-Shift-K	Preview a mail merge.
Alt-Shift-N	Merge a document.
Alt-Shift-M	Print the merged document.
Alt-Shift-E	Edit a mail merge data document.
Alt-Shift-F	Insert a merge field.

Table A-11: Printing and Previewing Keys

Key	Action
Ctrl-P	Print a document.
Alt-Ctrl-I	Switch to Print Preview.
Arrow keys	Move around the preview page when zoomed in.

Table A-11: Printing and Previewing Keys (continued)

Key	Action
Page Up or Page Down	Move by one preview page when zoomed out.
Ctrl-Home	Movc to the first preview page when zoomed out.
Ctrl-End	Move to the last preview page when zoomed out.

Table A-12: Field Keys

Key	Action
Alt-Shift-D	Insert a DATE field.
Alt-Shift-P	Insert a PAGE field.
Alt-Shift-T	Insert a TIME field.
Ctrl-F9	Insert an empty field and move the insertion point inside it.
F9	Update selected fields.
Shift-F9	Toggle display of field codes for whole document.
Ctrl-Shift-F9	Unlink a field.
F11	Go to next field.
Shift-F11	Go to previous field.
Ctrl-F11	Lock selected field.
Ctrl-Shift-F11	Unlock selected field.

Table A-13: Outlining Keys

Key	Action
Alt-Shift-Left	Promote a paragraph.
Alt-Shift-Right	Demote a paragraph.
Ctrl-Shift-N	Demote a heading to body text.
Alt-Shift-Up	Move selected paragraphs up.
Alt-Shift-Down	Move selected paragraphs down.
Alt-Shift-Plus	Expand text under a heading.
Alt-Shift-Minus	Collapse text under a heading.
Alt-Shift-A or the asterisk (*) key on the numeric keypad	Expand or collapse all text or headings.
Slash (/) key on the numeric keypad	Hide or display character formatting.
Alt-Shift-L	Show the first line of body text or all body text.
Alt-Shift-1	Show all headings with the Heading 1 style.
Alt-Shift-n	Show all headings up to Heading n.

Table A-14: Command Bar Keys

Key	Action
Shift-F10	Open a context menu.
F10 or Alt	Make the menu bar active or close an active menu. Once the menu bar is active, press the underlined letter of a menu or command to activate it.
Ctrl-Tab	Move to the next toolbar or menu bar.
Ctrl-Shift-Tab	Move to the previous toolbar or menu bar.
Arrow keys	Move between commands on an active menu bar.
Enter	Activate a selected command.
Home	Select the first command on an active menu or submenu.
End	Select the last command on an active menu or submenu.
Esc	Close a visible menu or submenu, leaving the menu bar active.
Ctrl-Alt-Hyphen	Pointer turns to minus sign. Open menu and click a command to remove from the menu.

Table A-15: Common Windows and Dialog Box Keys

Key	Action
Alt-Tab	Switch to the next program.
Alt-Shift-Tab	Switch to the previous program.
Ctrl-Esc or Windows logo key	Show the Windows Start menu.
Ctrl-W	Close the active document window.
Ctrl-F10	Maximize the document window.
Ctrl-F5	Restore the active document window.
Ctrl-F6	Switch to the next document window.
Ctrl-Shift-F6	Switch to the previous document window.
Alt-0	Open the folder list in the Open or Save As dialog box. Use the up and down arrow keys to select a folder from the list.
Alt-n	Choose a toolbar button in the Open or Save As dialog box. Numbering of buttons begins on the left.
F5	Update (refresh) the files visible in the Open or Save As dialog box.
Ctrl-Tab or y Ctrl-Page Down	Switch to the next tab in a dialog box.
Ctrl-Shift-Tab or Ctrl-Page Up	Switch to the previous tab in a dialog box.
Tab	Move to the next option on a dialog box.
Shift-Tab	Move to the previous option on a dialog box.
Arrow keys	Move between options in a selected drop-down list.
Space	Toggle a selected option.

Table A-15: Common Windows and Dialog Box Keys (continued)

Key	Action
Alt-letter key	Toggle an option using the underlined letter in its description.
Esc	Cancel a dialog. When a drop-down list is open, ESC closes the list instead.
Enter	Close a dialog box, accepting the default action suggested or any settings made.

Table A-16: Web Keys

Key	Action
Ctrl-K	Insert a hyperlink.
Alt-Left	Go back one page (if available).
Alt-Right	Go forward one page (if available).
F9	Refresh.

Table A-17: Cross-Reference and Footnote Keys

Key	Action
Alt-Shift-O	Mark a table of contents entry.
Alt-Shift-I	Mark a table of authorities entry.
Alt-Shift-X	Mark an index entry.
Alt-Ctrl-F	Insert a footnote.
Alt-Ctrl-D	Insert an endnote.

Table A-18: Office Assistant Keys

Key	Action
F1	Get Help from the Office Assistant.
Alt-F6	Make the Office Assistant balloon active.
Alt-n	Select from the topics the Office Assistant displays.
Alt-Down	See more topics.
Alt-Up	See previous topics.
Esc	Close an Office Assistant message or a tip window.
Alt-N	Display the next tip in a tip window.
Alt-B	Display the previous tip in a tip window.

Appendix B

Registry Keys

Word stores many settings in the Windows Registry, including file locations and many user options. The typical user will probably not find much value in manipulating Word's registry entries, as most settings can be changed using the Word interface. However, scanning the registry entries does provide an interesting look at how some of the program components are structured. Also, there are some advanced tasks that can only be performed in the Registry. For example, deleting Word's Data subkey resets many options set using Tools → Options to their default value, along with clearing the most recently used file list.

All of the keys listed in Table B-1 are found under the root entry: HKEY_CURRENT_USER\Software\Microsoft. This is by no means a complete list of all available Word-related registry entries, but it represents most of the ones that may be useful. Also, registry keys are added, deleted, and modified according to user options and installed software, so what you see here may not be exactly what you see in your Registry.

WARNING

Always make a backup copy of the Registry before making any changes. The Windows Registry Editor does not come with any safeguards and it is very easy to delete information critical to your system.

Table B-1: Word's Registry Keys

Key	Description
Office\9.0\Common	General key for common settings across all Office applications.
Office\9.0\Common\Assistant	Holds settings for the Office Assistant.
Office\9.0\Common\General	Holds settings for File locations, product IDs.
Office\9.0\Common\HelpViewer	Defines the position of the Help window.
Office\9.0\Common\Internet\FTP Sites	Holds settings for FTP locations defined in Office applications.
Office\9.0\Common\Open Find\Microsoft Word\MRU Searches	Holds the MRU list of recent searches.

Table B-1: Word's Registry Keys (continued)

Key	Description
Office\9.0\Common\Open Find\Microsoft Word\Saved Searches	Holds searches saved in Word's File → Open dialog.
Office\9.0\Common\Open Find\Microsoft Word\Settings	Holds MRU lists for the drop-down lists in many of Word's dialogs, including Tools → Templates and Add-Ins, Insert → Picture, File → Open, and File → Save As.
Office\9.0\Common\Open Find\Places	Holds settings for the Places Bar in Office's Open and Save As dialogs.
Office\9.0\Word	General Word key.
Office\9.0\Word\CustomizableAlerts	Specifies settings for Word's optional Customizable Alerts package. Download it at *http://officeupdate.microsoft.com/2000/downloadDetails/alerts.htm.*
Office\9.0\Word\Data	Holds user options and most recently used file list.
Office\9.0\Word\Options	Defines certain editable options, such as whether spelling and grammar are checked automatically and which program directory is used by Word. Also contains items added by the RegOptions macro.
Office\9.0\Word\Options\OutlookEditor	Determines whether Word is used as the email editor for Outlook.
Office\9.0\Word\Stationary	Sets the default template used for email created with Word.
Office\9.0\Word\Table of Authorities Categories	Holds category list for creating Tables of Authorities.
Office\9.0\Word\Wizards	Holds subkeys for wizards in Word that are created the first time the wizard is run and hold default wizard settings.
Office\9.0\Word\WebPage Wizard	Controls settings for the Web Page Wizard.
Word\Addins	Holds subkeys for certain add-ins registered with Word.
Shared Tools\Proofing Tools\Custom Dictionaries	Defines the custom dictionary file used with the spelling checker.
Shared Tools\Proofing Tools\Grammar\MSGrammar\2.0\1033	Holds subkeys that set the options and names of the grammar sets used by Word's grammar checker.

Appendix C

Converters and Filters

Previous versions of Word and many other applications do not fully support all of the features available in Word 2000. When Word opens or saves a document as something other than a *.doc* file, it uses text converters to change the file format to be more compatible with other applications. If a document contains graphics, Word uses graphic filters to open and save images.

Other Office applications use the same text converters and graphic filters as Word. All of these filters and converters are installed in the following locations:

- *Program Files\Common Files\Microsoft Shared\TextConv*
- *Program Files\Common Files\Microsoft Shared\Grphflt*

Text Converters

Table C-1 lists all of the text formats that are native to Word 2000 and need no conversion. Table C-2 lists all of the text converters supplied with Word.

Table C-1: Word 2000 Native Text Formats

Format	File Extension
Word 2000 and Word 97 for Windows	*.doc*
Word 98 for the Macintosh	*.doc*
HTML	*.htm and .html*
MS-DOS Text	*.txt*
MS-DOS Text with Line Breaks	*.txt*
Rich Text Format	*.rtf*
Text Only	*.txt*
Text with Line Breaks	*.txt*
Unicode Text	*.txt*
Word 6.0/95 for Windows and Macintosh	*.doc*
Word 4.x–5.1 for Macintosh (import only)	*.mcw*
Word 2.0 and 1.0 for Windows (import only)	*.doc*

Table C-2: Text Converters Supplied with Word 2000

Filename	Description
Dbase32.cnv	Opens files in Borland dBASE IV, III+, III, and II format.
Lotus32.cnv	Opens documents in Lotus 1-2-3 format. An export converter is not available.
Ami332.cnv	Opens and saves documents in Lotus AmiPro 3.x for Windows format.
Msimp32.dll *Mscthunk.dl* *Mswrd632.cnv* *Mswrd832.cnv*	Opens Word 2000, Word 97, Word 95, and Word 6.0 documents in Lotus Notes versions 4.x and 3.x.
Excel32.cnv	Opens Excel workbooks saved in Excel 97-2000, Excel 98 (Macintosh), Excel 97, Excel 95, and Excel 2.x–5.0.
Dbase32.cnv	Opens files in Microsoft FoxPro 2.6.
Write32.cnv	Opens and saves documents in Microsoft Write 3.1 and 3.0 for Windows.
Wrd6ex32.cnv	Saves documents in Word 6.0/95 binary file format with a *.doc* extension. (A converter is needed for importing.)
Doswrd32.cnv	Opens and saves documents in Word 3.x–6.0 for MS-DOS.
Macwrd32.cnv	Saves documents in Word 2.x format. (A converter is not needed for importing.)
Works332.cnv	Opens and saves documents in Microsoft Works 3.0 for Windows format.
Recovr32.cnv	Recovers text from damaged documents.
Rftdca.cnv	Opens and saves documents in Revisable-Form-Text Document Content Architecture (RFT-DCA) format.
Txtlyt32.cnv	Saves text documents with layout preserved.
Mpft432.cnv	Opens and saves documents in WordPerfect versions 4.2 and 4.1 for MS-DOS. The converter also allows you to install WordPerfect fonts.
Wpft632.cnv and *Wpft532.cnv*	Opens WordPerfect 6.x documents, and opens and saves WordPerfect 5.x documents.
Wrdstr32.cnv	Opens documents in WordStar 3.3–7.0 for MS-DOS and WordStar 1.0–2.0 for Windows. Allows you to also save documents in WordStar 7.0 and 4.0 for MS-DOS.

Graphics Filters

When Word tries to open a graphic in a native format, it preserves the format of the graphic. Table C-3 shows the graphics formats native to Word 2000. When Word tries to open a file in a nonnative format for which it has a filter, Word converts the graphic to Windows Metafile (*.wmf*) format. Table C-4 lists all of the graphics filters supplied with Word.

Table C-3: Word 2000 Native Graphic Formats

Format	File Extension
Graphics Interchange Format	*.gif*
Joint Photographic Experts Group	*.jpg* *.jpeg*
Macintosh PICT	*.pct*
Portable Network Graphics	*.png*
Windows bitmap	*.bmp*
Run-length encoded	*.rle*
Device-independent bitmap	*.dib*
Windows Enhanced Metafile	*.emf*
Windows Metafile	*.wmf*

Table C-4: Graphic Filters Supplied with Word 2000

Filename	Description
Cgmimp32.flt	Opens Computer Graphics Metafile (CGM) images that conform to CGM:1992 version 1.0.
Cdrimp32.flt	Opens CDR images from CorelDRAW versions 3.0–6.0.
Epsimp32.flt	Opens Encapsulated PostScript (EPS) images with embedded preview images in Tagged Image File Format (TIFF), WMF format, and PICT format. If no preview is embedded, a generic title page is used.
Emfimp32.flt	Converts Enhanced Metafile (EMF) images to WMF format.
Fpx32.flt	Opens FlashPix (FPX) and Picture It! (MIX) images. Converts a multiple-resolution image to a single-resolution image. You can choose which resolution to import.
Gifimp32.flt	Opens Graphics Interchange Format (GIF) images in versions Gif87a and Gif89a.
Jpegimp32.flt	Opens JPG images that conform to JPEG File Interchange Format version 6.0. The filter does not support JPEG Tagged Interchange Format (JTIF) images.
Pcdimp32.flt *Pcdlib32.dll*	Opens PCD images saved in Kodak Photo CD version 3.0. Converts a multiple-resolution image to a single-resolution image.
Pictim32.flt	Opens images created or edited in Microsoft Office for the Macintosh.
Pcximp32.flt	Supports all versions of PC Paintbrush (PCX) images through ZSoft version 3.0.
Png32.flt filter	Opens and saves PNG images conforming to the Portable Network Graphics Tenth Specification.
Tiffim32.flt	Opens Tagged Image File Format (TIFF) images and compressions that conform to TIFF Specification Revision versions 6.0 and 5.0.
Wpgimp32.flt *Wpgexp32.flt*	Opens and saves WPG images saved in WordPerfect versions 1.0, 1.0e, and 2.0.

Appendix D

Tip Reference

Index

B

C

D

E

F

G

H

I

N

O

P

Q

R

S

T

U

V

W

X

Z

About the Author

Walter Glenn has been working in the computer industry for nearly fifteen years, beginning as a PC and Macintosh technician and trainer. He has since formed his own business providing networking solutions for small and medium-sized companies. Recently, he has authored and co-authored several computer and networking related books, including *Windows 98 in a Nutshell* with Troy Mott and Tim O'Reilly (O'Reilly & Associates).

Colophon

Our look is the result of reader comments, our own experimentation, and feedback from distribution channels. Distinctive covers complement our distinctive approach to technical topics, breathing personality and life into potentially dry subjects.

The animal on the cover of *Word 2000 in a Nutshell* is a parakeet. The name "parakeet" is commonly applied to many small, colorful species of parrots that inhabit warm regions of the globe including tropical America, Australia and the Pacific, Southeast Asia, India, and Sri Lanka.

Parakeets range in size from about seven inches to two feet, and are found in many basic and hybrid colors. In the wild, parakeets are highly active birds that feed on seeds and travel in flocks, sometimes inflicting heavy damage on fields. The Carolina parakeet, the only parakeet native to the United States, became extinct in 1918, partly because it was hunted down as a scavenger of fruit crops.

Many kinds of parakeets are kept as pets, the most common being the shell parakeet, or Australian budgerigar (*Melopsittacus undulatus*). The name "budgerigar" is derived from an Australian aboriginal term meaning "good food." Budgerigars average seven to eight inches in length, and weigh about one ounce. They are often green in color and have yellow heads marked with bars and cheek spots. Males and females are similar in appearance, but may be distinguished by the color of the cere, the area above the nostrils, which is often blue in males and brownish in females.

As pets, parakeets need large cages and frequent friendly attention to become happily domesticated. With enough encouragement, some parakeets are able to mimic human speech, very occasionally mastering large vocabularies. Domestic parakeets generally live for eight to ten years, but have been known to survive as long as twenty-five years.

Madeleine Newell was the production editor and copyeditor for *Word 2000 in a Nutshell*. Colleen Gorman and Nancy Kotary provided quality control. Mary Sheehan provided production support. Brenda Miller wrote the index.

Hanna Dyer designed the cover of this book, based on a series design by Edie Freedman. The cover image is a 19th-century engraving from the Dover Pictorial

Archive. Emma Colby produced the cover layout with QuarkXPress 4.1 using Adobe's ITC Garamond font.

Alicia Cech designed the interior layout for this book, and Mike Sierra implemented the design in FrameMaker 5.5.6. The text font is Adobe Garamond and the heading font is ITC Franklin Gothic. The illustrations that appear in the book were produced by Robert Romano and Rhon Porter using Macromedia FreeHand 8 and Adobe Photoshop 5. This colophon was written by Madeleine Newell.

Whenever possible, our books use RepKover™, a durable and flexible lay-flat binding. If the page count exceeds RepKover's limit, perfect binding is used.

How to stay in touch with O'Reilly

1. Visit Our Award-Winning Site

http://www.oreilly.com/

★ "Top 100 Sites on the Web" —*PC Magazine*
★ "Top 5% Web sites" —*Point Communications*
★ "3-Star site" —*The McKinley Group*

Our web site contains a library of comprehensive product information (including book excerpts and tables of contents), downloadable software, background articles, interviews with technology leaders, links to relevant sites, book cover art, and more. File us in your Bookmarks or Hotlist!

2. Join Our Email Mailing Lists

New Product Releases

To receive automatic email with brief descriptions of all new O'Reilly products as they are released, send email to:
listproc@online.oreilly.com
Put the following information in the first line of your message (*not* in the Subject field):
subscribe oreilly-news

O'Reilly Events

If you'd also like us to send information about trade show events, special promotions, and other O'Reilly events, send email to:
listproc@online.oreilly.com
Put the following information in the first line of your message (*not* in the Subject field):
subscribe oreilly-events

3. Get Examples from Our Books via FTP

There are two ways to access an archive of example files from our books:

Regular FTP

- ftp to:
  ftp.oreilly.com
  (login: anonymous
  password: your email address)
- Point your web browser to:
  ftp://ftp.oreilly.com/

FTPMAIL

- Send an email message to:
  ftpmail@online.oreilly.com
  (Write "help" in the message body)

4. Contact Us via Email

order@oreilly.com
To place a book or software order online. Good for North American and international customers.

subscriptions@oreilly.com
To place an order for any of our newsletters or periodicals.

books@oreilly.com
General questions about any of our books.

software@oreilly.com
For general questions and product information about our software. Check out O'Reilly Software Online at **http://software.oreilly.com/** for software and technical support information. Registered O'Reilly software users send your questions to:
website-support@oreilly.com

cs@oreilly.com
For answers to problems regarding your order or our products.

booktech@oreilly.com
For book content technical questions or corrections.

proposals@oreilly.com
To submit new book or software proposals to our editors and product managers.

international@oreilly.com
For information about our international distributors or translation queries. For a list of our distributors outside of North America check out:
http://www.oreilly.com/www/order/country.html

5. Work with Us

Check out our website for current employment opportunites:
www.jobs@oreilly.com
Click on "Work with Us"

O'Reilly & Associates, Inc.
101 Morris Street, Sebastopol, CA 95472 USA
TEL 707-829-0515 or 800-998-9938
(6am to 5pm PST)
FAX 707-829-0104

International Distributors

UK, Europe, Middle East and Africa (except France, Germany, Austria, Switzerland, Luxembourg, Liechtenstein, and Eastern Europe)

INQUIRIES

O'Reilly UK Limited
4 Castle Street
Farnham
Surrey, GU9 7HS
United Kingdom
Telephone: 44-1252-711776
Fax: 44-1252-734211
Email: information@oreilly.co.uk

ORDERS

Wiley Distribution Services Ltd.
1 Oldlands Way
Bognor Regis
West Sussex PO22 9SA
United Kingdom
Telephone: 44-1243-779777
Fax: 44-1243-820250
Email: cs-books@wiley.co.uk

France

INQUIRIES

Éditions O'Reilly
18 rue Séguier
75006 Paris, France
Tel: 33-1-40-51-52-30
Fax: 33-1-40-51-52-31
Email: france@editions-oreilly.fr

ORDERS

GEODIF
61, Bd Saint-Germain
75240 Paris Cedex 05, France
Tel: 33-1-44-41-46-16 (French books)
Tel: 33-1-44-41-11-87 (English books)
Fax: 33-1-44-41-11-44
Email: distribution@eyrolles.com

Germany, Switzerland, Austria, Eastern Europe, Luxembourg, and Liechtenstein

INQUIRIES & ORDERS

O'Reilly Verlag
Balthasarstr. 81
D-50670 Köln
Germany
Telephone: 49-221-973160-91
Fax: 49-221-973160-8
Email: anfragen@oreilly.de (inquiries)
Email: order@oreilly.de (orders)

Canada (French language books)

Les Éditions Flammarion ltée
375, Avenue Laurier Ouest
Montréal (Québec) H2V 2K3
Tel: 00-1-514-277-8807
Fax: 00-1-514-278-2085
Email: info@flammarion.qc.ca

Hong Kong

City Discount Subscription Service, Ltd.
Unit D, 3rd Floor, Yan's Tower
27 Wong Chuk Hang Road
Aberdeen, Hong Kong
Tel: 852-2580-3539
Fax: 852-2580-6463
Email: citydis@ppn.com.hk

Korea

Hanbit Media, Inc.
Chungmu Bldg. 201
Yonnam-dong 568-33
Mapo-gu
Seoul, Korea
Tel: 822-325-0397
Fax: 822-325-9697
Email: hant93@chollian.dacom.co.kr

Philippines

Global Publishing
G/F Benavides Garden
1186 Benavides St.
Manila, Philippines
Tel: 632-254-8949/637-252-2582
Fax: 632-734-5060/632-252-2733
Email: globalp@pacific.net.ph

Taiwan

O'Reilly Taiwan
No. 3, Lane 131
Hang-Chow South Road
Section 1, Taipei, Taiwan
Tel: 886-2-23968990
Fax: 886-2-23968916
Email: taiwan@oreilly.com

China

O'Reilly Beijing
Room 2410
160, FuXingMenNeiDaJie
XiCheng District
Beijing
China PR 100031
Tel: 86-10-66412305
Fax: 86-10-86631007
Email: beijing@oreilly.com

India

Computer Bookshop (India) Pvt. Ltd.
190 Dr. D.N. Road, Fort
Bombay 400 001 India
Tel: 91-22-207-0989
Fax: 91-22-262-3551
Email: cbsbom@giasbm01.vsnl.net.in

Japan

O'Reilly Japan, Inc.
Yotsuya Y's Building
7 Banch 6, Honshio-cho
Shinjuku-ku
Tokyo 160-0003 Japan
Tel: 81-3-3356-5227
Fax: 81-3-3356-5261
Email: japan@oreilly.com

All Other Asian Countries

O'Reilly & Associates, Inc.
101 Morris Street
Sebastopol, CA 95472 USA
Tel: 707-829-0515
Fax: 707-829-0104
Email: order@oreilly.com

Australia

Woodslane Pty., Ltd.
7/5 Vuko Place
Warriewood NSW 2102
Australia
Tel: 61-2-9970-5111
Fax: 61-2-9970-5002
Email: info@woodslane.com.au

New Zealand

Woodslane New Zealand, Ltd.
21 Cooks Street (P.O. Box 575)
Waganui, New Zealand
Tel: 64-6-347-6543
Fax: 64-6-345-4840
Email: info@woodslane.com.au

Latin America

McGraw-Hill Interamericana
Editores, S.A. de C.V.
Cedro No. 512
Col. Atlampa
06450, Mexico, D.F.
Tel: 52-5-547-6777
Fax: 52-5-547-3336
Email: mcgraw-hill@infosel.net.mx